America's
TEST KITCHEN

ADDITIONAL COOKBOOKS AND DVD SETS AVAILABLE FROM THE PUBLISHERS OF COOK'S COUNTRY INCLUDE:

The *America's Test Kitchen* Library Series

The How Can It Be Gluten-Free Cookbook

The Make-Ahead Cook

The *America's Test Kitchen* Do-It-Yourself Cookbook

Slow Cooker Revolution

The Best Simple Recipes

Slow Cooker Revolution Volume 2: The Easy-Prep Edition

Comfort Food Makeovers

Cook's Country Blue Ribbon Desserts

From Our Grandmothers' Kitchens

Cook's Country Best Grilling Recipes

Cook's Country Annual Editions
from each year of publication (2005–2014)

From the Editors of *Cook's Illustrated*

The *Cook's Illustrated* Meat Book

The *Cook's Illustrated* Baking Book

The Science of Good Cooking

Cook's Illustrated Cookbook

The Best One-Dish Suppers

Soups, Stews & Chilis

The New Best Recipe

The Best Skillet Recipes

The Best Slow and Easy Recipes

The Best Chicken Recipes

The Best International Recipe

The Best Make-Ahead Recipe

The Best 30-Minute Recipe

The Best Light Recipe

The *Cook's Illustrated* Guide to
Grilling and Barbecue

Best American Side Dishes

Cover & Bake

Steaks, Chops, Roasts, and Ribs

Baking Illustrated

Perfect Vegetables

Italian Classics

The Best American Classics

1993–2014 *Cook's Illustrated* Master Index

Cook's Illustrated Annual Editions
from each year of publication (1993–2014)

America's Test Kitchen

The *America's Test Kitchen* New Family Cookbook

The Complete Cooking for Two Cookbook

The *America's Test Kitchen* Cooking School Cookbook

The Best of *America's Test Kitchen* (2007–2015 Editions)

Cooking for Two (2009–2013 Editions)

The *America's Test Kitchen* Family Baking Book

The *America's Test Kitchen* Family Cookbook

The *America's Test Kitchen* Healthy Family Cookbook

The *America's Test Kitchen* Quick Family Cookbook

The *America's Test Kitchen* Series Companion Cookbooks

America's Test Kitchen: The TV Companion Cookbook (2015)

America's Test Kitchen: The TV Companion Cookbook (2014)

America's Test Kitchen: The TV Companion Cookbook (2013)

America's Test Kitchen: The TV Companion Cookbook (2012)

America's Test Kitchen: The TV Companion Cookbook (2011)

The Complete *America's Test Kitchen* TV Show Cookbook (2010)

America's Test Kitchen: The TV Companion Cookbook (2009)

Behind the Scenes with *America's Test Kitchen* (2008)

Test Kitchen Favorites (2007)

Cooking at Home with *America's Test Kitchen* (2006)

America's Test Kitchen Live! (2005)

Inside *America's Test Kitchen* (2004)

Here in *America's Test Kitchen* (2003)

The *America's Test Kitchen* Cookbook (2002)

The *America's Test Kitchen* Series DVD Sets
(featuring each season's episodes from our hit
public television series)

The *America's Test Kitchen* 4-DVD Set (2002–2014 Seasons)

The *America's Test Kitchen* 2-DVD Set (2001 Season)

The *Cook's Country* TV Series Cookbooks and DVD Sets
(featuring each season's episodes from our hit
public television series)

The Complete *Cook's Country* TV Show Cookbook

The *Cook's Country* 2-DVD Set (Seasons 1–7)

Visit our online bookstore at CooksCountry.com to order any of our cookbooks and DVDs listed above. You can also order subscriptions, gift subscriptions, and any of our cookbooks and DVDs by calling 800-611-0759 inside the U.S., or 515-246-6911 if calling from outside the U.S.

$35.00

To get home delivery of *Cook's Country*, call 800-526-8447 inside the U.S., or 515-247-7571 if calling from outside the U.S., or subscribe online at CooksCountry.com.

2014 Recipe Index

Cook's Country

FEBRUARY/MARCH 2014

Pepperoni Pizza Monkey Bread

Skillet Chicken and Potatoes

Apple Pie with Cheddar Crust

Fried Chicken Sandwiches
Just 5 Minutes of Frying

Frosted Meatloaf
Meat 'n' Potatoes in One

Slow-Cooker Mulligatawny
Fewer Steps, Better Flavor

Tex-Mex Enchiladas
Oozy Cheese and Chile Gravy

Maryland Crab Fluff
Better than Crab Cakes

Testing Dish Towels
Which Fabric Works Best?

Stuffed Spareribs
American Classic Revived

Cooking Class: Baked Fish
Ten Steps to Perfection

Orange Kiss-Me Cake
Even the Rind Goes In

CooksCountry.com
$5.95 U.S./$6.95 CANADA

The dough pieces in this savory monkey bread are stuffed with salty, gooey pepperoni pizza toppings and then dipped in tomato sauce. Now that we've spent weeks in the test kitchen perfecting it, it's become our No. 1 favorite snack. PAGE 22

Cook's Country

Dear Country Cook,

Back in the 1950s, I grew up skiing in Vermont at Bromley Mountain, when skiing was not far removed from its beginnings: stretch pants, lace-up boots, and metal clasp bindings. Bromley still used an operating Poma lift. (Put the disk between your legs, the chain is pulled, and then one is violently yanked forward, into the air.) They also had J-bar lifts, J-shaped metal bars that you held on to with one hand, the short part of the J tucked up behind you. Bromley was and still is a wide-open sunny mountain, good for families.

There were sunny days in March with corn snow, when a small lake formed near the main lodge. There were days so cold that the trees were ice-shrouded and brittle at the top of the upper chairlift. And there were moments of sheer bliss, snaking one's way through fresh powder down a narrow black diamond trail on a sunny Saturday morning.

The best part of skiing, however, was coming home to our small cabin, to beef stew in a Dutch oven, a fire in the Franklin stove, and a game of cribbage before dinner. In those years, kids spent all day out of doors and then the family rejoined around the table with tales to tell: hunting in fall, skiing in winter, and fishing in spring.

Where else can we tell the stories of our lives?

Christopher Kimball
Founder and Editor, Cook's Country

North Conway, New Hampshire, 1946.

Cook'sCountry

Founder and Editor Christopher Kimball
Editorial Director Jack Bishop
Editorial Director, Magazines John Willoughby
Executive Editor Peggy Grodinsky
Managing Editor Scott Kathan
Senior Editors Lisa McManus, Bryan Roof, Diane Unger
Test Kitchen Director Erin McMurrer
Associate Editors Hannah Crowley,
Amy Graves, Rebeccah Marsters, Christie Morrison
Test Cooks Sarah Gabriel, Nick Iverson,
Ashley Moore, Cristin Walsh
Assistant Editor Shannon Friedmann Hatch
Copy Editors Nell Beram, Megan Ginsberg
Executive Assistant Christine Gordon
Test Kitchen Manager Leah Rovner
Senior Kitchen Assistants
Michelle Blodget, Meryl MacCormack
Kitchen Assistants
Maria Elena Delgado, Shane Drips, Ena Gudiel
Executive Producer Melissa Baldino
Co-Executive Producer Stephanie Stender
Production Assistant Kaitlin Hammond

Contributing Editors Erika Bruce,
Eva Katz, Jeremy Sauer
Consulting Editors Anne Mendelson, Meg Ragland
Science Editor Guy Crosby, PhD
Executive Food Editor, TV, Radio & Media
Bridget Lancaster

Managing Editor, Web Christine Liu
Senior Editor, Cooking School Mari Levine
Associate Editors, Web Eric Grzymkowski, Roger Metcalf
Assistant Editors, Web Jill Fisher, Charlotte Wilder
Senior Video Editor Nick Dakoulas

Design Director Amy Klee
Art Director Julie Cote
Deputy Art Director Susan Levin
Associate Art Director Lindsey Timko
Deputy Art Director, Marketing Jennifer Cox
Staff Photographer Daniel J. van Ackere
Color Food Photography Keller + Keller
Styling Catrine Kelty, Marie Piraino
Associate Art Directors, Marketing Melanie Gryboski,
Mariah Tarvainen
Designer, Marketing Judy Blomquist
Photo Editor Steve Klise

Vice President, Marketing David Mack
Circulation Director Doug Wicinski
Circulation & Fulfillment Manager Carrie Fethe
Partnership Marketing Manager Pamela Putprush
Marketing Assistant Marina Tomao

VP, Technology, Product Development Barry Kelly
Director, Project Management Alice Carpenter
Production & Traffic Coordinator Britt Dresser
Development Manager Mike Serio

Chief Operating Officer Rob Ristagno
Production Director Guy Rochford
Workflow & Digital Asset Manager Andrew Mannone
Senior Color & Imaging Specialist Lauren Pettapiece
Production & Imaging Specialists
Heather Dube, Lauren Robbins
Director of Sponsorship Sales Anne Traficante
Client Services Associate Kate May
Sponsorship Sales Representative Morgan Ryan
Customer Service Manager Jacqueline Valerio
Customer Service Representatives
Megan Hamner, Jessica Haskin,
Andrew Straaberg Finfrock

Retail Sales & Marketing Manager Emily Logan
Human Resources Manager Adele Shapiro
Publicity Deborah Broide

ON THE COVER: *Pizza Monkey Bread*, Keller + Keller,
Catrine Kelty
ILLUSTRATION: Greg Stevenson

Follow us on **Twitter**
twitter.com/TestKitchen

Find us on **Facebook**
facebook.com/CooksCountry

Contents

MARYLAND CRAB FLUFF, 17

SOUTHWESTERN APPLE AND RADISH SALAD, 11

ORANGE KISS-ME CAKE, 19

Features

Departments

Call for Cookies

Christmas 2013 has barely gone by, and where we live, the weather is still frightful. All the more reason we need a little Christmas cheer now.

Send it in the form of your best cookie recipes for our next Christmas Cookie Contest. Remember to include how you devised (or inherited) the recipe and its place in your family. Submit recipes and find contest details at **CooksCountry.com/cookiecontest**. The deadline for entries is April 30. If yours is our favorite cookie, you'll win a $1,000 grand prize; six finalists will get $100 each.

America's TEST KITCHEN
RECIPES THAT WORK®

America's Test Kitchen is a very real 2,500-square-foot kitchen located just outside Boston. It is the home of *Cook's Country* and *Cook's Illustrated* magazines and the workday destination of more than three dozen test cooks, editors, and cookware specialists. Our mission is to test recipes until we understand how and why they work and arrive at the best version. We also test kitchen equipment and supermarket ingredients in search of products that offer the best value and performance. You can watch us work by tuning in to *Cook's Country from America's Test Kitchen* (CooksCountry.com) and *America's Test Kitchen* (AmericasTestKitchen.com) on public television.

Ask Cook's Country

BY SARAH GABRIEL

I like to use my immersion blender to puree soups. Can I use it to whip cream and meringues, too?
Carly Eltringham, Little Rock, Ark.

When we tested immersion blenders several years ago, we found that most, including our winning KitchenAid 3-Speed Hand Blender, could handle whipping cream. We tried whipping a few egg whites alone in a bowl with the immersion blender, and though they got foamy pretty quickly, they never shaped up into a stable meringue, and a bit of liquid egg white always remained in the bottom of the bowl. We often use cream of tartar and sugar to stabilize whipped whites, so, wondering if the immersion blender would work better with some stabilizers, we tried again. Following the procedure that we use for angel food cake, we blended the whites with cream of tartar, and once they'd gained some volume, we slowly added the sugar. Unfortunately, the meringue still didn't turn out. According to our science editor, the immersion blender tears the proteins in egg whites into pieces that are too small to effectively coat the air bubbles and stabilize them to prevent collapse.

THE BOTTOM LINE: Whip out your immersion blender for whipped cream but not for meringues.

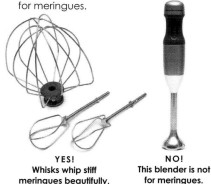

YES!
Whisks whip stiff meringues beautifully.

NO!
This blender is not for meringues.

Risotto recipes always call for a short-grained rice like Arborio. Since sushi rice is also short-grained, will it also work?
Yoshino Ueki, Burbank, Calif.

Whether the grains of a variety of rice will cook up sticky or separate is largely determined by the relative amounts of two starches: amylose and amylopectin. Varieties of rice with low levels of amylose and high levels of amylopectin cook up sticky, while those with high levels of amylose remain firm and produce more separate grains. Arborio, carnaroli, and sushi rice all have a greater proportion of amylopectin. The relative dryness of cooked sushi rice in contrast with the sauciness of risotto has to do with the vastly different liquid to rice proportions that recipes for each require (about equal parts for sushi rice and five or six times as much liquid as rice for risotto). So what would happen if we cooked sushi rice in a lot of liquid as we do for risotto? We headed to the kitchen to find out.

Following a test kitchen recipe for risotto, we added wine and broth in increments, and we noticed that the sushi rice was soaking up the liquid a little faster than risotto made with Arborio rice. When all was said and done, the two batches looked similarly creamy. When tasted side by side, the risotto made with sushi rice tasted good, but the grains lacked the firm center of risotto made with Arborio rice. It turns out that Arborio rice has a unique characteristic called chalk that causes the starch structures in the centers of the grains to deform in such a way that they remain firm after cooking. Because the sushi rice "risotto" lacked a distinguishing feature of risotto, we deemed the resulting dish tasty but not risotto.

THE BOTTOM LINE: Using sushi rice in a risotto recipe will yield a creamy, tasty dish, but the grains will lack the slight al dente bite that defines real risotto.

I baked bread from a test kitchen recipe but forgot to heat the milk. The loaves came out perfect, so is warm liquid optional?
Anthony Matteo, Manchester, N.H.

While we don't want you to think that you can just omit steps from recipes willy-nilly, the answer to your question is yes . . . sort of. Yeast is most active when warm (not hot), so we call for 110-degree liquid to ensure that the resulting dough is hospitable to the yeast. But using warm liquid isn't the only way to warm your dough; kneading either by hand or in a mixer creates friction, which warms the dough. If your kitchen and ingredients are already relatively warm, your dough may rise perfectly well without any help from warm liquid.

Also, our bread recipes call for instant or rapid-rise yeast, which is mixed with the dry ingredients. Instant and rapid-rise yeasts are dried more gently and in smaller particles than traditional active dry yeast, so there are more live cells and the smaller granules absorb water and begin working more quickly. Thus, the jump start from warm liquid is not essential. However, using the recommended temperature in a given recipe will make it more likely that the dough will rise in the amount of time specified, which eliminates some of the guesswork.

We made two loaves of sandwich bread, one with 110-degree milk (as per the recipe) and the other with milk straight from the refrigerator. Given the same hour-long first rise, the dough made with warm milk rose much higher. But in the second rise, the dough made with cold milk caught up, and both baked loaves turned out the same height. When we tasted them side by side, we noticed that the bread made with warm milk had a slightly stronger yeast flavor, which some tasters preferred.

THE BOTTOM LINE: When using recipes that call for instant or rapid-rise yeast, you don't need to use warm liquid, although it will speed the initial rise.

I read that placing foil over the surface of meat that's braising makes for more tender meat. Is this true?
Louis Hildago, San Antonio, Texas

We found reference to this "inverted foil lid" method for braising in Madeleine Kamman's 1971 classic *The Making of a Cook*. Once the meat and braising liquid are in the pot, Kamman has you press a sheet of foil directly on top of them and up the sides of the pot before putting on the lid and placing the pot in the oven. The foil lid allegedly increases the pressure, which "bears on the meat fibers and slowly pries them open." It didn't seem totally implausible to us. Look at pressure cookers: They have lids with rubber gaskets that prevent steam from escaping, thus increasing pressure inside the pot and raising the boiling point to as much as 250 degrees. So we know that hotter liquid can speed cooking, delivering tender pot roast in an hour or less. Could a mere sheet of foil have a similar effect?

To find out, we braised two pieces of meat of identical weight, using the same pot for the same amount of time, in the same oven, and we used the same amount of liquid, at the same temperature. Before sealing up the pot, we dropped in a gadget that would record the temperature inside the pot every 5 minutes for 2½ hours. When we compared the two, we saw that the pot with the foil lid heated slightly more quickly for the first 40 minutes, averaging 3 to 6 degrees higher than the foil-less pot. But the pots were within 1 degree of each other from the 40-minute mark until the 90-minute mark, when both reached 212 degrees, where they remained for the rest of cooking. The batches of meat were indistinguishable.

THE BOTTOM LINE: Don't waste your time and foil. Covering the meat with foil does not increase pressure or temperature in the pot or improve the meat.

I use sour cream occasionally on tacos or in cakes, but I never seem to use up the tub before it starts growing mold. Can I freeze it?
Bayard Lagacé, Toronto, Ontario

We'd never tried freezing sour cream before, so our first move was to put a tub of it in the freezer for a few days. Although it tasted OK after thawing, it looked broken, like a tub of white specks suspended in thick liquid. We tried whisking it to re-emulsify it, but that didn't work. But would its weird consistency be so noticeable if we mixed the sour cream into other things? When we stirred it into beef stroganoff, the texture didn't improve, leaving the sauce lumpy and broken. Asked how she liked the beef stroganoff made with previously frozen sour cream, one taster replied that she'd be happy to eat it . . . with her eyes closed. So frozen sour cream is no good on its own or stirred into sauce, but what about baked into a cake? Would the curdled-looking sour cream foul up a coffee cake? We baked two cakes, one with fresh sour cream and another with sour cream that had been frozen. Though the batter made with previously frozen sour cream looked curdled, once the cakes were baked, we couldn't tell the two apart.

THE BOTTOM LINE: You can freeze sour cream to bake with later, but because freezing causes it to separate, previously frozen sour cream is no good for other uses, such as finishing sauces or topping tacos.

LOOKS NASTY
Sour cream that's frozen and defrosted will break . . .

TASTES FINE
. . . but it works perfectly in baked goods like this Sock-It-to-Me Cake.

To ask us a cooking question, visit **CooksCountry.com/ask**. Or write to Ask *Cook's Country*, P.O. Box 470739, Brookline, MA 02447. Just try to stump us!

Kitchen Shortcuts

COMPILED BY CRISTIN WALSH

BETTER BAKING Frosting Fix
Jocelyn Kahn, Portland, Maine

When I'm filling a pastry bag with an especially soft frosting, I find that it may leak out through the tip before I'm ready to pipe. To prevent this, I devised a handy trick. Starting with the pastry tip placed securely in the bag, I twist the tip, which makes the bag twist to a close right above the tip, and then push the tip back toward the bag, creating a locked closure. After the bag is filled with frosting, I gently extend the tip and untwist.

COOL TIP Bread Protector
James Gallagher, Jamaica Plain, Mass.

I like to bake bread, and I often end up freezing a loaf or two. To prevent the crusts of the defrosted loaves from getting soggy, I place a paper towel in the plastic bag before freezing. When I take out the loaf to thaw, the paper towel absorbs any moisture from defrosting so that the bread doesn't get damp.

DOUBLE DUTY Custom Cupboard
Hilary Hughes, Brooklyn, N.Y.

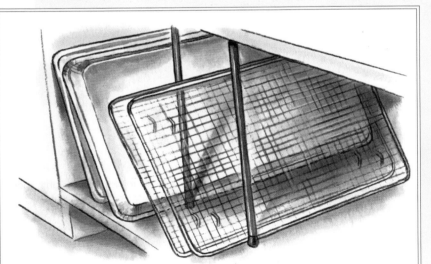

I use tension curtain rods to create better storage in my kitchen. I divide a deep shelf with a few rods placed vertically. This way, my cutting boards and baking sheets have separate storage spaces, and my kitchen is more organized.

Submit a tip online at CooksCountry.com/kitchenshortcuts or send a letter to Kitchen Shortcuts, *Cook's Country*, P.O. Box 470739, Brookline, MA 02447. Include your name, address, and phone number. If we publish your tip, you will receive a free one-year subscription to *Cook's Country*. Letters may be edited for clarity and length.

TIDY TIP Clean Transfer
Sharon Gudites, Great Falls, Mont.

Pouring dry ingredients into my mixer when making cookies or cakes can be a messy job. Rather than scatter flour everywhere, I first combine the dry ingredients on a paper plate. When I'm ready to add them to the mixer, I fold the plate to create a V shape that provides a straight path for the ingredients to follow into the mixer bowl. It's less mess and ensures that my baking measurements are accurate.

DOUBLE DUTY
Magic Beans
Jeremy Stevens, Santa Rosa, Calif.

Whenever I cook with garlic, the smell lingers on my fingers. To remove the smell, I take a few whole coffee beans and rub them back and forth in my hands. The oil released from the beans absorbs the smell. I rinse my hands afterward and they're garlic-free. This trick also makes other funky odors, like those from fish or onion, vanish.

TIDY TIP Clean Condiments
Erin Rice, Chicago, Ill.

To get the most out of my condiment bottles, I try to store them upside down in the fridge so that their contents funnel toward the opening. Unfortunately, if caps aren't shut tight or there's residue on the tops, they can make a mess of the refrigerator. I discovered that using a cut-up egg carton to hold the inverted bottles helps keep the fridge clean, plus the edges of the egg holders help my upside-down bottles stay upright.

SPEEDY PREP Single Servings
Jennifer Beck, Charlotte, N.C.

I like to drink smoothies for breakfast, but it's a hassle to prep several different kinds of fruit every morning. Instead, I found that I can prep for a week's worth of smoothies on Sunday by peeling and cutting up all the fruit and then portioning enough for one smoothie into each of five zipper-lock freezer bags. I freeze the portioned fruit and simply pull out a bag and blend its contents (usually with yogurt or juice) as needed. And with the fruit frozen solid, there's no need for ice, which can water down a smoothie.

Illustration: Ross MacDonald

Fried Chicken Sandwiches at Home

With just 5 minutes of frying—and a handful of our simple tricks—you'll be eating homemade fried chicken sandwiches that blow the feathers off any fast-food version. BY DIANE UNGER

M Y EYES WERE bloodshot, my back hurt, and my stomach was rumbling. I'd been on the highway for 5 hours when I saw a sign for a fast-food place that's famous for its fried chicken sandwiches. Since fried chicken is just about my favorite food on the planet, I decided to stop. I ordered my combo meal, and as I sat and chewed, I wondered why this place was so popular—the sandwich in my hand had none of the crunchy, flavorful appeal of real fried chicken. What's more, the bun was spongy, the lettuce was wilted, and the gloppy sauce tasted of nothing but salt. That sandwich was an insult to fried chicken, and it made me angry: I knew that I could do better.

Back in the test kitchen a week later, after I'd had time to cool off, I started my recipe development. I wanted my recipe to make four sandwiches, so I started experimenting with exactly how big the pieces of chicken should be. Whole breasts were too thick, so the coating (I was using a simple seasoned-flour dredge for now) burned in the oil before the meat was cooked through. Cutlets had the opposite problem: The delicate white meat overcooked by the time the coating took on sufficient browning. After a few days of testing, I landed on using two chicken breasts (6 to 8 ounces each) that I cut in half crosswise and gently pounded to an even ½-inch thickness. These pieces were perfectly done by the time the coating was nicely browned, and they were just the right size for a sandwich. I found that a mere 1½ inches of oil— peanut and vegetable both work—was enough to fry in.

In the test kitchen, we like to brine bone-in chicken—either in salty water or salty buttermilk—before frying it to ensure deep seasoning and to keep the meat juicy. But would brining be neces-sary for boneless breasts? I tested water and buttermilk brines against a simple 30-minute salt, and my tasters couldn't taste much difference; to keep the recipe as simple as possible, I'd go with the salting. Since I was rubbing the breasts with salt, I figured that I might as well add more flavor at the same time. We liked a combination of paprika, pepper, garlic powder, thyme, sage, and a little cayenne added to the salt. It was time to

Vary the toppings however you please—we like lettuce, onion, pickles, and flavored mayo—but sturdy, flavorful potato rolls are a must.

move on to the coating.

I knew that I wanted a flavorful, craggy coating that stayed on the chicken and could hold its crunch in a sandwich. I took care of the "flavor-ful" part of it by stirring a tablespoon of the salt-spice mixture into the flour. Dredging chicken in seasoned flour makes for a smooth coating. To create a craggy surface (more surface area means more potential for crunch), I added a

few tablespoons of water to the flour so that it would clump a little and add mass to the coating. Since I wasn't brining, I needed something wet and sticky to help the coating adhere. Beaten egg tasted too, well, eggy, but egg whites held on to the coating without mud-dying the flavor. Finally, a teaspoon of baking powder mixed into the flour— a tried-and-true test kitchen trick that makes fried coatings supercrispy—gave

the exterior extra crunch.

As for the buns—no small part of the sandwich experience—large kaiser or onion rolls tasted good but were simply too big. Hamburger buns were OK, but they tend to be flavorless and squishy—like the one at the fast-food place. I settled on potato rolls, which are flavorful, sturdy enough to hold a piece of hot chicken, and just the right size.

My fried chicken sandwiches were

already way better than the fast-food versions, but I wasn't done yet. I found that it was best to refrigerate the breaded breasts for 30 to 60 minutes on a cooling rack before frying. This gives the salt time to penetrate and also allows the coating to set up (because the chicken is elevated, the bottom won't get soggy) so that it adheres better. Plain mayonnaise was fine but not inspiring, so I created two easy, stir-together flavored mayos—one with dill pickles and mustard, the other with hot cherry peppers—to carry these sandwiches beyond good and into extraordinary.

The next time I'm tired and hungry on the highway, I'm going to step on the gas so that I can get home to make my own fried chicken sandwich.

FRIED CHICKEN SANDWICHES
Makes 4 sandwiches
Use a Dutch oven that holds 6 quarts or more. We like to serve these sandwiches topped with shredded iceberg lettuce, sliced onion, and dill pickle chips and slathered with one of our flavored mayonnaises (recipes follow).

- 1½ teaspoons kosher salt
- 1 teaspoon paprika
- 1 teaspoon pepper
- 1 teaspoon garlic powder
- ½ teaspoon dried thyme
- ½ teaspoon dried sage
- ¼ teaspoon cayenne pepper
- 2 (6- to 8-ounce) boneless, skinless chicken breasts, trimmed and halved crosswise
- 1½ cups all-purpose flour
- 1 teaspoon baking powder
- 3 tablespoons water
- 2 large egg whites, lightly beaten
- 2 quarts peanut or vegetable oil
- 4 potato sandwich rolls

1. Combine salt, paprika, pepper, garlic powder, thyme, sage, and cayenne in bowl. Measure out 1 tablespoon spice mixture and set aside. Pat chicken dry with paper towels. Using meat pounder, gently pound each chicken piece to even ½-inch thickness between 2 pieces of plastic wrap. Season chicken all over with remaining 2¾ teaspoons spice mixture.

2. Whisk flour, baking powder, and reserved 1 tablespoon spice mixture together in large bowl. Add water to flour mixture and rub together with your fingers until water is evenly incorporated and shaggy pieces form. Place egg whites in shallow dish.

3. Set wire rack in rimmed baking sheet. Working with 1 piece at a time, dip chicken in egg whites to thoroughly coat, letting excess drip back into dish, then dredge in flour mixture, pressing to adhere. Transfer chicken to prepared wire rack and refrigerate for at least 30 minutes or up to 1 hour.

4. Add oil to large Dutch oven until it measures about 1½ inches deep and heat over medium-high heat to 375 degrees. Add chicken to hot oil. Adjust burner, if necessary, to maintain oil temperature between 325 and 350 degrees. Fry, stirring gently to prevent pieces from sticking together, until chicken is golden brown and registers 160 degrees, 4 to 5 minutes, flipping halfway through frying. Transfer to clean wire rack and let cool for 5 minutes. Serve on rolls.

DILL PICKLE MAYONNAISE
Hellmann's Real Mayonnaise is our favorite nationally available mayonnaise.

- ½ cup dill pickle chips, patted dry and chopped fine, plus 1 teaspoon pickle brine
- ½ cup mayonnaise
- 1 tablespoon yellow mustard
- ½ teaspoon pepper

Combine all ingredients in bowl.

HOT CHERRY PEPPER MAYONNAISE
Hellmann's Real Mayonnaise is our favorite nationally available mayonnaise.

- 1 cup jarred hot cherry peppers, patted dry, stemmed, seeded, and chopped fine, plus 1 teaspoon brine
- ½ cup mayonnaise
- ½ teaspoon pepper

Combine all ingredients in bowl.

TEST KITCHEN TIP Clumpy Flour = Crunchier Coating
Seasoned flour is the traditional coating for fried chicken. We make it better by adding a little liquid to the seasoned flour. The flour clumps, which adds texture—and extra crunch—to the coating once it's fried.

PROBLEM: WHERE'S THE CRUNCH?
Dredging chicken in dry flour makes for a boring coating with minimal crunch.

SOLUTION: CLUMPY COATING
Moistening the dredging flour with water creates clumps that fry up extra-crunchy.

Mardi Gras Slaw

This slaw has a spicy kick and the colors of Mardi Gras. What it often lacks is properly softened cabbage and the right combination of components.

BY CRISTIN WALSH

MARDI GRAS SLAW is a loosely defined yet always tasty side dish—when it's done right, anyway. It's united by a few common denominators: cabbage; a spicy element; and the purple, gold, and green colors of Mardi Gras. Beyond these elements, the recipes that I found didn't agree on much. One called for adding red and green grapes, avocados, apples, and pecans. Several used carrots, yellow bell peppers, and onion. There was one recipe with poppy seed dressing, another with caraway seeds and olive oil. Most recipes used simple oil-and-vinegar dressings with a little mayonnaise whisked in.

My job was to sort through the options to make a spicy yet balanced slaw. I sliced, diced, and whisked, and after we tasted a half-dozen versions, I pinpointed another challenge: raw, hard cabbage. I'd get to that, but first I sifted through these initial results to decide what was in and what was out. I decided to keep thinly sliced red and green cabbage, yellow bell peppers, red onion, scallions, equal parts vegetable oil and cider vinegar, just a little mayonnaise, and—to season—salt, sugar, and cayenne.

I combined the vegetables with the dressing and was about to call my tasters when I changed my mind and let the slaw sit for a couple of hours, hoping to improve its texture. The cabbage softened considerably. Unfortunately, the moisture that it released in that time—reacting to the salt and sugar—watered down the dressing. The test kitchen has solved this problem in the past by salting the cabbage and letting it drain in a colander before dressing it. I hoped to avoid that extra step. Maybe, I thought, I could make a thicker, more concentrated dressing to take into account the inevitable watering down. Mayonnaise and oil struck me as redundant, so I tried one version of my slaw without the oil and a second without the mayo. The mayo lost this face-off. Without it, the dressing had a better texture, plus the slaw was more vibrant.

My Mardi Gras Slaw had a cayenne kick and no muting mayo, but it still tasted a little flat. A test kitchen recipe for Cajun spice rub inspired me to

This colorful slaw is dressed with a heavily seasoned vinaigrette.

reinforce the slaw with black pepper, sweet paprika, garlic powder, and dried thyme. I let this version marinate and meld for an hour. When we tasted it, my colleagues didn't throw beads or toot horns—but they did devour the slaw.

MARDI GRAS SLAW Serves 8 to 10

- ¼ cup vegetable oil
- ¼ cup cider vinegar
- 4 teaspoons sugar
- 2 teaspoons salt
- 2 teaspoons garlic powder
- ¾ teaspoon pepper
- ¼ teaspoon cayenne pepper
- ¼ teaspoon paprika
- ¼ teaspoon dried thyme
- ½ head red cabbage, cored and sliced thin (6 cups)
- ½ head green cabbage, cored and sliced thin (6 cups)
- 2 yellow bell peppers, stemmed, seeded, and sliced thin
- 6 scallions, sliced thin
- ½ cup thinly sliced red onion

Whisk oil, vinegar, sugar, salt, garlic powder, pepper, cayenne, paprika, and thyme together in large bowl until sugar has dissolved. Add red and green cabbage, bell peppers, scallions, and onion and toss to combine. Cover and refrigerate for at least 1 hour before serving.

Stuffed Spareribs

Roasted ribs are nothing new, but this version has a surprise inside. We set out to resurrect a forgotten American dish that sandwiches bread stuffing between two racks of roasted ribs. BY NICK IVERSON

I N MY CULINARY CAREER, I've stuffed chickens and turkeys. I've stuffed tomatoes and eggplant. I've even stuffed hamburgers and pizza. But spareribs? That was something completely new to me.

But as I found out after just 10 minutes in the test kitchen's cookbook library, stuffed spareribs are a tried-and-true American recipe. I discovered a half-dozen such recipes, including ones from *Joy of Cooking*, James Beard, and Betty Crocker—a sure sign that the recipe was once well-known. The recipes all followed the same blueprint: Two racks of ribs (despite "sparerib" in the name, two recipes called for baby backs) are rubbed with spices (often warm spices like cinnamon and nutmeg), tied together around a pile of fruit-and-bread stuffing, and roasted for an hour or two. I chose six recipes that used a variety of stuffings and prepared them in the test kitchen. First, the good news: My tasters and I could tell that stuffed spareribs were a solid concept, as the stuffing readily absorbed the flavorful pork juices. And now the bad: The stuffings were mushy and dense, tasters didn't love the spice rubs, and the ribs were chewy and undercooked.

From these initial tests I learned that spareribs—and not baby backs—were the way to go because they were bigger (and thus held more stuffing) and had more meat. But which kind of spareribs? I pitted "full" spareribs against St. Louis–style ribs, which are trimmed of fat, bone, and meat into an evenly shaped rack. Not surprisingly, we liked the St. Louis–style spareribs because they were easier to eat. As for seasoning the ribs, I decided to keep the rub basic—just salt, pepper, and brown sugar—and make a superflavorful stuffing to compensate. Baking the rib bundles for about 3 hours in a 325-degree oven, instead of the 1½ to 2 hours called for in most recipes, solved the undercooking problem. (I did have to flip the rib bundles halfway through.)

I moved on to the stuffing. Most of the stuffed spareribs recipes I had found used store-bought bread crumbs mixed with sautéed onion and celery, plus apple chunks and/or dried fruit; prunes, dates, dried cranberries, and raisins were all in the mix. In the test

Sweet, fruit-studded stuffing is an unexpected complement to rich, meaty spareribs.

kitchen, we usually prefer to make our own crumbs—it's hardly any work, and the flavor and texture are far superior to those of supermarket crumbs. But my homemade crumbs ended up soggy when roasted inside the ribs. I solved that problem by mixing the crumbs with butter and toasting them to golden brown in the oven before folding in the other ingredients. To be thorough, I tried making the stuffing with staled

bread cubes (the kind you'd use for poultry stuffing), but the cubes kept falling out of the rib bundle.

We had really liked the two chopped apples in one of the recipes from my initial tests, so I kept the ingredient—choosing Granny Smiths for their assertive apple-y tartness—but doubled the amount for more impact and lost the comparatively bland celery. I tested all manner of dried fruit; in the end,

we liked the complexity and richness of prunes. Fresh sage, minced garlic, and ground fennel rounded out the flavors, creating a sweet and savory stuffing that paired beautifully with the pork ribs.

My recipe was in the home stretch, but I had one more test to try. I wondered if I could skip the tying step and bake the two racks simply draped over a mound of stuffing. No can do: The stuffing burned on the baking sheet without the ribs to insulate it. When I tried moving the ribs to the bottom and piling the stuffing on top, I couldn't flip the racks for even cooking, and the stuffing didn't absorb much meaty flavor. What I did learn in my testing was that the bundles were the most secure and held more stuffing when the concave (bony) sides faced the stuffing and when they were arranged with one wide end over one narrow end (see "Stuffed Spareribs? Really?").

I'll forgive you if you think that stuffed spareribs sounds like a loony idea—I felt the same way when I first heard about the dish. But once we gave it a try, the combination of crusty, tender, savory ribs plus sweet-tart apples and earthy prunes won over even the most skeptical tasters. Beard wrote that stuffed spareribs were a "common dish . . . for over a century." Now I know why.

STUFFED SPARERIBS

Serves 6 to 8
Try to buy racks of ribs of equal size for this recipe, and make sure they're St. Louis–style. If any stuffing falls onto the baking sheet as you tie the racks together or flip them during cooking, stuff the filling back inside the bundle.

- 10 slices hearty white sandwich bread, torn into 1-inch pieces
- 4 tablespoons unsalted butter
  Salt and pepper
- 4 Granny Smith apples, peeled, cored, and cut into ¼-inch pieces
- 1 onion, chopped
- 1 cup pitted prunes, chopped
- 2 tablespoons minced fresh sage
- 5 garlic cloves, minced
- 1 teaspoon ground fennel
- 3 tablespoons packed brown sugar
- 2 (2½- to 3-pound) racks St. Louis–style spareribs, trimmed and membrane removed

1. Adjust oven rack to middle position and heat oven to 325 degrees. Pulse half of bread, 1 tablespoon butter, ½ teaspoon salt, and ¼ teaspoon pepper in food processor until finely ground, 10 to 15 pulses. Transfer to rimmed baking sheet. Repeat with remaining bread, 1 tablespoon butter, ½ teaspoon salt, and ¼ teaspoon pepper and add to sheet. Bake crumbs until golden brown, 15 to 20 minutes, stirring halfway through baking. Transfer to large bowl; set aside.

2. Meanwhile, melt remaining 2 tablespoons butter in 12-inch skillet over medium heat. Add apples, onion, 1 teaspoon salt, and ½ teaspoon pepper and cook until apples are soft and onion is translucent, 7 to 10 minutes. Add prunes, sage, garlic, and fennel and cook until fragrant, about 1 minute. Stir apple mixture into bread crumbs until well combined.

3. Line rimmed baking sheet with aluminum foil. Combine sugar, 1 tablespoon salt, and 1 tablespoon pepper in bowl. Pat ribs dry with paper towels and rub all over with sugar mixture. Lay five 20-inch-long pieces of kitchen twine about 3 inches apart crosswise on prepared sheet. Lay 1 rib rack, meat side down, across twine. Place stuffing mixture on top of rack and pack to uniform thickness. Place remaining rib rack, meat side up, on top of stuffing, arranging wider end of rack over tapered end of bottom rack to sandwich stuffing. Tie racks together and trim excess twine.

4. Roast ribs until tender and well browned, about 3 hours, flipping bundle halfway through roasting. Transfer ribs to carving board and let rest for 15 minutes. Cut ribs between bones, creating individual stuffed rib portions; discard twine. (Alternatively, discard twine and remove top rack of ribs. Transfer stuffing to platter. Cut ribs in between bones to separate and transfer to platter with stuffing.) Serve.

Stuffed Spareribs? Really?
It sounds like an awkward operation, but our technique makes it easy.

Two racks of **St. Louis–style spareribs**, with bone sides facing each other.

Pieces of **twine** are placed about 3 inches apart and tied securely.

Racks are **positioned** wide end to tapered end.

Bread and fruit **stuffing** is sandwiched between racks.

Illustration: Lauren Pettapiece

Sugar Snap Peas with Bacon and Shallots

Once we finessed the technique and the flavors, these peas proved a snap to make.

BY REBECCAH MARSTERS

These peas have a refreshing lemony kick.

I LIKE FRESH peas, and I like snow peas, so it's no surprise that I also like the crisp sweetness of sugar snap peas, a pea hybrid that's a cross between the two. When I looked up past test kitchen recipes for sugar snap peas, I found that we typically blanch them in boiling salted water, shock them in ice water, dry them, and then sauté them. This seemed like a lot of trouble, so I set out to simplify the process.

I decided to start by trying the sugar snap peas with another vegetable cooking method that we like: I'd steam them with a little water until they were bright green and starting to soften, and then I'd uncover them and sauté them with a pat of butter. When the water was gone and the sugar snaps were tender yet still slightly crunchy, I'd add a squirt of lemon to brighten them up. This simplified method worked nicely.

Cooking technique down, I turned to flavor. Sugar snaps are sweet—hence the name. And while good with just butter and lemon, wouldn't they be that much better with some savory contrast? After trying a few flavor combinations, I landed on bacon and shallots, additions that required that I adapt my method. This time, I started by sautéing four slices of bacon. I set the bacon aside and used the fat in the pan (goodbye butter) to sauté sliced shallots. When the shallots were browned, I tossed the snap peas into the pan and proceeded as before. At the end, I added the crumbled bacon with the lemon juice.

With the addition of bacon and shallots, the snap peas needed even more compensating brightness. Fresh lemon zest, added with the lemon juice and bacon, got me partway there, and when I introduced a handful of torn mint leaves, I struck the perfect balance between fresh and light and hearty and warming.

SUGAR SNAP PEAS WITH BACON AND SHALLOTS

Serves 4 to 6
You can use vegetable oil instead of bacon fat in step 2.

- 4 slices bacon
- 4 shallots, sliced thin
- 1½ pounds sugar snap peas, strings removed
- ¼ cup water
  Salt and pepper
- ½ cup fresh mint leaves, torn
- 1 teaspoon grated lemon zest plus 2 teaspoons juice

1. Cook bacon in 12-inch nonstick skillet over medium heat until crispy, 7 to 9 minutes. Transfer to paper towel–lined plate. When bacon is cool enough to handle, coarsely crumble and set aside.

2. Pour off all but 1 tablespoon fat from skillet and heat over medium-high heat until shimmering. Add shallots and cook until well browned, 3 to 5 minutes. Add snap peas, water, and 1¼ teaspoons salt and cook, covered, until snap peas are crisp-tender, 2 to 4 minutes, stirring halfway through cooking.

3. Uncover and continue to cook, stirring often, until liquid has evaporated and snap peas are tender, 1 to 3 minutes. Remove from heat and stir in mint, lemon zest and juice, and reserved bacon. Season with salt and pepper to taste. Serve.

Apple Pie with Cheddar Cheese Crust

If a slice of cheddar cheese makes apple pie even better,
how good could it be if we put the cheese right into the crust? BY CHRISTIE MORRISON

ACROSS NEW ENGLAND, you very often find a slice of cheddar cheese included with a wedge of warm apple pie on restaurant and diner menus. It's a powerful sweet-savory combination. And if a nibble of cheese eaten with a forkful of pie could be so satisfying, wouldn't it be even better if the cheese were baked right into the crust? I decided to find out.

I tracked down recipes and baked a few pies. Expecting assertive cheese flavor, I was disappointed that most of these pies came up short. Crusts that had decent cheese flavor were tough or greasy; the bottom crusts looked as though they had fried, rather than baked, in all the extra fat. And the pies with better texture tasted only faintly of cheese. The apple fillings were fairly standard, so for now I would use a simple recipe from the test kitchen's archive while I figured out the crust.

I took the best crust of the previous lot and gave it a closer look: The recipe called for 6 ounces (1½ cups) of cheddar, ¾ cup of butter, and 2½ cups of flour, and it relied on a food processor for ease. The crust was reasonably flaky, but we still found the cheese flavor underwhelming. Replacing the regular cheddar with extra-sharp helped, but less than I expected, so I decided to investigate how much cheese I could add before compromising the crust's structure and texture. I tested my working recipe with eight, 10, and 12 ounces (a full 3 cups) of extra-sharp cheddar. Not surprisingly, the more I added, the stronger the cheese flavor; alas, the pastry crust couldn't handle the onslaught. Though cheesy, the crust was now tough, crumbly, nearly impossible to roll, and once baked, it was greasy.

A good pie crust is all about balance: fat to flour to liquid. My crust was definitely out of whack. Since I was adding fat to the crust in the form of cheese, did I need to cut back on the butter? I couldn't back off enough to ever make 3 cups of cheese work, so I retested the crust with 2 cups and 2½ cups, at the same time reducing the butter from 12 tablespoons to as few as four. I found the right balance at 2 cups of cheese plus 8 tablespoons of butter. Not quite as flaky as a traditional pastry crust, this cheddar crust was tender but denser,

It looks like any other well-made apple pie . . . but the crust is packed with savory cheese.

with a mottled brown top from flecks of cheese and a noticeable cheddar flavor. For an even bigger impact, I borrowed an idea from—of all things—a test kitchen recipe for mac and cheese, adding a teaspoon of dry mustard. Odd for a pie, perhaps, but the spice added a complex, savory quality that really underlined the crust's cheese flavor. Similarly, we've found that a touch of cayenne—even in sweets—can cut

through richness and make flavors stand at attention. Just a smidgen did the job here without adding detectable heat.

Getting the crust right was only half of the equation. But since we have baked many an apple pie in the test kitchen, I had a head start on the filling. One problem with double-crust pies (like most apple pies) is the gap that forms between the top crust and the fruit. It develops as the raw apples break

down while baking—at the same time that steam pushes the crust up. We solve this by precooking the apples. I cooked 4 pounds of sliced apples—a combination of tart and sweet—with sugar, salt, cinnamon, and lemon zest until the apples were just tender, adding lemon juice at the end.

It's a mistake to pour hot filling into a chilled crust, as the butter in the crust must be cold to promote flakiness.

I'd need to let the apples cool first. I took the Dutch oven off the heat and let them cool right in the pot. Mistake. The fruit on the bottom continued to cook, overcook, that is, from the residual heat, and I inadvertently baked an apple*sauce* pie. So the next time, I spread the apple mixture on a baking sheet and let it sit for even, efficient cooling. After about 30 minutes, I assembled the pie.

I put the pie on a baking sheet, placed it on the bottom rack of a 425-degree oven, and set the timer for about 45 minutes (our usual protocol). When I checked the pie after about 25 minutes, I noticed that the crust was beginning to burn around the edges. It made sense: the milk solids in cheese contain natural sugars that caramelize (or burn) at high temperatures. Reducing the heat to 375 degrees kept the edges from burning, but now the bottom crust didn't brown. So I split the difference, baking the pie at 425 degrees for 20 minutes to set the bottom crust and then lowering the heat to 375 degrees for the last 35 to 45 minutes.

This time the bottom crust was nicely browned and properly cooked, the top crust flush against the fruit, and both were properly flaky. The filling was moist, with a sweet-tart flavor that complemented the cheese crust. My recipe was in apple pie order.

APPLE PIE WITH CHEDDAR CHEESE CRUST Serves 8

For the best flavor, be sure to use extra-sharp cheddar here. Freezing the butter for 15 minutes promotes flakiness in the crust—do not skip this step.

CRUST

- 2½ cups (12½ ounces) all-purpose flour
- 1 tablespoon granulated sugar
- 1 teaspoon salt
- 1 teaspoon dry mustard
- ⅛ teaspoon cayenne pepper
- 8 ounces extra-sharp cheddar cheese, shredded (2 cups)
- 8 tablespoons unsalted butter, cut into ¼-inch pieces and frozen for 15 minutes
- ⅓ cup ice water, plus extra as needed

FILLING

- 2 pounds Granny Smith, Empire, or Cortland apples, peeled, cored, halved, and sliced ¼ inch thick
- 2 pounds Golden Delicious, Jonagold, or Braeburn apples, peeled, cored, halved, and sliced ¼ inch thick
- 6 tablespoons (2⅔ ounces) granulated sugar
- ¼ cup packed (1¾ ounces) light brown sugar
- ½ teaspoon grated lemon zest plus 1 tablespoon juice
- ¼ teaspoon salt
- ⅛ teaspoon ground cinnamon

TEST KITCHEN TIP
Rapid Cooling

The hot apple filling must cool before it goes into the crust. If left to cool in the Dutch oven, even off the heat, the apples on the bottom will overcook and get mushy. We dump the filling onto a rimmed baking sheet, where the steam—and heat—can quickly dissipate.

---

1. FOR THE CRUST: Process flour, sugar, salt, mustard, and cayenne in food processor until combined, about 5 seconds. Scatter cheddar and butter over top and pulse until butter is size of large peas, about 10 pulses.

2. Pour half of ice water over flour mixture and pulse until incorporated, about 3 pulses. Repeat with remaining ice water. Pinch dough with your fingers; if dough feels dry and does not hold together, sprinkle 1 to 2 tablespoons extra ice water over mixture and pulse until dough forms large clumps and no dry flour remains, 3 to 5 pulses.

3. Divide dough in half and form each half into 4-inch disk. Wrap disks tightly in plastic wrap and refrigerate for 1 hour. Let chilled dough sit on counter to soften slightly, about 10 minutes, before rolling. (Wrapped dough can be refrigerated for up to 2 days or frozen for up to 1 month. If frozen, let dough thaw completely on counter before rolling.)

4. FOR THE FILLING: Stir apples, granulated sugar, brown sugar, lemon zest, salt, and cinnamon together in Dutch oven. Cover and cook over medium heat, stirring frequently, until apples are just tender but still hold their shape, 10 to 15 minutes. Off heat, stir in lemon juice. Spread apple mixture on rimmed baking sheet and let cool completely, about 30 minutes. (Filling can be refrigerated for up to 24 hours.)

5. Roll 1 disk of dough into 12-inch circle between 2 sheets of parchment paper or plastic. Loosely roll dough around rolling pin and gently unroll it onto 9-inch pie plate, letting excess dough hang over edge. Ease dough into plate by gently lifting edge of dough with your hand while pressing into plate bottom with your other hand. Trim overhang to ½ inch beyond lip of pie plate. Wrap dough-lined pie plate loosely in plastic and refrigerate until

---

TESTING SINGLE-SERVE POD COFFEE MAKERS

If convenience is key to getting your morning cup, it doesn't get much easier than single-serve pod coffee. The other major draw is choice: There are hundreds of varieties of pods for coffee, tea, chai, espresso, and hot chocolate. We rounded up five single-serve pod coffee makers costing from $50 to $199 and gave them a try, brewing coffee, tasting the results, and evaluating whether the machines were durable and easy to use. We also sent the coffee to an independent lab to check it against the "Golden Cup" standard established by the Specialty Coffee Association of America. One machine passed muster with the lab, held up well in user tests, and also satisfied our tasters: the quick, consistent, easy-to-use Cuisinart Single Serve Brewing System by Keurig. For the complete testing, go to CooksCountry.com/mar14. –AMY GRAVES

KEY Good ★★★ Fair ★★ Poor ★

RECOMMENDED

	CRITERIA	TESTERS' NOTES
CUISINART Single Serve Brewing System by Keurig **Model:** SS700 **Price:** $199 **Source:** wholelattelove.com **Pod Type:** K-Cups	Performance ★★★ Ease of Use ★★★ Coffee Flavor ★★½ 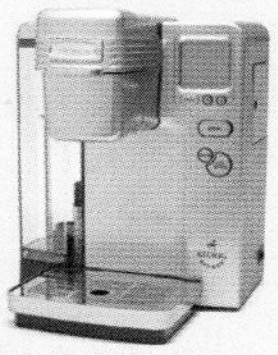	This machine was fast and intuitive. The controls let us set the temperature of the water, making coffee between 169 and 175 degrees. The "smooth" brew stayed within the optimal range for extraction and dissolved solids. The model's water reservoir holds 10 cups and lets users make seven 8-ounce cups before the machine's controls prompt refilling.

RECOMMENDED WITH RESERVATIONS

KEURIG Vue **Model:** V700 **Price:** $199 **Pod Type:** Vue cups	Performance ★★½ Ease of Use ★★★ Coffee Flavor ★½ 	This model brewed quickly at a consistently drinkable temperature, and the controls were easy to use without instruction. The machine's water reservoir holds 9½ cups and requires refilling after it makes five 8-ounce cups. The smaller pods that it uses are partially recyclable. The Vue's coffee passed lab tests, but tasters found the brew a tad weak. This model will not work with K-Cups.

NOT RECOMMENDED

BOSCH Tassimo T47 Single Cup Home Brewing System **Model:** TAS4702UC **Price:** $139.99 **Pod Type:** T Discs	Performance ★★ Ease of Use ★½ Coffee Flavor  ★★	This machine cost less and had a much smaller footprint than either the Cuisinart by Keurig or the Keurig Vue, and it matched their speed and temperature consistency. But its brew was overextracted, it took brute force to close the sprayer head, and the water reservoir held just 6 cups. Also, the standard-size K-Cups do not work in this machine, and many popular coffees are not available in the smaller pod that it requires.
BUNN My Café Single Cup Multi-Use Brewer **Model:** MCU **Price:** $159.99 **Pod Type:** K-Cups, Senseo pods, loose grounds	Performance ★★ Ease of Use ★½ Coffee Flavor ★½ 	With one of four different "drawers" that attach to the water sprayer, this machine can make coffee from loose grounds, K-Cups, or Senseo pods or dispense hot water. But testers struggled to get the attachments in place, and the machine held 14 ounces of water and brewed from all the water at once (requiring testers to mete out 8 ounces carefully). Though the machine brewed quickly and its beverage passed lab tests, the first cup was nearly tepid (at 155 degrees) and the eighth was too hot (181 degrees).

---

dough is firm, about 15 minutes.

6. Adjust oven rack to lowest position and heat oven to 425 degrees. Fill pie shell with apple mixture. Roll other disk of dough into 12-inch circle between 2 sheets of parchment or plastic. Loosely roll dough around rolling pin and gently unroll it onto filling.

7. Trim overhang to ½ inch beyond lip of pie plate. Pinch edges of top and bottom crusts firmly together. Tuck overhang under itself; folded edge should be flush with edge of pie plate. Crimp dough around edge of pie plate using your fingers. Cut four 2-inch slits in top of dough.

8. Set pie on foil or parchment-lined baking sheet and bake for 20 minutes. Reduce oven temperature to 375 degrees and continue to bake until crust is deep golden brown and filling is bubbling, 35 to 45 minutes. Transfer pie to wire rack and let cool for at least 1½ hours. Serve.

Tex-Mex Cheese Enchiladas

We hoped to duplicate Texans' favorite comfort food—minus the processed cheese and the deep frying.

BY CHRISTIE MORRISON

WHEN I TOLD a Texas-born coworker that I was developing a recipe for Tex-Mex cheese enchiladas, her face softened into a smile. "I miss Texas," she sighed. She described the enchiladas for me: oozing with cheese (usually yellow, often processed), wrapped in corn tortillas—never flour—and topped with brown chile gravy and onion, as she had last had them at Dart Bowl, a bowling alley in Austin. Lacking the meaty filling and tomato-enriched sauce that characterize Mexican enchiladas, Tex-Mex enchiladas are beloved for their relative simplicity. But as I discovered when I tried a slew of recipes, simplicity of flavor doesn't always mean "simple to prepare." I hoped to streamline the method where I could without sacrificing the dish's complex flavors.

The flavor backbone of cheese enchiladas is chile gravy, a cross between Mexican enchilada sauce and traditional Anglo brown gravy made from roux-thickened broth (see "What Is Chile Gravy?"). The sauce has deep, rich, complex flavor from the chiles, but it isn't usually fiery. The recipes that I tried employed a number of different methods to achieve flavor: hydrating ancho chiles before pureeing them with the thickened stock and aromatics; toasting and grinding chiles into a powder with other ingredients; and simply adding different amounts of commercial chili powder and spices to the oil or, more traditionally, lard and flour before whisking in broth. The pureed chile sauce had a slimy quality, and the sauces made with commercial chili powder couldn't compare with the ones I made with ancho chiles that I had toasted and ground myself. I found that two toasted chiles ground with a combination of garlic powder, cumin seeds, oregano, salt, and pepper gave my quick-cooking sauce smoky, slightly fruity flavor with just an edge of bitterness. To brighten this intense gravy, I added a few teaspoons of vinegar, an idea I had run across in *Cooking with Texas Highways* (so I felt good about my sauce's Texas cred).

My next challenge: cheese. Devotees argue that Tex-Mex cheese enchiladas must feature runny melted cheese that pools in the chile gravy, but I hoped to stay away from the nasty processed cheese that is often used in restaurant

There's no tomato here: This "gravy" gets its red color from toasted and ground ancho chiles.

enchiladas. After a few tests, I found that a mix of sharp cheddar and Monterey Jack gave me the right meeting point between good flavor and good meltability. I rolled about ¼ cup of the combined shredded cheeses in each tortilla with a tablespoon of chopped onion, reserving ½ cup of cheese to melt over the casserole. The cheeses melted nicely and at the same time had enough flavor to hold their own in the smoky gravy.

There was just one sticking point. Traditional recipes call for frying the corn tortillas in a few inches of oil to soften them and to keep them from getting soggy during baking. Aside from adding more fat to an already rich dish, this step involves a skillet filled with hot oil and the painstaking process of frying each tortilla separately. I wondered: Was it really necessary? I tested three different versions side by side: without any

oil, fried in oil, and brushed with oil and microwaved for 30 seconds. The naked tortillas were more difficult to roll, and the enchiladas quickly fell apart as they absorbed the sauce. Not surprisingly, the fried version held up well, but the extra oil left the sauce slick with puddles of grease. The microwave method, which required only 1½ tablespoons of oil for 12 tortillas and kept the enchiladas firm and intact without adding excess grease, was the clear winner.

Enchiladas are typically filled, sauced, and then quickly baked until the cheese melts and everything melds. I made a final dish of enchiladas and baked them until they were bubbling. Then I rounded up all the Texas-bred and cheese-enchilada-loving coworkers that I could find and anxiously watched them tuck in. One by one, they nodded their approval as they ate, the silence punctuated by smiles of recognition. "You bring the bowling ball," I told one. "I've got the enchiladas covered."

TEX-MEX CHEESE ENCHILADAS
Serves 6

Dried chiles vary in size and weight. You'll get a more accurate measure if you seed and tear them first; you need about ½ cup of prepped chiles. You'll lose some flavor, but you can substitute 2 tablespoons of ancho chile powder and 1 tablespoon of ground cumin for the whole ancho chiles and cumin seeds, decreasing the toasting time to 1 minute.

GRAVY
- **2** dried ancho chiles, stemmed, seeded, and torn into ½-inch pieces (½ cup)
- **1** tablespoon cumin seeds
- **1** tablespoon garlic powder
- **2** teaspoons dried oregano
- **3** tablespoons vegetable oil
- **3** tablespoons all-purpose flour
  Salt and pepper
- **2** cups chicken broth
- **2** teaspoons distilled white vinegar

ENCHILADAS
- **12** (6-inch) corn tortillas
- **1½** tablespoons vegetable oil
- **8** ounces Monterey Jack cheese, shredded (2 cups)
- **6** ounces sharp cheddar cheese, shredded (1½ cups)
- **1** onion, chopped fine

1. FOR THE GRAVY: Toast chiles and cumin in 12-inch skillet over medium-low heat, stirring frequently, until fragrant, about 2 minutes. Transfer to spice grinder and let cool for 5 minutes. Add garlic powder and oregano and grind to fine powder.

2. Heat oil in now-empty skillet over medium-high heat until shimmering. Whisk in flour, ½ teaspoon salt, ½ teaspoon pepper, and spice mixture and

cook until fragrant and slightly deepened in color, about 1 minute. Slowly whisk in broth and bring to simmer. Reduce heat to medium-low and cook, whisking frequently, until gravy has thickened and reduced to 1½ cups, about 5 minutes. Whisk in vinegar and season with salt and pepper to taste. Remove from heat, cover, and keep warm. (Sauce can be made up to 24 hours in advance. To reheat, add 2 tablespoons water and microwave until loose, 1 to 2 minutes, stirring halfway through microwaving.)

3. FOR THE ENCHILADAS: Adjust oven rack to middle position and heat oven to 450 degrees. Brush both sides of tortillas with oil. Stack tortillas, then wrap in damp dish towel. Place tortillas on plate and microwave until warm and pliable, about 1 minute.

4. Spread ½ cup gravy in bottom of 13 by 9-inch baking dish. Combine cheeses in bowl; set aside ½ cup cheese mixture for topping enchiladas. Place ¼ cup cheese mixture across center of each tortilla, then sprinkle each with 1 tablespoon onion. Tightly roll tortillas around filling and lay them seam side down in dish (2 columns of 6 tortillas will fit neatly across width of dish). Pour remaining 1 cup gravy over enchiladas, then sprinkle with reserved cheese mixture.

5. Cover dish with aluminum foil and bake until sauce is bubbling and cheese is melted, about 15 minutes. Let enchiladas cool for 10 minutes, then sprinkle with remaining onion. Serve.

What Is Chile Gravy?

Chile gravy is considered by many experts—and Texans—to be the defining food of Tex-Mex cuisine. Like beef or poultry gravy, it's based on broth thickened with a roux (usually vegetable oil or lard plus flour). Unlike those gravies, chile gravy gets its signature flavor not from meat drippings or fond but from spices plus ground ancho chiles (which are dried poblano peppers). Shortcut recipes often call for chili powder, but that shortcuts the flavor, too. Instead, we make our own chile powder by toasting the anchos and grinding them with cumin seeds, garlic powder, and dried oregano. Chile gravy should be dark, thick, and very flavorful; it's not that spicy, though.

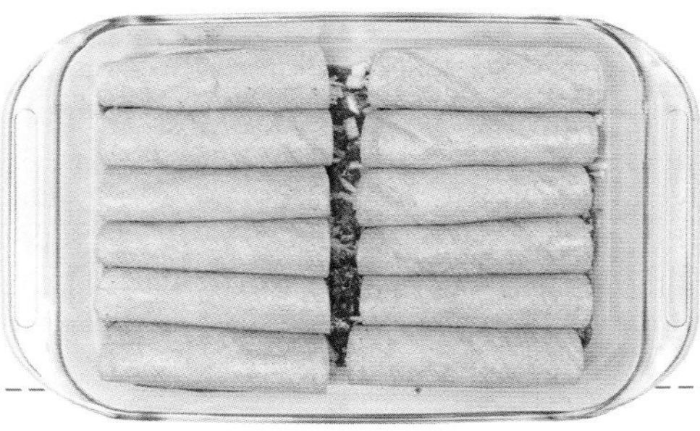

TEST KITCHEN TIP
Enchilada Orientation

The arrangement matters: After you have spread ½ cup of chile gravy in the 13 by 9-inch baking dish, fit the 12 enchiladas by creating two snug rows of six.

The American Table
The Great American Cheese Giveaway

How did Tex-Mex enchiladas, whose precursors are believed to date back to Mayan times, come to include that most reviled of modern processed foods, Velveeta? Tex-Mex food expert Robb Walsh reports a likely culprit on his website: the surplus agricultural commodity known as government cheese.

Queso fresco, the mild Mexican cheese traditionally used for enchiladas, was a scarce commodity in Texas supermarkets until the late 20th century. In plentiful supply, however, was the pasteurized processed American cheese that had been a staple of government-sponsored surplus food distribution programs for decades. When the federal government launched its food relief program in the midst of the Great Depression, long shelf life was deemed essential for the products that it handed out. So when the government purchased surplus agricultural commodities, it processed the more perishable items to ensure that they would survive transport and distribution. In 1933, the program's first year, it turned 11 million pounds of natural cheese into the foil-wrapped bricks that are still familiar today: The government used a method that closely resembled one that Kraft had recently developed for Velveeta.

Walsh's friend Richard Flores recalled that his Houston-based Latino family relied heavily on this processed cheese. His mother, aunts, grandmother, cousins, and neighbors all used it to make enchiladas and many other dishes. "You used what you had," he said. "What we had was American processed cheese." Government agencies even published cookbooks and booklets containing recipes that used surplus cheese, as did food banks and other charitable groups. One popular cookbook, *Cooking on Extended Benefits: The Unemployment Cookbook*, was published by a Pennsylvania food bank that served laid-off steelworkers in

the early 1980s. Its first printing of 6,000 copies sold out in a month. Government cheese's keeping qualities, mild flavor, and resistance to curdling when melted also made it appealing to school lunch programs, food banks, and home cooks. Tex-Mex restaurants also took note of Americans' growing fondness for the cheese and began to use it. The result? Today, Tex-Mex enchiladas with processed cheese are the iconic version.

SOUTHWESTERN APPLE AND RADISH SALAD Serves 4

- **2** tablespoons lime juice
- **1** tablespoon rice vinegar
- **1** tablespoon honey
- **1** teaspoon ground cumin
- **1** garlic clove, minced
  Salt and pepper
- **¼** cup olive oil
- **12** ounces radishes, trimmed, each cut into 6 wedges
- **1** Granny Smith apple, cored and cut into 2-inch-long matchsticks
- **½** cup thinly sliced red onion
- **2** avocados, halved, pitted, and cut into ¾-inch pieces
- **1** cup fresh cilantro leaves
- **4** ounces Cotija cheese, crumbled (1 cup)
- **⅓** cup pepitas, toasted

We like to serve this crunchy salad with enchiladas.

1. Whisk lime juice, vinegar, honey, cumin, garlic, ¾ teaspoon salt, and ¼ teaspoon pepper together in large bowl. Whisking constantly, slowly drizzle in oil until incorporated.

2. Add radishes, apple, and onion to dressing and toss to coat. Gently fold in avocados, cilantro, and Cotija. Season with salt and pepper to taste. Transfer to serving platter and sprinkle with pepitas. Serve.

Bringing Back Frosted Meatloaf

Meatloaf and mashed potatoes seem made for each other. This nearly forgotten classic makes the most of that match by actually joining them. BY NICK IVERSON

FROSTED MEATLOAF STARTED its life in America as a way to extend meat during the shortages brought about by World War II. It's nothing more than ordinary meatloaf that's "frosted," or coated, with mashed potatoes. Despite the dubious name and its wartime origins, the recipe took off; potatoes and meatloaf are, after all, a natural pair. I gathered and tested several recipes to see if its appeal had withstood the test of time.

The older recipes that I dusted off called for a meatloaf to be fully baked in a loaf pan, turned out into a baking dish, coated with mashed potatoes, and then returned to the oven to brown. Most modern recipes bypass the loaf pan, simply baking the meatloaf in a baking dish, frosting it, and returning it to the oven without having to switch vessels. This sounded like a smarter approach for those of us who'd rather not wrestle with a hot, slippery log of meat.

I prepared six of these recipes, and most were truly terrible, producing tasteless, dry meat framed by banks of potatoes that had slid off in a greasy avalanche. I was confident that I could fix the flavor and texture of the meatloaf, so my most pressing challenge was to find some way to make the potatoes adhere.

I started with a basic test kitchen meatloaf recipe that calls for baking the loaf free-form on a rack set over a rimmed baking sheet. It would let the grease drain, plus I wouldn't have to turn out the meatloaf to frost the top and sides. As I was putting together the meatloaf, I wondered if I could coat the raw loaf with the mashed potatoes to save myself a step. Failure—the fat and moisture that came out of the meatloaf as it cooked made the surface too slippery for the potatoes to stick to.

Could I borrow a page from the test kitchen glazed meatloaf recipe? It requires broiling an uncooked loaf to set the exterior, giving the glaze a tacky surface to stick to. Hoping that this method would help the spuds cling, I broiled the loaf; applied a simple ketchup-based glaze; broiled it again to set the glaze; and then baked the loaf, frosted it, and broiled it once more to brown the potatoes. The potatoes adhered, and this meatloaf was the best yet.

As my colleagues and I enjoyed slices of the tender, potato-coated meatloaf, we marvelled that a recipe born of deprivation turned out to be so satisfying.

FROSTED MEATLOAF Serves 6 to 8

If you don't have a ricer or a food mill, just mash the potatoes thoroughly.

- ¼ cup ketchup
- 1 tablespoon packed light brown sugar
- 1 tablespoon cider vinegar
- ½ teaspoon hot sauce
- 8 tablespoons unsalted butter
- 1 onion, chopped fine
- 3 garlic cloves, minced
- 17 square or 19 round saltines, crushed (⅔ cup)
- 1 cup whole milk
- 1 pound ground pork
- 2 large eggs plus 1 large yolk
- ⅓ cup minced fresh parsley
- 2 teaspoons Dijon mustard
- 2 teaspoons Worcestershire sauce
  Salt and pepper
- ½ teaspoon dried thyme
- 1 pound 90 percent lean ground beef
- 2 pounds russet potatoes, peeled and cut into 1-inch pieces

1. Adjust oven racks to upper-middle and lower-middle positions and heat broiler. Line rimmed baking sheet with aluminum foil, set wire rack in sheet, and place 14 by 6-inch piece of foil in center of rack. Whisk ketchup, sugar, vinegar, and hot sauce together in bowl; set aside glaze.

2. Melt 2 tablespoons butter in 10-inch skillet over medium heat. Add onion and cook until just softened, 3 to 5 minutes. Add garlic and cook until fragrant, about 30 seconds. Set aside off heat.

3. Combine saltines and ⅓ cup milk in large bowl and mash with fork until chunky paste forms. Add pork, eggs and yolk, parsley, mustard, Worcestershire, 1 teaspoon salt, ¾ teaspoon pepper, thyme, and onion mixture and knead with your hands until mostly combined. Add beef and knead until combined.

4. Transfer meat mixture to foil rectangle on wire rack and form into 9 by 6-inch loaf. Broil on upper-middle oven rack until well browned, 5 to 7 minutes. Brush glaze over top and sides of meatloaf, return to upper-middle rack, and broil until glaze begins to brown, 3 to 5 minutes. Move meatloaf to lower-middle oven rack, adjust oven temperature to 350 degrees, and bake until meatloaf registers 160 degrees, 40 to 45 minutes. Remove from oven.

5. Meanwhile, bring potatoes and 2 quarts water to boil in Dutch oven over high heat. Reduce heat to medium-low and simmer until potatoes are tender, 20 to 25 minutes; drain potatoes thoroughly in colander. Set ricer or food mill over now-empty pot and press or mill potatoes into pot. Stir 1 teaspoon salt, remaining 6 tablespoons butter, and remaining ⅔ cup milk into potatoes until combined.

6. Using offset spatula, spread mashed potatoes evenly over top and sides of meatloaf. Heat broiler and return meatloaf to lower-middle oven rack. Broil until potatoes are browned, about 15 minutes. Using foil as sling, transfer meatloaf to carving board and let rest for 15 minutes. Slice and serve.

A few rounds under the broiler ensures that both the glaze and the mashed potatoes adhere.

American Meat Institute, 1943.

During World War II, meat was rationed. Americans were encouraged to extend short supplies through many means including, here, a mashed potato "frosting."

Pasta with Roasted Garlic Sauce

Roasted garlic in the time it takes to cook pasta? Believe it. BY CRISTIN WALSH

IT'S HARD FOR me to even imagine that people used to use the term "garlic eater" as an ethnic slur. That's an *insult*? We adore garlic in the test kitchen, and roasting is right at the top of my own list of favorite ways of treating it. Roasting mellows, softens, and sweetens a head of garlic; the paste that results can be used in dozens of ways, including on pasta. But I don't always have the hour that it takes to roast garlic in the oven. I set out to develop a quick pasta dish with a silken sauce that could harness the same great flavor in short order.

I tested the handful of recipes I had found that attempted to do the same. One called for quickly roasting a head of garlic in a very hot oven, others for poaching peeled cloves on the stovetop in cream or milk. In both cases, the cloves were then pureed and tossed with pasta. Tasters described the garlic flavor from these approaches as variously "harsh," "faint," and even "nonexistent." Achieving a robust yet mellow garlic flavor with a short cooking time appeared to be an elusive goal.

Given how few recipes I could find for the pasta I had in mind, I looked for ideas in other recipes that use a lot of garlic. A fantastic chicken and roasted garlic recipe from the test kitchen calls for rubbing a roasted garlic paste under the chicken skin; maybe I could steal the paste method. The paste is made by cooking 50 peeled, whole garlic cloves (about four heads) in a little olive oil over medium-low heat. We let the cloves gently brown in a covered pan for 6-plus minutes—the lid speeds the cooking. The oil gets infused with garlic flavor, too. Then we puree the mixture. I followed the recipe, but instead of using the paste on chicken, I dumped it onto a pound of spaghetti. We liked the flavor a lot; despite the short cooking time, this method mellowed and sweetened the garlic. But the paste made for gritty pasta, and the ¼ cup of paste that the recipe produced wasn't nearly enough to sauce a pound of pasta. Still, I had my starting point. I just needed to turn this paste into a sauce.

To get the amount that I needed, I thought about thinning it with milk or cream. But the recipes I'd made earlier that required poaching the garlic in either of those ingredients resulted in subdued garlic flavor. Instead, after

Fifty cloves of garlic?! That's not as crazy as it sounds. The garlic develops mellow, roasty flavor.

I softened the garlic in oil, I tried pureeing it with a cup of chicken broth. It was still gritty. Maybe the cloves weren't cooking long enough to fully soften.

For my next try, after the garlic had browned in the oil, I added the broth directly to the pot and poached the garlic in it until the cloves gave way with a gentle poke, a mere 5 minutes extra. Not only did the grittiness disappear, but the simmering broth had also reduced slightly on the stove, which gave the sauce nice viscosity. The flavor was close but not perfect. A colleague suggested that I give the simmering mixture a shot in the arm with a little balsamic vinegar. Its sweetness and complexity, she thought, would mirror that of long-roasted garlic. Indeed, it did.

With a few more tweaks—some baby arugula, toasted walnuts, and a bit of grated Pecorino cheese—my dish was done, and it surpassed my expectations. Instead of an hour plus, the sauce had taken just 15 minutes—more than

enough time in which to cook the pasta, yet it tasted like my prized long-roasted garlic. I dished up bowls and then watched happily as tasters devoured the pasta. Garlic eaters? You bet.

PASTA WITH ROASTED GARLIC SAUCE, ARUGULA, AND WALNUTS Serves 4

It takes about four heads of garlic to yield 50 cloves, but you can use prepeeled.

- 50 garlic cloves, peeled (1 cup)
- 3 tablespoons extra-virgin olive oil, plus extra for drizzling
- 1 cup chicken broth
- 2 teaspoons balsamic vinegar
  Salt and pepper
- 1 pound spaghetti, linguine, or fettuccine
- 8 ounces (8 cups) baby arugula
- 1 cup walnuts, toasted and chopped
  Grated Pecorino Romano cheese

1. Combine garlic and oil in medium saucepan over medium-low heat. Cover and cook, stirring occasionally, until garlic is browned all over, 6 to 8 minutes. Add broth, vinegar, ¾ teaspoon salt, and ½ teaspoon pepper and bring to boil. Reduce heat to low and simmer, uncovered, until garlic is fork-tender, 5 to 7 minutes. Pour garlic mixture into food processor and process until smooth, about 1 minute.

2. Meanwhile, bring 4 quarts water to boil in large pot. Add pasta and 1 tablespoon salt and cook, stirring often, until al dente. Reserve ½ cup cooking water, then drain pasta and return it to pot. Add garlic sauce, arugula, and walnuts to pasta and toss to combine. Adjust consistency with reserved cooking water as needed. Season with salt and pepper to taste. Serve, drizzling individual servings with extra oil and passing Pecorino separately.

TEST KITCHEN TECHNIQUE
Speedy Stovetop "Roasting"

We love the mellow sweetness of roasted garlic, but we don't always have an hour to make it. Our stovetop method takes just 15 minutes. We sauté 50 cloves of garlic in olive oil in a covered pan for just 6 minutes or so. Later, we add balsamic vinegar, which helps mimic the complex, sweet flavor of oven-roasted garlic.

"ROASTED" GARLIC IN ABOUT 15 MINUTES

Better Brisket and Onions

Could a nod to Belgium elevate the classic American braised brisket?

BY JEREMY SAUER

BRISKET AND ONIONS is generally a simple dish: Brisket is braised with sliced onions in a broth fortified with bouillon cubes or powdered onion soup mix. Though variations abound—some recipes include ginger ale, ketchup, or red wine—the basic profile is consistent. Could a little "outside the box" thinking about the flavors elevate this dish? To this end, I turned to *carbonnade à la flamande*, a Flemish dish in which beef and browned onions are braised in Belgian beer to a deep, dark, malty finish—it's a beery, onion-heavy beef stew. Maybe I could translate its flavors into a fine sauce for sliced brisket.

Most carbonnade recipes—the test kitchen's included—use chuck stew meat that's browned and then braised in the onions and beer, plus thyme, flour, and tomato paste, until the meat is quiveringly tender. I started by swapping in a whole flat-cut brisket for an equal amount of stew meat, and searing the brisket before braising it in the sauce. I had to weigh down the brisket with a heavy Dutch oven in order to sear it well. Unfortunately, my simple switch didn't work. First, there was too much liquid in the stew—almost 4 cups, the right amount of broth for stew but too much sauce for a sliced brisket. Second, brisket's assertive, almost mineral-y taste needed a sauce with deeper, richer flavor. And third, since a brisket takes about an hour longer to braise than stew beef, the sliced onions were disintegrating by the time the brisket was tender.

Carbonnade recipes usually include beef or chicken broth in addition to beer, and they're thickened with flour. Dropping the amount of total liquid and cutting the flour to correspond was an obvious solution to produce the right amount of silky sauce for the brisket. I ended up with 1½ cups of liquid (equal parts chicken broth and beer) and 1½ tablespoons of flour.

I knew that it would take the brisket about 3 hours to braise in the oven and that it would be best to let it rest in the liquid for another hour so the meat could reabsorb some of the flavorful juices. For the sauce, I tested all sorts of beer—naturally, authentic Belgian ale was great, but I found that any wheat beer (such as Blue Moon) works well, as do lagers and pilsners. I did a

test with Budweiser and it was terrific. Even better, I lost the broth altogether and just used a full 12 ounces of beer for extra maltiness. I kept the herbal components standard—thyme sprigs and bay leaves—but included a tablespoon each of brown sugar and cider vinegar. A little Dijon added just before serving brought the sauce into focus.

As for the onions, I increased their amount and sliced them extra-thick to ensure they wouldn't cook down and disappear in the sauce. To boost the flavor even further, I tried something unusual: I pureed one of the raw onions before adding it to the sauce. The flavor was enhanced, and the pureed onion thickened the sauce, which in turn allowed me to use less flour for a cleaner, purer flavor. With a European influence and a couple of culinary tricks, I had created a recipe that combined two of my favorite things—beef and beer—into a fantastic new dish.

BRISKET CARBONNADE Serves 6

We like this recipe best when made with wheat beers, lagers, and pilsners.

- 4 large onions
- 1 (3½-pound) beef brisket, flat cut, fat trimmed to ¼ inch
- Salt and pepper
- 2 tablespoons vegetable oil
- 1 tablespoon tomato paste
- 2 garlic cloves, minced
- 1 tablespoon all-purpose flour
- 1½ cups beer
- 4 sprigs fresh thyme
- 2 bay leaves
- 1 tablespoon packed brown sugar
- 1 tablespoon cider vinegar
- 1 teaspoon Dijon mustard

1. Adjust oven rack to lower-middle position and heat oven to 325 degrees. Halve and slice 3 onions ½ inch thick. Puree remaining onion in food processor, about 10 seconds. Pat brisket dry with paper towels and season liberally with salt and pepper. Heat 1 tablespoon oil in 12-inch skillet over medium-high heat until just smoking. Place brisket in skillet, weigh down with Dutch oven or cast-iron skillet, and cook until well browned, about 4 minutes per side. Transfer brisket to 13 by 9-inch baking dish.

2. Heat remaining 1 tablespoon oil in now-empty skillet over medium heat

The sauce is made with beer and brightened with Dijon mustard and cider vinegar.

until shimmering. Add sliced onions and ½ teaspoon salt and cook, stirring occasionally, until soft and golden brown, about 15 minutes. Stir in tomato paste and garlic and cook until fragrant, about 30 seconds. Stir in flour until onions are evenly coated and flour is lightly browned, about 2 minutes. Stir in pureed onion and cook until mixture has thickened, about 2 minutes. Stir in beer, thyme sprigs, bay leaves, sugar, and vinegar, scraping up any browned bits. Increase heat to medium-high and bring to boil.

3. Pour onion mixture over brisket and cover dish tightly with aluminum foil. Bake until brisket is tender and fork easily slips in and out of meat, about 3 hours. Let brisket rest in liquid,

uncovered, for 1 hour.

4. Transfer brisket to carving board. Skim fat from top of sauce with large spoon and discard thyme sprigs and bay leaves. Whisk mustard into sauce and season with salt and pepper. Slice brisket against grain into ¼-inch-thick slices and return to dish with sauce. Serve.

TO MAKE AHEAD

Follow recipe through step 3. Remove brisket from sauce, discard thyme sprigs and bay leaves, whisk in mustard, return brisket to sauce, and let cool completely. Cover and refrigerate for up to 48 hours. To serve, defat sauce, slice brisket, return to sauce, and cover with aluminum foil. Bake at 350 degrees until brisket is heated through, about 1 hour.

Broccoli-Cheese Cornbread

Too much cottage cheese makes many versions of this deliciously hearty cornbread bland.
What is the best way to give it a shot in the arm? BY DIANE UNGER

BROCCOLI-CHEESE cornbread transforms a beloved side dish into something so substantial that it could practically stand as a meal. Most recipes keep it simple, calling for corn muffin mix, chopped onion, buttermilk, and frozen broccoli. But the key is cottage cheese, which makes for an especially moist cornbread that tastes like a cross between cornbread and spoon bread. To me, the idea of putting broccoli into cornbread sounded like a parental ploy to get a child to eat more vegetables. But after I made a few versions, I changed my mind. This concept definitely had promise.

That's not to say that these sample cornbreads were problem-free. As a group, they were wet rather than moist, and while you could see the broccoli, you couldn't taste it much, plus it tended to clump. What you *could* taste was raw, crunchy onion. Other than that onion, the recipes were on the bland side. (The cottage cheese didn't add much in the flavor department.) And while muffin mix was easy, it made the cornbread too sweet. With all these things in mind, I put together a new starting point and got down to work.

Since making cornbread from scratch is just a matter of stirring a handful of ingredients together, I opted to start with a basic cornbread recipe and nix the mix. As for the broccoli, I wanted to stick with frozen to avoid trimming, blanching, draining, and chopping fresh. We liked florets better than chopped frozen broccoli, but I did give the florets a quick chop so that they distributed more evenly in the batter. I discovered that if I thawed the florets and pressed them dry with paper towels before stirring them in, the cornbread wasn't quite so wet, which became even more important when I decided to use nearly twice the amount that some recipes call for.

At this point, I'd improved the texture and the broccoli flavor of the cornbread, but I hadn't repaired it

This hearty cornbread is fortified with broccoli, cheddar, and cottage cheese.

TEST KITCHEN TECHNIQUE
Building Flavor from the Bottom Up
Most recipes for this kind of cornbread call for stirring chopped raw onion into the batter—no wonder the onion tastes sharp and sulfurous. We found it better to sauté onion and garlic in the same skillet that we bake the cornbread in to create a savory base of flavor.

SAUTÉ AROMATICS
To build base flavor.

entirely. Wondering what to do next, I scanned my ingredient list thus far. Was the buttermilk really necessary on top of the cottage cheese? I made the recipe several times, decreasing the amount of buttermilk bit by bit, and eventually abandoned the buttermilk entirely, using just ¼ cup of milk instead. I had finally produced a perfectly moist—but not wet—cornbread.

Turning to the onion, I tried sautéing it in butter in a skillet. Much better. And it was just a small step from there to skipping the baking dish that I'd been using and baking the cornbread right in that skillet. Not only was it one less dish to wash but it gave the cornbread a crusty browned bottom and sides. While I was sautéing the onion for a test one morning, I threw in three minced garlic cloves. Garlic is unconventional for cornbread, yes, but it nicely underlined the savory qualities of this version.

My recipe was getting better, but it still lacked pizzazz. I'd seen recipes that called for additions of sharp cheddar cheese or hot sauce. I tried both. We liked 1½ cups of extra-sharp cheddar

stirred into the batter so much that I sprinkled more on top. A full tablespoon of hot sauce added a welcome punch.

This cornbread is substantial enough to serve as a light lunch on its own. It's versatile enough to pair with any soup, stew, or chili. And it's tasty enough that you'll make it time and again.

BROCCOLI-CHEESE CORNBREAD
Serves 8 to 10
Thaw the broccoli and press it as dry as possible before stirring it into the batter.

- 6 tablespoons unsalted butter
- 1 onion, chopped fine
- 3 garlic cloves, minced
- 1 cup (5 ounces) cornmeal
- 1 cup (5 ounces) all-purpose flour
- 2 tablespoons sugar
- 1 tablespoon baking powder
- ¾ teaspoon salt
- 8 ounces (1 cup) cottage cheese
- 3 large eggs
- ¼ cup milk
- 1 tablespoon hot sauce
- 12 ounces frozen broccoli florets, thawed, pressed dry with paper towels, and chopped coarse
- 8 ounces extra-sharp cheddar cheese, shredded (2 cups)

1. Adjust oven rack to middle position and heat oven to 375 degrees. Melt butter in 10-inch ovensafe nonstick skillet over medium-high heat. Add onion and cook until softened, about 5 minutes. Stir in garlic and cook until fragrant, about 30 seconds. Remove from heat; set aside.

2. Whisk cornmeal, flour, sugar, baking powder, and salt together in large bowl. Whisk cottage cheese, eggs, milk, and hot sauce together in separate bowl. Stir cottage cheese mixture into cornmeal mixture until combined. Stir broccoli, 1½ cups cheddar, and onion mixture into batter until thoroughly combined (batter will be thick).

3. Pour batter into now-empty skillet and smooth top with rubber spatula. Sprinkle remaining ½ cup cheddar evenly over top. Bake until cornbread is golden brown and toothpick inserted in center comes out clean, 40 to 45 minutes. Let cornbread cool in skillet on wire rack for 1 hour. Loosen edges of cornbread from skillet with spatula and slide out onto cutting board. Cut into wedges and serve.

Getting to Know Vinegars

More than just the yin to oil's yang in salad dressing, vinegar can help shape a perfect poached egg and save many a dish from terminal blandness. BY CHRISTIE MORRISON

Distilled White Vinegar
MULTITASKER

Buy a big jug of this neutral-tasting vinegar; you'll be turning to it for more than cooking. Made from grain alcohol that's distilled to produce a colorless liquid with high acidity, this kitchen stalwart doubles as a cleaning agent: Put some in a spray bottle and use it to wash wax, dirt, and chemicals from fruits and vegetables. Add a few tablespoons of vinegar to the water for eggs as they poach to keep the whites from threading.

Red Wine Vinegar
MOTHER OF ALL VINEGARS

Red wine usually becomes vinegar in one of two ways: A blob of cellulose and bacteria called a "mother" is added to wine to convert alcohol into acid, or wine and bacteria are combined in a machine that "aerates" them to feed the bacteria. Our favorite, Laurent du Clos Red Wine Vinegar, has a "clean, light, pleasant taste," according to our tasters, and a subtle sharpness that goes well in vinaigrettes.

White Wine Vinegar
BLANC SLATE

Crisp and acidic, with "subtle sweetness" and "lemony" flavors, white wine vinegar is what we use to brighten pan sauces for chicken and fish. We also turn to it in potato salad: Tossing hot potatoes in white wine vinegar is how we infuse our Dill Potato Salad with deep flavor: Find the recipe at **CooksCountry.com/ dillpotatosalad.** Our favorites are Colavita Aged White Wine Vinegar and Spectrum Naturals Organic White Wine Vinegar.

Cider Vinegar
YE OLDE STAPLE

Fruity and balanced, apple cider vinegar has been popular in the United States since colonial times; this vinegar is made from hard apple cider, a popular drink in that era. We use it every day in the test kitchen. Our favorite is Spectrum Naturals Organic Apple Cider Vinegar, Unfiltered; that it's unfiltered contributes to its "distinct apple flavor" and gives it an "assertive, tangy" quality.

Balsamic Vinegar
SWEET SYRUP

Traditional balsamic vinegar from Italy's Modena and Emilia-Romagna regions is aged in wooden barrels for years until the vinegar is sweet, syrupy, and expensive—up to $60 per ounce. Many cheaper versions bypass the aging and instead add colors or sweeteners; the price tag is lower but so is the quality. Our favorite supermarket balsamic vinegar—Lucini Gran Riserva Balsamico—contains no added sugars or colors. We like its "great complexity" and subtle acidity.

Sherry Vinegar
SPANISH TWIST

Sherry vinegar is made from sherry, a forti- fied wine. True *Vinagre de Jerez*, made in a small area of Spain, is aged for at least two years in oak barrels. Many sherry vinegars stocked in supermarkets are lesser-quality knockoffs. Sherry vinegar's flavors are "warm" and "toasty," with a "brown-sugary" sweetness. Use it to brighten pan sauces or to echo Spanish flavors in our Roasted Cauliflower with Paprika and Chorizo: **CooksCountry.com/ spanishcauliflower.**

Malt Vinegar
BRITISH MUSCLEMAN

Made from fermented malted barley— basically, unhopped beer—malt is a bit aggressive for most vinaigrettes. But when it comes to cutting through the oil of fried fish and chips and adding an intense, flavorful punch, there's nothing like it. We love its "savory," "beefy" flavor in our Roasted Salt-and-Vinegar Potatoes (**CooksCountry.com/vinegarpotatoes**), but it's not just for spuds. It's also the foun- dation of many chutneys and sauces.

Rice Vinegar
SUSHI SEASONER

Primarily used to season sushi rice, rice vinegar plays a role in stir-fries and satays, too. It's also called rice wine vinegar, but don't confuse it with rice wine. Rice vinegar is made from steamed rice that's blended with yeast and fermented into alcohol before being aerated to form vinegar. This vinegar has a characteristic "malty" sweetness and mild acidity. You can buy it seasoned or unseasoned; we prefer unseasoned because it's more versatile.

Chinese Black Vinegar
GRAIN SILO

Originating in China's Zhejiang province, black vinegar is made from sorghum, wheat, rice, or millet—sometimes in combination—and aged to develop its complex flavor. The flavors are hard to pin down, but our tasters suggested "woodsy" and "earthy," with hints of "warm spice" and herbs like tarragon. Balsamic or malt vinegars are good substi- tutes, though both lack black vinegar's complexity. Use black vinegar in dipping sauces and for braising meat.

Champagne Vinegar
OYSTER CHUM

This vinegar is made from the fermented juice of champagne grapes before second fermentation (the cause of the bubbles) occurs. The resulting vinegar has a "clean," "mineral-y" flavor that's usually more delicate than that of white wine vinegar (although our tasters had a hard time telling the difference). Champagne vinegar's light body and crispness make it a good base for fruit and herb vinegars. Splash it on vegetables or mix it with shal- lots in a mignonette sauce for oysters.

Fruit Vinegar
BOTTLED HARVEST

Raspberry vinegar has all but vanished from the cupboards of culinary trendset- ters, but we think that the pairing of sweet fruit with acidic vinegar is timeless. True fruit vinegars are made by fermenting fruit juice into wine and then letting it mingle with acid. Some fruit-flavored vinegars take a shortcut, infusing red wine, white wine, or champagne vinegars with macerated fruit or fruit purees. Use fruit vinegars in vinaigrettes or drizzled over grilled fruit.

Herb Vinegar
GARDEN IN A JAR

Unlike the other vinegars in this roundup, herb vinegars are infusions. Highly aromatic herbs like tarragon, sage, rosemary, or basil are added to warm (but not boiling) light-flavored vinegars, which are then set aside to steep for three to four weeks before the herbs are discarded. Figure on infusing every 2 cups of vinegar with about 1 cup of fresh herbs. Herb vinegars can add a fresh flavor to salad dressings and marinades and are a great way to use up extra herbs.

GAME-DAY BEER BRATS WITH ONION AND MUSTARD

ONE-PAN SHRIMP PAD THAI

SMOKY PORK AND WHITE BEAN STEW

CHICKEN PARMESAN SALAD

ONE-PAN SHRIMP PAD THAI Serves 4

✓ **WHY THIS RECIPE WORKS:** Pad thai sounds exotic, but it's fast and easy to make and requires just one skillet.

- 8 ounces (⅜-inch-wide) rice noodles
- ⅓ cup lime juice (3 limes)
- ⅓ cup packed brown sugar
- ¼ cup fish sauce
- 1 pound extra-large shrimp (21 to 25 per pound), peeled and deveined
- 2 tablespoons vegetable oil
- 4 garlic cloves, minced
- 8 ounces (4 cups) mung bean sprouts
- ¼ cup chopped fresh cilantro
- ¼ cup dry-roasted peanuts, chopped

1. Soak noodles in hot water until softened, stirring occasionally, about 15 minutes. Combine lime juice, sugar, and fish sauce in bowl. Pat shrimp dry with paper towels. Heat oil in 12-inch nonstick skillet over medium heat until just beginning to smoke. Add shrimp and garlic and cook, stirring occasionally, until shrimp are pink, about 4 minutes. Transfer to plate.

2. Return now-empty skillet to medium heat. Drain noodles and add to skillet. Cook until any residual moisture has evaporated, about 2 minutes. Add lime juice mixture and cook until thickened slightly, about 4 minutes. Add sprouts and shrimp to skillet and cook until shrimp are cooked through, about 3 minutes. Transfer to bowl, sprinkle with cilantro and peanuts, and serve.

TEST KITCHEN NOTE: Look for rice noodles at an Asian grocery store or in the international aisle of your supermarket.

GAME-DAY BEER BRATS WITH ONION AND MUSTARD Serves 4

✓ **WHY THIS RECIPE WORKS:** After searing the brats, we make a flavorful braising liquid from onion, mustard, and beer. Once the braising liquid has reduced, we use it as a condiment.

- 3 tablespoons vegetable oil
- 1½ pounds bratwurst (6 sausages)
- 1 onion, halved and sliced thin
  Salt and pepper
- 2 garlic cloves, minced
- 1 teaspoon caraway seeds
- 1½ cups beer
- ¼ cup whole-grain mustard
- 1 tablespoon honey
- 2 teaspoons cider vinegar

1. Heat 1 tablespoon oil in Dutch oven over medium heat until shimmering. Add bratwursts and cook until well browned all over, about 8 minutes. Transfer bratwursts to plate.

2. Heat remaining 2 tablespoons oil in now-empty pot over medium heat until shimmering. Add onion, ¼ teaspoon salt, and ¼ teaspoon pepper and cook, covered, until softened, about 5 minutes. Uncover and continue to cook, stirring occasionally, until onion is browned, about 4 minutes. Add garlic and caraway seeds and cook until fragrant, about 30 seconds.

3. Add beer, mustard, honey, vinegar, and bratwursts; cover; and cook until bratwursts are cooked through, 5 to 7 minutes. Transfer bratwursts to platter. Increase heat to medium-high and cook until onion mixture is thickened, about 5 minutes. Serve bratwursts topped with onion mixture.

TEST KITCHEN NOTE: Use an American lager. Serve on hoagie rolls.

CHICKEN PARMESAN SALAD Serves 4

✓ **WHY THIS RECIPE WORKS:** For a twist on the classic, we take the familiar crispy chicken breast and serve it with cherry tomatoes, peppery arugula, and little balls of fresh mozzarella (sold as *bocconcini*).

- 1 large egg
- 1 cup panko bread crumbs
  Salt and pepper
- 4 (4-ounce) chicken cutlets, ½ inch thick, trimmed
- 6 tablespoons vegetable oil
- ¼ cup pesto
- 1 teaspoon grated lemon zest plus 1 tablespoon juice
- 12 ounces cherry tomatoes, halved
- 5 ounces (5 cups) baby arugula
- 4 ounces bocconcini, halved (1 cup)

1. Beat egg in shallow dish. Combine panko, ¼ teaspoon salt, and ¼ teaspoon pepper in second shallow dish. Pat cutlets dry with paper towels and season with salt and pepper. Working with 1 cutlet at a time, dip cutlets in egg, then dredge in panko mixture, pressing to adhere. Heat 3 tablespoons oil in 12-inch nonstick skillet over medium heat until shimmering. Cook 2 cutlets until golden brown and crispy, about 2 minutes per side. Transfer to paper towel–lined plate. Repeat with remaining 3 tablespoons oil and remaining 2 cutlets. Tent loosely with aluminum foil and let rest for 5 minutes.

2. Whisk pesto and lemon zest and juice together in large bowl. Add tomatoes, arugula, and bocconcini and toss to combine. Season with salt and pepper to taste. Arrange salad on serving platter. Slice cutlets crosswise into ½-inch-wide strips and place over salad. Serve.

TEST KITCHEN NOTE: If you can't find bocconcini, cut a larger ball of fresh mozzarella into ½-inch pieces.

SMOKY PORK AND WHITE BEAN STEW Serves 4

✓ **WHY THIS RECIPE WORKS:** To make a quick stew, we use quick-cooking pork tenderloin, a particularly tender cut. Adding the beans in the last 5 minutes of cooking ensures that they won't blow out.

- 1 (12- to 16-ounce) pork tenderloin, trimmed and cut into 1-inch pieces
  Salt and pepper
- 3 tablespoons vegetable oil
- 1 onion, chopped
- 4 garlic cloves, minced
- 1 tablespoon smoked paprika
- 1 (28-ounce) can crushed tomatoes
- 3 cups chicken broth
- 1 (15-ounce) can white beans, rinsed
- ¼ cup chopped fresh parsley

1. Pat pork dry with paper towels and season with salt and pepper. Heat 2 tablespoons oil in Dutch oven over medium-high heat until just smoking. Add pork and cook until browned all over, 8 to 10 minutes. Transfer to plate.

2. Heat remaining 1 tablespoon oil in now-empty pot over medium heat until shimmering. Add onion and cook until softened and beginning to brown, about 4 minutes. Add garlic and paprika and cook until fragrant, about 30 seconds.

3. Add tomatoes, broth, and pork and any accumulated juices and bring to simmer. Reduce heat to medium-low, cover, and cook until pork is just cooked through, about 8 minutes. Add beans and cook until heated through, about 5 minutes. Stir in parsley. Season with salt and pepper to taste. Serve.

TEST KITCHEN NOTE: Make the stew spicier by using hot smoked paprika.

SWEET AND SPICY PORK TACOS

SPICE-RUBBED ROAST CHICKEN PARTS

FILETS MIGNONS WITH MUSHROOMS

SKILLET PENNE WITH CHICKPEAS AND CAULIFLOWER

SPICE-RUBBED ROAST CHICKEN PARTS Serves 4

✔ **WHY THIS RECIPE WORKS:** Thanks to the blender, the spice paste comes together quickly. We shave off more cooking time by using chicken parts instead of a whole chicken.

- ½ cup fresh mint leaves
- ⅓ cup olive oil
- 6 garlic cloves, peeled
  Salt and pepper
- 1 tablespoon ground cumin
- 1 tablespoon smoked paprika
- 1 tablespoon dried oregano
- 2 teaspoons grated lime zest plus ¼ cup juice (2 limes)
- 1 teaspoon minced habanero chile
- 3 pounds bone-in chicken pieces (split breasts cut in half, drumsticks, and/or thighs), trimmed

1. Adjust oven rack to lowest position and heat oven to 450 degrees. Line rimmed baking sheet with aluminum foil. Process mint, oil, garlic, 1 tablespoon salt, 1 tablespoon pepper, cumin, paprika, oregano, lime zest and juice, and habanero in blender to smooth paste, about 30 seconds. Transfer spice paste to 1-gallon zipper-lock bag. Add chicken to bag, seal, and gently toss to coat chicken evenly with paste.

2. Arrange chicken skin side up on prepared sheet. Roast until well browned and breasts register 160 degrees and drumsticks/thighs register 175 degrees, about 25 minutes. Transfer to platter and let rest for 5 minutes. Serve.

TEST KITCHEN NOTE: For milder heat, substitute jalapeño for the habanero. Serve with lime wedges.

SWEET AND SPICY PORK TACOS Serves 4 to 6

✔ **WHY THIS RECIPE WORKS:** Country-style ribs usually require long cooking to tenderize; to speed up the process, we chop them into smaller pieces and simmer them in sauce.

- 1½ pounds boneless country-style pork ribs, trimmed and cut crosswise into ¼-inch-thick slices
  Salt and pepper
- 2 tablespoons vegetable oil
- 1 onion, chopped
- 4 garlic cloves, minced
- 1 teaspoon ground cumin
- 2 (8-ounce) cans pineapple rings, drained with ½ cup juice reserved, rings cut into ½-inch pieces
- 2 tablespoons minced canned chipotle chile in adobo sauce
- ½ cup chopped fresh cilantro
- 12 (6-inch) corn tortillas, warmed

1. Season pork with salt and pepper. Heat 1 tablespoon oil in 12-inch nonstick skillet over medium-high heat until just smoking. Add pork and cook until no longer pink, about 5 minutes. Transfer to plate.

2. Heat remaining 1 tablespoon oil in now-empty skillet over medium heat until shimmering. Add onion and cook until softened and beginning to brown, about 4 minutes. Add garlic and cumin and cook until fragrant, 30 seconds. Add pork and any accumulated juices, pineapple and reserved juice, and chipotle. Bring to simmer, cover, and cook, stirring occasionally, until pork is cooked through and sauce has thickened, about 10 minutes. Stir in cilantro, season with salt and pepper to taste, and serve with tortillas.

TEST KITCHEN NOTE: Serve with lime wedges.

SKILLET PENNE WITH CHICKPEAS AND CAULIFLOWER Serves 4

✔ **WHY THIS RECIPE WORKS:** Browning the cauliflower and onion deepens the flavor of the sauce, and chickpeas add substance in the absence of meat.

- 3 tablespoons extra-virgin olive oil
- ½ head cauliflower (1 pound), cored and cut into 1-inch pieces
- ½ cup thinly sliced onion
  Salt and pepper
- 5 garlic cloves, minced
- 2 teaspoons dried oregano
- 1 (28-ounce) can crushed tomatoes
- 2¼ cups chicken broth
- 1 (14-ounce) can chickpeas, rinsed
- 12 ounces (3¾ cups) penne

1. Heat oil in 12-inch nonstick skillet over medium-high heat until shimmering. Add cauliflower, onion, and ½ teaspoon salt and cook until vegetables are spotty brown, about 8 minutes. Add garlic and oregano and cook until fragrant, about 30 seconds.

2. Add tomatoes, broth, chickpeas, pasta, ½ teaspoon salt, and ¼ teaspoon pepper and stir to combine. Bring to simmer, reduce heat to medium, cover, and cook until pasta is al dente, 15 to 17 minutes. Serve.

TEST KITCHEN NOTE: Sprinkle with extra oil, fresh basil, and Parmesan cheese to serve.

FILETS MIGNONS WITH MUSHROOMS Serves 4

✔ **WHY THIS RECIPE WORKS:** Covering the mushrooms speeds up the cooking time.

- 4 (6- to 8-ounce) center-cut filets mignons, trimmed
  Salt and pepper
- 3 tablespoons vegetable oil
- 1 pound cremini mushrooms, trimmed and quartered
- 1 shallot, minced
- 2 garlic cloves, minced
- 1 teaspoon minced fresh thyme
- ½ cup Marsala
- 2 teaspoons Worcestershire sauce
- 2 teaspoons lemon juice

1. Pat steaks dry with paper towels and season with salt and pepper. Heat 2 tablespoons oil in 12-inch skillet over medium-high heat until just smoking. Add steaks and cook until well browned and meat registers 125 degrees, about 6 minutes per side. Transfer steaks to platter and tent loosely with aluminum foil.

2. Heat remaining 1 tablespoon oil in now-empty skillet over medium heat until shimmering. Add mushrooms, ¼ teaspoon salt, and ¼ teaspoon pepper, cover, and cook until mushrooms release their juice, about 5 minutes. Uncover, increase heat to medium-high, and cook until moisture has evaporated and mushrooms are brown, about 5 minutes. Add shallot, garlic, and thyme and cook until fragrant, about 1 minute.

3. Stir in Marsala and Worcestershire, scraping up any browned bits, and cook until reduced by half, 3 to 5 minutes. Add lemon juice and any accumulated meat juices from platter. Season with salt and pepper to taste. Spoon sauce over steaks and serve.

Maryland Crab Fluff

What is better than a tasty crab cake? How about a tasty, *deep-fried* crab cake? Introducing Maryland crab fluff, the best crab cakes you've never had. BY DIANE UNGER AND CAROLYNN PURPURA MACKAY

WHILE CRAB CAKES are special occasion fare for most of us (good crabmeat is expensive, after all), along the crab-rich Maryland coast, and especially in Baltimore, many crab houses and fry shacks serve a more blue-collar, and possibly even more delicious, version: crab fluff. Crab fluff are battered and deep-fried Maryland crab cakes that usually come in a plastic basket with fries, coleslaw, tartar sauce, and ketchup. Crispy fried crab cakes? Sign us up.

We hit our cookbook library and gathered recipes for crab fluff. Every version started with a basic crab cake: lump crab meat, seasonings that were heavy on the Old Bay, an egg or two, a little mayo, and a minimal amount of saltine crumbs. But the batters were very different, ranging from heavy, pancakelike batters based on milk and flour; to beer batters that were more like fried-fish batter; to light tempura batters made with flour, baking powder, and seltzer.

When we tasted the different versions side by side, we preferred the lightness of the crab fluff that was dipped in the tempura-like batter before frying. But there were problems: The recipes called for huge crab cakes that held a lot of batter, so they took a long time to cook and were a bit greasy. Also, trying to dip a soft crab cake into a thin batter proved a serious challenge, as the cakes fell apart and the batter dripped all over the counter on the way to the frying pot.

Our first fix, cutting the size of each crab cake in half, from ½ cup to ¼ cup (we used a dry measuring cup to portion the cakes before battering), was an easy one. This allowed the cakes to fry faster and "cleaner," with less grease absorption. To make them easier and less messy to put together, we started thinking about the elements of crab fluff—the crab cake and the batter—as a whole instead of two separate entities: It seemed a little crazy, but what if we mixed the batter (the flour, baking powder, and seltzer) right into the crab cake ingredients (the crabmeat, saltines, egg, mayo, and seasonings) instead of dipping the cakes into the batter? We could tell in our first test that this idea had promise—the "raw" fluff were now much easier and neater to transfer to the hot oil, and they were nicely cohesive when cooked—but they were a little gummy and heavy. We tried using lighter cornstarch in place of some of the flour, but that didn't change much. In the end, we cut the flour back from 1½ cups to ½ cup and upped the crushed saltines, going from six crackers to 10.

This recipe, which had shifted from classic crab fluff to something more like crab-fluff fritters, was almost there, but we weren't quite done. We found that the mixture held together best when it was cold; after testing various times, it turned out that refrigerating the mix for at least 30 minutes before we portioned and fried it worked best. Spraying the dry measuring cup used to portion the fluff with vegetable oil spray meant that they slid out cleanly and safely into the hot oil. To give the fluff more flavor, we added sliced scallions, a little Dijon, and a tablespoon of hot sauce.

Crab fluff might not be fancy fare in Maryland, but these crispy, briny, sweet, almost delicate little cakes are so delicious that they'd suit any occasion at our houses.

MARYLAND CRAB FLUFF Makes 12
You can buy jumbo lump crabmeat fresh or pasteurized; the latter is slightly cheaper. Our favorite pasteurized crabmeat is Phillips Premium Crab Jumbo. Serve fluff with cocktail or tartar sauce.

- 10 square or 11 round saltines, crushed fine
- ½ cup all-purpose flour
- 1½ teaspoons Old Bay seasoning
- ½ teaspoon baking powder
- ⅛ teaspoon cayenne pepper
- ½ cup seltzer
- 2 scallions, sliced thin
- 1 large egg plus 1 large yolk
- 2 tablespoons mayonnaise
- 1 tablespoon Dijon mustard
- 1 tablespoon hot sauce
- 1 pound jumbo lump crabmeat, picked over for shells and pressed dry between paper towels
- 2 quarts peanut or vegetable oil

1. Whisk crushed saltines, flour, Old Bay, baking powder, and cayenne together in large bowl. Whisk seltzer, scallions, egg and yolk, mayonnaise, mustard, and hot sauce into saltine mixture until combined. Gently fold crabmeat into batter until well combined. Cover and refrigerate for at least 30 minutes or up to 2 hours.

2. Set wire rack in rimmed baking sheet and line half of rack with triple layer of paper towels. Add oil to large Dutch oven until it measures about 1½ inches deep and heat over medium-high heat to 350 degrees.

3. Spray ¼-cup dry measure with vegetable oil spray. Place 6 packed scoops of crab mixture in hot oil, using spoon to help dislodge batter from dry measure. Adjust burner, if necessary, to maintain oil temperature between 325 and 350 degrees. Fry until deep golden brown and hot throughout, about 5 minutes. Transfer crab fluff to paper towel–lined side of rack and let drain for 1 minute, then move to unlined side of rack. Return oil to 350 degrees and repeat with remaining crab mixture. Serve.

Our version of crab fluff combines crab cakes and batter to make mini crab fritters.

TEST KITCHEN TECHNIQUE
Safe Portioning into Hot Oil

First chill the batter so it's not too loose. Next, coat a ¼-cup dry measure with vegetable oil spray, scoop the batter, and gently nudge each fluff into the oil with a spoon.

Skillet Roast Chicken and Potatoes

Sure, this dish can be a "toss and roast" affair—if you don't mind eating flabby-skinned chicken and greasy, undercooked potatoes. BY REBECCAH MARSTERS

ALTHOUGH ROAST CHICKEN with potatoes is a common recipe in cookbooks, lots of people improvise when making it, tossing potato chunks in a roasting pan, plopping a bird on top, and roasting. Their nonchalance is a mistake, as this approach often leads to greasy, unevenly cooked potatoes and chicken with flabby skin. I liked the convenience of cooking meat and potatoes in one pan and sought a dish that would be quick enough for a midweek supper and delicious enough for a special meal.

I knew that I'd need a fairly hot oven to get the chicken skin brown and crisp, so I set the dial to 400 degrees. This would also help with my weeknight time frame, cooking a 4-pound bird in about an hour. For a quick, easy meal I was determined to use my everyday skillet. But as soon as I started prepping potatoes, I saw the problem: Even a roomy 12-inch skillet couldn't hold enough potatoes to feed four people.

We usually cut potatoes into chunks for roasting, but the only way I was going to get 2 pounds of them into my pan was with more height—I needed bigger pieces. After peeling and cutting potatoes into wedges, slices, and chunks and fitting them together like jigsaw puzzle pieces, I finally managed to squeeze an entire 2 pounds of Yukon Gold potatoes (our favorite variety for roasting) in a nonstick skillet by cutting them into hefty 1-inch-thick rounds.

After tossing the potatoes with oil and nestling them in the skillet, I seasoned the chicken with salt and pepper, tied the legs together for even cooking, and set the skillet in the oven. An hour later, the bird was golden brown and juicy, but the potatoes were neither fully cooked nor quite brown enough. Since I was using a skillet, why not give them a 10-minute head start on the stovetop before placing the bird on top and moving everything to the oven? These finished spuds had a deep-brown, caramelized crust on the bottom.

But . . . they were still undercooked. As I pondered the problem, I spied the last chicken that I had cooked resting on the cutting board, waiting to be carved—we usually allow 20 minutes so that the juices can redistribute; the potatoes sat alongside the bird. Hmm. For my next test, while the chicken rested, I returned the skillet (covered to trap steam) with the potatoes to the oven. By the time the chicken was ready to be served, the potatoes were perfectly tender.

To perk up the flavor, smoked paprika and thyme were great additions. I stirred these together with salt, pepper, lemon zest, and olive oil and rubbed the mixture all over the raw chicken and under its skin. A squeeze of lemon before serving added a welcome bright note. Fast, easy, simple, and delicious: This recipe has it all.

ONE-PAN ROAST CHICKEN AND POTATOES Serves 4

Use uniform, medium potatoes.

- 3 tablespoons olive oil
- 2 teaspoons minced fresh thyme
- 1½ teaspoons smoked paprika
- 1½ teaspoons grated lemon zest, plus lemon wedges for serving
  Salt and pepper
- 1 (4-pound) whole chicken, giblets discarded
- 2 pounds Yukon Gold potatoes, peeled, ends squared off, and sliced into 1-inch-thick rounds

1. Adjust oven rack to lower-middle position and heat oven to 400 degrees. Combine 2 tablespoons oil, thyme, paprika, lemon zest, 1 teaspoon salt, and ½ teaspoon pepper in bowl. Pat chicken dry with paper towels and use your fingers or handle of wooden spoon to carefully separate skin from breast. Rub oil mixture all over chicken and underneath skin of breast. Tie legs together with kitchen twine and tuck wingtips behind back.

2. Toss potatoes with remaining 1 tablespoon oil, 1½ teaspoons salt, and ½ teaspoon pepper. Arrange potatoes, flat sides down, in single layer in 12-inch ovensafe nonstick skillet. Place skillet over medium heat and cook potatoes, without moving them, until brown on bottom, 7 to 9 minutes (do not flip).

3. Place chicken, breast side up, on top of potatoes and transfer skillet to oven. Roast until breast registers 160 degrees and thighs register 175 degrees, 1 to 1¼ hours. Transfer chicken to carving board, tent loosely with aluminum foil, and let rest for 20 minutes.

4. Meanwhile, cover skillet, return potatoes to oven, and roast until tender, about 20 minutes. Carve chicken and serve with potatoes and lemon wedges.

Cutting the potatoes into flat disks helps them brown and provides a flat surface for the chicken.

TEST KITCHEN TECHNIQUE **Keys to Potatoes That Are Tender and Brown**
Potatoes don't cook at the same rate as a chicken. Here's how we got the dish to work.

ON THE STOVE Brown one side of the potatoes on the stovetop. Then top the spuds with the chicken and roast.

IN THE OVEN Once the chicken is done, set it aside, cover the pan, and return it to the oven to finish cooking the potatoes.

Orange Kiss-Me Cake

Mix an entire orange into cake batter—pulp, rind, pith, and all? Could that possibly taste good? BY SARAH GABRIEL

IN 1950, ONE LILY WUEBEL took home $25,000 in the Pillsbury Bake-Off for her unusual grand prize–winning Orange Kiss-Me Cake. She stuck an entire orange—peel, pulp, and all—in the blender with raisins and walnuts and then mixed the fruity paste into a simple cake batter. More than 60 years after its triumph, Orange Kiss-Me Cake still struck me as a fresh and unique recipe—a definite must-try.

Following the original recipe, I squeezed ⅓ cup of juice from the orange for drizzling over the baked cake. I ground up the rest of the orange in the blender as prescribed. I put together the basic batter (flour, sugar, baking soda, milk, butter, and eggs) in a mixer, stirred in the orange paste, and scooped the mixture into a baking dish. Some 40 minutes later, I drizzled the hot baked cake with the squeezed juice and sprinkled it with cinnamon sugar and walnuts. Like many snack cakes, this one had a humble appearance, but the intensely orangey aroma had me standing over the cooling cake, shifting from one foot to the other with impatience.

When we tasted it, we were amazed that the orange peel, with all that usually bitter white pith attached, had produced such delicious results. We loved the marmalade-like flavor, while the moist fruit and ground-up nuts made the cake uncommonly tender. I concluded that while the recipe could benefit from some adjustments, on the whole, that Lily Wuebel knew what she was about. On my list to tweak: Temper the sweetness, curb a mild gumminess, and bump up the orange flavor of the finishing drizzle/sprinkle. Also, I hoped to streamline the method.

Reducing the amount of sugar in the batter brought both sweetness and gumminess under control. The drop in sugar made the cake slightly less tender, but I simply added extra ground walnuts and restored the texture. So far so good.

Next I took on the sugar-and-chopped-walnut topping. Cutting back on cinnamon and adding orange zest proved a modest improvement, but for real orange flavor, I took drastic action: I added a second orange. I used its juice to double the amount that I was drizzling on the warm cake, which did bolster the flavor but also made the cake soggy. For my next try, I cooked down the juice from both oranges, thus doubling the flavor without adding extra liquid. To intensify the flavor further, I added strips of zest to the simmering juice, and a little sugar transformed it from juice into syrup. Now the cake was moist, tender, and saturated with orange. If I could only simplify the process . . .

The original recipe called for grinding the fruit and nuts in the blender and then making the batter separately in a mixer. In addition, the topping required finely chopped walnuts—did I have to chop them by hand? To begin, I switched from the blender to the food processor, hoping that it could handle all the cake-making tasks. After a few tries, I figured out that the most efficient method was to coarsely grind the sugar and nuts for both batter and topping in the processor. I removed ⅓ cup and mixed it with the orange zest and cinnamon to make the topping. I then added the orange pulp and peel and the raisins to the processor, followed by softened butter, the eggs and milk, and, finally, the dry ingredients.

Go ahead—kiss the cook. Now Orange Kiss-Me Cake is as easy to put together as it is delicious.

ORANGE KISS-ME CAKE
Serves 10 to 12
To prevent overbrowning, use a glass or ceramic baking dish.

- 2 oranges
- 2 cups (10 ounces) all-purpose flour
- 1¼ teaspoons salt
- 1 teaspoon baking soda
- 1 cup (7 ounces) plus 2 tablespoons sugar
- ¾ cup walnuts, toasted
- ¼ teaspoon ground cinnamon
- 1 cup golden raisins
- 8 tablespoons unsalted butter, softened
- 1 cup milk
- 2 large eggs

1. Adjust oven rack to middle position and heat oven to 350 degrees. Spray 13 by 9-inch baking dish with vegetable oil spray. Grate ½ teaspoon zest from 1 orange into small bowl. Remove three 2-inch strips zest from same orange with vegetable peeler; set aside.

2. Halve zested orange and squeeze juice into liquid measuring cup. Discard spent halves. Halve and squeeze second orange into same measuring cup, removing any seeds (you should have about ⅔ cup juice total). Set aside spent second orange halves for cake batter.

3. Whisk flour, salt, and baking soda together in bowl. Pulse 1 cup sugar and walnuts in food processor until walnuts are coarsely ground, about 10 pulses. Transfer ⅓ cup walnut mixture to bowl with grated zest, add cinnamon, and stir to combine; set aside.

4. Add raisins and reserved spent orange halves to remaining walnut mixture in food processor and process until paste forms, about 30 seconds. Add butter and process until combined, about 10 seconds. Add milk and eggs and process until combined, about 10 seconds, scraping down sides of bowl as needed. Add flour mixture and pulse until just combined, about 5 pulses.

5. Pour batter into prepared dish and smooth top with rubber spatula. Bake until toothpick inserted in center comes out clean, 30 to 35 minutes, rotating dish halfway through baking.

6. Meanwhile, combine reserved orange zest strips, orange juice, and remaining 2 tablespoons sugar in small saucepan. Bring to strong simmer over medium heat, stirring occasionally, and cook until syrupy and reduced to ¼ cup, 8 to 12 minutes; discard zest strips.

7. Immediately after removing cake from oven, drizzle with orange syrup, spreading evenly with rubber spatula. Let cake sit for 5 minutes to absorb syrup, then sprinkle with walnut-zest mixture. Let cake cool completely in dish on wire rack, about 2 hours. Serve.

Thick-skinned oranges like navels give a strong marmalade-like flavor, while smaller, thinner-skinned varieties make a milder-tasting cake.

Introducing Goetta

Strange but true: This midwestern breakfast favorite combines oats and meat.
Also true? It's really good. BY DIANE UNGER

GOETTA IS A German American breakfast food—a rich and hearty combination of oats and meat—that's popular in Ohio (primarily Cincinnati), Indiana, and Kentucky. Pronounced "GET-ta," it's eaten alongside eggs (much like sausage) and often served with applesauce, maple syrup, or ketchup. Though goetta is traditionally made from offal and other leftovers from butchering, today pork and/or beef is simmered with steel-cut (never rolled) oats in a lot of water—as if cooking a meaty oatmeal. Once the mixture has thickened, it's poured into a loaf pan and chilled for several hours. Slices are pan-fried, forming a thick crust that contrasts delectably with their creamy interiors. This sounded like just the sort of delicious heritage dish worth making in my own kitchen, so I set out to come up with a recipe to suit today's cooks.

To orient myself, I ordered goetta from Glier's, the largest purveyor in Kentucky. I fried it and served it alongside slices prepared from the few recipes that I could locate in cookbooks, a version from a colleague's mom, and several submissions from readers. One reader sent her recipe with a bag of Dorsel's Pinhead Oat Meal, the product that goetta aficionados swear by. These recipes called for a range of meats, raw and cooked, from pork shoulder, ground pork, and leftover pork of any sort to ground beef and beef chuck. The seasonings—largely limited to bay leaves, salt, and pepper—were very plain.

My tasters and I sat down to a hearty goetta breakfast and concluded that while these samples were tasty, there was room for improvement. The texture wasn't uniformly moist, and the flavor needed amping up. Also, I hoped to figure out how to make goetta more quickly. I pasted together the successful parts from these recipes as a baseline and began again. First up: meat options.

We adored a recipe that called for pork shoulder and used its braising liquid to cook the oatmeal. Unfortunately, it took several hours just to cook the pork shoulder. And while meat oddments are authentic to goetta, I'm not so adventurous so early in the day. I decided to keep the recipe simple by using either ground beef or pork. As I was getting ready to test these, the idea of breakfast sausage meat popped into

The best *goetta* is pan-fried in hot oil to create a flavorful, browned crust.

my head, and I tried that, too. Among the three, the sausage proved a convenient shortcut to moist, more flavorful goetta. To bolster the flavor further, I

sautéed finely chopped onion with ground sage, fennel, and allspice. Once the onion was soft, I added the water, sausage, and oats and proceeded as before. Now the flavor was robust.

But the steel-cut oats needed an awful long time to soften, release their starch, and thicken into the porridge that would set into firm slices. To speed things along, I tried replacing the standard steel-cut oats with old-fashioned rolled oats (don't do it unless you like mush) and quick-cooking steel-cut oats. The latter gave me the right appealingly nubby texture in half of the time.

After the mixture chilled, I fried a few slices in oil until the crusts were dark brown. Just the way to "goetta" great start to the day.

KEY INGREDIENT
Quick-Cooking Steel-Cut Oats
Regular steel-cut oats take too long to cook. Old-fashioned or rolled oats turn *goetta* to mush. Quick-cooking steel-cut oats are just right.

NO SUBSTITUTIONS

GOETTA Serves 6 to 8

Quick-cooking steel-cut oats (aka pinhead oats) are essential; don't substitute rolled oats. Chill *Goetta* for at least 3 hours before you slice it. Serve with eggs. Goetta is a great make-ahead dish: fry as much as you want, saving the rest for another day.

- 1 tablespoon unsalted butter
- 1 onion, chopped fine
- 1½ teaspoons ground sage
- 1 teaspoon ground fennel
- ¼ teaspoon ground allspice
- 1 pound bulk breakfast sausage
- 1¾ cups quick-cooking steel-cut oats
  Salt and pepper
- 2 tablespoons vegetable oil, plus extra as needed

1. Grease 8½ by 4½-inch nonstick loaf pan. Melt butter in Dutch oven over medium-high heat. Add onion and cook until lightly browned, about 5 minutes. Stir in sage, fennel, and allspice and cook until fragrant, about 30 seconds. Add 4¼ cups water and sausage and mash with potato masher until water and sausage are fully combined. Bring to boil and stir in oats. Cover, reduce heat to low, and simmer gently, stirring occasionally, for 15 minutes.

2. Uncover and maintain gentle simmer, stirring frequently, until mixture is very thick and rubber spatula dragged across bottom of pot leaves trail for about 3 seconds, 15 to 18 minutes. Season with salt and pepper to taste.

3. Transfer mixture to prepared pan. Smooth top and tap firmly on counter. Let cool completely, then cover with plastic wrap and refrigerate until fully chilled and firm, at least 3 hours or up to 2 days.

4. Run thin knife around edges of goetta, then briefly set bottom of pan in hot water to loosen goetta from pan. Turn out goetta onto cutting board. Cut desired number of ½-inch-thick slices from loaf. Heat oil in 12-inch nonstick skillet over medium heat until shimmering. Add up to 4 slices of goetta and cook until well browned, about 5 minutes per side. Transfer to wire rack and let drain. Repeat as needed. Serve. (Wrap any remaining goetta in plastic wrap and refrigerate for up to 3 days, or slice, wrap, and freeze for up to 1 month. To cook from frozen, reduce heat to medium-low and increase cooking time to 7 to 9 minutes per side.)

O'Brien Potatoes

Whether for breakfast, lunch, or dinner, we wanted these potatoes nicely browned and flavorful. BY CHRISTIE MORRISON

A CCORDING TO JAMES BEARD, O'Brien potatoes is "a turn-of-the-century dish that originated in Jack's, a great restaurant on Sixth Avenue in New York, where every celebrity in the theatre and sporting world ate when after-theatre suppers were still fashionable." Since then, this side dish has been appropriated by greasy spoons and frozen foods companies as a variation on breakfast potatoes, falling somewhere between hash browns and home fries on the spud spectrum. We're happy to eat O'Brien potatoes at any time of day—assuming they're made well.

The constants in the dish, I discovered, are potatoes, onion, and bell peppers. Beyond that, most recipes call for precooking the potatoes before chunking or slicing and then sautéing, while a few call for adding cream or cheese and are baked as casseroles. I cooked through some recipes, but the results were underwhelming: The pan-fried potatoes were starchy, less-crispy versions of home fries. The casseroles were dry and bland with muddied flavors. The best of the lot called for sautéing the raw potato pieces with the vegetables before adding water and braising on the stovetop. These potatoes were glazy with the reduced cooking liquid, had multimeal appeal, and required no precooking. I had my starting point.

I gathered 1½ pounds each of russets, Yukon Golds, and red potatoes. I peeled the russets and Yukons but not the red potatoes, because they have thin, tender skins. I cut the potatoes into ½-inch cubes, which I sautéed with a small diced onion and ½ cup each of finely chopped red and green bell pepper (I'd revisit these proportions later). When the onion and peppers were tender, I added a little water to the skillet, covered it, and cooked until the potatoes were tender, too. Then I removed the lid to let the water evaporate. The verdict? Tasters preferred the waxy firmness of the red potatoes—and I liked that I didn't have to peel them. But none of the potatoes had developed any browning, which limited the flavor.

I looked at the recipe again. Sautéing the vegetables at the beginning of cooking seemed unnecessary with 10 minutes of braising to follow. Would the sautéing time be better spent at the end of cooking, after the liquid had evaporated?

These flavorful spuds work equally well next to scrambled eggs or a steak.

I heated a little oil in the skillet, tossed in the potatoes and other vegetables, added the water, and covered the pan. When I removed the lid, I cooked everything for twice as long. The liquid evaporated after 5 minutes, leaving the oil behind. In another 5-plus minutes, the potatoes and vegetables were nicely browned.

Time to focus on the woeful lack of flavor. My finely chopped vegetables had cooked away to bland mush. How could I keep the flavor fresh after 20 minutes of cooking? I started by increasing the amount of each—a bigger onion and whole green and red bell peppers. To help them stand up to the heat, I cut the peppers into larger pieces, giving them a stronger presence in the dish and more

staying power during cooking. Now the dish was colorful and evenly browned.

But using more vegetables hadn't given the dish more depth of flavor. Replacing the water with chicken broth was an easy, though partial, fix. In the test kitchen, we often turn to *umami*-rich ingredients to add depth. After trying a few candidates, I landed on pungent, tangy Worcestershire sauce and was finally pleased with the dish's full flavor. A last sprinkling of sliced scallions gave the dish a fresh crunch.

Back in the day, O'Brien potatoes had to impress the celebrities at Jack's. The test kitchen cooks are a tougher crowd. Still, they declared my O'Brien Potatoes a rousing success—and as fit for dinner as for breakfast.

O'BRIEN POTATOES Serves 4

Use waxy red potatoes, which will hold their shape better than other varieties.

- 2 tablespoons vegetable oil
- 1½ pounds red potatoes, unpeeled, cut into ½-inch pieces
- 1 green bell pepper, stemmed, seeded, and cut into ½-inch pieces
- 1 red bell pepper, stemmed, seeded, and cut into ½-inch pieces
- 1 onion, chopped
- ½ cup chicken broth
- 2 teaspoons Worcestershire sauce
  Salt and pepper
- 4 scallions, sliced thin

1. Heat oil in 12-inch nonstick skillet over medium heat until shimmering. Add potatoes, bell peppers, and onion and stir to coat with oil. Stir in broth, Worcestershire, and 1½ teaspoons salt. Cover and cook until potatoes are tender, stirring occasionally, about 15 minutes.

2. Uncover and increase heat to medium-high. Cook, stirring occasionally, until liquid has evaporated and potatoes and bell peppers are spotty brown, about 12 minutes. Season with salt and pepper to taste. Stir in scallions. Serve.

TEST KITCHEN TECHNIQUE
Braise Before Browning
First, we cover the potatoes and simmer them in chicken broth so they can pick up flavor as they soften. Then we uncover the pan to let the broth evaporate and the vegetables brown for deeper flavor.

BRAISE
Cook the potatoes in flavorful broth so they soften before they're browned at the end.

Illustration: Lauren Pettapiece

Pizza Monkey Bread

As a fresh twist on sweet monkey bread, this pizza-flavored version is a knockout concept. Too bad most of the recipes we tried failed to execute it well. BY SARAH GABRIEL

L IKE THE MORE typical sweet monkey bread, pizza monkey bread is knobs of dough baked in a Bundt pan to form a golden-brown ring that you pull apart and eat with your fingers. But instead of being tossed in cinnamon sugar, the knobs are stuffed with salty, gooey pepperoni pizza fixings to form a crunchy-chewy snack. Combining the salty-spicy appeal of pepperoni pizza with something that looks really neat and is fun to pick apart with your fingers sounded to me like the ultimate snack food.

Pizza monkey bread, it turns out, is an Internet sensation. After days of trying to get a handle on the more than 2.6 million search results, plus cookbook versions, I had identified the major variables and had a lineup of recipes to test. While we didn't find any superstars in the first round, we learned a few things: Store-bought pizza dough had better flavor and texture than more widely used store-bought biscuit dough; punchy Parmesan gave melty mozzarella a welcome flavor boost; and we loved the pepperoni but not the grease that dripped down our chins when we bit into the bread. As for the sauce, it was better served alongside for dipping than baked into the pieces of dough (which made the bread sodden).

These initial tests also gave me a few procedural leads: For instance, two short rising periods were a boon to texture, and brushing the outside of each dough ball with oil made the pieces easier to pull apart once baked. I found that the easiest batches to assemble were the least satisfying, while the ones with the crispiest crusts and best molten cheesy pockets included a painstaking process of individually rolling out, stuffing, and pinching closed about two dozen knobs of dough. For pizza monkey bread to live up to its reputation in the blogosphere as the best thing to happen to pizza since delivery, it would need to be not only delicious but also doable.

I cobbled together a recipe using what I'd learned, grabbed a stack of Bundt pans, and headed back into the kitchen. First, I tried taking a cue from ravioli: I rolled out two balls of store-bought pizza dough into large rectangles, arranged small piles of filling (shredded mozzarella, grated Parmesan, sliced pepperoni, and dried oregano) between the two sheets of dough, pressed to seal around each pile, and then cut between the piles.

With pepperoni and melted cheese embedded in the dough, this fun-to-eat bubble bread isn't monkeying around.

No dice. Unlike ravioli dough, pizza dough either came apart at the seams or the filling poked through its thin walls. I could roll out the dough thicker, but then I'd have too few bundles.

Undeterred, I rolled out the dough balls into two large rectangles again, but this time I had cinnamon roll construction in mind. After the dough rectangles had rested briefly, I arranged the cheese, pepperoni, and oregano in a line near the long edge of each rectangle. I rolled up each rectangle to form a log, pinched the long seams and ends, and then cut each log in half. I continued cutting and pinching until I had cut each log into 12 pieces. Some of the cheese had escaped or gotten stuck in the seams when I pinched the ends closed, but this method was definitely simpler and seemed promising. I brushed the pan with olive oil, laid a layer of dough

pockets in the pan, brushed them with oil, and continued layering and brushing until I had used all the pieces. I let the bread rise for about 30 minutes. Then I baked it at 400 degrees until it was well browned. After turning it out, I saw that some cheese had leaked out, but otherwise the cheese was pleasantly gooey. The pepperoni was still greasy, but a colleague reminded me of a quick fix that we've used before: Microwave the

The American Table
March of the Munchies

Today it would be considered rude to invite friends over without providing munchies. Just over a century ago, though, our sense of propriety called for the reverse: In the Victorian era, snacking was considered filthy, vulgar, and low-class. Meals were to be eaten at the table, with the family, and at fixed times. Dinner was equated with the sanctity of the home. "It is to be deplored that eating on railway trains cannot be forbidden," etiquette expert Margaret Sangster wrote in *Harper's Bazar* in 1898. "Why a man should . . . deem it absolutely necessary to . . . disgust his fellow passengers by the munching of oranges, peanuts, bananas, and peppermint candy is one of the things that is past finding out."

The transformation of snacking into a "clean, innocent, even quaintly domestic" habit was largely accomplished through good PR, Abigail Carroll writes in *Three Squares: The Invention of the American Meal*. Food manufacturers managed the turnabout through packaging and branding. Peanuts, for instance, were originally sold in their shells, making them loud and messy to eat (the disparaging phrase "peanut gallery" referred to the cheap balcony seats where vaudeville fans noshed). In 1906, the founding of the Planters company marked the start of the nut's rehabilitation. Planters made peanuts neat, clean, and quiet by selling them preshelled and in bags. A decade later, the company's new mascot—a dapper peanut sporting white gloves, top hat, and monocle—suggested that peanuts weren't merely hygienic: They were glamorous.

Manufacturers also reached into American homes. Pretzels went from the bar to the bridge game to the kitchen, cozying up with Jell-O for pretzel salad, while potato chips gave crunch to home-baked cookies. By promulgating such recipes in magazines and advertisements, manufacturers made snacking acceptable and innocuous, Carroll explains. Slowly but surely, we became the nation of casual snackers that we are today.

pepperoni to render the grease and then drain it. It worked. Now I just had to devise a method to contain the cheese.

Shredded cheese spilled out when I cut the filled dough, so I tried cutting the cheese into batons. After rolling out the dough, I lined up the pepperoni, laid the batons end to end, and sprinkled the grated Parmesan alongside. This time the cheese stayed put. But a colleague who'd been watching me thought all that cheese-cutting looked needlessly fussy. "Try string cheese," she suggested. "It comes precut and is made from mozzarella." I dashed off to the store—and streamlined my recipe.

Back in the kitchen, while I was microwaving the pepperoni, I had another thought: Why not enlist the rendered pepperoni oil in place of some of the olive oil that I was using to brush the dough? I gave it a try. While the bread was baking, I put together a quick tomato sauce and enjoyed the even more potent pepperoni pizza aroma that filled the kitchen. When I turned the bread out, we found that the pepperoni oil had given the crust a gorgeously bronze hue. We pinched off pieces and dipped them in sauce. Judging by the flurry of hands reaching for seconds, this recipe was living up to the legend.

PIZZA MONKEY BREAD Serves 6 to 8

You will need all-purpose flour for dusting the counter. If the dough becomes slack or difficult to work with, refrigerate it for 10 minutes. Seal the open ends of the filled dough after each cut in order to keep the filling from leaking out. If your string cheese sticks are longer than 4½ inches, trim any overhang once you've placed the cheese on the dough.

MONKEY BREAD

- 2 (1-pound) balls pizza dough
- 4 ounces sliced pepperoni
- 3 tablespoons extra-virgin olive oil
- 1½ ounces Parmesan cheese, grated (¾ cup)
- ½ teaspoon dried oregano
- 8 (4½-inch) sticks mozzarella string cheese

TOMATO SAUCE

- 2 tablespoons extra-virgin olive oil
- 4 garlic cloves, minced
- 1 (28-ounce) can crushed tomatoes
- ½ teaspoon dried oregano
- ½ teaspoon salt
- ½ teaspoon pepper

1. FOR THE MONKEY BREAD: Line baking sheet with parchment paper and sprinkle with flour. Roll each dough ball into 10 by 6-inch rectangle on lightly floured counter, then transfer to prepared sheet. Cover with plastic wrap and let sit for 15 minutes.

2. Microwave pepperoni in bowl until fat is rendered, 60 to 90 seconds, stirring halfway through microwaving. Using tongs, transfer pepperoni to paper towel–lined plate, reserving pepperoni oil in bowl (you should have about 1 tablespoon). Pat pepperoni dry with paper towels. Stir olive oil into pepperoni oil. Brush 12-cup nonstick Bundt pan with 2 teaspoons oil mixture. Combine Parmesan and oregano in separate bowl.

3. Working with 1 dough rectangle at a time, return to lightly floured counter and roll into 18 by 9-inch rectangle with long edge parallel to counter edge, stretching corners as needed to make neat rectangle. Starting 2 inches from

long edge of dough nearest you, shingle half of pepperoni parallel to long edge. Lay 4 mozzarella sticks end to end on top of pepperoni. Sprinkle half of Parmesan mixture alongside mozzarella. Fold bottom 2-inch section of dough over filling and roll tightly toward opposite edge. Pinch seam and ends to seal. Repeat with remaining dough rectangle, remaining pepperoni, remaining 4 mozzarella sticks, and remaining Parmesan mixture.

4. Cut each log in half and pinch open ends to seal. Cut each log in half again, pinching open ends to seal. Cut each log into thirds, pinching open ends closed as you go. Place single layer of stuffed dough balls (about 6) ½ inch apart in prepared pan and brush tops and sides with one-fourth of oil mixture. Layer remaining dough balls in pan, brushing tops and sides with remaining oil mixture as you go. Cover pan with plastic and let rise at room temperature until slightly puffed, about 30 minutes. Adjust oven rack to lower-middle position and heat oven to 400 degrees.

5. FOR THE TOMATO SAUCE: Meanwhile, heat oil in small saucepan over medium heat until shimmering. Add garlic and cook until beginning to brown, about 90 seconds. Add tomatoes, oregano, salt, and pepper and bring to boil. Reduce heat to medium-low and simmer until slightly thickened, about 10 minutes. Remove from heat, cover, and set aside.

6. Bake until well browned, about 40 minutes, rotating pan halfway through baking. Transfer pan to wire rack and let cool for 10 minutes. Place serving platter on top of pan and invert. Let cool 10 minutes longer. Reheat sauce and transfer to serving bowl. Serve monkey bread with sauce.

TO MAKE AHEAD

Monkey bread can be assembled, covered with plastic wrap, and refrigerated for up to 24 hours. Let sit on counter for 20 minutes before baking, increasing time by 5 to 10 minutes.

STEP BY STEP **Constructing Pizza Monkey Bread**

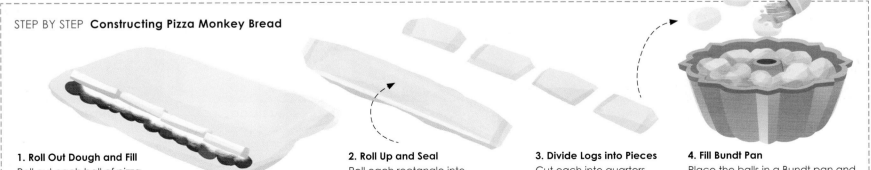

1. Roll Out Dough and Fill
Roll out each ball of pizza dough into a rectangle. Arrange pepperoni slices, mozzarella sticks, and seasoned Parmesan on dough.

2. Roll Up and Seal
Roll each rectangle into a log and pinch to seal the seam and ends.

3. Divide Logs into Pieces
Cut each into quarters, and quarters into thirds, for a total of 12 pieces. Seal open ends as you go.

4. Fill Bundt Pan
Place the balls in a Bundt pan and brush them with pepperoni oil for extra flavor and to make it easier to pull apart the baked bread.

Cooking Class Baking Whitefish Fillets

If cooking delicate whitefish fillets intimidates you, you're in good company. But armed with our foolproof baking method and some basic facts, you can make moist, flaky, flavorful fish like a pro. BY REBECCAH MARSTERS

All About Whitefish

Get It Straight
Whitefish is a marketing/fisheries term that encompasses many species of deepwater saltwater fish, all of which are mild-flavored and white-fleshed. It's a big group (sometimes lumped together as scrod) that includes cod, flounder, grouper, haddock, hake, halibut, pollock, sole, and many others. The term whitefish is often used to differentiate these species from oily fish, a designation that includes meatier, moister fish such as salmon, swordfish, and tuna. Confusingly, the word whitefish is used for a second and entirely different sort of fish (that we're *not* referring to on this page). That whitefish is freshwater fish that is often smoked, used for whitefish salad, and sold at Jewish delis.

Substitutions Are Fine
Are all whitefish created equal? In our baked fish recipe, we say that cod, halibut, and haddock can be used interchangeably (the thickness and weight must be the same), but the three do have different textures. Here's a quick rundown of some of the whitefish you may see at the market and how to prepare them: Flounder and sole are delicate and flaky and best sautéed; cod, haddock, and sea bass are medium-flaky and take to sautéing, baking, braising, or poaching; and grouper, halibut, and monkfish are firm and meaty and can handle any type of cooking.

SHOPPING The Right Address
It goes without saying that freshness and quality are paramount with seafood. With whole fish, you can check for bright eyes and gills and an overall shine. It's harder to know if fillets are fresh, so investigate your surroundings for clues. It's mostly common sense: The store should be clean, with a clean ocean scent; if it smells fishy or like ammonia, shop elsewhere. Whole fish should rest on lots of ice, not be sitting in puddles, while fillets should not be displayed directly on ice, as it could "burn" them. Rather, the fish should sit on a stainless-steel tray on top of the ice.

Fresh versus Frozen
Even if they look fresh, the fillets you buy at the store may have been previously frozen. That's not necessarily a bad thing. Fish that's flash-frozen at sea immediately after it's caught and then stored and thawed properly may actually be fresher than a never-frozen fillet that's been sitting around. By federal regulation, the store must label previously frozen seafood. In either case, look for fillets that appear moist and that aren't flaking into segments. And don't be afraid to ask at the fish counter which fish is the freshest.

Core Techniques

TEST KITCHEN TIPS FOR ANY WHITE-FISH FILLET RECIPE

Even Them Out
Fish fillets rarely come in perfect even pieces. Instead, each fillet may have a thick part and a thin one. To prevent the thin sections from overcooking before the thick sections are cooked through, we recommend folding the thin pieces under, thereby doubling the thickness and insulating them from drying out.

Add Fat
Whitefish is much leaner than oily fish. That's why many recipes call for adding fat in the form of butter, oil, bacon and/or bacon fat, or—as we do here—egg yolk–enriched mayonnaise.

Cook Gently
Without the natural oils and fats to protect them like those found in, say, salmon or mackerel,

leaner whitefish fillets are very easy to overcook. Avoid drying out your fillets by baking them gently and slowly. Our recipe calls for baking the fish for 30 to 40 minutes at a low 300 degrees.

Use a Thermometer
Skip the paring knife, which some cooks use to gauge when fillets are ready. (They make a cut in the middle of the fillets and peek inside. When the fish begins to flake yet is still juicy and it changes from translucent to just barely opaque, it's done.) For a far more exact and foolproof way to prevent overcooking, use your instant-read thermometer. Whitefish fillets are ready when they register 135 degrees at the thickest part.

STEP BY STEP Perfect Baked Fish

1. PREPARE RACK
Set a wire rack in a rimmed baking sheet and spray it with vegetable oil spray.
WHY? Elevating the fish prevents the fillets from stewing in their own juices on a baking sheet; spraying with oil keeps the delicate fish from sticking once it's cooked.

2. SAUTÉ AROMATICS
Soften the shallot, garlic, and thyme in butter on the stovetop.
WHY? Lots of flavor and rich butter help make mild whitefish sweet and flavorful.

3. BROWN PANKO
Add panko bread crumbs to the skillet and toast.
WHY? We use panko for good crunch. They won't brown in the oven because the temperature is too low, so we sauté them first, guaranteeing color and even more crunch.

4. LET CRUMBS COOL
Place the seasoned crumbs in a shallow dish and let them cool.
WHY? A shallow dish like a pie plate will make it easier to dredge the fish, and as the crumbs cool, they'll dry out slightly and get even crunchier.

5. MAKE BINDER
Combine mayonnaise, an egg yolk, lemon zest, and pepper in a bowl.
WHY? The bread crumbs need help sticking to the fish; the mayo and egg yolk act as glue and add richness, while the lemon and pepper add brightness.

CLASSIC BAKED FISH Serves 4

Haddock or halibut fillets are good alternatives to cod.

- 3 tablespoons unsalted butter
- 1 large shallot, minced
  Salt and pepper
- 1 garlic clove, minced
- 1 teaspoon minced fresh thyme
- ¾ cup panko bread crumbs
- 2 tablespoons minced fresh parsley
- 2 tablespoons mayonnaise
- 1 large egg yolk
- ½ teaspoon grated lemon zest
- 4 (6- to 8-ounce) skinless cod fillets, 1 to 1½ inches thick

1. Adjust oven rack to middle position and heat oven to 300 degrees. Set wire rack in rimmed baking sheet and spray with vegetable oil spray.

2. Melt butter in 12-inch skillet over medium heat. Add shallot and ½ teaspoon salt and cook until softened, about 3 minutes. Add garlic and thyme and cook until fragrant, about 30 seconds. Add panko and ¼ teaspoon pepper and cook, stirring frequently, until evenly browned, 5 to 7 minutes. Remove from heat and stir in parsley. Transfer panko mixture to shallow dish and let cool for 10 minutes.

3. Whisk mayonnaise, egg yolk, lemon zest, and ¼ teaspoon pepper together in bowl. Pat fillets dry with paper towels and season with salt and pepper. Brush tops of fillets evenly with mayonnaise mixture. Working with 1 fillet at a time, dredge coated side in panko mixture, pressing gently to adhere, and place crumb side up on prepared wire rack. Bake until centers are just opaque and fillets register 135 degrees, 30 to 40 minutes, rotating sheet halfway through baking. Serve.

Q&A

Just what *is* panko anyway?
Panko, a Japanese-style bread crumb that has gained great popularity in the United States in the past decade, has larger and fluffier crumbs than standard Western-style bread crumbs, hence greater crunch. It's made from loaves that are cooked by electric current. When we're using traditional bread crumbs, we always make them ourselves. But we like commercial panko a lot and often call for it. To see the results of our bread-crumb testing, go to CooksCountry.com/breadcrumbs.

Can I buy fish ahead of time?
We recommend cooking fish on the day you buy it. If you can't, unwrap it, pat it dry, and put it in a zipper-lock bag, pressing out the air. Set the package on a bed of ice or over a few reusable ice packs and place it in the back of the refrigerator, where it's coldest. Stored this way, the fish will keep one day longer.

THE BEST WAY TO STORE FISH
In plastic, on ice, in the back of the fridge.

6. DRY FISH
Pat the fillets dry with paper towels.
WHY? If the fillets are wet, the mayonnaise mixture won't adhere as well.

7. SEASON BIT BY BIT
Season the fillets with plenty of salt and pepper.
WHY? Mild whitefish needs plenty of seasoning. You've already seasoned the mayonnaise and the panko separately.

8. COAT FISH
Brush the tops of the fillets evenly with the mayo mixture and press them into the bread crumbs.
WHY? The mayonnaise helps the crumbs adhere. Don't bother coating the bottom of the fish, as those crumbs would just get soggy as the fish bakes.

9. BAKE FISH
Place the coated fillets on the wire rack that you've prepared and put them in a 300-degree oven.
WHY? A low oven cooks the fish gently, resulting in a greater margin of error, thus less chance of overcooking the fish.

10. TEMP FISH
Use a thermometer to take the temperature of the fillets after about 30 minutes; they're done when they are 135 degrees at the thickest part.
WHY? A thermometer is the best way to ensure that your fish doesn't overcook.

Slow Cooker Chicken Mulligatawny Soup

We set out to strip away complicated steps in this classic recipe without sacrificing complexity of flavor.

BY SARAH GABRIEL

MULLIGATAWNY SOUP, AN India-derived soup that returning British colonialists introduced to England, comes in several forms. It can be brothy or creamy, chunky or relatively smooth. There may be lentils, coconut flakes, or vegetables like potatoes, peppers, carrots, or tomatoes. It may contain meat from chicken to lamb—or no meat at all. While mulligatawny can be something of a shape-shifter, it's always recognizable thanks to the warming, spicy fragrance that it owes to combinations of curry powder, cumin, garam masala, coriander, ginger, and garlic. Mulligatawny soup seemed like the perfect thing to build in the slow cooker and come home to after a chilly day of errands.

To get my bearings, I made a favorite test kitchen recipe for chicken mulligatawny on the stovetop. I sautéed onions with flaked coconut and then added tomato paste, garlic, ginger, spices, flour (to thicken), carrots, celery, chicken broth, and bone-in split chicken breasts. Once the chicken was cooked, I let it cool and then shredded it. Meanwhile, I pureed the soup in a blender, returned it to the pot, added some lentils, simmered until the lentils were tender, and finally stirred in the shredded chicken. The soup was rich, smooth, and perfectly spicy, but I hoped to take a more hands-off approach with the slow cooker by eliminating the pureeing and skipping the into-the-pot, out-of-the-pot, back-into-the-pot rigmarole with the chicken.

For my first attempt at moving mulligatawny to the slow cooker, I kept a

We like to serve this flavorful soup with cilantro leaves, yogurt, and lime wedges.

stovetop step in order to sauté the base veggies and flaked coconut, bloom the spices, and cook the tomato paste and flour. After whisking in the broth and simmering to thicken it slightly, I emptied the pot into the slow cooker and added lentils and cut-up boneless, skinless chicken breasts. The results were mixed. The soup was very thin (the slow cooker doesn't allow for evaporation/concentration); my tasters didn't care for the bits of flaked coconut; and the cut-up chicken breasts, while easier to deal with than bone-in meat, were dry and tough. But we didn't mind the small chunks of onion, celery, and carrot, and the flavor was pretty good. I would have to make some adjustments to give the soup more body, find a way to get around the bits of coconut, and cook the chicken properly.

After fiddling with the amounts of chicken broth and flour, I found that decreasing the broth and upping the flour gave me the slightly velvety consistency I wanted. Trading the chicken breasts for boneless, skinless thighs cut into chunks led to properly cooked meat

in about 4½ hours without any fuss. I was on a roll. Next I tried to fix the problem of the coconut fragments by just omitting the flaked coconut altogether. With the now-thicker base and tender chunks of vegetables and chicken, my tasters and I found the soup much more pleasant, but we had to admit that the missing coconut left the spices without the sweet, nutty foil that made the stovetop version of mulligatawny so satisfying. What about coconut milk? It's smooth and might be able to provide the flavor that we were missing without forcing us to return to the blender for what I wanted to be a low-stress recipe.

I sautéed the aromatics, spices, and tomato paste for another batch, cooked the flour, and whisked in the broth. This time I subtracted 1¾ cups of broth and added a can of coconut milk to the thickened broth mixture and chicken in the slow cooker. When the soup was done, I put out some yogurt, cilantro, and lime wedges for garnishing and called over my tasters. Success. The flavor was full, complex, and, truth be told, amazingly delicious, but the recipe

was simple. "I would never guess this came from the slow cooker," one taster said as she slurped the last drop of soup. "It doesn't *taste* easy to make."

SLOW-COOKER CHICKEN MULLIGATAWNY SOUP Serves 8

Cut the carrots into ½-inch pieces or they won't cook through. If the carrots are more than ½ inch in diameter, halve or quarter them lengthwise.

- 3 tablespoons unsalted butter
- 2 onions, chopped
- 4 carrots, peeled and cut into ½-inch pieces
- 1 celery rib, minced
- 1½ tablespoons grated fresh ginger
- 4 garlic cloves, minced
- 1 tablespoon tomato paste
- 1 tablespoon curry powder
- 2 teaspoons garam masala
  Salt and pepper
- ¼ teaspoon cayenne pepper
- ⅓ cup all-purpose flour
- 5 cups chicken broth
- 1½ pounds boneless, skinless chicken thighs, trimmed and cut into 1½-inch pieces
- 1 (13.5-ounce) can coconut milk
- ½ cup brown lentils, picked over and rinsed
  Plain yogurt
  Chopped fresh cilantro leaves
  Lime wedges

1. Melt butter in large saucepan over medium heat. Add onions, carrots, and celery and cook until onions are softened and just beginning to brown, 10 to 14 minutes. Add ginger, garlic, tomato paste, curry powder, garam masala, 1 teaspoon salt, and cayenne and cook until fragrant, about 30 seconds. Stir in flour and cook for 1 minute. Slowly whisk in broth, scraping up any browned bits. Bring to boil, reduce heat to medium-low, and simmer until thickened, about 5 minutes. Transfer to slow cooker. Stir in chicken, coconut milk, and lentils.

2. Cover and cook until chicken and lentils are tender, 4 to 5 hours on low. Let sit, uncovered, for 5 minutes. Using large spoon, skim fat from surface of soup. Season soup with salt and pepper to taste. Ladle into serving bowls. Garnish with yogurt and cilantro. Serve with lime wedges.

Cooking for Two Salisbury Steak

We ejected one convenience product but discovered another that helped us resuscitate this old favorite.

BY REBECCAH MARSTERS

A MOIST BURGER with a nice seared crust topped with rich mushroom gravy sounds pretty good, right? The dish I just described is Salisbury steak. This misnomer (it's not a steak at all) just might be the reason that it has been relegated to TV dinners and cafeteria lunches. I wanted a recipe for Salisbury steak for two that didn't involve reaching into the freezer—or crashing the line at the local elementary school.

▶ Which beef broth should you buy? Visit CooksCountry.com/beefbroth to see our taste test.

I started by making a few standard Salisbury steak recipes, scaling down the portions to two servings. The good news was that the recipes were easy—most involved just shaping ground beef into ovals, pan-frying the patties, and serving them with a quick gravy. The bad news? They were all pretty unappetizing, even for cafeteria food. The meat was dry and tough, and most of the "gravies" were salty and goopy—not surprising, considering that they featured canned condensed soup.

My first step was to fix the texture of the meat. Here in the test kitchen we know that a panade helps keep ground meat moist and tender. It's usually a mixture of bread crumbs and milk, and it interrupts the protein structure of the ground meat, preventing it from toughening as it cooks. We use a panade in

meatloaf and meatballs, so why not in Salisbury steak? I soon discovered why not: A traditional panade made my Salisbury steak taste just like meatloaf. The solution came in the form of a side dish. One old recipe called for adding mashed potatoes to the meat mixture, and when I did the same, they acted just like a panade, but their flavor disappeared into the background. To make my fix even more convenient, I substituted instant potato flakes and milk for the mashed potatoes, and no one was the wiser.

Moving on to the sauce, naturally I wanted the mushroom gravy to be silky and flavorful. After cooking the patties in a 10-inch skillet (which was just the right size for two portions), I melted butter and browned sliced mushrooms and onion. I sprinkled in flour, added beef broth, and simmered the mixture until it thickened. Served with the steaks, it was decent enough— already better than canned soup—but it lacked depth and true beefiness.

Meat gravies from roasts are built from the drippings rendered while the

meat cooks, but my quick-cooking patties didn't render much fat. What if I cooked the "steaks" right in the sauce? For my next test, I browned the patties as before but didn't cook them all the way through. I made the gravy and then returned the patties to the pan, letting them finish cooking in the simmering sauce. The gravy was beefy and savory, and as a bonus, the meat was even more moist and tender than before—not to mention flavorful. To round out the gravy, I added a dollop of tomato paste, a supersavory ingredient that enhances meaty flavor, and I finished it off with a couple of tablespoons of ruby port— this was no lunchroom Salisbury steak, after all.

To unify and enrich the flavors of each, we finish cooking the patties right in the gravy.

KEY INGREDIENT Potato Flakes

Most Salisbury steak (and meatloaf) recipes employ a panade, a paste of milk and bread or crackers that helps keep the meat moist when it's cooked beyond medium. But a traditional panade made our Salisbury steak taste like meatloaf. We replaced the panade with 3 tablespoons of instant potato flakes. Our Salisbury steak stays moist and tastes like—whad'ya know?—Salisbury steak.

SIMPLE STARCH
Instant potato flakes keep the patties moist and tender.

SALISBURY STEAK FOR TWO Serves 2

You can use dry red wine or dry sherry in place of the port. Use wet hands to shape the patties in step 1.

- ¼ cup milk
- 3 tablespoons instant potato flakes
- 8 ounces 90 percent lean ground beef
  Salt and pepper
- 2 tablespoons unsalted butter
- ½ cup thinly sliced onion
- 8 ounces white mushrooms, trimmed and sliced thin
- 1 tablespoon all-purpose flour
- 2 teaspoons tomato paste
- 1 cup beef broth
- 2 tablespoons ruby port

1. Whisk milk and potato flakes together in large bowl. Add beef, ½ teaspoon salt, and ¼ teaspoon pepper and knead until combined. Shape into two ½-inch-thick oval patties. (Patties can be covered and refrigerated for up to 24 hours.)

2. Melt 1 tablespoon butter in 10-inch nonstick skillet over medium-high heat. Cook patties until well browned, 3 to 5 minutes per side. Transfer to plate.

3. Return now-empty skillet to medium-high heat, add onion and remaining 1 tablespoon butter, and cook until browned, about 5 minutes. Add mushrooms and ¼ teaspoon salt and cook until liquid has evaporated, 5 to 7 minutes. Stir in flour and tomato paste and cook for 2 minutes. Slowly whisk in broth and port and bring to simmer. Return patties to skillet, cover, reduce heat to medium-low, and cook until meat registers 160 degrees, 8 to 10 minutes, flipping patties halfway through cooking.

4. Transfer steaks to platter. Continue to simmer sauce until slightly thickened, 2 to 4 minutes. Season sauce with salt and pepper to taste. Pour sauce over steaks and serve.

DON'T MAKE THIS MISTAKE
Canned Mushroom Soup

Older recipes use canned condensed soup as the base of the gravy. We tried it—and didn't like it. It's much better to make a homemade gravy from the pan drippings, onion, mushrooms, port, and beef broth.

DON'T DO IT
Canned soup makes for gloppy sauce.

Recipe Makeover Chicken Pot Pie

We tried every trick in the book to make a low-fat pie crust that we'd actually want to eat. It took us weeks to find it, but an unlikely ingredient cracked the code. BY CRISTIN WALSH

ON A CHILLY winter evening, there's nothing I like better than homey, warming chicken pot pie. But at 650 calories and nearly 40 grams of fat per serving, I limit it to the rare treat. So I jumped at the chance to develop a recipe that would preserve all the dish's satisfaction but shed much of its calories and fat.

My benchmark was the test kitchen's fantastic full-fat version. I baked that pot pie, alongside several low-fat versions. None of these makeover pies was a success, so I'd start with our full-fat recipe and chip away at it, stealing good ideas wherever I found them. Normally, the butter and/or shortening in the crust accounts for much of the fat and calories. As for the filling, calories and fat chiefly come from whole milk and the roux, the butter and flour that are mixed together and used to thicken the filling.

I expected the crust to be the tougher challenge (literally and figuratively), so for now I'd use our full-fat crust and get the filling under control. Going with chicken breasts instead of fattier thighs was a no-brainer. To replace the whole milk, I tried a number of things, eventually concluding that a little low-fat sour cream whisked into the chicken broth did the best job of mimicking the creamy texture of chicken pot pie. Cornstarch had shown promise as a thickener in my first round, so I ran a few tests and eventually was able to whisk ¼ cup of it into the same amount of chicken broth to replace the roux. But I was still a long way from my target nutritional numbers.

Some low-fat recipes skimp on the chicken and replace the missing meat with extra carrots and potatoes. These versions had tasted like vegetable pot pie to me, but maybe the idea was workable

with meaty mushrooms. Accordingly, I sautéed 8 ounces of sliced white mushrooms with the usual chopped carrots, celery, and onion. And instead of 2 pounds of chicken, I used just 1½. The mushrooms were as hearty and meaty as I'd hoped, so while we knew that we weren't eating chicken, we didn't miss it either. But the rejiggered filling clearly needed some low-cal, low-fat flavor heavy hitters. I knew just what to do: I added a glug of soy sauce and some tomato paste, both of which have lots of *umami*, or meaty, savory flavors. Pleased, I turned to the real challenge: the crust.

A decent pie crust is the holy grail of low-fat recipes, so I wasn't surprised that most of the crusts in my first test had been crackerlike and almost inedible. After a few days of exhaustive testing without any butter or shortening whatsoever, I concluded that a flaky, tender, flavorful crust would require fat—not the 8 tablespoons of butter and 4 tablespoons of shortening of the original, of course, but some. Butter has the better flavor, so I tested it in various ratios and in combination with every low-fat dairy item that I'd seen in other

recipes: cream cheese, ricotta, yogurt, etc. To keep things easy, I made the dough in a food processor. Many crusts later, I discovered that an even unlikelier ingredient worked best of all: light mayonnaise (I got the idea when I saw a colleague baking a chocolate-mayonnaise cake). One-quarter cup of light mayo, combined with just 3 tablespoons of butter, gave me a reasonable, if slightly tougher, approximation of full-fat pie crust. To fix the texture, I swapped out a little of the flour for tenderizing cornstarch.

Pie crust accomplished, I calculated the numbers once again. They were still a smidge high. I couldn't compromise on the butter in the crust, so I revisited the filling. I concluded that the sour cream would have to go. Amazingly, when I served a sour cream–less chicken pot pie to my coworkers, we discovered that we liked the full-on clean chicken flavor. One last time, I put together crust and filling and baked a pie. With good chicken-y flavor, a reasonably tender and tasty crust, just 10 grams of fat, and fewer than 400 calories, this chicken pot pie hit the mark and then some.

The Numbers

All nutritional information is for one serving.

Traditional Chicken Pot Pie
CALORIES **650** FAT **38 g**
SATURATED FAT **18 g**

Cook's Country Reduced-Fat Chicken Pot Pie
CALORIES **390** FAT **10 g**
SATURATED FAT **4.5 g**

We cut down on fat in the filling by using sautéed mushrooms to replace some of the chicken.

REDUCED-FAT CHICKEN POT PIE
Serves 6
We like Hellmann's Light Mayonnaise.

CRUST
- 1¼ cups (6¼ ounces) all-purpose flour
- 2 tablespoons cornstarch
- ¼ teaspoon salt
- ¼ cup light mayonnaise
- 3 tablespoons unsalted butter, cut into ¼-inch pieces and chilled
- 2 tablespoons ice water
- 2 teaspoons whole milk

FILLING
- 2¾ cups chicken broth
- ¼ cup cornstarch
- 1 teaspoon vegetable oil
- 4 carrots, peeled and sliced ¼ inch thick
- 8 ounces white mushrooms, trimmed and sliced thin
- 1 onion, chopped fine
- 2 celery ribs, sliced ¼ inch thick
  Salt and pepper
- 3 garlic cloves, minced
- 2 teaspoons minced fresh thyme

Compare and Contrast

Our full-fat pie crust requires ½ cup of butter and ¼ cup of shortening, which adds 1,240 calories and 136 grams of fat. We were able to approximate its flavor and flakiness with just 3 tablespoons of butter and ¼ cup of light mayonnaise—a mere 360 calories and 37 grams of fat.

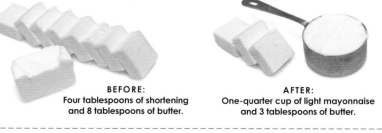

BEFORE:
Four tablespoons of shortening and 8 tablespoons of butter.

AFTER:
One-quarter cup of light mayonnaise and 3 tablespoons of butter.

1½ teaspoons tomato paste
2 bay leaves
1½ pounds boneless, skinless chicken breasts, trimmed and halved lengthwise
1 cup frozen peas
1 teaspoon soy sauce

1. FOR THE CRUST: Pulse flour, cornstarch, and salt in food processor until combined, about 3 pulses. Add mayonnaise and butter and pulse until mixture resembles coarse crumbs, about 10 pulses. Add water and pulse until dough looks wet and pebbly, about 10 pulses. Knead dough on lightly floured counter until smooth, about 10 seconds. Form dough into 4-inch disk, wrap tightly in plastic wrap, and refrigerate for 1 hour or up to 4 hours.

2. FOR THE FILLING: Whisk ¼ cup broth and cornstarch together in small bowl; set aside. Heat oil in Dutch oven over medium-high heat until shimmering. Add carrots, mushrooms, onion, celery, and 1½ teaspoons salt and cook until all liquid has evaporated and mushrooms begin to brown, 5 to 7 minutes. Add garlic, thyme, and tomato paste and cook until fragrant, about 30 seconds. Add bay leaves and remaining 2½ cups broth and bring to simmer. Submerge chicken in broth, reduce heat to low, cover, and cook until chicken registers 160 degrees, 8 to 12 minutes.

3. Transfer chicken to plate. Whisk cornstarch mixture into filling, return to boil, and cook until thickened, about 1 minute. Remove from heat and discard bay leaves. When chicken is cool enough to handle, shred into bite-size pieces, then stir into filling along with peas, soy sauce, and ½ teaspoon pepper. Season with salt and pepper to taste. (Filling may be refrigerated for up to 24 hours. Bring to a simmer and take off heat before proceeding with step 4.)

4. Adjust oven rack to upper-middle position and heat oven to 400 degrees. Transfer filling to 8-inch square baking dish. Roll dough into 9-inch square on lightly floured counter. Loosely roll dough around rolling pin and gently unroll it onto filling, letting excess dough hang over edge. Press overhanging dough onto side of dish to secure. Cut four 1-inch vent holes in crust and brush with milk. Bake until crust is golden and filling is bubbling up through vents, 25 to 30 minutes. Let cool for 30 minutes. Serve.

Commercial seasoned salts are OK, but if you have 5 minutes, you can make fresher, more interesting blends yourself.

BY NICK IVERSON

EVERY SUPERMARKET SELLS at least a few kinds of seasoned salt, and while I grew up with one of these store-bought mixes on the table at every meal, seasoned salts are incredibly easy to make—and when you make them yourself, they're fresher and you can tailor them to your tastes. My goal was to create a versatile seasoned salt that required nothing more than stirring together a few ingredients in a bowl but was superior to anything I could find in the supermarket. And given that a single version couldn't meet every need, I'd create four variations.

First I had to decide which kind of salt to use: table or kosher. I went with kosher salt, which has larger grains that are easier to evenly sprinkle over foods. Black pepper is a must in almost any seasoning blend, so I added some of that to my mix (freshly ground has much more potent, complex flavor). Since onion and garlic form the savory base of so many dishes, I incorporated them here in their dried forms; we preferred the rounder flavor of granulated garlic to garlic powder (which can be acrid), and we liked dehydrated onion, or onion flakes, better than onion powder. A few pinches of red pepper flakes gave the mix a welcome kick, and my All-Purpose Seasoned Salt Blend was set. My tasters and I approved this seasoned salt as a rub for raw chicken, beef, and pork; sprinkled onto steamed vegetables and raw avocado and tomato; or used at the table to season cooked meats, vegetables, eggs, rice, and pasta.

I created a Caribbean seasoned salt variation with the warm flavors of bay leaves, cloves, and nutmeg; the blend is great rubbed into roasts or steaks before cooking. A Greek-inspired version came together when I added dried thyme, basil, and oregano to the base seasoned salt; this salt works especially well as a rub for grilled lamb. Then I made a version of a Montreal seasoning blend, a mix for grilled meats that originated with the pickling blends brought to Montreal by Eastern European

These seasoned salts can be sprinkled on foods before, during, and after cooking.

immigrants. This salt is especially tasty on beef, pork, lamb, eggs, and salmon. And finally, I crafted a smoky blend that features hot smoked paprika, cumin, and chili powder and is fantastic in any Mexican or Tex-Mex dish—you'll never buy taco seasoning again. All these seasoned salts are terrific added to vinaigrettes or sprinkled over buttered popcorn or cooked eggs. Once you've got these salts in your pantry, you'll be writing to tell me all the uses you've found for them.

ALL-PURPOSE SEASONED SALT BLEND
Makes about ¼ cup
Store the salt blend for up to six weeks.

¼ cup kosher salt
1 tablespoon pepper
1 teaspoon granulated garlic
1 teaspoon onion flakes
¼ teaspoon red pepper flakes

Combine all ingredients in small bowl.

SUGGESTED USES: A rub for raw chicken or pork and sprinkled onto steamed vegetables or raw avocado, tomato, and cucumber.

CARIBBEAN SEASONED SALT BLEND
Grind 5 bay leaves and 1 teaspoon whole cloves in spice grinder until finely ground. Add bay leaf mixture and ½ teaspoon ground nutmeg to salt blend.
SUGGESTED USES: A rub for raw beef roasts and grilled steaks, chops, and fish.

GREEK SEASONED SALT BLEND
Add 1 teaspoon dried thyme, 1 teaspoon dried basil, and 1 teaspoon dried oregano to salt blend.
SUGGESTED USES: A rub for raw lamb, in vinaigrettes, and on eggs.

MONTREAL SEASONED SALT BLEND
Add 2 teaspoons dried rosemary, 1 teaspoon ground coriander, and 1 teaspoon caraway seeds to salt blend.
SUGGESTED USES: On beef (either as a rub or after cooking) and on salmon or other oily fish.

SMOKY SEASONED SALT BLEND
Add 1 tablespoon hot smoked paprika, 1 teaspoon ground cumin, and 1 teaspoon chili powder to salt blend.
SUGGESTED USES: A rub for meats in any Latin preparation, on popcorn or corn on the cob, and mixed into beans.

Equipment Review Dish Towels

Seeking: an absorbent, tough, and versatile towel. Must be handy, flexible, attractive, and willing to tackle multiple tasks. BY KATE SHANNON

KEY **Good** ★★★   **Fair** ★★   **Poor** ★

WHEN WE LAST scrutinized dish towels, the Now Designs Ripple Towel aced our tests. But at $8, it seemed a little expensive to use on the toughest tasks. Worse, readers complained that its seams sometimes unraveled after several washes. So we went back to the drawing board and bought new towels in a broad selection of sizes and textures from a kitchenware shop and low-priced restaurant suppliers. We even tested a new cloth diaper—one of our editors swears by them—and while we focused on cotton, which was strongly preferred in previous tests, we threw in one synthetic microfiber towel (the fabric is known for wicking moisture). With eight towels (priced from $2 to $8 per towel), including our old favorite, we went to work.

Whether we're using it to dry a dish or soak up a spill, first and foremost, a dish towel must be absorbent. To quantify absorbency, we dangled an inch of every towel into a tub of water for 15 minutes, weighing towels before and after. We did it again, this time dropping each towel on the surface of a tub of water to mimic wiping up a big spill. Microfiber excelled, while cotton towels ran the gamut. The worst towels seemed to almost repel water, floating lazily and taking a full minute to submerge. In the dangling test, we watched weaves acting like channels: Water zigzagged along herringbone, stepped up horizontal ribbing in fits and starts, traveled steadily up flat weaves, and stayed put in thick terry. The best towels had thinner areas that quickly transported water and thicker spongelike zones that held on to it.

We repeated our dangling test after putting the towels through 10 laundry cycles. Good news: All became dramatically more absorbent. Why? New textiles often contain leftover "sizing," a protective treatment that repels water. Two formerly middling towels became 100 percent more absorbent, taking in more than the former winner did when new. Nevertheless, the microfiber towel, as well as cotton towels with mixed textures, still held a clear advantage.

We often use dish towels as kitchen tools, enlisting them to squeeze out excess liquid from watery vegetables before cooking or to fill in for potholders, among other tasks. We put 10 ounces of defrosted frozen spinach into each towel and wrung the towels firmly. A few narrower towels were barely broad enough to contain even

HIGHLY RECOMMENDED		CRITERIA		TESTERS' NOTES
WILLIAMS-SONOMA Striped Towels, Set of 4 **Model:** 29-8845570 **Price:** $19.95 ($4.99 per towel) **Source:** williams-sonoma.com **Size (after washing):** 26 by 18.5 in (3.34 sq ft) **Material:** Cotton, alternating strips of basket and flat weave		Absorption Handling Durability	★★★ ★★★ ★★★	Goldilocks would like this towel: It's not too thick or too thin, too big or too small. Its fabric tightened, toughened, and grew more absorbent the more we used and washed it. Stripes camouflaged stains until they washed out and kept this sturdy towel looking fresh.
NOW DESIGNS Ripple Kitchen Towel, Set of 2 **Model:** 197545a **Price:** $16 ($8 per towel) **Source:** amazon.com **Size (after washing):** 25 by 18.25 in (3.17 sq ft) **Material:** Cotton, ribbed weave		Absorption Handling Durability	★★★ ★★ ★★★	Our previous winner still impressed with its streak-free drying, soft fabric, and excellent absorption. We'd heard complaints about unraveling but couldn't reproduce this in testing: After rigorous use and more than 26 laundry cycles, this towel showed no signs of fraying. One quibble: All that fluffy ribbing makes for a snug fit when drying tight corners.
RECOMMENDED WITH RESERVATIONS				
AUNT MARTHA'S Flour Sack Dish Towels, Set of 7 **Model:** TTS28 (28 x 28) **Price:** $15.99 ($2.28 per towel) **Size (after washing):** 26.25 by 26.25 in (4.79 sq ft) **Material:** Cotton flour sack, flat weave		Absorption Handling Durability	★★ ★★ ★★★	This traditional flour-sack towel was big but thin, fitting neatly inside a champagne flute. It dried without leaving behind lint and felt good in hand. It was terrific for squeezing spinach. However, big spills overwhelmed its flat weave, it was mediocre as an oven mitt, and shadowy stains persisted (although you can bleach it).
KUSHIES Washable Flat Diapers, Set of 6 **Model:** D-1026 **Price:** $19.99 ($3.33 per towel) **Size (after washing):** 28 by 24 in (4.67 sq ft) **Material:** Cotton, flat weave		Absorption Handling Durability	★★½ ★★ ★½	This cloth diaper was great for drying dishes, for squeezing vegetables, and as a potholder, but after washing, it felt like a baby blanket—flannel and fuzzy. At nearly 5 square feet, it was an awkward size for kitchen work. Stains hung on, but the cloth can be bleached.
NOT RECOMMENDED				
COTTON CRAFT Terry Waffle Weave Kitchen Towels, Set of 2 **Model:** X000D02AKH **Price:** $5.99 ($3 per towel) **Size (after washing):** 26.75 by 15.25 in (2.83 sq ft) **Material:** Cotton, lattice weave		Absorption Handling Durability	★½ ★½ ★½	Although its absorption improved after several washes, when new, this towel repelled liquid. Its thick lattice texture absorbed water where it touched rather than transporting liquid through the towel. Its label banned bleach and insisted that the towel be washed separately in cold water.
NOUVELLE LEGENDE Microfiber Kitchen Towels, Set of 2 **Model:** NL-MT-R-N-2 **Price:** $7.95 ($3.98 per towel) **Size (after washing):** 27.25 by 16 in (3.03 sq ft) **Material:** Microfiber, ribbed weave		Absorption Handling Durability	★★★ zero ★	This superabsorbent microfiber towel did many things well. But it turned from ivory to pea green after laundering, and testers hated its static feel. When pressed into service as a potholder, it smelled bad and felt alarmingly hot. It just doesn't seem like a dish towel to us.
KEEBLE OUTLETS Premium Dish Towels, 24-Ounce, Set of 12 **Model:** 24-ounce **Price:** $23.99 ($2 per towel) **Size (after washing):** 22.25 by 14 in (2.16 sq ft) **Material:** Cotton, herringbone weave		Absorption Handling Durability	★½ ★ ★	This ultrathin restaurant towel is cheap by the dozen, but its crisp appearance quickly went downhill, and its performance was underwhelming in every category. Small, floppy, and skimpy, the towel was gray, stained, and covered in lint by the end of testing.

that modest amount of food. Thicker towels were harder to squeeze than thin-to-medium-weight towels. We also used each towel to remove hot baking dishes filled with pie weights from a 450-degree oven. Bigger, thicker towels were harder to control, but the thinnest, smallest towels felt inadequate. (Warning: Microfiber is prone to melt; don't use it as a potholder. Also, never use a wet towel to handle a hot dish.) Our favorite midweight cotton towels readily folded into rectangles—about 10 by 7 inches—and felt secure while keeping our hands cool.

Testing the towels' maneuverability in tight spots, we dried slim, delicate

champagne flutes. No surprise that the thickest towels felt clumsy and made us fear dropping our glassware. Not so with thinner towels, which slipped into every cranny and dried thoroughly. The microfiber towel turned in another excellent performance, but we just couldn't overcome our dislike of its prickly, squeaky surface.

Finally, to test durability we poured on beet juice, mustard, wine, and oil and let the towels soak over a long weekend. Then we put them through 26 full laundry cycles to mimic six months of weekly washing. Within a few washes, towels started showing signs of wear and tear. By the end, nearly all the towels

had shrunk, but as long as they kept close to their original size and hemmed edges stayed flat and intact, we didn't fault them. On the plus side, midweight cotton towels with combination weaves seemed to grow thicker and sturdier.

In the end, the Williams-Sonoma Striped Towels ($19.95 for a set of four) emerged the clear winner. They featured cotton fabric with strips of basket weave alternating with flat weave, so they absorbed well without excessive bulk and only got tougher and thirstier with use. At more than 3 square feet, they're generous without being gigantic. And they cleaned up nicely. See the full testing chart at **CooksCountry.com/mar14.**

Taste Test Corn Tortillas

Our top pick has both flavor and flex, thanks to plenty of salt and an ingredient none of the other brands use. BY HANNAH CROWLEY

CORN TORTILLAS ARE a staple in Latin America, and as the Latino population in the United States grows, sales are booming in this country. Sales hit $2 billion in the States this year—up a whopping 35 percent from last year, according to IRi, a Chicago-based market research firm. While we love homemade corn tortillas, we usually rely on the convenience of store-bought. Good corn tortillas should be soft and pliable, with a fresh, light corn flavor. That's not what we found when last we evaluated national products—not even close. If popularity is surging, though, is it too much to hope that quality has also improved?

This time, as we surveyed the market, we found it dominated by Mexico-based Gruma Corporation, the world's largest manufacturer of corn tortillas. Gruma makes the majority of the tortillas sold in the States, including Mission and Guerrero, the two top-selling brands. Three of the seven products we tasted are made by Gruma.

We compared the tortillas in two blind taste tests, first assessing them warmed in an oven and served plain, and then pitting the top four products against one another in enchiladas. Commercial corn tortillas are made from specially treated corn flour, water, salt, binders, and preservatives. They can be yellow or white, depending on the variety of corn used; if a brand offered both, we tasted both. We asked tasters to judge both taste and texture.

When all the results were tallied, we had a winner—it's the first time that the test kitchen has been able to recommend a supermarket corn tortilla—and we found three others that we can recommend with reservations. (Clearly, tortilla quality has improved.)

Tasters faulted many of the tortillas for being either too sweet or bland. The sugar content, which ranged from 0 to 2.7 grams per serving, was from corn flour, added dextrose, or a combination. (Serving sizes ranged among products from one to three tortillas. To put them on an even playing field, we set an across-the-board serving size of 52 grams, and we based all our calculations on that.) Our winner had a hint of sweetness from its light, fresh corn flavor but no added sugar. Several products with added sugar were too sweet. Yet our last-place product had no added sugar; why did it tank? Tasters described it as "boring" and "flavorless."

So we checked sodium levels. Our winner had the most by far, with 120.5 milligrams per serving, while the product in second to last place had just 9 milligrams per serving; the other five ranged from 11 to 50 milligrams per serving. Yes, the winning product has 2½ to 13 times more salt than any other in our lineup. That sounds like a lot, but this amount of salt per serving is on par with the amount in an average slice of supermarket bread. And no one found our winning tortillas too salty. Actually, they were quite flavorful, which makes sense because salt is a flavor booster.

Texture is where supermarket corn tortillas can really go wrong; they're often crumbly and dry, and they break as you try to bend them around a filling. There's a reason for this: Corn is low in protein, which is needed to build strong, cohesive dough, and high in starch—particularly amylose (approximately 25% of total weight of starch), a form of starch that readily crystallizes, causing tortillas to stale. Manufacturers battle staleness with gums and stabilizers that tenderize and bond the corn flour, but this doesn't always work. So how did our winning product remain soft?

Our winner took a radical route to the top of the tasting. First, it has two to three times as much protein—6.3 grams per serving versus 2 to 3 grams in the other products. Our winner is the only product to add wheat gluten, which contains 75 percent protein, compared with 6.9 percent protein in corn flour. This extra protein binds with the water and makes the dough more cohesive and elastic, which in turn creates a softer, stronger tortilla. (This also means that unlike most corn tortillas, our winner is not gluten-free.) So what's the key to good texture in a supermarket corn tortilla? It's wheat.

Maria and Ricardo's Handmade Style Soft Corn Tortillas, Yellow ($2.99 for eight tortillas—by far the most expensive product in our lineup at 37 cents per tortilla)—rated highest with tasters on every criteria. These tortillas even had toasty brown griddle marks that contributed a pleasing nutty flavor and a homemade look. (The same company makes our lowest-ranking product, too.) For those who need gluten-free corn tortillas, our second-place finisher, Mission White Corn Tortillas, Restaurant Style, while lacking our winner's firm structure, is still a good option.

RECOMMENDED

TASTERS' NOTES

MARIA AND RICARDO'S
Handmade Style Soft
Corn Tortillas, Yellow
Price: $2.99 for 8 tortillas, 11.57 oz
(37 cents per tortilla)
Sodium: 120.5 mg
Protein: 6.3 g
Sugar: 0 g

These winning "tender yet substantial" tortillas wrapped enchilada fillings securely with the help of wheat gluten that kept them soft and pliable. "Clean" and "mellow," the tortillas had a light, cornlike sweetness with a hint of nuttiness, perhaps from the griddle marks that speckled each tortilla.

RECOMMENDED WITH RESERVATIONS

MISSION White Corn Tortillas, Restaurant Style
Price: $1.89 for 12 tortillas, 10 oz
(16 cents per tortilla)
Sodium: 11 mg
Protein: 2.2 g
Sugar: 2.2 g

These "mildly sweet" runner-up tortillas were "earthy," with good corn flavor and a drier yet more traditional texture (there is no added wheat gluten). Their "faint, stone-ground grit" was "pleasant," though some tasters complained that the tortillas were crumbly and disintegrated in the enchiladas.

GUERRERO White Corn Tortillas
Price: $1.79 for 30 tortillas, 25 oz
(6 cents per tortilla)
Sodium: 11 mg
Protein: 2.2 g
Sugar: 2.2 g

These tortillas had "more corn taste" than others, with a light "tang" and a sweetness that was like "fresh corn" to some tasters and like "raw pancake" to others. Tasters described the tortillas as a bit dry, with relatively thin sheets that could be "gritty."

LA BANDERITA Corn Tortillas, White (also sold as Olé)
Price: $2.49 for 30 tortillas, 27.5 oz
(8 cents per tortilla)
Sodium: 35 mg
Protein: 2 g
Sugar: 1 g (natural sugars and dextrose)

These tortillas separated into distinct layers—a quality that separated our tasters. Some found them "tender and flaky," whereas one groused, "Separates into sheets like toilet paper!" The cornlike sweetness also split tasters: One camp approved; the other judged the tortillas too sweet (this product adds dextrose).

NOT RECOMMENDED

LA BANDERITA Corn Tortillas, Yellow (also sold as Olé)
Price: $2.49 for 36 tortillas, 33 oz
(7 cents per tortilla)
Sodium: 35 mg
Protein: 2 g
Sugar: 1 g (natural sugars and dextrose)

Like their white-corn counterparts, these fragile tortillas flaked apart. Moreover, tasters found them "weirdly sweet" (maybe the added dextrose is to blame) and compared their flavor to "Pepto-Bismol" and "cough syrup."

MISSION White Corn Tortillas
Price: $1.99 for 10 tortillas, 6.92 oz
(20 cents per tortilla)
Sodium: 9 mg
Protein: 2.7 g
Sugar: 2.7 g

With a mere 9 milligrams of sodium per serving, these tortillas were "quite bland." Worse, we detected "metallic notes" and a "weird, off sweetness" (this product has the most sugar per serving of any in our lineup). The texture—"rubbery"—was also unappealing.

MARIA AND RICARDO'S Corn Tortillas
Price: $1.99 for 12 tortillas, 11 oz
(17 cents per tortilla)
Sodium: 15 mg
Protein: 2 g
Sugar: 0 g

These "bland," "boring" siblings of our winning product "didn't taste like corn"—or much else. They were dry, and they cracked when we rolled them up because they lack the tenderizers or gluten used by other corn tortilla brands.

DID YOU KNOW? All products reviewed by America's Test Kitchen, home of *Cook's Country* and *Cook's Illustrated* magazines, are independently chosen, researched, and reviewed by our editors. We buy products for testing at retail locations and do not accept unsolicited samples for testing. We do not accept or receive payment or consideration from product manufacturers or retailers. Manufacturers and retailers are not told in advance of publication which products we have recommended. We list suggested sources for recommended products as a convenience to our readers but do not endorse specific retailers.

Looking for a Recipe

Have you lost a recipe you treasure? Ask a reader. While you're at it, answer a reader. Post queries and finds at CooksCountry.com/magazines/home; click on **Looking for a Recipe** (or write to Looking for a Recipe, *Cook's Country*, P.O. Box 470739, Brookline, MA 02447). We'll share all your submissions online and one recipe on this page; please include your name and mailing address.

MATRIMONIAL BARS
Makes 16 bars
Debbie Allen, Glens Falls, N.Y.

Do not substitute quick or instant oats.

- 2 cups water
- 8 ounces pitted dates, chopped (1⅓ cups)
- 1 cup (5 ounces) all-purpose flour
- 1 cup packed (7 ounces) brown sugar
- 1 teaspoon ground cinnamon
- ½ teaspoon baking soda
- ¼ teaspoon salt
- 12 tablespoons unsalted butter, cut into ½-inch pieces
- 2 cups (6 ounces) old-fashioned rolled oats

1. Adjust oven rack to middle position and heat oven to 350 degrees. Make foil sling for 8-inch square baking pan by folding 2 long sheets of aluminum foil so each is 8 inches wide. Lay sheets of foil in pan perpendicular to each other, with extra foil hanging over edges of pan. Push foil into corners and up sides of pan, smoothing foil flush to pan. Spray with vegetable oil spray.

2. Combine water and dates in small saucepan and bring to boil over medium-high heat. Reduce heat to medium-low and simmer until dates are tender and liquid has been absorbed, 15 to 18 minutes.

3. Meanwhile, pulse flour, sugar, cinnamon, baking soda, and salt in food processor until combined, about 5 pulses. Add butter and pulse until mixture resembles coarse sand, about 15 pulses. Transfer to large bowl and stir in oats. Using your fingers, blend mixture until oats and flour mixture are well combined. Firmly press half of oat mixture evenly into bottom of prepared pan. Bake until lightly browned, about 10 minutes, rotating pan halfway through baking.

4. Process dates in now-empty food processor until smooth, about 1 minute. Spread date puree over crust. Sprinkle remaining oat mixture over date puree, pressing lightly to adhere. Bake until top is golden brown and filling is bubbling, 30 to 35 minutes, rotating pan halfway through baking. Transfer pan to wire rack and let bars cool completely. Using foil overhang, lift bars out of pan and slide off foil onto cutting board. Cut into 16 bars.

Haluski (Cabbage and Noodles)
Christie Matheson, Mount Carmel, Pa.

I grew up in a town with a large Polish community and have fond memories of a dish called *haluski*. It's made with sautéed cabbage, lots of butter, and soft, handmade egg noodles that are wider than anything you can buy. I used to eat haluski at a friend's house, with her dad's homemade kielbasa. I'd love to be able to make it for my family.

Lulu Paste
Pat Koerlin, Rapid City, S.D.

Despite the wacky name, lulu paste is a dip that I loved as a kid. It had a custard base that was whipped together with cream cheese, green peppers, and lots of onion. My mom always served it with Ritz Crackers or saltines. I'd like to have a recipe for it.

Vinegar Pie
Sarah Monroe, Wellesley, Mass.

I'm looking for a recipe for an old-fashioned vinegar pie that I first ate at a now-defunct restaurant called the Colonial Inn. It was a one-crust pie, with a custard filling that wasn't too sweet—the vinegar gave it a slight tang. Have you got a good recipe?

FIND THE ROOSTER!
A tiny version of this rooster has been hidden in the pages of this issue. Write to us with its location and we'll enter you in a random drawing. The first correct entry drawn will win our winning roasting pan, and each of the next five will receive a free one-year subscription to *Cook's Country*. To enter, visit **CooksCountry. com/rooster** by March 31, 2014, or write to Rooster FM14, *Cook's Country*, P.O. Box 470739, Brookline, MA 02447. Include your name and address. Lily Dioletto of Newark, California, found the rooster in the October/November 2013 issue on page 17 and won a set of our winning cake pans.

WEB EXTRAS
Free for 4 months online at **CooksCountry.com**

Beef Broth Tasting
Bread-Crumb Tasting
Chocolate Curls
Chocolate Layer Cake
Dill Potato Salad
Dish Towel Testing (full chart)
Roasted Cauliflower with Paprika and Chorizo
Roasted Salt-and-Vinegar Potatoes
Single-Serve Pod Coffee Makers Testing (full story and chart)

READ US ON iPAD.

Download the *Cook's Country* app for iPad and start a free trial subscription or purchase a single issue of the magazine. All issues are enhanced with full-color Cooking Mode slide shows that provide step-by-step instructions for completing recipes, plus expanded reviews and ratings. Go to **CooksCountry.com/iPad** to download our app through iTunes.

Follow us on **Twitter**
twitter.com/TestKitchen

Find us on **Facebook**
facebook.com/CooksCountry

Cherry-Chocolate Cake

Love eternal: The marriage of chocolate and cherries has stood the test of time.
To understand why, bake this fantastic cake.

To make this cake you will need:

- ⅓ cup cherry jam or preserves
- ½ cup (3½ ounces) sugar
- 2 large egg whites
- 2 tablespoons water
  Red food coloring
  Pinch salt
- 1 tablespoon kirsch or other cherry-flavored liqueur
- ½ teaspoon vanilla extract
- 2 (9-inch) chocolate cake layers*
- 1 (21-ounce) can cherry pie filling
  Chocolate curls*

FOR THE ICING: Microwave jam in small bowl until thin enough to pour, 35 to 45 seconds, stirring halfway through microwaving. Using rubber spatula, push jam through fine-mesh strainer set over bowl of stand mixer. Add sugar, egg whites, water, 3 to 4 drops food coloring, and salt to mixer bowl. Place over medium saucepan filled with 1 inch barely simmering water (bowl should not touch water). Cook, stirring constantly, until mixture registers 160 degrees, 5 to 10 minutes. Fit mixer with whisk; add kirsch and vanilla to icing. Whip icing on medium-high speed until stiff peaks form, 5 to 10 minutes.

TO ASSEMBLE: Place 1 cake layer on plate or pedestal. Spread cherry pie filling evenly over top, leaving ½-inch border around edge. Top with second cake layer. Spread icing evenly over top and sides of cake. Pile chocolate curls in center of cake. Serve.

▶ Go to **CooksCountry.com** for our **Chocolate Layer Cake** recipe and instructions for making **Chocolate Curls**.

Inside This Issue

Cook's Country

APRIL/MAY 2014

Hummingbird Cake

Spicy Deviled Short Ribs

Chicken Scaloppini

Five Easy Drop Biscuits
Better Butter Technique

Slow-Roasted Fresh Ham
Rich, Tender Pork Roast

Old-Fashioned Rice Pudding
The Secret? More Milk

Cream of Chicken Soup
New Idea Yields Deep Flavor

Tex-Mex Layered Beef Casserole

Italian Easter Pie
Lighter Is Better

Slow-Cooker Mashed Potatoes
Easy No-Drain Method

Thick and Chewy Chocolate Chip Cookies
Step-by-Step Cooking Class

Testing Dish Soaps
Do Foams Work Best?

CooksCountry.com
$5.95 U.S./$6.95 CANADA

*In the grand tradition of Southern layer cakes, **Hummingbird Cake** is rich, moist, and decadent. Maybe a bit too decadent. We intensified its fruit flavors and lightened it up without losing its classic charms.* PAGE 8

Dear Country Cook,

I grew up fly-fishing. My mother, the family's bespoke fisherman, took me on trips to lakes in Maine, and of course we fished the famous Battenkill in Vermont near our farm.

Fishing and cooking have a lot in common: observation and patience. Trout are choosy about which flies look particularly tasty. And it is no secret that only a patient fisherman will find success. Charging into a stream like a Christmas shopper on Black Friday is not conducive to good results.

A good cook waits patiently for a pie crust to set, for a steak to brown properly, and for bread dough to double in size. And as with fishing, one cooks just for the sheer joy of it. Each and every culinary expedition is its own reward.

And if you don't catch any fish, or if the cake doesn't rise, well, you can always get excited about next time.

Cordially,

Christopher Kimball
Founder and Editor, Cook's Country

Boy fishing with homemade pole, 1930s.

Cook's Country

Founder and Editor Christopher Kimball
Editorial Director Jack Bishop
Editorial Director, Magazines John Willoughby
Executive Editor Peggy Grodinsky
Managing Editor Scott Kathan
Executive Food Editor Bryan Roof
Senior Editors Hannah Crowley, Rebeccah Marsters,
Lisa McManus, Diane Unger
Test Kitchen Director Erin McMurrer
Associate Editors Shannon Friedmann Hatch,
Christie Morrison
Test Cooks Sarah Gabriel,
Ashley Moore, Cristin Walsh
Assistant Editor Lauren Savoie
Copy Editors Nell Beram, Megan Ginsberg
Executive Assistant Christine Gordon
Test Kitchen Manager Leah Rovner
Senior Kitchen Assistants
Michelle Blodget, Meryl MacCormack
Kitchen Assistants
Maria Elena Delgado, Shane Drips, Ena Gudiel
Executive Producer Melissa Baldino
Co-Executive Producer Stephanie Stender
Production Assistant Kaitlin Hammond

Contributing Editors Erika Bruce,
Eva Katz, Jeremy Sauer
Consulting Editors Anne Mendelson, Meg Ragland
Science Editor Guy Crosby, PhD
Executive Food Editor, TV, Radio & Media
Bridget Lancaster

Managing Editor, Web Christine Liu
Senior Editor, Cooking School Mari Levine
Associate Editors, Web Eric Grzymkowski, Roger Metcalf
Assistant Editors, Web Jill Fisher, Charlotte Wilder
Senior Video Editor Nick Dakoulas

Design Director Amy Klee
Art Director Julie Cote
Deputy Art Director Susan Levin
Associate Art Director Lindsey Timko
Deputy Art Director, Marketing Jennifer Cox
Staff Photographer Daniel J. van Ackere
Color Food Photography Keller + Keller
Styling Catrine Kelty, Marie Piraino
Associate Art Directors, Marketing Melanie Gryboski,
Mariah Tarvainen
Designer, Marketing Judy Blomquist
Photo Editor Steve Klise

Vice President, Marketing David Mack
Circulation Director Doug Wicinski
Circulation & Fulfillment Manager Carrie Fethe
Partnership Marketing Manager Pamela Putprush
Marketing Assistant Marina Tomao

VP, Technology, Product Development Barry Kelly
Director, Project Management Alice Carpenter
Project Manager Britt Dresser
Development Manager Mike Serio

Chief Operating Officer Rob Ristagno
Production Director Guy Rochford
Workflow & Digital Asset Manager Andrew Mannone
Senior Color & Imaging Specialist Lauren Pettapiece
Production & Imaging Specialists
Heather Dube, Lauren Robbins
Director of Sponsorship Sales Anne Traficante
Client Services Associate Kate May
Sponsorship Sales Representative Morgan Ryan
Customer Service Manager Jacqueline Valerio
Customer Service Representatives
Megan Hamner, Jessica Haskin,
Andrew Straaberg Finfrock

Retail Sales & Marketing Manager Emily Logan
Human Resources Manager Adele Shapiro
Publicity Deborah Broide

ON THE COVER: *Hummingbird Cake*, Keller + Keller,
Catrine Kelty
ILLUSTRATION: Greg Stevenson

Follow us on **Twitter**
twitter.com/TestKitchen

Find us on **Facebook**
facebook.com/CooksCountry

Cook's Country magazine (ISSN 1552-1990), number 56, is published bimonthly by Boston Common Press Limited Partnership, 17 Station St., Brookline, MA 02445. Copyright 2014 Boston Common Press Limited Partnership. Periodicals postage paid at Boston, MA, and additional mailing offices. USPS #023453. Publications Mail Agreement No. 40020778. Return undeliverable Canadian addresses to P.O. Box 875, Station A, Windsor, ON N9A 6P2. POSTMASTER: Send address changes to *Cook's Country*, P.O. Box 6018, Harlan, IA 51593-1518. For subscription and gift subscription orders, subscription inquiries, or change of address notices, visit AmericasTestKitchen.com/support, call 800-526-8447 in the U.S. or 515-248-7684 from outside the U.S., or write to us at *Cook's Country*, P.O. Box 6018, Harlan, IA 51593-1518. PRINTED IN THE USA.

Contents

ANADAMA BREAD, 10

HEARTY CREAM OF CHICKEN SOUP, 11

ASPARAGUS MIMOSA, 19

Features

Departments

Table for Two

You live in a two-person household. Should that mean that whenever you make lasagna for dinner, you're stuck eating the leftovers all week? No more.
In *The Complete Cooking for Two Cookbook*, we cut 650 of our favorite recipes down to size, including classic crowd-pleasers, great modern dishes, and international offerings; more than 150 of the recipes are ready in just 30 minutes or less. With color photos and informative notes from the test kitchen throughout, *The Complete Cooking for Two Cookbook* is the comprehensive kitchen manual that every small household needs. For more information, visit **AmericasTestKitchen.com/cookingfortwo.**

America's TEST KITCHEN
RECIPES THAT WORK®

America's Test Kitchen is a very real 2,500-square-foot kitchen located just outside Boston. It is the home of *Cook's Country* and *Cook's Illustrated* magazines and the workday destination of more than three dozen test cooks, editors, and cookware specialists. Our mission is to test recipes until we understand how and why they work and arrive at the best version. We also test kitchen equipment and supermarket ingredients in search of products that offer the best value and performance. You can watch us work by tuning in to *Cook's Country from America's Test Kitchen* (CooksCountry.com) and *America's Test Kitchen* (AmericasTestKitchen.com) on public television.

What's the difference between canned beef consommé and beef broth? Can I use them interchangeably?
Alex Dutton, Carson City, Nev.

In restaurant kitchens, consommé is meat broth that has been enriched and clarified using a "raft," an assemblage of egg whites and ground meat that forms, then floats on top of the pot as the broth simmers, and traps the proteins that cause cloudiness. Several canned soup companies market canned condensed "consommé" as well as broth. Comparing the ingredients listed on the labels of the two revealed that the main difference (assuming the same brand) is that the consommé includes gelatin and other additives to add body.

The two big national brands that offer both consommé and broth are Campbell's and Heinz. Tasting the consommé and broth from both brands side by side, we found that the consommé was more viscous at room temperature. Also, a few tasters noticed that soups made with consommé had a little more body than soups made with broth from the same brand, but the difference wasn't significant. We also found that we were able to swap out broth for consommé in recipes without much difference, save for one element: salt.

The commercial consommés were incredibly salty; we much prefer our recommended beef broth, Rachael Ray Stock-in-a-Box All-Natural Beef-Flavored Stock, for soups and all other recipes that call for beef broth. (Rachael Ray does not make consommé.)
THE BOTTOM LINE: Canned consommé is different from canned broth in that consommé typically contains gelatin and is saltier. You can use them interchangeably in most recipes if you correct the seasoning for the salty consommé.

Recipes for banana bread always call for very ripe or even brown bananas. Can I get away with a yellow or slightly green banana?
Susan Peters, Rochester, N.Y.

To answer your question, we made three loaves of banana bread, one with green, one with yellow, and one with brown bananas. The first hurdle was mashing: Mashing a ripe banana is a cinch, but to mash a green or even a yellow one, you really have to put your back into it (or use the food processor) to get a smooth puree. We did our best, and once we had baked the breads, we found, as we'd expected, that the riper the banana the more flavorful the bread.

I often use half of an avocado and save the rest for later. Can I keep the leftover half from turning brown?
Colby McHugh, Shaker Heights, Ohio

This is enough of a problem that a few companies have even designed gadgets that claim to keep leftover avocados green. (In our past tests they didn't succeed; see **CooksCountry.com/foodstoragegadgets**.) But if you start asking around, you'll find that nearly everyone has a solution. We put together a list of the most oft-cited methods—leave the pit in the avocado; rub lemon juice on the cut side; wrap it tightly in plastic wrap; seal out air by coating the cut side in oil—and started testing.

We know that cold slows enzymatic action, and when fruits and vegetables brown, it's an enzymatic process. Could we slow it down by refrigerating the avocados? Because each individual avocado browns at a different rate, we cut four avocados in half and put half of each in the refrigerator overnight. As we expected, the next day all the halves in the refrigerator were greener than their unrefrigerated mates. Once we'd established that chilling helps, we sliced four more avocados in half, treating one half of each with one of the aforementioned methods. We refrigerated them. At the 24-hour mark, all the treated halves were the same color as their corresponding untreated halves—obviously, none of these four methods made any difference.

BEST SOLUTION: VACUUM SEALER
Our favorite reasonably priced model, the FoodSaver V2240, keeps cut avocados green for a week.

NEXT BEST: LEMON WATER STORAGE
After 48 hours, this avocado (flipped over here to show the color) is still green.

Looking for other ideas, we called our science editor. Armed with his advice and three more cases of avocados, we spent two weeks doing everything from boiling avocados to dipping them in solutions made from crushed vitamin C tablets. Nothing worked, though we did inadvertently figure out how to make avocados brown faster. (You salt them.) We kept trying. Eventually, we were able to get nearly perfect green color at the 48-hour mark by leaving the avocado cut side down in a bowl of lemon juice and water. The drawback? The avocado was a little tart and slightly soft.

At this point, a colleague showed up to work one day with a box of vacuum-sealed peeled, pitted, and halved avocados from the grocery store. They were bright green—and stayed that way for a week in the fridge. What if we vacuum-sealed our own avocados? It worked (and cost less than buying them vacuum-sealed). A bowl of vacuum-sealed guacamole also stayed green for a week.
THE BOTTOM LINE: Vacuum sealing will keep leftover avocado halves and guacamole green for up to a week. Storing cut avocados submerged cut side down in lemon water in the refrigerator will maintain color for up to two days but may slightly affect texture and flavor.

What we didn't expect was that we'd discover a difference in the structure of the bread, too. Bread made with greenish bananas was "vegetal" and "astringent," according to some tasters, but also taller and drier, with a more open crumb, as opposed to the desirably moist, dense, compact crumb of banana bread made with ripe fruit. Yellow bananas with a few brown spots also lacked adequate banana flavor, but the vegetal taste was gone and the textural difference in the breads was small.

Our science editor explained that as bananas ripen, some of their starch is converted into sugar. Sugar behaves like a liquid in baked goods, moisturizing and tenderizing, so bread made with ripe bananas not only is the sweetest and has the most banana flavor but is also the most moist.
THE BOTTOM LINE: Use very ripe, or even overripe, bananas for baking. To speed ripening by a day or two, put underripe bananas in a paper bag with a ripe banana or any other ripe fruit (ripe fruits emit ethylene gas, which speeds ripening).

Why does foam form on top of the cooking water whenever I cook dried beans? Is there a way to prevent it? Do I need to skim it off?
Adrienne Hunter, Colorado Springs, Colo.

The foam that forms on the surface of the pot is caused by the release of water-soluble proteins from the beans. The proteins stabilize the walls of air bubbles that form as the water simmers, so instead of bursting, the bubbles join together and create foam. (Foam also forms on the surface when you boil many other foods, such as carrots or meat.) We prepared two pots of beans according to a favorite test kitchen method that requires soaking the dried beans overnight in salt water before cooking them. We drained off the brine and simmered the beans in fresh water until they were tender. Sure enough, foam formed. We skimmed it from one batch during cooking but not the other.

What did we find? Though we detected no difference in texture, three-quarters of our tasters found the skimmed beans "sweeter" or "milder." Our science editor explained that the skimmed beans probably tasted sweeter because "the proteins that stabilize the foam impart bitter taste."

Before putting your question to rest, we wondered whether the way that we prepared the beans affected the formation of foam. To find out, we did one more test, cooking three batches of beans side by side: one soaked in plain water overnight, one brined as we'd been doing, and one simmered from beans that had never been soaked. Both soaked and brined beans produced foam. The beans cooked from a dry state did not, but tasters didn't like their texture as much: It was less creamy and less evenly tender.
THE BOTTOM LINE: Soaking or brining dried beans means more foam formation when you simmer them, but it also improves the texture of the beans. Skimming off the foam improves the taste of the beans.

CURE FOR FOAM
Skim it off with a spoon.

To ask us a cooking question, visit **CooksCountry.com/ask**. Or write to Ask Cook's Country, P.O. Box 470739, Brookline, MA 02447. Just try to stump us!

Kitchen Shortcuts

COMPILED BY CRISTIN WALSH

BETTER BAKING
Stackable Bowls
Mary Francis Kerrington, Bay City, Mich.

Counter space is scarce in my kitchen, so when I'm making cookies or a cake, I use a few pieces of parchment paper to help stack bowls that I've filled with dry ingredients. I lay the parchment on top of the largest bowl and its ingredients, place another bowl on top of that, and so on. The parchment acts as a barrier, so I don't lose any ingredients and I don't dirty the bottoms of the stacked bowls. This method allows me to measure and organize all my ingredients before I get started.

TIDY TIP
Easy-Clean Food Processor
Angela Bolton, Grassy Creek, N.C.

I always loathed cleaning the lid of my food processor; with all the crevices and lips on the lid, it was nearly impossible to get clean. Fortunately, I've found a way around this annoyance. Whenever I use my food processor for something that doesn't require adding ingredients through the top chute, I create a barrier between the lid and the bowl with plastic wrap. When I'm done, I just throw away the dirty plastic and the lid is clean and ready to go.

TIDY TIP
Oh, What a Relief It Is
Chester Williams, Knoxville, Tenn.

Every once in a while my refrigerator needs a little freshening up. A great way to do this is by adding a tablet of Alka-Seltzer to 1 cup of water, letting it fizz, and leaving it in the closed fridge for 30 minutes. Alka-Seltzer contains sodium bicarbonate, a natural deodorizer. When I open the fridge back up, it smells fresh again.

HOT TIP
Easy Juicing
Jon Aberle, Glendale, N.J.

When I need a lot of lemon juice for a recipe, I use a handy trick to help me get the most juice from the lemons. I microwave them for 10 to 15 seconds. This softens the rind just enough to help me squeeze every last bit of juice out. And it makes my microwave smell clean to boot.

DOUBLE DUTY
Cake Comb
Linda Howe, Minnetonka, Minn.

I love to decorate cakes, and over the years I've discovered some unusual tools to help. Like chefs, I've looked to the hardware store for ideas. My favorite is a plastic square-notched plaster spreader. I use it to comb decorative grooves into the frosting. Not only does this tool make perfectly even lines on frosted cakes but it has multiple sizes of notches on each side to choose from.

NEAT TRICK Pomegranate Prep
Evan Robert Allen, Coral Gables, Fla.

Getting the seeds out of a pomegranate is easy now that I use the test kitchen's trick of bopping the backside of a halved pomegranate with a mallet. But what about separating the seeds from the white pith? The method I've found that works best is to dump all the seeds and pith into a bowl of water; the seeds sink but the pith floats to the surface, where it's easy to skim off with a strainer.

RECYCLE IT Ice Is Nice
Clarissa Simmons, Kansas City, Kan.

Last summer I was vacationing in a house that didn't have ice cube trays. I discovered that I could use polystyrene egg cartons to make ice cubes (I washed the trays first). The cubes were the right size, and with a little twist they came out of the carton easily.

Illustration: Ross MacDonald

Slow-Roasted Fresh Ham

If you love meaty, full-flavored pork dishes like ribs and pulled pork, fresh ham is destined to become your new favorite roast. BY DIANE UNGER

QUICK: WHAT COLOR is ham? It's pink, right? Well, mostly. All cured ham is indeed pink, but there's another ham—fresh ham—that is uncured, unsmoked, and, when cooked, as pale as a pork loin. Fresh ham starts with the same cut as cured ham—the rear leg of the hog—so it's basically just a big, bone-in, skin-on pork roast. I decided that a fresh ham would be just the thing for my Easter table this year.

As I began cooking my way through recipes, my tasters were immediately impressed by the tremendous meaty flavor of this cut. But the problems with cooking fresh hams quickly became evident. First, they are big—usually between 8 and 10 pounds—so it's hard to season the interior, especially with a thick, tough layer of skin covering much of the meat. Second, shank-end fresh hams (which are preferable to sirloin-end hams because they are easier to carve) are an uneven shape—one taster compared the shape to a ski boot—so it's difficult to get them to cook evenly. The fact that fresh hams are made up of different muscles (and lots of fat) that cook at different rates only compounds the problem. But the flavor payoff was so big that I was determined to figure out a foolproof way to cook fresh ham.

My first task was to establish the best way to season the ham. I tried brining it for a few days in a large plastic bucket. While the method did season the meat and help keep it moist, the bucket took up a lot of room—fine if you have a commercial walk-in refrigerator, but not so great for the home cook. Rubbing the roast with a salt mixture was a better approach: There's no bucket or sloshing brine, and—as long as you let the rubbed roast sit for at least 12 hours—the seasoning penetrates and, as with brining, helps the meat retain moisture during cooking. As long as I was seasoning the meat, I figured I might as well add some other flavors. After several tests, I ended up using a mixture of kosher salt, brown sugar, fresh rosemary, and fresh thyme. To get the seasonings even deeper into the blocky ham, I cut a large pocket in the meaty end and rubbed the seasoning right into it. Now I just needed to figure out how to cook the ham more evenly.

Most recipes agreed on a roasting temperature of around 325 degrees.

It looks like a cured ham until you start carving—the meat inside is white like a pork loin roast, but it's richer and more flavorful.

A relatively low oven is necessary to cook a cut this big all the way through without dehydrating or, worse, burning the exterior. I tried roasting the ham in all sorts of configurations: resting it on its flat bottom versus on its side; with water in the pan versus without; elevated versus simply sitting in the pan. I conducted these tests over the course of a week, and nothing was working: Most of the hams had some nicely cooked meat but also some that was over- or under-done. Most troublesome: I couldn't get the skin to render in the time required to cook the rest of the roast.

After more frustration than I care to admit, I made two decisions that saved this recipe (and my sanity): First, I removed the skin from the ham before cooking, leaving about ½ inch of fat (which I crosshatched so that it would render more efficiently) to add flavor to the ham. And second, I took a cue from some of the test kitchen's recipes for cured ham and cooked the fresh ham in an oven bag, elevated on a rack, until the meat reached 160 degrees. That took between 3½ and 5 hours, depending on the size of the ham. Then I let the ham rest, right in the bag, for an hour longer so that it could slowly finish cooking in the residual heat to perfect tenderness. Why do oven bags work? They create a moist environment that conducts heat more effectively than a dry oven does, so the ham reaches the cooking temperature more quickly and remains there longer. This helps break down fat and connective tissue into gelatin more efficiently, and gelatin helps keep meat moist. To get the ham to cook more evenly still, I tied kitchen twine around the widest part, forcing the ham into a more streamlined, regular shape.

All that was left was to develop a quick glaze that I could broil on the ham before serving. Of the several combinations I tried, tasters preferred a simple mixture of maple syrup, molasses, soy sauce, Dijon, and ground black pepper—and I liked that this glaze was an easy dump-and-stir affair.

Now that I had perfected the recipe in the test kitchen, I was excited to make it for my family. Once they got over their surprise that this "ham" was actually a roast, they were astonished at how good it tasted.

SLOW-ROASTED FRESH HAM
Serves 12 to 14
Use a turkey-size oven bag for this recipe.

- 1 (8- to 10-pound) bone-in, shank-end fresh ham
- ⅓ cup packed brown sugar
- ⅓ cup kosher salt
- 3 tablespoons minced fresh rosemary
- 1 tablespoon minced fresh thyme
- 1 large oven bag
- 2 tablespoons maple syrup
- 2 tablespoons molasses
- 1 tablespoon soy sauce
- 1 tablespoon Dijon mustard
- 1 teaspoon pepper

1. Place ham flat side down on cutting board. Using sharp knife, remove skin, leaving ½- to ¼-inch layer of fat intact. Cut 1-inch diagonal crosshatch pattern in fat, being careful not to cut into meat. Place ham on its side. Cut one 4-inch horizontal pocket about 2 inches deep in center of flat side of ham, being careful not to poke through opposite side.
2. Combine sugar, salt, rosemary, and

thyme in bowl. Rub half of sugar mixture in ham pocket. Tie 1 piece of kitchen twine tightly around base of ham. Rub exterior of ham with remaining sugar mixture. Wrap ham tightly in plastic wrap and refrigerate for at least 12 hours or up to 24 hours.
3. Adjust oven rack to lowest position and heat oven to 325 degrees. Set V-rack in large roasting pan. Unwrap ham and place in oven bag flat side down. Tie top of oven bag closed with kitchen twine. Place ham, flat side down, on V-rack and cut ½-inch slit in top of oven bag. Roast until thermometer inserted in center of ham, close to but not touching bone, registers 160 degrees, 3½ to 5 hours. Remove ham from oven and let rest in oven bag on V-rack for 1 hour. Heat oven to 450 degrees.
4. Whisk maple syrup, molasses, soy sauce, mustard, and pepper together in bowl. Cut off top of oven bag and push down with tongs, allowing accumulated juices to spill into roasting pan; discard oven bag. Leave ham sitting flat side down on V-rack.
5. Brush ham with half of glaze and roast for 10 minutes. Brush ham with remaining glaze, rotate pan, and roast until deep amber color, about 10 minutes longer. Move ham to carving board, flat side down, and let rest for 20 minutes. Pour pan juices into fat separator. Carve ham into ¼-inch-thick slices, arrange on platter, and moisten lightly with defatted pan juices. Serve, passing remaining pan juices separately.

TEST KITCHEN TECHNIQUE **How to Season Deeply and Cook Evenly**
We found two tricks for deep seasoning and even cooking of a fresh ham.

CUT a pocket in the meaty end and season the ham inside the pocket.

TIE twine around the base to create a more even shape, then season the exterior.

WHAT TO DO WITH LEFTOVERS
Ham and Sweet Potato Hash

This surprising combination is a surprise hit. BY DIANE UNGER

Like all hash, this one is better with an egg.

MAYBE YOU'RE LIKE me—a person who enjoys the leftovers even more than the original meal. With lots of tasty leftover Slow-Roasted Fresh Ham around, I got inspired to make a hash that would do justice to this superflavorful, tender, meaty pork.

The usual cubes of regular white potatoes weren't that interesting. But rich, earthy sweet potatoes proved the perfect foil to porky fresh ham. Jump-starting their cooking in the microwave ensured that the chunks of sweet potato cooked through in the hash in a relatively short time. Sliced red onion and minced garlic provided a good savory base, and a pinch of cayenne lifted the flavors without causing any burn damage. The hash was coming together nicely, yet something was missing . . . but what?

In the spring, I am so thankful for the return of fresh, local, green vegetables that I put asparagus in just about every dish I'm cooking. On a lark, I tried adding it to the hash. My tasters—though skeptical at first—were quick converts, as the asparagus proved surprisingly good paired with the leftover ham and sweet potatoes.

During several tests, I worked my way through the mechanics. After microwaving the peeled and cubed sweet potatoes, I heated a little vegetable oil in a skillet. In went the leftover ham, onion, garlic, cayenne, and parcooked sweet potatoes. After about 10 minutes, when the sweet potatoes were starting to brown, I added the asparagus and ¼ cup of the potent ham juices and covered the skillet. In less than 5 minutes, the asparagus was cooked to a perfect crisp-tender texture, and the hash was ready to be topped with eggs for a hearty, post-Easter breakfast.

HAM, ASPARAGUS, AND SWEET POTATO HASH
Serves 4
Serve this hash with fried or poached eggs. You can substitute chopped ham steak and chicken broth for the leftover Slow-Roasted Fresh Ham and its juices.

- 1½ pounds sweet potatoes, peeled and cut into ½-inch cubes
- 3 tablespoons vegetable oil Salt and pepper
- 2 cups chopped Slow-Roasted Fresh Ham plus ¼ cup leftover ham juices
- 1 red onion, halved and sliced thin
- 2 garlic cloves, minced
- ¼ teaspoon cayenne pepper
- 1 pound thin asparagus, trimmed and cut into 1-inch lengths
- ¼ cup minced fresh chives

1. Toss potatoes, 1 tablespoon oil, and ½ teaspoon salt together in large bowl. Microwave, covered, until potatoes are nearly tender, about 6 minutes, stirring halfway through microwaving.
2. Heat remaining 2 tablespoons oil in 12-inch nonstick skillet over medium-high heat until shimmering. Add ham, onion, garlic, cayenne, and precooked potatoes and cook, stirring occasionally, until potatoes are spotty brown and cooked through, about 10 minutes.
3. Stir in asparagus and ham juices, cover, and cook until asparagus is tender, about 4 minutes. Season with salt and pepper to taste, sprinkle with chives, and serve.

Potato-Tomato Gratin

For a sweeter, cleaner, lighter potato gratin, ditch the heavy cream and add tomatoes.

BY CRISTIN WALSH

THE POTATO GRATINS most of us know feature potatoes smothered in a rich, luscious blanket of milk and cream. Potato-tomato gratin almost is a different animal. While both types of gratin call for layering potatoes and employ cheese or bread-crumb toppings, the latter inserts a tomato layer and uses broth in place of milk and cream. Where traditional potato gratin is rib-sticking and luxe, potato-tomato gratin is sweeter, cleaner, and lighter—or so I had been told.

I collected recipes and set to work slicing, layering, and baking. To make the tomatoes less watery, some of these recipes called for salting and draining them or broiling them before layering them in the casserole. But as slicing so many potatoes and tomatoes was already laborious, I wasn't keen on even more steps. Unfortunately, the recipes that used untreated raw sliced tomatoes paid a price: When the dish came out of the oven, the potato slices stood in a pool of watery tomato juices, making the gratin a sloppy, washed-out mess.

> ▶ To learn which baking dish is best, visit **CooksCountry.com/ bakingdishes**, where you can read our testing story.

Keeping in mind my desire to use untreated tomatoes, I cherry-picked the more successful elements from this round of testing to find a starting point. I'd use plum tomatoes, which are less watery than other common varieties, and for cheese I'd go with a simple sprinkle of Parmesan, the classic gratin choice. As for the type of potato, while some of the recipes in the first testing used moderately starchy Yukon Golds and others opted for waxy red potatoes, the version made with high-starch russets—our usual choice for gratins—was by far the best, since their higher starch content caused them to soak up more of the tomato juices.

These decisions made, I set out to prepare another gratin. I sliced the raw plum tomatoes and arranged half of them in a baking dish, layering them with sliced potatoes and then the remaining tomatoes and sprinkling on salt and pepper as I went. After pouring chicken broth over the lot, I covered the gratin with foil and baked it in the steamy environment for 1 hour. Then I uncovered the dish, sprinkled on the

Kalamata olives, garlic, fresh thyme, and Gruyère cheese make this gratin incredibly flavorful.

Parmesan (I knew from experience to add it at the end, so the cheese wouldn't dry out before the potatoes were tender), and baked it until bubbling and brown, about another half-hour.

When I cut into this gratin, I could see that I hadn't made much progress: It remained watery. What if I tried baking the casserole uncovered from the start? My hope was that the extra liquid would evaporate and concentrate. This was an improvement but not a fix; a gratin made this way was still too wet. As I wondered what to try next, a colleague suggested an interesting, unconventional approach: Yes, watery tomatoes were the problem, but might they be the solution, too? "Skip the broth altogether," he advised. His

hypothesis? The potatoes would cook in the liquid released by the tomatoes alone. But would it work? Hallelujah, it did.

A bonus of using tomato "water" as my cooking medium was that instead of having a chicken broth background flavor, the gratin tasted intensely sweet, bright, and tomatoey. To boost the gratin's flavor further, I sandwiched in caramelized onions, which I'd made by slowly cooking thinly sliced onions in a little olive oil until soft, sweet, and brown and then adding some garlic. Excellent. For my next test, I stirred chopped olives into the onions, a quiet nod to the potato-tomato gratin's origins in Provence, France. Even better.

Daydreaming about delicious French food led to my final improvement: Taking a cue from what just may be the best cheese-topped dish on the planet—French onion soup, *bien sur*—I switched out the Parmesan for a generous sprinkling of nutty, potent Gruyère cheese.

At last, all was in harmony: bright tomatoes, sweet onions, salty olives, earthy potatoes, and tangy/nutty cheese. The gratin was not in the least watery, yet the potatoes were tender; the tomato slices on top had caramelized slightly, tasting sweet and becoming pleasantly chewy, like tomato candy of sorts; and the Gruyère was a pretty golden color. This lighter, brighter gratin was just as satisfying and possibly even more delicious than the usual one. We've a hunch it will be as popular in your home as it is in the test kitchen.

TEST KITCHEN TECHNIQUE **Layer by Layer and Row by Row**
Gratins are layered practically by definition. For our Potato-Tomato Gratin, in which the potato slices gently cook in the juices released by the tomatoes, it's critical that each potato layer adjoin a tomato layer.

- cheese
- tomato
- potato
- onion
- potato
- tomato

Holiday Green Bean Salad

We were looking for a side dish that we didn't have to worry about serving hot. With a little advance work, this salad is ready when you are. BY REBECCAH MARSTERS

POTATO-TOMATO GRATIN

Serves 6 to 8
A mandoline makes quick work of slicing the potatoes (tomatoes are better sliced by hand). We like the OXO Good Grips V-Blade Mandoline Slicer.

- 2 tablespoons olive oil
- 2 onions, halved and sliced thin
  Salt and pepper
- 2 garlic cloves, minced
- ¼ cup water
- ½ cup pitted kalamata olives, chopped
- 3 pounds plum tomatoes, cored and sliced ¼ inch thick
- 2 pounds russet potatoes, peeled and sliced ⅛ inch thick
- 2 teaspoons minced fresh thyme
- 8 ounces Gruyère cheese, shredded (2 cups)

1. Adjust oven rack to upper-middle position and heat oven to 400 degrees. Grease 13 by 9-inch baking dish. Heat oil in 12-inch skillet over medium heat until shimmering. Add onions, ½ teaspoon salt, and ¼ teaspoon pepper and cook, stirring frequently, until soft and golden brown, 15 to 20 minutes.

2. Add garlic and cook until fragrant, about 30 seconds. Add water and cook until nearly evaporated, scraping up any browned bits, about 2 minutes. Off heat, stir in olives; set aside.

3. Shingle half of tomatoes in even layer in prepared dish. Shingle half of potatoes over tomatoes and sprinkle 1 teaspoon thyme, ½ teaspoon salt, and ¼ teaspoon pepper over top. Spread onion mixture evenly over potatoes. Shingle remaining potatoes over onions. Shingle remaining tomatoes over potatoes. Sprinkle remaining 1 teaspoon thyme, ½ teaspoon salt, and ¼ teaspoon pepper over top.

4. Bake, uncovered, for 1 hour. Sprinkle with Gruyère and continue to bake until cheese is browned and bubbly and potatoes are completely tender, 25 to 30 minutes longer. Let cool for 30 minutes. Serve.

CHRISTMAS, EASTER, FOURTH of July, Thanksgiving—no matter the holiday, in my house green beans are on the table. But this Easter, I thought that it would be nice to come up with a recipe that I could serve cold or at room temperature to relieve some of the pressure of delivering everything hot to the table at the same time.

A little research unearthed many possibilities. As a starting point, I chose a diverse bunch of recipes—some called for cooking and chilling the beans, while others called for serving them raw and letting them soften in an acidic vinaigrette. Some recipes instructed the cook to leave the green beans whole, while the rest employed every manner of chopping, shredding, and fancy slicing. Seasonings ran the gamut from ginger and soy sauce to sage and rosemary. After an afternoon of cooking, I lined up an array of differing dishes for my tasters to try.

When it came to the cooking method (or lack thereof), beans that were boiled and immediately dressed turned muddy and drab after sitting in the acidic dressing. That was OK for me because I was secretly rooting for the raw beans—less work for the cook is never a bad thing on a holiday (or any day). But the raw beans didn't soften sufficiently in the dressing unless they were cut into paper-thin shreds; after I meticulously and laboriously sliced 2 pounds of beans, I knew that this procedure was a nonstarter. I opted instead for boiling and then shocking the beans, which means plunging them into ice water to immediately halt the cooking to preserve texture and color. Working with a handful of beans at a time and cutting them into 1½-inch pieces proved fast and efficient. As for the cooking, a few tests revealed that 6 minutes in boiling water, followed by the ice water dunk to halt the cooking, produced crisp-tender beans that could soak up the flavorful dressing.

Speaking of dressing, I cast about for fresh, bright flavors that would suit the arrival of spring. A combination of lemon juice and zest, shallot, mustard, garlic, and olive oil proved just the thing. I tried several herbs before landing on dill. When it came to the supporting players, sliced radishes brought color and peppery spice, while toasted almonds provided contrasting crunch.

I let the dressed salad sit for 30 minutes to give the flavors time to meld while

Let the dressed salad sit for 30 minutes before serving so the lemony dressing can permeate.

I readied the rest of the meal; the forgiving timing of my bean salad was a real plus. I scattered on the nuts just before serving so they'd retain their crunch. At last, my green beans were well seasoned, nicely cooked, bright, and beautiful. Scrawled one test cook on her final tasting sheet: "Delicious. Don't change a thing."

GREEN BEAN SALAD Serves 8

If you don't own a salad spinner, lay the green beans on a clean dish towel to dry in step 1. Our favorite Dijon is Grey Poupon Dijon Mustard. Substitute parsley for the dill, if you like.

- 2 pounds green beans, trimmed and cut into 1½-inch lengths
  Salt and pepper
- 1 shallot, minced
- 1 tablespoon Dijon mustard
- 1 teaspoon grated lemon zest plus 3 tablespoons juice
- 1 garlic clove, minced
- ¼ cup extra-virgin olive oil
- 8 radishes, trimmed and sliced thin
- 3 tablespoons minced fresh dill
- ½ cup sliced almonds, toasted

1. Bring 4 quarts water to boil in large pot. Fill large bowl halfway with ice and water. Add green beans and 1 tablespoon salt to boiling water and cook until crisp-tender, about 6 minutes. Drain green beans and place in ice bath to cool. Drain again, transfer to salad spinner, and spin dry. (Blanched, shocked, and dried green beans can be refrigerated for up to 2 days.)

2. Whisk shallot, mustard, lemon zest and juice, garlic, and 1½ teaspoons salt together in large bowl. Slowly whisk in oil until incorporated. Toss radishes, dill, and green beans with vinaigrette and let sit for 30 minutes or up to 2 hours, stirring occasionally. Stir almonds into salad. Season with salt and pepper to taste. Serve.

Hummingbird Cake

Somewhere this beloved Southern cake took a wrong turn. The combination of pineapples, bananas, and pecans should be fantastic. Instead, recipes yielded heavy, bland cakes. BY DIANE UNGER

I N 1978, A READER of *Southern Living* submitted a recipe to the magazine for a moist, three-layer, mildly spiced pineapple-banana cake slathered with cream cheese frosting and dotted with pecans. She called it "hummingbird cake" (see "The American Table"), and it struck an immediate chord. The cake continued a grand tradition of very sweet, bigger-than-life Southern layer cakes, and it went on to win blue ribbons, show up in countless bakery cases, and earn the devotion of home bakers from the Carolinas to Texas.

We tested the *Southern Living* recipe and several other versions—most of them not much different from that one. As we expected, hummingbird cake is very easy to put together (you don't need a mixer other than for the frosting) and tasted fine. That said, with four entire bananas, an 8-ounce can of pineapple, and 1½ cups of vegetable oil in the batter, the cake was heavy and greasy. Tasters bolted the first few bites, but not many could finish a slice. Plus, despite all that pineapple, the pineapple flavor was faint. The pecans didn't contribute much either. Finally, the original recipe called for stirring big chunks of banana into the batter. But in the baked cake, the chunks were mushy and the banana flavor limited: It was there when you bit into a chunk but nonexistent otherwise. These flaws seemed decidedly fixable, though, so I went into the test kitchen aiming to turn a good cake into a great one.

Starting with the published recipe, I began by changing the cake's dimensions, shifting from three 8-inch layers to two 9-inch ones. My motivation was practical: Few home bakers have three same-size cake pans, not to mention space on a cooling rack for three layers. Also, two layers meant one less pan to prep (grease, fit with parchment, grease again, and flour) and wash. I knocked a couple of the other easy problems out of the way right at the start as well. To bring out the flavor of the pecans, I toasted them before stirring them into the batter and sprinkling them over the top—a small change but a big improvement. And for better distribution, I mashed the (very ripe) bananas, as though I were making banana bread, and stirred the mash, rather than the chunks, into the batter. Now the banana

The toasted, chopped pecans on top echo the pecans inside the cake.

flavor was present in every bite.

Having maximized the banana flavor, I turned to amplifying the pineapple. The original recipe called for one 8-ounce can of crushed pineapple, including the juice. I tried straining out the juice (about ⅓ cup) and concentrating it by boiling it down and then adding the concentrated juice plus the pineapple solids to the cake batter. The pineapple flavor was better,

although I still wasn't over the moon. It took a mistake to send me there.

One afternoon, all I could find in the test kitchen pantry was a 20-ounce can of pineapple, so I measured my ⅓ cup of juice and weighed my 8 ounces of pineapple solids. The cake I made that day tasted truly, deeply tropical, but where had all that flavor come from? It doesn't take a genius to figure it out: The 8-ounce can of pineapple that

I'd been using didn't actually contain 8 ounces of fruit solids. When I measured it out later, I discovered that an 8-ounce can has just 3.6 ounces of pineapple solids; the rest is juice. By using a full 8 ounces of fruit, I'd inadvertently more than doubled the amount in the cake. Could I sneak in extra pineapple juice, too? I boiled down ⅔ cup of juice (the amount from two 8-ounce cans, from which I'd also get my fruit) and

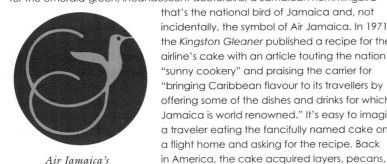
stirred it into the batter. The flavor of this cake was the most delicious yet.

Obviously, there was a price to pay: While the extra pineapple bolstered the flavor, it made the cake heavier and denser than ever. Turning to the oil to fix both faults, I cut back 1 tablespoon at a time. Eight test cakes later, I was using one-third less oil than at the start, and the cake was moist yet no longer greasy.

This lower-oil version was also lighter—but not light enough. To further lighten my cake, I took a look at the leavener. The original cake called for 1 teaspoon of baking soda. I knew from experience that too much soda produces baked goods with a metallic taste and, counterintuitively, less rise; introducing more wasn't an option. Instead, I'd try adding baking powder. I spent several days testing my cake with varying ratios of the two. Finally, with 1 teaspoon of baking soda and 2 teaspoons of powder, my cake was light, tall, and beautiful.

Turning to the frosting, I borrowed an unusual test kitchen method: In the past we've found that if you beat together softened cream cheese and butter, the frosting is soft and squishy, making the cake difficult to slice unless you chill it for many hours. Instead, I beat together the softened butter and the confectioners' sugar, adding the chilled cream cheese last, bit by bit; this way, the frosting was firmer and didn't squish out between the layers.

Now that we were tasting the frosted cake, we realized that the extra pineapple had pushed an already sweet cake over the edge. After a few frosting tests, I restored balance with a tangier cream cheese frosting—a simple matter of using less confectioners' sugar.

When my colleagues started to hover like hummingbirds whenever I was baking, I knew that my cake was ready to fly.

HUMMINGBIRD CAKE
Serves 12 to 16

Toast a total of 2 cups of pecans to divide between the cake and the frosting. The cake will slice more cleanly if you refrigerate it for at least 1 hour.

CAKE

- 2 (8-ounce) cans crushed pineapple in juice
- 3 cups (15 ounces) all-purpose flour
- 2 teaspoons baking powder
- 1 teaspoon baking soda
- 1 teaspoon ground cinnamon
- 1 teaspoon salt
- 2 cups (14 ounces) granulated sugar
- 3 large eggs
- 1 cup vegetable oil
- 4 very ripe large bananas, peeled and mashed (2 cups)
- 1½ cups pecans, toasted and chopped
- 2 teaspoons vanilla extract

FROSTING

- 20 tablespoons unsalted butter, softened
- 5 cups (20 ounces) confectioners' sugar
- 2½ teaspoons vanilla extract
- ½ teaspoon salt
- 20 ounces cream cheese, chilled and cut into 20 equal pieces
- ½ cup pecans, toasted and chopped

1. FOR THE CAKE: Adjust oven rack to middle position and heat oven to 350 degrees. Grease 2 light-colored 9-inch round cake pans, line with parchment paper, grease parchment, and flour pans. Drain pineapple in fine-mesh strainer set over bowl, pressing to remove juice. Pour juice into small saucepan and cook over medium heat until reduced to ⅓ cup, about 5 minutes; set aside.

2. Whisk flour, baking powder, baking soda, cinnamon, and salt together in bowl. Whisk sugar and eggs together in separate large bowl; whisk

TASTING CANNED CRUSHED PINEAPPLE

Buying a can of pineapple is a convenient way to eat the fruit without tangling with its spiky green fronds and eye-riddled peel. We use the crushed version in recipes that don't require whole rings or large chunks. But we had a question: If it's just fresh fruit, cut up and canned, are there noticeable differences from product to product? On supermarket shelves, we found three national products packed in pineapple juice (which we prefer to sugary syrup). We asked 21 test kitchen editors and cooks to taste each crushed pineapple in two blind taste tests, sampling them plain and in our Hummingbird Cake.

Our verdict: Brand matters. We can recommend two products with small, even chunks that tasted "almost like fresh" and gave the cake textural interest. The third product had a texture like that of "baby food." The U.S. Food and Drug Administration regulates the size of crushed pineapple, requiring "finely cut or finely shredded or grated or diced"; the definition apparently leaves lots of wiggle room.

There are more than 100 varieties of pineapple, so we checked in with the manufacturers of the products that we tasted and learned that the two we liked use Smooth Cayenne pineapples, while the product we disliked uses Queen Victorias. Both varieties are said to have excellent flavor when eaten fresh, but the Smooth Cayennes are prized for canning because they hold their shape well when processed—exactly what our tasters noticed.

Our top two products were also "perfectly sweet," with "fuller," "intense" flavor, while the bottom-ranking product tasted "flat." Nutrition labels revealed that the losing product had 2 to 3 fewer grams of naturally derived sugar per ½-cup serving. Experts we spoke with said that variety, processing, harvesting time, and postharvest storage and handling all affect flavor, as well.

In the end, Dole Crushed Pineapple in 100% Pineapple Juice, the least expensive product in our lineup, was lightly sweet yet tart, with recognizable pineapple chunks—just right for our baking and cooking needs. –HANNAH CROWLEY

RECOMMENDED

	TASTERS' NOTES
DOLE Crushed Pineapple in 100% Pineapple Juice **Price:** $1.99 for 20 oz ($0.10 per oz) **Sugar:** 16 g per ½-cup serving **Pineapple Variety:** Smooth Cayenne from the Philippines	Our top pick was "bright" and "perfectly sweet, but not cloyingly so," with "large tender chunks" and a "nice natural firmness"—"almost like fresh." In the cake, the pineapple pieces had a "pleasant" presence.
DEL MONTE Crushed Pineapple in 100% Juice **Price:** $2.63 for 20 oz ($0.13 per oz) **Sugar:** 15 g per ½-cup serving **Pineapple Variety:** Smooth Cayenne from the Philippines	This product was "sweet but not too sweet," with "bright, mild pineapple flavor." Its "nice and firm chunks" tasted "close" to fresh. They were "definitely" visible in the cake and made for a "pleasantly fruity background." A few tasters faulted the flavor for being too "subtle."

NOT RECOMMENDED

NATIVE FOREST 100% Organic Pineapple, Crushed **Price:** $3.45 for 14 oz ($0.25 per oz) **Sugar:** 13 g per ½-cup serving **Pineapple Variety:** Queen Victoria from Vietnam		This product was flat and "very mild," with "no complexity," and was even "tinny," according to a few tasters. But what really bugged us was the "pulverized to baby food" texture, which "totally changed" the cake. As one taster put it, "Where's the pineapple?"

in oil. Stir in bananas, pecans, vanilla, drained pineapple, and reduced pineapple juice. Stir in flour mixture until just combined.

3. Divide batter evenly between prepared pans and smooth tops with rubber spatula. Bake until dark golden brown on top and toothpick inserted in center comes out clean, 50 to 55 minutes, rotating pans halfway through baking. Let cakes cool in pans on wire rack for 20 minutes. Remove cakes from pans, discarding parchment, and let cool completely on rack, about 2 hours.

4. FOR THE FROSTING: Using stand mixer fitted with paddle, beat butter, sugar, vanilla, and salt together on low

speed until smooth; continue to mix for 2 minutes, scraping down bowl as needed. Increase speed to medium-low, add cream cheese 1 piece at a time, and mix until smooth; continue to mix for 2 minutes.

5. Place 1 cake layer on platter. Spread 2 cups frosting evenly over top, right to edge of cake. Top with second cake layer, press lightly to adhere, then spread 2 cups frosting evenly over top. Spread remaining frosting evenly over sides of cake. To smooth frosting, run edge of offset spatula around cake sides and over top. Sprinkle top of cake with pecans. Refrigerate cake for at least 1 hour before serving. (Cake can be refrigerated for up to 2 days.)

Rediscovering Anadama Bread

What's the secret to perfecting this old-fashioned cornmeal and molasses loaf? More of both.

BY REBECCAH MARSTERS

Colonial bakers had to guess when their bread was done; we use a thermometer.

A NADAMA BREAD IS a New England classic with two defining ingredients that have a centuries-old association with the region: cornmeal and molasses. I knew it as a child growing up in Massachusetts, but few of my fellow test cooks had even heard of it. I hoped to develop a version that lived up to my memories: moist and chewy, sturdy yet tender, faintly bitter yet sweet, and ever so slightly gritty.

All the recipes I found called for cornmeal, molasses, flour, and yeast, but beyond that, I had choices to make: all-purpose, bread, or whole-wheat flour? Butter or shortening? Water or milk? I chose an assortment of recipes and spent a day baking. The baking breads smelled amazing, but after they were cooled and sliced, we could barely taste the molasses and the cornmeal. I decided to pick a stripped-down recipe from this initial test, pack in more of both ingredients, and then test the other elements.

I started with a recipe that called for a typical ½ cup of cornmeal to produce two loaves. In succeeding tests, I added incrementally more cornmeal until I'd doubled the amount (with more than 1 cup, the bread was dense). But since cornmeal doesn't develop gluten the way that flour does, and breads need gluten for structure, by fixing a problem I'd inadvertently caused one: flat tops. Luckily, a little extra yeast restored the pretty domes. Older recipes for anadama bread often call for softening the cornmeal in hot liquid or cooking it into porridge before incorporating it. Leaving no stone unturned, I tried these methods but found them unnecessary.

Turning to the loaf's other signature ingredient, I started with 2 tablespoons of molasses and went up and up and up. At ½ cup of molasses and 1 cup of cornmeal, my anadama bread was a beautiful caramel-brown color—and it no longer had an identity crisis.

Next I did some side-by-side tests with flours: Whole-wheat made the bread heavy. Bread flour worked nicely, but so did all-purpose; I opted for the latter since most home cooks keep it on hand. As for milk, it made a softer bread, but we preferred the nicer chew of the bread made with water. Butter seemed truer to the bread's Colonial past than oil. Anadama bread is a basic, homey, old-fashioned loaf. Ultimately, simple was best.

ANADAMA BREAD Makes 2 loaves
This recipe is easily halved.

- 1 cup (5 ounces) cornmeal, plus extra for dusting
- 2 cups warm water (110 degrees)
- ½ cup molasses
- 5 tablespoons unsalted butter, melted
- 5½ cups (27½ ounces) all-purpose flour
- 1 tablespoon instant or rapid-rise yeast
- 2½ teaspoons salt

1. Grease large bowl. Grease two 8½ by 4½-inch loaf pans and dust with extra cornmeal. Whisk water, molasses, and melted butter in bowl or large measuring cup until combined.

2. Using stand mixer fitted with dough hook, mix flour, yeast, salt, and cornmeal on low speed until combined, about 5 seconds. Slowly add molasses mixture and knead until cohesive mass starts to form, about 2 minutes. Increase speed to medium-low and knead until dough is smooth and elastic, 6 to 8 minutes. (Dough should clear sides of bowl but will stick to bottom.) Turn out dough onto lightly floured counter and knead for 1 minute.

3. Transfer dough to prepared bowl and cover with plastic wrap. Let rise at room temperature until almost doubled in size and fingertip depression in dough springs back slowly, 1 to 1½ hours.

4. Gently press down on center of dough to deflate. Place dough on lightly floured counter and divide in half. Working with 1 half at a time, pat dough into 17 by 8-inch rectangle. With short side facing you, roll dough away from you into firm cylinder. Pinch seam closed. Place loaf seam side down in prepared pan, pressing gently into corners. Repeat with remaining dough.

5. Cover loaves loosely with plastic and let rise at room temperature until almost doubled in size, 1 to 1½ hours (tops of loaves should rise about 1 inch above lips of pans). About 20 minutes before dough is fully risen, adjust oven rack to lower-middle position and heat oven to 425 degrees.

6. Place pans in oven and reduce oven temperature to 375 degrees. Bake until crust is brown and bread registers 200 degrees, 35 to 45 minutes, switching and rotating pans halfway through baking. Turn out loaves onto wire rack and let cool completely before serving, about 2 hours.

TEST KITCHEN TECHNIQUE **Getting Anadama Bread into Shape**
Our anadama dough is easy to work with and requires no special tricks.

After the first rise, divide the dough in half and pat one piece of dough into a rectangle.

Roll the dough into a tight cylinder and pinch the seam closed.

Transfer the loaf, seam side down, to the prepared loaf pan. Repeat with the rest of the dough and bake.

Hearty Cream of Chicken Soup

Could we get deep, long-simmered chicken flavor on a weeknight timetable?
Yes, if we made the chicken skin do double duty. BY SARAH GABRIEL

I ONCE HOSTED A soup-only potluck, and I've made most every creamy soup in the book, from cream of broccoli to corn chowder. So it's safe to say that I'm a soup person. How is it, then, that cream of chicken soup has eluded me? I've eaten plenty of casseroles made with the canned version, but I've never had this soup as, well, soup. It was time to remedy that oversight.

I began by choosing a half-dozen recipes. They called for various thickeners (cream, roux, cornstarch) and chicken cuts (whole birds, just thighs or legs, just breasts). The simplest recipe called for simmering a chicken breast in store-bought broth, shredding the chicken, and then stirring it back into the broth with cream; I wasn't surprised that this soup was wan. The most complicated recipe was a two-day process calling for a double stock (you make stock and then make a second stock using the first stock in place of water); as you'd expect, this soup was rich and flavorful. But I needed a faster, simpler path.

At this point, I knew a few things. First, we preferred the texture of shredded white meat in the soup, so I'd use breasts. Second, it was clear that a roux was the easiest and best thickening method. Reducing a little sherry proved an easy path to enhanced depth. Lastly, I wanted this soup to be more substantial. To that end, I added potatoes and carrots, along with leeks for sweetness.

For my next test, I browned two bone-in, skin-on chicken breasts and set them aside while I sautéed the leeks in butter, stirred in flour, added the sherry, and cooked it down a bit. I whisked in chicken broth and then added diced potatoes, sliced carrots, and the browned chicken. I brought the soup to a boil and then simmered it until the chicken was cooked (about 20 minutes). I took out the chicken, shredded it, and returned it to the simmering pot when the vegetables were fully cooked, about 20 minutes later, along with some heavy cream. This soup was decent, but the chicken flavor wasn't great.

Since I wanted rich chicken flavor, I knew that I couldn't give up on the browning: The fond (the browned bits on the bottom of the pot) that searing creates is incredibly flavorful. And I knew that I couldn't leave the browned chicken in the pot the entire time to intensify the soup's flavor, because it

would overcook. Then I got a crazy idea: Could I take the skin off of the chicken and brown it alone to create fond, then leave it in through the cooking process to extract even more flavor? I gave it a try, using the skin from two breasts. Eyeing the chicken fat in the pot, I decided to use it to help build the roux. I left the skin in the pot, added butter, and sautéed the leeks in the tasty fats. Then I proceeded as before, eventually adding the breasts and simmering them until they registered 160 degrees.

I pulled the meat out to rest but continued to simmer the skin in the broth. When the meat cooled, I shredded it, removed the skin from the pot, stirred the cream and chicken into the soup, and collected my colleagues. We dipped in spoons, sipped, and agreed: Cream of chicken soup can be fast, hearty, and satisfying, after all.

HEARTY CREAM OF CHICKEN SOUP Serves 6

- 2 (12-ounce) bone-in split chicken breasts, skin removed and reserved, trimmed
  Salt and pepper
- 1 tablespoon water
- 1 pound leeks, white and light green parts only, halved lengthwise, sliced ¼ inch thick, and washed thoroughly (2½ cups)
- 2 tablespoons unsalted butter
- ½ cup all-purpose flour
- ⅓ cup dry sherry
- 8 cups chicken broth
- 12 ounces Yukon gold potatoes, peeled and cut into ¾-inch pieces
- 3 carrots, peeled and cut into ½-inch pieces
- 3 sprigs fresh thyme
- 1 bay leaf
- ½ cup heavy cream
- 3 tablespoons minced fresh chives

1. Season chicken with salt and pepper. Place water and chicken skin in Dutch oven and cook over medium-low heat with lid slightly ajar until enough fat has rendered from skin to coat bottom of pot, about 7 minutes.

2. Uncover pot, increase heat to medium, and continue to cook until skin has browned, about 3 minutes, flipping skin halfway through cooking. Add leeks and butter and cook until leeks are just softened, about 3 minutes. Stir in flour

and cook for 1 minute. Stir in sherry and cook until evaporated, about 1 minute.

3. Slowly whisk in broth until incorporated. Add potatoes, carrots, thyme sprigs, bay leaf, and chicken and bring to boil. Reduce heat to medium-low and simmer, uncovered, until chicken registers 160 degrees, 20 to 25 minutes.

4. Transfer chicken to plate and let cool for 20 minutes. While chicken cools, continue to simmer soup for 20 minutes. Using shallow spoon, skim grease and foam from surface of soup. Discard chicken bones and shred meat into 1-inch pieces. Discard chicken skin, thyme sprigs, and bay leaf. Off heat, stir in cream and chicken. Season with salt and pepper to taste. Sprinkle individual portions with chives and serve.

No dainty portions or fancy bowls here: This soup makes a rich, hearty, and satisfying supper.

TEST KITCHEN DISCOVERY
Building Chicken Flavor
We remove the skin from bone-in breasts, simmer it in water to render its fat, and then brown it to create flavorful fond.

SKIN IS IN
We brown just the chicken skin.

Deviled Beef Short Ribs

These rich, ultratender, spicy, crumb-coated short ribs sounded like a perfect late-winter dish. But the devil was in the details. BY JEREMY SAUER

WHEN THE COLD weather hits, my friends start thinking about sipping wine by the fire. Me? I start thinking about braised short ribs. But at winter's midpoint—after I've braised a rodeo's worth of ribs—I'm ready for something other than the standard onion-wine-broth braise. And that's why I was so excited to stumble across deviled short ribs. This throwback recipe from the 1960s calls for roasting (not braising) the ribs after they've been "deviled" with either a rub of dry mustard, black pepper, and spices or a marinade of prepared yellow mustard, black pepper, and seasonings. Once tender, the ribs are sprinkled with bread crumbs and broiled until the crumbs are crispy. I was sold on the idea, but after cooking my way through nearly a dozen versions of this recipe, one thing was clear: The devil is in the details.

Before I could figure out how to make short ribs taste devilish, though, I needed to figure out how best to cook them. Most recipes call for roasting the ribs, uncovered, in a moderate oven (anywhere from 350 to 425 degrees) for 3 to 5 hours, but I found this problematic, as the ribs never quite took on that silky quality that makes short ribs so appealing. Taking a cue from an old test kitchen technique, I turned down the oven to 325 degrees and roasted the ribs, meat side up, in a covered baking dish. The result was moist, tender, silky ribs in about 3 hours, though my tasters noted that a few pockets of fat remained. To make sure that the ribs were fully rendered, I cooked them meat side down so that the meat cooked in its own juices, resulting in ultratender and completely rendered ribs. With the cooking method settled, I could concentrate on making the flavor live up to its deviled name.

None of the initial recipes had been awful, but the seasonings were awfully meek: Maybe lots of mustard and black pepper were considered "devilish" 50 years ago, but they're not today. I needed to add a lot more fire to this dish. I decided I'd start by seasoning the ribs with just salt and pepper, roasting them, and then brushing them with an amped-up mixture of both prepared yellow mustard and dry mustard, a full tablespoon of black pepper, and a little cayenne near the end of cooking before

Jalapeño, yellow mustard, dry mustard, and cayenne make these rich, succulent short ribs especially devilish.

sprinkling on the crumbs. This immediately improved the dish's flavor and kick, but these ribs needed more depth—and they weren't close to making anyone sweat.

I tested my working recipe with both Dijon and brown mustards, but my tasters preferred the clarity of the traditional yellow mustard, so I'd have to add flavor in other ways. I tried all manner of citrus juices and zests, testing orange, lemon,

and lime against each other and in combination. My tasters ended up liking the pairing of orange juice and lemon zest best. Some brown sugar added roundness, and a couple of minced jalapeños really brought the brimstone. Combining these ingredients in the food processor ensured that the heat was evenly incorporated and that the mixture was thick enough to hold the crumbs.

All that was left was brushing on the

glaze, sprinkling on the bread crumbs (we liked panko for its superior crunch), and firing up the broiler. Unfortunately, the broiler was a no-go from the get-go. The crumbs on the exterior had a tendency to scorch, while those that were in contact with the glaze were gummy. Instead of using the broiler, I increased the oven temperature to 425 degrees. This browned the crumbs more evenly but didn't solve the gummy crumb problem. I hoped that I could fix this by brushing on the glaze and then roasting the ribs before coating them with the crumbs. It worked, and I found that I could actually glaze three times, for deeper flavor, before rolling the ribs in panko and roasting a final time to brown the crumbs.

I was almost there, but my tasters thought that the crumbs were unevenly browned and could use a little punching up. Changing course slightly, I opted to toast the crumbs in butter on the stovetop before coating the ribs and then serving them immediately. This allowed me to brown the crumbs perfectly while also adding a nutty sweetness from the butter and an herbal freshness from chopped parsley and lemon zest. Removed from the oven and rolled in the toasted crumbs before serving, these Deviled Beef Short Ribs definitely lived up to their name. And I didn't have to sell my soul to get them.

DEVILED BEEF SHORT RIBS
Serves 4 to 6
English-style short ribs contain a single rib bone. For a milder sauce, use only one jalapeño and discard the seeds.

- ⅔ cup yellow mustard
- ⅓ cup orange juice
- ⅓ cup packed light brown sugar
- 1–2 jalapeño chiles, stemmed, seeds reserved, and roughly chopped
- 4 teaspoons dry mustard
- 1 teaspoon grated lemon zest plus 1 tablespoon juice
  Salt and pepper
- ½ teaspoon cayenne pepper
- 5 pounds bone-in English-style short ribs, bones 4 to 5 inches long, 1 to 1½ inches of meat on top of bone, trimmed

- 2 tablespoons unsalted butter
- 1½ cups panko bread crumbs
- 1 tablespoon chopped fresh parsley

1. Adjust oven rack to middle position and heat oven to 325 degrees. Combine yellow mustard, orange juice, sugar, jalapeños and reserved seeds, dry mustard, lemon juice, and 2 teaspoons pepper in food processor and process until smooth, about 30 seconds; set aside. (Mustard mixture can be refrigerated for up to 1 week.)

2. Combine 1 tablespoon salt, 1 tablespoon pepper, and cayenne in bowl. Sprinkle ribs all over with spice mixture. Arrange ribs, meat side down, in 13 by 9-inch baking dish. Cover dish tightly with aluminum foil and roast until meat is nearly tender, about 3 hours.

3. Meanwhile, melt butter in 12-inch skillet over medium-high heat. Add panko and cook, stirring often, until golden brown, about 3 minutes. Off heat, stir in parsley and lemon zest and transfer to shallow dish.

4. Remove baking dish from oven and increase oven temperature to 425 degrees; transfer ribs to plate. Discard rendered fat and juices from dish. Brush meat (not bone) all over with one-fourth of mustard sauce and return ribs to dish, meat side up. Roast, uncovered, until beginning to brown, about 10 minutes. Brush meat again with one-third of remaining mustard sauce and continue to roast until well browned and completely tender, 10 to 15 minutes longer. Transfer ribs to serving platter, tent loosely with foil, and let rest for 15 minutes.

5. Brush meat once more with half of remaining mustard sauce and roll in panko mixture, taking care to entirely coat meat. Serve, passing remaining mustard sauce separately.

TEST KITCHEN TECHNIQUE **A Roasting-Braising Hybrid Method**
Most short rib recipes call for searing, then braising, and finally turning the braising liquid into a sauce. For Deviled Beef Short Ribs, we took a different road: We put the ribs in a baking dish, meat side down, and roasted them (covered) until tender, about 3 hours. The meat cooked in its own rendered fat and juices, giving us fully rendered, supertender short ribs without much hands-on work. To finish, we uncovered the ribs, brushed them with a glaze, roasted them meat side up, repeated, and then rolled them in toasted crumbs.

A foil cover traps steam for even, efficient cooking.

The ribs cook meat side down in their flavorful rendered juices and fat.

Illustration: Lauren Pettapiece

The American Table
Dinner with the Devil

There's no question that we give the devil his due when it comes to dining: Americans eat deviled eggs, devil's food cake, deviled ham, deviled ribs . . . We've by no means exhausted the list. Where does our culinary fascination with the dark side come from? The kitchen use of the term dates back more than 200 years, and although its precise meaning has evolved, "hot and spicy" are the constants—mostly.

The "devil" got its start in the kitchen as "a red-hot bit of meat" that was "loaded with kian" (cayenne), as British writer Peter Pindar described it way back in 1788. Often made from turkey gizzards that were scored, seasoned, and broiled, a devil was typically savored in the wee hours by 18th-century gentlemen hungry after a night of carousing.

Within 50 years, "deviled," now an adjective, was applied to any food that got the hot 'n' spicy treatment. A devil could be made from legs, rumps, kidneys, and backs of grouse, deer, calves, or sheep. Seasonings encompassed curry, mustard, anchovy, and truffle powder. Even a biscuit could be deviled. "The only indispensable attribute," Margaret Dods wrote in 1829 in *The Cook and Housewife's Manual*, "is scorching heat and tear-compelling pungency."

The occasional dose of spice was thought to revive jaded appetites and even to strengthen character. "If a man would keep the devil altogether out of him, he must have a little of the devil in him," Charles MacKay wrote in *The Gouty Philosopher* in 1864. "The homœopathists tell us that like kills like, and that poisons which create headache cure headache. Upon this principle a few globules of the essence of devil 'taken medicinally' at proper times, may weaken the devil in the blood."

Today, not every food with "devil" in its name scorches. Devil's food cake may have been named for its red tint, caused by a reaction of baking soda and cocoa, or to contrast with angel food cake. But more often than not, while it's said that he who sups with the devil needs a long spoon, we wonder if what would really help is a cooling spoonful of yogurt.

GREEN SALAD WITH ORANGES AND PISTACHIOS Serves 4 to 6
A fruity salad is a perfect counterpoint to our rich Deviled Beef Short Ribs. Use large oranges to ensure that you have enough juice for the dressing.

- 2 oranges
- 2 tablespoons cider vinegar
- 1 tablespoon honey
  Salt and pepper
- ½ teaspoon ground cumin
- ¼ cup extra-virgin olive oil
- 8 ounces (8 cups) mesclun
- ½ cup thinly sliced red onion
- ⅓ cup shelled pistachios, toasted and chopped

1. Grate 2 teaspoons zest from 1 orange; set aside. Cut away peel and pith from oranges. Holding fruit over large bowl, use paring knife to slice between membranes to release segments. Cut segments crosswise into ½-inch pieces and transfer to double layer of paper towels to drain. Squeeze membranes over bowl to release juice.

2. Pour off all but 2 tablespoons juice from bowl (reserve excess juice for another use). Add vinegar, honey, ¾ teaspoon salt, ½ teaspoon pepper, cumin, and reserved orange zest and whisk to combine. Whisking constantly, slowly drizzle in oil until incorporated. Add mesclun, onion, pistachios, and orange segments and toss to combine. Season with salt and pepper to taste. Serve.

The Best Fried Catfish

What's the secret to Mississippi's crunchy, perfectly seasoned fried catfish?
We went down to the delta's best fish joints to find out. BY CHRISTIE MORRISON

NOT TOO LONG ago, I was one of those northern naysayers who dismiss catfish as funny-looking bottom-feeders with a sometimes "pondy" taste. Then I visited the Mississippi delta. Mississippi is one of the biggest producers of farmed catfish in the United States, and the Mississippi River and its tributaries are still popular, productive destinations for catfish fishing. It's rare to visit a restaurant there that doesn't have fried catfish on the menu. The fish's firm texture (think grouper or sea bass) and mild flavor give it broad appeal, but for most aficionados, deep-fried catfish is the only way to go. I was convinced of that when I tried it prepared this way at the famed Ajax Diner in Oxford, Mississippi, and at Taylor Grocery in the nearby hamlet of Taylor. Both versions exemplified the best in fried catfish: crispy, thin cornmeal crusts; perfectly cooked, sweet meat; and just enough spice to make it interesting.

I peppered both restaurant owners with questions about their techniques. While neither Ajax Diner owner Randy Yates nor Taylor Grocery owner Lynn Hewlett would give up his secret formula, both men were willing to talk to me about their general approach. Yates dips his catfish in a mixture of buttermilk and egg and then dredges it in a blend of cornmeal and all-purpose flour; the result is a delicate yet crispy coating with just a hint of seasonings. Hewlett soaks the fish in ice water (to firm up the meat) before breading. His coating is also cornmeal-based, but instead of flour, he adds cream meal—a very finely ground cornmeal—and his own blend of spices for a bit of kick. His crust is crunchy and deeply flavored, making me wish that it wasn't impolite to use my fingers to pick up every crumb.

When I returned to the test kitchen, I cobbled together my best approximations of the two Mississippi versions that I'd tasted. Then, just to be sure that I was on the right track, I pitted these recipes against a few others that I found in our test kitchen library (including an all-cornmeal crust and one that called for "fish fry" coating). Tasters much preferred my Mississippi mock-ups: The Taylor Grocery coating came out ahead, while the Ajax Diner buttermilk wash scored big points for flavor. The all-cornmeal crust was too gritty, while the crusts using lots of all-purpose

A mixture of regular and finely ground cornmeal gives our coating superb crunch.

flour had the texture of cardboard and tended to flake off. Fish fry, a packaged blend of corn flour and spices, had a decent texture, but tasters didn't love the seasoning, which inevitably varies from brand to brand. Better to stick with a more neutral base and select my own seasonings.

We loved the cornmeal-slash-cream-meal crust, but cream meal is difficult to come by outside the South. Scouring the test kitchen pantry for a substitute, I spied masa harina—the finely ground cornmeal product used to make tortillas. When I mixed masa harina with the coarse cornmeal, its texture resembled the Taylor Grocery coating. Unfortunately, masa harina is not exactly a pantry staple in many homes, and I hated to call for it, especially when I needed such a small amount. My working recipe used 1⅓ cups of cornmeal

and ⅔ cup of masa harina, plus a few seasonings. I tried substituting an additional ⅔ cup of cornmeal, which I processed in a spice grinder, for the masa harina. After about 30 seconds, I had a pale yellow powder with the same lightness and grit as the masa harina. I pitted the cornmeal–masa harina version and the all-cornmeal version against each other; tasters couldn't tell the difference. I continued to tinker with the ratios to

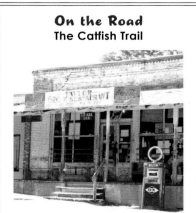

Look very carefully and you'll spy Taylor Grocery proprietor (and Taylor native) Lynn Hewlett on the far right. You can often find him there, sitting on his porch, finger-picking a tune on his Dobro guitar, and greeting regulars by name. Today, the 125-year-old store is a café that serves extraordinary fried catfish. To read more about it, and the rest of Christie's trip to Mississippi, visit **CooksCountry.com/catfishtrail**.

find the best texture and crunch. We declared equal parts of the coarse and the ground cornmeal—1 cup of each—the winner.

Just as important as crunch was the balanced blend of spices. While I was tempted to reach for a jar of Cajun seasoning, I knew from experience that brands vary widely, and the last thing I wanted was an overspiced, too-heavy-on-the-oregano blend. The fish that I had enjoyed most on my trip had plenty of salt and pepper, a hint of cayenne, and some garlic powder for backbone. After a few tries, I struck gold: 4 teaspoons of salt, 2 teaspoons each of pepper and granulated garlic, and a teaspoon of cayenne.

At this point the coating had won over tasters with its piquant flavor and crunch—if it would just stay put. I tested buttermilk, whole milk, and ice water—with and without egg—to determine which was the best glue for the crust. Not surprisingly, the ice water added no flavor, nor, in the end, did it noticeably firm up the fish. We liked the slight tang that buttermilk imparted and its texture (thicker than milk) helped the crust adhere, even without an egg. To bump up the flavor, I added a teaspoon of hot sauce to the buttermilk, and I simply gave the fish a quick dunk in the mixture before dredging it in the seasoned cornmeal.

The fillets spent about 8 minutes

> ▶ Fried catfish without sauce? That's like a teenager without a cell phone: unimaginable. For a recipe for our **Comeback Sauce**, go to CooksCountry.com/may14.

in 2 quarts of 350-degree oil. They emerged moist and tender, with a supercrunchy crust—which we liked so much that we wanted more of it. I got it by halving the fillets lengthwise, which yielded more surface area for extra coating, thus extra crunch. Also, the smaller pieces were easier to manage both in and out of the pot. The catfish "tenders" fried slightly faster than the whole fillets—in about 5 minutes—making it a snap to cook the second batch while the first batch was still piping hot.

As I tucked into a piece of fish and heard the satisfying crunch, I thought that my newfound friends in the delta would be pleased. Someday I'd like to make a return trip to this incredible area, but until then I can have a cornmeal-crusted reminder of my visit to Mississippi any time I want.

FRIED CATFISH Serves 4 to 6

Use a Dutch oven that holds 6 quarts or more. If your spice grinder is small, grind the cornmeal in batches or process it in a blender for 60 to 90 seconds. Serve with our Comeback Sauce (recipe is online).

- 2 cups buttermilk
- 1 teaspoon hot sauce
- 2 cups cornmeal
- 4 teaspoons salt
- 2 teaspoons pepper
- 2 teaspoons granulated garlic
- 1 teaspoon cayenne pepper
- 4 (6- to 8-ounce) catfish fillets, halved lengthwise along natural seam
- 2 quarts peanut or vegetable oil
  Lemon wedges

1. Set wire rack in rimmed baking sheet and line half of rack with triple layer of paper towels. Whisk buttermilk and hot sauce together in shallow dish. Process 1 cup cornmeal in spice grinder to fine powder, 30 to 45 seconds. Whisk salt, pepper, granulated garlic, cayenne, remaining 1 cup cornmeal, and ground cornmeal together in second shallow dish.

2. Pat fish dry with paper towels. Working with 1 piece of fish at a time, dip fish in buttermilk mixture, letting excess drip back into dish. Dredge fish in cornmeal mixture, shaking off excess, and transfer to large plate.

3. Add oil to large Dutch oven until it measures about 1½ inches deep and heat over medium-high heat to 350 degrees. Working with 4 pieces of fish at a time, add fish to hot oil. Adjust burner, if necessary, to maintain oil temperature between 325 and 350 degrees. Fry fish until golden brown and crispy, about 5 minutes. Transfer fish to paper towel–lined side of prepared rack and let drain for 1 minute, then move to unlined side of rack. Return oil to 350 degrees and repeat with remaining fish. Serve with lemon wedges.

TESTING CLIP-ON DIGITAL THERMOMETERS

Accuracy is paramount when cooking, as anyone with a faulty thermometer knows. A few degrees in the wrong direction can spell scorched sugar or soggy fried chicken. In the test kitchen, we use hands-free clip-on digital thermometers to monitor temperatures when deep-frying food, making candy, and—with some models—checking food in the oven without needing to open the oven door. We tested four models, priced from $24.99 to $59. We made French fries, fried chicken, and caramel sauce, evaluating the thermometers for accuracy, functionality, durability, and how well they fit a variety of pans. When all was said and done, we liked two of the four models that we tested. The Polder Classic Digital Thermometer/Timer is our Best Buy. But while the ThermoWorks ChefAlarm is more expensive than the others, its accuracy, easy interface, and promise of longevity are well worth it. (To read the full testing story, go to **CooksCountry.com/may14**.) –HANNAH CROWLEY

KEY Good ★★★   Fair ★★   Poor ★

HIGHLY RECOMMENDED

	CRITERIA		TESTERS' NOTES
THERMOWORKS ChefAlarm **Model:** TX-1100 **Price:** $59 **Source:** Thermoworks.com **Temperature Range:** -58°F to 572°F	Accuracy Functionality Pan Compatibility	★★★ ★★★ ★★★	This thermometer, with an oven-safe probe, was the most accurate among those we tested, plus it had an intuitive design. It's the only model we tested that can be calibrated; we also liked the programmable high- and low-temperature alarms, the adjustable brightness and volume, the on/off switch, and the small knob on the probe that stayed cool for over-the-pot adjustments.

RECOMMENDED

	CRITERIA		TESTERS' NOTES
POLDER Classic Digital Thermometer/Timer **Model:** THM-362-86RM **Price:** $24.99 **Source:** Polder.com **Temperature Range:** 32°F to 392°F *(BEST BUY)*	Accuracy Functionality Pan Compatibility	★★½ ★★½ ★★★	This basic thermometer doesn't have all the bells and whistles of our winner, but it has three key features: a timer, a programmable temperature alarm, and the ability to work in the oven. We also liked its on/off switch and flexible, plastic-coated cord. Most important: It was a very close second in accuracy.

RECOMMENDED WITH RESERVATIONS

	CRITERIA		TESTERS' NOTES
CDN Combo Probe Thermometer, Timer & Clock **Model:** DTTC-W **Price:** $24.99 **Temperature Range:** 14°F to 392°F	Accuracy Functionality Pan Compatibility	★½ ★★ ★★★	This thermometer was easy to read and kept a firm grip on all pots. But both models we tested averaged about 5 degrees off and weren't responsive with quickly changing temperatures. It has a timer, clock, and temperature alarm but no on/off button, so it beeps if it's jostled when not in use.

NOT RECOMMENDED

	CRITERIA		TESTERS' NOTES
MAVERICK Oil/Candy/Fryer Digital Thermometer **Model:** CT-03 **Price:** $34.99 **Temperature Range:** 130°F to 392°F	Accuracy Functionality Pan Compatibility	★½ ★ ★	We shouted "Timber!" every time we used this top-heavy timer, as it fell out of scorching hot oil, bubbling caramel, and a steaming *sous vide* machine. You can't use it in the oven, and while it does have a high-temperature alarm, you must select preset terms like "hard crack" instead of actual temperatures.

TEST KITCHEN TECHNIQUE
Halving Catfish

Before coating and frying the catfish, we cut the fillets in half lengthwise along their natural seams. Why? It's easier to manage the smaller pieces when frying, the strips cook faster and more evenly, and we get a better ratio of crunchy crust to flesh on every piece.

Getting to Know Radishes

There's a whole world of radishes beyond the tipped-and-tailed kind that are sold in plastic bags at the supermarket. BY CHRISTIE MORRISON

Cherry Belle Radish
SUPERMARKET STANDBY

The Cherry Belle is the radish you usually see at the supermarket. It's harvested in both spring and fall so it can be sold year-round, and its relatively sweet flavor and mild spiciness make it a go-to radish for all kinds of dishes—not just salads. This usually crisp radish softens and transforms in our Butter-Braised Vegetables recipe (**CooksCountry.com/butterbraisedveg**). With these and other thin-skinned spring radishes, good things come in small packages: Large specimens may be tough, woody, and hollow.

Black Spanish Radish
GOOD KEEPER

This large, black-skinned radish—inside it's white—looks a lot like a turnip; turnips and radishes are both in the *Cruciferae*, or mustard, family. Like other winter radishes, it's pungent and dry and has thicker skin than many more familiar radishes. It's a stalwart of Eastern European cooking—probably because it lasts for months in storage, especially in cold climates. Russians, for example, like to slather a mix of grated black radishes and sour cream on dark bread.

Easter Egg Radish
PASTEL BLOC

Because they are harvested in the spring, Easter Egg radishes are small—about an inch around. The name, from their pretty pastel colors, encompasses a grouping of similarly sized and flavored radishes, including Ruby, Plum Purple, and Snow Belle. All are mild and crunchy, with bright white flesh and subtle heat that builds as you eat them. If they start to soften, revive them (and all radishes) in a bowl of ice water for about an hour; this trick works with both whole and cut radishes.

White Icicle Radish
COOL CONTENDER

Featured as a "new" radish in a 1903 seed catalog, this heirloom radish is still in demand today. The name implies chill, but take a bite and watch out: The Icicle radish has a peppery flavor, sinus-clearing quality, and "slow-burning heat," our tasters said. You can eat the greens of the Icicle radish—or any radish, for that matter—raw in salad or sautéed briefly. Refrigerate the greens separately; otherwise, the leaves will pull moisture from the radishes.

French Breakfast Radish
BREAD AND BUTTERED

With its tapered, rosy-colored root and telltale white tip, the French Breakfast radish is easy to recognize. It's harvested primarily in the spring, when you'll find it at your local farmers' market. The French eat these radishes split and buttered—to balance the radishes' heat—with sea salt and bread, and we like their crunch in our Arugula, Radish, Mint, and Pea Salad (**CooksCountry. com/arugularadishsalad**).

Daikon
SUSHI SIDEKICK

The name of this big Asian radish—it can grow close to 2 feet long—means "large root" in Japanese. The taste is more sweet than spicy but the finish is peppery. Its juicy texture draws comparisons with water chestnuts and jícama. Daikon is the soft white pile of shredded stuff next to the wasabi on your sushi plate, and it's the bright yellow pickled slice that often accompanies Japanese or Korean food.

Watermelon Radish
SPITTING IMAGE

Cut into the thick, light-green skin of a Watermelon radish and you'll find a shocking fuchsia center—it's obvious where this (Eastern) radish got its (Western) name. Cut, these radishes look fabulous on a plate, which is probably why they are popular with chefs. The color fades when the radish is cooked, so we like it raw in salads or as crudités; it tastes sweet and mildly spicy. "This radish tastes like a carrot," one taster commented, "but it looks magical."

Snowball Radish
FAUX FROSTY

Despite the name, the Snowball is actually a spring radish. Its round root (all radishes are root vegetables) ranges in size from 1 to 3 inches. As with all radishes, look for firm roots with smooth skins—wrinkles and cracks are signs of age. This radish has a peppery heat, similar to that of spicy mustard: One of our tasters warned, "You think you're safe and then it hits you with a kicky bite."

Lime Radish
GREEN MONSTER

Slice into it and this Lime radish looks like a lime (some are greener than others). But that's where the similarity ends. Tasters compared its intense kick with that of wasabi or horseradish (mustard oils give radishes, horseradish, and wasabi heat). Dubbed a "silent killer" by one taster, Lime radish makes a mean kimchi or slaw to go with fatty meats. Store this radish, and most other varieties, in unsealed plastic bags in the refrigerator; they'll keep for about a week.

SHRIMP AND BACON PIZZA

PORK AND SUGAR SNAP PEA STIR-FRY

**STEAK TIPS WITH TOMATILLO SALSA
AND REFRIED BLACK BEANS**

**SAUTÉED BUFFALO CHICKEN BREASTS
WITH BLUE CHEESE TOASTS**

PORK AND SUGAR SNAP PEA STIR-FRY Serves 4

✅ **WHY THIS RECIPE WORKS:** Coating the pork strips with cornstarch gives them a velvety texture, keeps them moist, and helps the sauce adhere.

- 1 cup chicken broth
- 2 tablespoons soy sauce
- 5 teaspoons cornstarch
- 1 tablespoon Asian chili-garlic sauce
- 1 (12- to 16-ounce) pork tenderloin, cut crosswise into ½-inch-thick slices, each slice cut into ½-inch-thick strips
- 3 tablespoons vegetable oil
- 12 ounces sugar snap peas, strings removed
- 1 tablespoon grated fresh ginger
- 2 garlic cloves, minced
- ½ cup dry-roasted peanuts, chopped coarse

1. Whisk ½ cup broth, soy sauce, 2 teaspoons cornstarch, and chili-garlic sauce together in bowl; set aside. Toss pork, 1 tablespoon oil, and remaining 1 tablespoon cornstarch together in separate bowl. Heat 2 teaspoons oil in 12-inch nonstick skillet over medium-high heat until just smoking. Brown half of pork, 3 to 5 minutes; transfer to plate. Repeat with 2 teaspoons oil and remaining pork.

2. Add remaining 2 teaspoons oil and snap peas to now-empty skillet and cook until spotty brown, about 2 minutes. Add remaining ½ cup broth and cook, covered, until snap peas are just tender, about 2 minutes. Add ginger and garlic and cook until fragrant, about 30 seconds.

3. Whisk soy sauce mixture to recombine and add to skillet along with pork and any accumulated juices. Cook, stirring constantly, until slightly thickened, 1 to 2 minutes. Stir in peanuts. Serve.

TEST KITCHEN NOTE: Serve with steamed white rice.

SHRIMP AND BACON PIZZA Serves 4

✅ **WHY THIS RECIPE WORKS:** Buying peeled and deveined shrimp minimizes prep. Cutting the shrimp into smaller pieces ensures that they cook quickly.

- ¼ cup extra-virgin olive oil
- 4 slices bacon, cut into ½-inch pieces
- 12 ounces peeled and deveined jumbo shrimp (16 to 20 per pound), cut into ¾-inch pieces
- ½ cup thinly sliced red onion
- 2 garlic cloves, minced
- ½ teaspoon salt
- ¼ teaspoon pepper
- 1 pound pizza dough
- 6 ounces mozzarella cheese, shredded (1½ cups)
- 2 tablespoons minced fresh chives

1. Adjust oven rack to upper-middle position and heat oven to 500 degrees. Brush rimmed baking sheet with 2 tablespoons oil. Cook bacon in 10-inch nonstick skillet over medium-high heat until partially cooked through, about 3 minutes; transfer to paper towel–lined plate. Pat shrimp dry with paper towels and toss with onion, garlic, salt, pepper, and remaining 2 tablespoons oil.

2. On lightly floured counter, roll dough into 16 by 9-inch oval (about ¼ inch thick) and transfer to prepared sheet. Sprinkle mozzarella over dough. Spread shrimp mixture over cheese and top with bacon. Bake until shrimp are cooked through and crust is browned, about 13 minutes. Sprinkle with chives and let cool for 5 minutes. Serve.

TEST KITCHEN NOTE: Cook the bacon only partway in the skillet or it will overcook in the oven. Dry the shrimp thoroughly before combining them with the other ingredients.

SAUTÉED BUFFALO CHICKEN BREASTS WITH BLUE CHEESE TOASTS Serves 4

✅ **WHY THIS RECIPE WORKS:** Cooking the chicken in a combination of hot sauce and chicken broth infuses it with flavor.

- ¼ cup all-purpose flour
- 4 (6- to 8-ounce) boneless, skinless chicken breasts, trimmed
  Salt and pepper
- 1 tablespoon vegetable oil
- 1 cup chicken broth
- ⅓ cup hot sauce
- 4 tablespoons unsalted butter, softened
- 2 ounces blue cheese, crumbled (½ cup)
- 8 (¾-inch-thick) slices baguette
- ⅓ cup minced celery

1. Place flour in shallow dish. Season chicken with salt and pepper. Dredge chicken in flour, shaking off excess. Heat oil in 12-inch nonstick skillet over medium-high heat until just smoking. Cook chicken until golden brown, about 3 minutes per side. Add broth and hot sauce and bring to boil. Reduce heat to medium and simmer until chicken registers 160 degrees, 6 to 8 minutes. Transfer chicken to platter and tent loosely with aluminum foil.

2. Continue to simmer sauce until reduced to ¾ cup, about 1 minute. Off heat, whisk in 2 tablespoons butter. Season with salt and pepper to taste. Pour sauce over chicken and tent with foil.

3. Meanwhile, adjust oven rack 4 inches from broiler element and heat broiler. Combine blue cheese and remaining 2 tablespoons butter. Arrange bread on rimmed baking sheet and broil until golden, 1 to 2 minutes per side. Spread 1 side of toasts evenly with blue cheese mixture and broil until bubbly and spotty brown, 1 to 2 minutes. Sprinkle chicken with celery and serve with toasts.

STEAK TIPS WITH TOMATILLO SALSA AND REFRIED BLACK BEANS Serves 4

✅ **WHY THIS RECIPE WORKS:** Bright, tangy tomatillos balance the richness of the steak.

- 1 pound tomatillos, husks and stems removed, rinsed, dried, and halved
- 2 jalapeño chiles, stemmed, seeded, and minced
- ½ cup minced fresh cilantro
- 2 garlic cloves, minced
  Salt and pepper
- 1½ pounds sirloin steak tips, trimmed and cut into 1½-inch pieces
- 3 tablespoons vegetable oil
- 1 onion, chopped fine
- 1 teaspoon ground cumin
- 2 (15-ounce) cans black beans, rinsed

1. Pulse tomatillos in food processor until coarsely chopped, about 8 pulses. Transfer to fine-mesh strainer set over bowl and let drain for 5 minutes; reserve ¾ cup liquid. Combine half of jalapeños, ¼ cup cilantro, half of garlic, drained tomatillos, and ¼ cup reserved tomatillo liquid in bowl. Season with salt and pepper to taste.

2. Pat steak dry and season with salt and pepper. Heat 2 tablespoons oil in 12-inch nonstick skillet over medium-high heat until just smoking. Cook steak until browned all over and meat registers 125 degrees (for medium-rare), 6 to 8 minutes. Transfer to plate and tent loosely with aluminum foil. Add remaining 1 tablespoon oil and onion to now-empty skillet and cook over medium heat until just softened, about 2 minutes. Add cumin, remaining jalapeño, and remaining garlic and cook until fragrant, about 30 seconds. Add beans and remaining ½ cup reserved tomatillo liquid. Using potato masher, coarsely mash beans. Cook, stirring occasionally, until thickened, about 3 minutes. Stir in remaining ¼ cup cilantro. Season with salt and pepper to taste. Serve steak with beans and salsa.

THREE-CHEESE SKILLET MACARONI

SIRLOIN BURGERS AU POIVRE

PORK TENDERLOIN WITH CHERRY SAUCE

SKILLET CHICKEN WITH SPRING VEGETABLES

SIRLOIN BURGERS AU POIVRE Serves 4

✓ **WHY THIS RECIPE WORKS:** This is a riff on the classic steak au poivre, using ground sirloin instead of an expensive steak. We start making the creamy pan sauce while the burgers are in the oven.

- 1½ pounds 90 percent lean ground sirloin
- Salt and cracked peppercorns
- 3 tablespoons Dijon mustard
- 1 tablespoon unsalted butter
- ½ cup chicken broth
- ¼ cup dry red wine
- ½ cup heavy cream
- 2 tablespoons brandy
- 4 hamburger buns, toasted

1. Adjust oven rack to middle position and heat oven to 325 degrees. Set wire rack in rimmed baking sheet. Combine beef and ¾ teaspoon salt in bowl; shape into four ¾-inch-thick patties and press shallow divot in center of each. Brush each side of patties with 1 teaspoon mustard and press ½ teaspoon peppercorns onto each side.

2. Melt butter in 12-inch nonstick skillet over high heat. Cook patties until well browned, about 2 minutes per side. Transfer burgers to prepared wire rack and bake until burgers register 125 degrees (for medium-rare), about 5 minutes. Tent loosely with aluminum foil and let rest while preparing sauce.

3. Meanwhile, pour off fat from skillet and add broth and wine. Bring to boil over medium-high heat and cook, scraping up any browned bits, until thickened, about 4 minutes. Add cream and brandy, return to boil, and cook until reduced to ¼ cup, 3 to 5 minutes. Off heat, whisk in remaining 1 teaspoon mustard. Season with salt and pepper to taste. Place burgers on buns and spoon 1 tablespoon sauce over each. Serve.

THREE-CHEESE SKILLET MACARONI Serves 4

✓ **WHY THIS RECIPE WORKS:** Three potent cheeses give this mac and cheese layers of flavor, while canned evaporated milk keeps it creamy. Cooking the macaroni right in the sauce makes this a one-pan operation.

- 2 tablespoons unsalted butter
- ½ cup panko bread crumbs
- Salt and pepper
- 3¾ cups water
- 1 (12-ounce) can evaporated milk
- 12 ounces (3 cups) elbow macaroni
- 1 teaspoon cornstarch
- 6 ounces fontina cheese, shredded (1½ cups)
- 4 ounces Gorgonzola cheese, crumbled (1 cup)
- 2 ounces Parmesan cheese, grated (1 cup)

1. Melt butter in 12-inch nonstick skillet over medium-high heat. Add panko, ¼ teaspoon salt, and ¼ teaspoon pepper and cook, stirring frequently, until golden brown, about 5 minutes. Transfer to bowl and wipe out skillet.

2. Bring water, 1¼ cups evaporated milk, and ½ teaspoon salt to boil in now-empty skillet over medium-high heat. Add macaroni and cook, stirring often, until al dente, 8 to 10 minutes.

3. Whisk cornstarch and remaining ¼ cup evaporated milk together in bowl and stir into skillet. Simmer until slightly thickened, 1 to 2 minutes. Off heat, stir in cheeses 1 handful at a time, adjusting consistency with water as needed. Season with pepper to taste. Sprinkle with toasted panko. Serve.

TEST KITCHEN NOTE: The cornstarch helps keep the cheese from breaking.

SKILLET CHICKEN WITH SPRING VEGETABLES Serves 4

✓ **WHY THIS RECIPE WORKS:** Starting the asparagus in the microwave allows it to finish cooking in the tarragon pan sauce.

- 3 pounds bone-in chicken pieces (split breasts cut in half, drumsticks, and/or thighs), trimmed
- Salt and pepper
- 1 tablespoon vegetable oil
- ½ cup chicken broth
- ½ cup dry white wine
- 1 tablespoon minced fresh tarragon
- 1 pound asparagus, trimmed and cut on bias into 2-inch lengths
- 1 cup frozen peas
- 2 tablespoons unsalted butter
- 2 tablespoons minced fresh chives

1. Adjust oven rack to middle position and heat oven to 475 degrees. Season chicken with salt and pepper. Heat oil in 12-inch ovensafe skillet over medium-high heat until just smoking. Cook chicken, skin side down, until well browned, 6 to 10 minutes. Flip and cook until lightly browned on second side, about 2 minutes.

2. Add broth, wine, and 1½ teaspoons tarragon and transfer to oven. Roast until breasts register 160 degrees and drumsticks/thighs register 175 degrees, 12 to 15 minutes. Transfer chicken to platter and tent loosely with aluminum foil.

3. Meanwhile, microwave asparagus in covered bowl until just tender, about 3 minutes. Bring sauce to boil (skillet will be hot) over medium-high heat and cook until slightly thickened, about 3 minutes. Add peas and asparagus and cook until warmed through, about 1 minute. Off heat, whisk in butter, chives, and remaining 1½ teaspoons tarragon. Season with salt and pepper to taste. Pour vegetables and sauce over chicken. Serve.

PORK TENDERLOIN WITH CHERRY SAUCE Serves 4

✓ **WHY THIS RECIPE WORKS:** Searing pork tenderloin until browned and then letting it finish cooking in the oven makes this an easy, (mostly) hands-off meal.

- 2 (12- to 16-ounce) pork tenderloins, trimmed
- Salt and pepper
- 4 teaspoons vegetable oil
- 1 shallot, minced
- ¾ cup ruby port
- ¼ cup balsamic vinegar
- ¼ cup dried cherries, chopped
- 1 sprig fresh thyme
- 2 tablespoons unsalted butter

1. Adjust oven rack to middle position and heat oven to 450 degrees. Set wire rack in rimmed baking sheet. Pat pork dry with paper towels and season with salt and pepper. Heat oil in 12-inch skillet over medium-high heat until just smoking. Cook pork until browned on all sides, 5 to 7 minutes; transfer pork to prepared wire rack. Roast until meat registers 140 degrees, 14 to 18 minutes. Transfer to carving board, tent with aluminum foil, and let rest for 5 minutes.

2. Meanwhile, add shallot to now-empty skillet and cook until softened, about 1 minute. Add port, vinegar, cherries, and thyme sprig and bring to boil, scraping up any browned bits. Reduce heat to medium-low and simmer until reduced to about ½ cup, about 5 minutes. Off heat, discard thyme sprig and whisk in butter. Season with salt and pepper to taste. Slice pork, transfer to platter, and pour sauce over top. Serve.

TEST KITCHEN NOTE: Try dried cranberries in place of the cherries.

Old-Fashioned Rice Pudding

It requires just a handful of ingredients and dead-simple techniques. So why is it hard to make perfect rice pudding? BY CHRISTIE MORRISON

IN FLEMISH AND DUTCH folklore, heaven is a place where you eat rice pudding every day with a golden spoon. At first blush, that seems incongruous for such a humble sweet; on the other hand, if you ask me, good rice pudding tastes close to sublime. The list of ingredients is as basic as it gets: short- or long-grain rice, milk or cream, sugar, salt, and (usually, but not always) vanilla. Baked versions—rice puddings can be made on the stovetop or in the oven—often include a few eggs or just yolks. Some recipes gild the lily with citrus, cinnamon, and/or dried fruit. While the ingredients are more or less standard, the ratio of liquid to rice is not. And beyond oven versus stovetop, the techniques vary, too. Some recipes call for parboiling the rice; others call for adding it raw to the rest of the ingredients. With a sampling of recipes in hand, I got to work.

Given the variables, I wasn't surprised that these recipes produced variable results. Some puddings were creamy, others firmly set; some were thin and runny, others almost pasty. The starch from the rice, and in some recipes the eggs, is what thickens the pudding, and as the pudding cools, it continues to thicken. Helpfully, though, the assortment clarified what I wanted from the recipe: a homey, soft rice pudding. Instead of sugar or fancy flavoring, my pudding would taste like sweet cooked milk and pure vanilla. And it would be loose, not soupy, and cohesive but not gloppy, whether I ate it lukewarm or cold.

I put together a starting point: I'd use the stovetop method, as we preferred the creamy texture that it yielded to that of the firmer baked rice puddings. For now, I'd use 1 quart of milk, ½ cup of rice, ½ cup of sugar, vanilla, and a little salt, and I'd test the variables one by one. I was curious to see how the relative starch levels of short-, medium-, and long-grain rice would affect the consistency, as the shorter the grain the higher the starch. I was banking on short-grain Arborio, which is the key to risotto's creamy texture. Wrong. Deliciously thick and creamy right after cooking, the starchy rice made the pudding inedibly stodgy as it cooled. We liked both medium-grain and long-grain rice puddings, but since long-grain rice is a pantry staple and rice pudding is the ultimate in humble,

For perfect texture, we use double the usual amount of milk, and add some just before serving.

no-special-shopping-trips-required desserts, I opted for it.

Depending on the recipe you use, rice pudding calls for whole milk, cream, or half-and-half. In a side-by side test, we much preferred milk, which reduced and sweetened as the pudding cooked. The richer stuff didn't suit the simple spirit of the pudding. As for parcooking the rice, further tests showed that this was unnecessary. I simply combined everything in a pot and gently simmered the mixture, uncovered (so it wouldn't boil over), until the rice was tender.

Now my pudding was good, but heavenly? Hardly. And a nagging thought plagued me: "I am a professional test cook, yet my mother's rice pudding is much better than mine."

The pudding I remembered from childhood was looser and had a sweet, milky, truly wonderful flavor. I did the obvious thing: I rang home. Luckily, my mother was willing to share her secret. She used more milk, she told me matter-of-factly—twice as much as I'd been using: 2 entire quarts to the same ½ cup of rice. Nervously, I used her ratios to make my pudding and then asked my colleagues to judge the results.

Apparently mother *does* know best: More milk was the answer. But not quite as much as she said. With that amount, the flavor was a little weak and the pudding soupy. So I tested my recipe with gradually decreasing amounts of milk. After many tries, I got both flavor and texture right using 6 cups of milk

and adjusting the technique slightly: I cooked the pudding with 5½ cups of the milk. Then, whenever I was ready to eat the pudding—room temperature or cold—I stirred in another ½ cup of milk to loosen it. We loved this plain vanilla-scented pudding so much that I decided not to add other flavors. (That said, if you want to jazz up yours, try my variations.)

Unfussy, soothing, gently sweet, and plain in the nicest possible way, my rice pudding was finally transcendent. All I needed was a golden spoon.

OLD-FASHIONED RICE PUDDING
Serves 4 to 6
You can use 2 percent low-fat milk here (the consistency will be looser) but not skim.

- 6 cups whole milk
- ½ cup (3½ ounces) sugar
- ½ teaspoon salt
- ½ cup long-grain white rice
- 2 teaspoons vanilla extract

1. Combine 5½ cups milk, sugar, and salt in large saucepan and bring to boil over medium-high heat.

2. Stir in rice and reduce heat to low. Cook, adjusting heat to maintain gentle simmer and stirring occasionally to prevent scorching, until rice is soft and pudding has thickened to consistency of yogurt, 50 to 60 minutes. Stir in vanilla.

3. Transfer pudding to large bowl and let cool completely, about 2 hours, or let cool and refrigerate until cold, about 2 hours longer. Just before serving, stir in remaining ½ cup milk.

CINNAMON-RAISIN RICE PUDDING

In step 1, add 1 cinnamon stick to milk mixture. Combine ⅓ cup raisins and ⅓ cup water in bowl; cover and microwave for 1 minute. Let sit until softened, about 5 minutes; drain. Stir raisins into cooked rice pudding as it cools in step 3. Discard cinnamon stick.

COCONUT RICE PUDDING

In step 1, decrease milk to 3¾ cups and add 1¾ cups canned coconut milk. Stir ½ teaspoon ground cardamom into cooked rice pudding as it cools in step 3.

LEMONY RICE PUDDING

Stir 1 teaspoon grated lemon zest into cooked rice pudding as it cools in step 3.

Italian Easter Pie

This classic meat-and-cheese Easter pie is delicious—but overwhelming. We wanted to keep its virtues but make it fresher and lighter for modern-day appetites. BY DIANE UNGER

T ORTA RUSTICA (or *pizza rustica*) is a very large, very rich, and very delicious Italian meat-and-cheese pie that's typically eaten in Italian American homes for Easter lunch. Imagine a quiche crossed with a savory cheesecake—and the whole thing on steroids. It's eaten at room temperature or chilled, so it's the perfect dish to make ahead. Among the recipes I looked at to get the lay of the land were one that made an 11-plus-pound pie and another—jotted down in cursive on yellowing paper by my boss's grandmother—that called for 3 pounds of cheese, 3½ pounds of meat (sausage, prosciutto, and *sopressata*), and 17 eggs. For a single pie.

I continued to amass recipes—from the test kitchen library, a handful of grandmothers, and several Italian American colleagues. Everybody insisted that theirs was the best, and when I lined up seven rustic, double-crusted pies on the test kitchen counter for us to sample, the elasticity of this folk recipe became clear. Ricotta was pretty much a constant, but other than that the fillings varied widely, encompassing all manner of Italian cold cuts, sausages, and cheeses. Some recipes called for stirring in vegetables—assorted greens, red peppers, even eggplant—while a few fillings included sliced hard-cooked eggs. Crusts ranged from classic pie dough to yeast doughs to *pasta frolla*, which is a sweet, cookie-like Italian crust. As for top crusts, there were both latticework and plain.

Since most Italian immigrants came to America to escape grinding poverty, who can blame them for loading up their tortas with as many delicious things as they could afford? But by today's standards, it was too much of a good thing. As a group, these tortas were rich to the point of dense, and so overstuffed that many of the crusts couldn't adequately contain them. Plus, they required that a home cook procure just about the entire contents of an Italian delicatessen. For my version, I'd do some thoughtful pruning.

To begin with, rather than tussle with a large, cumbersome crust to fit a 13 by 9-inch casserole dish, as some of my test recipes required, I'd make my Easter torta in a deep cake pan. Also, in the interest of streamlining, I'd skip the lattice crust. To help offset the rich, heavy cheeses and meat, I'd include veg-

For many Italian American families, it wouldn't be Easter without a rich, generously proportioned *torta rustica*.

etables. I sketched out a recipe for a very stripped-down version of torta rustica and headed back into the test kitchen.

I began from the outside in—with the crust. Tasters damned pasta frolla with faint praise, calling it "interesting." I'd stick with a savory crust. A standard flaky pie crust proved flimsy for such a hefty torta and a yeast crust too much of a project, so I switched to an intriguing food processor crust from

my first round of testing. It reminded me of pasta dough because it used eggs, which made it elastic, and it called for kneading. Normally, kneading toughens pie crusts, but in this case it developed gluten, giving the crust structure, which, in turn, helped it hold the heavy filling. I tinkered with techniques and ratios and, after testing various fats, landed on a combination of butter, for flavor, and shortening, which made the dough

pliable and easy to handle. I rolled out a bottom crust, lined my cake pan, and turned to the filling.

Five different types of meat in one pie? Apparently, according to my first round of tests. In the interest of restraint and streamlining, I would limit myself to two. In truth, any number of combinations tasted delicious, but we went with hot Italian sausage and hot capicola; both are easy to find, plus their heat helped temper the very rich torta. As for cheeses, along with provolone—sliced and available at any deli counter and a classic for Easter pie—I used creamy, milky ricotta for the base and lots of Pecorino Romano for its salty, sharp edge. I mixed the ricotta and Pecorino with two eggs, but the provolone I'd simply layer in.

Greens brought much-needed lightness to this very rich pie. Among the several greens I tried, broccoli rabe was the favorite. Its slight bitterness made it the perfect partner for the filling. I simply chopped it, sautéed it briefly with garlic and sausage to imbue it with garlicky, meaty flavor, and then layered it into the torta with the provolone, the capicola, and the ricotta mixture.

At this point in my testing, I'd baked more than 30 pies; coworkers were jokingly calling me *nonna*. But I'd managed to make a torta rustica that was in delicious balance. No one could argue that it wasn't still big, rich, and celebratory, but now its cheesy creaminess was offset with a slight bitterness and heat, its heaviness relieved by greenery, and its sturdy crust a match for its heft. Finally, I had a torta rustica to call my own—and to share with you.

ITALIAN EASTER PIE Serves 12

Use a cake pan that's at least 2 inches deep. If your pan is light-colored, increase the baking time to 45 to 50 minutes. Substitute low-fat ricotta if you like. Note that the dough needs to rest in the refrigerator for at least an hour before you roll it out, and the baked pie must cool for about 4 hours.

DOUGH

- 3 large eggs
- 3 tablespoons cold water
- 3 cups (15 ounces) all-purpose flour
- 1¼ teaspoons salt
- 6 tablespoons unsalted butter, cut into ½-inch pieces and chilled
- 6 tablespoons vegetable shortening, cut into ½-inch pieces and chilled

FILLING

- 1 tablespoon olive oil
- 12 ounces broccoli rabe, trimmed and chopped
- 8 ounces hot Italian sausage, casings removed
- ¼ teaspoon salt
- 2 garlic cloves, minced
- 1 pound (2 cups) whole-milk ricotta cheese
- 4 ounces Pecorino Romano cheese, grated (2 cups)
- 2 large eggs
- 1 teaspoon pepper
- 8 ounces thinly sliced aged provolone cheese
- 6 ounces thinly sliced hot capicola

- 1 large egg yolk beaten with 1 tablespoon water

1. FOR THE DOUGH: Whisk eggs and cold water together in bowl; set aside. Process flour and salt in food processor until combined, about 3 seconds. Scatter butter and shortening over top and pulse until only pea-size pieces remain, about 10 pulses. Add egg mixture and pulse until dough ball forms, about 20 pulses. Turn out dough onto lightly floured counter and knead until smooth and elastic, about 20 turns. Divide dough into one 1-pound ball and one 10-ounce ball (roughly into two-thirds and one-third) and form each into 6-inch disk. Wrap disks tightly in plastic wrap and refrigerate for at least 1 hour or up to 24 hours.

2. FOR THE FILLING: Heat oil in 12-inch nonstick skillet over medium-high heat until shimmering. Add broccoli rabe, sausage, and salt and cook, breaking up sausage with spoon, until sausage is cooked through and broccoli rabe is tender, 5 to 7 minutes. Add garlic and cook until fragrant, about 30 seconds. Transfer to plate and let cool completely, about 15 minutes. Whisk ricotta, Pecorino, eggs, and pepper together in large bowl.

3. Adjust oven rack to middle position and heat oven to 375 degrees. Grease dark-colored 9-inch round cake pan. Roll 1-pound disk of dough into 14-inch circle on well-floured counter. Loosely roll dough around rolling pin and gently unroll it onto prepared pan, letting excess dough hang over edge. Ease dough into pan by gently lifting and supporting edge of dough with your hand while pressing into pan bottom and sides with your other hand. Leave overhanging dough in place.

4. Shingle half of provolone in bottom of dough-lined pan. Spread ricotta mixture over provolone. Scatter sausage mixture over ricotta mixture and press lightly into even layer. Shingle capicola over sausage mixture, followed by remaining provolone.

5. Roll remaining disk of dough into 10-inch circle on well-floured counter. Brush overhanging dough of bottom crust with egg wash. Loosely roll 10-inch circle around rolling pin and gently unroll it over filling. Trim overhanging top and bottom doughs to ½ inch beyond lip of pan and pinch firmly together. Fold overhanging dough inward so folded edge is flush with edge of pan. Crimp dough evenly around edge of pan with tines of fork.

6. Brush top of pie liberally with egg wash. Using paring knife, cut eight 1-inch vents in top of dough in circular pattern. Bake until filling registers 150 degrees halfway between edge and center of pie and crust is golden brown, 35 to 40 minutes. Transfer pie to wire rack and let cool for at least 4 hours or refrigerate for up to 2 days. Remove pie from pan, slice into wedges, and serve.

Asparagus Mimosa

This dish of steamed asparagus topped with grated hard-cooked eggs is a classic. Could we find a few tricks to make it even better?

BY REBECCAH MARSTERS

TO MAKE ASPARAGUS MIMOSA, you toss steamed asparagus with a mustardy dressing, fresh tarragon, and often capers and then shower it with bits of hard-cooked eggs (the bright egg shreds look like the flowers of the mimosa tree, hence the name). The recipe has been around for a long time, and it's well worth making. Still, when I tested it, I found a few kinks.

Since the traditional steaming technique requires a steamer basket and not everybody has one, I decided to boil the asparagus briefly instead. After about 5 minutes, I dropped the spears in ice water to stop them from cooking further. As they chilled, I made a vinaigrette from olive oil, red wine vinegar, tarragon, capers, and shallot; after a taste, I added a teaspoon of honey to round things out. I tossed the asparagus with the dressing and topped it with the hard-cooked eggs. More accurately, I attempted to sprinkle on the eggs. Unfortunately, a struggle with my fine-mesh strainer—the usual tool—meant that I got egg puree. When I traded in the strainer for the fine holes of a box grater, it was easy to produce properly fluffy grated eggs.

But the vinaigrette lacked body. To improve its consistency, I took a cue from the test kitchen's favorite egg salad recipe: I mashed one of the hard-cooked yolks right into the dressing. This thicker mixture, which had the consistency of a thin mayonnaise, coated the asparagus nicely. I salted my grated eggs so they wouldn't taste bland and sprinkled them over the asparagus. My recipe was ready. Bring on spring.

ASPARAGUS MIMOSA Serves 6 to 8

Use asparagus spears that are between ¼ and ½ inch in diameter.

- 2 pounds thin asparagus, trimmed
  Salt and pepper
- 2 tablespoons red wine vinegar
- 1 tablespoon minced shallot
- 1 tablespoon minced fresh tarragon
- 2 teaspoons Dijon mustard
- 1 teaspoon honey
- 2 large hard-cooked eggs
- 2 tablespoons extra-virgin olive oil
- 1 tablespoon capers, rinsed and chopped

One mashed yolk adds richness and body to the vinaigrette.

1. Bring 4 quarts water to boil in large pot. Fill large bowl halfway with ice and water. Add asparagus and 1 tablespoon salt to boiling water and cook until just tender, 4 to 6 minutes. Drain asparagus and transfer to ice bath. Drain again and pat dry with paper towels. Wipe out bowl. (The prepared asparagus can be refrigerated for up to 2 days.)

2. Whisk vinegar, shallot, tarragon, mustard, honey, ½ teaspoon salt, and ½ teaspoon pepper together in now-empty bowl. Halve 1 egg and add yolk to bowl, reserving white. Mash yolk with fork until incorporated into vinegar mixture. Slowly whisk in oil until incorporated; stir in capers. Add asparagus and toss to coat.

3. Grate remaining 1 egg and reserved white on small holes of box grater, then season with ¼ teaspoon salt. Transfer asparagus to serving platter and top with grated eggs. Serve.

> ▶ Learn how to hard-cook eggs—minus the nasty green tinge and rubbery texture. Visit CooksCountry.com/hardcookedeggs.

Southwestern Layered Beef Casserole

By adjusting the cooking method, carefully choosing the ingredients, and adding Tex-Mex flavors, we transformed this often-uninspired casserole. BY CHRISTIE MORRISON

SEARCH THE CASSEROLE chapter of any community or church cookbook and you're likely to find a recipe for layered beef casserole. While the number of layers may change, the composition is pretty consistent: ground beef; rice and/or potatoes; some sort of canned tomato; and vegetables including onions, green beans, corn, carrots, beans, or bell peppers. The beef typically goes in raw, and the other ingredients are layered so that everything (hopefully) cooks at the same rate. Unfortunately, we found when we tried a half-dozen of these recipes that the casserole's baffling lack of herbs, spices, or seasonings (most called for just salt and pepper) means that flavor takes a backseat to convenience—and you end up with a bland, messy hodgepodge.

Convinced that I could do better, I started with the beef. While putting raw beef right into the casserole was easiest, the fat rendered into the dish as it cooked and made it greasy. Browning the beef first rendered the fat, saved me 30 minutes of baking time, and added depth that this casserole was lacking. What's more, I discovered that stirring some tomato sauce into the beef helped keep it moist while it baked. For the vegetables, onion and green bell pepper (sautéed with the beef to build a flavorful base) were no-brainers. Beyond that, my tasters and I wanted a tasty, quick-cooking vegetable; corn fit the bill perfectly.

I had been trying to find a flavor direction for the casserole, and now I could see a clear course. Filled with ingredients common to enchiladas and burritos, this casserole had a compass that was pointing southwest. To spice

the dish up, I added chili powder, cumin, and coriander to the browning beef and vegetables. A can of pinto beans contributed heft and texture. For a touch of heat (and the necessary liquid to cook the starch), I substituted canned diced tomatoes with green chiles for the more traditional diced or stewed tomatoes.

As for the starch, rice was a better fit with my southwestern flavors than potatoes were. But in test after test, I bit into hard and even uncooked grains of rice. Adding more liquid didn't solve the problem, nor did extending the cooking time. I wondered if toasting the rice first in oil (as though making rice pilaf) might give the grains a head start on cooking. I toasted the rice to a golden brown, added it to the dish,

and finished and baked my casserole. This version yielded fully cooked grains of rice that stayed separate and had a fluffier texture. But why? Our science editor explained that acidic tomato juice can strengthen the pectin in the rice's cell walls, making the rice tough; sautéing the rice softens the cell walls, thereby counterbalancing the effect of the acid.

What covered dish could have any self-respect without cheese? Sprinkling on easy-melting Monterey Jack just before I added the corn helped bind the layers together, which made for a neater appearance. Requiring only about 30 minutes of hands-on time before I popped it into the oven, my casserole was still pretty low-fuss, but now it was chock-full of delicious flavors, too.

Our layers: rice, beef and sautéed vegetables, beans, cheese, corn, and scallions.

TEST KITCHEN DISCOVERY
Toast Rice for Even Cooking
Toasting the rice before assembling the casserole helps the rice cook through evenly and keeps the grains separate and fluffy.

PERFECTLY TOASTED
To help it cook evenly in the casserole, the rice should be toasted to deep golden.

SOUTHWESTERN LAYERED BEEF CASSEROLE Serves 6 to 8
To test the rice for doneness in step 3, scoop a small amount from the side of the casserole to sample. Serve with sour cream and lime wedges.

- 1 tablespoon vegetable oil
- ¾ cup long-grain white rice
- 1 (10-ounce) can Ro-tel Diced Tomatoes & Green Chilies
- ½ cup chicken broth
  Salt and pepper
- 1 pound 85 percent lean ground beef
- 1 onion, chopped fine
- 1 green bell pepper, stemmed, seeded, and chopped fine
- 1 tablespoon chili powder
- 2 garlic cloves, minced
- 1 teaspoon ground cumin
- 1 teaspoon ground coriander
- 1 (8-ounce) can tomato sauce
- 1 (15-ounce) can pinto beans, rinsed
- 6 ounces Monterey Jack cheese, shredded (1½ cups)
- 1 cup frozen corn, thawed
- 3 scallions, sliced thin on bias

1. Adjust oven rack to middle position and heat oven to 350 degrees. Grease 8-inch square baking dish. Heat oil in 12-inch skillet over medium-high heat until shimmering. Add rice and cook, stirring frequently, until deep golden, about 5 minutes. Transfer rice to prepared dish. Stir tomatoes and their juice, broth, ½ teaspoon salt, and ¼ teaspoon pepper into rice.

2. Wipe out now-empty skillet with paper towels. Add beef, onion, bell pepper, ½ teaspoon salt, and ¼ teaspoon pepper to skillet and cook over medium heat until beef is no longer pink and vegetables have softened, about 5 minutes. Stir in chili powder, garlic, cumin, and coriander and cook until fragrant, about 30 seconds. Stir in tomato sauce and cook until slightly thickened, about 2 minutes.

3. Add beef mixture to dish and spread evenly over rice. Layer beans, then Monterey Jack, and finally corn over beef. Spray 12-inch square of aluminum foil with vegetable oil spray and cover dish tightly with foil. Place on rimmed baking sheet and bake until liquid is absorbed and rice is tender, 60 to 70 minutes. Uncover, sprinkle with scallions, and let stand for 10 minutes. Serve.

Cheddar Olives

These small cocktail party nuggets have huge (salty, cheesy) flavor.
If we could just cut the grease . . . BY SARAH GABRIEL

RECENTLY, A COWORKER told me about a recipe for cheddar olives—pimento-stuffed cocktail olives swaddled in nuggets of cheesy biscuit dough—that his mom used to make. As soon as I heard about them, I had a feeling they would have the cheesy, pickle-y pluck to rival the usual pigs-in-a-blanket and mini-quiche party fare. After testing a few recipes, I saw clearly that while the idea was clever, the reality wasn't. At least not yet.

The cheesiest, most tender, and most delicious of the doughs liquefied in the oven, leaving the olives on top of greasy (but admittedly tasty) lumps of dough. The tidiest-looking cheddar olives stayed neatly tucked inside the dough after baking, but this dough was so dry and tough that some tasters peeled it off before eating the olives. Getting cheddar olives to be either tasty or neat was no problem. But could I have both?

With two sticks of butter and 4 cups of cheese in the dough, the problem with the tasty but messy recipe from the first round was too much fat. As for the dry yet neat dough, it contained less than a quarter of the cheese and butter and was held together by an egg, so neither its resilience nor its unappetizing texture was surprising. I decided to take a moderate approach: I used 7 (rather than 2 or 16) tablespoons of butter and 2 (rather than 1 or 4) cups of shredded cheese, plus one egg. That fixed the grease problem and helped the dough hold its shape yet still keep decent cheese flavor. Some chilling time prevented the butter from leaking out when I baked the olives. Much better.

Having gotten the major issues under control, I circled back to try some of the seasonings I'd seen in other recipes. After a few tests, I found that a teaspoon of Worcestershire sauce, along with some paprika and cayenne, improved the flavor. Move over, cocktail franks and mini quiches, and make room for just-try-to-stop-at-one cheddar olives.

CHEDDAR OLIVES

Makes 40 wrapped olives
Use regular-size, not colossal or queen, cocktail olives. The cheddar olives must chill for at least 1 hour before baking.

- 40 pimento-stuffed green olives, rinsed
- 1 cup (5 ounces) all-purpose flour
- ¾ teaspoon paprika
- ½ teaspoon pepper
- ⅛ teaspoon cayenne pepper
- 8 ounces extra-sharp cheddar cheese, shredded (2 cups)
- 7 tablespoons unsalted butter, cut into 7 pieces
- 1 large egg, lightly beaten
- 1 tablespoon water
- 1 teaspoon Worcestershire sauce

1. Spread olives on dish towel and roll around to dry. Pulse flour, paprika, pepper, and cayenne in food processor until combined, about 3 pulses. Add cheddar and butter and pulse until mixture resembles coarse crumbs, about 12 pulses. Add egg, water, and Worcestershire and process until dough ball forms, about 20 seconds.

2. Working with 2 teaspoons dough and 1 olive at a time, pat dough into 2-inch circle; place olive in center of dough; form dough around olive; and roll cheddar olive between your hands to make uniform ball. Place cheddar olives on large platter, cover tightly with plastic wrap, and refrigerate for 1 hour or up to 24 hours (or freeze to bake later).

3. Adjust oven racks to upper-middle and lower-middle positions and heat oven to 350 degrees. Line 2 rimmed baking sheets with parchment paper. Space cheddar olives evenly on prepared sheets. Bake until bottoms are well browned and tops are golden, 16 to 18 minutes (if baking from frozen, increase cooking time to about 25 minutes), switching and rotating sheets halfway through baking. Transfer cheddar olives to wire rack and let cool for about 30 minutes before serving.

They look like miniature biscuits, but take a bite: A surprise hides inside.

TEST KITCHEN TECHNIQUE
Shaping Cheddar Olives

After you've patted 2 teaspoons of dough into a circle, place an olive in the center and encase it in the dough.

Pork Ragu

Introducing the best pasta sauce you've probably never tried:
hearty, meaty, intensely flavored pork ragu. BY MATTHEW CARD

I N THIS COUNTRY, a ragu can be any meaty pasta sauce made from any variety or combination of meats (but it's usually beef and/or pork). It is the earthy, intense flavor of pure pork ragu—an Italian American staple—that I find most attractive. I gathered recipes and got to work developing my own.

I immediately discounted recipes that called for only quick-cooking pork sausage or lean pork loin—the spirit of this dish is long-simmered, deep flavors. The best recipe of the bunch from my initial survey included well-marbled pork shoulder for meaty flavor and a bony, collagen-rich cut for flavor and thickening. Pork shoulder is common enough, but the bony cuts—necks, shanks, and feet—are difficult to find in supermarkets. But without a bony cut in the mix, pork ragu lacks body and depth.

So what bony cuts of pork are easy to find? Ribs. I had four to choose from: country-style ribs, spareribs, St. Louis–style ribs, and baby back ribs. I decided to try them all.

Country-style ribs contain both white and dark meat. The batches that I made with them were either a little thin, because the white meat in the ribs couldn't simmer for very long without drying out, or they featured pork jerky. Spareribs' ungainly size made them too big to braise. Trimmer St. Louis–style ribs were more manageable, but they were still too big to brown in a pot, and browning them in the oven was a bit awkward. I had one more rib to try.

Baby back ribs are the leanest and most tender pork ribs. And they are reasonably sized—I could easily brown 2¼ to 2½ pounds (about two racks cut into

three-rib segments) in two batches in a large Dutch oven; as a bonus, I had to brown only the meat side to build a deep base of flavor. Two racks of baby backs made enough ragu to sauce 2 pounds of pasta—an appropriately hefty yield. This batch was so rich and meaty-tasting (after I stripped the cooked meat from the bones and returned it to the sauce) that I decided to forgo the pork shoulder and just go with the ribs. A mere 2 hours in a 300-degree oven (many recipes call for twice that cooking time) yielded fork-tender meat that pulled easily from the bones in bite-size shreds.

With the meat chosen, I moved on to the other elements. Italian-style sauces and braises are built on a foundation of vegetables called *soffritto*—chopped and sautéed onion, carrots, and celery. Since I had plenty of flavorful fat in the pot from searing the ribs, I used that to sauté the vegetables. But as I was chopping the vegetables, I paused to consider them. Onion and carrot were no-brainers. But could I swap out the celery for something more interesting? Since pork and fennel—an ingredient with a decidedly Italian accent—go so well together, I tried using chopped fennel in place of the celery. My tasters much preferred the sweeter, more complex version made with fennel. Seasoning the raw ribs with ground fennel echoed the bulb's anise flavor.

A handful of chopped garlic cloves is traditional, but peeling and chopping a dozen-odd cloves was time-consuming. For garlic flavor that didn't overpower the sauce, I lopped the top off a head of garlic and added it to the simmering sauce. Once the cloves were soft, I squeezed them into the pot, where

We like this substantial sauce best with wide noodles like pappardelle or tagliatelle.

their sweet flavor melded into the sauce.

As for wine, red easily bested white. I landed on 1 cup that I cooked down until nearly evaporated before I added the chicken broth, which we liked more than beef broth. Most recipes call for a quart or more of broth so that the meat is fully submerged, but then I had to reduce the sauce before serving. Instead, I opted for the minimum amount of liquid required—3 cups—to cover the meat (the bony tops of the ribs rose above the surface). This kept the sauce thick and potent.

With a handful of fresh herbs and a splash more wine added before serving, my ragu tasted meaty, balanced, and far more complex than its simple preparation would suggest.

PORK RAGU Makes about 8 cups

This recipe makes enough sauce to coat 2 pounds of pasta. Leftover sauce may be refrigerated for up to three days or frozen for up to one month.

    2   (2¼- to 2½-pound) racks baby
        back ribs, trimmed and each rack
        cut into fourths
    2   teaspoons ground fennel
        Kosher salt and pepper
    3   tablespoons olive oil
    1   large onion, chopped fine
    1   large fennel bulb, stalks discarded,
        bulb halved, cored, and chopped fine
    2   large carrots, peeled and chopped fine
    ¼   cup minced fresh sage
    1½ teaspoons minced fresh rosemary
    1   cup plus 2 tablespoons dry red wine

Chicken Scaloppini

Our goal? Perfectly cooked chicken and a flavorful sauce in about a half-hour.

BY CRISTIN WALSH

- 1 (28-ounce) can whole peeled tomatoes, drained and crushed coarse
- 3 cups chicken broth
- 1 garlic head, outer papery skins removed and top fourth of head cut off and discarded
- 1 pound pappardelle or tagliatelle
  Grated Parmesan cheese

1. Adjust oven rack to middle position and heat oven to 300 degrees. Sprinkle ribs with ground fennel and generously season with salt and pepper, pressing spices to adhere. Heat oil in Dutch oven over medium-high heat until just smoking. Add half of ribs, meat side down, and cook, without moving them, until meat is well browned, 6 to 8 minutes; transfer to plate. Repeat with remaining ribs; set aside.

2. Reduce heat to medium and add onion, fennel, carrots, 2 tablespoons sage, rosemary, and ½ teaspoon salt to now-empty pot. Cook, stirring occasionally and scraping up any browned bits, until vegetables are well browned and beginning to stick to pot bottom, 12 to 15 minutes.

3. Add 1 cup wine and cook until evaporated, about 5 minutes. Stir in tomatoes and broth and bring to simmer. Submerge garlic and ribs, meat side down, in liquid; add any accumulated juices from plate. Cover and transfer to oven. Cook until ribs are fork-tender, about 2 hours.

4. Remove pot from oven and transfer ribs and garlic to rimmed baking sheet. Using large spoon, skim any fat from surface of sauce. Once cool enough to handle, shred meat from bones; discard bones and gristle. Return meat to pot. Squeeze garlic from its skin into pot. Stir in remaining 2 tablespoons sage and remaining 2 tablespoons wine. Season with salt and pepper to taste.

5. Meanwhile, bring 4 quarts water to boil in large pot. Add pasta and 2 tablespoons salt and cook, stirring often, until al dente. Reserve ½ cup cooking water, then drain pasta and return it to pot. Add half of sauce and toss to combine, adjusting consistency with reserved cooking water as needed. Serve, passing Parmesan separately.

CHICKEN SCALOPPINI WITH mushrooms and peppers isn't rocket science—thin cutlets are floured, browned, and served with a sauce made from the fond plus vegetables, white wine, and broth. So why do so many recipes produce dry chicken?

I butchered cutlets, dredged them in flour, browned them, and set them in a low oven to keep warm while I made the sauce: I sautéed the vegetables, deglazed the pan, reduced the sauce, and finished it with a knob of butter. The technique seemed just right—but the cutlets were dry and leathery.

The problem was that the thin cutlets continued to cook in the just-warm oven for the 20 minutes or so that it took to make the sauce. Could I buck tradition and cook the sauce first?

In a word, yes: The sauce made without fond tasted just as good as the sauce made with it. But how? It turns out that the thin, lean cutlets weren't in the pan long enough to create many of the nice browned bits to start with—and if I left them in there long enough, they overcooked.

So one surprising trick later, I was enjoying tender chicken in rich sauce—plus the weekday-friendly cooking time.

CHICKEN SCALOPPINI WITH MUSHROOMS AND PEPPERS
Serves 4
The chicken breasts will be easier to slice in half if you freeze them for 15 minutes first.

- 3 (6- to 8-ounce) boneless, skinless chicken breasts, trimmed
  Salt and pepper
- 6 tablespoons vegetable oil
- 8 ounces white mushrooms, trimmed and quartered
- 1 red bell pepper, stemmed, seeded, and cut into thin matchsticks
- 1 shallot, sliced thin
- ¼ cup capers, rinsed
- 2 garlic cloves, minced
- 1¼ cups chicken broth
- ¾ cup white wine
- ¼ cup all-purpose flour
- 3 tablespoons unsalted butter, cut into 3 pieces
- 1 tablespoon chopped fresh parsley

1. Working with 1 breast at a time, starting on thick side, cut breasts in half horizontally. Using meat pounder, gently pound each cutlet into even

We make the sauce first so we don't have to hold the cooked cutlets in the oven, where they can overcook.

½-inch thickness between 2 pieces of plastic wrap. Pat cutlets dry with paper towels and season with salt and pepper; set aside.

2. Heat 2 tablespoons oil in 12-inch nonstick skillet over medium-high heat until just smoking. Add mushrooms, bell pepper, shallot, and ¼ teaspoon salt and cook until liquid has evaporated and vegetables begin to brown, 8 to 10 minutes. Add capers and garlic and cook until fragrant, about 1 minute. Add broth and wine and bring to boil, scraping up any browned bits. Cook until slightly thickened and mixture is reduced to 2 cups (measured with vegetables), about 8 minutes. Set aside in measuring cup. Wipe out skillet with paper towels.

3. Spread flour in shallow dish. Working with 1 cutlet at a time, dredge cutlets in flour, shaking off excess, and transfer to plate. Heat 2 tablespoons oil in now-empty skillet over medium-high heat until just smoking. Add 3 cutlets and cook until golden and cooked through, about 2 minutes per side. Transfer to platter and tent loosely with aluminum foil. Repeat with remaining 3 cutlets and remaining 2 tablespoons oil.

4. Discard any oil remaining in skillet. Return sauce to now-empty skillet and bring to boil. Once boiling, remove skillet from heat and whisk in butter. Stir in any accumulated juices from platter. Season with salt and pepper to taste. Spoon sauce and vegetables over chicken. Sprinkle with parsley. Serve.

Cooking Class How to Bake Thick and Chewy Chocolate Chip Cookies

There are two types of people in the world: those who like chewy cookies and those who like crunchy ones. Chewy chocolate chip cookie lovers, this is your lucky day. BY REBECCAH MARSTERS

Better Baking

ESSENTIAL GEAR Rimmed Baking Sheets

In the test kitchen, we use rimmed baking sheets—known as half sheet pans in restaurant kitchens—for baking cookies and biscuits and scones, roasting potatoes and other vegetables, and even cooking holiday roasts (usually with a wire cooling rack set inside to promote air circulation). Our favorite pan, from Wear-Ever, heats evenly, is sturdy and doesn't buckle at high temperatures or with heavy loads, and is roomy enough to accommodate most anything a home cook could throw at it. We recommend buying two of these pans: They are very durable and you'll find countless uses for them once you have them in your kitchen.

BAKE WITH THE BEST
Our favorite: Wear-Ever Half Size Heavy Duty Sheet Pan (13 gauge) by Vollrath ($21.79).

PRO TIP Faster Portioning

Our recipe instructs to shape each cookie by rolling 2 tablespoons of dough into a ball. This works well, but using a #30 ice cream scoop is a timesaver if you're baking a big batch.

KEY INGREDIENT Vanilla Extract

Is pure vanilla extract worth its expensive price tag? Well, yes and no. Pure extract came out on top in our recent taste test pitting pure versus imitation extracts, with one caveat: Many of the flavor compounds in pure vanilla are destroyed when baked at temperatures hotter than 300 degrees. But pure extract is far superior to imitation when used in uncooked and gently cooked recipes. So if you're buying only one bottle for many uses, go with pure extract. For all-purpose baking, our second place winner, CF Sauer Gold Medal Imitation Vanilla Extract, is just fine and much cheaper.

McCORMICK PURE VANILLA EXTRACT
Our taste test winner.

Core Techniques

TEST KITCHEN TIPS FOR ALL COOKIE RECIPES

Measure Ingredients Accurately

American home bakers have long liked to measure their ingredients by volume, but lately there has been a move toward weighing, a technique wholly endorsed by the test kitchen. We continue to include volume measurements for home cooks who don't own scales, but we also include weights of ingredients like flour and sugar.

Measuring by volume can create up to a 20 percent difference in the weight of the ingredient used. If you're measuring by volume, use the dip-and-sweep method for dry ingredients like flour and cocoa powder for the most consistent measurements: Dip a dry measuring cup into the container, fill it, and then sweep across the top with a straight edge (say, a butter knife or icing spatula) to get rid of the excess.

If you're using a scale, it's worth it to invest in a good one. Our favorite is the OXO Food Scale, which sells for about $50.

Rotate Pan

When set to "bake," most ovens heat from the bottom. So sheets baked concurrently on separate oven racks—standard for many recipes—will bake unevenly. We recommend that you bake one sheet of these cookies at a time. To guarantee even browning, rotate the baking sheet 180 degrees halfway through baking. If you have just one baking sheet, let it cool between batches or your cookies will spread too much.

STEP BY STEP Thick and Chewy Chocolate Chip Cookies

1. PREP
Line baking sheets with parchment paper and heat oven.
WHY? Parchment keeps the cookie bottoms from over-browning. Preheating to 325 degrees—slightly lower than the average temperature—yields chewier cookies.

2. COMBINE DRY INGREDIENTS
Using a whisk, combine the flour, baking soda, and salt.
WHY? Whisking will evenly distribute the leavener and salt in the dough. It also breaks up any clumps; sifting isn't necessary.

3. MELT BUTTER
Microwave unsalted butter until melted.
WHY? We use unsalted butter to better control the salt in the recipe, and we melt it to produce chewier cookies.

4. BEAT IN SUGAR
Beat the brown and white sugars with the melted butter for 2 minutes.
WHY? Using twice as much brown sugar as white makes for chewier cookies. Beating the butter with the sugars ensures that the sugars dissolve completely.

5. ADD EGGS
Beat in an egg, a yolk, and vanilla extract.
WHY? The back-of-the-bag chocolate chip cookie recipe calls for two whole eggs. With one less egg white, our cookie is denser and chewier.

THICK AND CHEWY CHOCOLATE CHIP COOKIES

Makes 24 cookies

To keep the cookies chewy longer, store them in an airtight container with a slice of sandwich bread.

- 2 cups plus 2 tablespoons (10⅔ ounces) all-purpose flour
- ½ teaspoon baking soda
- ½ teaspoon salt
- 12 tablespoons unsalted butter, melted and cooled
- 1 cup packed (7 ounces) light brown sugar
- ½ cup (3½ ounces) granulated sugar
- 1 large egg plus 1 large yolk
- 2 teaspoons vanilla extract
- 1½ cups (9 ounces) semisweet chocolate chips

1. Adjust oven rack to lower-middle position and heat oven to 325 degrees. Line 2 baking sheets with parchment paper. Combine flour, baking soda, and salt in bowl.

2. Using stand mixer fitted with paddle, beat melted butter, brown sugar, and granulated sugar on medium speed until smooth, about 2 minutes. Add egg and yolk and vanilla and beat until combined. Reduce speed to low and add flour mixture in 3 additions until just combined, scraping down bowl as needed. Stir in chocolate chips by hand.

3. Working with 2 tablespoons dough at a time, roll into balls and space them 2 inches apart on prepared sheets. Bake cookies, 1 sheet at a time, until edges are set and beginning to brown but centers are still soft and puffy, 15 to 20 minutes, rotating sheet halfway through baking. Let cookies cool on sheets for 10 minutes before serving.

Do's and Don'ts

DON'T Stint on Brown Sugar

Brown sugar produces chewier baked goods than white granulated sugar does. Not only is it moister but it also contains invert sugar, which granulated sugar has little of. Invert sugar is very hydroscopic; that means it pulls moisture from the air, even after the cookies are baked, helping them stay moist and chewy. We use twice as much brown sugar as white in this recipe.

DO Melt the Butter

Many recipes for cakes and cookies call for creaming together softened butter and sugar, which beats air into the mixture and yields tall, light baked goods. But our goal is good chew, so we melt the butter instead. The water contained in the melted butter becomes available to combine with the flour and form gluten. Too much gluten would make the cookies tough, but melted butter boosts gluten formation just enough to promote chew.

DO Plan Ahead

After you've made the dough, you can refrigerate it or roll the cookies and refrigerate the balls, in both cases for up to two days. For longer storage, shape the dough into balls; freeze them on a baking sheet; and store the frozen dough balls in layers, separated by parchment paper, for up to two months. Bake the cookies straight from the freezer, increasing the baking time by a minute or two.

6. ADD DRY INGREDIENTS
Slowly beat in the flour mixture.
WHY? Adding the dry ingredients gradually with the mixer on low helps them fully incorporate and prevents the flour from flying out of the bowl.

7. ADD CHIPS
Stir in chocolate chips by hand.
WHY? Stirring by hand prevents overworking the dough in the mixer, which would make the cookies tough.

8. SHAPE COOKIES
Roll the dough into balls.
WHY? Rolling the dough, rather than dropping it in mounds from a spoon, will yield thick, even cookies.

9. BAKE AND ROTATE
Bake one sheet of cookies at a time, rotating the sheet halfway through baking.
WHY? Baking one sheet at a time and rotating the pan ensures the most even browning in any oven.

10. LET COOL ON SHEET
Let the finished cookies cool on the baking sheet briefly.
WHY? Taking the cookies out when they're slightly underdone and letting them finish baking on the hot sheet ensures that they won't be overbaked and dry.

Cooking for Two Chicken and Sausage Gumbo

You can't make great gumbo without a long-cooked roux. Or can you?

BY CHRISTIE MORRISON

A ROUX IS a cooked blend of roughly equal parts flour and fat (usually oil, butter, or lard). When it's used to thicken cream sauces, gravies, or pan sauces, it is cooked for just a few minutes to rid the flour of its raw taste, until the color is blond or very pale brown. But dark roux—the kind used in gumbo—is cooked for up to an hour, until it is the color of an old penny. This roux—which gets very hot and requires almost constant stirring to keep the flour from burning—is what creates gumbo's defining deep, complex flavor and silky texture, and it's easier to justify making one if you're cooking a big batch. But a dark roux takes a lot of time and effort if it's just two of you hoping to enjoy gumbo on a weeknight. I wanted to find

a way to get the flavor and depth of a dark roux in less time. Was it possible, or was I grasping at straws?

I found two "shortcut" recipes in the test kitchen's archive of gumbo recipes. The first one calls for bringing vegetable oil to exactly 200 degrees before adding the flour and then stirring for about 20 minutes, until the roux reaches the correct color—not exactly fast, but 20 minutes is about half of the time called for in many other versions. The second in-house recipe calls for dry-toasting the flour in a skillet until it begins to brown, whisking in the oil, and then baking the roux in a 350-degree oven for about 45 minutes, until it is dark brown. But while mostly hands-off, this roux still took about 50 minutes before I could continue to make the gumbo on the stove.

While the stovetop method's shorter cooking time was appealing, its 20 minutes of constant stirring wasn't—not for two bowls of gumbo. And even with the small amount of roux I was making (2 tablespoons each of flour and oil), it took me upwards of 15 minutes of constant stirring to reach the right color. Using the oven to bake the roux would give me time to prep the rest of the dish, but I was loath to heat up the oven in addition to using the stovetop when I was trying to streamline the recipe for just two diners.

With the words "fast" and "easy" running through my head, I wondered: Could I make my dark brown roux in the microwave? I whisked the flour and oil together and microwaved the mixture, gradually adding time until it cooked through and browned completely. But the longer the roux stayed in the microwave, the harder it was to catch it before it burned, and after 5 minutes the mixture was insanely hot. To better control the cooking and browning, I browned the flour first on the stovetop in a dry pan for about 5 minutes, added the oil, and then microwaved the roux, covered, for just 2 minutes, stirring it after 1 minute to check the color. My roux was deeply brown in 7 minutes—with only 5 minutes of active cooking.

Now I could work on streamlining the rest of the stew. While all gumbos begin with sautéing the classic Cajun trio of onion, celery, and green bell

pepper with the roux, the rest of the gumbo is open to interpretation: chicken; pork or sausage; shrimp, lobster, oysters, or crab; wild game like rabbit; as well as such vegetables as tomato and okra. Clearly, my weeknight dinner for two had to have great flavor, but it wasn't the place for a pantheon of proteins; I would stick with the two meats that were simplest to handle: chicken and andouille sausage. I decided I would try to avoid browning the meats to save time. I added garlic and tomato paste for deeper flavor, as well as a bay leaf for earthy complexity.

One potential shortcut that turned out to be a nonstarter was using boneless, skinless chicken breasts. Despite the shorter cooking time of the breasts, my tasters were adamant that bone-in chicken thighs added vastly superior depth of flavor and meant moister meat. Since I wasn't browning the chicken, however, the skin didn't get a chance to render, leaving an extra-greasy gumbo at the finish. To solve the problem, I discarded the skin before cooking

the chicken. My tasters and I liked the texture of shredded, rather than cubed, chicken in the gumbo, so I used two forks to pull the cooked thighs into pieces.

To keep things proportioned for two servings, I substituted one cored, seeded, and chopped fresh tomato for the usual canned diced tomatoes and added it when the gumbo was almost finished. Using frozen sliced okra was a timesaver. The okra became just tender as it simmered in the gumbo, retaining a bit of bite and helping thicken the dish.

In less time than it usually takes to cook just the roux, I had a gumbo for two that had deep, complex flavor. It was so good that I almost wished I had leftovers.

CHICKEN AND SAUSAGE GUMBO FOR TWO

Serves 2

Serve gumbo over rice. Because microwave wattages vary, you may need to microwave the roux longer (or shorter) in step 1 to achieve a dark brown color.

Andouille sausage and dark roux add authentic Louisiana flavor to our streamlined gumbo.

TEST KITCHEN DISCOVERY
Faster Roux

Cooking a spattering roux on the stovetop for 45 minutes for just two portions is a nonstarter. We found two tricks that allowed us to shortcut the process and still wind up with a flavorful roux that nicely thickened our Chicken and Sausage Gumbo for Two.

DRY-TOAST THE FLOUR
Cook the flour in a saucepan until it's this shade of light brown.

MICROWAVE
Add the oil to the toasted flour and microwave until the roux is this shade of dark brown (about 2 minutes), stirring once halfway through.

One day we decided to ignore the standard instructions for drop biscuits. The result? Best biscuits ever. BY CRISTIN WALSH

THERE ARE TWO basic methods for making biscuits. Rolled biscuits require you to quite carefully incorporate butter or shortening into the dry ingredients, add the liquid (milk, cream, or buttermilk), gently knead into a cohesive dough, roll it out, and cut the biscuits. For drop biscuits, you just melt the butter or shortening, add it to the liquid, and stir this mixture into the dry ingredients. "Drop" this wetter batter onto a baking sheet to form biscuits and pop it into the oven. Done. But if drop biscuits are so easy, why are they often such a squat, gummy, tough disappointment?

Our drop biscuit recipe bakes up tall and tender every time. It calls for butter for flavor and buttermilk for gentle tang. All-purpose flour suits this style of biscuit just fine. Since you don't roll out the biscuits, you've less chance of overdeveloping the gluten and producing tough biscuits—no softer special flours needed. But our most interesting breakthrough was a lucky accident.

Most drop biscuit recipes call for cooled melted butter and room-temperature liquid (in our case buttermilk). When we developed this recipe, we adhered to those temperatures—mostly. On one occasion we got tired of waiting for the butter to cool or the buttermilk to warm up out of the fridge, and we just went ahead and combined the two, temperature be damned. The warm butter instantly clumped in the cold buttermilk, and no matter how much we subsequently whisked the mixture, the butter chunks wouldn't go away. Wondering what would happen if we proceeded regardless, we stirred the lumpy mixture into the dry ingredients and stuck the pan of biscuits in the oven. Amazingly, they came out higher and fluffier than those we'd been making with the ingredients at conventionally correct temperatures.

Why? The chunks of butter melted in the oven, giving off steam that created rise and resulted in especially light, fluffy biscuits. This interaction is more typical of rolled biscuits, as the pea-size chunks of chilled butter in rolled biscuit dough melt in the oven. By sheer luck, our much easier drop biscuit method gave us the same effect.

With this technique in hand, there's no limit on the delicious variations you can make.

This tasty variation is flavored with jarred pimentos and cheddar cheese.

BUTTERMILK DROP BISCUITS

Makes 12 biscuits

To refresh day-old biscuits, heat them in a 300-degree oven for 10 minutes.

- 2 cups (10 ounces) all-purpose flour
- 2 teaspoons baking powder
- ½ teaspoon baking soda
- 1 teaspoon sugar
- ¾ teaspoon salt
- 1 cup buttermilk, chilled
- 8 tablespoons unsalted butter, melted, plus 2 tablespoons unsalted butter

1. Adjust oven rack to middle position and heat oven to 475 degrees. Line rimmed baking sheet with parchment paper. Whisk flour, baking powder, baking soda, sugar, and salt together in large bowl. Stir buttermilk and melted butter together in 2-cup liquid measuring cup until butter forms clumps.

2. Add buttermilk mixture to flour mixture and stir with rubber spatula until just incorporated. Using greased ¼-cup dry measuring cup, drop level scoops of batter 1½ inches apart on prepared sheet. Bake until tops are golden brown, rotating sheet halfway through baking, 12 to 14 minutes.

3. Melt remaining 2 tablespoons butter and brush on biscuit tops. Transfer biscuits to wire rack and let cool for 5 minutes before serving.

CHEDDAR AND PIMENTO DROP BISCUITS

In step 1 add ¾ cup shredded extra-sharp cheddar cheese and ¼ cup finely chopped jarred pimentos to flour mixture.

MIXED HERB DROP BISCUITS

In step 1 add 2 tablespoons minced fresh basil, 2 tablespoons minced fresh parsley, and 2 teaspoons minced fresh oregano to flour mixture.

MUSTARD AND DILL DROP BISCUITS

In step 1 add 1 tablespoon minced fresh dill to flour mixture and 2 tablespoons whole-grain mustard to buttermilk mixture.

ROSEMARY AND OLIVE DROP BISCUITS

In step 1 add ¼ cup finely chopped pitted kalamata olives and 1½ teaspoons minced fresh rosemary to flour mixture.

- 2 (5- to 7-ounce) bone-in chicken thighs, skin removed, trimmed
  Salt and pepper
- 2 tablespoons all-purpose flour
- 2 tablespoons vegetable oil
- 1 small onion, chopped fine
- ½ cup finely chopped green bell pepper
- ¼ cup minced celery
- 1 tablespoon tomato paste
- 2 garlic cloves, minced
  Pinch cayenne pepper
- 1¾ cups chicken broth
- 1 bay leaf
- 4 ounces andouille sausage, halved lengthwise and sliced thin
- 1 tomato, cored, seeded, and chopped
- ¾ cup frozen sliced okra

1. Season chicken with salt and pepper; set aside. Toast flour in medium saucepan over medium heat, stirring constantly, until lightly browned, about 5 minutes. Transfer flour to bowl and whisk in oil. Microwave, covered, until roux is dark brown, about 2 minutes, stirring halfway through microwaving.

2. Transfer brown roux to now-empty pan. Stir in onion, bell pepper, and celery and cook over medium heat, stirring frequently, until softened, about 5 minutes. Stir in tomato paste, garlic, and cayenne and cook until fragrant, about 1 minute. Slowly whisk in broth, scraping up any browned bits. Add chicken and bay leaf to pan and bring to boil. Reduce heat to medium-low and simmer, covered, until chicken is tender, 20 to 25 minutes, stirring occasionally to prevent scorching.

3. Transfer chicken to plate and remove pan from heat. Skim fat from surface of gumbo with large spoon. When chicken is cool enough to handle, cut or shred into bite-size pieces and return to pan; discard bones.

4. Stir sausage, tomato, and okra into gumbo. Bring to simmer over medium heat and cook until heated through, about 7 minutes. Discard bay leaf, season with salt and pepper to taste, and serve. (Gumbo can be refrigerated for up to 3 days.)

Recipe Makeover Denver Omelet

We wanted a reduced-fat omelet that was better tasting (and less leathery) than the standard egg white omelet. BY CRISTIN WALSH

MAYBE ALL THOSE sporty folks high up in the mountains of Colorado burn off more calories and fat than the rest of us do. But while I love Denver omelets, with 400 calories and 31 grams of fat per serving, this breakfast slows me down before my day has even started. I hoped to slim down this diner classic—a buttery egg envelope enclosing diced onion, bell pepper, deli ham, and cheese—yet still have a dish that would satisfy hearty morning appetites.

I had a few tricks that I knew would get the calories down right off the bat. I'd trade full-fat cheese for a lower-fat version, swap high-in-saturated-fat butter for vegetable oil spray, and drop the yolks entirely to make an egg white omelet. Those decisions made, I sautéed the filling and set it aside. I poured six egg whites (to serve two people) in the same pan, and once they were set, I sprinkled in cheese. I arranged the sautéed vegetables and the ham over half of the omelet and folded it to enclose the filling.

It was a reasonable start, hitting close to my target nutrition numbers. But the egg whites were leathery and my Denver (aka western) omelet seemed puny. Although yolks account for much of the fat and calories in an egg (a large whole egg has 70 calories and 5 grams of fat, while an egg white has only 15 calories and no fat), they also make omelets tender. If I could somehow find calories to cut elsewhere, then maybe I could restore a yolk. That left the filling. After scrutinizing it, I tried swapping out some of the calorie-dense ham for additional low-calorie, good-for-you bell pepper. Nobody minded this change, so I reallocated some of the ham calories to the eggs and added back a single yolk to my recipe. I tasted the omelet again. Better but still a long way from actually good. Clearly I needed another yolk. I scanned the ingredient list: Would it be worth exchanging some of the cheese for another yolk? I made two omelets to taste side by side: the first with my lone yolk and the second with two yolks but less cheese. We preferred the latter.

With two whole eggs and four egg whites, my omelet was finally tender and richer-tasting. But it remained flimsy and unable to contain the plentiful filling. A coworker suggested that I try the blender: If you aerate the eggs, she said,

This extra-puffy omelet serves two people.

the omelet might appear more substantial. I gave it a whirl (literally), letting the eggs foam in the blender for about a minute. I was pleased with the fluffy yet somehow more substantial-seeming omelet that these blended eggs yielded.

But the fact remained that four fewer yolks meant the omelet simply couldn't contain the same amount of filling—it kept tumbling out. Eventually, I solved that problem by borrowing a technique used by short-order cooks. (They make enough Denver omelets to know.) I poured the blended eggs directly over the sautéed vegetables in the skillet, eliminating all distinction between egg and filling. When the eggs were almost set, I took them off the heat, sprinkled on the cheese, and covered the skillet until the cheese had melted in the residual heat. This omelet came out tender and puffy, and the spillovers were history. A dash of hot sauce, a sprinkle of parsley, and some minced garlic later, it was good to go. And given my slimmed-down breakfast—220 calories and 10 grams of fat—I was good to go, too.

TEST KITCHEN TECHNIQUE
Blend the Eggs
How do you get more from less? Put your eggs in the blender. With four fewer yolks in our omelet than usual for a full-fat version, we achieve the necessary volume by whirring the eggs for about a minute before cooking them.

USE THE BLENDER
Whir the eggs for a puffier omelet.

The Numbers
All nutritional information is for one serving.

Traditional Denver Omelet
CALORIES **400**
FAT **31 grams** SATURATED FAT **16 grams**

Cook's Country Reduced-Fat Denver Omelet
CALORIES **220**
FAT **10 grams** SATURATED FAT **4 grams**

REDUCED-FAT DENVER OMELET
Serves 2
If you can't find low-fat Monterey Jack cheese, substitute low-fat sharp cheddar.

- 1   small onion, chopped
- ½   cup chopped green bell pepper
- ½   cup chopped red bell pepper
- ¼   teaspoon salt
- ¼   teaspoon pepper
- 2   large eggs plus 4 large whites
- ½   teaspoon hot sauce
- 2   ounces thinly sliced deli ham, chopped fine
- 1   garlic clove, minced
- 1   ounce low-fat Monterey Jack cheese, shredded (¼ cup)
- 1   tablespoon minced fresh parsley

1. Spray 10-inch nonstick skillet liberally with vegetable oil spray. Add onion, green and red bell pepper, salt, and pepper and cook over medium heat until vegetables are just softened and lightly browned, about 5 minutes. While vegetables are cooking, process eggs and whites and hot sauce in blender until pale and foamy, about 1 minute.

2. Add ham and garlic to vegetables in skillet and cook until fragrant, about 1½ minutes. Pour egg mixture into skillet, stir to distribute vegetables, and cook until edges of omelet begin to set, 10 to 20 seconds. Pull cooked edges of omelet into center of skillet using rubber spatula, then tilt skillet to allow uncooked egg mixture to run to edge of pan. Repeat until omelet is just set but still moist on surface, 1 to 2 minutes.

3. Off heat, sprinkle Monterey Jack and parsley evenly over omelet, cover, and set aside until cheese is melted, about 1 minute. Run spatula around edges of omelet to loosen, shaking skillet gently to release. Using spatula, fold omelet in half, then cut in half crosswise. Serve immediately.

Slow Cooker Mashed Potatoes

Could we peel away some steps from this recipe and still end up with smashing results? BY SARAH GABRIEL

WHEN I FIRST came across a recipe for slow-cooker mashed potatoes, I was surprised by its similarity to conventional recipes: Potatoes are placed in the insert, covered with water, cooked until tender, and then drained, mashed, and mixed with butter and milk or cream. I gave it a try, and while it worked well enough, the only convenience it offered was that it didn't take up a burner on the stove. That would be somewhat helpful when I was cooking for a crowd, I guess, but what would be really helpful is nixing the draining step so I could cook, mash, and keep a big batch of potatoes hot throughout the meal without having to deal with moving the hot potatoes or dirtying extra dishes.

I did manage to find a few slow-cooker recipes that didn't call for draining the potatoes. The first recipe required cooking the potatoes in a few cups of milk, which seemed like a smart way to eliminate the draining, but the results were less than brilliant: The milk scorched and gave the potatoes an oddly sweet flavor. Another recipe called for cooking the potatoes in chicken broth, and while it didn't scorch like the milk, the broth made the potatoes taste like soup. The last recipe called for steaming chunked potatoes in a small amount of water (about ½ cup per pound). Unfortunately, the recipe didn't specify what size the chunks of potato should be. I tried 1-inch pieces, but they wound up overdone outside and underdone inside, plus pieces that weren't submerged were less done than pieces that were. And

to make matters worse, the pieces that weren't covered by the water had turned gray. On the bright side, the resulting mash was just about the right texture. Could I get all the potatoes to maintain their color and cook properly?

I wanted to be able to feed about a dozen people, so I'd need 5 pounds of potatoes. Using the steaming recipe's potato-to-water ratio, I put 2¾ cups of lightly salted water in the slow cooker. One-inch chunks had been undercooked in the middle, so I tried ¼-inch-thick slices. After 4 hours, the slices in or near the water on the bottom were perfect, but the slices on the top, away from the water, were discolored, dried out, and underdone. Thinly slicing the potatoes had given me even cooking within each slice, but I needed to figure out how to get all the slices to cook at the same rate and get rid of the discoloration.

For my next test, I pressed a sheet of greased parchment paper onto the top layer of potatoes, hoping that it might prevent discoloration by trapping steam close to the top layer of potatoes. Four hours later, I took off the lid and peeled back the paper. The parchment hadn't eliminated the discoloration, but the top layer of potato slices was cooked. I was making progress.

Peeled potatoes turn brown or gray because of an enzymatic process that happens when cut surfaces are exposed to oxygen. The enzymes are destroyed by heat, but because the slow cooker heats up slowly, the enzymes have plenty of time to do their dirty work. I tried

brushing the top layer of potatoes with butter to limit their exposure to oxygen. While this offered some improvement, it didn't solve the problem.

Getting the potatoes hot faster would give the enzymes less time to do damage before the heat destroyed them, but this was, hello, a slow-cooker recipe. I considered precooking the potatoes in the microwave, but the idea of wrestling 5 pounds of sliced potatoes in and out of the appliance was not appealing. Could simply heating up the water sufficiently jump-start cooking? I boiled the water and salt in a saucepan and then poured it over the sliced potatoes, stirred, and proceeded as before. The potatoes were evenly cooked after 4 hours, and while the top layer had darkened slightly, the potatoes looked normal once mashed.

I added the butter and ¼ cup of cream, but my tasters and I could hardly taste the latter. I added more little by little, and at 1 cup of cream the flavor was great but the mash was runny. After a few tests, I scrapped the cream entirely in favor of sour cream—just ½ cup provided plenty of flavor and creaminess. These potatoes were a huge hit in the test kitchen, and they'll be an even bigger hit with cooks who won't have to mash minutes before dinner is served.

These potatoes can be held on the slow cooker's "warm" setting for up to 2 hours.

SLOW-COOKER MASHED POTATOES Serves 10 to 12

The top layer of potatoes may discolor slightly, but this won't be noticeable after mashing. The mash may be held on the slow cooker's warm setting for up to 2 hours before serving. Loosen the potatoes with additional sour cream if needed.

- 5 pounds russet potatoes, peeled and sliced ¼ inch thick
- 2¾ cups water
  Salt and pepper
- 3 tablespoons unsalted butter, melted, plus 9 tablespoons cut into 9 pieces
- ½ cup sour cream
- 3 tablespoons minced fresh chives

1. Place potatoes in slow cooker. Bring water and 2½ teaspoons salt to boil in small saucepan. Pour boiling salted water over potatoes and stir to coat. Brush top layer of potatoes with melted butter. Press 16- by 12-inch sheet of parchment paper firmly onto potatoes, folding down edges as needed. Cover and cook until potatoes are completely tender, about 4 hours on high.

2. Discard parchment. Mash potatoes with potato masher until smooth. Stir in sour cream, chives, and remaining 9 tablespoons butter. Season with salt and pepper to taste. Serve.

KEY TECHNIQUES Mastering the Mash

BRUSH Coating the top layer of sliced potatoes with melted butter limits oxidation and discoloration.

COVER Pressing parchment paper onto the buttered potatoes helps ensure even cooking.

Equipment Review Liquid Dish Soap

Humans have been washing dishes for centuries.
Are innovations in dish soap making the job any easier? BY LAUREN SAVOIE

AS MUCH AS we love our dishwashers, when washing delicate china, wood cutting boards, sharp knives, and pots and pans, we still rely on soap and sponge. The last time we tested dish soaps, in 2007, we liked Method Go Naked Ultra Concentrated Dish Detergent best. But it was recently discontinued, so we are revisiting the subject.

We were surprised to find a host of new soaps designed for people who scrub dishes under a running tap rather than fill the sink with soapy water—the more traditional method. So we decided to include three such products: two with pumps that foam straight from the bottle, and one with a special motion-sensor system for germ-free dispensing. We also found an unusual dishwasher detergent/dish soap hybrid. Four of the seven products also make some claim to being environmentally friendly, so we pitted them against the benchmark for traditional liquid soaps—the national best seller Dawn Ultra.

In the kitchen, we gleefully made a mess, burning skillets with measured portions of hard-to-clean foods like béchamel sauce and chicken teriyaki. Controlling for the amount of soap, water temperature, and type of sponge, we washed the pans using both the fill-sink method and the rinse method, counting the strokes needed to get each pan clean. Our best soaps required fewer than 70 strokes, while others needed anywhere from 85 to 100. One soap consistently required more than 100 strokes and even then left a film of oil. What accounted for these differences?

Oil and water repel each other, so soap makes washing dishes easier because it contains surfactants, tadpole-shaped chemicals with water-loving heads and oil-loving tails that encourage water and fat to mix. Surfactants can be made from plants (for all-natural cleaners) or petroleum, but according to Brian Grady, director of the Institute of Applied Surfactant Research at the University of Oklahoma, the origin of surfactants doesn't determine the effectiveness of the soap. "There's no inherent advantage of one over the other," he said. "It comes down to the individual formula and overall quantity of surfactants."

We turned to a simple science project to measure the power of each product. Surfactants make water "wetter" by lowering its surface tension, allowing tightly packed water molecules to spread out and make room for dirt and grease. We mixed a measured solution of soap and water in plastic cups and suspended a strip of paper bag so that it was just touching the surface. A solution with strong surfactants (and therefore lower surface tension) will allow the water to climb the strip of paper; the higher it travels the stronger the surfactants.

After an hour, the two top-performing soaps climbed an average of more than 40 millimeters, while plain water traveled only 10 millimeters. Our poorest-performing soap (the same product that left dishes filmy with oil)

climbed just 11 millimeters. Despite the manufacturer's claims, it didn't work in the dishwasher either. We used the data from this test to calculate the strength of surfactants of each soap.

Scent also mattered to our testers, although we gave it less weight in our rankings than washing ability. We asked each soapmaker for its most popular fragrance and had 21 test kitchen staffers sniff each product mixed with water. Testers preferred lightly scented soaps.

All but one of our soaps performed reasonably well, though we're not sold on foams, even for tap runners. Our

recommended soaps worked no matter how we washed with them. In fact, all the products that we tested performed best when we used the fill-sink approach. Why? Since surfactants are dispersed throughout the water, the surfactants are cleaning your dishes even when you're not scrubbing.

In the end, one soap whipped both innovative products and traditional Dawn Ultra, no matter our washing technique, and we liked its smell, too. From now on, we'll use Mrs. Meyer's Clean Day Liquid Dish Soap when we have a sinkful of dirty dishes.

		CRITERIA		TESTERS' NOTES
HIGHLY RECOMMENDED				
MRS. MEYER'S Clean Day Liquid Dish Soap, Lavender **Price:** $3.99 for 16 oz ($0.25 per oz) **Strength:** 4.1 times more effective than water		Strength of Surfactants Cleaning Performance Scent	★★★ ★★★ ★★★	This "97% naturally-derived" dish soap cut through caked-on grime quickly and effortlessly. It cleaned burnt-on chicken teriyaki more than two times faster than other soaps that we tested, and testers loved its "clean," "herbal" lavender scent.
RECOMMENDED				
LYSOL No-Touch Kitchen System, Shimmering Berry **Price:** $10.39 for starter pack, including dispenser, batteries, and 8.5 oz of soap (starter pack: $1.22 per oz; soap refill: $0.47 per oz) **Strength:** 4.6 times more effective than water		Strength of Surfactants Cleaning Performance Scent	★★★ ★★★ ★½	While a few testers found this self-dispensing soap's "strong" berry scent "yummy," most likened it to something along the lines of "bad Jolly Ranchers." But its cleaning prowess was undeniable. The motion sensor base unit works cleanly and quickly and is particularly useful for those who prefer to wash dishes under running water. Even if its dispenser is expensive and a tad silly, there's no denying that this soap really works.
DAWN Platinum Erasing Dish Foam, Fresh Rapids **Price:** $3.27 for 10.1 oz ($0.32 per oz) **Strength:** 2.8 times more effective than water		Strength of Surfactants Cleaning Performance Scent	★★ ★★½ ★★★	A concentrated dish liquid that foams straight out of the pump, this soap scrubbed away burnt-on béchamel effortlessly, requiring an average of 71 strokes to clean. Testers compared its "pleasant," "mild" scent to "freshly cleaned laundry" and preferred it to the stronger but similar fragrance of Dawn Ultra.
DAWN Ultra, Original Scent **Price:** $2.97 for 24 oz ($0.12 per oz) **Strength:** 3.6 times more effective than water		Strength of Surfactants Cleaning Performance Scent	★★½ ★★ ★★	The nation's top-selling dish soap product, this traditional liquid soap worked reliably through all our tests, requiring an average of 80 strokes to clean dishes and performing particularly well when we soaked dirty dishes in a sinkful of its soapy water.
SEVENTH GENERATION Natural Dish Liquid, Free & Clear **Price:** $3.69 for 25 oz ($0.15 per oz) **Strength:** 3 times more effective than water		Strength of Surfactants Cleaning Performance Scent	★★ ★★ ★★	This environmentally friendly dish soap did a commendable job on all our dirty dishes, but some testers were perplexed by its lack of scent and color. "I wouldn't exactly object to using this stuff on my dishes," said one, "but I might not be convinced that they're actually clean."
RECOMMENDED WITH RESERVATIONS				
METHOD Power Foam Dish Soap, French Lavender **Price:** $4 for 16 oz ($0.25 per oz) **Strength:** 3.2 times more effective than water		Strength of Surfactants Cleaning Performance Scent	★★ ★½ ★	Testers were split on this innovative dish soap, designed for spraying directly onto dirty dishes. It washed well but needed double the soap to get the job done, and while some appreciated the spray function, others found it clunky and awkward to use.
NOT RECOMMENDED				
EARTH FRIENDLY PRODUCTS DuoDish, Organic Lavender **Price:** $4.49 for 25 oz ($0.18 per oz) **Strength:** 1.1 times more effective than water		Strength of Surfactants Cleaning Performance Scent	★ ★ ★★	We had high hopes for this all-natural soap meant for use in the dishwasher and the sink, but the product proved adept at neither. During our scrubbing tests, this detergent failed to dissolve in water, leaving stringy blobs of soap in the drain. In the dishwasher, it was no match for caked-on cheese and egg.

Taste Test Brown Mustard

Products awash in vinegar didn't cut the mustard with our tasters.

BY LAUREN SAVOIE

WHEN IT COMES to mustard, yellow tends to hog all the glory, zigzagging up ballpark franks and cornering the market on pretzel-stand squeeze bottles. But here at the test kitchen we like brown mustard, too, for its spicy, robust flavor. Unlike the yellow stuff, which gets its bright, mild character from white mustard seeds, brown mustard is made from the smaller, hotter brown seeds along with some of their bran, the tough outer layer of the seed that gives the mustard its speckled look. We use brown mustard to pack a punch when we're eating rich foods like pastrami, ham, or eggy breads. To find the best brown mustard, 21 test kitchen editors and cooks sampled seven nationally available products in three blind taste tests: plain, in deviled eggs, and with boiled hot dogs.

Which mustards didn't pass muster? Our tasters expected their spicy brown mustard to be, well, spicy. We wanted to feel the burn, and in every taste test, hotter mustards scored higher. Mustard's heat is a defense mechanism of the mustard plant against insects looking for something to chomp on; when its seeds are crushed, enzymes are freed and start to convert dormant chemicals into hot mustard oil. We measured the amount of mustard oil in each product, but surprisingly, the results didn't line up. Some of the hotter products that we preferred had plenty of mustard oil, but so did the product that ranked lowest, which tasters called "weak" and "wimpy." If we liked hotter mustards, why did one of our lowest-ranked products contain so much of the very compound that makes mustard hot?

A couple of the mustards boast "#1 grade mustard seed" on their ingredient lists, so we turned first to the quality of the seeds. But when we looked into it and found that all the mustards that we tested are made with top-grade seeds, whether stated or not, we realized that it was time to examine the mustard-making process. Mustard is created by mixing crushed seeds with a cold liquid (a cooler temperature is required to correctly activate the enzymes). Then

an acid is added to slow the formation of mustard oil, keeping the mustard from becoming blow-your-head-off spicy. The most common acid, used by every product that we tasted, is vinegar because of its three-pronged effect of taming heat, prolonging shelf life, and adding tang. But when there's too much vinegar, the formation of mustard oil is slowed too much, and the condiment loses its characteristic burn.

If more vinegar means less heat, we now understood why some products with lots of mustard oil fell flat and why tasters consistently rated overly tart products low in both heat and overall flavor. We measured each mustard's acidity to get at vinegar content and found that more acidic products, usually those with more vinegar, rated lowest in our taste tests. In sum: Mustards with both a high percentage of mustard oil and a moderate amount of vinegar came out on top and were praised for being complex and multidimensional. Our tasters also demanded mustards that were smooth and creamy and adhered well to hot dogs. Mustards that were gritty, chunky, or runny got lower scores.

In the end, Gulden's Spicy Brown Mustard took the top spot thanks to its bold heat, gentle tang, and smooth texture. That said, there are quite a few good brown mustards on the market, as we can recommend five of the seven that we tasted, and a sixth with some reservations.

So what should you do if one of our two bottom-ranking products is lurking at the back of your fridge? Use it in a recipe. When we enlisted our products as a condiment, distinctions among them were obvious and important, but when they were put to work as a supporting ingredient, unbalanced mustards were rounded out by other flavors. So when we sampled each mustard in a batch of deviled eggs, tasters could scarcely detect differences in either flavor or texture, even when we doubled the amount of mustard called for in the recipe.

RECOMMENDED

	TASTERS' NOTES
GULDEN'S Spicy Brown Mustard **Price:** $1.99 for 12 oz ($0.17 per oz) **Ingredients:** Vinegar, mustard seed, salt, spices, turmeric **Acidity:** 2.84% **Mustard Oil:** 0.014%	We liked Gulden's "bright," "classic" and familiar taste. On hot dogs, it was "complex" and "balanced" with a "smooth" texture that "goes great with the meat." As one taster summarized, it's "what brown mustard should taste like."
FRENCH'S Spicy Brown Mustard **Price:** $2.19 for 12 oz ($0.18 per oz) **Ingredients:** Distilled vinegar, #1 grade mustard seed, water, salt, spices, turmeric and natural flavors **Acidity:** 3.1% **Mustard Oil:** 0.02%	"Tastes like what I grew up with," said one taster. With "lots of bite" and "bold," "complex" flavors, French's earned high marks for its "full-frontal spiciness" and "punch of mustard heat." It led the pack on hot dogs, where we liked its "thick" and "creamy" texture.
BEAVER Deli Mustard **Price:** $3.50 for 12.5 oz ($0.28 per oz) **Ingredients:** Water, mustard seed, vinegars (white distilled, white wine and red wine), soybean oil, sugar, salt, white wine, grated horseradish roots, garlic, eggs, spices, xanthan and cellulose gums, sodium benzoate (preservative), citric acid, turmeric, high fructose corn syrup, lemon juice, calcium disodium EDTA (retains product freshness), artificial and natural flavors, annatto, red chili peppers, ginger **Acidity:** 2.6% **Mustard Oil:** 0.029%	A curveball in our lineup, Beaver was the only mustard we tested with whole seeds and an unusual ingredient list, full of additions like eggs, corn syrup, artificial flavors, and xanthan gum. Because of these characteristics, some of our tasters felt that this product was "a different animal." But most loved the "pleasant pop" of seeds in this "full-flavored," "well-balanced," "sweet and savory" mustard.
KOOPS' Spicy Brown Mustard **Price:** $3.39 for 12 oz ($0.28 per oz) **Ingredients:** Vinegar, water, mustard seed, salt, turmeric **Acidity:** 2.72% **Mustard Oil:** 0.009%	Koops' "smooth," "uniform" texture won many fans, and most tasters favorably likened its "mild" and "light" flavor to that of yellow mustard; it was similar to "what you would expect at any hot dog stand." However, a few tasters faulted its "simple" taste for being "barely there."
KOSCIUSKO Spicy Brown Mustard **Price:** $2.99 for 9 oz ($0.33 per oz) **Ingredients:** White distilled vinegar, #1 grade mustard seed, water, salt, spices **Acidity:** 3.56% **Mustard Oil:** 0.011%	"Sweet," "fruity" notes earned this "mild" mustard points with tasters who thought that its "mellow" flavor "might be good for kids." A few tasters were put off by its "thick," "hummuslike" consistency.

RECOMMENDED WITH RESERVATIONS

HEINZ Spicy Brown Mustard **Price:** $1.80 for 17.5 oz ($0.10 per oz) **Ingredients:** Distilled white vinegar, mustard seed, mustard bran, salt, spices, xanthan gum, turmeric, natural flavoring **Acidity:** 4.35% **Mustard Oil:** 0.007%	We picked up on an unusual array of flavors in this mustard, from "warm baking spices" like clove, allspice, and nutmeg to "curry," "minerals," and "berry flavors." While we've nothing against these flavors, per se, our tasters did find them out of place in a mustard.

NOT RECOMMENDED

EDEN FOODS Organic Brown Mustard **Price:** $2.78 for 9 oz ($0.31 per oz) **Ingredients:** Organic whole mustard seed, Eden organic apple cider vinegar, water, Eden sea salt **Acidity:** 3.23% **Mustard Oil:** 0.017%	"I'm not sure I'd know this was mustard without seeing it." "Whoa—vinegar superoverload!" With relatively high acidity and wimpy heat, this mustard tasted out of balance. While a few tasters favorably compared its consistency to that of "stone-ground," most found it "mealy," "sandy," and "gritty."

Heirloom Recipes

We're looking for recipes that you treasure—the ones that have been handed down in your family for a generation or more; that always come out for the holidays; that have earned a place at your table and in your heart, through many years of meals. Send us the recipes that spell home with a capital H. Visit **CooksCountry.com/magazines/home** (or write to Heirloom Recipes, *Cook's Country*, P.O. Box 470739, Brookline, MA 02447); click on Heirloom Recipes and tell us a little about the recipe. Include your name and mailing address. **If we print your recipe, you'll receive a free one-year subscription to *Cook's Country*.**

KÖNIGSBERGER KLOPSE
Serves 4 to 6

My great-grandmother taught her daughter and my mother to make these meatballs. Honestly, I wasn't crazy about them as a kid, but now I appreciate the unusual flavors—and their Prussian heritage. I like them with wide egg noodles to sop up the gravy and with sauerkraut to offset their richness.
–Diane Unger, Senior Editor

- 2 kaiser rolls, torn into ½-inch pieces
- 4 cups beef broth
- 1 cup sour cream
- 2 large egg yolks
- 2 anchovy fillets, rinsed and minced
- 2 pounds meatloaf mix
- 1 small onion, chopped fine
- 3 tablespoons capers, rinsed and chopped
- 3 tablespoons minced fresh parsley
  Salt and pepper
- 1 teaspoon ground allspice
- ½ teaspoon ground nutmeg
- 5 tablespoons unsalted butter
- ½ cup all-purpose flour
- 2 cups water
- 1 bay leaf
- 1 sprig fresh thyme
- 2 tablespoons Worcestershire sauce
- 1 teaspoon grated lemon zest

1. Pulse rolls, ½ cup broth, ¼ cup sour cream, egg yolks, and anchovies in food processor until well combined, about 10 pulses. Add meatloaf mix, onion, 1 tablespoon capers, 1 tablespoon parsley, 1½ teaspoons pepper, ½ teaspoon salt, ½ teaspoon allspice, and nutmeg and process until well combined, about 30 seconds. Transfer mixture to bowl, divide into twelve ½-cup portions, and form into meatballs with your wet hands.

2. Melt butter in Dutch oven over medium heat. Whisk in flour and remaining ½ teaspoon allspice and cook for 1 minute. Slowly whisk in water and remaining 3½ cups broth until incorporated. Add bay leaf and thyme sprig and bring to simmer. Add meatballs and return to simmer. Reduce heat to low, cover, and cook until meatballs register 160 degrees, 20 to 25 minutes. Using slotted spoon, transfer meatballs to a large, shallow casserole dish and tent loosely with aluminum foil.

3. While meatballs rest, bring sauce to boil over medium-high heat and cook until thickened and measures about 4 cups, 10 to 15 minutes. Off heat, whisk in Worcestershire, lemon zest, remaining ¾ cup sour cream, and remaining 2 tablespoons capers. Season with salt and pepper to taste. Discard bay leaf and thyme sprig. Pour sauce over meatballs and sprinkle with remaining 2 tablespoons parsley. Serve.

COMING NEXT ISSUE

In our June/July 2014 issue, we pull out the grill to perfect **Lemon Chicken**, **Burnt Ends**, and **Portobello Burgers**. Then we're back indoors to create the best **Peanut Butter Pie**, **Stuffed Tomatoes**, **Cherry Crisp**, **Shrimp Étouffée** . . . and much more.

FIND THE ROOSTER!

A tiny version of this rooster has been hidden in the pages of this issue. Write to us with its location and we'll enter you in a random drawing. The first correct entry drawn will win a set of our winning dish towels, and each of the next five will receive a free one-year subscription to *Cook's Country*. To enter, visit **CooksCountry.com/rooster** by May 31, 2014 or write to Rooster AM14, *Cook's Country*, P.O. Box 470739, Brookline, MA 02447. Include your name and address. Catherine Pease-Schafer of Millville, New Jersey, found the rooster in the December/January 2014 issue on page 7 and won our top-rated roasting pan.

WEB EXTRAS
Free for 4 months online at CooksCountry.com

Arugula, Radish, Mint, and Pea Salad
Baking Dishes Testing
Butter-Braised Vegetables
Clip-On Digital Thermometers Testing
Comeback Sauce
Food Storage Gadgets Testing
Hard-Cooked Eggs
Large-Batch Vanilla Frosting

READ US ON iPAD

Download the *Cook's Country* app for iPad and start a free trial subscription or purchase a single issue of the magazine. All issues are enhanced with full-color Cooking Mode slide shows that provide step-by-step instructions for completing recipes, plus expanded reviews and ratings. Go to **CooksCountry.com/iPad** to download our app through iTunes.

Follow us on **Twitter**
twitter.com/TestKitchen

Find us on **Facebook**
facebook.com/CooksCountry

Confetti Layer Cake

Skip the box. It's easy to make this whimsical (and delicious) three-layer cake.

To make this cake, you will need:

- ¾ cup rainbow sprinkles
- 6 large egg whites, room temperature
- ⅔ cup whole milk, room temperature
- 2 teaspoons vanilla extract
- 3 cups (12 ounces) cake flour
- 1½ cups (10½ ounces) sugar
- 4 teaspoons baking powder
- 1 teaspoon salt
- 16 tablespoons unsalted butter, cut into 16 pieces and softened
- 4–6 drops yellow food coloring
- 1 recipe Large-Batch Vanilla Frosting*

FOR THE CAKE: Adjust oven rack to middle position and heat oven to 350 degrees. Grease three 8-inch round cake pans, line with parchment paper, grease parchment, and flour pans.

Pulse ½ cup sprinkles in food processor until coarsely ground, 8 to 10 pulses; set aside. Whisk together egg whites, milk, and vanilla in bowl.

Using stand mixer fitted with paddle, mix flour, sugar, baking powder, and salt on low speed, about 30 seconds. With mixer running, add butter, 1 piece at a time, until incorporated and mixture resembles moist crumbs. Add all but ½ cup egg mixture and mix until just combined. Increase speed to medium-high and beat until light and fluffy, about 1 minute. Add remaining ½ cup egg mixture in slow stream. Scrape down bowl and beat on medium-high speed until well combined, about 15 seconds. Stir in ground sprinkles.

Divide batter evenly among prepared pans and smooth tops with rubber spatula. Bake

until toothpick inserted in center comes out clean, 21 to 25 minutes, rotating pans halfway through baking. Let cakes cool in pans on wire rack for 10 minutes. Remove cakes from pans, discarding parchment, and let cool completely on rack, about 2 hours.

TO ASSEMBLE: Mix food coloring into frosting. Place 1 cake layer on plate or pedestal. Spread ¾ cup frosting evenly over top. Top with second cake layer, then spread ¾ cup frosting evenly over top. Top with third cake layer, then spread remaining frosting evenly over top and sides. Press remaining ¼ cup sprinkles around bottom edge of cake. Serve.

▶ *Go to CooksCountry.com/may14 for our **Large-Batch Vanilla Frosting** recipe or use your own vanilla frosting recipe yielding 5 cups.

Inside This Issue

Cook's Country

JUNE/JULY 2014

Best Stuffed Tomatoes

Grill-Roasted Whole Chicken

Slow-Cooker Chicken Parm

Beef-Broccoli Stir-Fry for Two
Quicker, Easier, Better

Spice-Rubbed Pork Skewers
With Grilled Tomato Relish

Fire and Ice Salad
Southern Picnic Favorite

Easy Cherry Crisp
Think Outside the Oven

Peanut Butter Pie
No-Bake Summer Classic

Delta Hot Tamales
Mississippi Meets Mexico

Zucchini-Corn Salad
Grilled for Bold Taste

Make-Your-Own Pita Chips
Five Flavor Variations

Jalapeño Poppers
Bar Snack Comes Home

CooksCountry.com
$5.95 U.S./$6.95 CANADA

Stuffed tomatoes always sound delicious, but too often the tomatoes are leathery and the filling clumpy and bland. We figured out how to make a version with a tender tomato and a flavorful, well-integrated filling. PAGE 20

Dear Country Cook,

In our small town in Vermont, outdoor cooking is a simple affair. Just before sap season, we head out into the woods to tap trees. Lunch is cooked over an open fire using a cast-iron grate with short legs. Venison steaks or marinated kebabs with onions and peppers are typical fare.

Years ago, I went rabbit hunting in a high mountain swamp near Bromley Mountain on a cold day in January. Lunch was hot dogs grilled over an open fire in 3 feet of snow.

When the kids were little, we spent a week at a Montana dude ranch. The wranglers made baking powder biscuits in a cast-iron Dutch oven set into coals from the fire they used to grill the beefsteaks. Those were tasty biscuits!

Today, grilling and barbecue start with hundreds, if not thousands, of dollars of equipment. Even I use an expensive gas grill for everyday cooking—it's powerful and convenient.

But the simplicity of a wood fire, knowing hard from soft wood, getting the coals just right, and rigging up a spit—all these things make outdoor cooking what it should be: a return to simplicity.

Best of all, the fire is a conversation piece. You can sit around it and chat, keep warm, or just enjoy the embers, the last wisps of smoke, and the good company. Come to think of it, that pretty much sums up good cooking, too.

Cordially,

Christopher Kimball
Founder and Editor, Cook's Country

Campers grilling with a homemade spit, circa 1955.

Getty Images

Cook'sCountry

Founder and Editor Christopher Kimball
Editorial Director Jack Bishop
Editorial Director, Magazines John Willoughby
Managing Editor Scott Kathan
Executive Food Editor Bryan Roof
Senior Editors Hannah Crowley, Rebeccah Marsters, Lisa McManus, Diane Unger
Test Kitchen Director Erin McMurrer
Associate Editors Shannon Friedmann Hatch, Christie Morrison
Test Cooks Sarah Gabriel, Ashley Moore, Cristin Walsh
Assistant Editors Lauren Savoie, Kate Shannon
Senior Copy Editor Megan Ginsberg
Copy Editors Nell Beram, Krista Magnuson
Executive Assistant Christine Gordon
Test Kitchen Manager Leah Rovner
Senior Kitchen Assistants Michelle Blodget, Alexxa Grattan
Kitchen Assistants Maria Elena Delgado, Shane Drips, Ena Gudiel
Executive Producer Melissa Baldino
Co-Executive Producer Stephanie Stender
Associate Producer Kaitlin Hammond

Contributing Editors Erika Bruce, Eva Katz, Jeremy Sauer
Consulting Editors Anne Mendelson, Meg Ragland
Science Editor Guy Crosby, PhD
Executive Food Editor, TV, Radio & Media Bridget Lancaster

Managing Editor, Web Christine Liu
Senior Editor, Cooking School Mari Levine
Associate Editors, Web Jill Fisher, Eric Grzymkowski, Roger Metcalf
Assistant Editor, Web Charlotte Wilder
Senior Video Editor Nick Dakoulas

Design Director Amy Klee
Photography Director Julie Cote
Art Director Susan Levin
Associate Art Director Lindsey Timko
Art Director, Marketing Jennifer Cox
Staff Photographer Daniel J. van Ackere
Color Food Photography Keller + Keller
Styling Catrine Kelty, Marie Piraino
Associate Art Directors, Marketing Melanie Gryboski, Mariah Tarvainen
Designer, Marketing Judy Blomquist
Associate Art Director, Photography Steve Klise

Vice President, Marketing David Mack
Circulation Director Doug Wicinski
Circulation & Fulfillment Manager Carrie Fethe
Partnership Marketing Manager Pamela Putprush
Marketing Assistant Marina Tomao

Director, Project Management Alice Carpenter
Project Manager Britt Dresser
Development Manager Mike Serio

Chief Operating Officer Rob Ristagno
VP, Digital Products Fran Middleton
Production Director Guy Rochford
Workflow & Digital Asset Manager Andrew Mannone
Senior Color & Imaging Specialist Lauren Pettapiece
Production & Imaging Specialists Heather Dube, Lauren Robbins
Director of Sponsorship Sales Anne Traficante
Client Services Manager Kate Zebrowski
Sponsorship Sales Representative Morgan Ryan
Senior Controller Theresa Peterson
Customer Service Manager Jacqueline Valerio
Customer Service Representatives Jessica Haskin, Andrew Straaberg Finfrock, Juliet Tierney

Executive Director, Book Marketing Beth Ineson
Retail Sales & Marketing Manager Emily Logan
Human Resources Manager Adele Shapiro
Publicity Deborah Broide

ON THE COVER: *Stuffed Tomatoes*, Keller + Keller, Catrine Kelty
ILLUSTRATION: Greg Stevenson

Follow us on **Twitter**
twitter.com/TestKitchen

Find us on **Facebook**
facebook.com/CooksCountry

Cook's Country magazine (ISSN 1552-1990), number 57, is published bimonthly by Boston Common Press Limited Partnership, 17 Station St., Brookline, MA 02445. Copyright 2014 Boston Common Press Limited Partnership. Periodicals postage paid at Boston, MA, and additional mailing offices, USPS #023453. Publications Mail Agreement No. 40020778. Return undeliverable Canadian addresses to P.O. Box 875, Station A, Windsor, ON N9A 6P2. POSTMASTER: Send address changes to *Cook's Country*, P.O. Box 6018, Harlan, IA 51593-1518. For subscription and gift subscription orders, subscription inquiries, or change of address notices, visit AmericasTestKitchen.com/support, call 800-526-8447 in the U.S. or 515-248-7684 from outside the U.S., or write to us at *Cook's Country*, P.O. Box 6018, Harlan, IA 51593-1518. PRINTED IN THE USA.

Contents

JUNE/JULY 2014

LATIN FRIED CHICKEN, 18   GRILLED PORK SKEWERS, 17   PEANUT BUTTER PIE, 22

Features

Departments

The Test Kitchen's School Is in Session

Get personalized instruction from seasoned test cooks in the comfort of your own kitchen. At our online cooking school, you can take as many courses as you like (there are more than 125 in total), all for one monthly fee. Best of all, you study at your own pace. Visit **OnlineCookingSchool.com**.

America's TEST KITCHEN
RECIPES THAT WORK®

America's Test Kitchen is a very real 2,500-square-foot kitchen located just outside Boston. It is the home of *Cook's Country* and *Cook's Illustrated* magazines and the workday destination of more than three dozen test cooks, editors, and cookware specialists. Our mission is to test recipes until we understand how and why they work and arrive at the best version. We also test kitchen equipment and supermarket ingredients in search of products that offer the best value and performance. You can watch us work by tuning in to *Cook's Country from America's Test Kitchen* (CooksCountry.com) and *America's Test Kitchen* (AmericasTestKitchen.com) on public television.

BY SARAH GABRIEL

I have self-rising flour left over from a recipe—can I use it in muffins if I leave the leavener out?

Margaret Carver, Port Townsend, Wash.

Muffins can be leavened with baking powder, with baking soda, or with a combination of the two. We tested muffins in each category. For recipes that called for just one leavener, we tested the original recipe alongside the same recipe made with self-rising flour and no other leavener. For the muffins that contained both powder and soda, we tested the self-rising flour substitution in two ways: with self-rising flour and no added leavener at all, and again with just the baking powder omitted because self-rising flour contains baking powder but not baking soda. With self-rising flour in place of both powder and soda, the muffins came out slightly squat as well as pale and doughy-looking (baking soda helps with browning in addition to leavening). When used in tandem with baking soda, self-rising flour delivered muffins that were properly browned, but the domes still looked deflated and one batch had a flavor tasters described as "metallic" or "chemical-y." In recipes that called for only baking powder, self-rising flour didn't foul up the browning, but the muffins were still slightly squatter and much saltier than when made with all-purpose flour and baking powder. (The saltiness surprised us, but we should have looked more closely at the ingredient list on the package: Self-rising flour also contains salt.) The baking powder–only batch was the most promising, so we tried it one more time with self-rising flour, this time leaving out the salt as well as the baking powder. Though only one taster found the muffins overly salty, the domes were still squat. Not exactly what we would call a success.

THE BOTTOM LINE: Don't use self-rising flour in recipes that don't call for it.

I've read that you shouldn't add vanilla extract to pastry cream and pudding until after cooking. Is that really true?

Sally Staubach, Silver Spring, Md.

In short, yes. We made two batches of pastry cream, adding the vanilla to the half-and-half before simmering for the first batch and stirring the vanilla in after cooking for the second. Although the difference wasn't enormous, every taster noticed a slightly more potent vanilla flavor in the pastry cream to which we'd added the vanilla extract after cooking. The flavorful compounds in vanilla are volatile; simmering the vanilla extract with the half-and-half allowed more of the vanilla flavor to dissipate than simply stirring it into a bowl of already-cooked pastry cream. Would we get the same results with imitation vanilla? We repeated the test, this time using imitation vanilla, and found it much harder to detect any difference.

THE BOTTOM LINE: Add pure vanilla extract to puddings and pastry creams after cooking to preserve the most vanilla flavor.

I've noticed that some jalapeños are hotter than others. When I get a superspicy one, is there a way to temper the heat?

Andy LoPilato, Allston, Mass.

A quick way to turn down the heat on a hot pepper is to cut out the ribs and seeds, which contain a higher concentration of capsaicin (the compound that makes peppers hot). But what if that's not enough? This is a question on which opinions abound. Several sources suggested that cooking can calm your capsicums, while others argued that since capsaicin is heat stable, cooking the peppers won't temper spiciness at all. We also read in some sources that cooking hot peppers would make them even hotter.

To settle this, we gathered a few pounds of jalapeños and a team of adventurous tasters. Every individual pepper has a slightly different heat level, so in each test we compared two halves of the same fruit. We tried boiling the chiles in water and in milk, cooking them in oil, and roasting them. To our surprise, boiling the peppers in water or milk or cooking them in oil for 5 minutes did remove a significant amount of their burn, when compared with a raw piece of the same pepper. They were also quite soft—which might or might not be good, depending on how you intended to use them. Boiling or cooking in oil for just 2 minutes had less impact on texture and also less impact on heat. Roasting the jalapeños in the oven at 500 degrees for 5 minutes left the peppers still somewhat crunchy while also taking the edge off their heat.

THE BOTTOM LINE: Yes, cooking does tame chiles' heat. To lessen the burn while preserving the most texture, roast them for 5 minutes at 500 degrees.

FIRE FIGHTER
Quickly roasting jalapeños tames their heat while retaining most of their crunch.

I've heard that freezing ginger makes it easier to grate. Is that true?

Megan Foley, Cambridge, Mass.

To answer your question, we froze several pieces of ginger, then we had a group of testers each grate one frozen and one fresh piece on the same rasp-style grater. All the testers found the frozen ginger easier to grate—it didn't shred or break down like fresh ginger sometimes does with vigorous grating. We also found that the grater was much easier to clean after grating frozen ginger because the fibers neatly sheared crosswise and didn't leave frayed bits stuck in the grater. After precisely 30 seconds of grating, the piles of frozen ginger measured, on average, almost twice as much by volume as the fresh.

But when we weighed each sample, we found that the frozen ginger actually weighed much less (about 9 grams compared with about 14 grams for the fresh ginger), essentially because the frozen ginger made a fluffier pile. To get accurate volume measurements, we had to either let the grated ginger thaw or pack it gently into the measuring spoon.

THE BOTTOM LINE: Freezing ginger does make it easier to grate. It also makes it easier to clean the grater. When measuring grated frozen ginger by volume, pack it gently or let it thaw after grating.

GRATED FROZEN GINGER
Frozen ginger grates up taller and airier.

GRATED GINGER
Room-temperature ginger grates up dense and wet.

OUR FAVORITE RASP-STYLE GRATER
Microplane 8.5-Inch Classic Zester/Grater

I have amassed a bit of a collection of fancy salts. Can I substitute them for kosher or table salt in cooking and baking?

Judith Troka, Las Vegas, Nev.

We have found in previous tastings that salt, no matter how fancy, basically tastes like salt, with occasional traces of mild mineral flavors. Salts do differ considerably, however, in the size of their crystals. So to see how much difference a substitution would make in cooked dishes, we made chicken noodle soup, mashed potatoes, and chocolate chip cookies using table salt (very fine granules), Celtic sea salt (kosher salt–size granules), Maldon salt (large, flaky crystals), and coarse Himalayan pink salt (rock salt–size granules).

Since crystal size determines how much salt by weight is in a given amount by volume, to make a fair comparison we substituted by weight rather than by volume. For example, our first recipe, chicken noodle soup, called for 1 tablespoon of table salt, which weighs 19 grams. To get the same 19 grams of Maldon salt (which has much larger crystals), we had to use 3 full tablespoons. For the other salts, we needed about 20 percent more salt by volume to reach the required weight.

The soup recipe worked fine with each type of salt, though some tasters commented on slight "mineral-y" flavors in some batches. In the mashed potatoes, things started to unravel for the Himalayan pink salt. Its large, dense crystals didn't dissolve, leaving the potatoes bland in some places, studded with salty gravel in others. This salt was equally unsuccessful in chocolate chip cookies. Tasters didn't notice anything amiss, however, with the mashed potatoes and cookies made with Maldon or Celtic sea salt.

But there's also another factor to consider: price. At our local supermarket, table salt costs about $0.03 per ounce. Maldon and Celtic sea salt are both about 25 times that, at $0.79 and $0.74 per ounce, respectively, while the Himalayan pink salt came in at nearly $1.50 per ounce, 50 times the cost of plain old table salt. We'll save the spendy salts for finishing, where their unique textures and mineral flavors are actually noticeable.

THE BOTTOM LINE: Save the exotic salts for sprinkling on food just before serving.

To ask us a cooking question, visit **CooksCountry.com/ask**. Or write to Ask *Cook's Country*, P.O. Box 470739, Brookline, MA 02447. Just try to stump us!

Kitchen Shortcuts

COMPILED BY CRISTIN WALSH

COOL TRICK
Watermelon Ice Cubes
Kim Young, Hoffman Estates, Ill.

My kids love lemonade on hot days. To make it extra fun, I freeze diced watermelon to put in their glasses instead of ice cubes. The watermelon's water content helps it freeze easily, and my kids love eating the lemon-spiked watermelon when they've finished quenching their thirst.

COOL TIP
Ice Cream Saver
Jillian Merchant, Harwood, Md.

My freezer is stocked full of ice cream during the summer for impromptu sundae parties with my grandkids. To help save all those ice creams from getting freezer burn, I place a piece of parchment paper flush on top of the ice cream before putting the lids back and returning them to the freezer. No more icy ice creams.

CLEVER TIP
Greener Guacamole
Wayne Nichols, Milwaukee, Wis.

I found a trick to help keep guacamole looking fresh longer. Before storing the dip, pour an inch of water over the top. When you're ready to serve, just pour off the water; the guacamole is dense enough that it doesn't absorb the water. You'll have guacamole that looks like you just made it.

CLEVER TIP
Better Char
Jenny Moran, Atlanta, Ga.

I grill a lot during the summer. To get faster-cooking items to develop the char I want without overcooking them, I keep a spray bottle filled with cider on hand. Spraying grilling items with the sugary cider (away from the heat source) helps promote browning, plus it adds some extra flavor.

SMART TRICK
Berry Saver
Bill Stiles, Bellingham, Wash.

To extend the life of blueberries and strawberries, I wash them in a light white vinegar solution: 1 cup vinegar to 3 cups water. Then I dry them in a salad spinner and store them in a container with the lid slightly open to allow moisture to escape. The vinegar kills bacteria without imparting flavor. Now my berries stay fresher for longer.

DOUBLE DUTY
Label Helper
Melanie Madsen, Sioux Falls, S.D.

I've found a great tool for labeling containers of leftovers in my fridge: blue painter's tape. It comes off easily without leaving any adhesive behind, and I can rip just the right-size piece. Sometimes I'll even print reheating instructions on the tape.

HANDY TIP
Clean Straws
Sally Wilson, Redmond, Wash.

During the summer my kids use reusable plastic cups with straws, but the dishwasher does a lousy job of cleaning the straws. My trick is to use denture cleaner tablets to help get them clean. I fill a big glass with the directed amount of water, drop a denture cleaner tablet in, and add the straws (flipping them over after a few minutes so both ends get clean). The straws are as fresh as new in no time.

Submit a tip online at **CooksCountry.com/kitchenshortcuts** or send a letter to Kitchen Shortcuts, *Cook's Country*, P.O. Box 470739, Brookline, MA 02447. Include your name, address, and phone number. If we publish your tip, you will receive a free one-year subscription to *Cook's Country*. Letters may be edited for clarity and length.

Illustration: Ross MacDonald

Peach-Glazed Grilled Chicken

Too many recipes for peach-glazed grilled chicken give you chicken that's scorched or sickeningly sweet—or both. We wanted nicely glazed, unimpeachably peachy grilled chicken. BY SARAH GABRIEL

I GRILL CHICKEN ALMOST every day in the summer, so I'm always on the prowl for a new approach. Recently I came across one that seemed very promising: grilled peach chicken. After I noticed it once, I began to see it everywhere—in magazines, cookbooks, and all over the Internet. In its simplest form, it is no more than chicken breasts brushed with thinned-out peach preserves. More complicated recipes included purees of fresh raw or grilled peaches, along with tart relishes, various spices, and smoke. All of them promised something that I wanted to have on my weeknight dinner plate: tender chicken with a slightly sweet, nicely charred glaze featuring the delicate flavor of peaches. Time to get out the grill and start testing.

I knew from the start that I'd want to sprinkle the chicken with salt and pepper and let it sit for at least an hour before cooking it. This would not only season the chicken but also enable it to retain more moisture as it grilled. I also knew that I'd want some additional flavors of smoke and spice to counteract the overall sweetness of the preserves.

After my initial round of testing, though, it was clear that the main challenge would be balancing my desire for real peach flavor with the necessity of not incinerating dinner. Cooking the chicken covered in preserves from the start led to intense scorching, but just applying the glaze at the end didn't yield much flavor. I needed a way to cook the chicken in the peach preserves without exposing it to the open flames until it was almost done.

To achieve this, I set up a grill with all the charcoal on one side. I slathered the chicken with peach preserves mixed with a pinch of cayenne for heat, tossed a packet of wood chips on the charcoal to create some smoke, let the grill heat up, and then put the glazed raw chicken on the side with no coals, closed the lid, and crossed my fingers. About 30 minutes later, the chicken was nearly cooked inside, but the outside, while not scorched, was a sticky mess leading to torn chicken skin and a grill-cleaning session that I'd rather not talk about.

Maybe, I thought, the chicken shouldn't hit the grill at all until it was nearly cooked. Colleagues panned the idea of an oven or stovetop start ("I thought you said *grilled* chicken"), but what about starting the meat in a

To add real fruit flavor and a trace of heat, we grill a fresh peach and a jalapeño before adding them to the sauce.

disposable aluminum pan on the grill? I set up the grill again but this time with the charcoal spread evenly over the surface because flare-ups wouldn't be an issue. I then combined the peach preserves and a little cayenne in a 13 by 9-inch aluminum pan, added the salted chicken parts skin side down, and put the pan on the grill. After about 20 minutes, the chicken was nearly cooked. I rolled the pieces in the bubbling preserves and then transferred them to the grill grate. A couple of minutes per side got the chicken glazed, nicely browned, and cooked through. I was getting there.

The skin was a little rubbery, though, so I rejiggered the method, starting the chicken skin side down in the pan to render some fat before flipping the pieces skin side up to dry off and crisp up. This time, the skin came out quite crisp, shellacked with glaze, and perfectly brown. The glaze left in the pan was thinned out by the chicken juices, so I left it bubbling on the grill to reduce and concentrate before serving it alongside the chicken. At this point, I had the method down, but we all wanted a fresher, more summery flavor.

Fresh fruit was the obvious answer, so I added some peach halves to the pan along with the next batch of chicken, browning them at the end just like the

START IN PAN
Cook the chicken, peach, and jalapeño in a disposable roasting pan with peach preserves and cayenne.

SEAR ON GRATE
Move the chicken, peach, and jalapeño onto the grill grate to sear while the preserves caramelize in the pan.

COAT CHICKEN
Move just the chicken back to the pan, now off the grill, to coat with glaze and let rest.

MAKE SAUCE
Chop the peach and jalapeño and combine them with the reduced glaze and vinegar to make a serving sauce.

chicken. We tried using them in a few forms: mashed into the glaze left in the pan after I moved the chicken to the grate (this turned the sauce cloudy and goopy); sliced up and served alongside the chicken (good but not great); and chopped and then mixed into the remaining glaze, which we liked a lot. But the sauce still needed a little something; some heat, maybe? I tried one batch with extra cayenne and one batch with a jalapeño cooked just like the chicken and peach—in the pan and then browned on the grill. Chopped small and mixed into the sauce, the jalapeño added not just heat but vegetal and charred flavors that helped round out the sauce. Two tablespoons of cider vinegar added tang to balance the sauce's sweet fruitiness, smoke, and heat.

This was a recipe worthy of a place of pride in my summer repertoire.

PEACH-GLAZED GRILLED CHICKEN Serves 4

Leave the jalapeño whole for grilling. Note that the salted chicken needs to rest for 1 to 24 hours before grilling. Since the preserves cause the food to brown quickly in step 5, move the items around as necessary to manage any hot spots.

- 3 **pounds bone-in chicken pieces (split breasts cut in half crosswise, drumsticks, and/or thighs), trimmed Salt and pepper**
- 1 **cup wood chips**
- 1 **cup peach preserves**
- ⅛ **teaspoon cayenne pepper**
- 1 **(13 by 9-inch) disposable aluminum pan**
- 1 **peach, halved and pitted**
- 1 **jalapeño chile**
- 2 **tablespoons cider vinegar**

1. Pat chicken dry with paper towels and season with 2¼ teaspoons salt and 1 teaspoon pepper. Place in zipper-lock bag and refrigerate for at least 1 hour or up to 24 hours.

2. Just before grilling, soak wood chips in water for 15 minutes, then drain. Using large piece of heavy-duty aluminum foil, wrap soaked chips in foil packet and cut several vent holes in top. Whisk preserves and cayenne together in disposable pan. Place peach halves (cut side up), jalapeño, and chicken (skin side down) in pan.

3A. FOR A CHARCOAL GRILL: Open bottom vent halfway. Light large chimney starter filled with charcoal briquettes (6 quarts). When top coals are partially covered with ash, pour evenly over grill. Place wood chip packet on coals on 1 side of grill. Set cooking grate in place, cover, and open lid vent halfway. Heat grill until hot and wood chips are smoking, about 5 minutes.

3B. FOR A GAS GRILL: Remove cooking grate and place wood chip packet directly on primary burner. Set grate in place, turn all burners to high, cover, and heat grill until hot and wood chips are smoking, about 15 minutes. Turn all burners to medium. (Adjust burners as needed to maintain grill temperature between 350 and 375 degrees.)

4. Clean and oil cooking grate. Place disposable pan with chicken over side of grill opposite wood chip packet. Cover grill (position lid vent over chicken if using charcoal) and cook for 10 minutes. Flip chicken, and rotate pan 180 degrees. (Open top and bottom vents fully for charcoal grill.) Continue to cook, covered, until breasts register 155 degrees and drumsticks/thighs register 170 degrees, 10 to 14 minutes.

5. Flip chicken, peach halves, and jalapeño to coat with preserves, then transfer to grill grate (skin side down for chicken). Leave pan on grill to let preserves thicken and caramelize slightly around edges, 3 to 5 minutes, then remove pan from grill.

6. Meanwhile, cook chicken, peach halves, and jalapeño until well browned on first side, 2 to 5 minutes. Flip and continue to cook until chicken breasts register 160 degrees and drumsticks/thighs register 175 degrees and peach halves and jalapeño are well browned on second side, 2 to 5 minutes. Return chicken, skin side up, to pan with preserves, tent loosely with foil, and let rest for 10 minutes. Transfer peach and jalapeño to plate to cool slightly.

7. Remove any loose skin from peach halves and jalapeño (no need to remove all skin); then chop peach halves, seed and mince jalapeño, and transfer both to bowl. Arrange chicken on serving platter. Pour preserves from pan into bowl with chopped peach halves and jalapeño; stir in vinegar. Season glaze with salt and pepper to taste. Spoon glaze over chicken and serve.

TASTING PEACH PRESERVES

We like peach jam and preserves on toast, in desserts, and in barbecue glazes. To find the best peach spread, 21 staffers from America's Test Kitchen sampled five national products plain, in Peach Squares, and in Peach-Glazed Grilled Chicken.

First off, tasters marked down one product for being overly sweet. Yet when we checked nutrition labels, we found that it had the same amount of sugar as our top-ranking preserves—so why did tasters find one product too sugary and the other just right? Sugar in jam comes from both fruit and added sugars. The overly sweet product, Mrs. Miller's Peach Jam, is the only one that adds more sugar than peaches, and tasters found it lacking complexity and balance. Type of sugar was key, too—we preferred products made with granulated sugar to those sweetened with corn syrup or fruit concentrates, both of which tasters found cloying.

Texture was equally important; tasters liked preserves that were loose and spreadable and downgraded those that were superfirm. Here the culprit was pectin, a carbohydrate found naturally in fruit that makes jams thicken during cooking. Most manufacturers add powdered or liquid pectin, too, so we were interested to find that our top-rated product, American Spoon Red Haven Peach Preserves, contains no extra pectin. Among the products with added pectin, we preferred those that list it at the end of the ingredient list.

American Spoon Red Haven Peach Preserves was the standout winner for its bold, ripe peach taste and balanced sweetness. It's expensive, so we'll splurge on it when eating it on biscuits or toast. All products were fine for cooking. –LAUREN SAVOIE

HIGHLY RECOMMENDED

AMERICAN SPOON Red Haven Peach Preserves
Price: $9.95 for 9.5 oz ($1.05 per oz)
Ingredients: Peaches, sugar, lemon juice
Sugar: 9 g per tablespoon

TASTERS' NOTES
Tasters liked this product's "zesty," "tangy," "deep peach flavor" and found it "looser" and "spreadable," like "homemade" preserves. "Now I just need some Brie to go with it," said one taster.

RECOMMENDED

BEST BUY

BONNE MAMAN Peach Preserves
Price: $4.99 for 13 oz ($0.38 per oz)
Ingredients: Peaches, sugar, cane sugar, concentrated lemon juice, fruit pectin
Sugar: 13 g per tablespoon

Tasters liked these "thick," "chunky" preserves that had notes of "caramel" and large pieces of fruit that added "lots of peach flavor."

SMUCKER'S Peach Preserves
Price: $2.99 for 12 oz ($0.25 per oz)
Ingredients: Peaches, high-fructose corn syrup, corn syrup, fruit pectin, citric acid
Sugar: 12 g per tablespoon

This product was "milder" with a "good balance of acidity and sweetness." Most tasters said it was "tangier" and "fresh-tasting" but a small contingent found it too "jelly-like" and a bit cloying (it's the only product to add corn syrup).

ST. DALFOUR Golden Peach
Price: $4.29 for 10 oz ($0.43 per oz)
Ingredients: Peaches, sweetened only with fruit juice concentrates (grape and date), fruit pectin, lemon juice
Sugar: 8 g per tablespoon

Tasters liked this "soft and loose" product, which they noted "spreads better" on crackers. While many loved its "honey and flowery notes," some picked up on unexpected "raisin" and "wine" aftertastes from added date and grape fruit juice concentrates.

RECOMMENDED WITH RESERVATIONS

MRS. MILLER'S Homemade Peach Jam
Price: $3.75 for 8 oz ($0.47 per oz)
Ingredients: Sugar, peaches, water, pectin, lemon juice, citric acid
Sugar: 9 g per tablespoon

Tasters found pleasant "floral," "honey notes" and an attractive "vanilla" aftertaste in this jam, but some were put off by its "firm" texture and cloying sweetness that was compared to "canned peaches."

Burnt Ends

This brisket preparation, a favorite of barbecue masters, isn't really burnt; it's double-smoked and deeply charred. BY DIANE UNGER

THE BEST PART of any slow-smoked barbecue, be it ribs, brisket, or pulled pork, is the bark—the dark, smoky, crusty, crispy exterior. So it stands to reason that burnt ends, the bark-iest kind of barbecue there is, are my absolute favorite. Professional pit masters make their burnt ends by rubbing huge whole briskets (which can weigh 15 pounds or more) with salt, pepper, and sugar and smoking them for up to 12 hours, until tender. Then they divide each brisket into point and flat cuts; the leaner flat cut is sliced and served, while the fattier point cut is put back into the smoker to further render, tenderize, absorb more smoke, and form more tasty bark. After several hours, the almost-black point-cut briskets are hauled out, chopped up, sometimes sauced, and eaten as "burnt ends." They are, if I may say it, amazing.

But there are a few good reasons most home barbecuers don't make them: It's hard to find point cuts in supermarkets, and whole briskets are too big for most backyard grills and smokers. So my challenge was to try to make smoky, moist, tender burnt ends from lean flat-cut brisket—the wrong cut for the job—on a backyard kettle grill.

After slow-smoking four briskets on my first day of testing, I learned that it's hard to get good bark on a smoked flat-cut brisket without drying out the meat because there is so little fat to render and provide moisture. So how could I get meat that had great bark but was still moist? I tested two of the test kitchen's favorite techniques to help keep lean meats moist: salting and brining. After a few days of testing various intervals, I found that both methods work, but brining is faster: Just 6 hours of brining produced the same moist meat that it took salting 12 hours to achieve.

But the benefits of brining went only so far; when I smoked the briskets to tenderness (it took about 8 hours), cubed them, and put them back on the grill to get crusty and barky, the finished meat was dry. Was there a way to create the bark faster? Yes—cutting the brisket into long, 1½-inch-wide strips before brining exposed more surface area to "bark up" during the initial smoking. Cutting the meat into strips also cut the brining time from 6 hours to 2.

Some large problems remained. First of all, 8 hours of smoking meant

Cutting the brisket into pieces and building a long-smoking fire are keys to keeping the meat moist while creating a smoky, crusty exterior.

refueling the charcoal grill several times, which was a pain. Luckily for me, the test kitchen has developed a hybrid grill-to-oven method for both pulled pork and barbecued ribs that doesn't require any refueling—the meat stays on the grill only as long as one small pile of charcoal will throw heat, which is between 1 and 2 hours; we also place water pans in the grill to help moderate the temperature. At this point the meat goes into the

oven. I borrowed this technique and ended up with the following method: Cut the meat into strips, brine, smoke for roughly 2 hours, transfer the meat to a baking sheet, wrap tightly in foil to trap the steam, and bake at 275 degrees until tender, about 3 or 4 hours. Then I chopped the strips into chunks, tossed them with barbecue sauce (bottled for now), and called in my tasters.

"Pretty good . . . but not great" was

the consensus. The problem, unfortunately, was serious: The bark was too insubstantial. To fix it, I'd need to find a way to keep the strips of brisket on the grill longer without reloading the charcoal. I pinned my hopes on the Minion method, a barbecue circuit trick (named after the guy who came up with it, Jim Minion) where you place lit charcoal on a pile of unlit charcoal in your grill. After a few days of playing with the amounts and the timing, I was able to make it work by dumping 3 quarts of lit charcoal (plus a packet of soaked wood chips) on top of 3 quarts of unlit charcoal (and another packet of wood chips). This gave me a steady, smoky low heat for a full 3 hours—and cut the oven time to 2 hours.

I made sure to rest the brisket, right in the foil-covered pan, for an hour after it came out of the oven to maximize juiciness. And I made a quick, tasty sauce by cooking a mixture of ketchup, brown sugar, cider vinegar, seasonings, and the defatted brisket juices. These burnt ends had it all: moist, beefy brisket with a burnished, crusty exterior and flavorful sauce. Pit masters, take note.

BARBECUED BURNT ENDS
Serves 8 to 10

Look for a brisket with a significant fat cap. This recipe takes about 8 hours to prepare. The meat can be brined ahead of time, transferred to a zipper-lock bag, and refrigerated for up to a day. If you don't have ½ cup of juices from the rested brisket, supplement with beef broth.

BRISKET AND RUB
- 2 cups plus 1 tablespoon kosher salt
- ½ cup granulated sugar
- 1 (5- to 6-pound) beef brisket, flat cut, untrimmed
- ¼ cup packed brown sugar
- 2 tablespoons pepper
- 4 cups wood chips
- 1 (13 by 9-inch) disposable aluminum roasting pan (if using charcoal) or 2 (8½ by 6-inch) disposable aluminum pans (if using gas)

BARBECUE SAUCE
- ¾ cup ketchup
- ¼ cup packed brown sugar
- 2 tablespoons cider vinegar
- 2 tablespoons Worcestershire sauce
- 2 teaspoons granulated garlic
- ¼ teaspoon cayenne pepper

1. FOR THE BRISKET AND RUB: Dissolve 2 cups salt and granulated sugar in 4 quarts cold water in large container. Slice brisket with grain into 1½-inch-thick strips. Add brisket strips to brine, cover, and refrigerate for 2 hours. Remove brisket from brine and pat dry with paper towels.

2. Combine brown sugar, pepper, and remaining 1 tablespoon salt in bowl. Season brisket all over with rub. Just before grilling, soak wood chips in water for 15 minutes, then drain. Using 2 large pieces of heavy-duty aluminum foil, wrap soaked chips in 2 foil packets and cut several vent holes in tops.

3A. FOR A CHARCOAL GRILL: Open bottom vent halfway and place disposable pan filled with 2 quarts water on 1 side of grill, with long side of pan facing center of grill. Arrange 3 quarts unlit charcoal briquettes on opposite side of grill and place 1 wood chip packet on coals. Light large chimney starter halfway filled with charcoal briquettes (3 quarts). When top coals are partially covered with ash, pour evenly over unlit coals and wood chip packet. Place remaining wood chip packet on lit coals. Set cooking grate in place, cover, and open lid vent halfway. Heat grill until hot and wood chips are smoking, about 5 minutes.

3B. FOR A GAS GRILL: Add ½ cup ice cubes to 1 wood chip packet. Remove cooking grate and place both wood chip packets directly on primary burner; place disposable pans each filled with 2 cups water directly on secondary burner(s). Set grate in place, turn all burners to high, cover, and heat grill until hot and wood chips are smoking, about 15 minutes. Leave primary burner on high and turn off other burner(s). (Adjust primary burner as needed to maintain grill temperature of 275 to 300 degrees.)

4. Clean and oil cooking grate. Arrange brisket on cooler side of grill as far from heat source as possible. Cover (positioning lid vent over brisket for charcoal) and cook without opening for 3 hours.

5. Adjust oven rack to middle position and heat oven to 275 degrees. Remove brisket from grill and transfer to rimmed baking sheet. Cover sheet tightly with foil. Roast until fork slips easily in and out of meat and meat registers about 210 degrees, about 2 hours. Remove from oven, leave covered, and let rest for 1 hour. Remove foil, transfer brisket to carving board, and pour accumulated juices into fat separator.

6. FOR THE BARBECUE SAUCE: Combine ketchup, sugar, vinegar, Worcestershire, granulated garlic, cayenne, and ½ cup defatted brisket juices in medium saucepan. Bring to simmer over medium heat and cook until slightly thickened, about 5 minutes.

7. Cut brisket strips crosswise into 1- to 2-inch chunks. Combine brisket chunks and barbecue sauce in large bowl and toss to combine. Serve.

TEST KITCHEN TECHNIQUE
Cut Brisket into Strips
Slicing a flat-cut brisket into 1½-inch strips creates more surface area to facilitate brining, browning, and smoke absorption. We cube it just before serving.

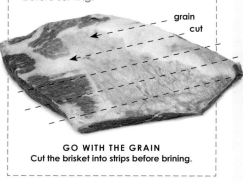

grain
cut

GO WITH THE GRAIN
Cut the brisket into strips before brining.

Texas Caviar

OK, it's not caviar. But this tangy black-eyed pea salad, a Texas tradition, is an ideal picnic dish.

BY CHRISTIE MORRISON

YOU WON'T FIND any beluga in this dish from the Lone Star State. Instead, the tongue-in-cheek moniker belongs to a salad of black-eyed peas created by Helen Corbitt, the "mother of modern Texas cooking." Corbitt made the salad famous during her stint as director of food services at the Zodiac Room restaurant at the Neiman Marcus store in Dallas. But the salad has come a long way since its 1940 debut. Corbitt's original version was nothing more than pickled black-eyed peas, as she called them—canned black-eyed peas, onions, and garlic marinated in a simple vinaigrette. Over the years, the dish has evolved to include herbs, bell peppers, chiles, and a range of other vegetables and legumes.

I knew where to begin. Armed with Corbitt's original recipe as well as four other versions from the test kitchen's library, I got busy slicing, dicing, and draining. No one recipe fully satisfied my tasters, but they rallied around the idea of simplicity; while Corbitt's recipe was a little too understated, we did like the idea of sticking to a small list of traditional ingredients. That meant opting for the convenience of canned beans over hours spent soaking and cooking dried beans. (Black-eyed peas aren't peas at all—they're beans.) To the base of canned black-eyed peas, I added scallions for a savory note, red and green bell peppers for earthy sweetness, a rib of celery for vegetal crunch, and two jalapeños for a bit of heat. (If you like things on the spicy side, don't remove all the seeds.) The final touch was ¼ cup each of fresh cilantro and parsley.

The real key to Texas caviar is the highly acidic dressing; after all, Corbitt didn't call her black-eyed peas "pickled" for nothing. I used a heavy hand with red wine vinegar and balanced it with vegetable oil until I had a punchy but not overaggressive dressing. I added a small amount of sugar to soften the burn and then let the finished salad sit for an hour to meld the flavors. It was delicious but, truth be told, even better the next day. One more virtue to appreciate.

This salad originated in Dallas back in 1940 as "pickled black-eyed peas."

TEXAS CAVIAR Serves 6
If you prefer a spicier salad, reserve and stir in some of the jalapeño seeds. Note that the salad needs to sit for at least an hour prior to serving. Texas caviar will keep in the refrigerator for at least five days.

- ⅓ cup red wine vinegar
- 3 tablespoons vegetable oil
- 1 tablespoon sugar
- 2 garlic cloves, minced
  Salt and pepper
- 2 (15.5-ounce) cans black-eyed peas, rinsed
- 6 scallions, sliced thin
- 1 red bell pepper, stemmed, seeded, and chopped
- 1 green bell pepper, stemmed, seeded, and chopped
- 2 jalapeño chiles, stemmed, seeded, and minced
- 1 celery rib, chopped fine
- ¼ cup chopped fresh cilantro
- ¼ cup chopped fresh parsley

1. Whisk vinegar, oil, sugar, garlic, 1 teaspoon salt, and ½ teaspoon pepper together in large bowl.

2. Add peas, scallions, bell peppers, jalapeños, celery, cilantro, and parsley and toss to combine. Season with salt and pepper to taste. Let sit for at least 1 hour before serving.

Grilled Portobello Mushroom Burgers

There's just one problem with most portobello mushroom burgers:
They have almost no resemblance to a burger. BY REBECCAH MARSTERS

After an initial grilling, we stuff the mushroom caps with a potent mixture of feta cheese, roasted red peppers, and sun-dried tomatoes. Then we put them back on the grill to heat through.

A S A BURGER lover, I take issue with anything masquerading under that name that's not made of ground beef—and up until now, that included portobello mushroom burgers. Don't get me wrong, I love portobellos, but most "burgers" made from them simply are not very good. Seeing no reason why that should be so, I set myself the goal of making portobello mushroom burgers that were worthy of the name.

Since smoke and char enhance any mushroom's meaty qualities, grilled recipes were my logical starting point. I foraged for recipes for grilled portobello burgers and came up with a promising selection. After firing up the grills, I assembled dozens of sandwiches for my tasters. While none of these burgers were bad, we had clear preferences. Cheese was in, and Asian ingredients were out—they just didn't feel right for a "burger." There were a couple of flavor-building tricks that we liked: marinating the portobello caps in a vinaigrette, and stuffing them with a savory filling. The biggest complaints were that most of the portobellos had a rubbery, tough "skin" on top, and they tasted muddy as opposed to pleasantly earthy. At this point, I had plenty of information to help me get cracking on my own version.

I began with an established test kitchen technique for portobellos: scraping out the dark brown gills on the underside of the mushrooms to prevent funky and muddy flavors. Then I put the caps into a zipper-lock bag with a simple mixture of olive oil, vinegar, garlic, salt, and pepper and let them soak for 30 minutes before heading to the grill. A few trial runs led me to the best cooking method: I grilled the caps gill side up over a medium-hot fire until the tops were nicely charred and they had released their liquid. Then I flipped them over to let the liquid drain and sear the other side. These mushrooms were seasoned throughout and had great grill flavor. Unfortunately, the tops were still slightly tough. To fix this, I turned to a technique we use for meat, crosshatching. Cutting a shallow crosshatch pattern into the tops of the mushrooms created a textured surface and thus eliminated the chewy "skin" on the exterior. As an added bonus, the crosshatched caps soaked up even more marinade.

As for the filling, I chose Mediterranean flavors to complement the simple marinade. I experimented with fillings featuring Parmesan, olives, capers, anchovies, and every other Mediterranean ingredient you can think of. After several rounds of testing, my tasters landed on a combination of chopped roasted red peppers and sun-dried tomatoes, plus feta cheese for a powerful, briny kick. After mixing the filling together, I went back out to the grill and quickly learned that stuffing the raw mushrooms was a nonstarter: The filling tumbled out as the mushrooms softened, and there was no way to flip them. I found it best to grill them as before, then transfer the cooked caps to a plate, add the filling, and place them back on the grill to quickly warm through.

I headed inside and placed the grilled, stuffed caps on buns with lettuce, a slice of onion, and a smear of mayo. "Good," my tasters said, "but you can do better." I swapped out the squishy burger buns for more substantial kaiser rolls, which I toasted on the grill after the mushrooms came off. In keeping with the Mediterranean theme, I added chopped fresh basil to the mayonnaise. Peppery baby arugula was an upgrade from ordinary lettuce, and the final coup came when I grilled rounds of red onion (brushed with the leftover mushroom marinade) until tender and sweet. After stacking a final batch of burgers, I bit in; they were juicy and rich, savory yet bright and fresh. I'm not giving up on beef, but these portobello burgers are an amazing alternative that will convert even the biggest skeptics—like me.

GRILLED PORTOBELLO BURGERS
Serves 4

Our favorite feta cheese is Mt. Vikos Traditional Feta from Greece. If the mushrooms absorb all the marinade, simply brush the onions with olive oil before grilling them in step 4.

- 4 portobello mushrooms (4 to 5 inches in diameter), stems and gills removed
- ½ cup extra-virgin olive oil
- 3 tablespoons red wine vinegar
- 1 garlic clove, minced
  Salt and pepper
- 4 ounces feta cheese, crumbled (1 cup)
- ½ cup jarred roasted red peppers, patted dry and chopped

TEST KITCHEN TECHNIQUE **Preparing Portobellos and Onions for the Grill**
A few easy tricks have a lot of impact.

SCORE THE CAP
Cut a shallow crosshatch into the top of each cap to minimize the rubbery texture.

SKEWER ONION SLICES
Use a toothpick to help hold the onion rounds together.

REMOVE THE STEM AND GILLS
Scrape out the muddy-tasting gills with a spoon.

½ cup oil-packed sun-dried toma-
    toes, patted dry and chopped
½ cup mayonnaise
½ cup chopped fresh basil
4 (½-inch-thick) slices red onion
4 kaiser rolls, split
1 ounce (1 cup) baby arugula

1. Using tip of paring knife, cut
½-inch crosshatch pattern on tops
of mushroom caps, ¹⁄₁₆ inch deep.
Combine oil, vinegar, garlic, 1 teaspoon salt, and ½ teaspoon pepper
in 1-gallon zipper-lock bag. Add
mushrooms, seal bag, turn to coat,
and let sit for at least 30 minutes or
up to 1 hour.

2. Combine feta, red peppers,
and sun-dried tomatoes in bowl.
Whisk mayonnaise and basil together
in separate bowl. Push 1 toothpick
horizontally through each onion slice
to keep rings intact while grilling.

3A. FOR A CHARCOAL GRILL:
Open bottom vent completely. Light
large chimney starter filled with
charcoal briquettes (6 quarts). When
top coals are partially covered with
ash, pour evenly over grill. Set cooking grate in place, cover, and open lid
vent completely. Heat grill until hot,
about 5 minutes.

3B. FOR A GAS GRILL: Turn all
burners to high, cover, and heat grill
until hot, about 15 minutes. Turn all
burners to medium-high.

4. Clean and oil cooking grate.
Remove mushrooms from marinade,
reserving excess. Brush onions all
over with reserved mushroom marinade. Place onions and mushrooms,
gill side up, on grill. Cook (covered
if using gas) until mushrooms have
released their liquid and are charred
on first side, 4 to 6 minutes. Flip
mushrooms and onions and continue
to cook (covered if using gas) until
mushrooms are charred on second
side, 3 to 5 minutes.

5. Transfer onions to platter;
remove toothpicks. Transfer mushrooms to platter, gill side up, and
divide feta mixture evenly among
caps, packing down with hand.
Return mushrooms to grill, feta side
up, and cook, covered, until heated
through, about 3 minutes.

6. Return mushrooms to platter
and tent with aluminum foil. Grill
rolls cut sides down until lightly
charred, about 1 minute. Spread
basil-mayonnaise on bun bottoms
and top each with 1 mushroom and
1 onion slice. Divide arugula evenly
among burgers, then cap with bun
tops. Serve.

Baked Jalapeño Poppers

An easier path to homemade jalapeño poppers starts with ditching the deep frying. BY DIANE UNGER

WITH A SPICED cream cheese
filling cutting through the heat
of the chile and a fried coating
adding richness and crunch,
jalapeño poppers are about the perfect
bar snack. Unfortunately, they have
remained largely found in bars because,
what with prepping the peppers and
mixing the filling, and then stuffing,
breading, and frying, they are so labor-
intensive. I wanted to find a better,
easier way to make poppers at home.

Eliminating the deep frying seemed
like the simplest way to streamline,
so I gathered six different recipes for
poppers cooked in the oven and got to
work. My tasters and I were surprised
that not a single recipe impressed us.
These poppers suffered from fillings that
were either bland, dry, and chalky, or
so runny they flowed out of the peppers
like cumin-scented lava. The peppers
themselves were mostly raw or so soft
they collapsed. I knew I could do better.

To control the texture of the jalapeños, I halved a dozen peppers (deep-
fried poppers are usually whole) and precooked them in a 500-degree oven for
about 5 minutes; this slightly softened
their flesh and drove off some of their
excess moisture. So far so good. For the
filling, I tested cutting the cream cheese
with various other melty cheeses that
would help bind it. I ended up using
equal parts cream cheese, mild cheddar,
and Monterey Jack, plus an egg yolk and
a few tablespoons of bread crumbs for
a creamy yet stable texture. Bacon, scallions, lime juice, and cumin proved an
unbeatable combination of seasonings.

Once the jalapeños were stuffed with
the flavorful filling, all they needed was
about 10 minutes at 450 degrees to
become tender, lightly browned, and
perfectly delicious.

With our easier recipe, you don't need to go to a bar for these spicy snacks.

BAKED JALAPEÑO POPPERS

Makes 24 poppers
Use a teaspoon to scrape the seeds and
ribs from the halved chiles.

6 slices bacon
12 jalapeño chiles, halved lengthwise
    with stems left intact,
    seeds and ribs removed
    Salt
4 ounces mild cheddar cheese,
    shredded (1 cup)
4 ounces Monterey Jack cheese,
    shredded (1 cup)
4 ounces cream cheese,
    softened
2 scallions, sliced thin
3 tablespoons minced fresh cilantro
2 tablespoons panko bread crumbs
1 large egg yolk
2 teaspoons lime juice
1 teaspoon ground cumin

1. Adjust oven rack to upper-middle
position and heat oven to 500 degrees.
Set wire rack in rimmed baking sheet.
Cook bacon in 12-inch nonstick skillet
over medium heat until crispy, 7 to
9 minutes. Transfer to paper towel–lined
plate. When bacon is cool enough to
handle, chop fine and set aside.

2. Season jalapeños with salt and
place cut side down on wire rack. Bake
until just beginning to soften, about
5 minutes. Remove jalapeños from
oven and reduce oven temperature to
450 degrees. When cool enough to
handle, flip jalapeños cut side up.

3. Mix cheddar, Monterey Jack,
cream cheese, scallions, cilantro, panko,
egg yolk, lime juice, cumin, and bacon
together in bowl until thoroughly combined. Divide cheese mixture among
jalapeños, pressing into cavities. Bake
until jalapeños are tender and filling is
lightly browned, 9 to 11 minutes. Let
cool for 5 minutes. Serve.

TO MAKE AHEAD

The filled and unbaked jalapeños can be
covered and refrigerated for up to 1 day.
Add 3 minutes to the baking time.

Delta Hot Tamales

Hot tamales—rich, spicy meat wrapped in a flavorful corn dough—are a bedrock favorite in the Mississippi delta. We set out to bring them into our home kitchen. BY CHRISTIE MORRISON

MOST OF US think of tamales—minced and seasoned meat packed inside a cornmeal dough, wrapped in corn husks, and steamed—as a Mexican dish. Historically, that's correct. But a spicy version has also become a specialty of Mississippi delta country. In the early 1900s, Mexican migrant workers helping with the cotton harvest brought with them traditional tamales of pork and cornmeal. These flavors were familiar to the local Mississippi workers even if the corn husk packaging wasn't. The tradition took root, and over the years it evolved to also allow beef, chicken, or turkey, plus a hearty dose of spices and a new cooking method—stewing, rather than steaming—to yield a spicy, moist tamale and plenty of cooking liquid to serve with it. Today they're sold all over the delta.

You're unlikely to find delta-style hot tamales outside Mississippi, though, so I went to the source, following the "Hot Tamale Trail" from Clarksdale to Greenville and sampling tamales in restaurants, blues clubs, and even people's homes.

While the tamales I tasted varied wildly in flavor and texture, the process of making them was similar. All started with beef—either round, brisket, or ground beef—which was browned with spices and fat (usually lard) before being chilled and then shaped into logs. As for the cornmeal, most sources began with the self-rising version (which comes with salt and baking powder mixed in) that they combined with spices and mixed into a firm batter or paste. After rolling the meat into the cornmeal or extruding it through a machine to make a corn dog–like cylinder, they rolled the tamales into moistened corn husks (or "shucks"). Finally, the tamales got packed, standing open side up, in layers in large pots, which were then filled with stewing liquid (heavily seasoned water or sometimes oil) for the final cooking.

I didn't meet a tamale that I didn't like during my time in the delta, but a few stood out. I liked those with some heat, and I liked the cornmeal batters that were fluffy and moist rather than dense or dry. I also liked those that had a more clingy sauce, so it would stick to the outside of the tamales and add more flavor. I returned to the test kitchen eager to do justice to this delta dish while keeping the recipe as streamlined as possible.

The spiced cooking liquid gets thickened and served as a sauce for the tamales.

Since tamales must be rolled by hand, I wanted to keep my precooking to a minimum. I opted to begin with ground beef rather than slow-cooking brisket or round. I whipped up a spice mix that came closest to the flavors I'd sampled in Mississippi: a combination of chili powder, paprika, cumin, cayenne, salt, and a touch of sugar for balance. Just as the tamale cooks down South did, I would add this mix to each component of the tamale (meat, cornmeal, and stewing liquid). Then I cobbled together a working recipe based on my delta experiences and some tamale recipes that I found in our library. I browned 1 pound of 85 percent lean ground beef with 1½ tablespoons of my spice mixture and then let it chill. Meanwhile, I processed 2½ cups of regular (not self-rising) cornmeal with 12 tablespoons of fat (vegetable shortening for now) and 1 tablespoon of baking powder, plus enough water to make a spreadable dough, about 1¼ cups.

I began to assemble the tamales in soaked corn husks that I'd softened in hot water. I spread a tablespoon of the cornmeal mixture on the husk and then tried to scoop and shape the ground beef. But the meat was loose, pebbly, and difficult to press into a log. What if I started with raw meat rather than cooked? Its sticky texture would be easy to shape into the necessary logs, and some of its flavorful fat would seep into the dough as it cooked.

This approach was much more successful, but after stewing the assembled tamales for 30 minutes so the dough would properly set, the meat was a bit dry. I wondered if adding a bit of the cornmeal mixture—like adding a panade of bread crumbs and liquid to meatballs—would keep the beef hydrated. I stirred ½ cup of the mixture into the ground beef and tried again. The meat filling was much more moist, but the beef still seemed tight. I recalled a pork pie recipe in which we kept the ground pork moist by adding some baking soda to the meat; would that work here? I added ½ teaspoon of baking soda combined with 2 tablespoons of water (to help it distribute evenly) to the ground beef before mixing in the spices and cornmeal. My tasters commented that the meat was decidedly more tender.

Mexican tamales are usually made with masa harina, which is very finely ground cornmeal made from hominy. Delta hot tamales, made with more coarsely ground cornmeal, have a rougher texture but an equally strong corn flavor. Traditional delta tamales mix good-quality lard with the cornmeal; sadly, the grocery store lard that's widely available often has an off-putting flavor. I had begun by substituting vegetable shortening for the lard, but it wasn't really satisfying. I decided to try using the same amount of butter—not a traditional ingredient in tamales, I know, but the kind of fat many people are likely to keep at home. When sampling the tamales side by side, tasters preferred those made with the butter. Interestingly, they couldn't taste a distinct butter flavor, but they all agreed that the tamales tasted more balanced.

Now I just needed to tweak the method for stewing my tamales. Traditional delta hot tamales are tied in groups of three to help them stand upright in a pot. My batch yielded about two dozen tamales, which required the space and height of a large saucepan to give them clearance to stew while covered. Unfortunately, the extra room

in the pot gave the trios of tamales room to topple. Tying the tamales in groups of six gave them more stability (and sped up the process). I added enough water to come within an inch of the tops of the tamales, stirred in the remaining spice mixture, and simmered the tamales until the cornmeal began to pull away from the husks and the beef was cooked through, about 30 minutes.

The resulting tamales were spicy and moist, but they needed some sauce. I remembered the thickened stewing liquid that I'd tasted at Larry's Hot Tamales in Clarksdale, and the way that it had just enough viscosity to cling to the tamales. To replicate it, I added a slurry of cornstarch and water to the stewing liquid after I removed the tamales and brought it to a simmer. I served up my tamales with the spicy, glazy sauce and took a bite. Ah yes. This was as close as I could come to being back in the delta without a plane ticket.

DELTA HOT TAMALES Serves 6 to 8

Use a saucepan that holds 4 quarts or more, with at least 5-inch sides. Corn husks can be found in the international aisle of grocery stores.

24	corn husks
1½	tablespoons chili powder
1	tablespoon paprika
1	tablespoon salt
2	teaspoons ground cumin
2	teaspoons sugar
¾	teaspoon pepper
¾	teaspoon cayenne pepper
2½	cups (12½ ounces) yellow cornmeal
1	tablespoon baking powder
12	tablespoons unsalted butter, cut into 12 pieces
½	teaspoon baking soda
1	pound 85 percent lean ground beef
2	garlic cloves, minced
2	tablespoons cornstarch combined with 2 tablespoons cold water

1. Place husks in large bowl and cover with hot water; soak until pliable, about 30 minutes. Combine chili powder, paprika, salt, cumin, sugar, pepper, and cayenne in bowl.

2. Pulse cornmeal and baking powder in food processor until combined, about

3 pulses. Add butter and 1½ tablespoons spice mixture and pulse to chop butter into small pieces, about 8 pulses. Add 1¼ cups water and process until dough forms, about 30 seconds. Reserve ½ cup cornmeal mixture. Divide remaining cornmeal mixture into 24 equal portions, about 1½ tablespoons each, and place on plate.

3. Dissolve baking soda in 2 tablespoons water in large bowl. Add beef, garlic, reserved ½ cup cornmeal mixture, and 1½ tablespoons spice mixture and knead with your hands until thoroughly combined. Divide meat mixture into 24 equal portions, about 1½ tablespoons each, and place on plate.

4. Remove husks from water and pat dry with dish towel. Working with 1 husk at a time, lay husk on counter, smooth side up, with long side parallel to counter edge and wide end oriented toward right. Using small offset spatula, spread 1 portion of cornmeal mixture in 3½-inch square over lower right corner of husk, flush to bottom edge but leaving ¼-inch border on right edge.

5. Place 1 portion of meat mixture in log across center of cornmeal (end to end), parallel to long side of husk. Roll husk away from you and over meat mixture so cornmeal mixture surrounds meat and forms cylinder; continue rolling to complete tamale. Fold tapered end (left side) of tamale up leaving top open. Using scissors, trim tapered end of tamale to align with filled end (if tapered end hangs over). Set tamales aside seam side down.

6. Stack tamales on their sides

in groups of 6 and tie into bundles with kitchen twine. Add remaining 2 tablespoons spice mixture to large saucepan. Stand tamales, open ends up, in pot (walls of pot should clear tops of tamales). Add about 5½ cups water to pot to come within 1 inch of tops of tamales, being careful not to pour water into tamales.

7. Bring tamales to boil. Cover, reduce heat to low to maintain gentle simmer, and cook until tamales are firm and beginning to pull away from husks, about 30 minutes. Using tongs and slotted spoon, carefully transfer tamales to serving platter and remove twine.

8. Return liquid to simmer over medium heat. Whisk in cornstarch slurry and cook until slightly thickened, about 1 minute. Serve sauce with tamales.

On the Road
The Hot Tamale Trail

Delta hot tamales are more than just Mississippi's version of a Mexican tamale—they are a rich culinary tradition that is as much a part of life in the delta as the blues. To learn how to make them, I packed my bags and flew to Clarksdale, Mississippi, to eat my way along the so-called Hot Tamale Trail. As I went, I got to know some of the home cooks and restaurateurs who have forgotten more about making hot tamales than I'll ever know. Visit **CooksCountry.com/ tamaletrail** to read more about my trip.

SHOPPING Corn Husks

Cooking the tamales in corn husks—which are available in most supermarkets near the dried chiles—adds a subtle depth of flavor. Working with the husks is actually quite easy, as they become pliable when soaked in hot water.

EASY TO FIND
Easy to use.

▶ Want to make tamales with parchment paper instead of husks? Find the recipe at **CooksCountry.com/july14**.

TEST KITCHEN TECHNIQUE **Make Bundles, and Bundle Them**
Yes, these tamales take time, but the technique is simple, and the payoff is worth the time.

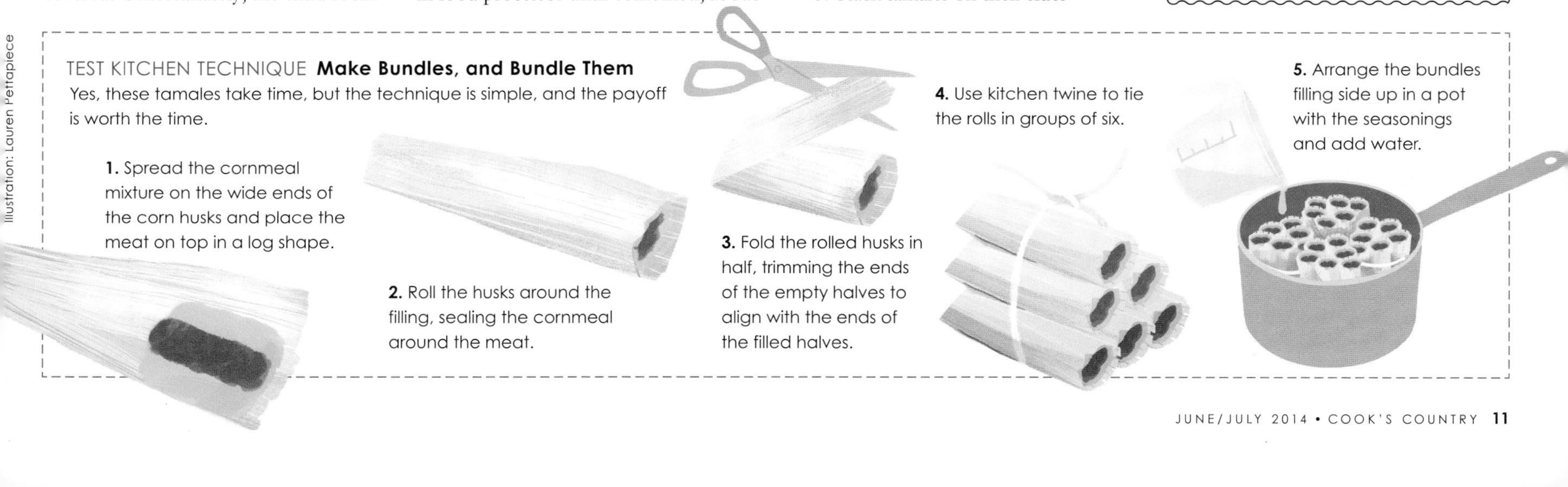

1. Spread the cornmeal mixture on the wide ends of the corn husks and place the meat on top in a log shape.

2. Roll the husks around the filling, sealing the cornmeal around the meat.

3. Fold the rolled husks in half, trimming the ends of the empty halves to align with the ends of the filled halves.

4. Use kitchen twine to tie the rolls in groups of six.

5. Arrange the bundles filling side up in a pot with the seasonings and add water.

Illustration: Lauren Pettapiece

Shrimp Étouffée

We wanted to cut down on the work of making this classic Creole seafood stew.
But did that have to mean shortchanging the flavor, too? BY REBECCAH MARSTERS

THERE'S NO LACK of good food in New Orleans, but the dish I came away remembering after a recent visit to the city was a simple cup of velvety, mildly spiced shrimp étouffée. The word means "smothered" in French, and the dish is named for the way the food is, well, smothered in a rich, thick sauce. When my vacation ended, I was unwilling to wait until my next trip to New Orleans to eat shrimp étouffée again. I'd need to come up with my own recipe.

Plenty have trod this path before, including superstars like John Besh, Emeril Lagasse, and Paul Prudhomme, as well as a plentiful supply of Louisianans with names like Billy Boy and Eula Mae. I picked a handful of existing recipes to begin my testing. All called for shrimp, garlic, cayenne or hot sauce, and what Louisianans dub the "holy trinity" (onion, celery, and green pepper). Most of the recipes included Worcestershire and called for thickening with roux, a cooked mixture of flour and fat; some used a long-cooked, deep red-brown roux and others a lighter, peanut butter–colored one. The fat might be oil, butter, or even crayfish fat (intriguing but definitely not at my local supermarket). Tomatoes were sometimes included, sometimes not. And the base of the sauce was variously water, chicken stock, beef broth, or shellfish stock, either homemade or store-bought.

The results of this first round of testing helped me sort through options and pinpoint challenges. First, the overcooked, rubbery shrimp would have to go. (Having cooked many a crustacean over the years in the test kitchen, I knew going forward to add them only in the last few minutes of cooking.) I'd use butter for the roux for its rich flavor, and the roux would be of medium tone, since the pale ones had no flavor and dark verged on acrid. I'd include canned diced tomatoes but no andouille; though we liked its smoky flavor, it upstaged the shrimp. And finally, I preferred the seafood stock to the other options, and I knew that I'd make my own, since recipes built with store-bought produced uninspired results. Given this, though, I'd have to work some magic to save time elsewhere.

> ▶ You can't have Shrimp Étouffée without rice. Find our recipe for fluffy, foolproof white rice at **CooksCountry.com/whiterice.**

Why is it better to buy shell-on shrimp? Because you can use the shells to make the easy shrimp stock that is the foundation of great étouffée.

Starting again, I peeled shell-on shrimp, set the meat aside for the étouffée, and sautéed the shells in butter with onion and celery. I added some spices, then water, and let everything simmer. Later, when I strained the mixture, its wonderful aroma and flavor proved that it was definitely worth the half-hour or so that it took to make homemade stock.

Now I buckled down and made the roux. Étouffée's complex flavors depend in part on roux, but that meant stirring constantly to keep it from burning. I melted a stick of butter in a pot, added ½ cup of flour, and stirred, and stirred, and stirred some more . . . A long 20 minutes later, the roux was the color of rich caramel and smelled like popcorn. I added onion, celery, and green pepper along with a few flavorings, including plenty of garlic; cooked the vegetables for about 10 minutes, until just softened;

and then introduced my seafood stock and tomatoes. At this point I let everything simmer for about 25 minutes, until the consistency was just right—neither watery nor gloppy. Only then did I add the shrimp and leave the pot to simmer a mere 5 minutes longer. Just before ladling out bowlfuls of stew, I stirred in sliced scallions.

The étouffée was quite good, but it was taking too long. Could I hurry the roux making without hurting its quality? I tried higher heat—and got burnt roux. I tried less flour—and got thin, weak étouffée. A few tests later, I made a happy discovery: If I first toasted the flour in a dry pot, adding the butter only after the flour started to brown—about 5 minutes—the roux cooked much faster. Once the butter was in the pot, I still needed to hover and stir, but now that took just 5 minutes or so, and the étouffée made from this sped-up roux was as good as before.

I dipped in a spoon, considered, and then reached for smoked paprika and a squirt of lemon juice, neither traditional but both terrific additions. Then I called in a special taster—a born-and-bred Southerner and self-proclaimed étouffée aficionado. After a nod of approval, he helped himself to seconds.

SHRIMP ÉTOUFFÉE Serves 4 to 6
You will need 3 cups of chopped onion and 1½ cups of chopped celery, which are divided between the shrimp stock and the étouffée. If you can't find shell-on shrimp, skip step 1 and substitute 3 cups of water, 1 (8-ounce) bottle of clam juice, and ¾ teaspoon of salt for the stock in step 3.

- 9 tablespoons unsalted butter, cut into 9 pieces
- 2 pounds extra-large shrimp (21 to 25 per pound), peeled and deveined, shells reserved
- 3 onions, chopped
- 3 celery ribs, chopped
  Salt and pepper
- 5 cups water
- 8 garlic cloves (2 peeled and smashed, 6 minced)
- 1 tablespoon peppercorns
- 3 bay leaves
- 2 sprigs fresh thyme, plus 1 teaspoon minced
- ½ cup all-purpose flour
- 1 green bell pepper, stemmed, seeded, and chopped
- 1 teaspoon smoked paprika
- ¼ teaspoon cayenne pepper
- 1 (14.5-ounce) can diced tomatoes
- 3 scallions, sliced thin
- 2 teaspoons Worcestershire sauce
  Cooked white rice
  Hot sauce
  Lemon wedges

1. Melt 1 tablespoon butter in Dutch oven over medium heat. Add shrimp shells, 2 cups onion, ½ cup celery, and 1 teaspoon salt and cook, stirring occasionally, until shells are spotty brown, about 10 minutes. Add water, smashed garlic, peppercorns, bay leaves, and thyme sprigs and bring to boil. Reduce heat to low, cover, and simmer for 30 minutes. Strain shrimp stock through fine-mesh strainer set over large bowl, pressing on solids to extract as much liquid as possible; discard solids. Wash and dry pot. (Stock can be refrigerated for 3 days or frozen for up to 1 month.)

2. Toast flour in now-empty pot over medium heat, stirring constantly, until just beginning to brown, about 5 minutes. Whisk in remaining 8 tablespoons butter until melted and combined with flour. Continue to cook, whisking constantly, until deep brown, 4 to 6 minutes.

3. Add bell pepper, remaining onion, remaining celery, 1 teaspoon salt, and ½ teaspoon pepper and cook, stirring often, until vegetables are softened, 10 to 12 minutes. Add paprika, cayenne, minced garlic, and minced thyme and cook until fragrant, about 1 minute. Stir in tomatoes and their juice and cook until dry, about 1 minute. Slowly whisk in 4 cups shrimp stock until incorporated (reserve any remaining stock for another use). Bring to boil, reduce heat to medium-low, and simmer until slightly thickened, about 25 minutes.

4. Season shrimp with salt and pepper, add to pot, and simmer until cooked through, about 5 minutes. Stir in scallions and Worcestershire. Season with salt and pepper to taste. Serve over rice with hot sauce and lemon wedges.

KEY DISCOVERY Faster Roux
If you first toast the flour until it's light brown, the roux takes only 5 minutes to cook.

DRY-TOAST THE FLOUR Until it's fragrant and just starting to brown.

COOK THE ROUX Until it's this shade of dark brown.

Grilled Zucchini and Corn Salad

To give this midsummer salad a needed boost of flavor, we decided to play with fire.

BY CHRISTIE MORRISON

CORN AND ZUCCHINI are both at their peak in midsummer, but even then, neither of them is exactly loaded with flavor. Corn is naturally sweet, yes, but it's a one-note sweetness, and zucchini's flavor is even more subtle. It seemed like the direct high heat of the grill might remedy this, since it would not only caramelize the sugars in the corn but help remove moisture from the zucchini as well as add flavorful char. I decided to take this salad to the grill.

Grilling shucked ears of corn over high heat gave them a nice char, and brushing them with oil kept the kernels moist. Once the corn cooled, I cut the charred kernels from the cobs and started on the zucchini.

I knew that the zucchini's moisture would inhibit browning, so I tried different ways of slicing the zucchini to get rid of some of it. In the end, cutting the planks ½ inch thick ensured that the flesh didn't turn to mush before the surfaces were fully charred, and slicing the cooked planks crosswise on the bias gave me bite-size pieces that mingled nicely with the corn kernels.

Grilling the vegetables got me halfway to my goal, but I still wanted more flavor. A few assertive ingredients—garlic, red pepper flakes, salt, and pepper—added to the oil made a quick marinade and dressing. I tossed the vegetables in the flavored oil before grilling and then dressed the warm grilled vegetables with the remaining oil, lemon juice, and fresh basil. A final sprinkle of crumbled feta added salty, creamy complexity to my now-flavorful corn and zucchini.

GRILLED ZUCCHINI AND CORN SALAD Serves 4
Serve warm or at room temperature.

- ⅓ cup extra-virgin olive oil
- 2 garlic cloves, minced
  Salt and pepper
- ¼ teaspoon red pepper flakes
- 2 ears corn, husks and silk removed
- 3 zucchini (8 ounces each), sliced lengthwise into ½-inch-thick planks
- 2 tablespoons chopped fresh basil
- 4 teaspoons lemon juice
- 2 ounces feta cheese, crumbled (½ cup)

Served warm or at room temperature, this salad is a natural picnic side dish.

1. Whisk oil, garlic, ½ teaspoon salt, ½ teaspoon pepper, and pepper flakes together in large bowl. Brush corn with 1 tablespoon oil mixture. Add zucchini to remaining oil mixture in bowl and toss to coat.

2A. FOR A CHARCOAL GRILL: Open bottom vent completely. Light large chimney starter filled with charcoal briquettes (6 quarts). When top coals are partially covered with ash, pour evenly over grill. Set cooking grate in place, cover, and open lid vent completely. Heat grill until hot, about 5 minutes.

2B. FOR A GAS GRILL: Turn all burners to high, cover, and heat grill until hot, about 15 minutes. Turn all burners to medium-high.

3. Clean and oil cooking grate. Place corn and zucchini on grill; reserve any oil mixture remaining in zucchini bowl. Grill, uncovered, turning corn every 2 to 3 minutes until kernels are lightly charred all over, 10 to 15 minutes total, and zucchini is well-browned and tender (not mushy), 4 to 8 minutes per side.

4. Transfer grilled vegetables to cutting board. Cut kernels from cobs. Cut zucchini on bias into ½-inch-thick slices. Add vegetables to bowl with reserved oil mixture. Add basil and lemon juice and toss to combine. Season with salt and pepper to taste. Transfer salad to platter and sprinkle with feta. Serve.

Rhode Island Johnnycakes

Golden brown and crispy outside, rich and creamy inside, these are much more than bland cornmeal pancakes. But to make them that good, we had to ignore the instructions. BY DIANE UNGER

BEING FROM NEW England, I had of course heard about Rhode Island johnnycakes. But they always sounded like more of a historical curiosity than a recipe worth seeking out to make at home. They're unleavened corn pancakes made from nothing but the stone-ground white cap flint corn that is native to Rhode Island (this tough corn is used for cornmeal) mixed with water or milk, salt, and a bit of sugar. The technique seems clunky: Mix cornmeal with salt and sugar, pour boiling liquid over it, stir, form, and cook. I didn't see where the deliciousness would come from.

But that idea changed completely when I attended the annual Johnny Cake Festival in West Kingston, Rhode Island. More specifically, it changed when I (finally) got to the front of the line at the Kenyon's Grist Mill booth, where cooks were flipping johnnycakes by the dozens on well-seasoned flat-top griddles the size of banquet tables. The cakes they piled on my plate were golden brown and crispy on the outside, creamy on the inside, and just thick enough that you got the perfect ratio of crispy exterior to soft, delicate, nutty, corn-flavored interior. Served with creamy maple butter, they were delicious—better than I had ever imagined.

This, admittedly, was the end rather than the beginning of my quest. Despite my misgivings, I had become intrigued by the history of these cakes and set out to learn what explained their popularity. I had already sampled versions from all over Rhode Island. Some, from the East Bay area, were thin and lacy; others, from the West Bay, were more like pancakes. I had preferred the thick ones because the thin ones ate more like crêpes and had little corn flavor. But even the thicker versions resembled disks of dried-out cornbread.

Now that I had tasted johnnycake greatness, I was determined to achieve it at home. I stocked up on a case of johnnycake meal at the Mill's quaint little store and made the drive back to Boston to get going. To start the cakes flipping, I searched out a handful of recipes, both old and new, including the one on the box of Kenyon's Johnny Cake Corn Meal. I was thrilled because I assumed I'd soon be eating cakes as excellent as those I'd enjoyed at the festival.

The technique used by virtually every

Not just for breakfast: These corn cakes are also a traditional (and delicious) side dish for soups and stews.

recipe I found was as simple as the ingredient list: Whisk together the dry ingredients, then pour boiling water over the top, mix again, and ladle out small dollops of batter onto a lightly greased griddle. Unfortunately, following these instructions resulted in johnnycakes that were nothing like the ones I was trying to re-create. Instead, I got a succession of cakes that were either gritty or sandy and either fell apart when I tried to turn

them or ended up with the consistency of wet cardboard. After a few frustrating attempts, I asked several other test cooks to also make the Kenyon's recipe. Not only were the textures of each of their cakes as unpleasant as mine but each was different.

What was the problem? What was I doing differently? I tried to recall exactly how the cooks at that stand back in Rhode Island had made their johnny-

cakes, and one factor did occur to me: I seemed to remember that the texture of their batter as it dropped onto the griddle looked different from mine. I went back over the photos I had taken, and sure enough, I found a picture of their batter in a saucepan, looking very much like mashed potatoes. Mine was much thinner. I figured I could probably get this texture if I used an approach more like that used in making polenta. Rather than pouring boiling water over the dry ingredients, what if I whisked the dry ingredients into the boiling water?

This turned out to be the key. When I switched to this method, I got consistent results every time and ended up with johnnycakes with a much smoother texture, without a hint of grittiness. It actually made perfect sense because the cornmeal was more thoroughly cooked before it went on the griddle, which got rid of the gritty or sandy qualities that resulted from batters with less fully cooked cornmeal. This approach gave me consistent cakes from batch to batch, and I also got very similar results even when I tested it with other brands of stone-ground cornmeal.

I had overcome a major hurdle, but I wasn't home free yet. I still was having problems with the thickness of the batter. The cooking method I was now using tended to make the batter too thick, since the cornmeal was cooking and therefore absorbing more water before it went on the griddle. Once again, I found the solution to this problem by ignoring the package instructions, which called for about equal parts cornmeal and water. I made batches with increasing amounts of water until I got a batter that cooked up into the proper creamy consistency: 2¾ cups water to 1 cup cornmeal. If I cooked this for about 30 seconds after whisking in the cornmeal and then let it sit for 15 minutes so the cornmeal absorbed even more water, it had the perfect consistency, like ploppable mashed potatoes. (I also found that, since this batter did thicken as it sat, I had to add a couple of tablespoons more water to the second batch in order to achieve the right consistency.)

Now I was almost there. But my johnnycakes were still not perfect, since they too often fell apart as I turned them. Like standing in line, this was a matter of patience. Attempting to cook johnnycakes as you would a standard flour pancake didn't work. Because the batter has no leavener, eggs, or flour, as regular pancake batter does, getting it to hold together is all about the cooking technique. The cakes need to be cooked for at least 6 minutes, and often as long as 8 minutes on the first side, so they form a crust that will hold the cake together when flipped. When you start to see a golden-brown crust forming around the edge of the pancake, then and only then is it time to flip. In addition, after flipping the cakes, you need to gently flatten them to about ¼ inch, at which height they will cook through by the time the second side has properly browned.

Now I had real johnnycakes—or at least the kind of cakes I had been working toward since that day at the festival. They were perfect just as is for a side dish, but for breakfast they needed a little something. Maple butter, made by simply mixing well-softened butter with pure maple syrup, was the easiest and best route to this final goal.

And you know what? The next time I called the tasters to try my johnnycakes topped with maple butter, they were very happy to stand in line for them.

RHODE ISLAND JOHNNYCAKES
Makes 12 johnnycakes

Johnnycakes are best served warm with maple butter (or maple syrup) for breakfast, or as a side dish for soups and stews. For authentic Rhode Island johnnycakes, we recommend using Kenyon's Johnny Cake Corn Meal, made from stone-ground white flint corn and available by mail order. Do not try to turn the johnnycakes too soon or they will fall apart. If you prefer crispier johnnycakes, press the pancakes thinner in step 5.

- 1 cup johnnycake meal or stone-ground cornmeal
- 2 teaspoons sugar
- ¾ teaspoon salt
- 2¾ cups water, plus extra hot water for thinning batter
- 2 tablespoons unsalted butter
- 2 tablespoons vegetable oil

1. Adjust oven rack to middle position and heat oven to 200 degrees. Set wire rack in rimmed baking sheet.

2. Whisk johnnycake meal, sugar, and salt together in bowl. Bring water to boil in large saucepan. Slowly whisk johnnycake meal mixture into boiling water until no lumps remain; continue to cook until thickened, about 30 seconds. Off heat, whisk in butter. Pour batter into bowl, cover with plastic wrap, and let sit until slightly firm, about 15 minutes.

3. Rewhisk batter until smooth. Batter should be consistency of ploppable mashed potatoes; if not, thin with 1 to 2 tablespoons extra hot water until mixture is able to drop easily from spoon.

4. Heat 1 tablespoon oil in 12-inch nonstick skillet over medium heat until shimmering (or heat nonstick griddle to 400 degrees). Using greased ¼-cup dry measuring cup, drop 6 evenly spaced scoops of batter into skillet, using spoon to help release batter from cup as needed. Cook johnnycakes, without moving them, until edges appear crispy and golden brown, 6 to 8 minutes.

5. Carefully flip johnnycakes and press with spatula to flatten into 2½- to 3-inch-diameter pancakes. Continue to cook until well browned on second side, 5 to 7 minutes. Transfer johnnycakes to prepared wire rack and place in oven to keep warm. Whisk 2 to 4 tablespoons extra hot water into remaining batter to return to correct consistency. Repeat cooking with remaining 1 tablespoon oil and remaining batter. Serve.

MAPLE BUTTER
Makes ¼ cup
Maple butter will keep, covered and refrigerated, for one week. Try it on roasted vegetables, corn bread, or pork chops, as well as johnnycakes.

- 4 tablespoons unsalted butter, softened
- 1 tablespoon pure maple syrup
- ¼ teaspoon salt

Whisk butter, maple syrup, and salt together in bowl until combined.

TEST KITCHEN TECHNIQUE **Shaping Johnnycakes**

1. Use a greased ¼-cup dry measuring cup to carefully portion the six mounds of batter into the hot pan.

2. When the edges are crispy and brown, carefully flip the cakes and gently flatten them with your spatula.

Getting to Know Oils

We use oils for many tasks in the test kitchen. But since no single oil is perfect for every task, we're offering a handy rundown of basic oils and their uses. BY CHRISTIE MORRISON

Vegetable Oil
PANTRY STAPLE

While it can be made from a number of different vegetable sources—from grains to seeds to beans—the vegetable oil in supermarkets is usually made from soybeans. This multipurpose oil has a high smoke point (the temperature at which the oil begins to break down), so it's great for shallow frying, sautéing, deep frying, and making mayonnaise and highly seasoned dressings and sauces. **BEST FOR:** Sautéing and frying.

Corn Oil
NEEDS HEAT

Like other RBD (refined, bleached, deodorized) oils such as vegetable and canola, corn oil is an inexpensive cooking oil with a high smoke point and neutral flavor when cooked. Unlike vegetable and canola oils, however, corn oil has an unpleasant "sour" and "pungent" flavor when used unheated in mayonnaise and dressings, so we don't recommend adding it to uncooked applications. **BEST FOR:** Deep frying.

Canola Oil
CLEVER ALIAS

First developed in Canada in the 1970s, canola is derived from rapeseed that produces oil low in acid and saturated fat. Its more marketable name, canola (Canada oil, low acid), distinguishes it from industrial rapeseed oil, which is toxic. Our winning all-purpose vegetable oil, Crisco Natural Blend Oil, is actually a blend of canola, sunflower, and soybean oils, which we use for everything but deep frying. **BEST FOR:** Sautéing.

Extra-Virgin Olive Oil
PRESSED PURE

Only oil from the first cold pressing of olives can be called extra-virgin olive oil. Depending on the type of olives it is made from, this rich-tasting oil can be grassy, peppery, or fruity, but its delicate flavors break down when heated. Add it to dishes after cooking, or save it for vinaigrettes. We love the "peppery finish" of Columela Extra Virgin Olive Oil. Store it in a cool, dry place out of sunlight. **BEST FOR:** Finishing drizzles and vinaigrettes.

Olive Oil
RE-PRESSED FRUIT

After extracting EVOO with the first press, producers apply heat or chemicals as they press the olives to extract more oil, yielding olive oils with progressively less olive flavor. ("Light" olive oil refers to its light flavor, rather than to lower levels of fat or calories.) Once olive oil is heated to 300 degrees, we find that there's little flavor difference between olive oil and vegetable oil. **BEST FOR:** Sautéing.

Grapeseed Oil
VINTNER'S BONUS

Pressed from the seeds of grapes and largely a byproduct of wine making, grapeseed oil is chemically extracted, largely because the seeds yield such a small amount of oil. While it has a neutral flavor and a high smoke point, grapeseed oil is high in polyunsaturated fat, which tends to break down quickly during cooking and leads to off-flavors. **BEST FOR:** Dressings and mayonnaise.

Coconut Oil
TASTE OF THE TROPICS

Coconut oil, once maligned for being high in saturated fat, has shorter-chain fatty acids that nutritionists suspect actually increase "good" HDL cholesterol. Solid at room temperature, coconut oil is a good nondairy substitute for butter in sautéing and baking. Refined coconut oil is virtually tasteless and odorless; virgin coconut oil has a strong coconut flavor. **BEST FOR:** Sautéing and baking.

Sésame Oil
ASIAN ELIXIR

Made from raw or toasted sesame seeds, this oil is a staple in Asian cooking. Plain sesame oil's high smoke point and neutral flavor make it a great cooking oil, and it can last for months at room temperature. Rich, nutty toasted sesame oil (shown here) is much darker and should be used in uncooked applications and refrigerated once opened. **BEST FOR:** Dressings and finishing stir-fries.

Palm Oil
SECRET SUBSTITUTE

Don't confuse palm kernel oil, which is very high in saturated fat and used in many processed foods, with palm oil, which is made from the palm fruit and is only moderately high in saturated fat. Palm oil's reddish tint comes from heart-healthy carotenoids. It's a common cooking oil in parts of Southeast Asia, Brazil, and Africa. **BEST FOR:** Sautéing.

Safflower Oil
FLOWER POWER

The oil that is extracted from the seeds of the *Carthamus tinctorius*, a thistle-like plant, is odorless, flavorless, and high in oleic acid; the seeds are an ancient crop once valued for making red and yellow dyes. Safflower oil is high in "healthy" polyunsaturated fat. **BEST FOR:** Dressings and sauces.

Peanut Oil
FRIED GOLD

Peanut oil has a high smoke point (between 450 and 475 degrees) and good flavor. While it costs about twice as much as vegetable or corn oil, it can withstand long periods at high heat without breaking down. Don't confuse it with unrefined peanut oil, which has a strong flavor and higher price tag; use the unrefined oil sparingly in quick-cooking stir-fries. **BEST FOR:** Deep frying.

Aromatic Nut Oils
POTENT DRIZZLE

Nut oils like walnut oil and hazelnut oil are extracted from pressings of raw or roasted nuts to yield oils that are nutty but delicate in flavor. Since heating breaks down the flavor compounds and causes them to become bitter, these oils are best used in dressings or as a finishing drizzle. The oils tend to go rancid quickly, so store them in the refrigerator. **BEST FOR:** Finishing drizzles and vinaigrettes.

**PRETZEL-CRUSTED CHICKEN FINGERS
WITH HONEY MUSTARD**

**GRILLED STEAK AND SWEET POTATO SALAD
WITH CHILE-LIME DRESSING**

BLACK BEAN, CORN, AND POBLANO QUESADILLAS

**GRILLED HOISIN-GLAZED PORK CHOPS
WITH PINEAPPLE SALSA**

GRILLED STEAK AND SWEET POTATO SALAD WITH CHILE-LIME DRESSING Serves 4

✔️ **WHY THIS RECIPE WORKS:** Cutting sweet potatoes into small pieces means they cook quickly and evenly in the microwave. Flank steak delivers big beefy flavor without a hefty price tag.

- 1 pound sweet potatoes, peeled and cut into ½-inch pieces
- ½ cup olive oil
  Salt and pepper
- 1 (1½-pound) flank steak, trimmed
- 2 tablespoons lime juice
- 2 tablespoons chopped fresh cilantro
- 1 tablespoon honey
- 1½ teaspoons minced canned chipotle chile in adobo sauce
- ½ teaspoon ground cumin
- 6 ounces (6 cups) baby arugula

1. Combine potatoes, 1 tablespoon oil, ½ teaspoon salt, and ¼ teaspoon pepper in bowl. Cover and microwave until potatoes are tender, about 6 minutes, stirring halfway through microwaving.

2. Pat steak dry with paper towels and season with salt and pepper. Heat 1 tablespoon oil in 12-inch nonstick skillet over medium-high heat until just smoking. Cook steak until well browned and meat registers 125 degrees (for medium-rare), 5 to 7 minutes per side. Transfer to carving board, tent loosely with foil, and let rest for 5 minutes.

3. Meanwhile, whisk lime juice, cilantro, honey, chipotle, cumin, remaining 6 tablespoons oil, ½ teaspoon salt, and ¼ teaspoon pepper together in large bowl. Add arugula and potatoes and toss to combine. Slice steak against grain on slight bias into ¼-inch-thick slices. Divide salad evenly among plates and top with sliced steak. Serve.

PRETZEL-CRUSTED CHICKEN FINGERS WITH HONEY MUSTARD Serves 4

✔️ **WHY THIS RECIPE WORKS:** Chicken tenderloins cook quickly, and there is no faster sauce than honey mustard.

- 6 ounces thin pretzel sticks
- ½ cup all-purpose flour
- 2 large eggs
- 2 tablespoons plus ½ cup Dijon mustard
- 3 tablespoons honey
- 1½ pounds chicken tenderloins, trimmed
  Salt and pepper
- 6 tablespoons vegetable oil

1. Process pretzels in food processor until finely ground, about 20 seconds (you should have about 1½ cups crumbs); transfer to shallow dish. Spread flour in second shallow dish. Beat eggs and 2 tablespoons mustard in third shallow dish. Whisk remaining ½ cup mustard with honey in bowl and set aside.

2. Pat chicken dry with paper towels and season with salt and pepper. Dredge chicken in flour, dip in egg mixture, then coat with pretzel crumbs, pressing gently to adhere.

3. Heat 3 tablespoons oil in 12-inch nonstick skillet over medium-high heat until shimmering. Cook half of tenderloins until golden brown and cooked through, about 5 minutes per side, adjusting heat if crust begins to burn. Transfer to paper towel–lined plate, discard oil, and wipe out skillet with paper towels. Repeat with remaining 3 tablespoons oil and remaining tenderloins. Serve tenderloins with honey mustard.

TEST KITCHEN NOTE: Use the thinner pretzel sticks, not the thicker rods, for this recipe.

GRILLED HOISIN-GLAZED PORK CHOPS WITH PINEAPPLE SALSA Serves 4

✔️ **WHY THIS RECIPE WORKS:** The sugar in the hoisin sauce encourages flavorful caramelization on the pork chops.

- ½ pineapple, peeled, cored, and cut into ½-inch-thick rings
- 2 tablespoons toasted sesame oil
- ½ cup hoisin sauce
- 3 tablespoons rice vinegar
- 8 (3- to 4-ounce) bone-in center-cut pork chops, ½ inch thick, trimmed
  Salt and pepper
- 3 scallions, sliced thin
- ¼ cup chopped fresh cilantro
- 1 jalapeño chile, stemmed, seeded, and minced
- 2 teaspoons grated fresh ginger

1. Brush pineapple all over with 1 tablespoon oil and grill, covered, over hot fire until charred, about 3 minutes per side. Transfer to cutting board.

2. Whisk hoisin and vinegar together in bowl. Transfer 3 tablespoons hoisin mixture to small bowl and set aside. Pat chops dry with paper towels and season with salt and pepper. Brush chops all over with remaining ½ cup hoisin mixture. Grill chops, covered, over hot fire until well browned and meat registers 140 degrees, about 3 minutes per side. Transfer chops to platter and brush with reserved 3 tablespoons hoisin mixture. Tent loosely with foil and let rest for 5 minutes.

3. When pineapple is cool enough to handle, chop into ½-inch pieces and combine with scallions, cilantro, jalapeño, ginger, and remaining 1 tablespoon oil in bowl. Season with salt and pepper to taste. Serve pork with pineapple salsa.

BLACK BEAN, CORN, AND POBLANO QUESADILLAS Serves 4

✔️ **WHY THIS RECIPE WORKS:** By seeding the poblano chile, we control the amount of heat in these quesadillas: Introduce the seeds for extra spice. Goat cheese adds an uncommon creamy and tangy profile.

- 4 ounces goat cheese, crumbled (1 cup)
- 4 ounces sharp cheddar cheese, shredded (1 cup)
- 3 tablespoons vegetable oil
- 1 onion, chopped fine
- 1 ear corn, kernels cut from cob
- 1 poblano chile, stemmed, seeded, and chopped
- 1 (15-ounce) can black beans, rinsed
- ½ cup water
  Salt and pepper
- 4 (10-inch) flour tortillas

1. Combine cheeses in bowl; set aside. Heat 2 tablespoons oil in 12-inch nonstick skillet over medium-high heat until shimmering. Add onion, corn, and poblano and cook until softened, about 7 minutes. Add beans and water and cook until water evaporates, about 1 minute. Off heat, coarsely mash mixture with potato masher. Season with salt and pepper to taste.

2. Spread one-quarter of bean mixture over half of each tortilla, leaving ½-inch border around edge. Top with one-quarter of cheese mixture and fold tortilla over filling, pressing firmly to seal. Wipe out skillet with paper towels.

3. Heat 1½ teaspoons oil in now-empty skillet over medium-high heat until shimmering. Cook 2 quesadillas at a time until golden brown and crispy, 1 to 2 minutes per side. Transfer to cutting board. Repeat with remaining 1½ teaspoons oil and remaining 2 quesadillas. Cut into wedges and serve.

TEST KITCHEN NOTE: Three-quarters of a cup of thawed frozen corn kernels can be substituted for the fresh.

GRILLED CHICKEN CAESAR PASTA SALAD

SOUTHEAST ASIAN GRILLED CHICKEN SANDWICHES WITH SPICY SLAW

GRILLED SHRIMP WITH COCONUT RICE SALAD

SKILLET SAUSAGE AND POTATOES WITH ARUGULA

SOUTHEAST ASIAN GRILLED CHICKEN SANDWICHES WITH SPICY SLAW Serves 4

✓ **WHY THIS RECIPE WORKS:** Store-bought coleslaw mix adds substance to this sandwich while saving on prep work.

- 2 tablespoons plus 2 teaspoons fish sauce
- 2 tablespoons vegetable oil
- 2 tablespoons packed brown sugar
- 4 teaspoons red curry paste
  Salt and pepper
- 8 (3- to 4-ounce) chicken cutlets, ½ inch thick, trimmed
- ½ cup mayonnaise
- 1 tablespoon lime juice
- 1 (11-ounce) bag green coleslaw mix
- 4 (6-inch) Italian sub rolls, split lengthwise

1. Whisk 2 tablespoons fish sauce, oil, sugar, 2 teaspoons curry paste, and ¼ teaspoon pepper together in bowl. Add cutlets and toss to coat.

2. Whisk mayonnaise, lime juice, remaining 2 teaspoons fish sauce, and remaining 2 teaspoons curry paste together in large bowl. Add coleslaw mix and toss to combine. Season with salt and pepper to taste.

3. Grill cutlets over hot fire until lightly charred and cooked through, about 4 minutes per side. Transfer to plate and tent loosely with foil. Grill rolls cut side down until toasted, about 1 minute. Divide cutlets and slaw evenly among rolls. Serve.

TEST KITCHEN NOTE: For a bit of extra heat, serve with Sriracha or your favorite hot sauce.

GRILLED CHICKEN CAESAR PASTA SALAD Serves 4

✓ **WHY THIS RECIPE WORKS:** Grilling both the lettuce and the chicken imparts great smoky flavor to this pasta salad.

- 1 pound fusilli, penne, or other short, tubular pasta
  Salt and pepper
- 1½ cups mayonnaise
- 1 ounce Parmesan cheese, grated (½ cup), plus extra for serving
- 2 tablespoons lemon juice
- 1 tablespoon Worcestershire sauce
- 2 garlic cloves, minced
- 6 tablespoons extra-virgin olive oil
- 4 (6- to 8-ounce) boneless, skinless chicken breasts, trimmed
- 2 romaine lettuce hearts (12 ounces), halved lengthwise through core

1. Bring 4 quarts water to boil in large pot. Add pasta and 1 tablespoon salt and cook, stirring often, until al dente. Drain pasta, rinse under cold water until cool, and drain again.

2. Whisk mayonnaise, Parmesan, lemon juice, Worcestershire, garlic, ½ teaspoon salt, and ½ teaspoon pepper together in large bowl. Slowly whisk in ¼ cup oil until incorporated. Add pasta and toss to combine. Season with salt and pepper to taste.

3. Brush chicken and lettuce with remaining 2 tablespoons oil and season with salt and pepper. Grill chicken and lettuce over hot fire until chicken is cooked through and lettuce is charred, about 5 minutes per side for chicken and 1 to 2 minutes per side for lettuce. Transfer chicken and lettuce to cutting board; tent loosely with foil and let rest for 5 minutes. Roughly chop lettuce, toss with pasta, and transfer to platter. Slice chicken crosswise into ½-inch-thick slices and arrange on top of pasta. Sprinkle with extra Parmesan and serve.

SKILLET SAUSAGE AND POTATOES WITH ARUGULA Serves 4

✓ **WHY THIS RECIPE WORKS:** Browning the potatoes in the sausage drippings adds lots of flavor to this quick dish.

- 6 ounces (6 cups) baby arugula
- 1 pound fingerling (or baby Yukon Gold) potatoes, unpeeled, halved lengthwise
- 2 tablespoons olive oil
- ¼ teaspoon salt
- 1½ pounds hot or sweet Italian sausage
- 1 tablespoon unsalted butter
- 2 garlic cloves, minced
- 1 teaspoon minced fresh rosemary
- ¼ teaspoon pepper
- 1 cup dry white wine

1. Arrange arugula on serving platter. Combine potatoes, 1 tablespoon oil, and salt in bowl. Cover and microwave until just tender, about 6 minutes, stirring halfway through microwaving. Heat remaining 1 tablespoon oil in 12-inch nonstick skillet over medium-high heat until just smoking. Cook sausages until browned on all sides, about 6 minutes. Transfer to plate.

2. Pour off all but 1 tablespoon fat from skillet and return to medium-high heat. Cook potatoes, cut side down, until golden brown, about 3 minutes. Add butter, garlic, rosemary, and pepper and cook until fragrant, about 30 seconds, stirring to combine. Arrange potatoes on top of arugula and tent loosely with foil.

3. Return now-empty skillet to medium-high heat, add sausages and wine, and bring to boil. Reduce heat to medium-low and simmer, covered, until sausages are cooked through, about 8 minutes. Transfer sausages to platter with potatoes and arugula, drizzle with wine sauce, and serve.

GRILLED SHRIMP WITH COCONUT RICE SALAD Serves 4

✓ **WHY THIS RECIPE WORKS:** We boil the rice in plenty of salted water until tender and then dry it on a dish towel so it can absorb more of the potent dressing.

- 1½ cups long-grain white rice
  Salt and pepper
- 6 tablespoons olive oil
- 3 tablespoons canned coconut milk
- 1 teaspoon grated lime zest plus 3 tablespoons juice (2 limes)
- 1 mango, peeled, pitted, and cut into ½-inch pieces
- 4 scallions, sliced thin
- 2 jalapeño chiles, stemmed, seeded, and minced
- 3 tablespoons chopped fresh mint
- 1½ pounds jumbo shrimp (16 to 20 per pound), peeled, deveined, and tails removed

1. Line rimmed baking sheet with clean dish towel. Bring 2 quarts water to boil in large saucepan. Add rice and 1 tablespoon salt and cook until just tender, 12 to 14 minutes. Drain rice, rinse under cold water until cool, and drain again; transfer to prepared sheet.

2. Whisk ¼ cup oil, coconut milk, lime zest and juice, ¾ teaspoon salt, and ½ teaspoon pepper together in large bowl. Transfer 2 tablespoons dressing to small bowl and set aside. Add mango, scallions, jalapeños, mint, and rice to remaining dressing and toss to combine. Season with salt and pepper to taste. Transfer to platter.

3. Pat shrimp dry with paper towels, toss with remaining 2 tablespoons oil, and season with salt and pepper. Thread shrimp onto four 12-inch metal skewers. Grill shrimp over hot fire until lightly charred and cooked through, about 2 minutes per side. Slide shrimp off skewers onto rice and drizzle with reserved dressing. Serve.

Grilled Pork Skewers

For tender, juicy, flavorful pork skewers, you need to pick the right cut and be bold when it comes to seasonings. BY ASHLEY MOORE

COMPARED WITH BEEF, chicken, and even shrimp, pork skewers get little love from grillers. Wondering why, I searched cookbooks for pork kebab recipes, selecting five that called for different cuts and took different approaches to grilling the meat. Unfortunately, they all came up short in two major areas: the texture of the meat (mushy, dry, and/or chewy) and the overall flavor (yawn). Now I knew why pork skewers aren't very popular.

The first matter of business was to decide what cut of pork to use. From our five-recipe test, it was clear that we weren't going to use pork shoulder because it would take too long to cook—kebabs should be a relatively fast weeknight meal. Cubed loin was prone to dry out, and tenderloin tended to be unpleasantly mushy. On a whim, I tried a cut that I hadn't found a recipe for: boneless country-style ribs, which are cut from the shoulder end of the loin. Good thought. These ribs cooked fairly quickly and were tender, yet had enough fat to keep them moist as well as contribute some serious flavor.

One of the more promising recipes from my initial batch had used a marinade of vegetable oil, plenty of salt, and warm spices, so I decided to start there. After several tests, I arrived at a tasty combination of oil, garlic, and lemon zest and a spice mixture of coriander, cumin, nutmeg, cinnamon, salt, and pepper. The salt made its way into the meat in just 30 minutes, so advance planning wasn't needed, but marinating for up to 24 hours had no adverse effects.

A colleague suggested using a little of my spice mix as the base of a basting sauce, so I took her advice and added 2 tablespoons of it to some butter and honey. I was ready for the grill.

I packed the cubed, marinated country-style ribs onto skewers and cooked them over a medium-hot fire for about 15 minutes (until the meat hit 140 degrees), basting and turning the skewers every few minutes. Through trial and error, I found that the best way to get all the pork to char and cook evenly was to loosely pack the meat on the skewers so that the pieces were just firmly touching but not compressed.

The nicely charred pork that came off these skewers was really good . . . but not quite great. I needed a sauce. With summer flavors in mind, I thought a tomato relish would play well off the warm, North African–inspired tastes of the spice mixture. I grilled skewers of cherry tomatoes alongside the pork, with a handful of scallions and two halved lemons. When the tomatoes, scallions, and lemon halves had picked up some decent char, I set them aside while the pork finished cooking.

When the tomatoes had cooled, I slid them off the skewers into a bowl, chopped the scallions and added them, squeezed in the grilled lemon juice, and added a bit of the basting mixture I had reserved. A few quick strokes with a potato masher transformed these ingredients into a bright, potent relish.

SPICE-GRILLED PORK SKEWERS WITH GRILLED TOMATO RELISH
Serves 4 to 6
You will need seven 12-inch metal skewers for this recipe.

- 2 lemons
- ¼ cup vegetable oil
- 5 garlic cloves, minced
- 1 tablespoon ground coriander
- 2 teaspoons ground cumin
  Salt and pepper
- ½ teaspoon ground nutmeg
- ½ teaspoon ground cinnamon
- 2 pounds boneless country-style pork ribs, trimmed and cut into 1-inch pieces
- 12 ounces cherry tomatoes
- 2 tablespoons unsalted butter
- 2 tablespoons honey
- 6 scallions

1. Grate 1 tablespoon zest from 1 lemon over large bowl. Halve both lemons and set aside. Add oil, garlic, coriander, cumin, 1½ teaspoons salt, ½ teaspoon pepper, nutmeg, and cinnamon to bowl with lemon zest and whisk together. Set aside 2 tablespoons marinade. Add pork to remaining marinade in bowl and refrigerate for at least 30 minutes or up to 24 hours.

2. Remove pork from marinade and thread onto four 12-inch metal skewers so pieces are touching; discard any remaining used marinade. Thread tomatoes onto three 12-inch metal skewers.

3. Combine butter, honey, and reserved marinade in small saucepan and cook over medium heat, whisking constantly, until butter is melted and mixture is fragrant, about 1 minute. Divide

The grilled tomatoes, scallions, and lemon juice get mashed (with honey and spices) into a potent relish to serve alongside the pork.

honey mixture evenly between 2 bowls. (Use 1 bowl for grilling pork in step 5 and second bowl for sauce in step 6.)

4A. FOR A CHARCOAL GRILL: Open bottom vent completely. Light large chimney starter filled with charcoal briquettes (6 quarts). When top coals are partially covered with ash, pour evenly over grill. Set cooking grate in place, cover, and open lid vent completely. Heat grill until hot, about 5 minutes.

4B. FOR A GAS GRILL: Turn all burners to high, cover, and heat grill until hot, about 15 minutes. Turn all burners to medium.

5. Clean and oil cooking grate. Place scallions, pork, tomatoes, and reserved lemon halves, cut side down, on grill. Grill pork (covered if using gas), turning every 2 minutes and basting with honey mixture reserved for grilling, until meat registers 140 degrees, 12 to 15 minutes. Grill scallions, tomatoes, and lemon halves until charred, turning scallions and tomatoes as needed to brown evenly, 5 to 10 minutes. Transfer items to platter as they finish grilling.

6. Tent pork loosely with aluminum foil and let rest while preparing tomato relish. Slide tomatoes from skewers into large bowl. Chop scallions and add to tomatoes along with honey mixture reserved for sauce; squeeze lemon halves into tomato mixture. Using potato masher, coarsely mash tomato mixture. Add any accumulated pork juices. Season with salt and pepper to taste. Serve tomato relish with pork.

Latin Fried Chicken

Adding Latin flavors—lime, garlic, and spices—to fried chicken sounds like a fantastic idea.
So why do most recipes mess it up? BY DIANE UNGER

MOST PEOPLE THINK of fried chicken as a Southern tradition. It is, of course, but if you venture even farther south, you'll find that countries like the Dominican Republic, Cuba, Guatemala, and El Salvador have strong fried chicken traditions of their own. While each nation puts its own spin on the dish, the constants of Latin fried chicken are a potent citrus-and-garlic marinade and a crunchy spiced coating. In the past 10 years several Latin-rooted fried chicken chains, El Pollo Loco and Pollo Campero most prominent among them, have established strong footholds in cities all across the United States. I was eager to explore this dish and create my own version.

I gathered a half-dozen recipes showcasing the possible variations in marinade and coating and got busy cooking. When the pots of bubbling oil had finally come to rest, my colleagues and I tasted these recipes alongside takeout from our local outpost of Pollo Campero. While none of this Latin fried chicken was bad, none of it was great either. The coatings were meekly seasoned and lacked crispiness, and the meat was sour or bland and was often dry. These failings made me even more determined to master this dish for the home cook.

My first order of business was to fix the dry, chalky texture of the chicken (the white meat was especially afflicted). Most of the recipes I'd found called for 6 to 24 hours of marinating in mixtures heavy on lime juice, vinegar, or both; the long exposure to the acid was denaturing the meat and making it dry and chalky when cooked—not to mention sour. To ensure juicy and moist meat, I tried brining the chicken for an hour; this fixed the texture problems, but it didn't let me imbue the meat with spice and citrus.

So I turned to salting, which has the same benefits as brining but allows the cook to incorporate more flavors. I started with a combination of salt and lime zest, thinking I could add lime flavor without the drawback of too much acid. But it didn't work: My tasters missed the bright pucker of the juice. After tinkering my way through 10-plus batches (using a simple seasoned-flour coating for now), I landed on a marinade of salt and pepper, a healthy dose

What makes this fried chicken different? A garlicky lime marinade, plenty of spice in the dredge, and an extra-crispy coating.

of garlic, cumin, hot smoked paprika, and dried oregano, plus lime zest and ¼ cup of lime juice for one cut-up chicken. Through several tests, I found that the lime juice added lots of flavor and caused no textural problems as long as I kept the marinating time between 1 and 2 hours.

Moving on to the coating, I wanted the classic Latin fried chicken version: thin and crispy with just enough spicing to complement the well-seasoned meat. A combination of flour cut with cornstarch made for a nice, light coating, but a test kitchen trick—the addition of just a teaspoon of baking powder to the flour mix—made it extra-crispy. I discovered that lightly beaten egg whites made the best "glue" to adhere the seasoned flour. Salt, pepper, granulated garlic, white pepper, cumin, and a pinch of cayenne added strong, but not overwhelming, flavor.

Finally, refrigerating the marinated, dredged chicken on a wire rack for at least 30 minutes (or up to 2 hours) before frying made sure the coating set up nicely and thus stayed put on the fried chicken.

Whether your idea of "South" is Savannah or San Salvador, this is one fried chicken recipe that you're definitely going to want to make.

LATIN FRIED CHICKEN Serves 4

Don't let the chicken marinate any longer than 2 hours or it will toughen from the lime juice. Use a Dutch oven that holds 6 quarts or more.

MARINADE

- 2 tablespoons kosher salt
- 6 garlic cloves, chopped coarse
- 1 tablespoon pepper
- 1 tablespoon ground cumin
- 2 teaspoons smoked paprika
- 2 teaspoons dried oregano
- 2 teaspoons grated lime zest plus ¼ cup juice (2 limes)
- 3 pounds bone-in chicken pieces (split breasts cut in half crosswise, drumsticks, thighs, and/or wings), trimmed

COATING

- 1¼ cups all-purpose flour
- ¾ cup cornstarch
- 1 tablespoon pepper
- 1 tablespoon granulated garlic
- 1 teaspoon baking powder
- 1 teaspoon white pepper
- 1 teaspoon kosher salt
- 1 teaspoon ground cumin
- ¼ teaspoon cayenne pepper
- 3 large egg whites, lightly beaten

- 3 quarts vegetable or peanut oil

1. FOR THE MARINADE: Combine salt, garlic, pepper, cumin, paprika, oregano, and lime zest and juice in bowl. Add chicken and turn to coat thoroughly. Cover with plastic wrap and refrigerate for at least 1 hour or up to 2 hours.

2. FOR THE COATING: Whisk flour, cornstarch, pepper, granulated garlic, baking powder, white pepper, salt, cumin, and cayenne together in bowl. Place egg whites in shallow dish.

3. Set wire rack in rimmed baking sheet. Remove chicken from marinade and scrape off solids. Pat chicken dry with paper towels. Working with 1 piece at a time, dip chicken into egg whites to thoroughly coat, letting excess drip back into dish. Dredge chicken in flour mixture, pressing to adhere. Transfer chicken to prepared wire rack and refrigerate for at least 30 minutes or up to 2 hours.

4. Add oil to large Dutch oven until it measures about 2 inches deep and heat over medium-high heat to 325 degrees. Add half of chicken to hot oil and fry until breasts register 160 degrees and drumsticks/thighs register 175 degrees, 13 to 16 minutes. Adjust burner, if necessary, to maintain oil temperature between 300 and 325 degrees. Transfer chicken to clean wire rack set in rimmed baking sheet. Return oil to 325 degrees and repeat with remaining chicken. Serve.

Fire and Ice Salad

Fire and ice are usually opposites, but in this fresh, easy summer salad they should be perfect complements. BY CRISTIN WALSH

THIS TRADITIONAL SOUTHERN picnic salad, made with tomatoes, onion, and cucumbers in a spicy, vinegary dressing that leaves the vegetables slightly pickled, is anything but subtle. To me, that means it's a perfect attention grabber for a hot summer day.

I collected recipes and headed to the kitchen. Alas, none of these salads grabbed our attention in a good way. Some were too sweet, with no heat, while others were too acidic, with vinegar dominating all the other flavors. Even worse, liquid from watery tomatoes and cucumbers diluted the dressing, muting its flavors so it made only a faint impression. I set to work to create a version of this salad worthy of its beguiling name.

I started with the obligatory trio of tomatoes, cucumbers, and onions, choosing red onions because of their mild, sweet flavor. I also opted to add green bell pepper for a pop of color and a little crunch. With the vegetables all set, I focused on the dressing.

Most dressings consisted of vinegar, sugar, salt and pepper, mustard seeds or powder, and something to provide some heat—be it cayenne, red pepper flakes, horseradish, or some combination of the three. Based on my initial tests, I used white wine vinegar for its mild acidity and chose dry mustard over mustard seeds because the powder had a more assertive and complex flavor. Tasters also preferred red pepper flakes as the heat source, since they provided an up-front spiciness that paired well with the tang of the vinegar. In addition, I increased the overall amount of the dressing, so there would be a better ratio of dressing to residual vegetable liquid. No more muted flavors.

Now for a little fine-tuning. To enhance the eye-opening effect of the dressing, I turned to another eye-opening tomato concoction, the Bloody Mary, and added a touch of celery salt. I tossed this now-potent dressing with the vegetables, and after an hour in the refrigerator, the flavors had melded. The tomatoes had slightly softened, yet the cucumbers were still crisp and cold; the red pepper flakes and dry mustard pinched your nose, while the vegetables took on a lightly pickled flavor. This salad

not only grabbed your attention but kept it for as long as you needed to finish your bowl.

A strong, vinegary dressing is the critical part of this bracing summer salad.

FIRE AND ICE SALAD Serves 6 to 8

It's important to refrigerate the dressed salad for at least 1 hour before serving so the tomatoes and cucumbers can release their juices and balance the dressing, as well as absorb the flavor. In fact it can sit for up to 24 hours, chilled, with no further dilution of flavor.

- ½ cup white wine vinegar
- 1 tablespoon sugar
- 2 teaspoons salt
- 1 teaspoon dry mustard
- ½ teaspoon celery salt
- ¼ teaspoon red pepper flakes
- ⅛ teaspoon pepper
- 2 pounds tomatoes, cored and cut into ½-inch-thick wedges
- 2 cucumbers, peeled and sliced ¼ inch thick
- 1 green bell pepper, stemmed, seeded, and sliced into thin matchsticks
- 1 red onion, halved and sliced thin

Whisk vinegar, sugar, salt, mustard, celery salt, pepper flakes, and pepper together in large bowl. Add tomatoes, cucumbers, bell pepper, and onion and toss to combine. Refrigerate salad for at least 1 hour or up to 24 hours. Serve.

Stuffed Tomatoes

Stuffed tomatoes always sound fantastic, but too often you end up with tasteless tomatoes and a lackluster stuffing that falls out in a clump. BY CHRISTIE MORRISON

RECIPES FOR STUFFED tomatoes run the gamut. The tomatoes can be raw or cooked and the fillings can be almost anything, from bread crumbs to custards to vegetables, grains, ground meat, and much more. I even found a recipe for dessert stuffed tomatoes served with ice cream. I selected a handful of recipes that represented a range of options, ordered a few cases of tomatoes, and went to work slicing off tops, hollowing out insides, and scooping in stuffings.

Several hours later, I lined up the array on the counter for my tasters. After sampling the lot, we found that we preferred baked tomatoes rather than raw. Baking concentrated the tomatoes' flavor, softened their texture (making them easier to eat), and helped meld the tomato case with the stuffing. As for that stuffing, I decided to use couscous as my base. I liked how its small grains absorbed some of the tomato juices, yet stayed moist and cohesive while the tomatoes baked. Lastly, we preferred recipes that included a crunchy element for contrast, often a bread-crumb topping. I'd include that, too.

This initial round of testing also clarified the problems I would face. First: Tomatoes are up to 94 percent water—juiciness is typically a virtue but not when flavors get watered down and stuffed tomatoes sit in pools of liquid. Second, in many cases there was no integration between the tomato casing and the stuffing, which often fell out on the plate as soon as you put knife to tomato. Finally, many of the stuffings were lackluster, striking me as relics of gardening club luncheons. I'd need to add some punch to mine.

I set to work. To concentrate the tomato flavor, clearly I needed to remove some of their liquid. I'd salt the cored tomatoes, a technique we often use to draw moisture out of watery vegetables. This did improve the tomatoes' flavor, but not enough; they lacked a little in sweetness. This reminded me that I had seen one recipe that called for sugaring, rather than salting, the tomatoes. I tested tomatoes sprinkled with sugar, salt, and a combination of the two. The combination worked nicely, producing stuffed tomatoes that were less watery and also delicately sweet.

At this point I started wondering about all the tomato pulp, flesh,

To keep our bread-crumb topping crisp, we bake the tomato caps alongside the stuffed tomatoes and re-top the tomatoes just before serving.

and juice that I had removed to make room for the filling. Throwing it away seemed just too wasteful, and it also seemed like adding it to the stuffing would help integrate the flavors of the dish. (Not to mention that much of the glutamate taste—umami—in a fresh tomato is found in the gel.) But when I chopped some of the tomato flesh and stirred it into the filling, it made the filling watery. Then it occurred to me

that since the couscous needed to be hydrated, maybe I could lose the traditional chicken broth and instead use the tomato liquids. Accordingly, I drained the pulp to extract the tomato juice and used that to plump the grains. The tomato flavor was intense and delicious.

I wanted to bolster the stuffing's flavor even more, so after a few trial runs, I added sautéed onion and garlic, chopped baby spinach, lemon zest,

and red pepper flakes. A little shredded cheese brought it all together. I tried a few types and landed on the nutty sweetness and meltability of Gruyère.

After only 20 minutes in a 375-degree oven, the tomatoes were just right. My knife sliced through cleanly, the stuffing stayed put, and the tomatoes were tender and sweet. All that was missing was a bit of crunch. To get it, I tossed panko bread crumbs with a little more shredded Gruyère. I topped each tomato with a sprinkling of the panko mixture before baking. But in the short baking time, the panko didn't brown. The next time, I pretoasted the panko in oil in a skillet before topping the tomatoes. Problem solved.

When I took this batch out of the oven and served it, I noticed a little tomato water pooling at the bottom of the baking dish. It seemed a shame to lose those flavorful liquids, so I took the opportunity to whisk in a spoonful of vinegar, and I dribbled the bright juices over the stuffed tomatoes. These tomatoes were so good that I couldn't resist developing a couple of variations.

KEY STEPS **Making Flavorful Stuffed Tomatoes**

One way to ensure bland stuffed tomatoes is to carelessly throw away the seeds and "jelly" you hollow out of each tomato—that pulp contains much of the tomatoes' savory flavor. We press the pulp to extract the tomato liquid, which we then use to boost the flavor of the couscous in the stuffing.

SCOOP
Use a melon baller to evenly and neatly hollow out the tomatoes.

PRESS THE PULP
Place the tomato pulp in a strainer and press it to extract the juice.

USE THE JUICE
The tomato juice takes the place of water or stock in hydrating the couscous.

STUFFED TOMATOES Serves 6

Look for large tomatoes, about 3 inches in diameter.

- **6 large vine-ripened tomatoes (8 to 10 ounces each)**
- **1 tablespoon sugar**
- **Kosher salt and pepper**
- **4½ tablespoons extra-virgin olive oil**
- **¼ cup panko bread crumbs**
- **3 ounces Gruyère cheese, shredded (¾ cup)**
- **1 onion, halved and sliced thin**
- **2 garlic cloves, minced**
- **⅛ teaspoon red pepper flakes**
- **8 ounces (8 cups) baby spinach, chopped coarse**
- **1 cup couscous**
- **½ teaspoon grated lemon zest**
- **1 tablespoon red wine vinegar**

1. Adjust oven rack to middle position and heat oven to 375 degrees. Cut top ½ inch off stem end of tomatoes and set aside. Using melon baller, scoop out tomato pulp and transfer to fine-mesh strainer set over bowl. Press on pulp with wooden spoon to extract juice; set aside juice and discard pulp. (You should have about ⅔ cup tomato juice; if not, add water as needed to equal ⅔ cup.)

2. Combine sugar and 1 tablespoon salt in bowl. Sprinkle each tomato cavity with 1 teaspoon sugar mixture, then turn tomatoes upside down on plate to drain for 30 minutes.

3. Combine 1½ teaspoons oil and panko in 10-inch skillet and toast over medium-high heat, stirring frequently, until golden brown, about 3 minutes. Transfer to bowl and let cool for 10 minutes. Stir in ¼ cup Gruyère.

4. Heat 2 tablespoons oil in now-empty skillet over medium heat until shimmering. Add onion and ½ teaspoon salt and cook until softened, 5 to 7 minutes. Stir in garlic and pepper flakes and cook until fragrant, about 30 seconds. Add spinach, 1 handful at a time, and cook until wilted, about 3 minutes. Stir in couscous, lemon zest, and reserved tomato juice. Cover, remove from heat, and let sit until couscous has absorbed liquid, about 7 minutes. Transfer couscous mixture to bowl and stir in remaining ½ cup Gruyère. Season with salt and pepper to taste.

5. Coat bottom of 13 by 9-inch baking dish with remaining 2 tablespoons oil. Blot tomato cavities dry with paper towels and season with salt and pepper. Pack each tomato with couscous mixture, about ½ cup per tomato, mounding excess. Top stuffed tomatoes with 1 heaping tablespoon panko mixture. Place tomatoes in prepared dish. Season reserved tops with salt and pepper and place in empty spaces in dish.

6. Bake, uncovered, until tomatoes have softened but still hold their shape, about 20 minutes. Using slotted spoon, transfer to serving platter. Whisk vinegar into oil remaining in dish, then drizzle over tomatoes. Place tops on tomatoes and serve.

STUFFED TOMATOES WITH BACON

Substitute shredded smoked cheddar for Gruyère. Stir 3 slices chopped, cooked bacon into cooked couscous mixture with cheddar in step 4.

STUFFED TOMATOES WITH CAPERS AND PINE NUTS

Substitute shredded mozzarella for Gruyère. Stir 2 tablespoons rinsed capers and 2 tablespoons toasted pine nuts into cooked couscous mixture with mozzarella in step 4.

STUFFED TOMATOES WITH CURRANTS AND PISTACHIOS

Substitute crumbled feta for Gruyère. Stir 2 tablespoons currants and 2 tablespoons chopped pistachios into cooked couscous mixture with feta in step 4.

STUFFED TOMATOES WITH OLIVES AND ORANGE

Substitute shredded Manchego for Gruyère. Substitute ¼ teaspoon grated orange zest for lemon zest. Stir ¼ cup pitted kalamata olives, chopped, into cooked couscous mixture with Manchego in step 4.

TESTING TOMATO CORERS

Tomato corers help you hollow out the stem and the tough core of a tomato. But do they work any better than a paring knife? We tested five models, all priced under $8, and rated each on speed, precision, and comfort compared with our winning paring knife, the Wüsthof Classic with PEtec (Precision Edge Technology), 3½-Inch ($39.95). Some were dull and uncomfortable or couldn't reach the whole core. But the best model, the Norpro Tomato Core It, was deft and lightweight; it made the cleanest, easiest cuts and has a rounded-off plastic handle that was comfortable in hands large and small. A knife works well, but this inexpensive corer cut our prep time in half—handy when you're working with large quantities of tomatoes for stuffing, canning, or making sauce. To read the full testing story, visit **CooksCountry.com/july14**. –HANNAH CROWLEY

KEY **Good** ★★★ **Fair** ★★ **Poor** ★

RECOMMENDED	CRITERIA	TESTERS' NOTES
NORPRO Tomato Core It **Model:** 1176 **Price:** $2.99 	**Speed** ★★★ **Precision** ★★★ **Comfort** ★★½	This lightweight winning corer has the best head-handle combination for comfort and sharp, neat scooping. It made tidy cuts and went through tomatoes twice as fast as a paring knife did.
MESSERMEISTER Pro-Touch Tomato Shark **Model:** Black: 800-151; red: 800-151/R **Price:** $7 	**Speed** ★★½ **Precision** ★★½ **Comfort** ★★★	This corer had the best handle: big, grippy, and comfortable. But it had a slightly duller serrated edge than our winner, so we had to use a bit more force, though not enough to mangle our tomatoes.
RECOMMENDED WITH RESERVATIONS		
UPDATE INTERNATIONAL Tomato Stem Corer **Model:** TSC-4 **Price:** $1.79 	**Speed** ★★★ **Precision** ★★★ **Comfort** ★	This cheap, deft little corer expertly sliced through tomato flesh, but the flat metal handle was sharp, too, and dug into our hands after a while. We found this tool useful for projects with five tomatoes or fewer but would likely just use a knife.
CHEF'N StemGem **Model:** 102-138-005 **Price:** $7.84 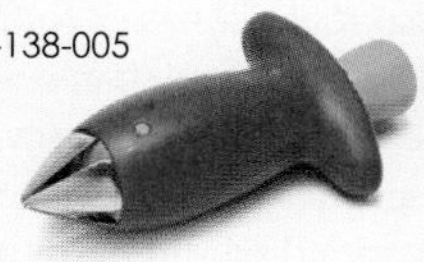	**Speed** ★½ **Precision** ★★ **Comfort** ★★★	This huller's pincer-style prongs plucked out the stem with an easy twist, but it couldn't retrieve bits of core left deeper in the body of the tomato. This tool works best with small tomatoes and strawberries.
NOT RECOMMENDED		
KUCHENPROFI Tomato & Strawberry Corer **Model:** 914002800 **Price:** $7.80 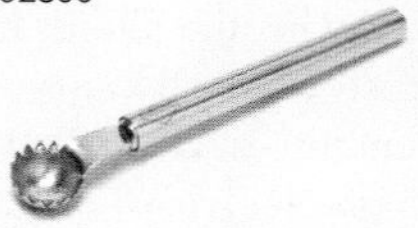	**Speed** ★★ **Precision** ★½ **Comfort** ★½	This corer was the dullest and turned out ragged tomatoes because we had to use more force to push through the skin. It also had a thin, round handle made of smooth metal that was slippery and cramped our hands.

Peanut Butter Pie

Smooth, creamy peanut butter seems like a natural for pie. But keeping its flavor strong
while creating a light, almost airy texture took some doing. BY CRISTIN WALSH

WITH ITS SMOOTH, creamy texture and robust peanut flavor, it's no surprise that peanut butter was pressed into service as a pie filling by some nameless Southern cook back in the early 1970s. Since then, peanut butter pie—a mousselike peanut butter filling nestled in a crumb crust and topped with whipped cream or chocolate sauce—has gone on to become a fixture on picnic tables all over the country. Some recipes call for cooking the peanut butter with eggs, dairy, and sweeteners to create a pudding-style filling, while others take the even easier (and more popular) route of simply combining peanut butter with cream cheese and confectioners' sugar in a no-bake filling.

For my initial testing, I tried both styles of pie. Tasters appreciated the relatively light texture of the ones with pudding-style fillings, but the pies lacked rich peanut butter flavor and were often so loose that they were unsliceable. The no-cook fillings, on the other hand, had good peanut butter flavor, but they were too dense and either too sweet or too tangy.

Given the stronger peanut butter flavor of the no-cook fillings, I decided to go that route with my pie. I started out with a relatively standard version, mixing together 6 ounces of cream cheese, ½ cup of peanut butter, and ¾ cup of confectioners' sugar in a stand mixer until well combined and then folding in ¾ cup of whipped cream for lightness. It wasn't a bad start, since the whipped cream was helping lighten the otherwise thick texture, but the flavor of the cream cheese obscured the big peanut flavor I was looking for. After several days spent testing various ratios, I finally landed on an additional ¼ cup of peanut butter.

This was a significant enough jump in the amount of peanut butter that its flavor was in the forefront, but not so much that it obliterated the slight tang of the cream cheese.

Now I turned to the filling's texture. The problem with combining cream cheese and peanut butter is that, independently, each feels rather thick and heavy in the mouth; put them together and that effect is compounded. Though the whipped cream did lighten the texture of the filling somewhat, the

▶ Which creamy peanut butter is best? Read our taste test at CooksCountry.com/creamypeanutbutter.

filling was still too heavy. But what if I added some cream to the initial mixture and turned up the mixer speed so that it would aerate more during mixing? (Having a more liquid initial mixture would also make it easier to fold in the whipped cream later, so less aeration would be lost.) I lined up several pies for tasting, each with a different amount of cream added to the initial mixture, and waited. Tasters preferred the pie with 3 tablespoons of cream, which had a lighter, more mousselike texture than previous versions did.

Satisfied with the filling, I moved on to the crust. I had all kinds of suggestions from coworkers, including, "Did you try a pretzel crust?" The pretzel crusts I tried were either sandy and

We beat peanut butter, cream cheese, confectioners' sugar, and just a little cream together to make a light, flavorful base that stands up straight and slices cleanly.

falling apart or required so much butter to stay together that they were too rich for this pie. After many tests and much discussion, I opted to stick with an already proven test kitchen recipe: the graham cracker crumb crust. But to enhance the peanut butter flavor, I swapped out the granulated sugar that's typical in graham cracker crumb crusts for brown sugar; its caramel notes played off the peanut butter beautifully.

Now for the fun part: the toppings. Chocolate sauce was a real contender, but it turned out that it distracted too much from the peanut butter flavor I had worked so hard to bring to the fore. Instead, I went with a whipped cream topping, since it added some textural lightness without introducing

a distracting flavor. I decided to play up the salty-sweet peanut taste even more by scattering honey-roasted peanuts over both the baked crust and the top of the chilled pie. (Despite the time it takes to make them, homemade candied peanuts were preferred by tasters who thought the honey-roasted nuts were a little too salty. A recipe for candied peanuts follows.)

Now I had it: With its creamy and light filling, whipped cream topping, crunchy candied peanuts, and graham cracker crumb crust, this was a fully grown-up, fully delicious dessert.

PEANUT BUTTER PIE Serves 8

All-natural peanut butters will work in this recipe. You can use our Homemade Candied Peanuts (recipe follows) in place of the honey-roasted peanuts.

- 9 whole graham crackers, broken into 1-inch pieces
- 3 tablespoons packed light brown sugar
- 5 tablespoons unsalted butter, melted
- ½ cup honey-roasted peanuts, chopped
- ¾ cup (3 ounces) plus 2 tablespoons confectioners' sugar
- ¾ cup creamy peanut butter
- 6 ounces cream cheese, softened
- 1¾ cups heavy cream
- 1 teaspoon vanilla extract

1. Adjust oven rack to middle position and heat oven to 325 degrees. Grease 9-inch pie plate. Process graham crackers and brown sugar in food processor until finely ground, about 30 seconds. Add melted butter and pulse until combined, about 8 pulses.

2. Transfer crumbs to prepared plate. Using bottom of dry measuring cup, press crumbs into bottom and up sides of plate. Bake until crust is fragrant and beginning to brown, 12 to 14 minutes, rotating plate halfway through baking. Let crust cool completely on wire rack, about 30 minutes. Spread ⅓ cup peanuts evenly over bottom of cooled crust.

3. Using stand mixer fitted with whisk, mix ¾ cup confectioners' sugar, peanut butter, cream cheese, and 3 tablespoons cream on low speed until combined, about 1 minute. Increase speed to medium-high and whip until fluffy, about 1 minute. Transfer to large bowl; set aside.

4. In now-empty mixer bowl, whip ¾ cup cream on medium-low speed

until foamy, about 1 minute. Increase speed to high and whip until stiff peaks form, 1 to 3 minutes. Gently fold whipped cream into peanut butter mixture in 2 additions until no white streaks remain. Spoon filling into crust and spread into even layer.

5. In now-empty mixer bowl, whip vanilla, remaining cream, and remaining 2 tablespoons confectioners' sugar on medium-low speed until foamy, about 1 minute. Increase speed to high and whip until stiff peaks form, 1 to 3 minutes. Spread whipped cream evenly over filling. Refrigerate until set, about 2 hours. Sprinkle with remaining peanuts. Serve.

PEANUT BUTTER PIE WITH CHOCOLATE GRAHAM CRUST
In step 1, substitute chocolate graham crackers for graham crackers.

HOMEMADE CANDIED PEANUTS Makes about ½ cup

- ½ cup dry-roasted peanuts
- 2 tablespoons granulated sugar
- 2 tablespoons water
- ¼ teaspoon salt

1. Line baking sheet with parchment paper. Bring all ingredients to boil in medium saucepan over medium heat. Cook, stirring constantly, until water evaporates and sugar appears dry, opaque, and somewhat crystallized and evenly coats peanuts, about 5 minutes.

2. Reduce heat to low and continue to stir peanuts until sugar turns amber color, about 2 minutes longer. Transfer peanuts to prepared sheet and spread in even layer. Let cool completely, about 10 minutes.

Cherry Crisp

To speed up and streamline our cherry crisp, we had to think outside the oven. BY SARAH GABRIEL

SINCE THE BYWORD for fruit crisps is "easy," when I decided to create a recipe for cherry crisp, I started with easy-to-find sweet (rather than sour) cherries. And hoping to avoid having to invest the time to pit fresh ones, I tested frozen. Fortunately, when mixed with sugar and baked, they were hard to tell from fresh.

But there was a problem with all the recipes I found. Unless the filling was stiff and gloppy (no thanks), it boiled up over the streusel topping, making it soggy. Dried cherries did absorb some of the juice in the looser fillings, but not enough. Prebaking the topping did work, but between baking the topping for 25 minutes and the filling for 45 minutes, plus shuffling the baking dish in and out of the oven to add the topping, this crisp was taking way too long.

Maybe cooking the filling in a skillet on the stove would bring it to a boil—and therefore thicken the cornstarch—faster. I combined the frozen cherries, sugar, and flavorings in a skillet, and then cooked them until the cherries thawed (about 7 minutes). I added the dried cherries, simmered them for a few minutes, and then stirred in the cornstarch. Just 2 minutes later, the filling was fully thickened; I had done in 12 minutes what had previously taken 45. I added the topping that I'd baked in the oven and returned the pan to the heat for a minute to join the two. The filling was perfectly thickened, and the topping was glazed with syrup on the edge but still crunchy. But wait: Could I do this all in one pan?

After a few failures, I figured out that by putting some of the almonds in the pan first to toast, and then adding the rest of the topping ingredients, I could cook the topping in the skillet in about 15 minutes. Only one pan was dirtied, plus the whole thing took only 40 minutes start to finish. Mission accomplished.

NO-BAKE CHERRY CRISP
Serves 6
There's no need to thaw the cherries.

TOPPING
- ¾ cup sliced almonds
- ⅔ cup (3⅓ ounces) all-purpose flour
- ¼ cup packed (1¾ ounces) light brown sugar
- ¼ cup (1¾ ounces) granulated sugar
- ½ teaspoon vanilla extract

We figured out how to cook both filling and topping in a skillet, while keeping the topping crisp.

- ¼ teaspoon ground cinnamon
- ¼ teaspoon salt
- 6 tablespoons unsalted butter, melted

FILLING
- ⅓ cup (2⅓ ounces) granulated sugar
- 1 tablespoon cornstarch
- 2 pounds frozen sweet cherries
- 1 tablespoon lemon juice
- 1 teaspoon vanilla extract
- ½ teaspoon salt
- ¼ teaspoon almond extract
- ⅔ cup dried cherries

1. FOR THE TOPPING: Finely chop ¼ cup almonds. Combine flour, brown sugar, granulated sugar, vanilla, cinnamon, salt, and chopped almonds in bowl. Stir in melted butter until mixture resembles wet sand and no dry flour remains.

2. Toast remaining ½ cup almonds in 10-inch nonstick skillet over medium-low heat until just beginning to brown, about 4 minutes. Add flour mixture and cook, stirring constantly, until lightly browned, 6 to 8 minutes; transfer to plate to cool. Wipe out skillet.

3. FOR THE FILLING: Combine 2 tablespoons sugar and cornstarch in small bowl; set aside. Combine cherries, lemon juice, vanilla, salt, almond extract, and remaining sugar in now-empty skillet. Cover and cook over medium heat until cherries thaw and release their juice, about 7 minutes, stirring halfway through cooking. Uncover, stir in dried cherries, and simmer until cherries are very tender, about 3 minutes.

4. Stir in cornstarch mixture and simmer, stirring constantly, until thickened, 1 to 3 minutes. Remove skillet from heat and distribute topping evenly over filling. Return skillet to medium-low heat and cook until filling is bubbling around edges, about 3 minutes. Remove from heat; let cool for at least 30 minutes before serving.

Cooking Class Grilled Whole Chicken

Whole birds spend more time on the grill, which means more grill flavor. But all too often you end up with flabby skin, fierce flare-ups, and bland, unevenly cooked meat. Here's how to get it right. BY REBECCAH MARSTERS

SHOPPING Picking the Right Bird
With all the different terms you find on chicken packages, it can be hard to know exactly what you're buying. Our cheat sheet will help you choose the right bird.

Choose Air-Chilled
During water chilling, chickens absorb water and plump, taking on up to 14 percent of their body weight—weight that you're paying for by the pound. Water chilling can also cause spongy meat and washed-out flavor. Look for air-chilled birds instead; they have a better texture and more flavor.

The Best Birds?
Mary's Free Range Air Chilled Chicken (also sold as Pitman's) and Bell & Evans Air Chilled Premium Fresh Chicken were the winners of a recent test kitchen taste test.

Avoid Injected or Enhanced
These chickens have been injected with a solution of chicken broth, salt, and flavorings that plump the meat but can also make it spongy, and again, inflate cost.

Natural Chickens?
Any claims about antibiotics aren't strictly regulated, so unless the bird's organic, take these with a grain of salt. Natural and all-natural just mean that no synthetic substances have been added to the meat.

ESSENTIAL GEAR Kitchen Shears
Breaking down a chicken is quite easy to do, but a good pair of kitchen shears is essential. A recent testing helped us understand the important features of this tool. The blades should be sharp and strong enough to cut through bones without warping, but precise enough for delicate tasks. High-carbon stainless steel stays sharp for a long time, and microserrations on the blades anchor the shears to whatever you're cutting, preventing dangerous slips. We also like shears that allow us to adjust the tension. By the end of our testing, we'd found a winning pair that works for both righties and lefties, plus a more affordable pair that doesn't have adjustable tension but met all our other requirements.

THE ULTIMATE SHEARS
Shun Classic Kitchen Shears ($49.95).

OUR BEST BUY
J.A. Henckels International Kitchen Shears—Take Apart ($14.95).

Core Techniques

Flatten It Out
A whole chicken needs more time on the grill than chicken parts do. But grilled in its natural shape, a whole bird cooks unevenly, and it is hard to get the skin crispy all over. Butterflying and flattening the bird not only cuts down on cooking time (it's still longer than parts) but also means all the skin is in contact with the grill at once.

Salt Under the Skin
Brining chicken seasons the meat and helps keep it moist, but the added water means the skin will not crisp as well. Rubbing salt under the chicken skin seasons the meat deeply and keeps the skin dry so it can more easily render and crisp. We added lemon zest to the salt here, but herbs and spice rubs also work well.

Prevent Flare-ups
The cause of most flare-ups is fat dripping onto the fire and igniting. Trimming excess fat from the bird is one way to minimize flare-ups, but another culprit can be excess oil or sugar from marinades or sauces. If you marinate your chicken before grilling, make sure to pat it dry thoroughly. Better yet, use dry seasonings or rubs as we do here, and add sauce only after grilling. And if you do have flare-ups, just move the chicken to the side of the grill with no coals until the flare-ups die.

Go Slow to Render
Even when grilled chicken looks pleasantly charred, biting into it can reveal rubbery skin and pockets of fat. Chicken skin needs relatively high heat to crisp, but before this can happen, the fat underneath the skin must render and the moisture must evaporate. Starting the birds on the cooler side of the grill provides moderate heat and ample time for the subcutaneous fat to melt out and for evaporation to occur. Only after the chickens are cooked and the skin is golden and rendered do we slide them over the hot fire to sear.

STEP BY STEP Ten Steps to Grilled Whole Chicken

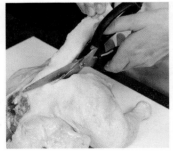

1. BREAK IT DOWN
Use kitchen shears to remove the backbone from the chicken and open it up like a book.
WHY? Butterflying the chicken means all the skin is on the same side so it can crisp up on the grill.

2. POUND IT OUT
Use a meat pounder to gently pound the breasts to an even thickness.
WHY? Pounding the bird creates a flat surface to encourage even browning and cooking.

3. SEASON UNDER SKIN
Rub a mixture of lemon zest, salt, and pepper under the chicken skin and then season the bird all over with salt and pepper.
WHY? Getting the seasonings in direct contact with the meat helps them permeate and prevents them from burning.

4. REST UNCOVERED
Place the chickens on a rack set in a rimmed baking sheet and refrigerate, uncovered, for at least an hour.
WHY? The salt mixture needs time to penetrate; leaving the birds uncovered helps dry out the skin so it crisps on the grill.

5. MAKE LONG-BURNING FIRE
Pour lit coals on one side of the bottom grate and top them with unlit charcoal.
WHY? Using both lit and unlit charcoal creates a longer-burning fire so there's enough heat left to sear the chickens after an hour of gentle cooking.

GRILLED BUTTERFLIED LEMON CHICKEN Serves 8

- 2 (4-pound) whole chickens, giblets discarded
- 5 lemons
  Salt and pepper
- 1 (13 by 9-inch) disposable aluminum pan (if using charcoal)
- 1 garlic clove, minced
- 2 tablespoons minced fresh parsley
- 2 teaspoons Dijon mustard
- 1 teaspoon sugar
- ⅔ cup extra-virgin olive oil

1. Set wire rack in rimmed baking sheet. Working with 1 chicken at a time, place chicken breast side down on cutting board. Using kitchen shears, cut through bones on either side of backbone; discard backbone. Trim chicken of excess fat and skin. Flip chicken over and press on breastbone to flatten. Cover chicken with plastic wrap and pound breasts with meat pounder to even thickness.

2. Grate 2 teaspoons zest from 1 lemon (halve and reserve lemon) and mix with 2 teaspoons salt and 1 teaspoon pepper in bowl. Pat chickens dry with paper towels and, using your fingers or handle of wooden spoon, gently loosen skin covering breasts and thighs. Rub zest mixture under skin, then season exterior of chicken with salt and pepper. Tuck wingtips behind breasts and transfer chickens to prepared rack. Refrigerate, uncovered, for at least 1 hour or up to 24 hours.

3A. FOR A CHARCOAL GRILL: Open bottom vent completely and place disposable pan on 1 side of grill with long side of pan facing center of grill. Light large chimney starter filled with charcoal briquettes (6 quarts). When top coals are partially covered with ash, pour evenly over other half of grill (opposite disposable pan). Scatter 20 unlit coals on top of lit coals. Set cooking grate in place, cover, and open lid vent completely. Heat grill until hot, about 5 minutes.

3B. FOR A GAS GRILL: Turn all burners to high, cover, and heat grill until hot, about 15 minutes. Leave primary burner on high and turn other burner(s) to low. (Adjust primary burner as needed to maintain grill temperature of 350 to 375 degrees.)

4. Clean and oil cooking grate. Halve remaining 4 lemons and place, along with reserved lemon halves, cut side down on hotter side of grill. Place chickens skin side down on cooler side of grill, with legs pointing toward fire; cover, placing lid vent over chickens on charcoal grill.

5. Grill lemons until deep brown and caramelized, 5 to 8 minutes; transfer to bowl. Continue to grill chickens, covered, until breasts register 160 degrees and thighs register 175 degrees, 40 to 50 minutes longer. Slide chickens to hotter side of grill and cook, uncovered, until skin is well browned, 2 to 4 minutes. Transfer chickens to carving board skin side up, tent loosely with aluminum foil, and let rest for 15 minutes.

6. Meanwhile, squeeze ⅓ cup juice from grilled lemons into bowl. (Cut any unsqueezed lemons into wedges for serving.) Using flat side of knife, mash garlic and ½ teaspoon salt into paste and add to bowl with lemon juice. Whisk in parsley, mustard, sugar, and ½ teaspoon pepper. Slowly whisk in oil until emulsified.

7. Carve chickens, transfer to serving platter, and pour ⅓ cup vinaigrette over chicken. Serve, passing remaining vinaigrette and grilled lemon wedges separately.

6. GRILL LEMONS
Place the lemons cut side down over the hotter side of the grill.
WHY? For maximum lemon flavor without the bitterness and pucker of raw lemons, caramelizing the citrus on the grill concentrates the juices and mellows the tang.

7. COOK GENTLY
Place the chickens skin side down on the cooler side of the grill with the legs nearest the heat.
WHY? Moderate heat allows the skin to render without flare-ups, and pointing the legs toward the fire means the delicate white meat won't overcook.

8. SEAR HOT
Once the skin is golden and the chickens are cooked through, slide them to the hotter side of the grill for a few minutes.
WHY? Once the fat has rendered, the hot fire will crisp the skin and develop flavorful char.

9. LET REST
Tent the chickens loosely with foil and let them rest for 15 minutes.
WHY? Resting the birds allows the juices to redistribute for more moist and flavorful meat.

10. MAKE SAUCE, SERVE
Use the juice from the grilled lemons to make a garlicky vinaigrette for the chicken.
WHY? The smoky lemon juice makes a delicious base for the bold vinaigrette.

Slow Cooker Chicken Parmesan

Sometimes the trick to putting together a great dish is taking it apart. BY SARAH GABRIEL

CHICKEN PARMESAN MAY seem simple at first glance, but a closer look shows that between the breading, frying, assembling, and baking, it's actually a substantial project. Because I love the dish but don't fancy spending all day making it, I was hoping the slow cooker might be able to offer an easier approach. I collected a stack of slow-cooker recipes and headed into the test kitchen to try my luck.

I found three basic approaches: Some recipes keep the initial breading and frying step. Others bread the boneless chicken breasts and put them in the cooker raw. And still others dispense with breading altogether, adding unadorned chicken breasts to the cooker with jarred pasta sauce. I quickly found that breading and frying before loading the chicken and sauce in the cooker simply didn't work—the crumb coating got bloated and soggy. The same held true for the chicken that was breaded but not fried. Unadorned chicken breasts didn't have the displeasing pasty coating . . . but they didn't really taste like chicken Parmesan either.

One thing all the recipes shared was that they called for 5 to 8 hours of cooking, which is way too long for boneless chicken breasts. Also common to all the recipes was thin and flavorless sauce; once the chicken released its juice, the sauces became watery and bland. Still, most of the problems, while serious, seemed fixable.

The crunchy, cheesy crumbs go on only after the chicken is cooked.

> **Go to CooksCountry. com/breadcrumbs** to find out which bread crumbs we like best.

Solving the overcooking issue was easy. I loaded six boneless, skinless chicken breasts in the slow cooker with a jar of our favorite pasta sauce, covered it, and cooked the chicken on low, taking the temperature of the meat every half-hour after the 2-hour mark. The breasts were perfectly done—and just as moist as if I'd baked or poached them—after 3 to 4 hours on low (160 degrees is the target temperature; we give a range of times because each slow cooker heats differently).

Next up were the soggy coating and washed-out sauce. Breading and frying before slow cooking didn't make any sense to me—it was too much work, and the coating got soggy—but the other

two obvious options (breading but not frying, and skipping the breading altogether) weren't going to cut it either. Could I cook the breading separately and then coat the cooked chicken in toasted bread crumbs? I toasted a few cups of panko bread crumbs with olive oil in a skillet and then added basil, parsley, dried oregano, salt, and pepper. When the chicken was finished cooking, I rolled the breasts in the crumb mixture and then returned them to the cooker, sprinkled them with cheese, and covered the turned-off cooker to melt the cheese. After 15 minutes the cheese was nicely melted, but the crumbs were soggy. Maybe this recipe wasn't going to work after all?

But then a colleague suggested trying to reverse the crumbs and cheese. It sounded odd, but I gave it a try, placing the cheese over the cooked chicken in the turned-off cooker, letting it sit covered until the cheese melted, and then sprinkling the crumbs on top just before serving. To my happy surprise, this deconstructed approach worked beautifully, giving the cheesy chicken breasts

plenty of toasty flavor and crunch. As a bonus, I needed only about one-third as much of the crumb mixture to top the chicken. Now I just had to fix the watered-down sauce.

I knew that the juice released by the chicken would thin the sauce, so I figured that starting with an extra-thick sauce would give me the right consistency in the end. I got to work building a thicker sauce, sautéing chopped onion with a lot of tomato paste and generous amounts of garlic, red pepper flakes, and oregano. When the onions were soft and the tomato paste had browned a bit, I added this mixture to the slow cooker along with a can of well-drained diced tomatoes. To thicken the sauce further, I stirred in a mixture of cornstarch and water before adding the chicken. After about 3½ hours, I sprinkled in a little chopped basil, added the cheese, and covered the cooker until it melted. I scattered the toasted bread crumbs over the cheese and called my hungry tasters. "Did this really come out of the slow cooker?" one of them asked; that's my benchmark for slow-cooker success.

SLOW-COOKER CHICKEN PARMESAN
Serves 6
The red pepper flakes are optional.

- 6 (6- to 8-ounce) boneless, skinless chicken breasts, trimmed
  Salt and pepper
- 5 teaspoons olive oil
- 1 onion, chopped
- 1 (6-ounce) can tomato paste
- 4 garlic cloves, minced
- ¾ teaspoon dried oregano
- ⅛ teaspoon red pepper flakes
- 1 (28-ounce) can diced tomatoes, drained
- 1 tablespoon cornstarch
- 1 tablespoon water
- 6 ounces mozzarella cheese, shredded (1½ cups)
- ¼ cup grated Parmesan cheese
- 3 tablespoons chopped fresh basil
- ⅓ cup panko bread crumbs
- 1 tablespoon minced fresh parsley

1. Season chicken with salt and pepper. Heat 1 tablespoon oil in 12-inch nonstick skillet over medium-high heat until shimmering. Add onion, tomato paste, garlic, ½ teaspoon oregano, pepper flakes, ¼ teaspoon salt, and ¼ teaspoon pepper and cook until onions are softened and tomato paste is rust-colored, about 4 minutes.

2. Transfer tomato paste mixture to slow cooker and stir in tomatoes. Dissolve cornstarch in water and stir into tomato mixture. Shingle breasts on top of tomato mixture with tapered ends pointing toward control panel. Cover and cook until chicken registers 160 degrees, 3 to 4 hours on low.

3. Combine mozzarella and 2 tablespoons Parmesan in bowl. Sprinkle chicken with 2 tablespoons basil, followed by mozzarella mixture. Cover and let sit in turned-off cooker until cheese is melted, about 15 minutes.

4. Meanwhile, combine panko and remaining 2 teaspoons oil in 12-inch nonstick skillet over medium heat and cook, stirring often, until well browned, 3 to 5 minutes. Transfer panko to bowl, let cool for 5 minutes, then stir in parsley, remaining 2 tablespoons Parmesan, remaining 1 tablespoon basil, remaining ¼ teaspoon oregano, ⅛ teaspoon salt, and ⅛ teaspoon pepper. Sprinkle panko mixture over cheese. Serve.

To streamline this dish for two, we had to reduce not just the portion size but also the ingredient list.

BY REBECCAH MARSTERS

LIKE MANY HOME COOKS, sometimes I'm willing to go the extra mile and spend hours preparing dinner, and other times I'm motivated by speed and convenience—not to mention the growling stomach and dropping blood sugar that signal pressing hunger. For the latter scenario, I had in mind a recipe for beef and broccoli stir-fry for two that didn't require too much time or too many specialty ingredients.

The test kitchen has developed a few recipes for this stir-fry over the years, and I used a basic one as my starting point. This recipe uses flank steak because it has great flavor, with just enough chew, and it's easy to slice thin. The problem, though, is that even the smallest flank steak I found weighed about a pound (and most of them are twice that). This means that, while the dish was very tasty, when all was said and done, I had more than half of a flank steak left over, not to mention a few containers of Asian condiments missing only a few teaspoons—so much for streamlining. To make this stir-fry work for two, I'd have to find a more appropriate cut of meat and winnow the ingredient list.

With flank steak out, I explored my options for smaller cuts of beef at the butcher counter. A tender filet mignon worked well but was awfully pricey for a stir-fry. I had decent results with flavorful steak tips, too, but their wide grain and inconsistent size made them difficult to thinly slice into bite-size pieces. In the end, I chose blade steak. It was tender, flavorful, and affordable. Its only drawback is a tough line of gristle running through the center, but that was easy to remove since I was slicing the steak anyway.

The test kitchen's method for this dish is straightforward. First, marinate the sliced meat in soy sauce and sugar to season it deeply; the salt in the soy sauce travels into the meat, while the sugar helps create a tasty seared crust on the beef because sugar browns faster than meat. After browning the meat in batches and removing it, we add the vegetables to the hot skillet and steam them, covered, with a little water until they're almost tender. Garlic, scallion whites, and ginger go in next, then the browned beef, and finally the sauce—a mixture of soy sauce, chili-garlic paste,

hoisin sauce, and a little water.

With only two portions of meat, I could easily brown it all in one batch before removing it from the skillet. After that, the broccoli florets needed only a few minutes to steam and soften. A pinch of red pepper flakes lent just enough kick to heighten the other flavors without making the dish overly spicy. So far so good. Now for the sauce.

After trying various pared-down sauce combinations, I ditched the flavorless water and "specialty" chili-garlic and hoisin sauces and landed on a potent combination of soy sauce, sesame oil, sugar, and orange juice, whisked together with a little cornstarch. I finished the dish with the sliced scallion greens and some nutty, crunchy toasted sesame seeds. In less time than it takes for takeout to be delivered to my door, supper was on the table.

SESAME BEEF AND BROCCOLI STIR-FRY FOR TWO
Freezing the beef for 15 minutes makes it easier to slice thin. After trimming the steak, you should have about 8 ounces of sliced meat. A rasp-style grater makes quick work of grating the ginger. Toast the sesame seeds in a small skillet over medium-low heat, stirring often, until lightly browned and fragrant, 3 to 5 minutes. Serve with rice.

10 ounces beef blade steak, trimmed, halved lengthwise, then cut crosswise into 1/8-inch-thick slices
2 tablespoons soy sauce
2 teaspoons sugar
2 scallions, white parts minced, green parts sliced thin on bias
1 tablespoon vegetable oil
1½ teaspoons grated fresh ginger
1 garlic clove, minced
   Pinch red pepper flakes
6 tablespoons orange juice
1 tablespoon toasted sesame oil
2 teaspoons cornstarch
6 ounces broccoli florets, cut into 1½-inch pieces
⅓ cup water
2 teaspoons sesame seeds, toasted

1. Combine beef, 1 teaspoon soy sauce, and ½ teaspoon sugar in bowl; let sit for 10 minutes. Combine scallion whites, ½ teaspoon vegetable

No exotic ingredients here: The flavorful sauce is made from soy sauce, sesame oil, sugar, orange juice, and cornstarch.

oil, ginger, garlic, and pepper flakes in second bowl. Whisk orange juice, sesame oil, cornstarch, remaining 5 teaspoons soy sauce, and remaining 1½ teaspoons sugar together in third bowl.

2. Heat 1 teaspoon vegetable oil in 12-inch nonstick skillet over medium-high heat until just smoking. Add beef in single layer, breaking up any clumps, and cook without stirring for 1 minute. Stir and continue to cook until beef is browned all over, 1 to 2 minutes. Transfer beef to clean bowl.

3. Add remaining 1½ teaspoons vegetable oil to now-empty skillet

and return to medium-high heat. Add broccoli and water and cook, covered, until nearly tender, about 2 minutes. Push broccoli to sides of skillet. Add scallion mixture to center and cook, mashing mixture into skillet, until fragrant, about 30 seconds. Stir mixture into broccoli.

4. Return beef and any accumulated juices to skillet and stir to combine. Whisk orange juice mixture to recombine and add to skillet. Cook, stirring constantly, until slightly thickened, about 1 minute. Sprinkle with sesame seeds and scallion greens. Serve.

KEY TECHNIQUE
Trimming Blade Steak
Blade steak is tender, flavorful, and affordable, but it's got a line of gristle running through the center of each steak. The gristle is easy to remove: Simply cut the steak in half on one side of the gristle and remove it with your next cut.

CUT IT OUT
Remove and discard the chewy line of gristle in the middle of the steak before slicing the meat into bite-size pieces.

Recipe Makeover   Breakfast Casserole

Everyone loves a rich, cheesy, sausage-stuffed breakfast casserole—at least until they see the fat and calorie content. We set out to retool this favorite.

BY CRISTIN WALSH

WHENEVER I HAVE to feed a crowd for breakfast, I turn to an easy, hearty classic that pleases everybody: breakfast casserole. For this dish, chopped vegetables and potatoes, breakfast meats, and cheese are baked in a custard of eggs and half-and-half or cream until the filling is set and the casserole is nicely browned. What's not to like? Well, perhaps the fact that a single serving contains 610 calories and 43 grams of fat.

I began by making the test kitchen's favorite full-fat version of this dish. I diced 2 pounds of Yukon Gold potatoes and parcooked them in boiling water, and then I tossed them with 8 ounces of shredded cheddar cheese and 12 ounces of chopped chorizo, along with sautéed onions and red bell pepper. I evenly spread this mixture in a baking dish, poured a custard mixture of 2 cups of half-and-half and eight whole eggs over the top, and then baked it until it was lightly browned. The finished dish had plenty of flavor, all right, but this was one heavy breakfast.

Right off the bat, I swapped out the most obvious high-calorie ingredients. Lean Canadian bacon took the place of the chorizo, and full-fat cheddar was exchanged for a lower-fat counterpart. Though the robust flavor of the dish was slightly diminished, it still seemed like a good start. I decided to focus next on the custard.

My initial plan was to switch whole eggs for egg whites, but that turned out to be a disaster: My whites-only casserole came out of the oven flat and meager in flavor as well as texture. I tried various ratios of whole eggs and egg whites but finally concluded that the plentiful filling needed the structure and richness that the whole eggs provided. Next I tried switching the half-and-half for lower-fat dairy substitutes. I auditioned low-fat sour cream, cottage cheese, and fat-free milk, but in the end, whole milk combined with whole eggs was the only option that gave me enough flavor and also provided enough fat to keep the custard from breaking as it cooked. I hadn't shaved as many calories as I had hoped, so I returned to the filling.

The Numbers

All nutritional information is for one serving.

Traditional Potato and Egg Breakfast Casserole
CALORIES **610**
FAT **43 g**   SATURATED FAT **21 g**

***Cook's Country* Reduced-Fat Potato and Egg Breakfast Casserole**
CALORIES **330**
FAT **14 g**   SATURATED FAT **6 g**

I decided to try trading a few of the potatoes in the filling for meaty-tasting mushrooms to get me closer to my target nutritional numbers. I tossed sliced mushrooms in with the parcooked potatoes and chopped pepper and onions for the filling, added the custard, and baked. Unfortunately, liquid leached from the mushrooms, ruining the texture of the custard.

I thought about precooking the mushrooms, but adding a step was going to steer this recipe too far away from "easy." I tried sautéing the mushrooms and potatoes together, but the potatoes cooked unevenly. I added the onions and red pepper to the skillet, hoping that their moisture would help steam the potatoes. This did help, but not enough. At this point, a coworker suggested covering the skillet during the initial 5 minutes of cooking to steam the potatoes. It worked. The potatoes were tender and evenly cooked, and the mushrooms' moisture had evaporated during the 10 minutes that the skillet was uncovered. The custard was still just a little loose, though, so I added in 3 tablespoons of cornstarch. This would thicken the filling without my having to introduce any extra egg yolks or cheese, both of which would add calories along with their thickening power. This time the custard baked up just right.

I was now close to the target numbers and the flavor was good, but there was room for one more adjustment to boost flavor and cut a few calories. I swapped

Canadian bacon and plenty of vegetables help cut the fat and calories in this tasty casserole.

out 4 ounces of the low-fat cheddar for 1 ounce of Parmesan, which is made from skim milk and therefore naturally lower in fat. This went a long way toward upping the rich flavor of the casserole, plus the swap saved calories. Now I had a hearty, creamy casserole that I could proudly serve to any guests—no need for them to know it's much better for them.

REDUCED-FAT POTATO AND EGG BREAKFAST CASSEROLE

Serves 8

We prefer Cracker Barrel Reduced Fat Sharp Cheddar Cheese.

- 1 teaspoon vegetable oil
- 1½ pounds Yukon Gold potatoes, peeled and cut into ½-inch pieces
- 8 ounces white mushrooms, trimmed and sliced thin
- 2 onions, chopped fine
- 1 red bell pepper, stemmed, seeded, and chopped
  Salt and pepper
- 12 ounces Canadian bacon, chopped
- 6 scallions, sliced thin
- 4 ounces low-fat cheddar cheese, shredded (1 cup)
- 8 large eggs
- 2 cups whole milk
- 3 tablespoons cornstarch
- 1 ounce Parmesan cheese, grated (½ cup)

1. Adjust oven rack to middle position and heat oven to 350 degrees. Spray 13 by 9-inch baking dish with vegetable oil spray. Heat oil in 12-inch nonstick skillet over medium-high heat until shimmering. Add potatoes, mushrooms, onions, bell pepper, and ½ teaspoons salt; cover; and cook for 5 minutes. Uncover and continue to cook until liquid has evaporated and vegetables are tender, about 10 minutes.

2. Transfer vegetable mixture to prepared dish and let cool for 10 minutes. Stir in bacon, scallions, and cheddar. Whisk eggs, milk, cornstarch, ½ teaspoon pepper, and ¼ teaspoon salt together in large bowl. Pour egg mixture over vegetable mixture. Sprinkle casserole with Parmesan. Bake until eggs have set and top is lightly browned, 30 to 40 minutes, rotating dish halfway through baking. Let cool for 20 minutes before serving.

TO MAKE AHEAD

Cooked, cooled vegetable and egg mixtures can be refrigerated separately for up to 24 hours.

Our DIY pita chips require just a few minutes of work for a big payoff.

BY ASHLEY MOORE

SURE YOU CAN buy pita chips for your next party, but homemade are much better, plus you can customize the flavors and avoid salt overload. Not to mention that they're very easy. The only tricky points are how to efficiently cut and flavor the chips and how to ensure that the spices actually stick to those chips. Fortunately, the test kitchen has figured out techniques to help with both.

To cut the pita rounds into chips, we first separate each round into its two component layers for thinner, crispier chips. Then we stack them up and cut through the stack, making eight wedges from each 8-inch pita round. But wait—back up. Don't make the same mistake that I did the first time and cut all the rounds into wedges before you've flavored them. By brushing the rounds before cutting, you have to brush only eight rounds on just one side instead of brushing 64 individual wedges.

Here's how we do it: After we've separated each pita into two, we brush the rounds generously with oil (we like olive oil for its robust flavor). At that point, we sprinkle on the flavorings and only then do we stack them seasoned side up and cut them. A bonus—once stacked and pressed, the pita rounds absorb the seasoned oil from the rounds above and below, so they're seasoned on all sides.

We arrange the wedges on two rimmed baking sheets in a single layer

We offer four savory and one sweet variation to make sure all your dipping needs are covered.

to ensure that they'll bake evenly. Many recipes instruct the cook to flip each chip halfway through for better browning. Don't bother. We've found that the heat from the rimmed baking sheet browns the bottoms perfectly well while the tops naturally crisp from the oven's heat. It's less work, which is nice, and this no-flip method has a second advantage—you needn't worry that the seasonings will be dislodged and end up

on the baking sheet.

Master recipe in hand, I developed four variations, three savory and one sweet. The savory ones are terrific munched on their own or with dips such as hummus or roasted red pepper–feta, depending on the variation. I sent pitas to the Mediterranean Sea for my rosemary-Parmesan variation. Next, they made a few stops in America, transforming into Buttermilk-Ranch Pita Chips

and Chili-Spiced Pita Chips. If you crave sweet snacks, try my Cinnamon-Sugar Pita Chips; I replaced the olive oil with melted butter, producing something that tasted like a fantastic cross between that childhood favorite, cinnamon toast, and a salty, crunchy potato chip.

SALT AND OLIVE OIL PITA CHIPS
Serves 8

Use whole-wheat pita bread, if you like. You can also substitute vegetable oil for the olive oil.

- 4 (8-inch) pita breads
- ½ cup extra-virgin olive oil
- 1 teaspoon kosher salt

1. Adjust oven racks to upper-middle and lower-middle positions and heat oven to 350 degrees. Using kitchen shears, cut around perimeter of each pita and separate into 2 thin rounds.

2. Working with 1 round at a time, brush cut side generously with oil and sprinkle with salt. Stack rounds on top of one another, cut side up, as you go. Using chef's knife, cut pita stack into 8 wedges. Spread wedges, cut side up and in single layer, on 2 rimmed baking sheets. Bake until wedges are golden brown and crisp, about 15 minutes, rotating and switching sheets halfway through baking. Let cool before serving.

BUTTERMILK-RANCH PITA CHIPS
Mix 1 tablespoon buttermilk powder, 2 teaspoons dried dill, ¼ teaspoon garlic powder, and ¼ teaspoon onion powder with salt before sprinkling on chips.

CHILI-SPICED PITA CHIPS
Mix 1 tablespoon chili powder, ½ teaspoon garlic powder, and pinch cayenne with salt before sprinkling on chips.

CINNAMON-SUGAR PITA CHIPS
Substitute 8 tablespoons melted unsalted butter for olive oil. Decrease salt to ¼ teaspoon. Mix 3 tablespoons sugar and 1 tablespoon cinnamon with salt before sprinkling on chips.

ROSEMARY-PARMESAN PITA CHIPS
Decrease salt to ½ teaspoon. Mix ½ cup grated Parmesan and 2 tablespoons minced fresh rosemary with salt before sprinkling on chips.

TEST KITCHEN DISCOVERY
Easier Seasoning
Instead of cutting the pitas and oiling and seasoning each wedge (as most recipes instruct), we brush oil and seasonings onto the pita halves, stack them, and then cut them into wedges.

SEASON FIRST
Then cut the stacked, halved pitas into wedges.

TEST KITCHEN TECHNIQUE **Every Chip in Its Place**
If tossed on haphazardly, 64 chips (the amount we make in these recipes) will never fit onto two rimmed baking sheets without overlapping. It takes a few minutes to arrange the pita wedges head-to-tail like this, but you'll gain the time back by not having to bake an extra batch.

A SMART ARRANGEMENT
This setup allows you to bake 64 chips on just two sheets.

Equipment Review Grill Spatulas

Is there one all-purpose model that's nimble enough for a grillful of burgers and sturdy enough to flip heavy swordfish steaks? BY ADAM RIED

GRILL SPATULAS ARE long-handled turners designed to keep your hands away from the flames while grilling. In our lineup of eight models priced from $10.99 to almost $41, we hoped that at least one would pass all our tests—turning large swordfish steaks, grilled pizzas, and closely packed hamburgers—with assurance, proving to be comfortable, secure, and maneuverable enough for any job.

Wondering if a dedicated grill spatula was even really necessary, we also tested our favorite indoor metal spatula, the Wüsthof Gourmet Turner/Fish Spatula ($44.95). Quickly it became apparent that a long handle and a larger head were essential, so we set the indoor model aside.

Ideally, a spatula head will be wide enough to support the pizzas and broad swordfish steaks but not too large to maneuver between crowded burgers. Extra-wide heads of about 5 inches were great with swordfish steaks but a liability with crowded burgers: Testers had to ease the corners of these spatula heads under the burgers, requiring concentration and finesse. (If you're grilling just a couple of burgers with ample space between them, practically any long-handled spatula will turn them without incident.) Conversely the OXO, with the narrowest head of the bunch at 3⅜ inches, made it easy to turn the burgers but left some testers feeling less sure while turning the broad swordfish. Spatulas with heads of medium width, roughly 4 inches, offered the best compromise of support and dexterity.

The spatulas' handles were no less important. We included people of varying heights and strengths among our testers because some of the spatulas seemed quite hefty. That turned out to be a good call because those who were taller, with larger hands, didn't notice variations in weight, grip size, and position. But for smaller testers, heavy spatulas felt like baseball bats, and thick handle grips, or grips that required you to hold the very end of the handle, were awkward and unwieldy.

All testers agreed, however, on handle grip shape and material. Rounded grips without any edges were universally comfortable, and everyone favored plastic and wood over the metal grip, from Rösle, which got hot if left right next to the body of the grill.

Testers were also unanimous in their enthusiasm for the offset handle of the

Weber, the only such design in the lineup. The handle was set 45 degrees above the head, providing extra clearance between the griller's hand and the grill. Testers felt that this design improved leverage and gave the Weber a remarkably nimble feel, far and away the best of the bunch.

So which spatula handled swordfish, pizza, and bunches of burgers with equal aplomb? None worked perfectly (hence none fall into the Highly Recommended category), but one stood out as the best possible compromise, the Weber

Original Stainless Steel Spatula. Its midsize head got all the jobs done, and its nimble offset handle and comfortable, rounded plastic grip made it the class leader, hands down. As an added bonus, this was among the least expensive of the grill spatulas in our testing.

RECOMMENDED

WEBER Original Stainless Steel Spatula
Model: 306620
Price: $14.99
Source: weber.com
Weight: 7 oz **Handle Grip Length:** 7⅞ in
Overall Handle Length: 13 in (including offset)
Head Width: 3¾ in

CRITERIA	
Performance	★★½
Ease of Use	★★★

TESTERS' NOTES: Testers of all sizes loved this spatula's slim, rounded, offset handle, remarking on the agility, sense of control, and confidence that it inspired. Particularly when the grill is really packed, this is your spatula. Its relatively small head was also able to lift and move large swordfish steaks, but we noticed a bit of flex where the steaks weren't completely supported.

OXO Good Grips BBQ Turner
Model: 19091
Price: $10.99
Source: oxo.com
Weight: 7⅝ oz **Handle Grip Length:** 8⅞ in
Overall Handle Length: 12¾ in
Head Width: 3⅜ in

CRITERIA	
Performance	★★½
Ease of Use	★★½

TESTERS' NOTES: This spatula's slim, rounded, soft-grip handle worked well for all testers, especially testers with smaller hands, who called it "supercomfortable" and noted that it allowed their hands to "get closer to the food for more control." Because the handle extended almost straight out from the head, this spatula wasn't quite as maneuverable as the Weber.

RECOMMENDED WITH RESERVATIONS

CHARCOAL COMPANION Big Head Spatula
Model: CC1032
Price: $17.47
Weight: 12¼ oz **Handle Grip Length:** 13¾ in
Overall Handle Length: 13¾ in
Head Width: 5 in

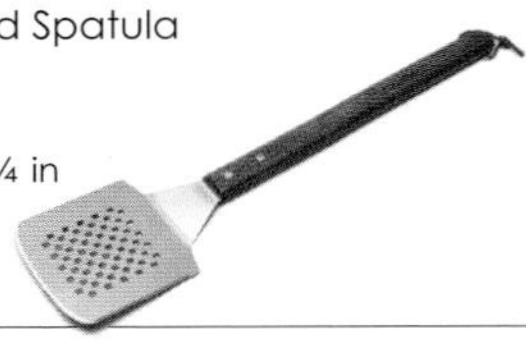

CRITERIA	
Performance	★★½
Ease of Use	★★

TESTERS' NOTES: This spatula's wide head offered good support for swordfish and pizza but wasn't well suited to a crowded grill, forcing testers to work mostly with the corners. Opinion about the wood handle was divided; testers with smaller hands found this spatula easier to maneuver than larger models.

STEVEN RAICHLEN Best of Barbecue Stainless Steel Spatula
Model: SR8110
Price: $17.09
Weight: 17 oz **Handle Grip Length:** 5¾ in
Overall Handle Length: 12¾ in
(excluding bottle opener)
Head Width: 5⅛ in

CRITERIA	
Performance	★★½
Ease of Use	★★

TESTERS' NOTES: The large head offered great support for swordfish and pizza, but it struck smaller testers as heavy, and in tandem with the short handle grip made this spatula feel unbalanced (it was the heaviest in the test). That large head also pushed burgers on a crowded grill every which way.

NOT RECOMMENDED

RÖSLE Barbecue Turner
Model: 12365
Price: $40.95
Weight: 13⅞ oz **Handle Grip Length:** 5½ in
Overall Handle Length: 11⅓ in
Head Width: 4¼ in

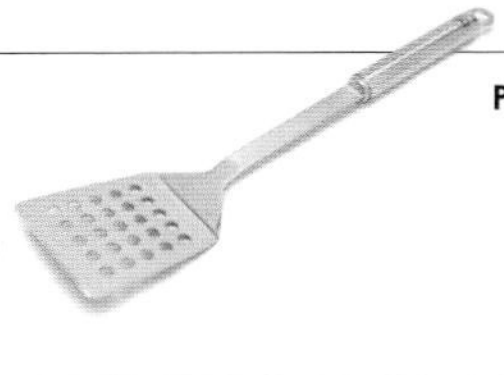

CRITERIA	
Performance	★★
Ease of Use	★½

TESTERS' NOTES: This expensive tool (it's more than twice the price of the others) was flawed. The weighty head and short handle grip felt out of balance, especially to smaller testers. The handle grip, which was metal, got hot if we accidentally left it too close to the grill body.

CHAR-BROIL 2-in-1 Spatula Combo with Knife
Model: 8419589
Price: $19.99
Weight: 13⅜ oz **Handle Grip Length:** 11¼ in
Overall Handle Length: 14 in
Head Width: 4 in

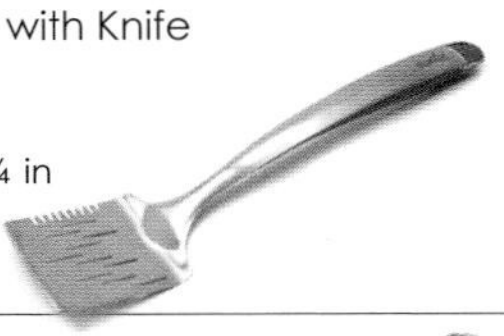

CRITERIA	
Performance	★★
Ease of Use	★½

TESTERS' NOTES: Testers with small hands found the metal edges on the handle uncomfortable, and the features made no sense. The deep serrations were dull and useless, and the integrated knife was relatively long (almost 5 inches), making it a poor choice for nicking meat to check doneness.

MR. BAR-B-Q Finger Grip Spatula
Model: 02150X
Price: $11.23
Weight: 10⅝ oz **Handle Grip Length:** 13 in
Overall Handle Length: 13 in
Head Width: 3¹⁵/₁₆ in

CRITERIA	
Performance	★★
Ease of Use	★

TESTERS' NOTES: Testers with smaller hands disliked the positioning of the finger indentations on the handle because they impaired leverage. And every tester was puzzled by the extra-deep, pointy serrations on one side, which seemed more appropriate for fending off a yeti on attack than any cooking task.

GRILL DADDY Heat Shield Pro Spatula
Model: GQ52611WB
Price: $19.99
Weight: 16 oz **Handle Grip Length:** 6¼ in
Overall Handle Length: 19 in (fully extended)
Head Width: 4 in

CRITERIA	
Performance	★★
Ease of Use	★

TESTERS' NOTES: The quality was poor and the extra features were silly. The head (which is interchangeable with other components, available separately at extra cost) wobbled like crazy. The handle grip felt bulky to smaller testers, and its loose, swiveling "heat shield" was far more nuisance than help.

Taste Test Lemonade

A small brand squeezes past the big names. BY LAUREN SAVOIE

FEW IMAGES ARE more representative of American can-do spirit than the childhood lemonade stand. And there's a good reason why lemonade is the choice of these budding entrepreneurs: It's very simple to make. So why is it so hard to find a great-tasting supermarket version?

When we last tasted lemonade, we recommended just three of the nine we sampled. All of those had ingredient lists that stuck closely to the bare-bones traditional recipe of water, lemon juice, and sugar, without preservatives or artificial flavors. We praised our winner, Newman's Own Organic Virgin Lemonade, for its big flavor and short ingredient list. In the years since, though, more brands have taken a stab at "simpler" supermarket lemonade. One brand even includes the word in its moniker—Simply Lemonade, introduced by the Coca-Cola Company in 2006, has just four ingredients and now outsells every other lemonade by 300 percent. A smaller brand, Natalie's Orchid Island Juice Company, also caught our attention for its locally sourced ingredients and straightforward recipe.

To see if these newcomers might have elevated store-bought lemonade, we pitted them against our previous winner and the four top-selling nationally available products from the frozen, refrigerated, and bottled soft drink sections of the supermarket.

Tasters wanted big lemon flavor and gave high scores to tart lemonades and low marks to products that seemed overly sweet. Tartness in lemonade nearly always comes from citric acid, usually lemon juice, so it was no surprise that tasters preferred products with more than 10 percent lemon juice, calling them the tartest and freshest. Our top choice reported a whopping 20 percent juice, while lemonades at the bottom of our ranking pulled only single digits or, in the case of one product, 0 percent (it's made tart with chemical citric acid instead of lemon juice). But there was one noticeable exception: Turkey Hill, which plummeted to the very bottom of our ranking, boasted a moderate 10 percent fruit juice. When we measured each lemonade's acidity to understand lemon juice's impact on taste, things started to line up. While other lemonades define "juice" as strictly juice from lemons, Turkey Hill uses a citrus blend that includes sweeter citrus like orange, which dampens the pleasantly puckering taste of lemon.

Since tasters rated sweet products low, we looked into sugar, too. In grams, our favorite lemonades had the most sugar—because our winning products have lots of lemon juice, more sugar is needed to balance the acidity. But when we checked out ingredient labels for type of sweetener used, we made a key discovery: Three out of four of our recommended products used sucrose, while all our least favorite products used corn syrup. Tasters were put off by the sappy texture of lemonades sweetened with corn syrup and found those made with sucrose more crisp and refreshing.

While we were looking at ingredient labels, we noticed something else: Just as in our previous testing, scores dropped as ingredient lists got longer. Our top pick contains just three simple ingredients—water, lemon juice, and pure cane sugar—while lemonades at the bottom of our ranking are filled with preservatives and artificial flavors. Luckily, there's an easy way to escape products riddled by additives without poring over ingredient labels: Avoid unrefrigerated lemonades. The citric acid in lemon juice is a natural preservative, so if you're storing lemonade only short-term in the fridge, no chemicals are needed. Both of the brands we picked from the unrefrigerated soft-drink aisle were loaded with artificial stuff because they're formulated for a longer shelf life. But if you do need to plan ahead, we found one frozen lemonade concentrate that was great-tasting and preservative-free and, with a shelf life of two years, it's the best option when you want to stock up.

In the end, Natalie's Natural Lemonade earned the top spot in our ranking. When we compared it with our recipe for homemade lemonade, it was clear why. With the most lemon juice and shortest ingredient list in our lineup, Natalie's is the only product that comes close to the 25 percent lemon juice and 29 grams of sugar we prefer in our homemade recipe. Our tasters praised this lemonade for its balanced tang and clean, fresh-squeezed flavor, but when we pressed manufacturers for more details about how they process their lemonade, we found that Natalie's doesn't just taste homemade; it's made like it, too. Unlike most major manufacturers, Natalie's keeps no inventory. Instead, Florida lemons are squeezed, blended with sugar and water, and bottled within 24 hours after receiving each order. This also means, however, that the availability of Natalie's fluctuates seasonally as demand for lemonade trickles out in colder months. It's also available in only 32 states while our runner-up, top-selling brand Simply Lemonade, is found nationally year-round. When we can't find our winner on supermarket shelves, we'll be reaching for Simply Lemonade, but for a perfectly tart refreshing drink that satisfies summer cravings, Natalie's is worth the hunt.

Fresher in the Fridge (or Freezer)

Among other discoveries we made while studying lemonade was a very simple one: If you find it on the supermarket shelf, it contains preservatives and you'll taste the chemistry. For fresher flavor, stick with the refrigerated or frozen lemonade.

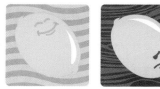

IN THE FRIDGE   **ON THE SHELF**

RECOMMENDED

	TASTERS' NOTES
NATALIE'S Natural Lemonade **Price:** $3.25 for 64 fl oz (5 cents per fl oz) **Category:** Refrigerated **Percentage Juice:** 20% **Acidity:** 0.88* **Sugar:** 33 g per 8-oz serving	Tasters loved the "supertart," "fresh lemon" flavor of this small-batch lemonade, which contains 20 percent lemon juice—far more than any other in our lineup. It was "tangy" and "refreshing."
SIMPLY LEMONADE **Price:** $3.49 for 59 fl oz (6 cents per fl oz) **Category:** Refrigerated **Percentage Juice:** 11% **Acidity:** 0.62 **Sugar:** 28 g per 8-oz serving	"Tastes like childhood," remarked one happy taster. This lemonade was "clean" and "bright," with a "good balance of sweet and tart."
MINUTE MAID Premium Frozen Lemonade Concentrate **Price:** $1.89 for 12 fl oz (3 cents per fl oz, reconstituted) **Category:** Frozen **Percentage Juice:** 15% **Acidity:** 0.69 **Sugar:** 27 g per 8-oz serving	Tasters favorably compared this "bright," "lemony" frozen concentrated lemonade to "fresh-squeezed," though a few found it "a little watery." "Simple, tried, and true," said one taster.

RECOMMENDED WITH RESERVATIONS

NEWMAN'S OWN Organic Virgin Lemonade **Price:** $2.99 for 59 fl oz (5 cents per fl oz) **Category:** Refrigerated **Percentage Juice:** 15% **Acidity:** 0.66 **Sugar:** 27 g per 8-oz serving	Tasters praised our previous winner for its "balanced" flavor and visible pulp, but some were turned off by a lingering "metallic," "bitter" aftertaste.

NOT RECOMMENDED

MINUTE MAID Lemonade **Price:** $1.67 for 67.6 fl oz (2 cents per fl oz) **Category:** Shelf-stable **Percentage Juice:** 3% **Acidity:** 0.47 **Sugar:** 27 g per 8-oz serving	"Bland city" and "weak" were among the ways tasters described this "watered down" and "cloyingly sweet" bottled lemonade. To us, it tasted more "engineered" and "cheap" than its frozen counterpart.
COUNTRY TIME Lemonade **Price:** $1.50 for 67.6 fl oz (2 cents per fl oz) **Category:** Shelf-stable **Percentage Juice:** 0% **Acidity:** 0.62 **Sugar:** 24 g per 8-oz serving	"I wouldn't drink this if I was stranded in the desert," one taster said. Others picked up on a "fake" flavor and strong "chemical aroma," which isn't surprising: This product contains citric acid but no lemon juice.
TURKEY HILL Lemonade **Price:** $1.89 for 64 fl oz (3 cents per fl oz) **Category:** Refrigerated **Percentage Juice:** 10% **Acidity:** 0.35 **Sugar:** 26 g per 8-oz serving	With the lowest acidity in our ranking, this lemonade was a "sugar overload" for our tasters who compared its "sick, sticky sweetness" to "lemon frosting."

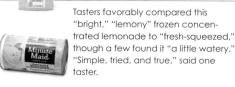

*Acidity is expressed as grams of citric acid per 100 ml of lemonade

Heirloom Recipes

We're looking for recipes that you treasure—the ones that have been handed down in your family for a generation or more; that always come out for the holidays; that have earned a place at your table and in your heart, through many years of meals. Send us the recipes that spell home to you. Visit CooksCountry.com/magazines/home (or write to Heirloom Recipes, *Cook's Country*, P.O. Box 470739, Brookline, MA 02447); click on Heirloom Recipes and tell us a little about the recipe. Include your name and mailing address. **If we print your recipe, you'll receive a free one-year subscription to *Cook's Country*.**

GREEK BUTTER COOKIES

Makes 20 cookies

"This shortbread-like butter cookie recipe comes from a junior high school friend of mine of Greek heritage. It's been in my mom's recipe box, handwritten on a coffee-stained 3 by 5-inch recipe card, for over 40 years. I still make these cookies a lot, and although you can eat them on the day they're made, my family prefers them after they've aged for a few days."

–Diane Unger, Senior Editor

- 2 cups (10 ounces) all-purpose flour
- ½ cup blanched sliced almonds, toasted and chopped fine
- ½ teaspoon salt
- 16 tablespoons unsalted butter, softened
- ¼ cup (1¾ ounces) granulated sugar
- 1 large egg yolk
- 1 tablespoon brandy
- 2 teaspoons vanilla extract
- 1 teaspoon grated orange zest
- ¼ cup (1 ounce) confectioners' sugar

1. Combine flour, almonds, and salt in bowl; set aside. Using stand mixer fitted with paddle, beat butter on medium-high speed until pale and fluffy, about 3 minutes. Add granulated sugar, egg yolk, brandy, vanilla, and orange zest and beat until incorporated.

2. Reduce speed to low, add flour mixture in 3 additions, and mix until just combined, scraping down bowl as needed. Turn out dough onto lightly floured counter and knead until cohesive ball forms. Wrap dough in plastic wrap and refrigerate for 30 minutes.

3. Adjust oven racks to upper-middle and lower-middle positions and heat oven to 300 degrees. Line 2 rimmed baking sheets with parchment paper. Working with 1 heaping tablespoon dough at a time, roll into 20 balls and space them 2 inches apart on prepared sheets (10 per sheet).

4. Bake until bottom edges are very lightly browned, 20 to 25 minutes, switching and rotating sheets halfway through baking. Let cookies cool on

sheets for 5 minutes, then transfer to wire rack. Let cookies cool completely. Sift confectioners' sugar over cookies before serving. (Cookies can be stored at room temperature for up to 1 week.)

COMING NEXT ISSUE

Our **August/September 2014** issue features regional favorites from all over the United States. We've got **Kentucky Bourbon Chicken, New Orleans Muffuletta, Iowa Loose Meat Sandwiches, New England Bar Pizza,** and **Huevos Rancheros,** not to mention **Dakota Fruit Kuchen.** Don't miss the trip.

FIND THE ROOSTER!

A tiny version of this rooster has been hidden in the pages of this issue. Write to us with its location and we'll enter you in a random drawing. The first correct entry drawn will win a set of our winning dish towels, and each of the next five will receive a free one-year subscription to *Cook's Country*. To enter, visit CooksCountry.com/rooster by July 31, 2014, or write to Rooster JJ14, *Cook's Country*, P.O. Box 470739, Brookline, MA 02447. Include your name and address. Robert Barello of Macomb, Michigan, found the rooster in the February/March 2014 issue on page 21 and won our top-rated roasting pan.

WEB EXTRAS

Free for 4 months online at
CooksCountry.com

Bread-Crumb Tasting
Chiffon Layer Cake
Creamy Peanut Butter Tasting
Delta Hot Tamales with Parchment Paper
Large-Batch Lightly Sweetened
    Whipped Cream
Tomato Corers Testing (full story)
White Rice

READ US ON iPAD

Download the *Cook's Country* app for iPad and start a free trial subscription or purchase a single issue of the magazine. All issues are enhanced with full-color Cooking Mode slide shows that provide step-by-step instructions for completing recipes, plus expanded reviews and ratings. Go to CooksCountry.com/iPad to download our app through iTunes.

Follow us on **Pinterest**
pinterest.com/TestKitchen

Follow us on **Twitter**
twitter.com/TestKitchen

Find us on **Facebook**
facebook.com/CooksCountry

Summer Berry Chiffon Cake

Show your colors using summer's most vibrant fruits—
blueberries, raspberries, and strawberries—in this light and airy cake.

To make this cake, you will need:

- ½ cup (3½ ounces) sugar
- 2 tablespoons plus 1 teaspoon low- or no-sugar-needed fruit pectin
- 8¾ ounces (1¾ cups) blueberries
- 7½ ounces strawberries, hulled and quartered (1¼ cups)
- 6¼ ounces (1¼ cups) raspberries
- 1 (9-inch) round chiffon or sponge cake*
- 4 cups lightly sweetened whipped cream*

FOR THE FILLING: Whisk ¼ cup sugar and 1 tablespoon pectin together in small saucepan. Add 1½ cups blueberries and mash well with potato masher. Bring mixture to boil over medium heat and cook, stirring frequently, until starting to thicken, about 2 minutes. Strain mixture through fine-mesh strainer set over bowl, pressing on solids to extract juice; discard solids. Cover with plastic wrap and refrigerate until set, about 2 hours. Rinse saucepan and repeat mashing and cooking process with remaining ¼ cup sugar, remaining 4 teaspoons pectin, 1 cup strawberries, and 1 cup raspberries. Strain and press over separate bowl (discard solids), cover with plastic, and refrigerate until set, about 2 hours.

TO ASSEMBLE: Using long serrated knife, cut 2 horizontal lines around sides of cake; then, following scored lines, cut cake into 3 even layers. Place 1 cake layer on platter. Spread blueberry filling evenly over top, followed by 1½ cups whipped cream. Top with second cake layer, press lightly to adhere, then spread strawberry-raspberry filling evenly over top, followed by 1½ cups whipped cream. Top with remaining cake layer and spread remaining 1 cup whipped cream on top (do not frost sides). Toss remaining ¼ cup blueberries, ¼ cup strawberries, and ¼ cup raspberries together and arrange in small pile in center of cake. Serve.

▶ *Go to CooksCountry.com/july14 for our **Chiffon Layer Cake** and **Large-Batch Lightly Sweetened Whipped Cream** recipes.

Inside This Issue

Cook's Country

AUGUST/SEPTEMBER 2014

Tex-Mex Huevos Rancheros

Thick-Cut BBQ Pork Chops

Smoky Bourbon Chicken

Watermelon-Feta Salad
Savory Summer Side Dish

Easy Tomato Gazpacho
Both Creamy and Crunchy

Tasting Frozen Pizzas
Does Price Matter?

Grill-Roasted Peppers
New Technique, Better Texture

Lower-Fat French Silk Pie
Still Tastes Rich and Silky

Dakota Peach Kuchen
Dessert, Snack, Breakfast

Whole-Wheat Blueberry Muffins
Good, Not Just Good for You

Iowa Loose Meat Sandwiches
Ground Beef Classic

CooksCountry.com
$5.95 U.S./$6.95 CANADA

*The classic Tex-Mex dish of **Huevos Rancheros** is wildly popular, but it's also a lot of work for the home cook. Or at least it was, until we spent a couple of weeks in the test kitchen figuring out how to make it simpler.* PAGE 14

Cook's Country

Dear Country Cook,

Los Angeles may be the center of the automobile universe, but our small Vermont town has a similarly enthusiastic love of pickups. Just go to Hathaway's Drive-In in Hoosick Falls, across the border in New York, and see all the pickups parked backward, with folding chairs set up on the flatbeds. Phones are still rarely used in our town; two pickups pull up next to one another on the town road, heading in different directions, and one catches up on local news.

A pickup is also a good spot to store baling twine; miscellaneous tools such as hammers, pliers, and crowbars; a 30.06 rifle during the season; binoculars at all times for counting the number of points on a rack; and limitless accessories for dealing with transportation emergencies—towing straps, jumper cables, and chains.

A pickup is also a hay wagon, a moving van, and a livestock trailer. It can handle a good load of sand, horse manure, sawdust, and a 250-gallon sap tank. In a pinch, it makes a decent "Just Married" getaway vehicle and has lots of surface area for advertising one's point of view, as in my favorite bumper sticker, "Possum: The Other White Meat."

And, if worse comes to worst, you can move your belongings onto the flatbed and park on a back road while you sort out life's difficulties. This also works during winter months—just get a fiberglass truck cap and you're all set. You can even lock up your valuables.

In fact, almost everything can be done in a pickup truck. You can even drive somewhere in it!

Cordially,

Christopher Kimball
Founder and Editor, Cook's Country

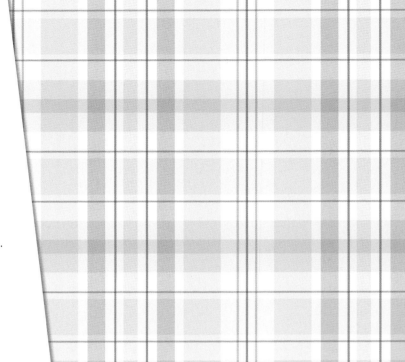

Drive-Thru Grocery and Liquor Store, Los Angeles, 1949

Cook'sCountry

Founder and Editor Christopher Kimball
Editorial Director Jack Bishop
Editorial Director, Magazines John Willoughby
Executive Editor Tucker Shaw
Managing Editor Scott Kathan
Executive Food Editor Bryan Roof
Senior Editors Hannah Crowley, Rebeccah Marsters, Lisa McManus, Diane Unger
Test Kitchen Director Erin McMurrer
Associate Editors Shannon Friedmann Hatch, Christie Morrison
Test Cooks Morgan Bolling, Sarah Gabriel, Ashley Moore, Cristin Walsh
Assistant Editors Lauren Savoie, Kate Shannon
Senior Copy Editor Megan Ginsberg
Copy Editors Nell Beram, Krista Magnuson
Executive Assistant Christine Gordon
Test Kitchen Manager Leah Rovner
Senior Kitchen Assistants Michelle Blodget, Alexxa Grattan
Kitchen Assistants Maria Elena Delgado, Shane Drips, Ena Gudiel
Executive Producer Melissa Baldino
Co-Executive Producer Stephanie Stender
Associate Producer Kaitlin Hammond

Contributing Editors Erika Bruce, Eva Katz, Jeremy Sauer
Consulting Editors Anne Mendelson, Meg Ragland
Science Editor Guy Crosby, PhD
Executive Food Editor, TV, Radio & Media Bridget Lancaster

Managing Editor, Web Christine Liu
Senior Editor, Cooking School Mari Levine
Associate Editors, Web Jill Fisher, Eric Grzymkowski, Roger Metcalf
Assistant Editor, Web Charlotte Wilder
Senior Video Editor Nick Dakoulas

Design Director Amy Klee
Photography Director Julie Cote
Art Director Susan Levin
Associate Art Director Lindsey Timko
Art Director, Marketing Jennifer Cox
Staff Photographer Daniel J. van Ackere
Color Food Photography Keller + Keller
Styling Catrine Kelty, Marie Piraino
Associate Art Director, Marketing Melanie Gryboski
Designer, Marketing Judy Blomquist
Associate Art Director, Photography Steve Klise

Vice President, Marketing David Mack
Circulation Director Doug Wicinski
Circulation & Fulfillment Manager Carrie Fethe
Partnership Marketing Manager Pamela Putprush
Marketing Assistant Marina Tomao

Director, Project Management Alice Carpenter
Project Manager Britt Dresser
Development Manager Mike Serio

Chief Operating Officer Rob Ristagno
VP, Digital Products Fran Middleton
Production Director Guy Rochford
Workflow & Digital Asset Manager Andrew Mannone
Senior Color & Imaging Specialist Lauren Pettapiece
Production & Imaging Specialists Heather Dube, Lauren Robbins
VP, New Business Development Michael Burton
Director of Sponsorship Sales Anne Traficante
Client Services Manager Kate Zebrowski
Senior Controller Theresa Peterson
Customer Service Manager Amy Bootier
Customer Service Representatives Jessica Haskin, Andrew Straaberg Finfrock, Juliet Tierney

Director, Retail Book Program Beth Ineson
Retail Sales & Marketing Manager Emily Logan
Human Resources Manager Adele Shapiro
Publicity Deborah Broide

ON THE COVER: *Huevos Rancheros*, Keller + Keller, Catrine Kelty
ILLUSTRATION: Greg Stevenson

Follow us on **Pinterest**
pinterest.com/TestKitchen

Follow us on **Twitter**
twitter.com/TestKitchen

Find us on **Facebook**
facebook.com/CooksCountry

Cook's Country magazine (ISSN 1552-1990), number 58, is published bimonthly by Boston Common Press Limited Partnership, 17 Station St., Brookline, MA 02445. Copyright 2014 Boston Common Press Limited Partnership. Periodicals postage paid at Boston, MA, and additional mailing offices, USPS #023453. Publications Mail Agreement No. 40020778. Return undeliverable Canadian addresses to P.O. Box 875, Station A, Windsor, ON N9A 6P2. POSTMASTER: Send address changes to Cook's Country, P.O. Box 6018, Harlan, IA 51593-1518. For subscription and gift subscription orders, subscription inquiries, or change of address notices, visit AmericasTestKitchen.com/support, call 800-526-8447 in the U.S. or 515-248-7684 from outside the U.S., or write to us at Cook's Country, P.O. Box 6018, Harlan, IA 51593-1518. PRINTED IN THE USA.

Contents

IOWA LOOSE MEAT SANDWICHES, 18

WATERMELON SALAD, 23 FASTER SMOKED PORK CHOPS, 10

Features

Departments

Follow Us: Pinterest.com/testkitchen

We love our Pinterest community, and we hope you'll join in the fun. Explore our boards for recipe inspiration and look out for new pins every day.

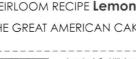

Ask Cook's Country

BY CHRISTIE MORRISON

Many recipes for white sauce tell me that I should scald the milk before adding it to the roux. How does the milk's temperature affect the sauce?
Janice Kavanagh, Charlottesville, Va.

A white sauce or béchamel is one of the French mother sauces. Classically, equal amounts of flour and fat (usually butter) are cooked to allow the fat to encase the starch granules before milk is whisked in and the sauce is brought to a boil to thicken it. Older recipes often call for scalding the milk before adding it to the roux. Theories abound regarding the reason for doing this. Some sources insist that it prevents heat shock, a phenomenon in which milk proteins separate and curdle when the cold milk comes in contact with hot roux. Others suggest that it's done to protect the starch in the flour from losing its thickening potential. Julia Child claimed that hot milk plus vigorous whisking is the only way to get a lump-free white sauce.

To test this claim, we made Child's recipe for béchamel using cold milk (straight from the refrigerator), room-temperature milk (about 65 degrees), and just-boiling milk. We streamed the milk into each sample while whisking vigorously, brought the mixture to a boil, and then cooked the mixture (while whisking frequently) for a full 2 minutes, as per her instructions. We then strained the sauce through a fine-mesh strainer to catch any lumps of flour.

In multiple tests, we found very little difference in the amount of clumping that occurred in the cold and room-temperature milks—both were fairly smooth, with minimal lumping. The hot milk, however, yielded significantly more lumps despite the same amount of vigorous whisking. Could the classic recipe be wrong?

Our science editor explained that in order to form a really smooth, lump-free sauce, the starch granules in the roux must disperse completely in the liquid milk before they start to absorb water and gelatinize. Adding cold milk to the roux gives the fat-coated starch granules time to disperse before the fat melts away from the granules and they begin to absorb water and gelatinize. Adding hot milk quickly melts some of the fat, so some of the granules become exposed to the hot liquid before they are completely dispersed, causing them to become wet on the surface and stick together to form lumps.

THE BOTTOM LINE: There's no reason to scald the milk for white sauce unless you're trying to infuse it with other flavors (onion or herbs, for instance). Not only does the scalding process take extra time, but using cold or room-temperature milk actually gives you a smoother sauce—and one less pot to wash.

What's the difference between vanilla and French vanilla?
Connie Sprowl, Tunkhannock, Pa.

French vanilla isn't a variety of vanilla (those come from Madagascar, Tahiti, and Mexico), but rather a technique used in ice cream making. While American (also known as Philadelphia) vanilla ice cream is an uncooked mixture of cream, milk, sugar, and vanilla, French vanilla ice cream begins with a cooked custard containing egg yolks. The presence of egg yolks gives French vanilla ice cream a denser, richer texture and smooth consistency, as well as a yellowish color. The vanilla flavor, however, is no different from that of ice cream made with a similar amount and type of vanilla using the Philadelphia technique.
THE BOTTOM LINE: French vanilla can be marketing hype—or it can signify the use of eggs and thus a different textural style of ice cream.

NO PASSPORT REQUIRED
"French vanilla" means the ice cream contains eggs—or it means nothing at all.

I've seen bartenders slapping herbs before adding them to cocktails. Is this just for show? Why do they do this?
Laurie Miles, Ipswich, Mass.

To get to the bottom of this question, we asked Tom Schlesinger-Guidelli, the manager of Island Creek Oyster Bar in Boston, Massachusetts, and an expert in mixology, "Does slapping herbs affect the flavor, or is it the herbal equivalent of twirling cocktail shakers and juggling whiskey bottles?" He replied that it does indeed affect the herb's flavor and isn't just a flashy gimmick. "It can be a light pressing or a slap," he explained. "Depending on the type of herb, it breaks the outer cell structure of the herb, releasing the aroma. As much of what we

One of your recipes calls for garam masala, but I'm having trouble finding it in my grocery store. Is there an easy substitution?
Pat McGinnis, Shallotte, N.C.

This Indian spice blend (*garam* means "warm" and *masala* means "spice blend") varies from brand to brand, but most blends consist of the same basic spices: black pepper, cardamom, coriander, cinnamon, and chiles. Additional spices like cumin, fennel, and/or nutmeg show up on occasion to round out the flavors. Our favorite product, McCormick Gourmet Collection Garam Masala, sticks to the core ingredients with a heavy note of cardamom. While this and other commercial garam masala mixtures have become increasingly common on supermarket shelves, they aren't nearly as ubiquitous as curry powder, another Indian spice blend. So to find an easy substitute, we mixed together six different ratios of the five basic spices and compared them with McCormick's in rice pilaf and chicken mulligatawny. The blend that mimicked the flavors of McCormick's most closely was as follows.

HOMEMADE GARAM MASALA
Makes about 3 tablespoons
To achieve a powder of uniform consistency, be sure to use finely ground black pepper (a spice grinder works like a charm).

3½	teaspoons finely ground pepper
2	teaspoons ground coriander
1½	teaspoons ground cardamom
1	teaspoon ground cumin
1	teaspoon ground cinnamon

Combine all ingredients in bowl.

THE BOTTOM LINE: It's easy to create a reasonable substitute for garam masala with ingredients that are probably already in your spice rack.

taste actually comes through a sense of smell, enhancing the aromatized ingredient of the drink will highlight that on the palate."

Makes sense, but how does it translate to cooking? We compared basil and mint leaves in a Caprese-type salad, using raw, untouched leaves in one sample and slapping or rubbing the leaves used in the second sample. Tasters noticed a marked difference in the strength of flavor and aroma in the slapped herbs before they were mixed into the salad, but once they mingled with the other ingredients, the enhanced flavor was lost.
THE BOTTOM LINE: Slapping herbs can enhance the flavor and aroma of herb garnishes, but if you're mixing the herbs into a dish, there's no need for violence.

I recently quick-pickled some radishes. When I opened the jar, the funky smell was overwhelming. Are they safe to eat?
Meredith McRae, Arlington, Mass.

While it's always a good idea to be alert to off-smells, particularly with home canning and pickling, in this case it's a false alarm. Radishes belong to the family Brassicaceae, more commonly known as cruciferous vegetables, which also includes daikon, turnips, and cauliflower. When the cells of cruciferous vegetables are damaged or disrupted in some way (chopping, slicing, the early stages of cooking), they release an enzyme that converts compounds called glucosinolates into other compounds called isothiocyanates and nitriles. The nitriles are the predominant product formed under acidic conditions, such as pickling. Radishes, along with daikon and turnips, contain particular glucosinolates that produce rather evil-smelling nitriles in the presence of an acid like vinegar. Cooking radishes can deactivate the enzyme. Unfortunately, a cooked radish is a soft radish and not ideal for pickling. We tried blanching the radishes briefly in boiling water to deactivate the enzyme, but in order to maintain the crunch, the cooking time had to be short, so the smell remained.
THE BOTTOM LINE: Funky odors go hand-in-hand with certain pickled crucifers. But the smell dissipates quickly and the pickles should taste fine.

To ask us a cooking question, visit **CooksCountry.com/ask**. Or write to Ask *Cook's Country*, P.O. Box 470739, Brookline, MA 02447. Just try to stump us!

Kitchen Shortcuts

COMPILED BY CRISTIN WALSH

CLEVER TIP
Jam Dressing
Angela Colastanti, Chester Springs, Pa.

I make a variety of homemade jams every year. To savor every last morsel of them, I add olive oil, red wine vinegar, Dijon mustard, and herbs/spices when the jam jar is nearly empty, screw the lid on, and shake away. In seconds I have delicious fruity salad dressing, and nothing is wasted from my homemade jams.

SMART TRICK
Cleaner Pounding
Kevin Moran, Fort Rock, Ark.

I love the idea of pounding chicken cutlets inside a plastic zipper-lock bag to keep my cutting board, counter, and meat pounder clean of raw chicken. But the bag used to tear every time I tried it. I discovered that adding just a few tablespoons of water to the bag along with the meat reduces friction and prevents the bag from tearing. This also works great with pork or veal cutlets.

HOT TIP
Quicker Pizza Refresher
Michelle Poulin, Auburn, Maine

Microwaving cold pizza makes the crust soggy, and reheating it in the oven takes almost 30 minutes. The best way I've found to reheat cold pizza is to put a few slices in a cold skillet, cover it, and turn the burner to low. About 8 minutes in the pan gives the cheese time to melt while the bottom crisps perfectly. No more soggy slices.

DOUBLE DUTY
Vegetable Scrubber
Sherry Hopkins, Morgantown, W. Va.

I grow lots of fresh vegetables in my home garden. To clean carrots, leeks, potatoes—really any sturdy root—I use body-scrubbing/loofah gloves that I buy at the dollar store. Used in a bowl of water, these gloves make quick work of scrubbing the vegetables clean.

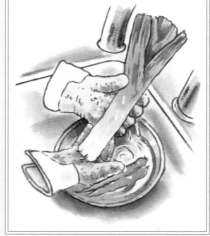

DOUBLE DUTY **Banana Bonus**
Christi Walsh, Annapolis, Md.

Did you know that you can use a banana peel to polish tarnished silverware? After you enjoy a banana, rub the inside of the peel along the silver and you'll see the magic happen. Just wipe it off with a clean cloth afterward to have sparkling silverware again. It doesn't work with really dark spots, but this trick works great with lightly tarnished utensils.

COOL TRICK **Cooling Soup**
Virginia Mark, Pasadena, Calif.

Cooling down soups can take too much time. I speed up the cooling process by freezing cubes of chicken stock in an ice cube tray. Whenever I make a soup, I just omit some of the stock in the recipe and add it back in with the frozen cubes of stock when I need to cool the soup.

HOT TIP
Frosting Fixer
Gary DiLisio, Franklin, Mass.

I make a lot of cakes and have noticed that sometimes the frosting is too stiff to smooth out easily. When this happens, I run my offset spatula under very hot water for a few seconds, quickly wipe it dry, and even out the frosting while the spatula is still warm. The heat softens the frosting, making it easy to get a neat, even layer.

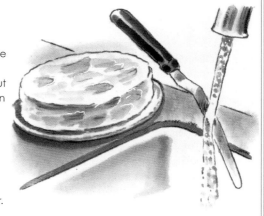

Submit a tip online at **CooksCountry.com/kitchenshortcuts** or send a letter to Kitchen Shortcuts, *Cook's Country*, P.O. Box 470739, Brookline, MA 02447. Include your name, address, and phone number. If we publish your tip, you will receive a free one-year subscription to *Cook's Country*. Letters may be edited for clarity and length.

New Orleans Muffuletta Sandwiches

This Italian cold-cut sandwich is a New Orleans classic. Could we make an easy, delicious version at home?

BY REBECCAH MARSTERS

LOOKING FOR A quick lunch in the French Quarter of New Orleans? Check out Central Grocery on Decatur Street. The signature—and only—sandwich served there is the muffuletta, a hefty round of seeded bread stuffed with Italian meats, cheeses, and olive spread. And just like every signature sandwich, it's got an origin story to match. In 1906, Salvatore Lupo, the owner of Central Grocery, noticed Sicilian immigrants on their lunch breaks eating meals of meats, cheeses, olives, and bread. The enterprising grocer decided to save the workers some trouble by putting all the components together in a convenient, handheld sandwich. Thus was born the muffuletta, named after the round Sicilian bread it's made on and served at Central Grocery—and elsewhere all over the city—ever since.

On my last trip to New Orleans, I stopped in at Central Grocery to sample a muffuletta at its place of origin. The sandwich was salty and spicy, with the tangy olive salad balancing the generous swath of meat and cheese in the middle and savory oil seeping into the bread. The bread itself was sturdy but soft, chewy but not crusty, and topped with plenty of sesame seeds. I decided right then that I would try to replicate this sandwich in the test kitchen.

The muffuletta recipes I found were fairly similar. The meats and cheeses varied only slightly—I ended up using a pretty standard grouping of salami, mortadella, and capicola with provolone cheese—but the bread selection was all over the place (muffuletta bread is hard to find outside New Orleans), as were the recipes for the olive salad that is the heart and soul of this sandwich. Since none of the salads seemed spot on, I went to the source, ordering a jar from Central Grocery. When it arrived, I perused the ingredient list and got to work. Olives, both black and green, were key, and opting for the pimento-stuffed variety added more flavor. Capers, vinegar, oil, and garlic followed. The next six items—celery, cauliflower, carrots, sweet peppers, onions, and pepperoncini—brought to mind bottled *giardiniera*, a spicy Italian-style mixed vegetable pickle, which conveniently combines all those ingredients in one jar. My first round of tests showed that if the olive salad was too coarse, it wouldn't hold the sandwich together properly,

Alternating layers of meats and cheese helps create a more stable sandwich that's easier to eat.

so I reached for the food processor and pulsed olives (I used twice as many green as kalamata, since the latter are far saltier and the sandwich tends to be on the oversalty side), giardiniera, capers (rinsed to control the salt), red wine vinegar, and fresh garlic. Judging by the flavor of the Central Grocery version, the "spices" included oregano and thyme, so I threw in both. To flavor and bind the salad, I stirred in plenty of olive

oil. After assembling a sandwich (with store-bought Italian bread for now) and tasting, I knew I'd nailed it.

It was time to figure out what bread to use. Through the course of my testing, I had tried every iteration of supermarket bread, but none was working. A *boule* was too crusty and turned into a soggy mess, focaccia was too fluffy and not nearly thick enough, and sourdough bread just had the wrong flavor. I finally

had a breakthrough when one of my coworkers commented that the giant sandwich reminded her of a calzone—what about store-bought pizza dough? After a trip to the supermarket and some experimentation, I learned that a 1-pound ball of dough was the perfect size for a sandwich cut in quarters, but if I was going to the trouble, I figured I might as well serve a crowd—two balls of dough meant that I could feed eight or more with about the same amount of work. One hour of rising on the counter was plenty, and a brushing of egg wash followed by a sprinkling of sesame seeds before baking gave the finished loaves an extra touch of authenticity.

After the loaves cooled, it was time to assemble. The flavor and texture of my ersatz homemade bread were spot on, and after plenty of tumbling olive salad and wayward cold cuts, I found the best method of construction: After splitting the loaves horizontally, I spread olive salad on the cut sides of both the tops and the bottoms, which effectively "glued" everything together. Alternating layers of cheeses and meats created more stability, and finally, weighting the sandwiches for an hour rendered them compact and sliceable as well as helped the oil soak into the bread. I assembled, pressed, and sliced my muffulettas one more time; salty meats, briny olives, creamy cheese, and fresh, chewy bread, all in a convenient, handheld package? Mr. Lupo would be proud.

NEW ORLEANS MUFFULETTAS
Serves 8

You will need one 16-ounce jar of *giardiniera* to yield 2 cups drained; our favorite brand is Pastene. If you like a spicier sandwich, increase the amount of pepper flakes to ½ teaspoon.

- 2 (1-pound) balls pizza dough
- 2 cups drained jarred giardiniera
- 1 cup pimento-stuffed green olives
- ½ cup pitted kalamata olives
- 2 tablespoons capers, rinsed
- 1 tablespoon red wine vinegar
- 1 garlic clove, minced
- ½ teaspoon dried oregano
- ¼ teaspoon red pepper flakes
- ¼ teaspoon dried thyme
- ½ cup extra-virgin olive oil
- ¼ cup chopped fresh parsley
- 1 large egg, lightly beaten
- 5 teaspoons sesame seeds
- 4 ounces thinly sliced Genoa salami
- 6 ounces thinly sliced aged provolone cheese
- 6 ounces thinly sliced mortadella
- 4 ounces thinly sliced hot capicola

1. Form dough balls into 2 tight round balls on oiled baking sheet, cover loosely with greased plastic wrap, and let sit at room temperature for 1 hour.

2. Meanwhile, pulse giardiniera, green olives, kalamata olives, capers, vinegar, garlic, oregano, pepper flakes, and thyme in food processor until coarsely chopped, about 6 pulses, scraping down sides of bowl as needed. Transfer to bowl and stir in oil and parsley. Let sit at room temperature for 30 minutes. (Olive salad can be refrigerated for up to 1 week.)

3. Adjust oven rack to middle position and heat oven to 425 degrees.

Keeping dough balls on sheet, flatten each into 7-inch disk. Brush tops of disks with egg and sprinkle with sesame seeds. Bake until golden brown and loaves sound hollow when tapped, 18 to 20 minutes, rotating sheet halfway through baking. Transfer loaves to wire rack and let cool completely, about 1 hour. (Loaves can be wrapped in plastic and stored at room temperature for up to 24 hours.)

4. Slice loaves in half horizontally. Spread one-fourth of olive salad on cut side of each loaf top and bottom, pressing firmly with rubber spatula to compact. Layer 2 ounces salami, 1½ ounces provolone, 3 ounces mortadella, 1½ ounces provolone, and 2 ounces capicola in order on each loaf bottom. Cap with loaf tops and individually wrap sandwiches tightly in plastic.

5. Place baking sheet on top of sandwiches and weigh down with heavy Dutch oven or two 5-pound bags of flour or sugar for 1 hour, flipping sandwiches halfway through pressing. Unwrap and slice each sandwich into quarters and serve. (Pressed, wrapped sandwiches can be refrigerated for up to 24 hours. Bring to room temperature before serving.)

TEST KITCHEN TECHNIQUE Easy Homemade Muffuletta Bread
Starting with store-bought pizza dough means no mixing or kneading—just shape, rest, top, and bake.

1. Shape two store-bought pizza doughs into tight balls, place on baking sheet, cover with plastic wrap, and let rise for 1 hour.

2. Flatten balls into 7-inch disks, brush with beaten egg, sprinkle with sesame seeds, and bake.

3. Let loaves cool on wire rack for 1 hour and then slice horizontally like burger buns.

The American Table
Fellow Submarine

Though its olive salad and namesake round loaf make the muffuletta unique, it still lands firmly in the camp of that old American favorite, the submarine, or sub. Like the muffuletta, subs are to a large extent defined by the bread they're eaten on. Until the late 19th century, the American sandwich was a between-two-slices affair. But in 1893 at the Chicago World's Fair, the "Columbia roll"—basically a whole loaf of bread, so named because the Fair's formal name was The World's Columbia Exposition—made its debut. When this was married to the Italian cold cut sandwich popularized here by Italian immigrants in the late 19th century, the sub was born. It soon spread through the United States, acquiring different names as it went. We've found some 15 names for it, from relatively widespread ones like the hero to more intensely regional names like the bomber (upstate New York); the Garibaldi (Madison, Wisconsin— named for the Italian patriot); the

Sub scene, 1955 Saturday Evening Post.

torpedo (New Jersey, New York, and parts of the Midwest); the grinder (New England—slang for workers who ground the hulls of ships before repainting); the zeppelin (eastern Pennsylvania); the gondola (central Illinois); the hoagie (Philadelphia—from Hog Island Shipyard workers in World War II); and the wedgie (southeastern New York). Whatever the name, they all consist of a collection of meats, cheeses, and other ingredients—as few as three and as many as 30— stuffed into a loaf of bread.

A Salad That's a Glue

A food processor turns everyday ingredients into a potent condiment that holds the sandwich together.

KEY STEP Press for Success
Pressing the assembled sandwiches for an hour helps the olive salad properly soak into the bread.

A WEIGHTY SOLUTION
If you don't have a heavy Dutch oven, use two 5-pound bags of flour or sugar to weigh down the wrapped muffulettas.

Smoky Bourbon Chicken

This combination sounded perfect. All we had to do was figure out how to infuse smoke and bourbon flavors while keeping the chicken from drying out. BY CRISTIN WALSH

Slashing the meat creates more surface area to soak up the marinade and smoke. The skewers make the chicken halves easier to flip on the grill.

TEST KITCHEN TECHNIQUE **How to Cut a Chicken in Half**

1. REMOVE BACKBONE Using poultry shears, cut through bones on both sides of backbone; discard backbone.

2. CUT THROUGH BREAST Flip chicken over and use chef's knife to halve chicken through center of breastbone.

IT USED TO be that bourbon was thought of only as a drink. While that may be its highest and best use, this classic American spirit has long been used in cooking, too. It seems to have started with adding a shot or two to barbecue sauces and has progressed to recipes like smoky bourbon chicken. This sounded to me like a perfect combination of Southern flavors, so I decided to develop my own version.

I found plenty of recipes for this dish, but their approaches were all over the map. I tried them all and got varied results. In the end, none were very successful; all featured either dried-out chicken or meek bourbon flavor or both.

My first decision, based on that first round of testing, was to use two whole chickens but split them rather than leave them whole, so I could cook each half skin side up for crispier skin.

The next issue I tackled was the bourbon flavor. Recipes that relied on either a pregrill bourbon brine or a postgrill coating with a bourbon-spiked barbecue sauce had failed to imbue much of that flavor. But using a marinade, with its concentrated flavor components, had yielded promising results. I cobbled together a marinade that, along with bourbon, used brown sugar, shallots, garlic, and soy sauce. After an hour of marinating, I set up a grill fire with areas of high direct heat and lower indirect heat, put a foil packet containing a cup of soaked wood chips on top of the hot coals, and then put the chicken on the cooler side of the grill and covered it. An hour later the chicken halves were ready, with mixed results. I did get good bourbon flavor, but the marinade was lacking balance and impact.

I decided to try a method we'd used before, cutting slashes into the meat to create more surface area to absorb flavors. When I tried this, I definitely got more flavor into the chicken. But I still didn't feel that the marinade was living up to its potential, so I called our science editor for some advice. He explained that soy sauce has aroma compounds that can be intensified when heated, and heating the marinade for a mere minute right after I mixed it together could potentially improve the overall flavor in the chicken. Accordingly, for my next version I brought the marinade to a boil in a saucepan, let it cool to room temperature, and then added the chicken. Bingo.

This batch of chicken had smokiness, a pleasantly bold bourbon flavor, and deep, well-rounded seasoning.

Now I was ready to deal with the dryness. Since I was already marinating with a potent combination including soy sauce, brining didn't seem like the right approach. I turned instead to a staple of barbecue recipes: a mopping sauce. Mopping sauces are applied during grilling to long-cooking recipes, such as ribs. They help keep the meat moist by preventing the surface temperature from going above 212 degrees. In addition, since smoke is attracted to moisture, keeping the chicken skin damp should enhance the smoky flavor. I put another batch of chicken on the grill and diligently basted every 15 minutes until the skin was a deep mahogany (an added effect of the constant basting) and the chicken had come to the right temperature. After I brought the chicken inside, tasters gathered around the carving board, eagerly looking at the impressively dark, browned chicken halves. This time, heads nodded in agreement: The bourbon flavor was definitely there, as was smoke, and the chicken was moist. Finally chicken, bourbon, and smoke had met in a recipe that was not just good, but smokin' good.

SMOKED BOURBON CHICKEN
Serves 4

Use a bourbon you'd be happy drinking. Use all the basting liquid in step 5.

- 1¼ cups bourbon
- 1¼ cups soy sauce
- ½ cup packed brown sugar
- 1 shallot, minced
- 4 garlic cloves, minced
- 2 teaspoons pepper
- 2 (3½- to 4-pound) whole chickens, giblets discarded
- 1 cup wood chips
- 4 (12-inch) wooden skewers

1. Bring bourbon, soy sauce, sugar, shallot, garlic, and pepper to boil in medium saucepan over medium-high heat and cook for 1 minute. Remove from heat and let cool completely. Set aside ¾ cup bourbon mixture for basting chicken. (Bourbon mixture can be refrigerated up to 3 days in advance.)

2. With chickens breast side down, using kitchen shears, cut through bones on both sides of backbones; discard

Grilled Potato Salad

We wanted a grilled potato salad that didn't require preboiling the potatoes.

BY REBECCAH MARSTERS

backbones. Flip chickens over and, using chef's knife, split chickens in half lengthwise through centers of breastbones. Cut ½-inch-deep slits across breasts, thighs, and legs, about ½ inch apart. Tuck wingtips behind backs. Divide chicken halves between two 1-gallon zipper-lock bags and divide remaining bourbon mixture between bags. Seal bags, turn to distribute marinade, and refrigerate for at least 1 hour or up to 24 hours, flipping occasionally.

3. Just before grilling, soak wood chips in water for 15 minutes, then drain. Using large piece of heavy-duty aluminum foil, wrap soaked chips in foil packet and cut several vent holes in top. Remove chicken halves from marinade and pat dry with paper towels; discard marinade. Insert 1 skewer lengthwise through thickest part of breast down through thigh of each chicken half.

4A. FOR A CHARCOAL GRILL: Open bottom vent halfway. Light large chimney starter filled with charcoal briquettes (6 quarts). When top coals are partially covered with ash, pour into steeply banked pile against side of grill. Place wood chip packet on coals. Set cooking grate in place, cover, and open lid vent halfway. Heat grill until hot and wood chips are smoking, about 5 minutes.

4B. FOR A GAS GRILL: Remove cooking grate and place wood chip packet directly on primary burner. Set grate in place, turn all burners to high, cover, and heat grill until hot and wood chips are smoking, about 15 minutes. Leave primary burner on high and turn off other burners. (Adjust primary burner as needed to maintain grill temperature between 350 to 375 degrees.)

5. Clean and oil cooking grate. Place chicken halves skin side up on cooler side of grill with legs pointing toward fire. Cover and cook, basting every 15 minutes with reserved bourbon mixture, until breasts register 160 degrees and thighs register 175 degrees, 75 to 90 minutes, switching placement of chicken halves after 45 minutes. (All of bourbon mixture should be used.) Transfer chicken to carving board, tent loosely with foil, and let rest for 20 minutes. Carve and serve.

WHEN I GET out the grill, I like to use it for everything I'm cooking, so grilled potato salad is right up my alley. For ease, I looked for recipes that did not call for precooking the potatoes. One called for grilling whole unpeeled potatoes, but that took over an hour, and the leathery skins were nearly inedible. Another recipe simply required cooking cubed potatoes over a medium fire, which gave me nicely charred and surprisingly tender potatoes. But standing over the grill turning dozens of tiny potato cubes was too laborious. Looking for a middle ground, I tried halving small red potatoes and grilling them directly. This worked perfectly, giving me potatoes with nice smoky flavor that were also crisp outside and tender inside.

For even more smokiness, I decided to grill the onions along with the potatoes and add a bit of smoky chipotle chile to my vinaigrette. As a final touch, I sautéed some bacon and stirred it into the salad at the last minute. Not wanting to waste the bacon fat, I tried tossing the potatoes with it instead of olive oil. Perfect.

SMOKY POTATO SALAD
Serves 8

Use small red potatoes 1½ to 2 inches in diameter. If you don't have 2 tablespoons of fat in the skillet after frying the bacon, add olive oil to make up the difference.

- 6 slices bacon
- 3 tablespoons red wine vinegar
- 2 tablespoons mayonnaise
- 2 teaspoons minced canned chipotle chile in adobo sauce
  Salt and pepper
- 3 tablespoons olive oil, plus extra for brushing
- 3 pounds small red potatoes, unpeeled, halved
- 1 large onion, sliced into ½-inch-thick rounds
- 4 scallions, sliced thin

1. Cook bacon in 12-inch skillet over medium heat until crisp, 7 to 9 minutes; transfer to paper towel–lined plate. Set aside 2 tablespoons bacon fat. When cool enough to handle, crumble bacon and set aside. Whisk vinegar, mayonnaise, chipotle, ½ teaspoon salt, and ½ teaspoon pepper together in large bowl. Slowly whisk in 3 tablespoons oil until

Using the grill from start to finish yields smoky potatoes that are tender inside and crisp outside.

combined; set aside dressing.

2A. FOR A CHARCOAL GRILL: Open bottom vent completely. Light large chimney starter three-quarters filled with charcoal briquettes (4½ quarts). When top coals are partially covered with ash, pour evenly over grill. Set cooking grate in place, cover, and open lid vent completely. Heat grill until hot, about 5 minutes.

2B. FOR A GAS GRILL: Turn all burners to high, cover, and heat grill until hot, about 15 minutes. Turn all burners to medium.

3. Clean and oil cooking grate. Toss potatoes with reserved bacon fat and ½ teaspoon salt. Push toothpick horizontally through each onion round to keep rings intact while grilling. Brush onion

rounds lightly with extra oil and season with salt and pepper. Place potatoes, cut side down, and onion rounds on grill and cook, covered, until charred on first side, 10 to 14 minutes.

4. Flip potatoes and onion rounds and continue to cook, covered, until well browned all over and potatoes are easily pierced with tip of paring knife, 10 to 16 minutes longer. Transfer potatoes and onion rounds to rimmed baking sheet and let cool slightly.

5. When cool enough to handle, halve potatoes; remove toothpicks and coarsely chop onion rounds. Add potatoes, onion, scallions, and bacon to dressing and toss to combine. Season with salt and pepper to taste. Serve warm or at room temperature.

Pasta with Raw Tomato Sauce

Summer's tomatoes are most flavorful eaten raw.
But could we get the texture of a sauce with no cooking? BY ASHLEY MOORE

IN THE HEART of summer when perfectly ripe tomatoes taste so unbelievably good, it almost seems like a crime to cook them. But there's a limit to the number of sliced tomatoes one person can eat. That's where pasta with raw tomato sauce comes in.

I found plenty of recipes for this summer sauce, all of which called for very different approaches. One recipe called for heating oil on the stovetop and pouring it over seasoned tomatoes to quickly wilt them. The result was a fragrant tomato mixture with absolutely no ability to cling to the pasta as a sauce should. Another recipe called for marinating tomatoes in sugar, vinegar, oil, and aromatics for a few hours before processing them through a food mill. This resulted in a sweet-and-sour tomato soup that had my tasters wondering if I had tricked them by making gazpacho. I wanted the mixture thick enough to cling nicely to the pasta, but not so thin that it would seem like a soup.

I first concentrated on figuring out how to avoid a thin, watery sauce. For this, I turned to a trick that the test kitchen often uses when faced with this challenge: salting the tomatoes. This technique extracts liquid from the tomatoes and softens their flesh. After many tests, I figured out that an hour was the optimal time to let seasoned tomatoes sit. It was shocking to see that 2 pounds of tomatoes released a full cup of liquid. Along the way, I also figured out that if I added garlic and fresh oregano to the mix along with the salt, their flavors would mellow nicely and also be somewhat absorbed by the tomatoes.

It was time to focus on how to transform my drained tomatoes into a sauce. I tried mashing them. This gave them a pretty good texture, but they were too mealy. What would it be like if I mashed half of the mixture? Good idea. Now the sauce was the ideal combination of crushed tomatoes surrounded by newly released tomato liquid, with just the right amount of chunkiness.

But I found myself wondering what to do with the drained tomato liquid. I was not about to toss it out because I knew it had a ton of flavor. One of my test kitchen colleagues had a thought: What if I used this liquid to cook the pasta? Diluted by the amount of water used to cook pasta in the traditional method, it wouldn't have much of an

Mashing half of the macerated (but still raw) tomatoes helps create a proper saucy consistency.

effect. But we have a skillet method of cooking pasta that requires much less liquid; the pasta absorbs the water as it cooks and is never drained. Using this as my guide, I combined the tomato liquid with enough water to bring the total amount to 4 cups (enough for 1 pound of pasta with our skillet method) in a 12-inch skillet. I stirred in 1 pound of pasta and cooked it until the pasta was al dente and most of the liquid was gone.

After stirring the mashed and reserved tomatoes into the now-cooked pasta, I was relieved to see a sauce—but it needed to be just a little thicker. I knew that stirring the pasta as it cooked would release its natural starches, which would in turn thicken the sauce. There wasn't room enough to do this in the skillet,

though, so I switched to a Dutch oven and stirred the pasta frequently as it cooked. When the liquid was all gone, the pasta was cooked well, infused with tomato flavor, and coated with a light rose–colored tomato sheen. Once again I stirred in the tomatoes. There was a strong tomato presence now, created by

not only the chunks and mashed tomatoes but also the subtly flavored pasta. I stirred in some basil, Parmesan cheese, and extra-virgin olive oil and finally had what I had dreamed of: a sauce with all the fresh, bright flavor of raw tomatoes.

PASTA WITH RAW TOMATO SAUCE
Serves 4
Use the ripest tomatoes you can find.

- **2** pounds very ripe tomatoes, cored and cut into ½-inch pieces
- **1½** tablespoons chopped fresh oregano
- **2** teaspoons plus 2 tablespoons extra-virgin olive oil, plus extra for serving
- **2** garlic cloves, minced
  Salt and pepper
- **¼** teaspoon sugar
- **3** cups water
- **1** pound short pasta, such as campanelle, penne, or fusilli
- **½** cup fresh basil leaves, torn
- **1** ounce Parmesan cheese, grated (½ cup), plus extra for serving

1. Combine tomatoes, oregano, 2 teaspoons oil, garlic, 1½ teaspoons salt, and sugar in large bowl. Let sit until tomatoes soften and release their juice, at least 1 hour or up to 3 hours.

2. Drain tomato mixture in fine-mesh strainer set over bowl and reserve juice. (You should have 1 cup tomato juice; if not, add water as needed to equal 1 cup.) Divide drained tomato mixture evenly between 2 bowls. Using potato masher, mash 1 bowl of tomato mixture to pulp.

3. Combine water, pasta, and reserved tomato juice in Dutch oven. Cover, place over medium-high heat, and cook at vigorous simmer, stirring often, until pasta is al dente and liquid has nearly evaporated, 12 to 15 minutes. Off heat, stir in basil, Parmesan, mashed and unmashed tomato mixtures, and remaining 2 tablespoons oil. Season with salt and pepper to taste. Serve with extra oil and extra Parmesan.

TEST KITCHEN DISCOVERY
Cook the Pasta in Tomato Water
After macerating the chopped tomatoes in salt, sugar, garlic, oregano, and olive oil, we drain out a cup of the flavorful juice. This juice is combined with water to cook the pasta, which infuses the noodles with subtle tomato flavor.

Zucchini Fritters

Zucchini fritters can be bland and soggy. We developed a crisp but tender version that packs a potent punch of flavor. BY SARAH GABRIEL

ZUCCHINI FRITTERS FALL somewhere on the spectrum between pancakes and latkes. To make them, shredded zucchini is bound with a seasoned flour and egg batter that sometimes includes cheese. Thick batters and large volumes of frying oil yield crunchier, more fritter-like fritters. Loose, eggy batters cooked in less oil yield more pancake-like results. Both styles can be delicious, and if you're a gardener, zucchini fritters are perfect for transforming surplus squashes from burden to benefit. If you're not a gardener, zucchini fritters are a good reason to befriend one.

I gathered a slew of zucchini fritter recipes, a box grater, and a pile of zucchini and hit the kitchen in search of the best way to turn zucchini into something spectacular. Many recipes called for squeezing the water out of the shredded zucchini, which ended up being a prerequisite: Unsqueezed zucchini resulted in wet, mushy fritters. Flour and egg was the standard base, but too much batter and not enough zucchini made the fritters dense and tough. One egg and ½ cup of flour seemed like a good starting point for 1½ pounds of zucchini. I tried a variety of add-ins and my tasters settled on feta, mint, and dill. I combined all these elements in one recipe and cooked the batter in oil in a nonstick skillet. I was aiming for something in between the pancake-y style and the crispy, fried style, but what I got was a little soggy and disappointing. Even after squeezing, the zucchini was releasing too much moisture into the batter.

To dry out the batter, I tried wringing out the shredded zucchini in a dish towel. That got rid of a little more water than simply squeezing the zucchini by the handful—especially when I salted the zucchini first—but it still didn't yield crispy fritters. Short of using a dehydrator, I couldn't think of a way to get more liquid out of the zucchini, so I changed gears and looked for something to add to the batter to soak up the remaining excess liquid.

Using more flour just made the fritters denser and tougher. Maybe what I needed wasn't more starch but a different starch. Cornstarch can soak up about twice as much liquid as flour can, so I tried a few different amounts. Six tablespoons of cornstarch worked perfectly; now the batter was amply stiff and the fritters were moist and tender inside but lightly crisped outside. My tasters liked them, but they wanted a sauce on the side.

Yogurt sauces are often served with this dish, but we already had creamy cheese inside the fritters. What my fritters needed was something bright, like marinara sauce, except fresher-tasting and slightly more exotic. We hadn't used citrus in the fritters, but maybe we'd like it in the sauce. After a few tries, I settled on a simple sauce made by sautéing scallion whites and then adding orange juice and brown sugar and cooking it until syrupy. Then I introduced coriander, orange zest, and canned diced tomatoes and simmered briefly. The sweet-tart flavors of the tomato and orange worked well together, and the coriander contributed a warm backbone. I called my tasters. This time, everyone took a plate and used the fritters to mop up dollops of sauce. After all the plate swabbing and seconds grabbing was over, I asked for comments. The first one was, "When are you making this again?"

ZUCCHINI FRITTERS
Makes 12 fritters

We prefer to use young, small zucchini—about 1½ inches in diameter. If you use larger zucchini, you may drain off more liquid in step 2.

SAUCE
- 2 tablespoons unsalted butter
- 2 scallions, white and green parts separated and sliced thin
- ¼ teaspoon salt
- ½ teaspoon grated orange zest plus ¼ cup juice
- 1 teaspoon packed brown sugar
- ¼ teaspoon ground coriander
- 1 (14.5-ounce) can diced tomatoes

FRITTERS
- 1½ pounds zucchini
- 1½ teaspoons salt
- 6 tablespoons cornstarch
- 6 ounces feta cheese, crumbled (1½ cups)
- 1 large egg, lightly beaten
- 2 tablespoons minced fresh mint
- 2 tablespoons minced fresh dill
- 2 garlic cloves, minced
- 1 teaspoon pepper
- ¼ cup vegetable oil

Our simple tomato sauce is flavored with scallions, orange, and coriander.

1. FOR THE SAUCE: Melt butter in medium saucepan over medium heat. Continue to cook, swirling pan constantly, until butter is dark golden brown and has nutty aroma, 1 to 3 minutes. Add scallion whites and salt and cook until softened, about 2 minutes. Stir in orange juice and sugar and cook until syrupy, about 3 minutes. Add coriander and cook until fragrant, about 30 seconds. Stir in tomatoes and their juice and orange zest and cook until slightly thickened, about 8 minutes. Remove from heat. Stir in scallion greens, cover, and keep warm.

2. FOR THE FRITTERS: Line large bowl with clean dish towel. Grate zucchini on large holes of box grater into prepared bowl. Stir in salt and let sit for 10 minutes. Gather ends of towel to form bundle and twist to squeeze zucchini as dry as possible (you should squeeze off about 1 cup liquid). Discard liquid and return zucchini to bowl (without towel). Stir cornstarch into zucchini until fully incorporated. Stir in feta, egg, mint, dill, garlic, and pepper.

3. Heat 2 tablespoons oil in 12-inch nonstick skillet over medium-high heat until shimmering. Using ¼-cup dry measuring cup, drop 6 scant ¼-cup portions of batter into pan. Gently press each fritter to 2½-inch diameter using back of spoon or rubber spatula. Cook until well browned and slightly crisp, about 4 minutes per side. Let drain on paper towels, 30 seconds per side, then transfer to wire rack. Repeat with remaining 2 tablespoons oil and remaining batter. Serve with sauce.

Faster Smoked Pork Chops

Long-cooked barbecue is great, but we wanted that deep smoke flavor (and tender meat) in less than an hour. BY CHRISTIE MORRISON

ORDINARILY, GOOD BARBECUE comes to those who wait. When it comes to big cuts of meat like brisket and pork shoulder, with lots of marbling and connective tissue to break down, a long, slow stay over indirect heat and smoke is definitely the way to go. But other cuts of meat, like center-cut pork chops, are leaner, with less connective tissue, so they dry out and get tough if they spend too long on the grill. This means that they aren't suited to the low-and-slow barbecue approach. As a big barbecue fan, though, I wanted to find a way to quick-grill chops so they would come off the grill still moist and tender, but with that long-smoked barbecue flavor. In other words, I wanted the best of both worlds: tenderness and smoke.

Before I headed to the grill, I needed to choose my chop. What makes blade chops great for longer cooking—their connective tissue and mix of light and dark meat—makes them a nonstarter for quick grilling. Leaner rib or center-cut chops, which come from the tender loin section of the pig, made more sense. I also opted for a thick-cut chop, about 1½ inches thick, so the outside wouldn't begin to dry out before the center cooked through.

A couple of other things were givens. When it comes to grilling, we like to brine thick-cut chops in a salt and sugar solution to season them and keep them juicy, and this would be no exception. Most barbecue recipes call for adding a spice rub to the meat before smoking; I settled on a simple mix of salt, pepper, and sugar to perk up the flavor and increase browning.

I also knew that I would want a basic and relatively mild barbecue sauce to reinforce the smoky flavor of the chops without overpowering the mild pork, so I set about creating this before the grilling began. I gathered the usual suspects—ketchup, molasses, mustard, Worcestershire, and a healthy dose of apple cider vinegar for punch. Then I sautéed some onion (grated to avoid chunks in the sauce) in a bit of oil to take off the raw edge and bloomed garlic, chili powder, and cayenne in the same pan to intensify their flavors. The sauce simmered for about 10 minutes, reducing to a thick but pourable sauce that I hoped would be able to pull double duty—as a glaze and a serving sauce.

These thick, meaty center-cut chops soak up lots of sultry smoke flavor.

For the grilling, I set up my grill for a half-grill fire, which calls for piling the coals on one side to create a hotter side and a cooler side. To add some smoke, I soaked 2 cups of wood chips before folding them into a foil packet and placing them over the pile of coals. I put my brined and dried pork chops on the hotter side and seared them well. Then I brushed them with barbecue sauce and transferred them to the cooler side to cook the rest of the way, flipping them and brushing them with more sauce after about 4 minutes. All told, the grilling took only about 15 minutes.

Unfortunately, what I made up for in speed, I lost in smoky flavor. The wood chips had barely caught fire by the time the chops were done. With such a short cooking time, I needed more smoke from the get-go. For my next test, I scattered the wood chips directly over the coals, which definitely increased the smoke output and the resulting smoky flavor in the chops. Keeping the grill covered, despite the relatively short cooking time, trapped more smoke inside, yielding even better flavor and a noticeable smoke ring.

This time the chops were well seasoned and smoky, and the sauce caramelized into a thick, spicy glaze. My smoke-grilled pork chops might not be authentic barbecue, but with results this tasty after just 15 minutes on the grill, I was content with a well-seasoned, nicely smoky knock-off.

QUICK SMOKED PORK CHOPS
Serves 4 to 6

If the pork is enhanced (injected with a salt solution), do not brine. Use the large holes of a box grater to grate the onion for the barbecue sauce. Wood chunks are not recommended for this recipe because they take too long to begin to smoke.

PORK
- 3 tablespoons plus 2 teaspoons sugar
  Salt and pepper
- 4 (12- to 14-ounce) bone-in pork rib or center-cut chops, 1½ inches thick, trimmed
- 2 cups wood chips

BARBECUE SAUCE
- 1 teaspoon vegetable oil
- ¼ cup grated onion
- 1 garlic clove, minced
- 1 teaspoon chili powder
- ¼ teaspoon cayenne pepper
- 1 cup ketchup
- ¼ cup molasses
- 3 tablespoons cider vinegar
- 2 tablespoons Worcestershire sauce
- 2 tablespoons Dijon mustard

1. FOR THE PORK: Dissolve 3 tablespoons sugar and 3 tablespoons salt in 1½ quarts cold water in large container. Submerge chops in brine, cover, and refrigerate for 1 hour. Combine remaining 2 teaspoons sugar, 1 teaspoon salt, and 1 teaspoon pepper in bowl; set aside. Just before grilling, soak wood chips in water for 15 minutes, then drain.

2. FOR THE BARBECUE SAUCE: Meanwhile, heat oil in small saucepan over medium heat until shimmering. Add onion and cook until softened, about 3 minutes. Stir in garlic, chili powder, and cayenne and cook until fragrant, about 30 seconds. Whisk in ketchup, molasses, vinegar, Worcestershire, and mustard. Bring to simmer, reduce heat to medium-low and cook, stirring occasionally, until sauce is reduced to 1½ cups, 7 to 10 minutes. Set aside ¾ cup barbecue sauce for serving.

3A. FOR A CHARCOAL GRILL: Open bottom vent completely. Light large chimney starter filled with charcoal briquettes (6 quarts). When top coals are partially covered with ash, pour evenly over half of grill. Scatter soaked wood chips over coals. Set cooking grate in place, cover, and open lid vent completely. Heat grill until hot and wood chips are smoking, about 5 minutes.

3B. FOR A GAS GRILL: Using large piece of heavy-duty foil, wrap soaked chips in foil packet and cut several vent holes in top. Remove cooking grate and place wood chip packet directly on primary burner. Set grate in place, turn all burners to high, cover, and heat grill until hot and wood chips are smoking, about 15 minutes. Leave primary burner on high and turn off other burner(s).

4. Clean and oil cooking grate. Remove pork from brine and pat dry with paper towels. Season chops all over with spice mixture. Grill chops over hotter side of grill, covered (positioning lid vent over chops if using charcoal), until well browned, 3 to 5 minutes per side.

5. Brush each chop with about 1 tablespoon barbecue sauce and flip sauce side down onto cooler side of grill. Grill, covered, until sauce begins to tighten, about 3 minutes. Brush chops with remaining barbecue sauce, and flip sauce side down. Continue to grill, covered, until meat near but not touching bone registers 140 degrees, about 3 minutes. Transfer chops to platter, tent loosely with foil, and let rest for 5 to 10 minutes. Serve chops with reserved barbecue sauce.

Smoke Flavor Faster

To build intense smoke flavor on a compressed timetable, we sear the chops directly over the smoking wood chips, where they soak up smoke flavor fast. Then we finish cooking the chops on a cooler part of the grill.

Gazpacho

It may seem contradictory, but for our version of this cold summer favorite, we wanted a gazpacho that was at once creamy and crunchy. BY DIANE UNGER

ALTHOUGH GAZPACHO originated in southern Spain as a white soup based on bread and garlic, today the name generally refers to a cold tomato-based version. It typically contains cucumbers, bell peppers, onions or shallots, and garlic along with the tomatoes. But there are seemingly endless variations that differ primarily in texture. Some recipes call for hand-chopping the vegetables, creating a salsa-like consistency. Others turn to either the blender or the food processor, giving the soup a more homogenous texture. Then there is the more traditional Spanish approach, in which a creamier texture is created by thickening the soup with a slice of bread and emulsifying it with fruity olive oil.

After making all three styles of gazpacho, my tasters and I decided we wanted something in between. We liked the creamy texture of the soups thickened with bread and olive oil, but we also wanted bits of vegetables for crunchy contrast. I set out to make a version that satisfied everybody.

Cutting all the vegetables into tiny pieces would take too much effort. Instead, I cut them all into large chunks, pulsed them in the food processor to pieces somewhere between ¼ and ½ inch long, and then returned 2 cups of the vegetables to the processor to puree until smooth. The combination of the slightly processed and fully processed base, when mixed with tomato juice, gave me a nice mix of smooth and chunky. But it still didn't have the perfect creamy texture.

To make the gazpacho creamier, I tore up a slice of bread and added it to the 2 cups of vegetables I was pureeing fully. When that mixture was completely smooth, I slowly drizzled in ½ cup of extra-virgin olive oil while the machine ran. Now the texture was not just smooth but creamy and rich with crunchy bits of vegetables.

But I noticed a faint but distinctive sour undertone. I consulted our science editor, who explained that pureeing shallots and garlic releases too many molecules of an enzyme that then combines with other molecules to create a harsh, sulfurous taste. The solution was simple: I minced the garlic and shallot and stirred them in at the end.

High-quality extra-virgin olive oil makes a big difference in this recipe.

GAZPACHO Serves 4 to 6

Campbell's makes our favorite tomato juice. The traditional garnish is more of the same vegetables that are in the soup.

- 12 ounces vine-ripened tomatoes, cored and quartered
- 1 red bell pepper (8 ounces), stemmed, seeded, and cut into 1-inch pieces
- 1 cucumber (8 ounces), halved lengthwise, seeded, and cut into 1-inch pieces
- 2½ cups tomato juice
- 2½ tablespoons sherry vinegar
- 1 teaspoon hot sauce
   Salt and pepper
- 1 slice hearty white sandwich bread, torn into pieces
- ¼ cup extra-virgin olive oil, plus extra for serving
- 1 shallot, minced
- 1 garlic clove, minced

1. Pulse tomatoes in food processor until broken into ½- to ¼-inch pieces, about 12 pulses; transfer to large bowl. Pulse bell pepper and cucumber in now-empty processor until broken down into ½- to ¼-inch pieces, about 8 pulses; add to bowl with tomatoes. Stir in tomato juice, vinegar, hot sauce, 1 teaspoon salt, and ½ teaspoon pepper.

2. Process bread and 2 cups tomato mixture in now-empty processor until smooth, about 1 minute. With processor running, slowly drizzle in oil until incorporated. Return pureed tomato mixture to bowl with remaining tomato mixture and stir in shallot and garlic. Cover and refrigerate gazpacho for at least 4 hours or up to 2 days.

3. Season with salt and pepper to taste. Ladle gazpacho into chilled bowls and drizzle with extra oil. Serve.

Illustration: Lauren Renaplece

Introducing New England Bar Pizza

With a thin, crisp crust and melty cheese on top, New England bar pizza is appealing . . . even before you know about the "laced" edges. BY CRISTIN WALSH

SITUATED BETWEEN BOSTON and the shoulder of Cape Cod is a stretch of mostly suburban towns collectively known as the South Shore. While this region has a rich cultural history dating back to Colonial times, pizza fanatics know it as the spiritual home of New England bar pizza.

Truthfully, I had never heard of this pizza—despite living just 20 miles away—until a colleague who grew up on the South Shore lovingly described the pies at her favorite pizza place, the family-owned and -operated Lynwood Café in Randolph, Massachusetts. She described their pizza as having a tender, thin crust with a crisp underside, a fresh and potent sauce, and plenty of browned, bubbly cheese on top. When I mentioned that I was contemplating a visit, her expression turned very serious: "You have to get a pie with laced edges," she said. A secret, off-menu option, a "laced" pizza has sauce and cheese spread beyond the dough's lip, where it sinks between the dough and this pizza's signature lipped pan, resulting in a well-charred edge where the cheese and sauce crisp and caramelize into a delicious, crackly lace.

With my mouth practically watering, I wasted no time in driving down to the Lynwood Café. After looking over the menu, which hasn't changed in over 60 years (the Lynwood hasn't changed much since its start in 1949), I ordered a cheese pizza and their signature pie, the baked bean special, which is loaded with Boston baked beans, onions, and salami. While I waited, I had a chance to speak with Steve, the fourth generation of his family to work there. I tried my best to squeeze some trade secrets out of Steve, but he preferred to let the pizza speak for itself. It spoke loud and clear; it was love at first bite. And the baked bean version, odd as it sounded, was delicious.

I headed to the test kitchen determined to replicate New England bar pizza with the few clues I had. I tried the handful of copycat recipes I found online, but they were poor imitations, with crusts that were too chewy or too thick and that lacked the defining crisp bottom. Sauces were ho-hum. The best cheese toppings used equal amounts of cheddar (for robust flavor) and mozzarella (for easy melting).

Getting the dough right was

No doughy bits: Cooking this pizza in an oiled pan gives it a crisp, deeply-browned crust.

paramount. It had to be tender yet crisp—not chewy like most pizza crust. I decided to start by baking the test kitchen's thin-crust pizza dough recipe in cake pans (since most home cooks don't have rimmed pizza pans). The recipe calls for mixing bread flour, sugar, instant yeast, and water in the food processor to form a ball. The dough rests until the flour is hydrated and then oil and salt are processed in; the dough

rises at room temperature for about 2 hours before shaping. Once it had risen, I divided the dough in half, rolled each piece out, and pressed the dough into two 9-inch round cake pans, making a ¼-inch lip up the sides. I spooned on a quick tomato sauce and sprinkled a mix of mozzarella and cheddar over top. Following the original recipe, I baked the pizzas on a pizza stone on the top rack of a 500-degree oven.

The resulting pizzas were promising, if not quite right. The dough was a little too chewy on the edges, and the bottom wasn't perfectly crisp all over, although the cake pans seemed to work well as baking vessels. For a more tender dough, I switched to all-purpose flour instead of the bread flour; the all-purpose flour is lower in protein and thus creates less gluten and chew. But how could I get the bottom

On the Road
Baked Bean Pizza?

The Lynwood Café in Randolph, Mass., has a lot of character, and a few characters too. Standard pizza toppings share the menu with local favorites like linguica (a Portuguese sausage) and the house special: Baked beans, onions and salami. Sounds odd, but the sweet-spicy combo of beans and meat makes this pizza work. To read more about my trip and the Lynwood's history (and for a link to the recipe variation for baked bean pizza), visit **CooksCountry.com/ lynwoodcafe.**

Place your order.

appropriately crisp?

I tried adding lots of olive oil to the pans, which helped a bit. But the real solution was placing the oven rack at the lowest position, closest to the heating element. Moving the pizzas away from the reflected heat at the top of the oven meant that the cheese took longer to brown, which allowed extra time for the pizza's bottom to crisp. The extra baking time also meant that I no longer needed the pizza stone, another plus. Now the pizzas were tender and nicely browned with crisp bottom crusts—just as they are at the Lynwood.

I turned to the sauce. Simplicity was the key here, and that meant an uncooked sauce. Working to replicate the Lynwood's straightforward yet flavorful version, I processed one can of diced tomatoes together with a touch of olive oil, dried oregano, sugar, salt, pepper, and pepper flakes and ladled ⅓ cup of the sauce over each pan of dough. Equal parts sharp cheddar and mozzarella made for the perfect cheesy topping. To get that authentic "lacing" on the crust, I brushed the sauce and sprinkled the cheese over the edge where the dough met the pans. These pizzas, finally, tasted a lot like what had made me swoon in Randolph.

Is the world ready to fall in love with New England bar pizza? With this recipe, I think it just might be.

NEW ENGLAND BAR PIZZA
Serves 4
Clean the food processor in between making the dough and the pizza sauce. You will have some sauce left over; reserve it for another use. Use sharp cheddar cheese, not extra-sharp (which makes the pizzas too greasy).

DOUGH
1⅔	cups (8⅓ ounces) all-purpose flour
1	tablespoon sugar
1	teaspoon instant or rapid-rise yeast
⅔	cup water
1½	teaspoons extra-virgin olive oil
¾	teaspoon salt

SAUCE
1	(14.5-ounce) can diced tomatoes
1	teaspoon extra-virgin olive oil
½	teaspoon dried oregano
½	teaspoon sugar
¼	teaspoon salt
⅛	teaspoon pepper
⅛	teaspoon red pepper flakes

TOPPING
4	ounces sharp cheddar cheese, shredded (1 cup)
4	ounces whole-milk mozzarella, shredded (1 cup)
1	tablespoon extra-virgin olive oil

1. FOR THE DOUGH: Process flour, sugar, and yeast in food processor until combined, about 3 seconds. With processor running, slowly add water; process dough until just combined and no dry flour remains, about 10 seconds. Let dough stand for 10 minutes. Add oil and salt to dough and process until dough forms satiny, sticky ball that clears sides of workbowl, 30 to 60 seconds.

2. Transfer dough to lightly oiled counter and knead until smooth, about 1 minute. Shape dough into tight ball and place in greased bowl. Cover with plastic wrap and let rise at room temperature until almost doubled in size, 2 to 2½ hours.

3. FOR THE SAUCE: Process all ingredients in clean, dry food processor until smooth, about 30 seconds; set sauce aside. (Sauce can be refrigerated for up to 2 days or frozen for up to 1 month.)

4. FOR THE TOPPING: Adjust oven rack to lowest position and heat oven to 500 degrees. Combine cheddar and mozzarella in bowl. Using pastry brush, grease bottom and sides of 2 dark-colored 9-inch round cake pans with 1½ teaspoons oil each.

5. Transfer dough to lightly floured counter, divide in half, and snap into balls. Gently flatten 1 dough ball into 6-inch disk using your fingertips. Using rolling pin, roll disk into 10-inch round. Transfer dough to prepared pan and press into corners, forcing ¼-inch lip of dough up sides of pan. Repeat with remaining dough ball.

6. Spread ⅓ cup sauce in thin layer over entire surface of 1 dough. Using pastry brush, brush sauce over lip of dough. Sprinkle 1 cup cheese mixture evenly over pizza, including lip. Repeat with remaining dough, ⅓ cup sauce, and remaining 1 cup cheese mixture.

7. Bake until crust is browned and cheese is bubbly and beginning to brown, about 12 minutes, switching and rotating pans halfway through baking. To remove pizzas from pans, run offset spatula along top edge of pizza crust. Once loosened, slide spatula underneath pizza and slide pizza onto wire rack. Let cool for 5 minutes. Slice and serve.

Watercress Salad

Peppery watercress needs other strong flavors for balance. BY BRYAN ROOF

TO MAKE WATERCRESS work in a salad, you first have to add sweetness (we use honey) to temper its bite. Then you need potent ingredients like the Dijon, lemon, dill, and fresh cheese we use here, to create a bold and bright salad.

Cucumber and radishes give this salad crunch.

WATERCRESS AND CUCUMBER SALAD WITH LEMON VINAIGRETTE
Serves 4 to 6
You can substitute crumbled goat cheese or feta for the farmer's cheese.

1	small shallot, minced
2	teaspoons honey
	Salt and pepper
½	teaspoon Dijon mustard
¼	teaspoon grated lemon zest plus 2½ tablespoons juice
2½	tablespoons extra-virgin olive oil
8	ounces (8 cups) watercress
1	seedless English cucumber, peeled, halved lengthwise, and sliced thin
6	radishes, trimmed, each cut into 6 wedges
⅓	cup shelled pistachios, toasted and chopped
¼	cup coarsely chopped fresh dill
2	ounces farmer's cheese, crumbled (½ cup)

1. Whisk shallot, honey, ¾ teaspoon salt, ½ teaspoon pepper, mustard, and lemon zest and juice together in large bowl. Whisking constantly, slowly drizzle in oil until incorporated.

2. Add watercress, cucumber, radishes, pistachios, and dill and toss to combine. Season with salt and pepper to taste. Transfer to platter and sprinkle with farmer's cheese. Serve.

TEST KITCHEN TECHNIQUE **Making New England Bar Pizza at Home**
You don't have to travel to Randolph, Massachusetts, for this one. We've mastered the "laced" edges and the crisp crust, and you can, too.

This "Lace" Isn't Fancy
We spread the sauce and cheese to the very edge of the pans, where they caramelize into a delicious "lace."

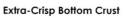

Extra-Crisp Bottom Crust
We bake the pizzas in oiled cake pans on the bottom rack of a 500-degree oven.

Huevos Rancheros

This lively Tex-Mex breakfast—fried eggs served with tortillas, cheese, and a rich tomato-and-chile sauce— typically takes a lot of work. We set out to simplify. BY MATTHEW CARD

THERE ARE THOSE who throw off the sheets for a sweet stack of fluffy pancakes or a syrup-soaked waffle, but I am not one of them. Instead, I stir for savory—think corned beef hash, bacon and eggs, or my favorite breakfast: huevos rancheros. I find the dish's fine-tuned combination of sunny-side up eggs, spicy sauce, tender tortillas, and rich cheese unbeatable (especially once it's all doused in hot sauce).

However, preparing the dish's numerous components requires more effort and attention to detail than I am usually willing to commit to first thing in the morning. Is there an easy (or at least *easier*) way to make huevos rancheros?

Huevos rancheros wended its way northward from Mexico through the border states before becoming near-ubiquitous on breakfast menus around the United States. Perhaps because of its wayward migration, there's no singularly defined version. The tortillas remain constant, of course, but the eggs can be fried or poached, and sauces range from simple salsas and pico de gallo to both red and green moles and, finally, enchilada-style or ranchero sauces. After preparing a few promising recipes, I preferred this latter sauce, which is traditionally made from roasted tomatoes, onion, garlic, chiles, and seasonings.

Instead of just browning the vegetables in a skillet, though, I wanted to replicate the deep char that Mexican cooks get using a cast-iron (or earthenware) griddle called a *comal*. In the past, the test kitchen has turned to the broiler for this type of aggressive searing, so that's where I started, too. But broiling requires frequent stirring and close attention to avoid incineration (speckled charring is perfect, burning not so much). The last thing I wanted to do first thing in the morning was prepare anything requiring such high-wire focus.

Instead of broiling, I wondered if a hot oven might give me similar results. I tossed the sauce components—by this point, I had narrowed it down to diced canned tomatoes (drained), onion, jalapeño chiles, and garlic—with salt, pepper, and olive oil and roasted the mix on a rimmed baking sheet at temperatures ranging from 400 to 500 degrees. The high end of the spectrum did the trick, browning the vegetables

We roast the tomatoes, onion, garlic, and chiles with oil and chili powder to give the sauce deep, intense flavor.

and concentrating their flavor in the same fashion as broiling—just a lot more conveniently (it requires only one quick stir midway through to ensure even browning). Sure, it took a little longer to roast than to broil—about 40 minutes all said—but I put that time to good use making coffee and reading the newspaper.

While some recipes call for dried chiles (usually pasilla or ancho), I knew

that the stemming, toasting, soaking, and pureeing would be too much work here. I tested standard chili powder and was pleased to find that 3 tablespoons contributed the kick I wanted, especially when I added it to the vegetables before roasting so it could toast and intensify in the oven's high, dry heat. In an attempt to simplify my recipe, I made a batch in which I omitted the fresh jalapeños from the mix and added a can of green chiles

instead. The sauce tasted great with the canned chiles, which required no effort besides popping the lid off the can. To fine-tune the sauce, I added a tablespoon each of brown sugar and fresh lime juice.

In my early batches, I pureed the sauce to a smooth, silky consistency. It tasted right, but there was little textural contrast to the eggs. Why not leave the sauce chunky? Straight from the oven,

TEST KITCHEN TECHNIQUE
Roast the Vegetables; Bake the Eggs

To evoke the charred flavors in traditional huevos rancheros, we roast vegetables in a hot oven before layering them into a baking dish with cheese sprinkled over. Cracking eggs into wells in the mixture allows us to bake eight servings at once—no more standing at the stove frying egg after egg for an impatient crowd.

it was too thick—more side dish than sauce—so I mixed it with a portion of the tangy liquid I'd drained from the tomatoes. This batch proved the best to date and was easier, too. With about 5 minutes of hands-on prep and 40 minutes of oven time, I had a terrific-tasting sauce for my eggs.

The eggs for huevos rancheros are usually fried sunny-side up. Ever tried frying eight eggs at once? It's nearly impossible unless you're a line cook. The first egg in the pan is largely set by the time the last egg is cracked and chances are high that at least one of the yolks cracks in the haste of getting the eggs into the pan. The same problems hold true for poached eggs.

Looking afield for inspiration, I remembered a colorfully named Italian dish called "eggs in purgatory" in which eggs are poached directly in a pan of simmering sauce. I transferred the thick sauce to my largest skillet, brought it to a simmer, cracked eight eggs into divots that I had dimpled into the sauce, and covered the pan. Ten minutes later, I had well-cooked eggs, but the dish looked a mess: The sauce was nearly entirely covered under a shaggy mess of amoeba-shaped eggs. A skillet was simply too small to accommodate both sauce and eggs for four.

I had roasted the sauce in the oven, so why not cook the eggs there too? A 13 by 9-inch baking dish provided far more real estate than a skillet and I easily nestled eight eggs in the sauce in two tidy rows. I first left the oven at the temperature at which I had roasted the vegetables—500 degrees—but the eggs cooked unevenly. A much better temperature was 400 degrees; within 13 to 16 minutes, the eggs were just set (and they continued to cook a little further via carryover cooking).

Garnishes for huevos rancheros range broadly and after trying a host of options, I settled on a blend of scallions and cilantro to brighten the sauce and some spicy pepper Jack cheese and avocado to complement it. Finally, I had a recipe for huevos rancheros that didn't require waking before dawn or an armload of ingredients to prepare.

HUEVOS RANCHEROS Serves 4

Use a heavyweight rimmed baking sheet; flimsy sheets will warp. Our winning sheet is the Wear-Ever Half Size Heavy Duty Sheet Pan (13 gauge) by Vollrath. Serve with refried beans and hot sauce.

- 2 (28-ounce) cans diced tomatoes
- 1 tablespoon packed brown sugar
- 1 tablespoon lime juice
- 1 onion, chopped
- ½ cup chopped canned green chiles
- ¼ cup extra-virgin olive oil
- 3 tablespoons chili powder
- 4 garlic cloves, sliced thin
  Salt and pepper
- 4 ounces pepper Jack cheese, shredded (1 cup)
- 8 large eggs
- 1 avocado, halved, pitted, and diced
- 3 scallions, sliced thin
- ⅓ cup minced fresh cilantro
- 8 (6-inch) corn tortillas, warmed

1. Adjust oven rack to middle position and heat oven to 500 degrees. Line rimmed baking sheet with parchment paper. Drain tomatoes in fine-mesh strainer set over bowl, pressing with rubber spatula to extract as much juice as possible. Reserve 1¾ cups tomato juice and discard remainder. Whisk sugar and lime juice into reserved tomato juice and set aside.

2. In separate bowl, combine onion, chiles, oil, chili powder, garlic, ½ teaspoon salt, and drained tomatoes. Transfer tomato mixture to prepared baking sheet and spread in even layer to edges of sheet. Roast until charred in spots, 35 to 40 minutes, stirring and redistributing into even layer halfway through baking. Reduce oven temperature to 400 degrees.

3. Transfer roasted tomato mixture to 13 by 9-inch baking dish and stir in tomato juice mixture. Season with salt and pepper to taste, then spread into even layer. Sprinkle pepper Jack over tomato mixture. Using spoon, hollow out 8 holes in tomato mixture in 2 rows. Crack 1 egg into each hole. Season eggs with salt and pepper.

4. Bake until whites are just beginning to set but still have some movement when dish is shaken, 13 to 16 minutes. Transfer dish to wire rack, tent loosely with aluminum foil, and let sit for 5 minutes. Spoon avocado over top, then sprinkle with scallions and cilantro. Serve with warm tortillas.

TESTING TORTILLA WARMERS

Tortilla warmers promise to keep tortillas warm longer than wrapping them in a dish towel or aluminum foil. To see if any are worth buying, we gathered five, priced from around $6 to $45, made of plastic, terra-cotta, ceramic, and fabric. We loaded them with different sizes and amounts of tortillas to see what fit and then heated tortillas in each warmer and timed how long it took for the tortillas to cool.

The two plastic warmers chilled first at 20 minutes and then the foil packet at 45 minutes. The terra-cotta and ceramic warmers kept tortillas warm for 50 minutes and 1 hour, respectively, but any longer and the tortillas became dry or soggy.

One model remained: After 30 seconds in the microwave, the IMUSA 12" Cloth Tortilla Warmer kept tortillas warm for an hour and a half and fit enough for a fiesta. The secret is its layered sides: Two layers of fabric sandwich a sheet of plastic; the plastic and outer layer of fabric insulate and the internal layer of fabric wicks away moisture from the tortillas but holds it nearby, creating a warm, moist environment. It keeps tortillas hot and pliable two times longer than foil. –HANNAH CROWLEY

KEY **Good ★★★** **Fair ★★** **Poor ★**

	CRITERIA		TESTERS' NOTES
HIGHLY RECOMMENDED			
IMUSA 12" Cloth Tortilla Warmer **Model:** MEXI-10004 **Price:** $19.99 **Material:** Cloth and plastic **Diameter:** 12 in **Works In:** Microwave	Heat Retention ★★★ Tortilla Compatibility ★★★		After a 30-second stint in the microwave, this brightly colored fabric warmer kept tortillas hot for just shy of an hour and a half and fit even the largest wraps. It looks like a circular pocket and has triple layered sides with two layers of fabric sandwiching a sheet of insulating plastic; the fabric wicks moisture from the tortillas but holds it close, so they stay soft and pliable, not soggy.
RECOMMENDED			
RSVP INTERNATIONAL Stoneware Tortilla Warmer, 10 Inch **Model:** MAIZ-10W **Price:** $44.95 **Material:** Stoneware **Diameter:** 10 in **Works In:** Microwave and oven	Heat Retention ★★ Tortilla Compatibility ★★½		This attractive ceramic warmer would dress up any table and kept tortillas warm for an hour, surpassing the foil packet. Longer and testers noted dry tortillas at the top of the stack and soggy ones on the bottom. It fit tortillas 9½ inches wide and smaller and is large enough to be used for pancakes and other flatbreads, too.
RECOMMENDED WITH RESERVATIONS			
FOX RUN Tortilla Warmer **Model:** 3943 **Price:** $21.58 **Material:** Terra-cotta **Diameter:** 8.5 in **Works In:** Microwave and oven	Heat Retention ★★ Tortilla Compatibility ★★		This warmer beat our aluminum foil method, keeping tortillas warm for 50 minutes, and we like that it's an attractive serving dish. At an hour, however, its lukewarm tortillas began to harden at the top and become mushy on the bottom; it fits tortillas 8 inches or less across.
NOT RECOMMENDED			
NORDIC WARE Microwave Safe Tortilla Warmer **Model:** 67300 **Price:** $7.97 **Material:** Plastic **Diameter:** 10 in **Works In:** Microwave	Heat Retention ★ Tortilla Compatibility ★★		Tortillas zapped in this warmer for 30 seconds were lukewarm at 20 minutes; when we upped the time to the recommended maximum—45 seconds—they were lukewarm at 40 minutes, but soggy on the bottom. And even though the warmer is 10 inches across, its thicker sides meant anything bigger than 9½ inches didn't fit.
IMUSA 8" Tortilla Warmer **Model:** MEXI-1000-TORTW **Price:** $5.99 **Material:** Plastic **Diameter:** 8 in **Works In:** Microwave	Heat Retention ★ Tortilla Compatibility ★		Tortillas microwaved in this warmer for 30 seconds were lukewarm in 20 minutes; when we upped the time to the recommended maximum—60 seconds—they were lukewarm at 40 minutes, but unevenly cooked: dry on the top and soggy on the bottom—not worth the trouble. Also, tortillas wider than 8 inches didn't fit.

TO MAKE AHEAD

The sauce can be made 24 hours in advance. Microwave until hot, about 2 minutes (stirring halfway), before transferring to baking dish and proceeding with recipe.

Getting to Know Corn Products

The United States produces 32 percent of the world's corn—three times as much as any other nation. With all that corn, it's little wonder that we use it in so many ways. BY CHRISTIE MORRISON

Popcorn
CONCESSION OBSESSION

Kernels of popping corn consist of a moist, starchy center sealed inside a tough, dried hull. Whether you use a microwave, air popper, or stovetop, heating the kernels softens the starch and turns the moisture into steam, which increases pressure inside until the hull pops into a "flake." For the best results, we prefer stovetop popcorn. Try our recipe for Parmesan-Pepper Popcorn: **CooksCountry.com/parmpepperpopcorn**.

Cornstarch
PURE STARCH

This thickener is made from the dried, ground corn endosperm (which contains starch and protein). When using it to thicken sauces, we first mix it with liquid to form a slurry; otherwise, the cornstarch will clump. We've found that cornstarch, when added to marinades, can also be used to protect lean meats like pork from overcooking; it helps form a protective sheath around the meat that insulates it from high temperatures.

Corn Syrup
SWEET STUFF

Don't confuse corn syrup with high-fructose corn syrup—a much sweeter product that is used in processed foods. Corn syrup, which is about 45 percent as sweet as sugar, is very thick and doesn't crystallize like maple syrup or honey, which is why it's often used in candy making. We use dark corn syrup to add deep, sweet flavor to our Southern Pecan Praline Pie: **CooksCountry.com/pecanpralinepie**.

Bourbon
PROOF POSITIVE

In order for whiskey to be called bourbon, its fermented grain mash (which also includes wheat, rye, and malted barley) must be at least 51 percent corn and produced in the United States. The mash is mixed with water and yeast, fermented, distilled, and then aged in charred oak barrels that impart lots of nuanced flavors. Bourbon can be a great addition to sauces and marinades, as in our recipe for Smoked Bourbon Chicken (page 6).

Corn Oil
FRY COOK

A relatively modern invention, corn oil was refined for cooking in 1910 and introduced to the commercial market as Mazola in 1911. While the oil is bleached and deodorized, some trace amounts of flavor compounds remain, giving room-temperature corn oil a mild corn flavor that doesn't meld well in mayonnaise or vinaigrettes. Heating changes the compounds, however, making corn oil a good choice for sautéing and frying.

Sweet Corn
BABY MAIZE

While most corn produced in the United States is grown to maturity and sold as a grain for livestock, milling, or human consumption, sweet corn is harvested in its immature "milk stage" while the kernels are smooth, plump, and filled with a milk-like juice; then it's cooked and eaten as a vegetable. New varieties of "supersweet" corn have made it less important to cook corn as quickly as possible after harvesting.

Hominy
POSOLE STAR

Hominy, an essential ingredient in posole, is dried corn that has been soaked or cooked in an alkaline solution of water and calcium hydroxide to remove the germ and hull; it has a distinctive flavor and soft, almost chewy texture. The resulting kernels are large—about twice their original size. Hominy is a great addition to soups, or use it in bean salads. Try hominy in our version of posole: **CooksCountry.com/posole**.

Cornmeal
GROUND CONTROL

Cornmeal is ground processed corn kernels and can be yellow, white, or blue depending on the type of corn. Stone-ground cornmeal has a rustic, coarse texture due to the rough grinding surface of stone; compare this texture with the fine, uniform grind that comes from the smooth steel rollers that companies like Quaker use. We like the clean flavor and "fine sand texture" of Arrowhead Mills Organic Yellow Cornmeal.

Polenta
IDENTITY CRISIS

Italian polenta is a porridge made with water or stock and coarsely ground corn-meal. You can buy imported "polenta," but you'll often pay twice as much as you would for medium or coarsely ground cornmeal, which is the same thing. We are not fans of the bland instant and quick-cooking dried versions. Visit **CooksCountry.com/bakedpolenta** for our mostly hands-off oven recipe.

Grits
SOUTHERN STALWART

Another form of ground cornmeal, grits usually have a coarser grain than most packaged cornmeal. Some large-scale cornmeal producers use the same corn to make grits and cornmeal, while artisan companies might use softer dent corn for grits and tougher flint corn for cornmeal or polenta. We love the "nice chew" and "intense" corn flavor of Anson Mills Pencil Cob Grits.

Masa Harina
TORTILLA BASE

The ancient Aztecs invented masa harina, and their basic method is still used today: Corn is heated in an alkaline solution containing calcium hydroxide (the Aztecs used limewater or ash) and then rinsed, dried, and ground. Then it's dried again and ground into the fine powder known as masa harina or masa seca. This process enables this variation of cornmeal—the main ingredient in corn tortillas—to form a malleable dough when mixed with water.

30-MINUTE SUPPER

SEARED SCALLOPS WITH SPINACH, FENNEL,
AND GRAPEFRUIT SALAD

30-MINUTE SUPPER

HAM, BRIE, AND APPLE PANINI

30-MINUTE SUPPER

SKILLET ZITI WITH SAUSAGE AND SUMMER SQUASH

30-MINUTE SUPPER

PORK TENDERLOIN WITH CORN, TOMATO,
AND GOAT CHEESE SALAD

HAM, BRIE, AND APPLE PANINI Serves 4

✓ **WHY THIS RECIPE WORKS:** The combination of smoky ham and almonds, tart apple, and creamy Brie makes for a satisfying dinner sandwich. A heavy Dutch oven turns a stovetop grill pan into a panini press.

- 6 tablespoons mayonnaise
- ¼ cup smoked almonds, chopped fine
- 2 teaspoons minced fresh tarragon
  Salt and pepper
- 8 (½-inch-thick) slices rustic bread
- 8 ounces thinly sliced deli Black Forest ham
- 1 Granny Smith apple, cored, halved, and sliced thin
- 1 (8-ounce) wheel Brie cheese, halved, each half cut into 8 slices

1. Combine mayonnaise, almonds, tarragon, ¼ teaspoon salt, and ¼ teaspoon pepper in bowl. Spread mayonnaise mixture evenly on 1 side of 4 bread slices. Arrange ham, apple, and Brie in even layers over mayonnaise. Top with remaining 4 bread slices.

2. Heat 12-inch grill pan or nonstick skillet over medium heat until hot, about 1 minute. Place 2 sandwiches in pan, cheese side down, and weigh down with Dutch oven. Cook sandwiches until golden brown and cheese is melted, about 5 minutes per side. Transfer to wire rack and repeat with remaining 2 sandwiches. Serve.

TEST KITCHEN NOTE: Wrap the bottom of your Dutch oven in aluminum foil for easy cleanup.

SEARED SCALLOPS WITH SPINACH, FENNEL, AND GRAPEFRUIT SALAD Serves 4

✓ **WHY THIS RECIPE WORKS:** Searing the scallops for just 3 minutes enhances their flavor without overcooking them.

- ¼ cup extra-virgin olive oil
- 2 tablespoons cider vinegar
- 1 tablespoon Dijon mustard
  Salt and pepper
- 6 ounces (6 cups) baby spinach
- 1 fennel bulb, stalks discarded, bulb halved, cored, and sliced thin
- 1 red grapefruit, segmented
- 1½ pounds large sea scallops, tendons removed

1. Whisk 2 tablespoons oil, vinegar, mustard, ½ teaspoon salt, and ½ teaspoon pepper together in large bowl. Add spinach, fennel, and grapefruit and toss to combine. Transfer salad to platter.

2. Pat scallops dry with paper towels and season with salt and pepper. Heat 1 tablespoon oil in 12-inch nonstick skillet over medium-high heat until just smoking. Add half of scallops in single layer and cook without moving them until well browned, about 1½ minutes per side. Transfer scallops to plate and tent loosely with foil. Repeat with remaining 1 tablespoon oil and remaining scallops. Arrange scallops over salad. Serve.

TEST KITCHEN NOTE: To segment the grapefruit, cut away the peel and pith. Holding the fruit over a bowl, use a paring knife to slice between the membranes to release the segments.

PORK TENDERLOIN WITH CORN, TOMATO, AND GOAT CHEESE SALAD Serves 4

✓ **WHY THIS RECIPE WORKS:** Searing pork tenderloin until browned and then letting it finish cooking in the oven makes this an easy, (mostly) hands-off meal. We char fresh corn kernels in the same skillet we use to sear the pork before combining them with tomatoes, arugula, a lemony dressing, and tangy goat cheese.

- 2 (12-ounce) pork tenderloins, trimmed
  Salt and pepper
- ¼ cup extra-virgin olive oil
- 2 scallions, sliced thin
- 2 tablespoons lemon juice
- 5 ears corn, kernels cut from cobs
- 8 ounces grape tomatoes, halved
- 2 ounces (2 cups) baby arugula, chopped
- 4 ounces goat cheese, crumbled (1 cup)

1. Adjust oven rack to middle position and heat oven to 450 degrees. Set wire rack in rimmed baking sheet. Pat pork dry with paper towels and season with salt and pepper. Heat 1 tablespoon oil in 12-inch nonstick skillet over medium-high heat until shimmering. Cook pork until browned on all sides, 5 to 7 minutes; transfer pork to prepared wire rack. Roast until meat registers 140 degrees, 14 to 18 minutes. Transfer to carving board, tent with foil, and let rest for 5 minutes.

2. Meanwhile, whisk 2 tablespoons oil, scallions, lemon juice, ¾ teaspoon salt, and ½ teaspoon pepper together in large bowl. Heat remaining 1 tablespoon oil in now-empty skillet over medium-high heat until shimmering. Add corn and cook, stirring occasionally, until spotty brown, about 5 minutes; transfer to bowl with dressing. Add tomatoes and arugula to bowl and toss to combine. Transfer salad to platter and sprinkle with goat cheese. Slice pork ½ inch thick and serve with salad.

SKILLET ZITI WITH SAUSAGE AND SUMMER SQUASH Serves 4

✓ **WHY THIS RECIPE WORKS:** Cooking the pasta right in the sauce infuses it with flavor and restricts the cooking to one pan.

- 12 ounces sweet Italian sausage, casings removed and sausage broken into 1-inch pieces
- 1 pound yellow summer squash, halved lengthwise and sliced ¼ inch thick
- 2½ cups chicken broth
- 1 (14.5-ounce) can diced tomatoes
- 12 ounces (3¾ cups) ziti
  Salt and pepper
- 2 ounces Parmesan cheese, grated (1 cup)
- ½ cup torn fresh basil

1. Cook sausage in 12-inch nonstick skillet over medium-high heat, stirring occasionally, until lightly browned, about 5 minutes. Add squash and cook until beginning to brown, about 3 minutes.

2. Add broth, tomatoes and their juice, pasta, and ½ teaspoon salt to skillet and bring to boil. Reduce heat to medium-low, cover, and simmer, stirring occasionally, until pasta is al dente, about 15 minutes.

3. Stir ½ cup Parmesan into pasta. Season with salt and pepper to taste. Top with remaining ½ cup Parmesan, cover, remove from heat, and let stand until cheese is melted, about 1 minute. Sprinkle with basil and serve.

TEST KITCHEN NOTE: You can substitute hot Italian sausage for the sweet.

GRILLED TURKEY PITAS WITH CUCUMBER SALAD

THAI-STYLE CHICKEN AND SWEET POTATO CURRY

**PAN-SEARED CHICKEN BREASTS
WITH CHICKPEA SALAD**

GRILLED STEAK AND VEGETABLE SALAD

THAI-STYLE CHICKEN AND SWEET POTATO CURRY Serves 4

✓ **WHY THIS RECIPE WORKS:** Blooming the spices in the fat rendered from the chicken helps unify the diverse flavors of this dish.

- 6 (5- to 7-ounce) bone-in chicken thighs, trimmed
  Salt and pepper
- 3 tablespoons red curry paste
- 1 pound sweet potatoes, peeled and cut into ½-inch pieces
- 1 (13.5-ounce) can coconut milk
- 2 tablespoons fish sauce
- 4 scallions, sliced thin on bias
- ¼ cup dry-roasted peanuts, crushed
- 2 tablespoons minced fresh cilantro

1. Pat chicken dry with paper towels and season with salt and pepper. Place chicken skin side down in 12-inch nonstick skillet. Cover and set skillet over medium-high heat and cook until skin is browned, about 7 minutes. Flip chicken and cook on second side until lightly browned, about 1½ minutes. Transfer chicken to plate and discard all but 1 tablespoon fat.

2. Add curry paste to skillet and cook until fragrant, about 30 seconds. Stir in potatoes, coconut milk, and fish sauce, scraping up any browned bits. Return chicken and any accumulated juices to skillet, skin side up. Bring to simmer, reduce heat to medium-low, cover, and cook until chicken registers 175 degrees, about 12 minutes. Transfer chicken to platter. Season sauce with salt and pepper to taste. Spoon sauce and potatoes over chicken. Sprinkle scallions, peanuts, and cilantro over top. Serve.

TEST KITCHEN NOTE: Serve with rice and lime wedges.

GRILLED TURKEY PITAS WITH CUCUMBER SALAD Serves 4

✓ **WHY THIS RECIPE WORKS:** Feta cheese adds flavor and richness to lean ground turkey, and a fresh cucumber salad with kalamata olives continues the Mediterranean flavor profile.

- 1 cucumber, peeled, halved lengthwise, seeded, and sliced thin
- 4 ounces feta cheese, crumbled (1 cup)
- ½ cup pitted kalamata olives, chopped, plus 2 teaspoons brine
- ¼ cup mayonnaise
- 4 scallions, white and green parts separated and sliced thin
  Salt and pepper
- 1½ pounds ground turkey
- 2 tablespoons chopped fresh oregano
- 2 (8-inch) pita breads, halved

1. Combine cucumber, ¼ cup feta, olives and brine, mayonnaise, and scallion greens in bowl. Season with salt and pepper to taste. Knead turkey, oregano, remaining ¾ cup feta, scallion whites, 1 teaspoon salt, and ½ teaspoon pepper together in second bowl. Shape turkey mixture into 4 (½-inch-thick) oval patties and press shallow divot in center of each.

2. Grill over medium-hot fire until burgers register 160 degrees, 5 to 7 minutes per side. Transfer to plate. Grill pita bread until warmed through, about 30 seconds per side. Place 1 burger in each pita along with one-quarter of cucumber salad. Serve.

TEST KITCHEN NOTE: Making a divot in the center of each burger lets the burgers cook up flat.

GRILLED STEAK AND VEGETABLE SALAD Serves 4

✓ **WHY THIS RECIPE WORKS:** Grilling the steaks and vegetables adds lots of smoky flavor to this summer-inspired salad.

- ¼ cup extra-virgin olive oil, plus extra for drizzling
- ¼ cup red wine vinegar
- 2 garlic cloves, minced
- 2 teaspoons minced fresh thyme
- 1 teaspoon Dijon mustard
  Salt and pepper
- 2 zucchini, sliced lengthwise into ½-inch-thick planks
- 2 red bell peppers, halved, stemmed, and seeded
- 2 (12-ounce) boneless strip steaks, about 1 inch thick
- 2 tomatoes, cored and cut into ½-inch wedges

1. Whisk oil, vinegar, garlic, thyme, mustard, ¾ teaspoon salt, and ½ teaspoon pepper together in large bowl. Brush zucchini and bell peppers with 2 tablespoons vinaigrette; set aside remaining vinaigrette.

2. Pat steaks dry with paper towels and season with salt and pepper. Place steaks and vegetables on grill over hot fire. Grill steaks until meat registers 125 degrees (for medium-rare), 4 to 8 minutes per side, and vegetables until well browned, about 4 minutes per side. Transfer vegetables and steaks to carving board, tent steaks loosely with foil, and let rest for 5 minutes.

3. Cut vegetables into 1-inch pieces. Add vegetables and tomatoes to reserved vinaigrette and toss gently to combine; divide vegetables evenly among dinner plates. Slice steaks ¼ inch thick and arrange on top of vegetables. Drizzle with extra oil. Serve.

TEST KITCHEN NOTE: Our favorite red wine vinegar is Laurent du Clos Red Wine Vinegar.

PAN-SEARED CHICKEN BREASTS WITH CHICKPEA SALAD
Serves 4

✓ **WHY THIS RECIPE WORKS:** Reserving a few tablespoons of the dressing for drizzling on the chicken before serving helps reinforce the smoky, tangy flavors of the chickpea salad.

- 5 tablespoons extra-virgin olive oil
- ¼ cup lemon juice (2 lemons)
- 1 teaspoon honey
- 1 teaspoon smoked paprika
- ½ teaspoon ground cumin
  Salt and pepper
- 2 (14-ounce) cans chickpeas, rinsed
- ½ red onion, sliced thin
- ¼ cup torn fresh mint
- 4 (6-ounce) boneless, skinless chicken breasts, trimmed

1. Whisk ¼ cup oil, lemon juice, honey, paprika, cumin, ½ teaspoon salt, and ½ teaspoon pepper together in bowl. Set aside 3 tablespoons dressing. Add chickpeas, onion, and mint to remaining dressing in bowl. Season with salt and pepper to taste.

2. Pat chicken dry with paper towels and season with salt and pepper. Heat remaining 1 tablespoon oil in 12-inch nonstick skillet over medium-high heat until just smoking. Cook chicken until golden brown and meat registers 160 degrees, about 6 minutes per side. Transfer chicken to carving board, tent loosely with foil, and let rest for 5 minutes.

3. Transfer chickpea salad to platter and top with chicken. Drizzle reserved dressing over chicken. Serve.

TEST KITCHEN NOTE: Smoked sweet or smoked hot paprika can be used interchangeably in this recipe.

Strawberry Chiffon Pie

Could we pack this dessert with strawberry flavor and still keep its signature light-as-air texture?

BY REBECCAH MARSTERS

WHEN CHIFFON PIES first showed up in the early 20th century (at which point they were called, among other names, fairy tarts and soufflé pies), they were made by mixing pudding with egg whites and baking the resulting mixture. Later, gelatin became the favored thickening agent. But whatever the technique, the defining characteristic of these pies (which were usually flavored with some type of fruit) has always been their superlight, almost fluffy texture. Strawberry is my favorite flavor for this type of pie, so after searching out recipes old and new, I made five of the most promising and called my tasters to sample them. Overall, the fillings were stiff and rubbery, and most lacked strawberry flavor, as they had just a bit of fruit stirred in at the end. Plus, many of the pies tasted too lean, almost as if they were trying to be healthful.

The crusts, on the other hand, were mostly successful. We particularly liked one made from shortbread cookies and toasted almonds; its nutty flavor and crunchy texture were well suited to the fluffy fruit pie.

Now back to those unsatisfying fillings. For flavor, I knew that simply stirring in sliced strawberries wasn't going to cut it, but the versions that had achieved better flavor by pureeing the fruit had an unpleasant texture. To solve this, I made my own strawberry juice by pureeing fresh berries and forcing them through a fine-mesh strainer until I had a full cup of smooth, deeply flavorful ruby liquid to add to the filling.

The pie with the best texture in the initial round supplemented the traditional gelatin with cornstarch for firm setting and sliceability without the bounce factor, a tactic that seemed worth borrowing. The pie I made using this approach had a good texture, but again, it felt lean. Fat seemed the obvious antidote, and when I looked back at some of the old recipes, I found the solution: While most relied solely on whipped egg whites for lift, some used whipped cream as well. For my next test, I whipped the egg whites as before and then poured chilled cream into the empty mixer bowl. After folding the whipped cream into the berry–egg white mixture, I poured my enriched filling into the crust, chilled it, and waited.

I had finally made headway; the filling was as fluffy as ever but now had a velvety texture from the added fat and almost tasted like strawberry ice cream—in pie form. To strengthen the berry flavor a bit more while also adding visual appeal, I folded sliced strawberries into the finished filling right before pouring it into the crust. Finally, a generous splash of lemon juice enhanced the sweet-tart berries.

STRAWBERRY CHIFFON PIE

Serves 8

You will need about 3 pints of fresh strawberries for this recipe.

CRUST
- 1 (5.3-ounce) box shortbread cookies, broken into 1-inch pieces
- 2 tablespoons sugar
- ¼ teaspoon salt
- ½ cup slivered almonds, toasted
- 2 tablespoons unsalted butter, melted

FILLING
- 2 teaspoons unflavored gelatin
- 2 tablespoons water
- 12 ounces strawberries, hulled (2½ cups), plus 8 ounces strawberries, hulled, halved, and sliced thin (1⅓ cups)
- ¾ cup (5¼ ounces) plus 2 tablespoons sugar
- 2 tablespoons cornstarch
- ¼ teaspoon salt
- 2 tablespoons lemon juice
- 2 large egg whites
- ⅛ teaspoon cream of tartar
- ½ cup heavy cream, chilled

1. FOR THE CRUST: Adjust oven rack to middle position and heat oven to 325 degrees. Grease 9-inch pie plate. Process cookies, sugar, and salt in food processor until finely ground, about 1 minute. Add almonds and pulse until coarsely chopped, about 8 pulses. Add melted butter and pulse until combined, about 10 pulses. Transfer crumb mixture to pie plate. Using bottom of dry measuring cup, press crumbs evenly into bottom and up sides of plate. Bake until crust is golden brown, 18 to 20 minutes, rotating halfway through baking. Let crust cool completely on wire rack, about 30 minutes. (Crust can be wrapped in plastic and stored at room temperature for up to 24 hours.)

2. FOR THE FILLING: Sprinkle gelatin over water in small bowl and let sit until gelatin softens, about 5 minutes. Process hulled whole strawberries in food processor until completely smooth, about 1 minute. Transfer to fine-mesh strainer set over medium bowl and press on solids to extract 1 cup of juice; discard solids. Whisk ¾ cup sugar, cornstarch, salt, and strawberry juice together in small saucepan.

3. Bring juice mixture to simmer over medium heat, stirring constantly. Cook until slightly thickened, about 1 minute. Off heat, whisk in gelatin mixture until dissolved. Transfer to large bowl, stir in lemon juice, and let cool completely, about 30 minutes, stirring occasionally.

4. Using stand mixer fitted with whisk, whip egg whites and cream of tartar on medium-low speed until foamy, about 1 minute. Increase speed to medium-high and whip whites to soft, billowy mounds, about 1 minute. Gradually add remaining 2 tablespoons sugar and whip until glossy, stiff peaks form, 2 to 3 minutes. Whisk one-third of meringue into cooled strawberry mixture until smooth. Fold remaining meringue into strawberry mixture until only few white streaks remain.

5. In now-empty mixer bowl, whip cream on medium-low speed until foamy, about 1 minute. Increase speed to high and whip until stiff peaks form, 1 to 3 minutes. Gently fold whipped cream into strawberry mixture until no white streaks remain. Fold in sliced strawberries. Spoon filling into crust and spread into even layer using back of spoon. Refrigerate pie for at least 3 hours or up to 24 hours. Serve.

For the best flavor and texture, we make our own "strawberry jelly" from fresh berries.

Iowa Loose Meat Sandwiches

If you don't think a steamed ground beef sandwich can be delicious, one bite of this simple, savory midwestern classic will quickly change your mind. CHRISTIE MORRISON

THE LOOSE MEAT sandwich—a simple affair of steamed ground beef topped with mustard, pickles, and onions and served on a soft hamburger bun—is a low-key midwestern classic. In earlier days, it was ubiquitous throughout the states of Iowa, Minnesota, Nebraska, Illinois, and Kansas. If you ask folks in central Iowa, this beloved sandwich is properly called a Maid-Rite, after the Maid-Rite chain that made it famous. In other states, though, you might find it sold under different aliases: a tavern, a steamer, a Big T, and a tastee, to name a few.

Whatever you call it, the sandwich can still be found in a handful of diners and small restaurants around the central Midwest, and Iowa claims some 30 remaining Maid-Rite franchises. But the easiest way to get your hands on a loose meat sandwich is to make it yourself. I figured it was time for us to give it a try.

In addition to my usual recipe research, I asked John "Doc" Willoughby, *Cook's Country*'s editorial director and a native of Grundy Center, Iowa, to help me understand the beauty (and simplicity) of the sandwich. Doc was a regular at Hulne's Maid-Rite in his hometown until it closed some 40 years ago. After that, he had to get his loose meat fix at Taylor's Maid-Rite in nearby Marshalltown, which is still open today. The recipe hasn't changed substantially since its debut there in 1928. As all Maid-Rites used to do, Taylor's grinds its meat daily and uses a large steam box to cook and hold the lightly seasoned meat. As for the seasonings, that's something of a mystery. Plenty of aficionados on the Internet claim to have nailed the formula, but there's little consensus. Most agree on the basics: salt and pepper. Beyond that, some call for sugar, Worcestershire sauce, mustard, beef bouillon, soy sauce, or paprika. The beef has no sauce, per se—nothing to really bind it together. In fact, the sandwich is served with a spoon to scoop up all the beef that escapes from the wax paper wrapping.

After trying a few of the most promising recipes, I quickly determined that less is more with this sandwich. Starting with 85 percent lean ground beef was important. The fat added flavor and helped keep the beef from drying out during cooking—particularly important since it is cooked to a full brown "well."

The savory, mild beef gets a flavor boost from yellow mustard, onion, and tangy pickles.

Even with the higher-fat beef, though, intense flavors like those of Worcestershire and steak sauce were overwhelming. They disguised the beef's flavor, as did spices like paprika. One flavor we did like, however, was mustard. Dry mustard, added in small amounts, provided a faint tang, and a little sugar helped balance the flavors and enhance the beef's subtle sweetness. While cooking the beef in beef broth or bouillon sounded like a promising way to boost meaty flavor, it ended up being a wash; we used such a small amount that we couldn't taste a significant difference.

The trickiest part of the loose meat sandwich, I found, was not the ingredient list but the cooking. Since I couldn't reproduce the classic steam box

contraption, I needed to find another way to achieve the same essential pebbly beef texture. While a few recipes called for browning the beef over high heat, fans insist that a true Maid-Rite is never browned (so much for adding more flavor through the Maillard reaction). One version called for cooking the beef over a double boiler, while others simmered it with a little water in a skillet. The double boiler didn't seem the most practical way to go. I found that as long as I kept the heat low and gently simmered the beef in water with the salt, pepper, sugar, and dry mustard, I was able to cook the beef in the skillet in just 5 minutes. The resulting meat was surprisingly tender and juicy, and there was just enough residual fat and liquid in

the pan to keep the meat moist.

No Maid-Rite sandwich is complete without a healthy dose of chopped onion and dill pickle slices. Some recipes call for cooking onion with the meat, but the resulting mixture tasted too much like meatloaf. Yet raw onion was too harsh. Seeking a compromise, I stirred the onion into the finished beef and let it sit, covered, to steam and soften just slightly. Since I was serving the sandwiches with prepared yellow mustard anyway, I streamlined the recipe and swapped a tablespoon of prepared mustard for the dry mustard in the beef mixture.

One thing all Maid-Rite fans agree on is the bun. The only way to serve this sandwich is on a soft white hamburger bun. And don't think you can eat this on the fly; with loose pebbles of beef falling from the bun with each bite, you need to be hunkered over a table if you don't want to miss the good stuff. Though tasters had been initially skeptical of the extraordinarily plain, very messy sandwich, by the time I put out my final version, there were plenty of Maid-Rite fans in the crowd.

IOWA LOOSE MEAT SANDWICHES Serves 4

Do not substitute leaner ground beef in this recipe or the sandwich will be dry.

- 1 pound 85 percent lean ground beef
- ¼ cup water
- 1 tablespoon yellow mustard, plus extra for serving
- 1 teaspoon sugar
- 1 teaspoon salt
- 1 teaspoon pepper
- ½ cup finely chopped onion
- 4 hamburger buns
  Sliced dill pickles

1. Combine beef, water, mustard, sugar, salt, and pepper in 10-inch skillet. Bring to simmer over medium heat, breaking up meat with spoon. Reduce heat to medium-low to maintain gentle simmer and cook, stirring frequently, until meat is no longer pink, about 5 minutes. Stir in onion, cover, and remove from heat; keep warm while preparing buns.

2. Spread extra mustard on bun bottoms then, using slotted spoon, mound beef mixture over top. Cap with pickles and bun tops. Serve.

Grill-Roasted Peppers

Roasting red peppers transforms their juicy crunch to smoky tenderness. But to get real flavor into the peppers, we had to come up with a whole new approach. BY CHRISTIE MORRISON

A S A GENERAL rule, we try to avoid blackening foods. But when it comes to bell peppers, that's the best way to soften the flesh and impart smoky flavor. And while a broiler will do the job, it doesn't compare with the fire of a grill. Most recipes for grill-roasted peppers are simple: Place whole peppers on the cooking grate and grill, turning as needed, until the skins are completely black and the flesh is tender. At that point, put the peppers in a covered bowl so they steam, which further softens them and makes it easier to remove the charred skins.

This tried-and-true method works fine, but as I grilled my way through dozens of peppers, I found that it wasn't perfect. It was hard to get the texture of the peppers just right; often they were not quite soft enough in the center, but if I left them on long enough to remedy that, the outer portion ended up a little mushy. I wanted to fix this; plus, I wondered if I could infuse the peppers with more flavor while I was at it.

Olive oil enhanced with garlic and herbs seemed like a perfect way to amp up the flavor. But brushing such a mixture onto the outsides of the peppers would make little difference, since the skin is removed before eating. What might work, I thought, was applying the oil mixture to the insides of the peppers, where the flesh is exposed and the oil could penetrate. For my next round of testing, I removed the stems and seeds from the peppers and then tossed them with garlic-infused olive oil. To prevent flare-ups from the oil, I decided to grill the peppers (with the remaining garlic-infused oil) in a foil-covered 13 by 9-inch disposable aluminum pan. I let the peppers steam in the aromatic oil, shaking and turning the pan once to prevent the contents from burning. After about 15 minutes, the peppers became tender and started to wilt, at which point I drained them of any excess juice and oil and placed them directly on the hot grates to char. They flattened out on the grates, which promoted even charring (a problem with the curves and crannies of raw peppers). After another 15 minutes over direct heat, the peppers had blackened completely.

While the peppers were grilling, I examined the oil left behind in the pan. The steaming peppers had released liquid into the oil-garlic mixture, adding

Serve these peppers as a side dish for grilled meats and poultry, use them to top sandwiches or burgers, or add them to salads and antipasti.

flavor and loosening it considerably. I transferred the mixture to a bowl and whisked in some sherry vinegar to make a flavorful vinaigrette.

I returned the charred peppers to the now-empty, cool disposable pan and let them steam under foil until they were cool enough to handle. After scraping the charred skins from the peppers (rinsing washes away flavor), I cut the pieces into quarters and took a bite. The peppers were tender but not mushy, and they were infused with heady garlic flavor that complemented the intensified sweetness. I tossed the bunch into the vinaigrette and set out a plate of the finished peppers. My tasters all agreed that the new method was even better than the old.

TEST KITCHEN TECHNIQUE
Steam and Then Sear

We first steam the peppers in garlicky olive oil and their own juices. Then we sear the peppers and serve them with a vinaigrette made from the infused oil.

GRILL-ROASTED PEPPERS Serves 4

These peppers can be refrigerated for up to five days.

- ¼ cup extra-virgin olive oil
- 3 garlic cloves, peeled and smashed
  Salt and pepper
- 1 (13 by 9-inch) disposable aluminum pan
- 6 red bell peppers
- 1 tablespoon sherry vinegar

1. Combine oil, garlic, ½ teaspoon salt, and ¼ teaspoon pepper in disposable pan. Using paring knife, cut around stems of peppers and remove cores and seeds. Place peppers in pan and turn to coat with oil. Cover pan tightly with aluminum foil.

2A. FOR A CHARCOAL GRILL: Open bottom vent completely. Light large chimney starter filled with charcoal briquettes (6 quarts). When top coals are partially covered with ash, pour evenly over half of grill. Set cooking grate in place, cover, and open lid vent completely. Heat grill until hot, about 5 minutes.

2B. FOR A GAS GRILL: Turn all burners to high, cover, and heat grill until hot, about 15 minutes. Turn all burners to medium-high.

3. Clean and oil cooking grate. Place pan on grill (over hotter side for charcoal) and cook, covered, until peppers are just tender and skins begin to blister, 10 to 15 minutes, rotating and shaking pan halfway through cooking.

4. Remove pan from heat and carefully remove foil (reserve foil to use later). Using tongs, remove peppers from pan, allowing juices to drip back into pan, and place on grill (over hotter side for charcoal). Grill peppers, covered, turning every few minutes until skins are blackened, 10 to 15 minutes.

5. Transfer juices and garlic in pan to medium bowl and whisk in vinegar. Remove peppers from grill, return to now-empty pan, and cover tightly with foil. Let peppers steam for 5 minutes. Using spoon, scrape blackened skin off each pepper. Quarter peppers lengthwise, add to vinaigrette in bowl, and toss to combine. Season with salt and pepper to taste, and serve.

▶ Want to jazz up your peppers with fresh herbs? Visit CooksCountry.com/sept14 for our recipe for **Grill-Roasted Peppers with Rosemary**.

Dakota Peach Kuchen

Kuchen, the official state dessert of South Dakota, features layers of sweet yeasted dough, luscious fruit, and rich custard. And it's easier to make than it looks. BY NICK IVERSON

I GREW UP IN South Dakota, which means I grew up eating fruit kuchen. My dad, who did most of the baking in our family, made it not only for special occasions but also just to have around the house for dessert, as a snack in the afternoon, or even for breakfast. Most other families we knew did the same thing.

Like many other classic Dakota dishes, fruit kuchen was brought to the United States by German immigrants who began to settle in the Dakotas in the late 1800s. In German, kuchen (pronounced "KOO-kin") simply means "cake," and it can refer to any number of sweet confections. But in the Dakotas, kuchen has just one meaning: a sweet yeasted dough layered with fresh or canned fruit, custard, and a sprinkle of cinnamon and baked in a cake pan. I made it my mission to introduce my fellow test cooks to this wonderful pastry.

To get started, I ordered samples from several bakeries back home and baked my father's own kuchen recipe. As you might imagine with a dish this popular, not all kuchen are the same. There are two distinct types of crust—a short, almost biscuit-like crust and the softer, richer style that I was more accustomed to. As for the fruit (peaches are the most popular option), some versions used fresh but most went for canned. After sampling, we knew that we preferred the more tender dough, and fresh fruit rather than canned. Of course, we also noted some problems, even with my dad's version, which was the most popular. (No nepotism here—this was a blind tasting.) The peaches wept as they baked, leaving a pool of moisture, and the custard had a rather strong eggy flavor. And though the crust was pretty good, it seemed a bit too lean. Clearly some fine-tuning was in order.

To remedy the crust's leanness, I added a second egg and switched from the melted butter–oil combination that the recipe called for to all melted butter. But when I followed the standard procedure (combining the dry and wet ingredients separately and then mixing the wet into the dry), the dough was a sticky mess. Nevertheless, I let it rise, shaped it as best I could, and baked it just to see what it tasted like. No surprise: When it came out of the oven, it did have a really nice, buttery-rich flavor, but it was squat with virtually no structure.

I consulted our science editor, who

While peach kuchen is the standard, cherry and berry versions are also popular.

explained that adding a relatively large amount of fat, like the butter, at the same time as the other wet ingredients inhibited gluten development, which accounted for my dense, squat crust. So for my next attempt, I decided to slowly add softened butter to the dough after the other wet ingredients had been thoroughly mixed, hoping that this would give the milk and flour an opportunity to form gluten before the proteins

became coated with fat from the butter. I gave it a try, mixing the dry ingredients, adding the milk and eggs, and then mixing that combination thoroughly in the stand mixer before finally adding the butter. I let it proof on the counter and came back after an hour to find a nice, puffy ball of dough—a good sign that I had solved my structural problems. But all that butter still made the dough extremely sticky and hard to shape.

Looking for a remedy, I borrowed a technique usually reserved for pie dough. Because the butter incorporated into the dough was now at room temperature, it was on the verge of melting. Putting the dough in the refrigerator would harden the butter and consequently firm up the dough. After the large ball of dough proofed on the counter, I cut it into two smaller balls and put both in the refrigerator. After an hour the dough was soft and supple, a dream to work with. I rolled the balls into disks, put them in 9-inch round cake pans, and let them come back up to room temperature. In the meantime, I would evaluate the custard filling.

My dad's custard was dead simple, containing 2 eggs, 1¼ cups of cream, and 1 cup of sugar. But it also had the offending eggy flavor. Luckily, that eggy flavor is found primarily in egg whites, so separating one of the eggs and adding only the yolk lessened the egginess while still providing thickening power. Straining the finished custard got rid of lumps, and for extra flavor, I added a bit of vanilla and a good ¼ cup of butter.

With the dough and the custard all set, it was time to deal with the weeping peaches. I knew from experience that mixing the fruit with some sugar would pull out some of the moisture. After a number of tests, I determined that 25 minutes in a colander was enough time to get rid of just enough juice.

Now I could assemble the kuchen. Once the dough had come to room temperature, I pressed down the center, leaving a border around the edge for the crust, and then layered in the sliced peaches and poured the custard over the top. I gave both pans a dusting of cinnamon before baking. Once the kuchens cooled, I called my tasters. The crust was rich, tender, and a deep brown, the peaches full of flavor, and the custard smooth and delicately sweet.

Dad would be proud.

DAKOTA PEACH KUCHEN
Makes two 9-inch kuchens

The dough will need 2 hours to rise plus 1 hour to chill in the refrigerator. We developed this recipe using dark cake pans; if your pans are light, increase the baking time in step 7 to 55 to 60 minutes.

CRUST
- ½ cup whole milk
- 2 large eggs
- 2½ cups (12½ ounces) all-purpose flour
- 1 tablespoon sugar
- 2 teaspoons instant or rapid-rise yeast
- ½ teaspoon salt
- 8 tablespoons unsalted butter, cut into 8 pieces and softened

FRUIT AND CUSTARD
- 1 pound fresh peaches, peeled, halved, pitted, and cut into ½-inch wedges or 12 ounces frozen sliced peaches, thawed
- 2 tablespoons plus ¾ cup (5¼ ounces) sugar
- 1 large egg plus 1 large yolk
- ¼ teaspoon salt
- 1¼ cups heavy cream
- 4 tablespoons unsalted butter, cut into 4 pieces
- ½ teaspoon vanilla extract
- ¼ teaspoon ground cinnamon

1. FOR THE CRUST: Grease large bowl. Whisk milk and eggs in 2-cup liquid measuring cup until combined. Using stand mixer fitted with dough hook, mix flour, sugar, yeast, and salt on medium-low speed until combined, about 5 seconds. With mixer running, slowly add milk mixture and knead until dough forms, about 1 minute.

2. With mixer still running, add butter 1 piece at a time until incorporated. Continue kneading until dough clears sides of bowl but still sticks to bottom, 8 to 12 minutes (dough should be soft and sticky).

3. Transfer dough to greased bowl, cover with plastic wrap, and let rise on counter until doubled in size, about 1 hour. Punch down dough and divide into 2 equal balls. Wrap each ball in plastic, transfer to refrigerator, and let rest for at least 1 hour or up to 24 hours.

4. Grease two dark-colored 9-inch round cake pans. Roll chilled doughs into two 9-inch disks on lightly floured counter. Transfer to prepared pans, pushing dough to edges of pans. Cover pans loosely with plastic and let rise on counter until puffy, about 1 hour. Adjust oven rack to middle position and heat oven to 350 degrees.

5. FOR THE FRUIT AND CUSTARD: Meanwhile, toss peaches with 2 tablespoons sugar in bowl, then transfer to colander set in sink; let sit for 25 minutes. Whisk remaining ¾ cup sugar, egg and yolk, and salt in medium bowl until combined. Heat cream in medium saucepan over medium heat until just beginning to simmer.

6. Slowly whisk hot cream into egg mixture. Transfer cream mixture back to saucepan and cook over medium-low heat, stirring constantly, until mixture thickens and coats back of spoon, 3 to 5 minutes. Strain custard through fine-mesh strainer set over medium bowl. Whisk in butter and vanilla and transfer to refrigerator to cool until dough is ready. (Custard can be made up to 24 hours in advance but does not need to be fully chilled before going into crust.)

7. Leaving 1-inch border all around, press down centers of doughs with bottom of dry measuring cup to deflate and create wells for peaches and custard. Arrange peaches, evenly spaced, in circular pattern in depressed dough bottoms, avoiding border. Pour custard evenly over peaches in each pan, about 1 cup per pan (you may have a few tablespoons extra). Sprinkle with cinnamon. Bake until crusts are golden brown and centers jiggle slightly when shaken, 35 to 40 minutes, switching and rotating pans halfway through baking. Let cool completely. Remove kuchens from pans using flexible spatula. Slice and serve.

 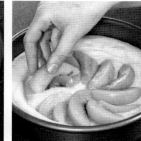
TASTING GRAPEFRUIT JUICE

To find out which grapefruit juice is best, we rounded up five nationally available brands and poured glasses for 21 America's Test Kitchen staffers.

Tasters preferred not-from-concentrate products for their fuller body and fresher tang and favored juices that struck a balance between sweet and bitter—20 to 25 grams of sugar per 8-ounce serving was the preferred range for the best flavor.

Since none of the juices contain added sugars, sweetness is determined by the type of fruit used. One overly tart juice is made with all white grapefruits, and many tasters found it too "pithy." Another juice was too sweet; it's made with pink and Ruby Red grapefruits but also concentrates from fruits like grapes and apples.

Our favorite juice, Natalie's 100% Florida Grapefruit Juice, uses a mix of citrusy pink grapefruits and sweet Ruby Reds; the result is a juice that is "balanced" and "drinkable," sweet but not cloyingly so, and bitter but not astringent.

Visit CooksCountry.com/sept14 to read the full tasting story. –LAUREN SAVOIE

HIGHLY RECOMMENDED

NATALIE'S 100% Florida Grapefruit Juice
Price: $5.60 for 64 oz ($0.09 per oz)
From Concentrate: No
Sugar: 22 g per 8-oz serving
Fruit: Pink and Ruby Red grapefruits

TASTERS' NOTES: Our top pick was "zippy" and "bright," with a "clean and refreshing" crispness that many tasters likened to "fresh-squeezed." "Not too sweet," with "just enough sour," this "drinkable" juice was perfectly "balanced."

FLORIDA'S NATURAL Ruby Red Grapefruit Juice
Price: $2.99 for 59 oz ($0.05 per oz)
From Concentrate: No
Sugar: 20 g per 8-oz serving
Fruit: Proprietary

Tasters enjoyed the "floral," almost "tropical" notes in this "nicely balanced," "fresh-tasting" grapefruit juice. "This is what I want to wake up to," said one taster.

RECOMMENDED

SIMPLY GRAPEFRUIT
Price: $4.19 for 59 oz ($0.07 per oz)
From Concentrate: No
Sugar: 25 g per 8-oz serving
Fruit: Proprietary

This juice was "refreshing," "well balanced," and "lightly floral," with hints of "mango" and "guava." Most tasters liked its "bright and fresh" "fruity" sweetness, though a few found this juice "more like orange than grapefruit."

RECOMMENDED WITH RESERVATIONS

OCEAN SPRAY 100% Juice White Grapefruit
Price: $2.50 for 60 oz ($0.04 per oz)
From Concentrate: Yes
Sugar: 17 g per 8-oz serving
Fruit: White grapefruit

Most tasters agreed that this product was "for the disciplined juice drinker." While many loved the "sour" and "very tart" bite to this juice, its "astringent" bitterness was too "harsh" for some tasters. A few disliked its "watered-down" consistency.

NOT RECOMMENDED

OCEAN SPRAY 100% Juice Ruby Red Grapefruit
Price: $2.50 for 60 oz ($0.04 per oz)
From Concentrate: Yes
Sugar: 26 g per 8-oz serving
Fruit: Ruby Red and pink grapefruits, grapes, apples

"Grapefruit juice? Is this a joke?" asked one taster. This product, which also uses grape and apple juices, tasted more like "fruit punch," with its "candy-like" "syrupy" sweetness.

Whole-Wheat Blueberry Muffins

Is it possible to create tender, light muffins using flavorful, healthy 100 percent whole-wheat flour? Common wisdom says no, but we weren't convinced. BY ASHLEY MOORE

IN THE PAST few years, baking with whole-wheat flour has become increasingly popular. Not only is it better for you nutritionally, providing more fiber and bran, but it also provides a unique sweet, nutty flavor that white flour simply can't match. Unfortunately, baked goods that use solely whole-wheat flour (as opposed to a mixture of whole-wheat and white) too often emerge from the oven with a dense, almost brick-like texture. As a fan of the flavor of whole wheat, though, I was on a mission to make a 100 percent whole-wheat blueberry muffin that was just as tender and light as its white all-purpose alternative.

I pored over "healthy" cookbooks for five recipes that would knock the socks off my tasters. I was going to show them that these muffins weren't as dry, dense, and squat as people had said they were. Well, not so fast. The five-recipe test I did was pretty underwhelming. Some of the muffins were overly greasy, one tasted "soapy," another tasted bitter, one was disguised as a scone, and another was so sweet that we thought we were eating a cupcake from our neighborhood bakery.

But there was one recipe that gave me some inspiration. It used whole-wheat flour, brown sugar, baking powder, baking soda, buttermilk, and vegetable oil. Tasters preferred this recipe out of all five because it was surprisingly moist.

Unfortunately, it was also pretty dense and quite squat, common side effects of baking with whole-wheat flour.

At this point, I decided to abandon other people's recipes and instead look back at the test kitchen's own standard blueberry muffin, which is made with all-purpose flour. Maybe there was something there that would help me.

Interestingly, this recipe had similar ingredients to the one that gave the best results in the five-recipe test, but there were also differences. It used white sugar instead of brown, used one leavener (baking powder) where the other used two (baking soda in addition to powder), included an egg in the recipe, and used melted butter in addition to vegetable oil. I baked up a batch of muffins from our classic recipe, simply substituting 100 percent whole-wheat flour for the all-purpose flour in the original. Quite surprisingly, these muffins were better—lighter in texture and much more tender—than any of those made with the best of the recipes supposedly designed for whole wheat.

I was at a loss to figure out why, so I turned to our science editor for some insight. He immediately saw a number of reasons for the success of this muffin.

First, there is an unusually high amount of liquid in this recipe—not just the cup of buttermilk, but also 1½ cups of blueberries, two eggs, and 4 tablespoons each of melted butter and vegetable oil. This high water content, he explained, produces more steam during baking, which serves as another kind of leavening. The liquid also softens the bran in the whole wheat, which helps create a lighter, more tender, less dense muffin. The combination of melted butter and oil also reduces gluten development and helps tenderize the muffin. Likewise, the acid from the buttermilk lowers the pH, again inhibiting gluten development and therefore producing a more tender muffin.

Looking at the two recipes, our science editor also suggested that I might get even better results if I took a hint from the five-recipe test winner and tried using baking soda in addition to baking powder. The whole-wheat flour, he figured, could use that additional leavening power. Sure enough, when I did a side-by-side test of my working recipe using just baking powder versus powder plus soda, there was a clear difference. The

How do you make light, fluffy, whole-wheat muffins? Use more liquid and two leaveners.

muffins that used both leaveners were lighter in texture, the top was domed, and they were more golden brown in color. Our science editor explained that the baking soda was helping neutralize the acid in the buttermilk, which in turn allowed the baking powder to function more effectively. Without the added baking soda, much of the baking soda already in the baking powder was being neutralized and losing its leavening power.

Inspired by this, I decided to do a couple more side-by-side tests comparing elements from the two recipes. First I tried muffins made with brown versus white sugar. As it turned out, the combination of brown sugar and whole-wheat flour made a sour muffin with traces of bitterness that tasters didn't enjoy. White sugar it would be. Next

I compared muffins made with buttermilk, yogurt, and sour cream, respectively. The sour cream produced an unappealingly pasty and tangy muffin, but yogurt and buttermilk were both good. Given that result, I chose to stick with the original buttermilk.

I was satisfied with the texture and flavor of this muffin, but there was still one thing missing: a satisfying topping. Because these muffins were relatively low in sugar, tasters felt that they could benefit from a bit of extra sweetness before baking. I turned to our trusty streusel topping and it satisfied us all. After a few tweaks to the butter, sugar, and flour ratios, we eventually had a crumbly, slightly sweet topping for our now light and delicate 100 percent whole-wheat blueberry muffin. (And, yes, you read that correctly).

Watermelon Salad

For this unconventional savory fruit salad, we turned to a trick more often used with vegetables. BY REBECCAH MARSTERS

WHOLE-WHEAT BLUEBERRY MUFFINS Makes 12 Muffins

Do not overmix the batter. You can substitute frozen (unthawed) blueberries for fresh in this recipe.

STREUSEL

- 3 tablespoons granulated sugar
- 3 tablespoons packed brown sugar
- 3 tablespoons whole-wheat flour
  Pinch salt
- 2 tablespoons unsalted butter, melted

MUFFINS

- 3 cups (16½ ounces) whole-wheat flour
- 2½ teaspoons baking powder
- ½ teaspoon baking soda
- 1 teaspoon salt
- 1 cup (7 ounces) granulated sugar
- 2 large eggs
- 4 tablespoons unsalted butter, melted
- ¼ cup vegetable oil
- 1¼ cups buttermilk
- 1½ teaspoons vanilla extract
- 7½ ounces (1½ cups) blueberries

1. **FOR THE STREUSEL:** Combine granulated sugar, brown sugar, flour, and salt in bowl. Add melted butter and toss with fork until evenly moistened and mixture forms large chunks with some pea-size pieces throughout; set aside.

2. **FOR THE MUFFINS:** Adjust oven rack to middle position and heat oven to 400 degrees. Spray 12-cup muffin tin, including top, generously with vegetable oil spray. Whisk flour, baking powder, baking soda, and salt together in large bowl. Whisk sugar, eggs, melted butter, and oil together in separate bowl until combined, about 30 seconds. Whisk buttermilk and vanilla into sugar mixture until combined.

3. Stir sugar mixture into flour mixture until just combined. Gently stir in blueberries until incorporated. Using heaping ¼-cup dry measuring cup, divide batter evenly among prepared muffin cups (cups will be filled to rim); sprinkle muffin tops evenly with streusel.

4. Bake until golden brown and toothpick inserted in center comes out with few crumbs attached, 18 to 20 minutes, rotating muffin tin halfway through baking. Let muffins cool in muffin tin on wire rack for 5 minutes. Remove muffins from muffin tin and let cool 5 minutes longer. Serve.

IT'S HARD TO beat the simple pleasure of biting into a juicy slice of watermelon, but I was recently served a dish that took watermelon to a new place: a savory salad. In this salad, briny olives and feta cheese were the perfect foils for the sweet melon. Inspired, I headed into the kitchen to make my own version.

I was able to dig up quite a few recipes for salads featuring watermelon, olives, and feta, so I took them into the kitchen for a trial run. None of these salads was an outright failure, but my tasters repeatedly complained of watery salad and bland melon. One salad featured two elements that I thought worked well—cucumber and shallot—so I decided to use them in my version, too. To temper the shallot, I quickly soaked it in a little white wine vinegar (spiked with red pepper flakes and sugar for extra flavor); when the shallot had softened, I drained it and used the flavorful vinegar as the base of my vinaigrette. I tossed the melon and cucumber with chopped kalamata olives and a handful of torn basil for freshness. A sprinkling of feta and we were ready to taste.

The flavors were spot on, but wateriness still plagued the salad, and the watermelon tasted a bit lackluster. Here in the test kitchen we have a trick to deal with watery coleslaw: We salt the cabbage and let it sit before using it. The salt draws moisture out of the cabbage so it can drain away in a colander instead of diluting the dressed slaw. I tried the same technique with the watermelon, salting it and letting it drain for 30 minutes before assembling the salad. This technique successfully banished excess liquid, and the watermelon took on a pleasantly firm texture.

But with the melon so heavily seasoned with salt, I'd lost the balance of salty and sweet—the very backbone of this dish. The solution was simple: I'd use sugar instead of salt. Macerating the watermelon cubes in granulated sugar drew out almost as much moisture as the salt, re-creating the textural improvement but without interfering with the overall flavor of the dish. In fact, the sugar enhanced the flavor and brought the whole salad into focus.

This sweet and savory salad is fantastic alongside grilled meats or as part of a brunch spread.

WATERMELON SALAD Serves 4 to 6

You'll need 3 pounds of watermelon.

- 6 cups seedless watermelon, cut into 1-inch pieces
- 1½ teaspoons sugar
- 1 shallot, sliced into thin rings
- 3 tablespoons white wine vinegar
- ¼ teaspoon red pepper flakes
  Salt and pepper
- 1 English cucumber, peeled, quartered lengthwise, seeded, and cut into ½-inch pieces
- 3 tablespoons extra-virgin olive oil
- ½ cup pitted kalamata olives, chopped coarse
- ½ cup fresh basil leaves, torn
- 3 ounces feta cheese, crumbled (¾ cup)

1. Toss watermelon with 1 teaspoon sugar in large bowl, transfer to colander set in sink, and let drain for 30 minutes. Wipe out bowl. Combine shallot, vinegar, pepper flakes, ¼ teaspoon salt, and remaining ½ teaspoon sugar in separate bowl and let sit while watermelon drains.

2. Pat cucumber and drained watermelon dry with paper towels and transfer to now-empty bowl. Using fork, remove shallot from vinegar mixture and add to bowl with watermelon. Add ½ teaspoon pepper and ¼ teaspoon salt to vinegar mixture and slowly whisk in oil until incorporated. Add dressing and olives to bowl with watermelon and toss to combine. Refrigerate for at least 30 minutes or up to 4 hours.

3. Add basil to salad and toss to combine. Season with salt and pepper to taste. Transfer to serving platter and sprinkle with feta. Serve.

Cooking Class Macaroni and Cheese

Why suffer through stodgy, gritty, greasy, or bland mac and cheese? We can steer you toward a delicious, foolproof homemade version that's fast enough for a weeknight. BY REBECCAH MARSTERS

CLASSIC MACARONI AND CHEESE
Serves 6 to 8

The test kitchen's favorite elbow macaroni is Barilla Elbows. Serve with hot sauce and/or celery salt.

3	slices hearty white sandwich bread, torn into quarters
2	tablespoons unsalted butter, cut into 4 pieces and chilled, plus 5 tablespoons unsalted butter
1	pound elbow macaroni
	Salt
6	tablespoons all-purpose flour
1½	teaspoons dry mustard
¼	teaspoon cayenne pepper
5	cups whole milk
8	ounces Monterey Jack cheese, shredded (2 cups)
8	ounces sharp cheddar cheese, shredded (2 cups)

1. Adjust oven rack to lower-middle position and heat broiler. Pulse bread and chilled butter in food processor until coarsely ground, 7 to 10 pulses; set aside.

2. Bring 4 quarts water to boil in Dutch oven. Add macaroni and 1 tablespoon salt and cook, stirring often, until tender. Drain macaroni and set aside in colander.

3. Melt remaining 5 tablespoons butter in now-empty pot over medium-high heat. Whisk in flour, mustard, cayenne, and 1 teaspoon salt and cook for 1 minute. Slowly whisk in milk until smooth. Bring mixture to boil, reduce heat to medium, and cook, whisking occasionally, until thickened to consistency of heavy cream, about 5 minutes. Off heat, whisk in cheeses until fully melted. Add macaroni and cook over medium-low heat, stirring constantly, until steaming and heated through, about 6 minutes.

4. Pour mixture into 13 by 9-inch broiler-safe baking dish. Top with bread-crumb mixture and broil until crumbs are deep golden brown, 3 to 5 minutes, rotating dish if necessary for even browning. Let rest for 5 minutes. Serve.

STEP BY STEP **Classic Macaroni and Cheese**

1. MAKE BREAD CRUMBS
Pulse the bread and chilled butter in a food processor until the pieces are no larger than ⅛ inch.
WHY? Homemade bread crumbs have better flavor and texture than commercial versions, and using the food processor produces even crumbs quickly.

2. BOIL PASTA
Add the macaroni and salt to 4 quarts of boiling water, cook until the macaroni is tender, and drain.
WHY? Plenty of water ensures evenly cooked macaroni, and salt seasons it throughout.

3. MAKE ROUX
Melt the butter in the now-empty pot, add flour and spices, and stir until the roux is golden brown and fragrant.
WHY? Cooking the roux eliminates the raw flour taste while adding toasty depth. Blooming the spices maximizes their flavor.

4. SLOWLY ADD DAIRY
Whisk in the milk in a steady stream until the mixture is smooth.
WHY? Dumping in the milk all at once can cause the roux to clump, resulting in a lumpy sauce.

5. BOIL AND THEN SIMMER
Bring the sauce to a boil, reduce the heat, and simmer until it's the consistency of heavy cream.
WHY? Flour needs to be heated to at least 190 degrees to activate its thickening power, and continuing to simmer the sauce further thickens it.

Core Techniques

Mind the Cheese(s)

For creamy sauce with deep flavor, two cheeses are better than one. Sharp cheddar gives our sauce good cheese flavor, while high-moisture, easy-melting Monterey Jack ensures a smooth texture. The amount of cheese matters, too. We've found that a pound of cheese to a pound of pasta is the right ratio for a dish that's rich and full-flavored but not cloying or stringy. Finally, don't be tempted to use preshredded cheese: It has added coatings that can negatively affect texture.

Make Your Own Crumbs

When we want a delicately crisp, buttery topping, homemade crumbs—which are easy to make in the food processor—are the way to go. After a run under the broiler, the topping is flavorful, golden, and crisp. And while some sources claim otherwise, we've found that fresh—not stale—bread makes the best crumbs.

Cook the Pasta Correctly

While we usually stress the idea of cooking pasta until just al dente for a pleasantly firm texture, we discovered that undercooked pasta can be too firm to readily absorb any of the cheese sauce. On the other hand, if the pasta is cooked until it's completely soft, it will be soggy in the finished dish and won't absorb any of the moisture from the cheese sauce, making for a loose, runny casserole. For perfectly tender, flavorful pasta and a thick but creamy sauce, cook the pasta until it's past al dente and just tender. Bite into one noodle: It should be fully tender all the way through but not bloated or mushy.

Make a True Roux

A roux—a mixture of flour and fat—is the customary thickener for white sauces, like the one that binds this (and most) macaroni and cheese. In addition to thickening the sauce, the roux contributes flavor and color. The longer the roux cooks, the darker its color and the more pronounced its flavor, but its thickening power decreases. In this recipe, we make a medium, or "blond," roux, which should be golden in color and smell like toasting nuts or popcorn; this should take about 1 minute.

Mac and Cheese Primer

One of the best things about macaroni and cheese is that you can make nearly endless variations. Here are four of the test kitchen's favorite recipes for this dish.

The Classic: Classic macaroni and cheese (like this recipe) features a Mornay sauce (béchamel with cheese added) and a bread-crumb topping.

The Weeknight Warrior: We've developed a technique for getting homemade macaroni and cheese on the table fast. We simmer uncooked macaroni in a mixture of water and evaporated milk and then add lots of shredded cheese for flavor and a cornstarch slurry for thickening. After it's topped with bread crumbs, our skillet mac and cheese goes right from stovetop to table in the same pan. Find our recipe for Skillet Macaroni and Cheese at **CooksCountry.com/skilletmacandcheese**.

The Heavy Hitter: Custard-based macaroni and cheese is enriched with eggs and baked into a cheesy casserole. For our version, we toss mild cheddar with cornstarch to prevent it from breaking and reserve the flavorful sharp cheddar for the top of the dish. We use cream instead of milk to further guard against broken sauce, and we include extra yolks to produce mac and cheese that's rich, smooth, and creamy. For our recipe, visit **CooksCountry.com/macandcheesecasserole**.

Reduced-Fat: We found four ways to reduce the fat (and calories) in our macaroni and cheese recipe. We replaced full-fat cheddar cheese with low-fat cheddar and substituted 2 percent milk for whole milk. A can of 2 percent evaporated milk added creaminess, and cornstarch replaced the butter roux. Find the recipe at **CooksCountry.com/reducedfatmacandcheese**.

ESSENTIAL GEAR **Broiler-Safe Baking Dish**

Our favorite 13 by 9-inch Pyrex baking dish is a real workhorse—but it can't go under the broiler. For recipes like our Classic Macaroni and Cheese, we needed an alternate choice. We tested baking dishes made from steel, cast iron, ceramic, and porcelain and liked the light weight of the latter two materials best. We looked for a baking dish that had the same shape and proportions as the Pyrex, and large, easy-to-grasp handles. Our winner stood up to the heat and was effortless to whisk in and out of the oven, even piping hot.

OUR FAVORITE
Porcelain Lasagna Baking Dish
from HIC ($37.49)

6. WHISK IN CHEESE

Remove the pot from the heat and add both cheeses, whisking until they're completely melted.
WHY? Adding the cheeses off heat prevents them from scorching and breaking; the hot sauce has plenty of residual heat to fully melt the cheeses.

7. COOK ON STOVETOP

Add the boiled, drained macaroni to the cheese sauce and cook it until it's heated through.
WHY? Since the dish isn't baked, the sauce and the macaroni must be fully cooked and piping hot when they go into the baking dish.

8. TOP WITH CRUMBS

Transfer the macaroni to a broiler-safe baking dish and sprinkle evenly with the bread-crumb mixture.
WHY? Adding the bread crumbs right before broiling prevents them from becoming soggy.

9. BROIL

Place the dish on the lower-middle rack underneath the preheated broiler for 3 to 5 minutes.
WHY? The topping needs only a few minutes to become golden brown and crunchy under the broiler.

10. LET REST AND THEN SERVE

After removing the dish from the oven, let it rest for 5 minutes before serving.
WHY? Straight from the oven, the casserole is scalding hot; letting it sit allows it to cool while the sauce thickens to the perfect consistency.

Slow Cooker Carne Adovada

As long as we were adapting this delicious New Mexican pork stew for the slow cooker, we decided to streamline the recipe, too. BY DIANE UNGER

CARNE ADOVADA IS a classic New Mexican dish made from chunks of pork shoulder stewed in a thick, red chile sauce seasoned with onions, garlic, oregano, and lime juice. It's saucy enough to be served over rice or in a bowl with toasted corn tortillas, but the meat can also be used as a filling for tacos or burritos. Traditional recipes start with dried New Mexican chiles that are toasted and ground to a powder in order to add a deep, fruity, complex flavor.

Our test kitchen has a wonderful carne adovada recipe that blends chili powder, raisins, and brewed coffee to mimic the unique flavor of New Mexican chiles. I wanted to figure out how to translate that stovetop-to-oven recipe for the slow cooker. Should be easy, right?

Following our recipe, I diligently browned the chunks of pork in two batches, a process that takes about 25 minutes and coats the stovetop with a fine layer of pork fat. I finished the rest of the prep—which included sautéing onions; blooming spices; cooking them down with the chili powder, raisins, and coffee; and then pureeing all that in a blender—and 40 minutes later my pork and sauce were ready for the slow cooker. Mind you, I hadn't even had my morning coffee yet. For me, the allure of using a slow cooker is its ability to make life easier. Sure, coming home to a great meal is lovely, but not if I have to put in more than an hour's work before I head out to my day job.

As it turned out, all that work wasn't worth the effort. The flavor was OK, but generally speaking, the dish didn't have the depth of the stovetop-to-oven method, since the slow cooker's moist environment and the dish's long cooking time tend to mute flavor. I needed to figure out a way to make this work in the slow cooker and streamline the recipe while I was at it.

The first step I hoped to get rid of was browning all that meat, which was messy as well as time-consuming. A side-by-side tasting showed that, thanks to the assertive flavor of the sauce, browning was not essential to the overall flavor of the dish. But tasters did find that the version with browned meat had a sort of meaty, earthy taste that the unbrowned version lacked, so I looked for something to bring it back. In the test kitchen, we often use soy sauce, which is

This rich stew has a pleasantly bitter, spicy flavor that works well with white rice or tortillas.

rich in the savory taste known as umami, to bolster meatiness. Sure enough, tossing the meat in 3 tablespoons of soy sauce before cooking brought back the meaty flavor that tasters were missing.

My next question was whether I needed to dirty a skillet sautéing the onions and spices. I knew that blooming spices like chili powder in oil brings out and mellows the flavor, but wouldn't it be easier to fall back on my microwave? Another side-by-side test revealed that there was very little flavor difference between the two approaches, plus it was a lot easier to transfer the onion mixture to the blender from a bowl rather than from a large skillet.

Next I wondered if I could eliminate blending the sauce before it went into the slow cooker; turns out I couldn't. In yet another side-by-side test, this time of pureed versus unpureed sauce, the pureed stuff won hands down: The sauce was thicker, coated the meat better, and was free of bloated raisins. This was one corner I couldn't cut.

Now I had the flavor I wanted, but the texture wasn't right—it was way

too thin. I asked our science editor why this might be happening, and he explained that it had to do with the way that flour, the only thickener in the dish, behaves when it's cooked over a long period of time at a low temperature. (My slow-cooker version cooks at just over 200 degrees for some 5 to 6 hours, while the original version cooked in a 350-degree oven for about 2 hours.) The slow-cooking process, our science editor explained, was gradually breaking down the starch granules that had swollen and thickened the liquid; as the swollen granules exploded like bursting balloons, their thickening power was greatly reduced.

Rather than fight against the chemistry of flour and liquid, I decided to tinker with the relative quantities of both. The original recipe called for 2½ cups of chicken broth along with ½ cup of brewed coffee. After testing gradually decreasing amounts, I settled on only ¾ cup of broth, but for flavor purposes I left the amount of coffee the same. At the same time, I also increased the flour from ¼ to ⅓ cup. Together, these

two adjustments gave me the rich, thick broth I was looking for.

As a final step, I freshened up the flavor by finishing the stew with cilantro and lime zest and juice after the meat was fully tender. Now I had an adovada that was a fit rival to my previous favorite version, but with a lot less work.

SLOW-COOKER CARNE ADOVADA Serves 6 to 8
Pork butt roast is often labeled Boston butt in the supermarket. Serve the finished dish over rice or with warm corn tortillas.

- 1 (4- to 5-pound) boneless pork butt roast, pulled apart at seams, trimmed, and cut into 1½-inch pieces
  Salt and pepper
- 3 tablespoons soy sauce
- 2 onions, chopped
- ½ cup chili powder
- 6 garlic cloves, minced
- 3 tablespoons vegetable oil
- 1 tablespoon minced canned chipotle chile in adobo sauce
- 2 teaspoons dried oregano
- ¾ cup chicken broth
- ½ cup brewed coffee
- ⅓ cup all-purpose flour
- ¼ cup raisins
- ¼ cup minced fresh cilantro
- 1 teaspoon grated lime zest plus 1 tablespoon juice

1. Season pork with salt and pepper. Combine pork and soy sauce in slow cooker. Combine onions, chili powder, garlic, oil, chipotle, oregano, and 1 teaspoon salt in bowl. Microwave, covered, until onions have softened and mixture is fragrant, about 7 minutes, stirring halfway through microwaving.

2. Puree broth, coffee, flour, raisins, and onion mixture in blender until smooth, about 1 minute. Stir sauce into slow cooker, then scrape down any sauce from sides of cooker with rubber spatula. Cover and cook until pork is tender, 5 to 6 hours on high or 6 to 7 hours on low.

3. Turn off slow cooker, let stew settle for 5 minutes, then remove fat from surface using large spoon. Stir in cilantro and lime zest and juice. Let sit for 15 minutes to thicken slightly. Season with salt and pepper to taste. Serve.

Recipe Makeover French Silk Pie

This pie is all about over-the-top decadence. Could we maintain the appeal while cutting the fat and calories? BY CRISTIN WALSH

WHEN BETTY COOPER won the 1951 Pillsbury Bake-Off with her recipe for French silk pie, it was lauded as the ultimate in dessert decadence. Wondering if what was considered decadent then would still play today, I prepared her original recipe—and yes, it was indeed decadent. The filling is made by creaming two sticks of butter with 1 cup of sugar and stirring in 3 ounces of melted unsweetened chocolate and four eggs.

This pie is delicious, but a single serving has 490 calories and 36 grams of fat. Could I keep the decadence while cutting the calorie and fat load?

I found a few low-fat recipes for French silk pie, but none of them were very good. The problems? Weak chocolate flavor and fillings so rubbery they ate like Jell-O. Instead of trying to fix these fundamentally flawed versions, I decided to start with Mrs. Cooper's original recipe and chip away at the fat and calories any way that I could.

My starting point was obvious: the two sticks of butter. In the past, the test kitchen has successfully replaced butter with reduced-fat cream cheese in desserts, so I gave that a try here. The numbers were good—with this switch, the recipe went from 36 to 18 grams of fat. But the cream cheese made the pie too sour. To mitigate the sourness (while keeping the cream cheese), I tried using bittersweet chocolate instead of unsweetened, hoping the sugar would balance the cream cheese's heavy tang. This swap immediately made the pie more palatable. It got even better when I doubled the amount of chocolate to 6 ounces. When I went to compute the nutritional information, I was surprised to find that unsweetened chocolate has significantly more fat than bittersweet, so although I was adding calories (because of the sugar in bittersweet chocolate), the fat numbers were a wash. The switch in chocolate allowed me to drop the sugar from 1 cup to ½ cup.

The pie tasted good and I had made solid progress on reducing the fat calories . . . but not enough. Four whole eggs give the original pie a silken texture; I tried making a pie with no eggs, but the filling was too dense. To lighten it back up, I tried whipping three egg whites into a meringue with ¼ cup of sugar and then folding them in. Now the filling was silky, but it was still a bit

too soft without the butter to firm it up when chilled. An easy fix was to add a little gelatin for stability and set. Now the filling had a light, creamy texture.

As for the crust, I knew that low-fat pastry crusts were terrible so I decided to go with the test kitchen's low-fat crumb crust recipe that uses crushed graham crackers, 3 tablespoons of butter, 3 tablespoons of sugar, and 1 ounce of low-fat cream cheese (which I was already using). But as the recipe stood, I wasn't cutting enough calories. I tried replacing the graham crackers with crushed Cheerios, cornflakes, ladyfingers, and low-calorie cookies, but the crusts were sandy or too hard or shrunk during baking. I was at my wit's end when a fellow test cook suggested trying crisp breadsticks, which are low in calories and fat and have a neutral flavor. Surprisingly, when crushed into crumbs and pressed into a pie plate, they were sturdy and perfectly complemented the intense chocolaty filling.

My tasters loved this pie's rich flavor and light, fluffy texture—and I loved its much healthier profile.

We use reduced-fat cream cheese to bind both the filling and the crust.

The Numbers
Nutritional information is for one slice.
Traditional French Silk Pie
CALORIES **490**
FAT **36 g** SATURATED FAT **21 g**

Cook's Country Reduced-Fat French Silk Pie
CALORIES **320**
FAT **16 g** SATURATED FAT **9 g**

sugar in food processor to fine crumbs, about 30 seconds. Add butter and cream cheese and pulse until combined, about 8 pulses. Using bottom of dry measuring cup, press crumbs into bottom and up sides of pie plate. Bake until crust is fragrant and beginning to brown, 15 to 20 minutes, rotating plate halfway through baking. Let crust cool completely on wire rack, about 30 minutes.

2. FOR THE FILLING: Sprinkle gelatin over ¼ cup milk in small bowl and let sit until gelatin softens, about 5 minutes. Whisk cream cheese, ½ cup sugar, and vanilla in large bowl until smooth. Combine chocolate and remaining ¼ cup milk in medium bowl and microwave at 50 percent power, stirring occasionally, until melted, about 90 seconds. Microwave gelatin mixture until melted, about 10 seconds. Stir gelatin mixture into chocolate mixture. Whisk chocolate mixture into cream cheese mixture until smooth.

3. Using stand mixer fitted with whisk, whip egg whites and cream of tartar on medium-low speed until foamy, about 1 minute. Increase speed to medium-high and whip whites to soft, billowy mounds, about 1 minute. Gradually add remaining ¼ cup sugar and whip until glossy, stiff peaks form, 2 to 3 minutes. Gently fold whipped egg whites into chocolate mixture in 2 additions until no white streaks remain. Pour filling into crust. Refrigerate until set, at least 3 hours or up to 24 hours. Serve.

REDUCED-FAT FRENCH SILK PIE
Serves 8
Purchase cracker-style breadsticks for the crust, not the soft, freshly baked variety.

CRUST
- 4 ounces crisp breadsticks
- 3 tablespoons sugar
- 3 tablespoons unsalted butter, melted
- 1 ounce ⅓ less fat cream cheese (neufchatel), softened

FILLING
- 2 teaspoons unflavored gelatin
- ½ cup 2 percent low-fat milk
- 7 ounces ⅓ less fat cream cheese (neufchatel), softened
- ¾ cup (5¼ ounces) sugar
- 1 teaspoon vanilla extract
- 6 ounces bittersweet chocolate, chopped
- 3 large egg whites
- ¼ teaspoon cream of tartar

1. FOR THE CRUST: Adjust oven rack to middle position and heat oven to 350 degrees. Spray 9-inch pie plate with vegetable oil spray. Process breadsticks and

KEY INGREDIENT
Breadsticks
A mixture of ground breadsticks, sugar, butter, and reduced-fat cream cheese makes for a crisp, tasty lower-fat crust.

Cooking for Two Maryland Crab Cakes

Too many crab cakes are tightly bound with bready fillers. We wanted a crab cake that could barely keep it together. BY CHRISTIE MORRISON

A REALLY GOOD crab cake is all about the crab, as any Marylander worth her salt could tell you. With its lands hugging the Chesapeake Bay, the state is home to the famous blue crab and its sweet, tender meat. It's small wonder, then, that Maryland crab cakes contain little else—namely crushed saltines, Old Bay seasoning, mustard, and just enough mayonnaise to hold them together. I wanted our version to combine a stripped-down ingredient list with a virtually hands-off cooking method that would make these crab cakes a great meal for two, even if you're not using impeccably fresh crab from Chesapeake Bay.

I knew from previous recipes that, when it comes to crab cakes, there is no substitute for jumbo lump crabmeat—other varieties of crabmeat are inferior. Of course, we also prefer fresh crabmeat to pasteurized, but sadly, the fresh stuff is pricey and not always available. A recent test kitchen tasting found that a few brands of pasteurized crabmeat (available canned or in the refrigerated section of most supermarkets) are promising alternatives to fresh. The downside? The pasteurized versions occasionally have a noticeably "fishy" flavor and odor that fresh crabmeat lacks. To combat this, our science editor suggested soaking the crabmeat in milk for a short amount of time. The casein in milk, he explained, would bind to the compound in the crabmeat that gives it the fishy odor; when the crabmeat was later drained, the milk would take the fishy compound with it. Sure enough,

after a 20-minute soak in milk, the crabmeat had completely lost its fishiness.

Fortunately, fresh and pasteurized crabmeats are available in 8-ounce containers—the perfect amount for two large crab cakes. I patted the milk-soaked crabmeat dry with paper towels to prevent extra moisture from watering down the crab cakes. I knew that mayonnaise was a necessary glue, and that Dijon mustard added both moisture and sharp, tangy flavor. A teaspoon of hot sauce and ½ teaspoon of Old Bay seasoning added heat and spice, respectively, without overpowering the mild crab. I eschewed the hard crunch of celery and raw flavor of chopped onions (two frequent crab cake additions) for the bright flavor of minced scallions. Since these would be stand-alone, no-sauce-necessary, dinner-worthy crab cakes, I added a tablespoon of melted butter for extra richness.

Now that my flavors were balanced, I needed to bulk up the cakes to make them shapeable; as currently constructed, the mixture wouldn't stay bound into cakes. For the bread component, Maryland crab cakes usually stick to a moderate amount of crushed saltines. I found that 2 tablespoons of crushed saltines added some cohesion without being noticeable.

Still, my crab cakes weren't holding together very well, and I thought I knew the reason. Most crab cake recipes (yielding four cakes) use one whole egg or an egg yolk to glue the ingredients together. Thinking that a yolk would make my smaller batch of two cakes too

We drop these tender crab cakes into a buttered skillet and broil them: No flipping required.

wet and eggy, I omitted it. But when I tested another batch with a yolk (and an extra tablespoon of crushed saltines to balance the additional moisture), it was clear that the yolk was necessary; the cakes held together much better and were much easier to handle. And they tasted better, too. Chilling the cakes before cooking made them more firm,

and thus they held their shape better through cooking.

Even with a chilling step, however, these tasty, tender crab cakes were a bit too delicate. Instead of pan-frying the cakes (which would involve flipping—and most likely destroying—them), I did what many Marylanders do: I broiled the crab cakes. I placed the chilled cakes in a 10-inch skillet that I coated with softened butter and slid them under the preheated broiler until the tops were golden and the interior was thoroughly cooked. The only problem? My tasters complained that the bottoms of the crab cakes were soggy. So for my next test, I dipped the bottoms of the cakes in some crushed saltine crackers before I refrigerated them. The crackers (which I was already using inside the cakes) eliminated the sogginess and effectively fried in the butter to form a crispy, sturdy, tasty bottom crust.

These crab cakes are chock-full of crabmeat and not lacking in richness, so one crab cake will make a filling meal. But that doesn't mean you won't wish you could have another one . . .

Big Cake, Big Flavor
What makes our Maryland Crab Cakes for Two better than other crab cakes? Deliberate design and careful construction.

Chunks of Crabmeat
We soak lump crabmeat in milk to produce a cleaner flavor, and we handle it gently so each crab cake has large chunks.

Chopped Scallions
The scallions add bright color and sharp flavor. Unlike onions, they require no precooking.

Crushed Saltines
A layer of cracker crumbs makes for a crisp, crunchy bottom crust.

INSIDE STORY.

MARYLAND CRAB CAKES FOR TWO

Fresh crabmeat may be hard to come by, but its flavor is superior to that of pasteurized. If your crabmeat smells clean and fresh when you open the package, skip the soaking process in step 1. These crab cakes make for a nice entrée when served with a salad.

- 8 ounces lump crabmeat, picked over for shells
- 1 cup milk
- 7 square or 8 round saltines
- 2 scallions, minced
- 1 tablespoon unsalted butter, melted, plus 1 teaspoon softened
- 1 large egg yolk
- 1 tablespoon mayonnaise
- 2 teaspoons Dijon mustard
- 1 teaspoon hot sauce
- ½ teaspoon Old Bay seasoning
  Lemon wedges

1. Place crabmeat and milk in bowl, making sure crabmeat is totally submerged. Cover and refrigerate for at least 20 minutes. Drain crabmeat in fine-mesh strainer, pressing firmly to strain milk but being careful not to break up lumps of crabmeat.

2. Transfer crabmeat to paper towel–lined plate and dry well with paper towels. Place saltines in zipper-lock bag and crush to fine crumbs with rolling pin. Using rubber spatula, gently combine scallions, melted butter, egg yolk, mayonnaise, mustard, hot sauce, Old Bay, crabmeat, and 3 tablespoons saltine crumbs in bowl.

3. Divide mixture into 2 equal portions and shape into tight balls. Press 1 side of each ball into remaining saltine crumbs, flattening saltine side slightly while keeping opposite side rounded, then place crumb side down on plate. Cover with plastic wrap and refrigerate for at least 1 hour or up to 8 hours.

4. Adjust oven rack 6 inches from broiler element and heat broiler. Grease 10-inch skillet with softened butter. Transfer crab cakes to prepared pan, crumb side down. Broil until crab cakes are golden brown on top and centers register 140 degrees, 12 to 15 minutes. Serve with lemon wedges.

What are the secrets to transforming a can of humble white beans into an elegant appetizer? The food processor and some key mix-ins.

BY ASHLEY MOORE

IF YOU ARE ever looking for me at a party, I can be found standing around the hors d'oeuvres table. Needless to say, that means I have had my fair share of bean dips—most often hummus. But I've also had some white bean dips (made from cannellini or navy beans) that had promise. I decided to come up with a really good dip recipe for white bean dip, with rich flavor and a just-right texture.

I had a good starting point in a recipe we published a while back: a white bean spread that served as the base for a tomato bruschetta. It included a little lemon juice, along with some garlic and rosemary, and it called for processing half of the beans, which resulted in a coarse, chunky spread. I took out a food processor and gave it a whirl. My colleagues enjoyed the flavor profile of this "dip" but found its chunky texture a drawback, more suited to its previous use as a spread than as a dip. I needed to find a way to keep the potent flavor but lighten up the texture.

I started by adding different amounts of water to the dip (I was using one 15-ounce can of beans, drained and rinsed), resulting in some very loose catastrophes. Two tablespoons of water ended up creating just the right consistency, but now my dip was too lean in flavor. I added more extra-virgin olive oil and decided to use another tablespoon for drizzling right before serving, adding a final little burst of richness. The oil and water together help achieve a rich yet loose dip, perfect for any chip. I also processed the dip longer and included all the beans in this step, rather than just half, to give the dip a smooth texture.

Inspired by the success of this white bean dip, I decided to create four variations using potent ingredients like capers, goat cheese, green chiles, and sun-dried tomatoes. Now I have an even better reason to hang around the hors d'oeuvres table.

Creamy white beans are a good backdrop for potent add-ins like garlic and rosemary.

GARLIC AND ROSEMARY WHITE BEAN DIP
Makes 1¼ cups

Serve this dip with slices of toasted baguette or tortilla chips, or use it as a spread for sandwiches. You can make the dip up to 24 hours in advance, but wait to drizzle it with oil until right before serving.

- 1 (15-ounce) can cannellini beans, rinsed
- ¼ cup extra-virgin olive oil
- 2 tablespoons water
- 2 teaspoons lemon juice
- 1 teaspoon minced fresh rosemary
- 1 small garlic clove, minced
  Salt and pepper
  Pinch cayenne pepper

1. Process beans, 3 tablespoons oil, water, lemon juice, rosemary, garlic, ¼ teaspoon salt, ¼ teaspoon pepper, and cayenne in food processor until smooth, about 45 seconds, scraping down sides of bowl as needed.

2. Transfer to serving bowl, cover, and let stand at room temperature for at least 30 minutes. Season with salt and pepper to taste. Drizzle with remaining 1 tablespoon oil and serve.

CAPER AND TARRAGON WHITE BEAN DIP

Substitute 2 teaspoons minced fresh tarragon for rosemary; omit salt; and add 3 tablespoons rinsed capers to food processor with beans.

GOAT CHEESE AND LEMON WHITE BEAN DIP

Substitute minced fresh thyme for rosemary and add 1 cup crumbled goat cheese and 2 teaspoons grated lemon zest to food processor with beans.

GREEN CHILE AND CILANTRO WHITE BEAN DIP

Omit water; increase lemon juice to 1 tablespoon and cayenne to ⅛ teaspoon. Substitute 3 tablespoons minced fresh cilantro for rosemary. Add ½ cup patted dry canned green chiles and 2 tablespoons sour cream to food processor with beans.

SUN-DRIED TOMATO AND FETA WHITE BEAN DIP

Increase water to ¼ cup, substitute minced fresh oregano for rosemary, reduce salt to ⅛ teaspoon, and add ½ cup crumbled feta cheese and ¼ cup oil-packed sun-dried tomatoes to food processor with beans.

Equipment Review Vacuum Sealers

With the next generation of home vacuum sealers out, could we find one that keeps food fresh without sucking our wallets dry? BY HANNAH CROWLEY

VACUUM SEALERS ARE great for storing food. We use them at the test kitchen to help store hundreds of pounds of food weekly. They're popular at home, too, among hunters and fishermen freezing their hauls, as well as among bulk shoppers, gardeners, and farmers' market frequenters. They work by pulling air away and creating a tight seal around the food, blocking it from elements that hasten deterioration. We wrote about vacuum sealers a few years ago, but of the eight models we tested, only the winner, the Weston Pro 2300, still exists. Ours is still chugging along, sealing hundreds of pounds of meat weekly, but at $500, its cost and size make it impractical for most home cooks.

Fortunately, a new wave of sealers offers less expensive options, so we set ourselves a price cap of $200 and bought seven models to test, ranging from about $50 to $199. We sealed and froze strawberries, ground coffee, steaks, chicken, and individual portions of lasagna and monitored them for signs of freezer burn. We also portioned and sealed pretzels and cereal and stored them in the pantry, sampling them periodically to gauge freshness.

We have good news to report: In our previous testing, only our winning model kept food freezer-burn-free for two months. This time at two months, food from six of the seven sealers still looked good. But eventually, a pattern emerged. Sealers come in two basic styles—heat seal or valve seal—and the latter lost their seals faster. Valve sealers use what look like extra-sturdy plastic storage bags; you zip the food in and the sealer then sucks the air out through a valve on the bag. We were intrigued by valve versions; they're typically smaller, quieter, and cheaper. But they aren't as foolproof because their bags are made of thick, often brittle plastic. It's difficult to be certain they're closed, and once they are, a firm jostle can break the seal. One valve sealer proved successful; at two and a half months a few packets had loosened seals but most still looked great, thanks to a small plastic clamp that you run over the zipper to definitively close the bag before sealing. Heat sealers, on the other hand, work by pulling away the surrounding air and closing off the plastic by melting it shut. With these sealers, it was easy to be sure the bags were closed—was the plastic melted or not?

The second factor was power.

Vacuum strength is measured in inches of mercury (inHg); a higher number means a stronger suction. There's a reason the Pro 2300 weighs a whopping 26 pounds: It houses a large motor that pulls 28 inHg of vacuum power. Not every manufacturer shared its sealer's strength, but with those in our testing that did, we found a range from 11 to 23 inHg and the machine with the strongest vacuum kept food the freshest because less air was left in its bags. Stronger vacuums went hand in hand with larger motors, and for heat sealers a larger motor can support a more powerful seal bar—the chamber that heats up and seals

off the plastic. A powerful seal bar heats up faster to quickly seal at maximum suction and seals more consistently, as it can power through small wrinkles and specks of errant food or liquid.

Also important: a manual pulse. Automatic pulse mode is too strong and crushed delicate items in its quest to vacate the air. Manual mode allows control over the vacuum, so you can stop it before it crunches your food. Our winning sealer had a responsive pulse mode, a large motor, and a powerful vacuum. It kept frozen food looking fresh and pantry items crisp for three months and counting. The compact Weston Professional

Advantage Vacuum Sealer ($189.99) is the home version of our favorite Pro 2300. The Pro 2300 has the muscle to seal hundreds of pounds of meat daily, and if money and space aren't an issue, it's still the best sealer we've tested, but for home use, the Weston Professional Advantage Vacuum Sealer has the muscle, seal quality, durability, and smaller footprint we require. The one valve sealer we liked, the Waring Pro Pistol Vac Professional Vacuum Sealer System, kept the majority of its food fresh for at least three months, and at nearly $70, it's a great choice for the occasional home sealer; we're naming it our Best Buy.

	CRITERIA		TESTERS' NOTES
HIGHLY RECOMMENDED			
WESTON Professional Advantage Vacuum Sealer **Model:** 65-0501-W **Price:** $189.99 **Vacuum Strength:** 23 inHg **Style:** Heat	Performance ★★★ Easy to Use ★★★		This compact, powerful heat-sealing model kept food fresh for three months and counting. Its intuitive interface has a responsive pulse mode and bright blue lights that indicate its progress. It works with a wide variety of bags, canisters, and rolls that were the cheapest of any sealer in our lineup.
RECOMMENDED			
WARING PRO Pistol Vac Professional Vacuum Sealer System **Model:** PVS1000 **Price:** $69.95 **Vacuum Strength:** 18 inHg **Style:** Valve	Performance ★★½ Easy to Use ★★★	BEST BUY	This compact handheld model was the only valve sealer we liked. The key to its success is a 2-inch plastic clamp that you run over the zipper to make sure it's closed. Most of its food looked great at three months, and while you have to charge the sealer, you don't have to rest 15 seconds between seals as you do with heat sealers.
RECOMMENDED WITH RESERVATIONS			
FOODSAVER 2-in-1 Vacuum Sealer System **Model:** V4865 **Price:** $199 **Vacuum Strength:** Proprietary **Style:** Heat	Performance ★★ Easy to Use ★★½		This heat sealer has two unique features: first, a sensor that automatically grabs, vacuums, and seals bags and, second, a roll storage compartment with a built-in plastic slicer that tidily cuts bags to size. Both are handy, but we found this sealer to be bulky, and some of its seals had loosened by month three.
FOODSAVER Vacuum Sealing System **Model:** V2244 **Price:** $79.99 **Vacuum Strength:** Proprietary **Style:** Heat	Performance ★★½ Easy to Use ★★		This entry-level heat sealer is light, small, and quiet and, more important, held its own against pricier models, keeping food freezer-burn-free for three months and counting. While we didn't have any issues, the light plastic frame had us concerned about its durability.
SEAL-A-MEAL Vacuum Food Sealer **Model:** FSSMSL0160-000 **Price:** $49.99 **Vacuum Strength:** 11 inHg **Style:** Heat	Performance ★★ Easy to Use ★½		This small, basic heat sealer is the only model you still have to press on while it initiates the seal, but it's a gentle push. It has no manual pulse mode, so it crunched pretzels and cereal into crumbs. That said, it kept frozen food ice-free just as long as models that cost four times its price, three months and counting.
NOT RECOMMENDED			
OLISO Frisper PRO-1000 Vacuum Sealer Starter Kit **Model:** PRO-1000 **Price:** $179.99 **Vacuum Strength:** 18 inHg **Style:** Heat	Performance ★½ Easy to Use ★		This heat sealer punctures a small hole in its zippered bags to extract the air and then seals off a circle around the pin prick–size vent. Its zippers were thick and hard to close, and only half of its frozen food looked good at three months. The pantry items were stale. The company makes a plastic clamp to help close the bags, but it's sold separately; at this price, it should be standard.
SOUSVIDE Supreme Zip Sealer **Model:** VS0500 **Price:** $74.99 **Vacuum Strength:** 17 inHg **Style:** Valve	Performance ½ Easy to Use ★		The size of a computer mouse, this valve sealer was easy to use but it was near impossible to tell if its bags were sealed. Testers fiddled with the zippers until they were certain they were closed, only to find the bags drawing air when they vacuumed them. After two weeks food was stale or covered in frost.

Taste Test Frozen Pepperoni Pizza

Frozen pizza has a bad rep, but a slew of new "artisanal" options promise pizzeria quality from the freezer aisle. Can any product deliver? BY LAUREN SAVOIE

ASSOCIATED WITH CASH-STRAPPED college students and undiscerning children, frozen pizza doesn't exactly have a reputation for quality. Still, it's not hard to see why more than 1.3 billion frozen pies were sold in the United States last year: It's a cheap and convenient meal that comes in an endless array of options. We've noticed a trend of manufacturers trying to cash in on the current "artisanal" pizza craze by offering "brick oven" or "fire baked" frozen products that promise a more gourmet, pizzeria-style pie. We wondered: Does this mean there's better frozen pizza out there?

We've tasted frozen cheese pizza before, but recently we learned that pepperoni is equally, if not more, popular. So for this tasting, we focused on pepperoni and assembled a lineup of seven pizzas—three artisanal-style pies, three national best sellers, and the pepperoni version from California Pizza Kitchen (a brand we've liked in the past).

To find out why we liked what we did, we analyzed the pizzas from the top down, starting with the pepperoni, which was almost a nonissue: Every product had sufficiently plentiful and flavorful pepperoni for our tasters.

Cheese, though, was a bit more contentious. Tasters liked clean, traditional, milky mozzarellas, and four of the seven products delivered. Of the three that we didn't like, one product tasted sooty from the addition of smoked gouda. Worse, another product's cheese was so waxen that some tasters called it "prison pizza." The label showed that it's not even real cheese but a substitute made

from palm and soybean oils—yuck.

When we got to the sauce, the gap between good and bad was even wider. Our tasters preferred herby sauces with strong tomato flavor and balanced tang. Overly sweet sauces earned low marks for tasting "cheap" and processed. We also wanted a moderate amount of sauce; some pizzas were so saucy that the sauce soaked right through the crust, making the dough "gummy."

Pizza aficionados will tell you that great pizza is all about the crust, so it's not surprising that this was the most important element to our tasters. And newer artisanal-style crusts won by a landslide. Tasters thought that they held the weight of the toppings better and actually resembled "real" pizza.

What does "real" pizza look like? First, a crust we could hold on to. Nearly all our bottom-ranked pizzas were covered from edge to edge with sauce and cheese, while artisanal-style pizzas gave us a solid rim of crust to wrap our hands around. Second, artisanal crusts were thicker. When we measured their crusts, our preferred pizzas were 14 to 20 millimeters at their thickest edge, while bottom-ranked pies were a paltry 5 to 10 millimeters. Thin crusts were veritable crackers—"dried out" and "cardboardy." We preferred crusts with an "airy" chew reminiscent of pizzeria-quality dough.

Looks aside, are artisanal-style crusts made differently? Frozen pizza cooks in two stages: It's parbaked at the factory and finished at home. We asked manufacturers about their methods, but they were tight-lipped. However, when we examined the underside of each pizza straight from the freezer, we found a clue about artisanal pies. Top-ranked products showed visible char marks and browning on their crusts, while lower-scoring pies had pale undersides that hardly looked baked at all. We could tell right out of the box that our preferred products were baked more thoroughly at the factory, and this produced a much better crust.

They're baked differently at home, too. We compared each product's instructions and noticed that pies baked at lower temperatures for longer outperformed those that cooked shorter and hotter. Why? According to our science editor, temperature matters more than time when it comes to moisture loss. Higher temperatures conduct heat into

the bottom of the pizza faster, causing the crust to lose more water and turn brittle, while products that baked lower and slower emerged evenly tender. We tried cooking bottom-ranking products like their winning counterparts, and while this did improve their texture slightly, they were too thin and dried out from the get-go to fully recover.

In the end, tasters overwhelmingly preferred artisanal-style crusts: The three we included earned gold, silver, and bronze in our rankings, with a

new product by best-selling brand DiGiorno taking top honors. Pizzeria! by DiGiorno Primo Pepperoni won over skeptics with meaty pepperoni, milky mozzarella, and, most important, a chewy and tender crust. But good crust comes at a price: Our recommended pizzas are nearly twice the cost of bottom-ranked products, and about on par with a delivery pie of the same size. Still, we think that a premium-quality frozen pizza is worth the extra dough, so we'll reach for Pizzeria! by DiGiorno.

The Flip Side
Our favorite frozen pizzas are cooked more thoroughly at the factory to give their bottom crusts more char and flavor.

TOP-RANKED = BROWN

LOWEST-RANKED = PALE

RECOMMENDED

PIZZERIA! BY DIGIORNO
Primo Pepperoni
Price: $8.49 for 18.7 oz
($0.45 per oz)
Crust Thickness: 20.9 mm

TASTERS' NOTES

With a "thick," "crisp and airy" crust, this product delivered its promise of a "classic," "pizzeria-like" pie. Tasters praised DiGiorno's "very meaty" pepperoni and "herby," "zesty" sauce, which "balanced sweet and tangy," resulting in an all-around "vibrant" pizza.

FRESCHETTA Brick Oven Crust Pepperoni and Italian Style Cheese
Price: $7.99 for 22.7 oz
($0.35 per oz)
Crust Thickness: 14.8 mm

Tasters enjoyed the "smoky" taste of this product's "really porky," "spicier" pepperoni and compared its "crispy" crust to "fresh delivery pizza." Many noticed the "heft" to this pizza's crust, which didn't wilt under its "earthy," "fruity" sauce.

RED BARON Fire Baked Pepperoni Pizza
Price: $6.49 for 19.86 oz
($0.33 per oz)
Crust Thickness: 14.2 mm

This pizza's "rich," "very saucy" topping held up nicely on its "crispy," "tender" crust. A few tasters found this product's sauce "overly sweet," but most were pleased with its "nice spicy flavor."

RECOMMENDED WITH RESERVATIONS

TOMBSTONE Original Pepperoni Pizza
Price: $3.67 for 21.6 oz
($0.17 per oz)
Crust Thickness: 8.1 mm

While many tasters were won over by this pizza's "very cheesy" topping and "meaty" sauce (which was speckled with extra crumbles of pepperoni), others compared its crust to "bad elementary school" pizza: "soggy and bready" in some parts and "dry and stale" in others.

NOT RECOMMENDED

TOTINO'S Party Pizza Classic Pepperoni
Price: $1.36 for 9.8 oz
($0.14 per oz)
Crust Thickness: 9.6 mm

"Grease bomb!" Tasters were put off by the "gross" amount of oil on this pizza, which turned its crust "soggy," "mushy," and "bland." Worse, this pizza uses a cheese substitute that tasters found "pale," "anemic," and "grainy."

JACK'S Original Pepperoni Pizza
Price: $3.99 for 16.5 oz
($0.24 per oz)
Crust Thickness: 5.4 mm

This pizza's cheese had an "off, funky, sour" flavor, and its "sweet," "superwet" sauce was closer to "ketchup" than tomato. Tasters were equally put off by the "limp" crust, which was "floppy and gummy" like a "cracker that is getting soggy."

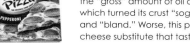

CALIFORNIA PIZZA KITCHEN Crispy Thin Crust Signature Pepperoni
Price: $7.69 for 17 oz
($0.45 per oz)
Crust Thickness: 10.0 mm

One taster unfavorably compared this product to bottled Italian dressing: "too herby," "overly seasoned," and dotted with "watery" unripe tomato chunks. Gouda cheese added a "weird smoky flavor," and the crust was "thin and dry" like "stale bread."

Heirloom Recipe

We're looking for recipes that you treasure—the ones that have been handed down in your family for a generation or more; that always come out for the holidays; that have earned a place at your table and in your heart, through many years of meals. Send us the recipes that spell home to you. Visit **CooksCountry.com/magazines/home** (or write to Heirloom Recipes, *Cook's Country*, P.O. Box 470739, Brookline, MA 02447); click on Heirloom Recipes and tell us a little about the recipe. Include your name and mailing address. **If we print your recipe, you'll receive a free one-year subscription to *Cook's Country*.**

LEMON BISQUE Serves 12

"Whenever my mother, grandmother, cousin, aunt, or just about anyone living in our small village in Pennsylvania made a ham dinner, the dessert was always lemon bisque. The light fluffiness of the filling and the tartness of the lemon made it the crowning touch."

Cheryl Morrison, Elysburg, Pa.

It's important to refrigerate the evaporated milk overnight to ensure that it will be cold enough to whip properly. Use a food processor to grind the graham crackers.

- ¾ cup (5¼ ounces) sugar
- 1 (3-ounce) package lemon-flavored gelatin
- 1 cup boiling water
- 1 tablespoon grated lemon zest plus ¼ cup juice (2 lemons)
- 8 whole graham crackers, ground (1 cup)
- 1 (12-ounce) can evaporated milk, chilled

1. Dissolve sugar and gelatin in boiling water in bowl. Stir in lemon zest and juice. Refrigerate until mixture is thickened but not completely set, about 1½ hours.

2. Grease 13 by 9-inch baking dish with vegetable oil spray and coat with ½ cup ground crackers. Using stand mixer fitted with whisk, whip evaporated milk on medium-high speed until stiff peaks form, about 5 minutes. Transfer mixture to large bowl. Using clean, dry mixer bowl and whisk attachment, whip chilled gelatin mixture on medium-high speed until thickened and light lemon colored, about 4 minutes.

3. Using large spatula, fold gelatin mixture into whipped evaporated milk until no yellow streaks remain. Transfer mixture to prepared dish and smooth top. Sprinkle remaining ½ cup ground crackers evenly over top. Cover and refrigerate until fully chilled and set, at least 4 hours or up to 24 hours. Serve.

COMING NEXT ISSUE

In our **October/November 2014** issue, you'll find a Thanksgiving menu that includes **Turkey (Breast) in a Pot**, **Old-Fashioned Cracker Stuffing**, **Creamed Kale**, and **Maple Syrup Pie**. But that's just a start. We also bring you the best recipes for **Beef Pot Pie**, **Ballpark Pretzels**, **Potato Biscuits**, **Bee Sting Cake**, and many more. Plus, we test salted butters and innovative slow cookers to find out which are the best. See you then.

FIND THE ROOSTER!

A tiny version of this rooster has been hidden in the pages of this issue. Write to us with its location and we'll enter you in a random drawing. The first correct entry drawn will win our winning vacuum sealer, and each of the next five will receive a free one-year subscription to *Cook's Country*. To enter, visit **CooksCountry.com/rooster** by September 31, 2014, or write to Rooster AS14, *Cook's Country*, P.O. Box 470739, Brookline, MA 02447. Include your name and address. Betty Toth of Downers Grove, Illinois, found the rooster in the April/May 2014 issue on page 18 and won our winning dish towels.

WEB EXTRAS

Free for 4 months online at **CooksCountry.com**

Baked Polenta
Grapefruit Juice Tasting (full story)
Grill-Roasted Peppers with Rosemary
Large-Batch Lightly Sweetened Whipped Cream
Macaroni and Cheese Casserole
New England Bar Pizza with Baked Beans and Salami
Parmesan-Pepper Popcorn
Posole
Reduced-Fat Macaroni and Cheese
Skillet Macaroni and Cheese
Southern Pecan Praline Pie

READ US ON iPad

Download the *Cook's Country* app for iPad and start a free trial subscription or purchase a single issue of the magazine. All issues are enhanced with full-color Cooking Mode slide shows that provide step-by-step instructions for completing recipes, plus expanded reviews and ratings. Go to **CooksCountry.com/iPad** to download our app through iTunes.

Follow us on **Pinterest**
pinterest.com/TestKitchen

Follow us on **Twitter**
twitter.com/TestKitchen

Find us on **Facebook**
facebook.com/CooksCountry

RC = Recipe Card

Blackberry-Key Lime Trifle

Our laid-back, late-summer blackberry trifle is inspired
by the refreshing flavors of Key lime pie.

To make this cake, you will need:

- ¼ cup (1¾ ounces) granulated sugar
- 1 tablespoon grated lime zest plus 1 cup juice (8 limes), plus 5 limes sliced ⅛ inch thick
- 8 ounces cream cheese, softened
- 1 (14-ounce) can sweetened condensed milk
- ⅓ cup instant vanilla pudding mix
- 1 teaspoon vanilla extract
- 12 whole graham crackers, broken in half
- 1 recipe Large-Batch Lightly Sweetened Whipped Cream*
- 30 ounces (6 cups) blackberries

FOR THE FILLING: Process sugar and lime zest in food processor until sugar turns bright green, about 30 seconds. Set aside 2 teaspoons lime sugar. Add cream cheese to remaining lime sugar and process until combined, about 30 seconds. Add condensed milk and pudding mix and process until smooth, about 30 seconds, scraping down sides of bowl as needed. With processor running, add lime juice and vanilla and process until thoroughly combined, about 30 seconds. Transfer custard to bowl, cover with plastic wrap, and refrigerate until thickened, about 1 hour.

TO ASSEMBLE: Shingle 12 cracker halves along bottom of 3½-quart trifle dish or glass bowl. Arrange half of lime slices upright around bottom of dish, wedged between cracker halves and wall of dish. Spread 1½ cups custard in even layer over cracker halves, followed by 2 cups whipped cream. Sprinkle 5 cups blackberries in even layer over whipped cream. Shingle 11 cracker halves over blackberries along edge of trifle and place remaining 1 cracker half in center. Arrange remaining lime slices upright around dish. Spread remaining custard over cracker halves, followed by remaining 2 cups whipped cream. Cover with plastic and refrigerate for at least 6 hours or up to 24 hours. Just before serving, arrange remaining 1 cup blackberries in center of trifle and sprinkle top of trifle with reserved lime sugar.

▶ *Go to **CooksCountry.com/largebatchwhippedcream** for our **Large-Batch Lightly Sweetened Whipped Cream** recipe or use your own lightly sweetened whipped cream recipe yielding 4 cups.

Inside This Issue

New England Bar Pizza **13**

Smoked Bourbon Chicken **6**

Skillet Ziti with Sausage **RC**

Strawberry Chiffon Pie **17**

Crab Cakes for Two **29**

Grill-Roasted Peppers **19**

Seared Scallop Spinach Salad **RC**

Quick Smoked Pork Chops **10**

Easy White Bean Dips **29**

Smoky Potato Salad **7**

Thai-Style Chicken Curry **RC**

Pasta with Raw Tomato Sauce **8**

New Orleans Muffulettas **5**

Watermelon Salad **23**

Dakota Peach Kuchen **21**

Iowa Loose Meat Sandwiches **18**

Pan-Seared Chicken Breasts **RC**

Grilled Steak Salad **RC**

Reduced-Fat French Silk Pie **27**

Whole-Wheat Blueberry Muffins **23**

Gazpacho **11**

Ham, Brie, and Apple Panini **RC**

Slow-Cooker Carne Adovada **26**

Zucchini Fritters **9**

Pork Tenderloin with Corn **RC**

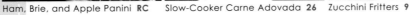

Cook's Country

CooksCountry.com
$5.95 U.S./$6.95 CANADA

*An old North Woods favorite, **Maple Syrup Pie** seemed worthy of revival. But first we had to cut back on its over-the-top sweetness, make sure it would slice easily, and boost that deep, rich maple flavor.* PAGE 8

7 25274 05251 6

Cook's Country

Dear Country Cook,

Old photos tell stories. My family album includes a snapshot of myself at age 12 at a ranch in Montana. I was dressed in jeans, cowboy hat, and boots—quite comfortable in the local gear—whereas my father stood awkwardly in a flannel shirt and chinos, both likely purchased at Brooks Brothers. My mother, however, shines through our early Vermont photos, happily settled into Bean boots, Elmer Fudd hat, and red flannel jacket, pouring sap into a holding tank or hunched down outside a barn talking to one of the Bentleys.

What, then, does one make of the photo below? At first glance, it says that we had larger families and that dad, although he never cooked indoors, was always in charge of carving. What strikes me more, however, is that it is a true family photo.

These days, family photos look like a motley collection of individuals. In our town, being a Bentley, Woodcock, Skidmore, or Wilcox was one's first sense of identity, more important than whether you operated a backhoe, drove a dump truck, or milked cows for a living. Many of my childhood friends were named Junior or Sonny—it was the last name that counted.

So when we look at our family photo from this Thanksgiving, let's seek out what we have in common beyond the turkey and fixings, even if we don't all have the same last name.

Cordially,

Christopher Kimball
Founder and Editor, Cook's Country

The Baker family of Joliet, Illinois, celebrates Thanksgiving in the late 1940s.

Cook's Country

Founder and Editor Christopher Kimball
Editorial Director Jack Bishop
Editorial Director, Magazines John Willoughby
Executive Editor Tucker Shaw
Managing Editor Scott Kathan
Executive Food Editor Bryan Roof
Senior Editors Hannah Crowley, Rebeccah Marsters, Lisa McManus, Diane Unger
Test Kitchen Director Erin McMurrer
Associate Editors Shannon Friedmann Hatch, Christie Morrison
Test Cooks Morgan Bolling, Aaron Furmanek, Ashley Moore, Cristin Walsh
Assistant Editors Lauren Savoie, Kate Shannon
Senior Copy Editor Megan Ginsberg
Copy Editor Krista Magnuson
Executive Assistant Christine Gordon
Test Kitchen Manager Leah Rovner
Senior Kitchen Assistants Michelle Blodget, Alexxa Grattan
Kitchen Assistants Maria Elena Delgado, Ena Gudiel
Executive Producer Melissa Baldino
Co-Executive Producer Stephanie Stender
Associate Producer Kaitlin Hammond

Contributing Editors Erika Bruce, Eva Katz, Jeremy Sauer
Consulting Editors Anne Mendelson, Meg Ragland
Science Editor Guy Crosby, PhD
Executive Food Editor, TV, Radio & Media Bridget Lancaster

Managing Editor, Web Christine Liu
Senior Editor, Cooking School Mari Levine
Associate Editors, Web Jill Fisher, Roger Metcalf
Assistant Editor, Web Charlotte Wilder
Senior Video Editor Nick Dakoulas

Design Director Amy Klee
Photography Director Julie Cote
Art Director Susan Levin
Associate Art Director Lindsey Timko
Art Director, Marketing Jennifer Cox
Staff Photographer Daniel J. van Ackere
Color Food Photography Keller + Keller
Styling Catrine Kelty, Marie Piraino
Associate Art Director, Marketing Melanie Gryboski
Designer, Marketing Judy Blomquist
Associate Art Director, Photography Steve Klise

Vice President, Marketing David Mack
Circulation Director Doug Wicinski
Circulation & Fulfillment Manager Carrie Fethe
Partnership Marketing Manager Pamela Putprush
Marketing Assistant Marina Tomao

Director, Project Management Alice Carpenter
Project Manager Britt Dresser
Development Manager Mike Serio

Chief Operating Officer Rob Ristagno
VP, Digital Products Fran Middleton
VP, New Product Development Michael Burton
Production Director Guy Rochford
Workflow & Digital Asset Manager Andrew Mannone
Senior Color & Imaging Specialist Lauren Pettapiece
Production & Imaging Specialists Heather Dube, Lauren Robbins
Client Services Manager Kate Zebrowski
Senior Controller Theresa Peterson
Customer Loyalty & Support Manager Amy Bootier
Customer Loyalty & Support Reps Jessica Haskin, Andrew Straaberg Finfrock, Juliet Tierney

Director, Retail Book Program Beth Ineson
Retail Sales & Marketing Manager Emily Logan
Human Resources Manager Adele Shapiro
Publicity Deborah Broide

ON THE COVER: *Maple Syrup Pie*, Keller + Keller, Catrine Kelty
ILLUSTRATION: Greg Stevenson

Follow us on **Pinterest**
pinterest.com/TestKitchen

Follow us on **Twitter**
twitter.com/TestKitchen

Find us on **Facebook**
facebook.com/CooksCountry

Cook's Country magazine (ISSN 1552-1990), number 59, is published bimonthly by Boston Common Press Limited Partnership, 17 Station St., Brookline, MA 02445. Copyright 2014 Boston Common Press Limited Partnership. Periodicals postage paid at Boston, MA, and additional mailing offices, USPS #023453. Publications Mail Agreement No. 40020778. Return undeliverable Canadian addresses to P.O. Box 875, Station A, Windsor, ON N9A 6P2. POSTMASTER: Send address changes to *Cook's Country*, P.O. Box 6018, Harlan, IA 51593-1518. For subscription and gift subscription orders, subscription inquiries, or change of address notices, visit AmericasTestKitchen.com/support, call 800-526-8447 in the U.S. or 515-248-7684 from outside the U.S., or write to us at *Cook's Country*, P.O. Box 6018, Harlan, IA 51593-1518. PRINTED IN THE USA.

Contents

SOUTH CAROLINA SHRIMP BURGERS, 10

CIDER-GLAZED ROOT VEGETABLES, 6

BEE STING CAKE, 22

Features

Departments

Get a Jump on Supper

Most make-ahead cookbooks just focus on stocking the freezer, but our latest title, *The Make-Ahead Cook*, takes a new approach with eight creative strategies. We'll show you how a little advance work can save you tons of time and reap huge benefits: delicious meals on your schedule. We've done the planning for you, leaving nothing to chance. Order online at **americastestkitchen.com/MakeAheadCook**.

America's TEST KITCHEN
RECIPES THAT WORK®

America's Test Kitchen is a very real 2,500-square-foot kitchen located just outside Boston. It is the home of *Cook's Country* and *Cook's Illustrated* magazines and the workday destination of more than three dozen test cooks, editors, and cookware specialists. Our mission is to test recipes until we understand how and why they work and arrive at the best version. We also test kitchen equipment and supermarket ingredients in search of products that offer the best value and performance. You can watch us work by tuning in to *Cook's Country from America's Test Kitchen* (CooksCountry.com) and *America's Test Kitchen* (AmericasTestKitchen.com) on public television.

Ask Cook's Country

BY CHRISTIE MORRISON

How can I tell if a whole honeydew melon will be sweet?
Donna Hunter, Middleboro, Mass.

Most melons, including honeydew, are nonclimacteric fruits. These fruits need to ripen (i.e., sweeten, soften, and develop aromas) while they're still on the vine, obtaining nutrients from the plant and developing their sugars. The sugars present in the fruit at the time of harvest are the endgame; the fruit won't get any sweeter after it's picked. A melon may continue to soften just slightly, however, as other enzymes break down, and it may give off an aroma, but neither softness nor aroma is an accurate indicator of sweetness.

When a honeydew is harvested at full slip (when the fruit easily and naturally pulls away from the stem), it can be as high as 15 percent sugar by weight. At full maturity, these melons are also soft—an attribute not compatible with shipping. So commercial melons that need to travel long distances are usually harvested before full slip, at half slip, or at three-quarters slip. These melons aren't as soft, so they can withstand transport, but they're also not as sweet, usually hovering somewhere between 8 and 12 percent sugar content.

We tested the sugar content of honeydews from a local supermarket to see just how sweet the melons were. Using a refractometer, we tested the juice of 15 melons. The sugar content ranged from 7 to 12 percent, with an average of 10.25 percent. The sweetest melons had creamy yellowish-white skin with no green cast. When we pressed the flower end of the fruit (opposite the stem), they felt slightly springy. We found no correlation between aroma and sweetness in the melons we tested.

THE BOTTOM LINE: Whenever possible, buy local melons harvested at their peak. Short of that, look for melons with a creamy yellow skin and no traces of green, and make sure the blossom end is soft and springy when pressed.

BLOSSOM END
If it's soft and springy, the melon should be sweet.

Can I get a good sear on a steak in a nonstick skillet? Will there be enough fond to make a pan sauce?
Chad Hayes, Rutland, Vt.

Browning meats adds flavor because of a chemical reaction known as the Maillard reaction: When food is heated, the amino acids react with certain sugars to produce new flavor compounds, which multiply rapidly both on the meat and on the cooking vessel where they are in contact.

Because nonstick pans are coated with a moisture-repelling coating, these flavor compounds have nothing to bond to on the pan, so they must bind to the meat instead. In theory, nonstick pans would be better for browning.

To test this theory in the kitchen, we prepared the same recipe for pan-seared steaks in both nonstick and conventional versions of our winning All-Clad skillet, heating the pans over medium-high heat with a tablespoon of oil and using four strip steaks of equal thickness and weight that were the same temperature out of the refrigerator. After 4 minutes of cooking per side, each steak had an evenly browned crust that released easily. The only difference we could see was in the brown bits left behind. The nonstick pan was clean, with just a few specks clinging to the bottom. The conventional skillet, on the other hand, featured a golden-brown imprint of each steak—precisely what makes for a tasty pan sauce.

THE BOTTOM LINE: Nonstick skillets are fine for searing steaks, but you won't have enough fond to build a flavorful pan sauce. Serve steaks seared in a nonstick skillet with a compound butter or a no-cook sauce like chimichurri or salsa verde.

FOND = FLAVOR FOR PAN SAUCES
The nonstick pan (left) doesn't have much fond; the traditional-finish pan does.

Does pricking eggs before cooking result in hard-cooked eggs that are easier to peel?
Liz Sutherland, Cupertino, Calif.

Many sources recommend pricking uncooked eggs with a pushpin before cooking and then dunking the cooked eggs in cold water to make peeling easier. The popular theory for why this method works is that the opening allows water and air to seep in between the egg's white and membrane, making peeling easier.

We hard-cooked a dozen eggs for a side-by-side test—one-third pricked with a pushpin through the wide end; one-third pricked in the narrow end; and one-third following our test kitchen peeling procedure, which calls for unpricked, drained, cooked eggs to be returned to the dry pan and shaken vigorously to crack the shell—and then transferred each group to an ice bath to chill before peeling. The eggs pricked in the narrow end were the hardest to peel, and the eggs pricked in the wide end weren't much easier.

By far the least tedious method was our preferred drain, shake, and dunk routine. It's much simpler than pricking a hole in each egg and you don't run the risk of the eggs springing a leak while they cook.

THE BOTTOM LINE: The pin-prick method isn't all it's cracked up to be. Leave your pushpins in the bulletin board.

Can I make caramelized onions from onions that were chopped a few days ago?
Bob Burnham, Olympia, Wash.

To find out, we caramelized four batches of onions that had been stored from one to four days after chopping. We found very little difference in the onions stored for up to two days. However, beyond that we noticed a marked difference in both the flavor and texture of the onions. Onions that had been stored for at least three days began to brown sooner than the fresher onions and tended to take at least 5 fewer minutes to caramelize. But instead of the moist, jammy texture of caramelized onions made with recently chopped onions, these older onions cooked into distinct pieces that had an unpleasant, dry, leathery texture and lacked sweetness.

Our science editor explained that chopping the onions damages their cells and allows water to leak out during storage. This surface water quickly evaporates during cooking, causing the onions to dry out faster than onions that are cooked immediately after chopping. As for the flavor difference, chopping also causes the enzymes that create the pungent taste in onions to be released and become active. These reactions occur immediately but continue over time, so the chopped onions will develop more pungency the longer they are stored. So, it's not that the older onions are less sweet, but rather that other flavor compounds are more prominent.

THE BOTTOM LINE: You can caramelize onions that have been chopped up to two days in advance.

What is the difference between sweet Hungarian paprika and Spanish paprika? Can I use them interchangeably?
Tim Boucher, Aurora, Colo.

All varieties of paprika are made from grinding and regrinding chile pods (and sometimes the seeds and stems as well) to a fine powder. The plant varieties used are all members of the chile family but differ slightly in pod size and color (capsanthin), the latter of which determines the color of the paprika produced. Hungarian paprika is a dark, deep crimson, while Spanish paprika has a lighter, slightly orange tint. In Hungary, paprika is produced in six different grades, from very mild to pungent and hot (the most commonly exported is *édesnemes*, or noble sweet). Spanish *pimentón*, as it is also known, is available in its sweet form, as well as in two varieties of smoked paprika: sweet and hot.

We tested the two types of sweet, nonsmoked paprika in side-by-side tests of chicken paprikash, the Hungarian dish that uses a whopping ¼ cup of paprika for both its flavor and thickening power, and paprika potatoes. Tasters didn't notice much of a difference in the potatoes, where just a few teaspoons of paprika seasoned the skillet-fried spuds, but they were able to detect the nuances of each variety in the paprikash. "Earthy" and "intense" were terms used to describe the Hungarian spice. "More what I want from paprika," said another taster. Other tasters described the Spanish version as "brighter," "a little tangy," and "slightly smoky," with a "hint of heat."

THE BOTTOM LINE: Yes, you can use either variety in most recipes that call for sweet paprika. Use whichever type you prefer.

To ask us a cooking question, visit **CooksCountry.com/ask**. Or write to Ask Cook's Country, P.O. Box 470739, Brookline, MA 02447. Just try to stump us!

Kitchen Shortcuts

COMPILED BY SHANNON FRIEDMANN HATCH AND CRISTIN WALSH

CLEVER TIP
Save the Stems
Kate Elton, Bloomfield Hills, Mich.

Whenever I cook with mushrooms, I remove the stems but don't discard them as the recipe suggests. Instead, I toss them with olive oil, salt, pepper, and whatever fresh herbs I have on hand and roast them. I then chop the roasted stems and add them to everything from pizza to scrambled eggs for a boost of flavor.

CLEVER TIP
Dish ID
Micki Cesario, Fort Wayne, Ind.

I've always struggled with how to label the food I bring to potlucks and get-togethers. Recently, it dawned on me that I could use a dry-erase marker and write directly on the plate or dish. It makes for easy identification at the table, and easy cleanup later.

DOUBLE DUTY
Do the Mashed Potato (Ricer)
Candace Carrothers, Trenton, Ontario

Mashing ripe bananas for a recipe isn't hard, but it is time-consuming. I've started using my potato ricer to speed up the process. It's quick and it also produces a smoother end result.

EASY CLEANUP
Groove-y Idea
Tom Higgins,
Glendale, Ariz.

I love using my grill pan, but it can be a pain to clean. I've found that the handle of my wooden spoon fits perfectly between the pan's grooves to help dislodge any stuck-on food, and the wood is soft enough that it won't damage the pan's surface.

CLEVER TIP
Quicker Meatballs
Kelly Thome, Melrose, Mass.

My family loves meatballs, so I often make a big batch. Rather than scoop and roll each one, I press the meat mixture into a square pan and then cut it into even portions. From there, I can quickly form each meatball before cooking.

TIDY TIP
Can-Do
Louis Thabault, South Burlington, Vt.

I've learned that if I puncture the bottom of a can of cranberry sauce with a church key while I'm emptying it through the open end, the can's contents will slide right out. This also works great for pumpkin puree, or even sticky pie filling.

SMART TRICK
Memory Key
Vic Miller, Colorado Springs, Colo.

I often make a bagged lunch to bring to work—only to forget it at home in the fridge. I've started placing my keys with it; that way, I can't leave the house unless I have my lunch.

Submit a tip online at **CooksCountry.com/kitchenshortcuts** or send a letter to Kitchen Shortcuts, *Cook's Country*, P.O. Box 470739, Brookline, MA 02447. Include your name, address, and phone number. If we publish your tip, you will receive a free one-year subscription to *Cook's Country*. Letters may be edited for clarity and length.

Illustration: Ross MacDonald

Turkey in a Pot

After deciding to cook a turkey breast instead of a whole turkey,
we looked to an unlikely source for our Thanksgiving inspiration—France. BY DIANE UNGER

FIRST, DISPENSE WITH the obvious: Serving a turkey breast instead of a whole turkey changes the look of the Thanksgiving table. But consider how quickly that photo op fades once carving commences. The breast, alone, is much easier to cook and to carve. This year, I was willing to forgo the full bird for a moist, perfect breast—if only I could figure out how.

Of course, roasting is the usual method for cooking a turkey breast. But I had another idea. Cooking a whole bird in a pot is a French technique in which poultry is cooked over low heat in a covered pot for an extended period of time; it produces very moist, tender meat. A whole chicken is the most common choice, but I wondered if that same technique would work with a bone-in turkey breast. My goal was a tender, moist turkey breast with crispy skin plus a delicious gravy to seal the deal.

Bone-in turkey breasts tend to vary in size, weighing anywhere from 5 to 10 pounds. After several initial tests, I figured out that 6 to 7 pounds was the ideal size; it's large enough to feed a small crowd (up to eight people), but small enough to fit into a 7-quart Dutch oven, particularly if the rib bones are trimmed.

As we had found when we cooked a whole chicken using this method, browning the turkey breast was an essential step in developing deep flavor. Due to the shape of the breast, it took a little finagling, but I was able to brown the breast in around 15 minutes, tilting it on its sides to brown all over. My next step, after removing the browned breast from the pot, was to add some diced onion, carrot, and celery to the same pot, along with garlic, thyme, and a bay leaf. This would not only begin building a gravy but also add moisture to the pot for deglazing the flavorful fond left from the browning. When the vegetables were well browned (for even more flavor), I set the turkey breast over the vegetables, meaty side up, and then covered the pot with foil and a tight lid and transferred it to a low oven. (I already knew that the low 250-degree temperature would turn out moister turkey than higher temperatures would.) The turkey breast took between 1½ and 1¾ hours to come up to the target temperature of 155 degrees.

Our covered cooking method ensures moist, juicy meat and flavorful gravy.

The meat was moist and juicy, but unfortunately, the skin, although well browned, was nowhere near as crispy as I wanted it—not surprising, since the turkey had been steaming in the pot. To fix the flabby skin issue, I turned to the broiler. For my next test, I pulled the turkey out of the oven at 155 degrees, waited for the broiler to come up to temperature, brushed the skin with melted butter to help browning, and

returned my potted turkey, still on the middle rack, to the broiler. With a close eye through the glass oven door, I let the turkey brown for about 10 minutes (broilers vary, so some took as little as 8 minutes, while others took about 15 minutes). The skin that had been flabby before now had a lovely crispy texture. With the meat tender and juicy and the skin crispy, all that was left was to focus on the gravy.

Initially, I tried straining and defatting the juices left in the pot and then thickening them with either a roux (a cooked mixture of flour and butter) or a slurry (a mixture of flour and water). But the resulting gravy lacked complexity. For my next try, I took a new approach. After removing the turkey from the pot, I reduced the pan juices until they had all but evaporated, concentrating the turkey flavor and producing a mahogany fond on the bottom of the pot. I stirred some flour into this rich mixture to make a roux and then added a full quart of chicken broth to the pot. I brought the mixture to a simmer and cooked it until the mixture had reduced and concentrated, which took about 15 minutes. After straining and seasoning, I finally had it all: perfectly cooked, incredibly moist and tender meat; crispy skin; and intensely flavored gravy, all from one pot. Satisfied, I gathered my tasters. Their opinion? "Tastes like Thanksgiving should taste."

TURKEY IN A POT WITH GRAVY
Serves 6 to 8

Try to purchase a turkey breast with the wings already removed so it's sure to fit into your pot. Otherwise, remove the wings before proceeding with the recipe. A carving fork works well for turning the turkey and removing it from the pot.

- 1 (7-pound) bone-in whole turkey breast, wings discarded, trimmed
  Salt and pepper
- 2 tablespoons olive oil
- 1 onion, chopped
- 1 carrot, chopped
- 1 celery rib, chopped
- 6 garlic cloves, crushed and peeled
- 1 teaspoon minced fresh thyme
- 1 bay leaf
- 1 tablespoon unsalted butter, melted
- ¼ cup all-purpose flour
- 4 cups chicken broth

1. Adjust oven rack to middle position and heat oven to 250 degrees. Using kitchen shears, trim any rib bones that extend beyond underside of turkey breast. (If any backbone pieces are still attached to underside of turkey, remove them.) Pat turkey dry with paper towels and season with salt and pepper.

2. Heat oil in large Dutch oven over medium-high heat until just smoking. Add turkey, skin side down, and cook until well browned, 12 to 16 minutes, rolling it from side to side as needed for even browning. Transfer turkey to plate and set aside. Pour off all but 2 tablespoons fat from pot. Add onion, carrot, celery, garlic, thyme, and bay leaf to pot and cook until vegetables are well browned, 7 to 10 minutes.

3. Return turkey and accumulated juices to pot, skin side up. Off heat, place large sheet of aluminum foil over pot and

TEST KITCHEN TECHNIQUE
Sear, Braise, and Broil
Our three-step cooking method makes for juicy, tender meat and nicely browned skin every time.

1. SEAR for deeper flavor.

2. COVER AND BRAISE breast, skin side down, to cook it gently.

3. BROIL to brown the skin.

press edges to seal, then cover tightly with lid. Transfer pot to oven and cook until thickest part of breast registers 155 degrees, 1½ to 1¾ hours.

4. Remove pot from oven and heat broiler. Uncover pot (handles will be very hot) and brush turkey with melted butter. When broiler is heated, return pot to oven and broil until skin is golden brown, 8 to 15 minutes, rotating pot as needed for even browning. Remove pot from oven. Transfer turkey to carving board, tent loosely with foil, and let rest while making gravy.

5. Place pot over medium-high heat, bring to boil, and cook until almost all liquid has evaporated, 8 to 15 minutes. Stir in flour and cook until lightly browned, about 2 minutes. Slowly whisk in broth and bring to boil. Reduce heat to medium and cook at strong simmer, stirring often, until gravy is thickened and measures about 2 cups, 15 to 18 minutes. Strain gravy through fine-mesh strainer set over medium saucepan; discard solids. Season gravy with salt and pepper to taste. Carve turkey. Rewarm gravy and serve with turkey.

Old-Fashioned Cracker Dressing

In 19th-century America, crackers often stood in for bread in stuffings and dressings. Was this tradition worth reviving? BY DIANE UNGER

THOUGH IT MIGHT seem strange to contemporary cooks, the idea of using crackers as a dressing base isn't a new one. In earlier times, practical home cooks frequently pressed "pilot" or "common" crackers—pantry staples in the 1800s—into service.

Today's versions are made with crushed saltines or even buttery Ritz Crackers, and several tests revealed that toasting the crackers before crushing them kept them from going soggy, leaving a solid base for additions of celery, onions, and sausage.

A heavy dressing can weigh down a holiday dinner, so I looked for ways to lighten this dish. Though I was skeptical of cutting back on butter, a few tests proved that I could use it judiciously without significantly sacrificing flavor. A half-cup of white wine added a touch of acidity for brightness. Chopped cranberries and pecans brought a celebratory note; fresh sage and thyme cemented this dressing's seasonal flavors.

Rich but restrained, with a soft but not mushy texture, this cracker dressing wasn't just an easy pantry dish; it was one that I'd be proud to have on my Thanksgiving table.

CRACKER DRESSING WITH DRIED CRANBERRIES AND PECANS
Serves 8 to 10

The easiest way to crush the saltines is to place them in a 1-gallon zipper-lock bag and roll over them with a rolling pin. Do this in two batches. Swanson Chicken Stock is our favorite chicken broth.

- 5 tablespoons unsalted butter
- 1 pound saltines, coarsely crushed
- 1 pound bulk breakfast sausage
- 2 pounds onions, chopped fine
- ½ cup dry white wine
- 1 cup dried cranberries, chopped
- 1 cup pecans, toasted and chopped
- 4 celery ribs, chopped
- 2 large eggs, lightly beaten
- ¼ cup minced fresh sage
- 2 tablespoons minced fresh thyme
- 2 teaspoons pepper
- 1 teaspoon salt
- 4½ cups chicken broth

Dried cranberries add a burst of seasonal flavor.

1. Adjust oven rack to middle position and heat oven to 350 degrees. Grease 13 by 9-inch baking dish with 1 tablespoon butter. Line rimmed baking sheet with parchment paper. Spread crushed saltines in even layer on prepared sheet. Bake until very lightly golden, 10 to 12 minutes; set aside. Increase oven temperature to 425 degrees.

2. Cook sausage in 12-inch nonstick skillet over medium heat, breaking up pieces with spoon, until no longer pink, about 10 minutes. Transfer to large bowl. Melt 2 tablespoons butter in now-empty skillet over medium heat. Add onions and cook until softened and lightly browned, 12 to 15 minutes. Add wine and cook until nearly evaporated, about 3 minutes. Transfer mixture to bowl with sausage. Stir in cranberries, pecans, celery, eggs, sage, thyme, pepper, salt, and crushed saltines until combined. Stir in broth until incorporated.

3. Transfer stuffing to prepared dish and lightly press into even layer, leaving top somewhat craggy. Melt remaining 2 tablespoons butter in microwave and brush over top of dressing. Bake until golden brown and crisp on top, 35 to 40 minutes. Let cool for 15 minutes. Serve.

Cider-Glazed Root Vegetables

To brighten up the flavors of fall vegetables, we gave them a stiff shot of hard cider.

BY CRISTIN WALSH

A diced tart apple—stirred in at the end—echoes and reinforces the bright cider flavor.

APPLE CIDER AND root vegetables are New England fall classics. So it's no surprise that many cooks in the region have come up with dishes in which the sweet, earthy richness of the root vegetables is enhanced by a glaze featuring the bright, sweet-tart cider. Unfortunately, when I tried a handful of those recipes, the results were uniformly bland. The glazes were overly sweet and the apple flavor was nearly undetectable. The vegetables themselves were often too hard or unevenly cooked. This recipe was in desperate need of a revamp.

Piecing together our favorite elements from these initial recipes, I began by poaching a combination of parsnips, turnips, carrots, and shallots in 2½ cups of cider, 3 tablespoons of butter, and a bit of salt in a covered skillet. I then took off the lid and let the liquid reduce to a glaze. For a bright hit of acidity at the end, I stirred in 2 teaspoons of cider vinegar, which also enhanced the cider flavor.

The dish wasn't a bad start, but there were issues to resolve. I had cut all the vegetables (aside from the shallots, which were halved) in the same ¾-inch pieces, but while the parsnips and turnips were tender, the carrots remained undercooked. I dropped the carrot size down to ½-inch pieces for the next round. Much better; now the vegetables were all evenly cooked. But could I coax even more flavor from them? Rather than starting the vegetables in the cider, I sautéed them in butter until they began to brown and caramelize and then deglazed the pan with the cider, scraping the browned bits into the liquid. This moved the vegetables' sweet flavors to the forefront and added a nice complexity to the dish.

The vegetables had great flavor now, but the glaze was still a bit wan. On a whim, I made a batch in which I swapped out regular cider for hard—that is, alcoholic—apple cider. The results were surprising: Tasters unanimously preferred the crisp, clean flavor of the hard cider glaze, which they felt provided more apple flavor, although it was a little on the tart side. When I tried it again, this time adding a few tablespoons of sugar to combat the tartness, the glaze got rave reviews. To enhance the apple flavor even more, I added a diced Granny Smith apple toward the

end of the glaze reduction so it would soften but still retain some crunch. Delicious. The Granny Smith brightened up the sweet glaze, putting it solidly in tune with the earthy vegetables. The only thing the dish needed was an herb to add another fresh flavor; tasters preferred the slight anise flavor of tarragon, a classic pairing with apple.

CIDER-GLAZED ROOT VEGETABLES WITH APPLE AND TARRAGON Serves 8

If you prefer to use an equal amount of nonalcoholic sparkling or regular cider, reduce the sugar to 1 tablespoon.

- 4 tablespoons unsalted butter
- 1 pound carrots, peeled and cut into ½-inch pieces
- 12 ounces parsnips, peeled and cut into ¾-inch pieces
- 12 ounces turnips, peeled and cut into ¾-inch pieces
- 3 shallots, peeled and halved
- 2½ cups hard cider
- 3 tablespoons sugar
  Salt and pepper
- 1 Granny Smith apple, cored and cut into ½-inch pieces
- 2 tablespoons chopped fresh tarragon
- 2 teaspoons cider vinegar

1. Melt 1 tablespoon butter in 12-inch skillet over medium-high heat. Add carrots, parsnips, turnips, and shallots and cook until lightly browned, about 5 minutes. Add cider, sugar, 1½ teaspoons salt, and remaining 3 tablespoons butter and bring to boil. Reduce heat to medium-low, cover, and cook until vegetables are just tender, 7 to 10 minutes, stirring occasionally.

2. Uncover, increase heat to medium, and cook until vegetables are fully tender, about 13 minutes, stirring occasionally. Stir in apple and continue to cook until cider is syrupy and apple is just tender, about 2 minutes longer. Off heat, stir in tarragon and vinegar. Season with salt and pepper to taste. Transfer to serving dish and pour any remaining glaze over vegetables. Serve.

CIDER-GLAZED ROOT VEGETABLES WITH POMEGRANATE AND CILANTRO

Substitute chopped fresh cilantro for tarragon and add ¼ cup pomegranate seeds along with cilantro and vinegar.

TASTE TEST Hard Apple Cider

Hard cider was the most popular drink in colonial America, as it was typically safer to drink than water. This drink is having a revival, and to find the best one, we invited 21 staffers from America's Test Kitchen to taste four nationally available ciders. We tasted them plain and cooked into cider-glazed root vegetables.

Sweeter ciders were rated highly for tasting "fresher" and "fruitier," while the lone dry cider in our lineup tasted muted. Sweetness was also important in cooking, as the dry cider tasted "boozy" and "sour" in the vegetables. Angry Orchard Crisp Apple Cider won the top spot for its strong apple sweetness and refreshing, juicy complexity. Ciders from Strongbow and Woodchuck were also recommended. For the full tasting story and results chart, visit **CooksCountry. com/nov14.** –LAUREN SAVOIE

RECOMMENDED

Angry Orchard   Strongbow   Woodchuck

Creamed Kale with Chestnuts

This hearty green makes a great substitute for more common creamed spinach—but not if it has a heavy coating of stodgy sauce. BY REBECCAH MARSTERS

W E'VE ALL HEARD of creamed spinach, but when I happened upon recipes for creamed kale, I was intrigued.

The recipes that I found were split between those that called for simmering prewilted greens in cream until the dish thickened and those that called for using a béchamel, a traditional white sauce of milk thickened with a flour-and-butter roux. Hoping to keep this side dish as streamlined as possible, I balked at the prospect of pulling out multiple pans to make a sauce and sauté piles of greens. Happily, when I lined up five different dishes featuring representatives from both camps, my tasters and I unanimously preferred the simplicity of the ones made with cream. The béchamel-based versions turned out pasty and cloyingly rich. We also favored a simple flavor profile, with shallots and garlic as supporting players and a hint of red pepper flakes for heat, though we did like the chestnuts that one recipe called for. To feed a crowd of eight, I'd need a hefty 3½ pounds of kale. So with a mountain of greens in front of me, I got to work.

After several attempts to cram all the stemmed, chopped greens into my Dutch oven at once, I learned that a gradual approach is better. By introducing the greens a few handfuls at a time and letting each addition wilt before following with the next, I was able to fit all the kale in one pot. A couple of cups of chicken broth at the bottom of the pot kept it from drying out while contributing savory flavor. I also quickly learned that if I added the aromatics to the kale in the pot, they never fully cooked and ended up tasting steamed and harsh. For my next batch, I moved the wilted kale to a bowl, melted some butter in the pot, and only then added sliced shallots. Letting the chestnuts sauté with the aromatics and a bit of salt and pepper gave the convenient jarred product homemade flavor, and adding the garlic and red pepper flakes later prevented them from burning.

Now for the cream. Preliminary tests showed that 1½ cups of heavy cream were just enough to give the kale richness and a silky texture without going overboard. But before adding the dairy, I used some more chicken broth to deglaze the pan, scraping up the tasty fond left over from the

sautéed aromatics. After that, I poured in the cream, brought it to a boil, and added the kale back to the pot to warm through.

I had made progress with this last attempt, but for a truly celebratory meal this dish was missing one thing: cheese. A cup of grated Parmesan added nutty complexity and thickened the sauce, helping it cling to the kale.

This dish received no complaints, but in the end, two simple tricks helped it sing. First, freshly grated nutmeg: Just a pinch stirred in with the cheese was the perfect warm-spice complement to the sweet cream and slightly bitter kale. Finally, a squeeze of lemon right before serving brightened everything up. These creamy greens were ready for their debut.

Earthy kale gets dressed up for the holidays with a rich cream sauce and meaty chestnuts.

KEY INGREDIENT Chestnuts

The chestnuts that add a celebratory note to this dish can be found in 7- and 14-ounce jars in most grocery stores, especially around the holidays. Look for roasted, peeled chestnuts, not chestnuts packed in syrup or water. Skip the water chestnuts, which aren't nuts at all, and save the raw, unpeeled chestnuts for the open fire.

CREAMED KALE WITH CHESTNUTS
Serves 8

You will need approximately six bunches of curly kale for this recipe (it cooks down considerably). If you wash the kale before you cook it, be sure to dry it thoroughly, as overly wet kale will alter the recipe's cooking times. Buy chestnuts that are roasted and peeled and not packed in water or syrup. This recipe is easily cut in half to serve four; wilting the kale in step 1 will take only about half of the time.

- 2¾ cups chicken broth
  Salt and pepper
- 3½ pounds curly kale, stemmed and chopped
- 4 tablespoons unsalted butter
- 3 cups (14 ounces) peeled cooked chestnuts
- 5 shallots, sliced into thin rings
- 4 garlic cloves, minced
- ½ teaspoon red pepper flakes
- 1½ cups heavy cream
- 2 ounces Parmesan cheese, grated (1 cup)
- ¼ teaspoon ground nutmeg
  Lemon wedges

1. Bring 2 cups broth and ¾ teaspoon salt to boil in large Dutch oven over high heat. Gradually add kale, covering pot and letting each addition wilt to make room before adding more, using tongs to turn and stir (this will take about 10 minutes). When all kale has been added to pot, reduce heat to medium-high, cover, and cook, stirring occasionally, until kale is fully wilted and bottom of pot is nearly dry, 5 to 10 minutes; transfer kale to bowl. Wipe out pot with paper towels.

2. Melt butter in now-empty pot over medium heat. Add chestnuts, shallots, 1 teaspoon salt, and 1 teaspoon pepper and cook, uncovered, until shallots have softened, 5 to 7 minutes. Add garlic and pepper flakes and cook until fragrant, about 30 seconds. Add remaining ¾ cup broth and bring to boil, scraping up any browned bits. Add cream and return to boil.

3. Add kale and cook, stirring occasionally, until slightly thickened, 7 to 9 minutes. Off heat, stir in Parmesan and nutmeg. Season with salt and pepper to taste. Transfer to serving dish. Serve with lemon wedges.

Maple Syrup Pie

We wanted to take this classic New England pie back to its roots, with real maple flavor. But we wanted pie, not candy. BY REBECCAH MARSTERS

EVERY YEAR, THE holiday feast includes the obligatory parade of pies: apple, pumpkin, pecan . . . Nothing against these heavy hitters, but I was on the prowl for a new pie for my holiday table. When a coworker suggested maple syrup pie, I jumped.

Maple syrup pie was once common in the syrup-producing northern regions of the country and in Canada. No mystery there; if you have a surplus of syrup, why not make a pie with it? What was a mystery, though, was why so many of the recipes I found used brown sugar, white sugar, or even sweetened condensed milk in addition to the syrup, which ought to be sweet enough.

I did find a few recipes that relied solely on syrup as a sweetener. I baked a couple of these alongside a few of the sugar-supplemented recipes and called my tasters. Some pies had so much dairy and egg that they were essentially custard pies with a whiff of maple flavor, while others used so much brown sugar that they were dense and chewy, like a pecan pie without the nuts—but light on maple flavor. The pie with the most maple flavor had syrup as its only sweetener—a full 2 cups. The flavor was there, but the pie was granular and much too sweet—like the leaf-shaped maple sugar candies I ate as a kid. Fine for candy, but too much for a slice of pie.

▶ Visit CooksCountry. com/singlepiecrust for our recipe for **Classic Single-Crust Pie Dough**.

Far from wasted experiments, these early tests helped me home in on what I wanted: a sweet but balanced pie with major maple flavor.

I started with the proportions from our favorite pie in the initial test, using 2 cups of maple syrup, three eggs, 4 tablespoons of butter, and ½ cup of cream, along with 1 tablespoon of flour for thickening. (I also added salt, which none of the recipes called for.) The procedure involved cooking the syrup and cream on the stovetop, whisking in the butter and flour and then stirring in the eggs after the mixture cooled a bit.

The process wasn't too cumbersome, but other recipes simply called for whisking all the ingredients together and pouring them into the pie shell. I hoped this easier method would work, so using the test kitchen's favorite single-crust pie dough, I baked two pies: one with a cooked filling and one simply stirred

A surprise ingredient—vinegar—allows us to use enough syrup for big maple flavor without tooth-aching sweetness.

together. Both pies emerged from the oven bronzed and beautiful, but after they cooled and we tasted them, it was clear that the cooked filling was more consistent, its maple flavor was more concentrated, and it sliced much more neatly. The good news was that since the filling was still warm when it went into the oven, it cooked faster than the stir-and-bake version, so time-wise it was nearly a draw.

With the technique settled, I moved on to the pie's other issues. Besides the overbearing sweetness, a few tasters also noticed a slight starchiness in the filling. I tried a side-by-side test of flour versus cornstarch for thickening. All the recipes I'd found called for flour, which is more traditional, but I discovered that cornstarch produced a creamier pie, and a few tests showed that 2 tablespoons was the right amount for optimal sliceability.

To prevent clumping, we usually mix cornstarch with a room-temperature liquid to make a slurry before adding it to hot liquids. (Clumping occurs when hot water wets the surface of the starch granules and forms a gel, causing the granules to stick together.) But after a chat with our science editor, I learned that the high proportion of sugar in the simmering syrup mixture actually binds the water, meaning it can't form a gel on the surface of the granules. The upshot? I could add the cornstarch directly to the saucepan without it clumping.

Moving on to the sweetness surfeit: Since maple syrup equals maple flavor, I was hesitant to decrease the amount. Luckily, I found that if I backed down by just ¼ cup of syrup, the sweetness ebbed slightly with no noticeable difference in flavor. I couldn't decrease the sweetness any more, but maybe I could balance it. I wondered if additional richness would help, providing a foil for the sugar and coaxing the maple flavor to the fore—fat carries flavor, after all. Increasing the cream and butter helped balance the sweetness, as did adding two egg yolks for even more richness.

I was making headway. My pie was still sweet, but tasters were polishing off whole slices now. To add the final note to this pie, I turned to a trick that we use for fruit desserts here in the test kitchen: adding acid. Citrus didn't seem right for this nonfruit pie, so I tried vinegar. I stirred 2 teaspoons of vinegar into the filling before baking (I chose cider vinegar for its mellow tang), and when we tasted the vinegar-spiced next to a plain pie, the verdict was unanimous. Without guessing my secret ingredient, tasters noted that the pie with the vinegar had more pronounced maple flavor and was brighter and more balanced overall. That sounded like a mission accomplished to me.

MAPLE SYRUP PIE Serves 8

Our favorite store-bought crust is Wholly Wholesome 9" Certified Organic Traditional Bake at Home Rolled Pie Dough. Serve with unsweetened whipped cream or crème fraîche.

- 1 (9-inch) pie dough round
- 1¾ cups pure maple syrup
- ⅔ cup heavy cream
- ¼ teaspoon salt
- 5 tablespoons unsalted butter
- 2 tablespoons cornstarch
- 3 large eggs plus 2 large yolks
- 2 teaspoons cider vinegar

1. Adjust oven rack to middle position and heat oven to 375 degrees. Grease 9-inch pie plate. Roll dough into 12-inch circle on lightly floured counter. Loosely roll dough around rolling pin and gently unroll it onto prepared pie plate, letting excess dough hang over edge. Ease dough into plate by gently lifting edge of dough with your hand while pressing into plate bottom with your other hand.

2. Trim overhang to ½ inch beyond lip of pie plate. Tuck overhang under itself; folded edge should be flush with edge of pie plate. Crimp dough evenly around edge of pie using your fingers. Wrap dough-lined pie plate loosely in plastic and freeze until dough is firm, about 15 minutes.

3. Line chilled pie shell with parchment paper or double layer of aluminum foil, covering edges to prevent burning, and fill with pie weights. Bake until edges are light golden brown, 18 to 25 minutes, rotating pie plate halfway through baking. Remove parchment and weights and continue to bake until center begins to look opaque and slightly drier, 3 to 6 minutes. Remove from oven and let cool for at least 30 minutes. (Baked, cooled crust can be wrapped in plastic and stored at room temperature for up to 24 hours.)

4. Reduce oven temperature to 350 degrees. Bring maple syrup, cream, and salt to boil in medium saucepan. Add butter and whisk until melted. Reduce heat to medium-low and whisk in cornstarch. Bring to simmer and cook for 1 minute, whisking frequently. Transfer to large bowl and let cool at least 30 minutes. Whisk in eggs and yolks and vinegar until smooth. (Cooled filling can be refrigerated for up to 24 hours. Whisk to recombine and proceed with step 5, increasing baking time to 55 to 65 minutes.)

5. Place cooled crust on rimmed baking sheet, and pour filling into crust. Bake until just set, 35 to 45 minutes. Let pie cool completely on wire rack, about 2 hours. Transfer to refrigerator and chill until fully set, at least 2 hours or up to 24 hours. Serve cold or at room temperature.

Backstory
Making the Grade

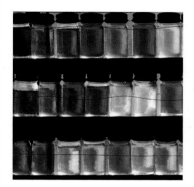

Maple syrup labels have confounded consumers for years: Why are some syrups marked Grade A and others Grade B when both products are high quality? The system, based on syrup color, made sense for early 20th-century cooks who often turned to maple syrup as a substitute for expensive cane sugar. Lighter syrup, the easiest swap, was given the highest grade.

Matthew Gordon of the Vermont Maple Sugar Makers Association acknowledges that contemporary consumers "understandably thought that Grade B was somehow inferior." He's joined the International Maple Syrup Institute in a push for more descriptive labels like "Grade A: Golden Color with Delicate Taste," or "Grade A: Amber with Rich Taste." While just a handful of producers have adopted the new system, Gordon expects the rest of the industry to follow suit in coming years.

TESTING INNOVATIVE DISH DRYING RACKS

We've noticed a trend of new dish drying racks with extra features—could any improve on the basic wire basket/plastic mat?

We tested five innovative dish racks (priced from nearly $25 to $64) against the standard basket and mat ($18.37). We compared footprints and counted utensil trays, plate slots, and cup holders. We looked at how the racks could be positioned and loaded them with dinner dishes for a family of four to evaluate capacity.

Testers found only one unacceptable. Of the rest, even the basic basket model has admirable capacity and, at $18, an unbeatable price. But two solved lingering problems. The first, Progressive Prepworks Collapsible Over-the-Sink Dish Drainer ($24.99), was the best for small spaces. It's too petite for pots and pans but fit smaller dishes and has expandable arms that pull out to suspend it over a sink while in use; it folds flat for easy storage and is dishwasher-safe—a great option for tight spaces.

The second innovative rack testers singled out was the Simple Human Steel Frame Dishrack ($63.57); it's large, handsome, and pricey. It fit pots and pans and has extra features like a wineglass holder and a knife block. For dish drying needs large or small, these two innovative racks offer smart solutions. Go to CooksCountry.com/nov14 for the full testing story and chart. –HANNAH CROWLEY

KEY Good ★★★ Fair ★★ Poor ★

RECOMMENDED		CRITERIA		TESTERS' NOTES
SIMPLE HUMAN Steel Frame Dishrack **Model:** KT1154 **Price:** $63.57 **Dimensions:** 19.7 x 13 x 12 in **Positioning:** Right side, long or short way **Feature(s):** Knife block, wineglass holders, drip tray, swiveling drain spout	BEST LARGE	Capacity ★★★ Design ★★½		This large rack has two roomy utensil holders, a seven-slot knife block, and a ledge that can hang four wineglasses upside down so they dry spot-free. Its swiveling spout efficiently drained off water, and little raised feet hold it up off the counter.
PROGRESSIVE Prepworks Collapsible Over-the-Sink Dish Drainer **Model:** CDD-20GY **Price:** $24.99 **Dimensions:** 16.5 x 12.4 x 5 in (1.8 in high collapsed) **Positioning:** Left or right side, long or short way **Feature(s):** Folds flat, extendable arms for over-sink suspension	BEST SMALL	Capacity ★★½ Design ★★★		This smart collapsible rack is too small for a pile of pots and pans but readily fit smaller items. It folds flat for easy storage and can be used on the counter (on a dishcloth) or suspended over the sink, thanks to expandable arms. It's the best choice for small spaces or light loads.
RUBBERMAID Antimicrobial Sink Drainer, Large and Antimicrobial Drain Board, Large **Model:** Drainer, 6032. Mat, 1180. **Price:** $10.99 for basket, $7.38 for mat, $18.37 total **Dimensions:** 17.5 x 13.4 x 6.7 in **Positioning:** Left or right side, long way only **Feature(s):** N/A	BEST BUY	Capacity ★★★ Design ★★		This affordable old standard isn't flashy, but it fit dishes for a family of four, including larger items like a baking sheet, saucepan, and skillet; it has the most plate slots and cup holders and a basic utensil holder. Its angled mat tidily drained off water, but its slant only allows the rack to be positioned lengthwise.

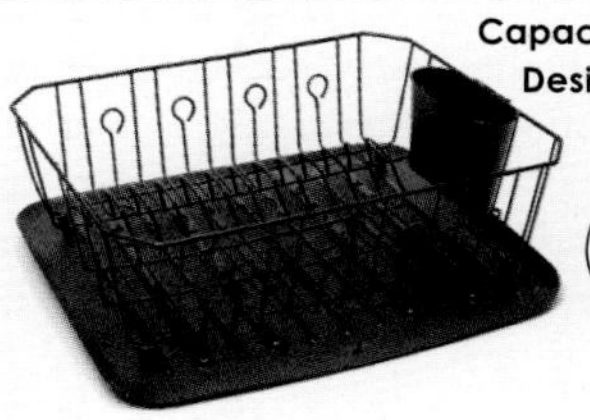

CRÈME FRAÎCHE

Makes 1 cup

Don't use ultrapasteurized or UHT cream for this recipe—organic pasteurized cream works best. The ideal temperature for the crème fraîche to culture is 75 degrees. It will work at lower temperatures but may take up to 36 hours.

- 1 cup pasteurized heavy cream, room temperature
- 2 tablespoons buttermilk, room temperature

Combine cream and buttermilk in 1-pint jar. Cover jar with triple layer of cheesecloth and secure with rubber band. Let sit in warm place (about 75 degrees) until thickened but still pourable, 12 to 24 hours. Stir to recombine. Serve. (Crème fraîche can be refrigerated for up to 1 month.)

South Carolina Shrimp Burgers

To capture the big shrimp flavor in this beloved Lowcountry dish, we had to make the most of a sticky situation. BY CHRISTIE MORRISON WITH NICK IVERSON

NEW ENGLAND HAS the lobster roll and Maryland is the undisputed home of crab cakes, but when it comes to shrimp burgers, it's time to head to South Carolina. The coastal fishing village of Beaufort, to be precise, home to a shrimp festival ("Dance your shrimp tails off and come with an empty stomach!") and a spate of restaurants that offer their unique take on the shrimp burger.

Of all the shrimp burgers in Beaufort, one of the most memorable can be found at the Shrimp Shack, a Beaufort institution since 1978. Robert "Captain Bob" Upton, a local fisherman, and his wife, Hilda Upton, opened the Shack in his front yard that year, after a particularly poor fishing season. Daughters Hilda "Sis" Godley and Julie Madlinger run the place now, using local shrimp and Captain Bob's recipe.

Unlike some other shrimp burgers in town, the Shrimp Shack's burger was almost pure shrimp, with no bready fillers to get in the way of the clean, sweet shrimp flavor. It eschewed additional ingredients like bell peppers and Old Bay, which some of the Shack's competitors used to excess. Sis and her longtime staff—Necie and Mildred—scooped out the shrimp mixture, patted it into a thin patty, and then dredged it in flour before dropping it carefully into the deep-fryer.

There was nothing fancy about this burger, but it boasted a delightful juxtaposition of warm, crispy outside and moist inside studded with tender pieces of juicy shrimp, and it was served on a plain burger bun with either mayonnaise or tartar sauce.

Inspired by the shrimp burgers in Beaufort, I gathered all the shrimp burger recipes I could find. Most began with raw shrimp, though several used cooked and a few used tiny rock shrimp. Binders ran the gamut from mayonnaise, eggs, egg whites, and baking powder to panades made from crackers, bread crumbs, and cornbread. Onion, shallot, or scallion were popular additions, as were bell pepper, celery, and herbs. Every recipe called for pan-frying the burgers.

A few initial tests helped eliminate cooked or rock shrimp as options; both became rubbery during cooking and were nothing like the tender shrimp that I had enjoyed at the Shrimp Shack. Since I liked the idea of having substantial chunks of shrimp in the burgers, I took raw, peeled large shrimp and chopped them into ½-inch pieces. It made an awful mess on my cutting board, and the resulting pieces seemed too disparate, lacking. I pulled out the food processor for the next batch and pulsed the shrimp into coarse pieces. Even coarsely chopped in the processor, the shrimp developed a sticky quality that helped the mixture hold together.

For my next test, I took about a third of the shrimp and processed it until it was finely chopped, and then I added the rest of the shrimp and pulsed it just a few times to coarsely chop it. This gave me a sticky mixture of both smooth and chunky shrimp that held together remarkably well when I portioned it into individual burgers . . . but it fell apart when subjected to the heat of the skillet. Clearly the burgers needed some additional binding.

I tested my shrimp mixture with different "glues" to flavor and bind it. Adding an egg made the mixture too loose and dulled the shrimp flavor, and since the burgers weren't lacking in structure or moisture, a bready panade was unnecessary. Two tablespoons of mayonnaise did the trick, and tasters liked the added tang. I used salt, pepper, and cayenne to season the burgers and then tested onion, shallot, and scallion, respectively, to add depth. Tasters liked the freshness of scallions.

The sweet shrimp flavor is front and center in these crispy, panko-coated burgers.

The Shrimp Shack has a deep-fryer at the ready, so it's easy for the workers to fry the burgers. Trying to simplify things for the home cook meant pan-frying, but could we achieve the same crispy crust without the fryer?

I tried lightly dredging the burgers in either flour or cornstarch, but neither developed a crispy coating without a substantial amount of oil. I wondered if I could cheat by starting with a crispy coating of bread crumbs or panko and brown it to mimic the crispy coating of the deep-fried shrimp burger.

Since the test kitchen prefers light, crispy panko bread crumbs to traditional dried bread crumbs, I decided to start there. The light crunch of the panko seemed promising, but when I pressed the burgers into the flaky crumbs, the result looked more like crab cake than burger. Pulsing the panko in the food processor first yielded a finer, more consistent crumb that evenly coated the patties and quickly browned in just 3 tablespoons of oil in the skillet. Crust achieved.

While many shrimp burgers in Beaufort are dressed with nothing more than a smear of mayonnaise, I wanted to introduce a subtle tang with some fresh tartar sauce. An easy sauce of mayonnaise, chopped dill pickles, capers, and shallot came together in a flash to add brightness to the salty-sweet shrimp burgers. They'll never take the place of a trip to the Shrimp Shack, but these burgers would tide me over.

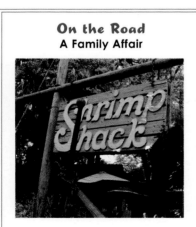

SHRIMP BURGERS Serves 4

We prefer untreated shrimp—those without added sodium or preservatives like sodium tripolyphosphate (STPP). Most frozen shrimp have been treated (the ingredient list should tell you). If you're using untreated shrimp, increase the amount of salt to ½ teaspoon. If you're purchasing shell-on shrimp, you should buy about 1½ pounds.

TARTAR SAUCE

- ¾ cup mayonnaise
- 3 tablespoons finely chopped dill pickles plus 1 teaspoon brine
- 1 small shallot, minced
- 1 tablespoon capers, rinsed and chopped fine
- ¼ teaspoon pepper

BURGERS

- 1 cup panko bread crumbs
- 1¼ pounds peeled and deveined large shrimp (26 to 30 per pound), tails removed
- 2 tablespoons mayonnaise
- ¼ teaspoon pepper
- ⅛ teaspoon salt
- ⅛ teaspoon cayenne pepper
- 3 scallions, chopped fine
- 3 tablespoons vegetable oil
- 4 hamburger buns
- 4 leaves Bibb lettuce

1. FOR THE TARTAR SAUCE: Combine all ingredients in bowl and refrigerate until needed.

2. FOR THE BURGERS: Pulse panko in food processor until finely ground, about 15 pulses; transfer to shallow dish. Place one-third of shrimp (1 cup), mayonnaise, pepper, salt, and cayenne in now-empty processor and pulse until shrimp are finely chopped, about 8 pulses. Add remaining two-thirds of shrimp (2 cups) to shrimp mixture in processor and pulse until coarsely chopped, about 4 pulses, scraping down sides of bowl as needed. Transfer shrimp mixture to bowl and stir in scallions.

3. Divide shrimp mixture into four ¾-inch-thick patties (about ½ cup each). Working with 1 patty at a time, dredge both sides of patties in panko, pressing lightly to adhere, and transfer to plate.

4. Heat oil in 12-inch nonstick skillet over medium heat until shimmering. Place patties in skillet and cook until golden brown on first side, 3 to 5 minutes. Carefully flip and continue to cook until shrimp registers 140 to 145 degrees and second side is golden brown, 3 to 5 minutes longer. Transfer burgers to paper towel–lined plate and let drain, about 30 seconds per side. Spread tartar sauce on bun bottoms, then place burgers and lettuce on top. Cover with bun tops. Serve.

Senate Navy Bean Soup

A mainstay in the U.S. Senate dining room for more than a century, this simple bean soup was in dire need of reform. BY CHRISTIE MORRISON

TALK ABOUT GRIDLOCK: The debate over the origins of Senate Bean Soup shows no signs of resolving itself (see "Soupy Start"). But the dish has been on the menu at the U.S. Capitol cafeteria for more than a century.

Turns out this white bean and potato soup with ham hock, aromatic vegetables, and butter makes for a filling meal. But it's also dull. I wanted to stay true to the simple ingredient list but add flavor to inspire even the weariest lawmaker.

First, I doubled up on ham hocks. Next, I ditched the butter for vegetable oil so the vegetable flavor was cleaner. A few whole cloves, removed before serving the soup, added a gentle infusion of spice. And instead of stirring precooked mashed potatoes into the beans, as some recipes suggest, I added cut-up potatoes right to the soup pot and then mashed them to thicken the soup.

You can take my word that this soup is improved, or we can put it to a vote.

SENATE NAVY BEAN SOUP

Serves 6 to 8

The finished texture of the soup should be creamy but not too thick. We use whole cloves because ground cloves turn the soup an unsightly gray color.

- Salt and pepper
- 1 pound (2½ cups) navy beans, picked over and rinsed
- 1 tablespoon vegetable oil
- 1 onion, chopped fine
- 2 celery ribs, chopped fine
- 2 garlic cloves, minced
- 3 whole cloves
- 2 (12-ounce) smoked ham hocks
- 8 ounces russet potatoes, peeled and cut into ¼-inch pieces
- 1 tablespoon cider vinegar

1. Dissolve 3 tablespoons salt in 4 quarts cold water in large container. Add beans and soak at room temperature for at least 8 hours or up to 24 hours. Drain and rinse well.

2. Heat oil in Dutch oven over medium heat until shimmering. Add onion, celery, and 1 teaspoon salt and cook until softened, 8 to 10 minutes. Stir in garlic and cook until fragrant, about 30 seconds. Transfer onion mixture to bowl.

3. Insert cloves into skin of 1 ham hock. Add 8 cups water, ham hocks,

This hearty, satisfying soup derives much of its flavor from smoked ham hocks.

and beans to now-empty pot and bring to boil over high heat. Reduce heat to medium-low and simmer, covered with lid slightly ajar, until beans are tender, 45 to 60 minutes, stirring occasionally.

4. Stir potatoes and onion mixture into soup and simmer, uncovered, until potatoes are tender, 10 to 15 minutes; remove pot from heat. Transfer ham hocks to cutting board and let cool slightly. Discard cloves, then shred meat, discarding bones and skin.

5. Using potato masher, gently mash beans and potatoes until soup is creamy and lightly thickened, 8 to 10 strokes. Add ½ teaspoon pepper and shredded meat and return to simmer over medium heat. Stir in vinegar. Season with salt and pepper to taste. Serve.

Backstory
Soupy Start

The origins of Senate Bean Soup are muddy, according to Senate Historian Don Ritchie. "Some accounts attribute it to Idaho Senator Fred Dubois (b. 1851) (pictured), who . . . pushed a resolution to require the bean soup on the menu every day. The other story attributes it to Minnesota Senator Knute Nelson (b. 1843), who got the Rules committee to adopt a resolution in 1907. It's possible that both stories are true."

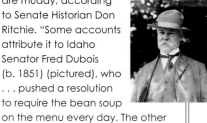

Ballpark Pretzels

Professional bakers have their tricks, but you can make warm, salty, chewy pretzels at home, too.

BY CRISTIN WALSH

WITH THEIR MAHOGANY-BROWN crusts, tender insides, and salty bite, soft pretzels are pretty much irresistible. Something this good shouldn't be available only on those rare occasions when I make it to a ball game (or fair, or New York City street cart). I decided I'd learn how to make these pretzels at home.

I found plenty of recipes and whittled down the list to several promising candidates. All followed the same process of making a dough with flour, water, a sweetener, salt, and yeast. The dough was left to rise and then twisted into the classic pretzel shape. From there, recipes varied: Some called for baking the pretzels straight away; others required a boil in water first.

After mixing, proofing, rolling, shaping, boiling, and baking an abundance of pretzels, I called my tasters to weigh in. While the test revealed one step as essential—the prebake boil for a chewy interior—the rest was up in the air. Most of these "made at home" pretzels were dull. And even the best-tasting lacked that essential pretzel element: a deep mahogany crust.

I wasn't surprised. I knew that professional bakers get that dark mahogany exterior with its distinctive flavor by treating the dough with lye, which helps a small piece of dough, like a pretzel, achieve a rich brown exterior during a relatively short baking time (see "An Easy Fix for a Caustic Challenge"). Of course, most home cooks don't have lye on hand, nor would they want to. It's tricky to work with—abrasive and caustic. But every home cook has, knowingly or not, worked with a more subdued and friendlier alkali: baking soda. Could I achieve a beautiful brown pretzel crust at home with this common ingredient?

Choosing the best of the tested recipes as my launching point, I stirred 1½ cups of warm water, 2 tablespoons of oil, 2 tablespoons of sugar, and 2 teaspoons of yeast in a mixing bowl until the yeast was activated and the mixture was foamy. To that I added 3¾ cups of all-purpose flour and some salt and then used a dough hook to knead until I had a silky-smooth dough. I set the dough aside to rest, and after it had doubled in size, about an hour later, I started shaping pretzels.

When 12 pretzels were twisted and pressed, I heated a solution of 1 cup of

A quick dunk in a boiling baking soda solution produces a shiny, brown exterior and a dense, chewy middle.

baking soda and 4 cups of water in a pot, dipped the pretzels into the simmering solution a few at a time (a surprisingly easy process), and then divided them among two greased baking sheets and sprinkled them with kosher salt (so-called pretzel salt, which has larger crystals, works well, too). After baking at 425 degrees for 15 minutes, the pretzels were nicely darkened and shiny on the outside, exactly what I had hoped for.

Unfortunately, their beauty was only crust-deep. The exterior had an unpleasant soapy flavor and the inside was bland and too tender. As one taster put it, "There's no chew!" and another added, "It's like a dinner roll pretzel." What's more, the pretzels were sticking to the baking sheets. To get the pretzels off the sheets, I had to tear them to shreds.

I decided to change direction and work from the inside out, addressing the

poor interior texture and flavor first. I wondered if bread flour, with its higher gluten content, could provide more of that distinctive chew that tasters were looking for. Answer: Yes. A test showed that it had a nice chew yet was still soft. And to combat the dinner roll flavor, I tested various sweeteners, thinking that something other than white sugar might provide more complexity. Dark brown sugar beat out light brown sugar, white sugar, and honey; tasters felt that dark brown sugar most closely mimicked the sweet, subtly malty flavor that pretzels at the ballpark have.

On to the exterior issues, specifically the challenges created by the baking-soda solution. It was clear that the previously tested ratio of 1 cup baking soda to 4 cups water was too strong and was leaving that unpleasant soapy residual taste on the crust. I dipped four different batches in four different baking-soda-and-water solutions of varying strengths. I found that the solution that created the best dark crust with no off-putting flavor was relatively weak, with only ¼ cup baking soda to 4 cups water.

▶ To find out which yellow mustard came out on top in our recent taste test, visit CooksCountry.com/yellowmustard.

But one problem remained: The baking-soda-and-water solution made the surface of the pretzels especially sticky, causing them to cement themselves to the baking sheet. I tried creating a barrier between the baking sheet and pretzels by sprinkling salt on the greased sheets before placing the boiled pretzels on them. Though tasters raved about the added seasoning, which covered all sides of the pretzel, it didn't prevent the pretzels from staying glued to the metal surface. In the end, the answer was simple: A 5-minute rest on a wire rack to allow the bottoms of the pretzels to dry off postsimmer prevented sticking.

Making pretzels requires more effort than opening a Cracker Jack box, but the delicious reward of a ballpark pretzel at home makes the extra effort worth it. Serve them warm with a side of mustard and you're ready to play ball.

BALLPARK PRETZELS Makes 12 pretzels

We use kosher salt on the exterior of our pretzels, but coarse pretzel salt may be substituted. However, be sure to still use kosher salt in the dough. Keep in mind that the dough needs to rise for 60 minutes, and then the shaped pretzels require a 20-minute rise before boiling and baking. These pretzels are best served warm, with mustard.

- 1½ cups warm water (110 degrees)
- 3 tablespoons vegetable oil
- 2 tablespoons packed dark brown sugar
- 2 teaspoons instant or rapid-rise yeast
- 3¾ cups (20⅔ ounces) bread flour
  Kosher salt
- ¼ cup baking soda

1. Lightly grease large bowl. In bowl of stand mixer, combine warm water, 2 tablespoons oil, sugar, and yeast and let sit until foamy, about 3 minutes. Combine flour and 4 teaspoons salt in separate bowl. Add flour mixture to yeast mixture. Fit stand mixer with dough hook and knead on low speed until dough comes together and clears sides of bowl, 4 to 6 minutes.

2. Turn out dough onto lightly floured counter and knead by hand until smooth, about 1 minute. Transfer dough to greased bowl and cover with plastic wrap. Let dough rise at room temperature until almost doubled in size, about 60 minutes.

3. Gently press center of dough to deflate. Transfer dough to lightly greased counter, divide into 12 equal pieces, and cover with plastic.

4. Lightly flour 2 rimmed baking sheets. Working with 1 piece of dough at a time, roll into 22-inch-long rope. Shape rope into U with 2-inch-wide bottom curve and ends facing away

from you. Crisscross ropes in middle of U, then fold ends toward bottom of U. Firmly press ends into bottom curve of U 1 inch apart to form pretzel shape. Transfer pretzels to prepared sheets, knot side up, 6 pretzels per sheet. Cover pretzels loosely with plastic and let rise at room temperature until slightly puffy, about 20 minutes.

5. Adjust oven racks to upper-middle and lower-middle positions and heat oven to 425 degrees. Dissolve baking soda in 4 cups water in Dutch oven and bring to boil over medium-high heat. Using slotted spatula, transfer 4 pretzels, knot side down, to boiling water and cook for 30 seconds, flipping halfway through cooking. Transfer pretzels to wire rack, knot side up, and repeat with remaining 8 pretzels in 2 additional batches. Let pretzels rest for 5 minutes.

6. Wipe flour from sheets and grease with remaining 1 tablespoon oil. Sprinkle each sheet with ½ teaspoon salt. Transfer pretzels to prepared sheets, knot side up, 6 pretzels per sheet. Sprinkle 1 teaspoon salt evenly over pretzels.

7. Bake pretzels until mahogany brown and any yellowish color around seams has faded, 15 to 20 minutes, switching and rotating sheets halfway through baking. Transfer pretzels to wire rack and let cool for 10 minutes. Serve.

TO MAKE AHEAD

The pretzels are best eaten the day they are baked but will keep at room temperature in an airtight container for up to 2 days. Freeze pretzels, wrapped well in plastic wrap, for up to 1 month. To reheat room-temperature pretzels, brush tops lightly with water, sprinkle with salt, and toast on baking sheet at 300 degrees for 5 minutes. Let frozen pretzels thaw before reheating.

An Easy Fix for a Caustic Challenge

Commercial pretzel makers spray unbaked pretzels with lye, a strong alkali, to promote browning and create a shiny crust. Or do they? We consulted our science editor, who told us that while manufacturers call the sprayed solution "food-grade lye," it's not really lye at all . . . it's actually sodium hydroxide. True lye is created by soaking ashes in water, while sodium hydroxide is created in a chemical plant—and other than being powerful alkalis, the two have nothing in common. Here's the good news: The baking process neutralizes the caustic sodium hydroxide after it has done its work, making pretzels safe to eat. We neutralized the issue altogether in our recipe, using a more common (and less caustic) alkali, baking soda. By quickly boiling our pretzels in a solution of baking soda and water before they hit the oven, we accomplish two critical tasks: We introduce a thin layer of alkali for browning and shininess, and we set the exterior crust to ensure a dense, chewy interior.

TEST KITCHEN TECHNIQUE **Shape Shifter**
Pretzel dough is fairly dry, so instead of working on a surface dusted with flour, we've found that rolling and shaping pretzels is easier and neater on a kitchen counter that's been lightly greased with vegetable oil. To achieve an even thickness when rolling the balls into ropes, use both hands. Start in the center and work your way toward the ends, using a gentle rocking motion.

1. DIVIDE the dough into quarters.

2. SEPARATE each quarter into thirds.

3. FORM the dough into 12 equal-size balls.

4. ROLL each ball into a 22-inch rope.

5. BEND the rope into a U-shape with the ends facing away from you.

6. CROSS the rope ends in the middle of the U, then cross them again.

7. FOLD the ends over the top toward the bottom of the U.

8. PRESS the ends firmly into the bottom of the curve, about 1 inch apart.

Illustration: Lauren Pettapiece

Beef Pot Pie

Meaty stew under a flaky crust—beef pot pie is as comforting as it gets.
Could we revive, and reinvigorate, this satisfying one-dish dinner? BY MATTHEW CARD

BEEF POT PIE hits all the marks for classic comfort food: bite-size bits of fork-tender meat, sweet peas, soft carrots, silky gravy, and flaky crust. It's a soothing, satisfying one-dish meal that is at once humble and a bit dressed up.

But beef pot pie is easier to eat than to create. Between the rigmarole of preparing the filling—essentially rich and refined beef stew—and the crust and then waiting for it to bake, this dish takes some doing to get it to the table. I wanted a pitch-perfect rendition that would work every time and not take all day to prepare.

Most recipes for beef pot pie call for a predictable set of components: beef, vegetables, gravy, and a top crust. But there were variables. Which cut of meat? What vegetables? What other flavors? What type of crust?

I whipped up a few existing recipes for survey's sake and quickly settled on chuck roast as the best cut for flavor, texture, and economy (short-rib meat tasted terrific but broke the budget; tri-tip cooked up tough and brought a liver-like flavor; and cuts from the round didn't have enough fat to braise well). But the recipes were sadly one-dimensional, tasting of little beyond the beef. This dish needed some punch.

In recent recipe development, the test kitchen has found that for many stews, not all the meat needs to be browned to impart deep flavor—browning just a portion of the meat can suffice if it's cut small enough to increase surface area and browned deeply. Would the technique work here? To find out, I made two batches of my starting-point recipe: I browned all the meat in one, and only half in the other. The difference between the two was surprisingly slight.

After browning the beef, I did the same to the onions and carrots before adding minced garlic, dry red wine, and tomato paste for acidity, sweetness, and body. (I'd save the peas until later so that they didn't turn to mush.) Beef broth proved just the right base for the gravy, which I thickened with 3 tablespoons of flour, briefly cooked to eliminate the raw flour taste.

I had the structure of this dish in place, but it still tasted plain. I needed to turn up the flavor. After trying several test kitchen flavor-boosting favorites, including anchovies, miso paste, and

The umami flavor of the beef is enhanced with sautéed mushrooms, tomato paste, beef broth, soy sauce, and Worcestershire.

dried porcini mushrooms, I zeroed in on a few sautéed cremini mushrooms, a splash of soy sauce, and a stiff shot of tangy Worcestershire sauce, beef's best friend, to give this pie some added muscle. A bit of chopped thyme and a bay leaf added a welcome herbal note.

Back to that crust. I was initially inclined to cap this pie with a fluffy biscuit-style topping, but the dough just sucked up moisture like a sponge,

rendering the cooked biscuits gummy and unappealing. No thanks. I decided that for convenience's sake, store-bought pie dough was the best way forward.

Laying raw pie dough over hot filling, though, proved to be a problem—the warm stew rendered the dough too limp to effectively shape, and it just sagged into the filling. Patience was the salve: transferring the filling to a pie plate and letting it cool for 30 minutes before

capping it with the dough allowed me to carefully crimp the dough around the inside edge and create a tidy pie. A few slits in the center of the pie gave the steam an escape route, ensuring a crisp, flaky crust.

An egg wash for gloss and a dusting of salt, pepper, and chopped thyme were the final savory touches on this beef pot pie that looked every bit as good as it tasted.

BEEF POT PIE Serves 6

You should have about 1¾ pounds of meat after trimming. Note that only half of the meat is browned. You can use button mushrooms instead of the cremini. Our favorite store-bought crust is Wholly Wholesome 9" Certified Organic Traditional Bake at Home Rolled Pie Dough.

- 1 (2¼-pound) boneless beef chuck-eye roast, trimmed and cut into ¾-inch pieces
  Salt and pepper
- 3 tablespoons vegetable oil
- 4 ounces cremini mushrooms, trimmed and quartered
- 1 onion, chopped fine
- 2 carrots, peeled and cut into ½-inch pieces
- 2 tablespoons tomato paste
- 4 garlic cloves, minced
- ½ cup dry red wine
- 3 tablespoons all-purpose flour
- 1¾ cups beef broth
- 1 tablespoon soy sauce
- 1 tablespoon Worcestershire sauce
- 1 bay leaf
- 1 cup frozen peas
- 1½ teaspoons chopped fresh thyme
- 1 large egg, lightly beaten
- 1 (9-inch) store-bought pie dough round

1. Adjust oven rack to lower-middle position and heat oven to 350 degrees. Pat beef dry with paper towels and season with salt and pepper. Heat 1½ tablespoons oil in Dutch oven over medium-high heat until just smoking. Add half of beef and cook until well browned all over, 7 to 10 minutes. Using slotted spoon, transfer beef to bowl with remaining uncooked beef.

2. Add remaining 1½ tablespoons oil to now-empty pot and reduce heat to medium. Add mushrooms, onion, and carrots and cook until vegetables are lightly browned, about 5 minutes, scraping up any browned bits. Stir in tomato paste and garlic and cook until fragrant, about 30 seconds.

3. Stir in wine and cook until evaporated, about 2 minutes. Stir in flour until vegetables are well coated and cook for 1 minute. Stir in broth, soy sauce, Worcestershire, and bay leaf until combined. Add beef and bring to simmer. Cover and transfer to oven. Cook until beef is tender, about 1¼ hours.

4. Remove filling from oven and increase oven temperature to 400 degrees. Transfer filling to 9-inch deep-dish pie plate; discard bay leaf. Let filling cool, uncovered, for 30 minutes. Stir in peas and 1 teaspoon chopped thyme. Season with salt and pepper to taste.

5. Brush rim and interior lip of pie plate with egg. Top filling with pie dough so dough overhangs edges of pie plate slightly. Fold overhanging pie dough inward so folded edge is flush with inner edge of pie plate. Crimp dough evenly around edge of pie using your fingers.

6. Using paring knife, cut ½-inch hole in center of pie. Cut six ½-inch slits around hole, halfway between center and edge of pie. Brush dough with remaining egg, then season with salt, pepper, and remaining ½ teaspoon chopped thyme. Transfer pie to rimmed baking sheet and bake until crust is golden brown, about 30 minutes. Transfer pie to cooling rack and let cool for 20 minutes. Serve.

The American Table
Frozen Pot Pies

Frozen food entrepreneur E. Gordon Male developed and sold the first commercial frozen pot pies at Pearson's Bakery in Oak Park, Illinois, in 1944. The pies, frozen raw to be baked off at home, were a hit, and large-scale food processors noticed. A spike in home freezer ownership in the postwar years, along with improvements in automation, transportation, and distribution meant that by 1953, giants like Swanson and Banquet were in on the game. They produced more than 50,000 frozen pot pies a day—chicken, turkey, beef, and tuna. By 1955 the pot pie was the second-biggest moneymaker in the frozen food business, just behind orange juice concentrate.

With 50-odd companies producing frozen meat pies, quality varied widely and consumers complained. Enter the U.S. Department of Agriculture, which set minimum meat content guidelines for pot pies in 1956. The most recent edition of the agency's labeling policy book requires that pies be 25 percent meat.

The future of frozen pot pie? It's bright. According to trade publication *The National Provisioner*, while the overall frozen meal sector is slowly declining, pot pie revenues are up: Americans spent more than $500 million on them in 2012.

1955 advertisement for pot pies.

Bibb Lettuce Salad with Pear

Delicate greens call for careful dressing. We wanted to find the right balance. BY MORGAN BOLLING

BIBB LETTUCE, A tender variety of butterhead lettuce, is often passed over for sturdier salad greens like romaine or iceberg. This is a shame, as Bibb lettuce has a delicate crunch and a sweet, refreshing flavor. In a salad, it calls for a sharp but not over-powering dressing.

Our standard vinaigrette calls for a 3:1 ratio of oil to vinegar, but after a few tastings with colleagues, I found that a 2:1 ratio, along with sharp additions of shallot and Dijon mustard, worked best for this salad. We preferred the bolder flavor of extra-virgin olive oil to canola or vegetable oil and liked the sweet-tart punch of apple cider vinegar in the dressing. To soften the acidic edges from the vinegar, I whisked in some plain yogurt, which gave the dressing a creamy cling that was just right.

For a sweet element, I tested sliced pear, apple, and orange; tasters voted for the subtle floral flavor and soft texture of the pear. I added sliced radishes for spice, toasted walnuts for crunch, and sliced scallions for freshness, and suddenly my tasters were coming back for seconds.

BIBB LETTUCE SALAD WITH YOGURT-DIJON DRESSING
Serves 4

Use a slightly firm pear for this salad; very ripe pears will fall apart.

- ¼ cup extra-virgin olive oil
- 1 small shallot, minced
- 2 tablespoons plain yogurt
- 2 tablespoons Dijon mustard
- 2 tablespoons cider vinegar
  Salt and pepper
- 1 head Bibb lettuce (8 ounces), leaves separated and torn
- 4 radishes, trimmed and sliced thin
- 1 Bosc pear, halved, cored, and sliced thin
- ½ cup walnuts, toasted and chopped coarse
- 3 scallions, sliced thin on bias

Whisk oil, shallot, yogurt, mustard, vinegar, ½ teaspoon salt, and ½ teaspoon pepper together in small bowl. Combine lettuce, radishes, pear, walnuts, and scallions in large bowl. Toss salad with half of dressing. Season with salt and pepper to taste. Serve, passing remaining dressing separately.

Pear and radishes nicely complement the sweet lettuce.

Getting to Know Flours

In spite of its name, all-purpose flour isn't the best choice for every task. Here is a primer on common flours and the best ways to use them. BY CHRISTIE MORRISON

All-Purpose Flour
WORKHORSE

All-purpose flour is a workhorse because its protein content (between 10 and 11.7 percent) is high enough to provide structure to sandwich breads yet low enough to produce a tender crumb in many cakes. We prefer unbleached flour: We've found that some bleached flours carry off-flavors. Our favorite all-purpose flours are made by King Arthur and Pillsbury.

Whole-Wheat Flour
COMPLETE KERNEL

Whole-wheat flour contains the entire wheat kernel, including the germ, which means that it's higher in fiber, fat, and protein than all-purpose flour. Because the protein in the germ doesn't form gluten, whole-wheat flour is often bolstered with all-purpose flour or bread flour in baking recipes. Whole-wheat flour is prone to rancidity; store it in a zipper-lock bag in the freezer.

Cake Flour
TENDER CRUMB

Cake flour creates a finer, more delicate crumb than all-purpose flour. While all-purpose flour is used to provide structure in many sheet and layer cakes, we like to use lower-protein (6 to 8 percent) cake flour for more delicate cakes like angel food and pound cakes. You can substitute ⅞ cup of all-purpose flour and 2 tablespoons of cornstarch for every cup of cake flour called for.

Pastry Flour
INDUSTRY INSIDER

Primarily used by professional bakers, pastry flour is a soft wheat flour with a protein content between those of all-purpose flour and cake flour. It's used for pastries like Danish and tarts and for butter-rich shortbread; it produces a fine crumb in baked goods. We've found that in most recipes, all-purpose or cake flour (used singularly or in combination) can approximate pastry flour's effect.

Semolina
PEEL DUSTER

This staple in dried pasta making comes from coarsely ground durum wheat, a hard winter wheat that is high in gluten. In addition to featuring in pasta, semolina is used to make bread, couscous, puddings, and Roman-style gnocchi. The test kitchen sometimes uses it in pizza making to keep pizza from sticking to the peel (it doesn't char as easily as flour and will let the pizza release without sticking).

Rice Flour
SIZE MATTERS

Both brown and white rice flours are fairly high in protein (5 to 7 percent) for nonwheat flours and help provide structure in gluten-free baked goods. Be aware that the coarseness of the grind will affect its performance in recipes; coarse flours can impart grittiness to baked goods. While white rice flour will keep in your pantry, brown rice flour should be stored in the refrigerator.

Bread Flour
PROTEIN HEAVYWEIGHT

With a protein percentage of 12 to 14, bread flour is the highest-protein flour available. It's aces at developing gluten, which in turn gives great structure and chew to rustic breads like ciabatta and our seven-grain Dakota Bread (**CooksCountry.com/dakotabread**). We've also turned to bread flour in some of our pizza crusts; the gluten gives the crust elasticity and chew.

Nut Flours
FINE GRIND

While grinding nuts produces a fine powder akin to flour, it's not a straight substitute for flour because nuts don't contain the proteins that produce gluten, which gives structure to most baked goods. We often add nut flours to regular flour to flavor and tenderize cookies like madeleines. These flours are expensive and prone to rancidity, so make them last by storing them in the freezer.

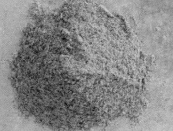

Self-Rising Flour
POWDER KEG

Self-rising flour has leavener and salt already added. It has a protein content similar to that of cake flour and is often used in biscuits and quick breads. Don't substitute self-rising flour for other flours in recipes. However, in recipes that call for self-rising flour, you can substitute cake flour and add your own leavener and salt (1½ teaspoons of baking powder and ½ teaspoon of salt for every cup of flour).

Buckwheat Flour
WHEATLESS WONDER

Don't be fooled by its name: Gluten-free buckwheat isn't related to wheat at all. It's an herb, more closely related to rhubarb or sorrel than to wheat. Buckwheat flour is made by grinding its triangular seeds, which contribute a dark color and earthy flavor. With a protein content of 13 percent, it adds structure to buckwheat crêpes, soba noodles, and the Russian pancakes known as blini.

Instant Flour
TWICE COOKED

Instant flour (Wondra is the most common brand) is finely ground, low-protein flour that is able to dissolve instantly (with very few lumps) in hot or cold liquids like sauces, gravies, and soups. This is due to pregelatinization, a process in which the flour is effectively precooked and then dried. Instant flour is also used as a coating for fried chicken or fish, as the tiny particles distribute evenly into thin crusts.

Chickpea Flour
GLUTEN-FREE GRAB

Also known as *besan*, garbanzo flour, or gram flour, beany-tasting chickpea flour is made from ground raw or roasted chickpeas. It's a common ingredient in Indian, Middle Eastern, and European cooking and is used to make unleavened crêpes called *socca*, as well as *pakoras* and *pappadams*. Because of its high protein content (20 percent), chickpea flour is often used in savory gluten-free baking.

30-MINUTE SUPPER

**CRISPY CHICKEN
WITH SAUTÉED RADISHES, SPINACH, AND BACON**

30-MINUTE SUPPER

**BOURBON-BUTTER STEAK TIPS
WITH MAPLE MASHED SWEET POTATOES**

30-MINUTE SUPPER

FIG, GORGONZOLA, AND PROSCIUTTO PIZZA

30-MINUTE SUPPER

LINGUINE WITH WHITE CLAM SAUCE

BOURBON-BUTTER STEAK TIPS WITH MAPLE MASHED SWEET POTATOES Serves 4

✔ **WHY THIS RECIPE WORKS:** To build layers of flavor, we make the bourbon pan sauce in the skillet after cooking the steak tips.

- 2 pounds sweet potatoes, peeled and cut into ½-inch pieces
- 3 tablespoons vegetable oil
- Salt and pepper
- ¼ cup heavy cream
- ¼ cup maple syrup
- 1½ pounds sirloin steak tips, trimmed and cut into 2-inch chunks
- ½ cup bourbon
- 2 teaspoons cider vinegar
- 2 tablespoons unsalted butter
- 1 tablespoon chopped fresh chives

1. Combine potatoes, 2 tablespoons oil, 1 teaspoon salt, and ½ teaspoon pepper in large bowl. Cover and microwave until potatoes are tender, about 10 minutes, stirring halfway through cooking. Add cream and 3 tablespoons maple syrup and mash until smooth; cover and set aside.

2. Meanwhile, pat steak tips dry with paper towels and season with salt and pepper. Heat remaining 1 tablespoon oil in 12-inch skillet over medium-high heat until just smoking. Add steak and cook until well browned all over and meat registers 125 degrees (for medium-rare), 6 to 8 minutes. Transfer to platter and tent loosely with foil.

3. Off heat, add bourbon, vinegar, and remaining 1 tablespoon maple syrup to skillet; return to medium-high heat and cook until slightly thickened, about 3 minutes, scraping up any browned bits. Off heat, whisk in butter and season with salt and pepper to taste. Return steak and any accumulated juices to skillet and toss to coat. Sprinkle with chives and serve with mashed potatoes.

CRISPY CHICKEN WITH SAUTÉED RADISHES, SPINACH, AND BACON Serves 4

✔ **WHY THIS RECIPE WORKS:** Cooking the chicken in rendered bacon fat ensures both crisp skin and a subtle smoky flavor.

- 3 pounds bone-in chicken pieces (split breasts cut in half crosswise, drumsticks, and/or thighs), trimmed
- Salt and pepper
- 2 slices bacon, chopped fine
- 10 ounces radishes, trimmed and quartered
- 10 ounces (10 cups) baby spinach
- 2 garlic cloves, minced
- 2 teaspoons lemon juice, plus lemon wedges for serving

1. Adjust oven rack to middle position and heat oven to 450 degrees. Pat chicken dry with paper towels and season with salt and pepper. Cook bacon in ovensafe 12-inch skillet over medium-high heat until crisp, about 5 minutes. Using slotted spoon, transfer bacon to paper towel–lined plate, leaving rendered fat behind.

2. Add chicken to skillet, skin side down, and cook until well browned, about 5 minutes. Flip chicken, transfer skillet to oven, and roast until breasts register 160 degrees and drumsticks/thighs register 175 degrees, about 15 minutes. Transfer chicken to plate and tent loosely with foil.

3. Discard all but 1 tablespoon fat from skillet and return to medium-high heat. Add radishes and ½ teaspoon salt and cook until tender, about 2 minutes. Stir in spinach and garlic and cook until wilted, about 2 minutes. Off heat, stir in bacon and lemon juice. Transfer to serving platter and top with chicken. Serve with lemon wedges.

TEST KITCHEN NOTE: To ensure crispy chicken skin, resist the urge to move the chicken while browning it in step 2.

LINGUINE WITH WHITE CLAM SAUCE Serves 4

✔ **WHY THIS RECIPE WORKS:** For this quick weeknight meal, we opted for the convenience of canned chopped clams. Butter, stirred in at the end, enriches the clam sauce and provides a velvety texture.

- 2 shallots, minced
- 2 tablespoons extra-virgin olive oil
- 4 garlic cloves, minced
- 2 (6.5-ounce) cans chopped clams
- 1 cup chicken broth
- 1 (8-ounce) bottle clam juice
- 2 tablespoons unsalted butter
- Salt and pepper
- 1 pound linguine
- 2 tablespoons minced fresh parsley

1. Cook shallots, oil, and garlic in 12-inch skillet over medium heat until shallot is just golden and garlic is fragrant, about 2 minutes. Add clams and their juice, broth, and bottled clam juice; increase heat to medium-high; and bring to boil. Cook until sauce is reduced to 2 cups, about 15 minutes. Off heat, whisk in butter and season with salt and pepper to taste.

2. Meanwhile, bring 4 quarts water to boil in large pot. Add linguine and 1 tablespoon salt to boiling water and cook, stirring often, until al dente. Reserve ½ cup cooking water, then drain linguine and return it to pot. Add sauce and parsley to linguine and toss to combine. Adjust consistency with reserved cooking water as needed. Season with salt and pepper to taste. Serve.

TEST KITCHEN NOTE: Our favorite clam juice is Bar Harbor Clam Juice. For a little brightness, serve with lemon wedges and red pepper flakes.

FIG, GORGONZOLA, AND PROSCIUTTO PIZZA Serves 4

✔ **WHY THIS RECIPE WORKS:** An oiled baking sheet helps ensure a crisp—not floppy—pizza crust.

- ¼ cup olive oil
- 1 tablespoon balsamic vinegar
- Salt and pepper
- 1 pound pizza dough
- ¼ cup fig jam
- 3 ounces Gorgonzola cheese, crumbled (¾ cup)
- 2 ounces (2 cups) baby arugula
- 4 thin slices prosciutto, torn into 1-inch pieces

1. Adjust oven rack to upper-middle position and heat oven to 500 degrees. Brush rimmed baking sheet with 2 tablespoons oil. Whisk vinegar, ½ teaspoon salt, ½ teaspoon pepper, and 1 tablespoon oil together in bowl.

2. Roll dough into 16 by 10-inch oval on lightly floured counter, about ¼ inch thick. Transfer dough to prepared sheet and brush with remaining 1 tablespoon oil. Brush dough with jam and sprinkle with Gorgonzola, leaving ½-inch border.

3. Bake until cheese is melted and crust is browned, about 10 minutes, rotating sheet halfway through baking. Let pizza cool for 5 minutes. Toss arugula with vinaigrette. Distribute arugula and prosciutto over pizza. Serve.

TEST KITCHEN NOTE: Fresh pizza dough can be found in the refrigerated section of most grocery stores.

HOISIN-GLAZED PORK TENDERLOIN

SALMON TACOS WITH LATIN SLAW

SAUSAGE AND RED PEPPER POLENTA LASAGNA

CHICKEN TIKKA MASALA

SALMON TACOS WITH LATIN SLAW Serves 4

✓ **WHY THIS RECIPE WORKS:** Skin-on salmon fillets hold together during cooking, and the skin helps keep the fish moist.

- 3 cups (8¼ ounces) coleslaw mix
- 1 small red onion, halved and sliced thin
- ½ cup fresh cilantro leaves
- 2 tablespoons lime juice
  Salt and pepper
- ¼ cup sour cream
- 1 teaspoon chili powder
- 2 (6-ounce) skin-on salmon fillets, 1 to 1½ inches thick
- 1 tablespoon vegetable oil
- 8 (6-inch) corn tortillas, warmed

1. Combine coleslaw mix, onion, ¼ cup cilantro, 5 teaspoons lime juice, ½ teaspoon salt, and ¼ teaspoon pepper in bowl. Whisk sour cream, remaining 1 teaspoon lime juice, ¼ teaspoon salt, and ¼ teaspoon pepper together in separate bowl. Combine chili powder, ¾ teaspoon salt, and ¼ teaspoon pepper; season salmon with spice mixture.

2. Heat oil in 12-inch nonstick skillet over medium heat until shimmering. Cook salmon, skin side up, until well browned, 4 to 6 minutes. Flip and continue to cook until salmon registers 125 degrees (for medium-rare), 4 to 6 minutes. Transfer salmon to plate and let cool slightly, about 2 minutes. Using 2 forks, flake fish into 1-inch pieces; discard skin. Divide fish evenly among tortillas. Top with coleslaw mixture, sour cream mixture, and remaining ¼ cup cilantro. Serve.

TEST KITCHEN NOTE: Our favorite chili powder is Morton & Bassett Chili Powder.

HOISIN-GLAZED PORK TENDERLOIN Serves 4

✓ **WHY THIS RECIPE WORKS:** A potent Asian-style glaze means you don't have to marinate the meat.

- 2 (12-ounce) pork tenderloins, trimmed
  Salt and pepper
- ¾ cup chicken broth
- ¼ cup hoisin sauce
- 1 tablespoon packed brown sugar
- 1 tablespoon ketchup
- 2 teaspoons soy sauce
- 1 tablespoon vegetable oil
- 2 scallions, sliced thin on bias
- 1 teaspoon sesame seeds, toasted

1. Pound tenderloins between 2 sheets of plastic wrap to 1-inch thickness. Pat tenderloins dry with paper towels and season with salt and pepper. Whisk broth, hoisin, sugar, ketchup, and soy sauce together in bowl.

2. Heat oil in 12-inch nonstick skillet over medium heat until shimmering. Cook tenderloins until well browned on both sides and meat registers 140 degrees, about 7 minutes per side. Add hoisin mixture and simmer until slightly thickened, 2 to 5 minutes, turning tenderloins to coat.

3. Remove skillet from heat and let pork rest in sauce for 5 minutes, then slice ½ inch thick. Serve, drizzled with glaze and sprinkled with scallions and sesame seeds.

TEST KITCHEN NOTE: Buy tenderloins that are of equal size and weight so they cook at the same rate; make sure they are no larger than 12 ounces, as bigger tenderloins won't fit in the skillet together.

CHICKEN TIKKA MASALA Serves 4

✓ **WHY THIS RECIPE WORKS:** Thanks to garam masala, we didn't need to use half of the spice cabinet to flavor our chicken. We save time by cooking cubed chicken right in the flavorful tomato sauce and then stirring in heavy cream at the end.

- 1 tablespoon garam masala
  Salt and pepper
- 4 (6- to 8-ounce) boneless, skinless chicken breasts, trimmed and cut into 1-inch cubes
- 2 tablespoons vegetable oil
- 1 onion, chopped fine
- 2 tablespoons grated fresh ginger
- 3 garlic cloves, minced
- 1 (28-ounce) can crushed tomatoes
- ¼ cup heavy cream
- ¼ cup fresh cilantro leaves

1. Combine garam masala, 1½ teaspoons salt, and ½ teaspoon pepper in bowl. Toss chicken with 1 tablespoon oil and 1 tablespoon spice mixture in separate bowl.

2. Heat remaining 1 tablespoon oil in 12-inch nonstick skillet over medium-high heat until shimmering. Add onion and cook until beginning to brown, about 5 minutes. Stir in ginger, garlic, and remaining 2 teaspoons spice mixture and cook until fragrant, abut 30 seconds. Add tomatoes and chicken and simmer until slightly thickened and chicken is cooked through, about 10 minutes. Off heat, stir in cream. Season with salt and pepper to taste. Sprinkle with cilantro. Serve.

TEST KITCHEN NOTE: Garam masala is an Indian seasoning made from warm spices like clove, cinnamon, pepper, cardamom, and cumin. Our taste test winner is McCormick Gourmet Collection Garam Masala.

SAUSAGE AND RED PEPPER POLENTA LASAGNA Serves 4

✓ **WHY THIS RECIPE WORKS:** Precooked polenta, simply sliced and placed in a single layer in the casserole dish, helps save cooking time and absorbs the rich flavors of the sauce.

- 1 pound hot Italian sausage, casings removed
- 1½ cups jarred roasted red peppers, rinsed, patted dry, and sliced into ¼-inch-thick strips
- 1 onion, halved and sliced thin
  Salt and pepper
- 3 garlic cloves, minced
- 1 teaspoon minced fresh rosemary
- 1 (14.5-ounce) can diced tomatoes
- 1 (18-ounce) tube precooked polenta, sliced into ⅓-inch-thick rounds
- 4 ounces mozzarella cheese, shredded (1 cup)
- ¼ cup chopped fresh basil

1. Adjust oven rack to middle position and heat oven to 450 degrees. Cook sausage, red peppers, onion, and ¼ teaspoon salt in 12-inch skillet over medium-high heat, breaking up sausage with spoon, until vegetables are lightly browned, about 8 minutes. Add garlic and rosemary and cook until fragrant, about 30 seconds. Stir in tomatoes and their juice and cook until slightly thickened, about 5 minutes. Season with salt and pepper to taste.

2. Spread 2 cups meat sauce in 13 by 9-inch baking dish. Arrange polenta in single layer over sauce, then top with remaining 2 cups sauce. Sprinkle mozzarella over top. Bake until polenta is heated through and cheese is melted, 10 to 15 minutes. Sprinkle with basil. Serve.

TEST KITCHEN NOTE: Our favorite supermarket mozzarella is Galbani (formerly Sorrento) Whole Milk Mozzarella.

Chicken Chow Mein

We were determined to rescue this Chinese American restaurant classic from its depressing gloppy, bland state. BY ASHLEY MOORE

LIKE MANY DISHES you'll find in Chinese restaurants in America, chow mein has deep roots in China, where *chao mian* ("fried noodles" in Mandarin) has been around for centuries. When Chinese immigrants arrived in California in the 19th century, they brought along the dish, and Americans have been dining on it ever since. But chow mein has changed over the years—based on ingredient availability and local tastes—and not always for the better.

I wanted to get to the heart of this simple dish. I called Martin Yan, the respected Chinese chef, to get his advice. "The vegetables should be consistent in shape and size," he counseled, "and not too much sauce." Most important, he said, was that the noodles, vegetables, and meat should be constantly "moving about the wok."

I experimented with several recipes. The basic mechanics were similar from version to version: Boil the noodles and set them aside; sear the marinated chicken and remove it from the pan; add the vegetables to stir-fry; work in the chicken, sauce, and noodles; and serve. After making five iterations, it was clear that there were problems: inconsistent vegetables, dry meat, and pasty sauce.

After settling on egg noodles as my base (see "Fresh Egg Noodles"), I cut mushrooms, carrots, and celery into similar-size pieces so the finished dish would be easy to eat and then gave them a little extra time to soften in the skillet. Scallion whites, garlic, and fresh ginger added sharp edges.

I addressed the dry chicken with a technique that we've used before in the test kitchen: soaking the chicken in a solution of water and baking soda, which helps break the meat down and results in tender, juicy chunks. (The solution gets washed off before cooking to prevent soapy flavors.) I followed this with a quick soak in rice wine and cornstarch, which helps the meat retain moisture. These tricks worked so well that I found that I could streamline the recipe and keep the chicken in the pan the whole time without it drying out.

Turning to the sauce, I followed the lead of most recipes and used savory chicken broth and soy sauce as a base. Oyster sauce was a must for its meaty back notes, and Chinese rice wine added sweet brightness. The key to avoiding a gloppy sauce was using just 1 tablespoon of cornstarch to thicken. Delicious.

CHICKEN CHOW MEIN
Serves 4

Purchase thin, round fresh Chinese egg noodles, not flat and/or dried noodles, or substitute 6 ounces of dried chow mein, ramen, or wheat vermicelli.

- 1 (9-ounce) package fresh Chinese noodles
- 1 tablespoon toasted sesame oil
- 1 teaspoon baking soda
- 2 (6-ounce) boneless, skinless chicken breasts, trimmed and cut crosswise into ¼-inch-thick slices
- 3 tablespoons Chinese rice wine or dry sherry
- 1 tablespoon cornstarch
- ½ cup chicken broth
- 3 tablespoons soy sauce
- 3 tablespoons oyster sauce
- ¼ teaspoon white pepper
- 2 tablespoons vegetable oil
- 6 ounces shiitake mushrooms, stemmed and sliced thin
- 1 carrot, peeled and cut into 2-inch matchsticks
- 2 celery ribs, cut on bias into ¼-inch-thick slices
- 4 scallions, white and green parts separated and sliced thin
- 3 garlic cloves, minced
- 1 tablespoon grated fresh ginger
- 4 ounces (2 cups) mung bean sprouts

Our lighter, brighter chow mein goes easy on the cornstarch and heavy on the mushrooms, scallions, garlic, and ginger.

1. Bring 4 quarts water to boil in large pot. Add noodles to boiling water and cook until tender, 2 to 4 minutes. Drain noodles, rinse thoroughly with cold water, then drain again. Toss noodles with sesame oil in bowl; set aside.

2. Meanwhile, dissolve baking soda in ½ cup cold water in second bowl. Add chicken and let sit at room temperature for 15 minutes. Drain chicken, rinse under cold water, then drain again. Pat chicken dry with paper towels. Combine 1 tablespoon rice wine, 2 teaspoons cornstarch, and chicken in bowl; set aside.

3. Whisk broth, soy sauce, oyster sauce, pepper, remaining 2 tablespoons rice wine, and remaining 1 teaspoon cornstarch together in bowl; set aside.

4. Heat oil in 12-inch nonstick skillet over high heat until just smoking. Add chicken and cook, stirring frequently, until opaque, about 2 minutes. Add mushrooms and carrot and cook, stirring frequently, until tender, about 2 minutes. Add celery and cook until crisp-tender, about 1 minute. Add scallion whites, garlic, and ginger and cook until fragrant, about 30 seconds.

5. Whisk broth mixture to recombine, then add to skillet and cook until thickened and chicken is cooked through, about 2 minutes. Add bean sprouts and noodles and toss until sauce evenly coats noodles, about 1 minute. Transfer to platter and sprinkle with scallion greens. Serve.

KEY INGREDIENT
Fresh Egg Noodles

You'll find chow mein in Chinese restaurants prepared with wheat noodles, Italian pastas, ramen noodles, or egg noodles. But our tasters preferred fresh Chinese egg noodles, available in the Asian section of most grocery stores.

FRESH CHINESE EGG NOODLES
The best choice for chow mein.

Potato Biscuits

The science was promising, but the biscuits were disappointing. We found an unlikely solution in a convenience product. BY REBECCAH MARSTERS

Potato not only adds a subtle savory flavor but also helps tenderize these biscuits.

ANYONE WHO LOVES a good biscuit, as I do, can quickly list its requisite qualities: light, flaky, tender, and rich. Here at the test kitchen we've made every manner of biscuit—or so I thought, until I came across a recipe for a particular breed of stamped biscuits using mashed potatoes. A resourceful idea, to be sure, but wouldn't adding heavy, wet mashed potatoes to biscuit dough work against producing a light biscuit? I needed to find out.

I fished around for more recipes, ultimately coming up with a handful that called for leftover mashed potatoes and several that built the cooking and mashing of the spuds right into the recipe. After baking up a few of each, I had my answer: Most of these potato biscuits were squat and heavy, resembling crackers more than the high, light biscuits I love. Those that used leftover mashed potatoes had inherent problems—how much butter or cream was in the mash? What kind of potatoes were used?

There were too many variables. The results were more consistent in recipes that used fresh mashed potatoes, but something about this approach bothered me. Biscuits are by nature one of the quickest, easiest baked goods out there—cooking, draining, mashing, and then cooling potatoes didn't fit into that time line. Were potato biscuits even worth salvaging? I took a break from the kitchen and hit the books.

A little research unearthed the potential benefits: Adding potato to baked goods, whether bread, rolls, or, yes, biscuits, is said to produce a superlatively tender texture. How? Gluten, the protein that makes bread products chewy, is formed when the proteins in wheat flour mix with liquid and link together. Granules of potato starch interrupt the protein structure, meaning less gluten is formed, resulting in extra tenderness in the finished product. Interesting.

But how could I reap the benefits of potato starch without the moisture of the potatoes wreaking havoc on the biscuits? In the end, I found my answer in a box: instant mashed potatoes. Dehydrated potato flakes have all the starch of whole potatoes but are devoid of water and much more consistent than real spuds. Best of all, they're instant—absolutely perfect for my speedy biscuit time line.

I started off working with my favorite test kitchen stamped biscuit recipe, which calls for combining all-purpose flour, sugar, salt, baking powder, and baking soda in the food processor, cutting in butter and shortening, and then stirring in buttermilk before rolling and stamping out the biscuits. After starting the biscuits in a hot oven for maximum rise, you reduce the temperature slightly and let them gently finish baking. Finally, when they're hot from the oven, you brush the tops of the biscuits with melted butter for extra richness and gloss. A few experiments revealed that for every 2 tablespoons of potato flakes I added, I needed to subtract 1 tablespoon of flour from the recipe to give the biscuit dough the proper texture. Working in increments, I got all the way up to ¾ cup of potato flakes, which produced an incredibly flaky biscuit—any more than that and flaky began to border on crumbly.

> ▶ Visit CooksCountry.com/nov14 for a variation for **Potato Biscuits with Bacon.**

These biscuits were delicious, no doubt, but there were a few skeptics in the test kitchen who questioned whether mine were any better than regular biscuits. To prove my case, I whipped up another batch of potato biscuits and laid them out next to a freshly baked tray of traditional buttermilk biscuits. The results? Both were good, but tasters appreciated the lighter, flakier texture of the ones made with potato flakes. The one complaint: My biscuits weren't quite as tall as the traditional ones. Since potato starch has no gluten, my dough had less structure, so the biscuits couldn't rise quite as high. Luckily, an extra teaspoon of baking powder did the trick, making tender *and* tall biscuits, and there were no more doubters to be found.

To pair with the subtly earthy flavor of the potato, I added fresh chives to the biscuits. This batch went over so well that I developed a couple of variations, turning to other classic potato pairings. I added sharp cheddar cheese and sliced scallions to one, and to the other, crispy, salty, crumbled bacon. Just when I thought a biscuit was a biscuit, I found a reason to rekindle my love.

Backstory
Flaking Out

It was 1953 and chemical engineers James Cording and Miles J. Willard had a challenge: a potato glut. Cording and Willard, working for the Department of Agriculture in Wyndmoor, Pennsylvania, set out to find a way to preserve the bounty by creating a potato product that was shelf-stable, lightweight, and pleasant to eat—something the military, for example, could use for rations. After many gluey failures, they developed the three-step "Philadelphia Cook": The potatoes are cooked at 150 to 165 degrees for 20 minutes to gelatinize the starch, then cooled and cooked again in a steam cooker to separate the potato cells without rupturing them (ruptured cells make paste, not mash). Finally, the potatoes are dried and broken into flakes. The result: easy-to-rehydrate, shelf-stable, light potatoes. Cording and Willard were granted a patent for the process in 1956. Today, about 10 percent of the U.S. potato crop is dehydrated, most for use in military, school, and food aid programs here and abroad.

POTATO BISCUITS WITH CHIVES

Makes 12 biscuits

We like the texture of biscuits made with both butter and shortening, but if you prefer to use all butter, omit the shortening and use 12 tablespoons of chilled butter in step 1.

2½	cups (12½ ounces) all-purpose flour
¾	cup instant potato flakes
⅓	cup chopped fresh chives
4	teaspoons baking powder
½	teaspoon baking soda
1	tablespoon sugar
1	teaspoon salt
8	tablespoons unsalted butter, cut into ½-inch pieces and chilled, plus 2 tablespoons unsalted butter, melted
4	tablespoons vegetable shortening, cut into ½-inch pieces and chilled
1¼	cups buttermilk, chilled

1. Adjust oven rack to middle position and heat oven to 450 degrees. Line rimmed baking sheet with parchment paper. Process flour, potato flakes, chives, baking powder, baking soda, sugar, and salt in food processor until combined, about 15 seconds. Add chilled butter and shortening and pulse until mixture resembles coarse crumbs, 7 to 9 pulses.

2. Transfer flour mixture to large bowl. Stir in buttermilk with rubber spatula until combined, turning and pressing until no dry flour remains. Turn out dough onto lightly floured surface and knead briefly, 8 to 10 times, to form smooth, cohesive ball. Roll out dough into 9-inch circle, about ¾ inch thick.

3. Using floured 2½-inch round cutter, stamp out 8 to 9 biscuits and arrange upside down on prepared sheet. Gather dough scraps and gently pat into ¾-inch-thick circle. Stamp out remaining 3 to 4 biscuits and transfer to sheet.

4. Bake until biscuits begin to rise, about 5 minutes, then rotate sheet and reduce oven temperature to 400 degrees. Continue to bake until golden brown, 10 to 12 minutes longer. Brush biscuit tops with melted butter. Transfer to wire rack and let cool for 5 minutes before serving.

POTATO BISCUITS WITH CHEDDAR AND SCALLIONS

Omit chives and process ¾ cup shredded extra-sharp cheddar cheese and 4 thinly sliced scallions with flour in step 1.

Marinated Mushrooms

Simply dropping raw mushrooms into a marinade won't do. We show you the trick to the best marinated mushrooms you've ever tasted. BY DIANE UNGER

WHAT I LOVE most about marinated mushrooms—aside from how their garlicky vinaigrette perfectly accents the mushrooms' inherent meaty, savory flavor—is their versatility. They're great as a side dish for a holiday, a barbecue, and everything in between; on salads and sandwiches; and in pasta or egg dishes (to name just a few uses).

In order to make my own version, I had to know how other cooks have approached marinated mushrooms. So I gathered and prepared a handful of recipes. I quickly discovered that recipes calling for raw mushrooms had some issues—namely watery dressings (because the mushrooms release liquid as they break down in the dressing), an overall lack of flavor, and a flabby texture.

The recipe that my tasters liked most called for roasting the mushrooms whole on a rimmed baking sheet until they browned and released their liquid and then tossing them with a potent dressing. But roasting took a while, and I had to keep opening the oven door to check on how they were coming along. Cooking them in a skillet was faster, and it was easier to monitor their progress—plus, I could make the "marinade" right in the skillet. I started cooking the mushrooms covered to encourage them to release their liquid, and then I uncovered the pan so the liquid could evaporate. At this point I added sliced shallot, garlic, oregano, and red pepper flakes to the skillet and then poured in a mixture of red wine vinegar and water, which I let reduce and concentrate in flavor.

I took the skillet off the burner and let the mushrooms cool right in the liquid; then I refrigerated them. These mushrooms were good but not quite great. Since the cooking liquid was heavy on the vinegar, I thought I could add oil and mustard to transform it into a vinaigrette. This worked well, and now the mushrooms were everything I wanted them to be: tender and full of flavor.

MARINATED MUSHROOMS

Makes about 4 cups

Try to find small mushrooms, about 1¼ inches in diameter, for this recipe. If your mushrooms are larger, halve or quarter them before cooking. You can substitute minced fresh chives or tarragon for the parsley.

Serve these mushrooms on an appetizer platter, on salads or sandwiches, or as a side dish.

½	cup extra-virgin olive oil
2	pounds small white mushrooms, trimmed
	Salt and pepper
1	large shallot, sliced thin
3	garlic cloves, crushed and peeled
1	teaspoon dried oregano
¼	teaspoon red pepper flakes
¾	cup red wine vinegar
½	cup water
1	tablespoon Dijon mustard
2	tablespoons minced fresh parsley

1. Heat 2 tablespoons oil in 12-inch nonstick skillet over medium-high heat until just smoking. Add mushrooms and 1 teaspoon salt and cook, covered and stirring occasionally, until mushrooms release their liquid and begin to soften, about 10 minutes. Uncover and continue to cook, stirring occasionally, until skillet is dry and mushrooms are lightly browned, 5 to 7 minutes.

2. Add shallot, garlic, oregano, and pepper flakes and cook until fragrant, about 1 minute. Stir in vinegar and water and bring to boil. Cook until liquid reduces by half, about 5 minutes.

3. Whisk mustard, remaining 6 tablespoons oil, ¼ teaspoon salt, and ¼ teaspoon pepper together in medium bowl. Add mushroom mixture and stir to combine. Let cool completely. Stir in parsley. Cover and refrigerate until chilled, at least 1 hour. Season with salt and pepper to taste before serving. (Mushrooms can be refrigerated for up to 5 days.)

Cheese-Stuffed Meatballs

Stuffing meatballs with cheese is easy. But keeping them stuffed?
That's a different story. BY JEREMY SAUER

I ALWAYS THOUGHT MEATBALLS were . . . well, just meatballs. But when I stumbled across a recipe for cheese-stuffed meatballs, it proved too tempting to resist. I had to give it a shot.

The premise is simple: Throw together some meatballs, stuff them with cheese, brown them in a skillet, and then braise them in a tomato sauce. But though the premise may be simple, the execution is anything but. Nearly every meatball I stuffed ruptured gloriously in the skillet, releasing a spurting, sputtering stream of molten cheese. My first task was clear: I needed a sturdier meatball.

On my next round, I took extra care to completely encase the cheese in the meat mixture, using damp hands to smooth the exterior and prevent any cracking. This helped, but the meatballs were still too loose—cracks formed and the cheese had an easy exit route.

Clearly, I had to rethink the recipe. For generations, the basic meatball recipe has called for a panade, a paste made from bread and milk to help bind the meat and add moisture. But a panade makes for a soft, delicate meatball that's loath to hold on to the cheese inside. Since the panade is insurance against dry, overcooked meatballs, what if I just lost the panade and didn't overcook the meatballs? A quick test proved that panade-less meatballs also crumbled as they cooked, releasing a torrent of cheese. Clearly the meatballs needed some ballast. I tried using just bread crumbs—in this case, crispy, Japanese-style panko bread crumbs—in place of the panade. Success: When mixed into the meat and egg mixture, the bread crumbs (with no added liquid) provided the firmness needed to keep the cheese contained.

With the texture of the meatballs in place, it was time to tackle their flavor. Many recipes supplement the beef with pork or veal, but to complement the richness of the cheese, I wanted something more assertive. Adding a bit of Italian sausage to the mix did the trick. Minced garlic, chopped basil, and a bit of grated Parmesan cheese rounded out the flavors nicely.

Next I dealt with the cheese filling. After I tested seven cheeses, mozzarella was the clear winner. The only hassle was cutting perfect ½-inch cubes of cheese from a block of mozzarella. A colleague suggested string cheese. Sure enough, three sticks of string cheese yielded the perfect amount.

On to the sauce. Meatballs and sauce have an important symbiotic relationship: The meatballs flavor the sauce as the sauce gently poaches the meatballs. Without a panade, I knew that the meatballs couldn't spend very long in the sauce without toughening, so I had to make the most of the limited time.

I started by browning the meatballs to build some flavor in the pan. Then, after removing the meatballs, I added chopped onion and cooked it until golden. Next, garlic and a teaspoon of oregano, cooked until fragrant. I stirred in a large can of crushed tomatoes, rather than diced tomatoes (too watery) or tomato sauce (too "cooked"-tasting), and a bit of Parmesan for added richness. After returning the meatballs to the pan, a few minutes of simmering was all I needed for perfectly cooked stuffed meatballs in a flavorful sauce.

STUFFED MEATBALLS WITH MARINARA Serves 6

To minimize sticking, use slightly wet hands to roll and form the meatballs in step 2. This recipe makes enough sauce to coat 1 pound of pasta; these meatballs also make great subs.

- ¾ cup panko bread crumbs
- 1½ ounces Parmesan cheese, grated (¾ cup)
- 2 large eggs
- ¼ cup chopped fresh basil
- 3 garlic cloves, minced
  Salt and pepper
- 4 ounces sweet Italian sausage, casings removed
- 1¼ pounds 85 percent lean ground beef
- 3 (4½-inch-long) sticks mozzarella string cheese
- 2 tablespoons olive oil
- ½ cup finely chopped onion
- 1 teaspoon dried oregano
- 1 (28-ounce) can crushed tomatoes

1. Combine panko, ½ cup Parmesan, eggs, 2 tablespoons basil, half of garlic, 1 teaspoon salt, and ½ teaspoon pepper in large bowl. Add sausage and knead with your hands until incorporated into panko mixture. Add beef and knead until just incorporated. (Do not overmix or meatballs will be tough.) Using greased ¼-cup dry measuring cup, divide meat mixture into 15 portions and place on plate.

2. Cut mozzarella sticks crosswise into fifteen ¾-inch cubes (each stick should yield 5 cubes). Place 1 mozzarella cube in center of each meat portion and pinch meat around cheese to enclose. Roll meat between wet hands to form completely sealed meatball. Place stuffed meatballs on plate and refrigerate for 30 minutes or cover and refrigerate for up to 24 hours.

3. Heat oil in 12-inch nonstick skillet over medium-high heat until just smoking. Add meatballs and cook until browned on 1 side, about 3 minutes. Flip meatballs and cook until browned on opposite side, about 3 minutes. Transfer meatballs to plate. (Sides of meatballs will still appear raw.)

4. Discard all but 1 tablespoon fat from skillet and return to medium heat. Add onion and cook until just softened and beginning to brown, about 2 minutes. Add oregano and remaining garlic and cook until fragrant, about 30 seconds. Stir in tomatoes, remaining ¼ cup Parmesan, ¾ teaspoon salt, and ½ teaspoon pepper.

5. Nestle meatballs in sauce with 1 browned side up and bring to boil. Reduce heat to medium-low, cover, and simmer for 4 minutes. Flip meatballs so second browned side is up. Cover and continue to cook for 4 minutes. Remove skillet from heat and let rest, covered, for 5 minutes. Sprinkle with remaining 2 tablespoons basil. Serve.

Omitting the liquid from the panade makes for stronger meatballs that hold their shape, which prevents the cheese from leaking out during cooking.

Kielbasa Casserole

This Polish American casserole too often starts with canned soup.
We wanted to make it from scratch but keep it simple. BY CAROLYNN PURPURA MACKAY

A T A RECENT gathering, I was introduced to kielbasa casserole, a Polish American dish popular in Chicago and other areas of the Midwest that combines kielbasa, potatoes, and sauerkraut in a creamy sauce. It wasn't pretty, but with ingredients like these, I knew it had potential.

Some digging uncovered plenty of recipes for this casserole, all variations on the same idea: Mix sliced potatoes, kielbasa, and sauerkraut with a can of condensed cream of potato soup in a casserole dish, bake for about an hour, and serve. I made several versions—with different varieties of potatoes and different additions including tomato and apple—but found them all underwhelming. They were easy to prepare but dull and gloppy. I wasn't too surprised; condensed soup is frequently to blame for these symptoms.

Luckily for me, the test kitchen has had great success replacing problematic condensed soup in casseroles in the past. I started my next version using a tried-and-true substitute: 1 cup of half-and-half and 3 cups of chicken stock whisked into onion cooked with flour for thickening. I then stirred in cubed russet potatoes (my early tests showed that fluffy russets were best), kielbasa, sauerkraut, and a tablespoon of yellow mustard. I baked the casserole, covered, until the potatoes were tender, about 45 minutes. It was already a huge improvement over the gloppy condensed soup version, but I couldn't claim victory yet. The kielbasa—which is sold precooked—was overdone and spongy, and the sauce lacked complexity. What's more, the flavors of sauerkraut and mustard were almost undetectable. The dish was bland.

To bolster the flavor, I reduced the amount of half-and-half to ½ cup (and supplemented it with ½ cup more chicken stock). I also browned the kielbasa to add flavor and then sautéed the

We build flavor by slicing and browning the kielbasa before it goes into the casserole.

onion in the kielbasa-flavored oil along with some caraway seeds, which I'd seen used in some recipes. I doubled the mustard and, at the urging of my tasters, stirred in a couple of teaspoons of fresh dill for another dose of flavor. Finally, rather than risk overcooking the kielbasa

in the oven, I parbaked the casserole to soften the potatoes and then (carefully) stirred in the kielbasa near the end to reduce its cooking time.

I was close to the goal line. The flavor was complex and the kielbasa texture was markedly improved. But stirring the kielbasa into the hot casserole dish was unwieldy. Was there a way to reduce the oven time so that all the ingredients could be added to the casserole dish at once without overcooking the kielbasa? Yes. Giving the potatoes a head start on the stovetop—just 15 minutes did the trick—allowed me to combine all the casserole ingredients in one stir and bake for just 15 minutes.

I felt triumphant, but I knew that my dish needed one last thing—texture. Why

not a crunchy topping? Bread crumbs crisped in the oven added just the right touch. A last sprinkle of fresh dill over the top and my casserole was complete.

KIELBASA CASSEROLE Serves 8 to 10

Wellshire Farms Smoked Polska Kielbasa is our favorite kielbasa. Use russet potatoes here for the best texture.

- 3 tablespoons vegetable oil
- 1½ pounds kielbasa sausage, halved lengthwise and sliced crosswise ½ inch thick
- 1 onion, chopped fine
  Salt and pepper
- ⅛ teaspoon caraway seeds
- ¼ cup all-purpose flour
- 3½ cups chicken broth
- ½ cup half-and-half
- 2 pounds russet potatoes, peeled and cut into ½-inch pieces
- 3 slices hearty white sandwich bread, torn into 1-inch pieces
- 1 pound sauerkraut, squeezed dry (1½ cups)
- 2 tablespoons yellow mustard
- 1 tablespoon chopped fresh dill

1. Adjust oven rack to middle position and heat oven to 400 degrees. Heat 2 tablespoons oil in Dutch oven over medium heat until just smoking. Add kielbasa and cook, stirring occasionally, until spotty brown, about 5 minutes. Using slotted spoon, transfer kielbasa to paper towel–lined plate, leaving fat in pot.

2. Add onion, 1¼ teaspoons salt, ½ teaspoon pepper, and caraway seeds to fat in pot and cook until just softened, about 3 minutes. Stir in flour to coat onion and cook for 1 minute. Slowly whisk in broth and half-and-half until incorporated. Add potatoes and bring to boil. Reduce heat to medium-low and simmer, stirring occasionally, until potatoes are just tender, about 15 minutes.

3. Meanwhile, pulse bread, remaining 1 tablespoon oil, ½ teaspoon salt, and ¼ teaspoon pepper in food processor until coarsely ground, about 7 pulses; set aside.

4. Off heat, stir sauerkraut, mustard, 2 teaspoons dill, and kielbasa into pot. Transfer mixture to 13 by 9-inch baking dish and sprinkle bread crumbs evenly over top. Bake until crumbs are golden brown and edges of casserole are bubbling, 12 to 15 minutes. Sprinkle with remaining 1 teaspoon dill. Let cool for 15 minutes. Serve.

KEY INGREDIENT **Kielbasa**
The test kitchen's taste test winning product, Wellshire Farms Smoked Polska Kielbasa, does not contain nitrates or nitrites and thus lacks the pink hue of most other kielbasas. Our tasters praised this all-pork kielbasa's "deeply smoked" and "distinctive garlicky" flavor. The natural pork casing also provides a satisfying "snap" when you bite into it.

TOP ROPE
Wellshire Farms makes our favorite kielbasa.

Bee Sting Cake

A bread-like base, a custard filling, and a crown with crunch—there's a lot to like about this gorgeous cake. We set out to re-create the buzz that once surrounded it. BY REBECCAH MARSTERS

UNLESS YOU'RE LUCKY enough to be of a certain age and to have grown up in Queens, N.Y., or the Manhattan neighborhood of Yorkville, where it was once a core item in the local German bakeries (or you're a total cake geek who reads every baking blog you can find), you probably haven't heard of *bienenstich*, or bee sting cake. It's a brioche-like cake filled with pastry cream under an almond-honey crown. This dessert is so irresistible, as the story goes, that the baker who first made it was stung by a bee that flew in his open window, lured by the sugary-sweet topping.

Recipes for the cake aren't easy to find—in American cookbooks, at least—but I managed to dig up a few that seemed promising. All concurred on a few points. First, bee sting cake always contains flour, milk, sugar, yeast, and butter, but measurements diverge from recipe to recipe. Second, the topping always includes honey, butter, and sliced almonds, but some versions supplement the honey with brown or white sugar, and a few throw in cream. The vanilla pastry cream is undisputed, so I'd just need to perfect it.

With these parameters set, I was ready to bake. At the end of a marathon day of mixing, kneading, baking, and filling, I lined up five versions of bee sting cake, and even before taking a bite, I could see the appeal. Whether square or round, tall or squat, each cake had a burnished, deep-brown crown of almonds on top. But my tasters did have a few requests. They preferred a lightly sweetened cake but wished it were a little richer. They wanted a cream filling that didn't run and a light, crunchy topping rather than a gooey one. Finally, round cakes were preferred to square.

Back in the kitchen, I used our favorite cake from the initial test as a starting point, baking it without a topping for now. While most of the recipes call for creaming the butter and sugar together in the stand mixer as you would for cake batter, I found that this sticky dough was better suited to the test kitchen's brioche method: mixing the dry ingredients (flour, salt, yeast, and a bit of sugar), adding the milk and eggs, and then kneading in the softened butter 1 tablespoon at a time. Traditional yeasted doughs need two rises—one right after

The sweet, crackly topping is spread on the brioche-like cake before baking.

mixing and one after shaping. This cake was no exception, so after letting the dough rise for about an hour, I pressed it into a cake pan, pierced it all over with a fork to eliminate the largest air bubbles, and let it sit until it was puffy. About half an hour in a 350-degree oven did the trick.

Now for a bit more decadence. I upped the butter in my recipe until the cake tasted sufficiently rich and then

added an extra egg yolk for good measure. This once-good base was now great. Time to top it. I melted butter and honey together on the stovetop and stirred in sliced almonds before spreading the mixture over the proofed dough in the pan. This topping turned out a bit chewy, but a few tests showed that adding just 2 tablespoons of granulated sugar took care of that problem—with this addition, the almonds came out shiny and pleasingly

brown with a delicate crunch.

Now for the filling. Most of the pastry creams in the initial recipes were runny and soaked right into the cakes, all but disappearing, and those that had the right texture were spread too thin. I'd begin with the test kitchen's existing pastry cream recipe. Doubling the amount of filling in most bee sting cakes, I combined six egg yolks with ½ cup of sugar, a touch of salt, and

After the dough's initial rise, cake construction can begin. Here's how it works:

1. When the dough has doubled in size, press it into a pan, poke it all over with a fork, let it rise again, and cover it with the warm almond topping.

2. Bake the cake and let it cool. Then use a long serrated knife to split it in half horizontally.

3. Spread the chilled pastry cream over the bottom half of the cake.

4. Cut the top half of the cake into wedges and place them, one at a time, on top of the pastry cream to reconstruct the top layer.

¼ cup of cornstarch. I tempered the yolks by slowly stirring hot milk into the egg mixture, and then I cooked the custard on the stovetop until it thickened. I whisked in a few tablespoons of butter and a splash of vanilla and then chilled the pastry cream before layering it into my cooled, split cake. All was well—until I sliced into it. This cake tasted good, but my double layer of pastry cream oozed out the sides and onto the plate. Cutting through the crunchy topping required so much force that it displaced all the soft cream inside.

Obviously if I wanted extra filling (and I did), I'd have to make it extra-sturdy. Sometimes in the test kitchen we stabilize whipped cream with gelatin, so I tried the same thing here, dissolving a teaspoon of bloomed gelatin in the pastry cream. This worked well, but creating clean slices was still a challenge. Luckily, one of the original recipes I'd found, from baker Nick Malgieri, offered an ingenious trick: After spreading the pastry cream onto the bottom cake layer, he sliced the cake top into wedges before layering it on top of the pastry cream. The idea was that this would make it easy to slice through the filling and bottom layer, using the top layer as a guide. When I tried it, the slices came out neat and tidy, and the pastry cream stayed put.

Tender, lightly sweet cake; thick, creamy filling; and a crisp almond-brittle topping—was it irresistible? I sure thought so, and I'd be keeping the window shut just in case.

BEE STING CAKE Serves 12

We developed this cake using a light-colored cake pan, which we prefer for this recipe. If your pan is dark, start checking the cake after 25 minutes in step 7. If the sides of your cake pan are less than 2½ inches high, bake the cake on a foil-lined rimmed baking sheet to catch drips. Plan ahead: The pastry cream and dough require at least 3 hours of prep time.

PASTRY CREAM
- 1 teaspoon unflavored gelatin
- 1 tablespoon water
- 6 large egg yolks
- ½ cup (3½ ounces) sugar
- ¼ teaspoon salt
- 1¾ cups milk
- ¼ cup (1 ounce) cornstarch
- 2 tablespoons unsalted butter
- 1 tablespoon vanilla extract

CAKE
- ¾ cup milk
- 1 large egg plus 2 large yolks
- 2¾ cups (13¾ ounces) all-purpose flour
- ¼ cup (1¾ ounces) sugar
- 2¼ teaspoons instant or rapid-rise yeast
- ½ teaspoon salt
- 8 tablespoons unsalted butter, cut into 8 pieces and softened

TOPPING
- 4 tablespoons unsalted butter
- ¼ cup honey
- 2 tablespoons sugar
- ⅛ teaspoon salt
- ⅔ cup blanched sliced almonds

1. FOR THE PASTRY CREAM: Sprinkle gelatin over water in small bowl and let sit until gelatin softens, about 5 minutes. Whisk egg yolks, sugar, and salt in medium bowl until pale yellow. Whisk ¼ cup milk and cornstarch into egg mixture until smooth. Heat remaining 1½ cups milk in medium saucepan over medium heat until hot but not simmering. Slowly whisk hot milk into egg mixture.

2. Transfer egg mixture back to saucepan and cook over medium-low heat, whisking constantly, until mixture thickens to pudding consistency, about 5 minutes. Off heat, vigorously whisk in gelatin mixture until dissolved. (If pastry cream is lumpy, strain through fine-mesh strainer.) Transfer pastry cream to clean bowl and whisk in butter and vanilla. Cover and refrigerate until firm, at least 3 hours or up to 24 hours.

3. FOR THE CAKE: Grease large bowl. Whisk milk and egg and yolks together in 2-cup liquid measuring cup until combined. Using stand mixer fitted with dough hook, mix flour, sugar, yeast, and salt together on medium-low speed until combined, about 5 seconds. With mixer running, slowly add milk mixture and knead until cohesive dough forms and no dry flour remains, 3 to 5 minutes, scraping down bowl and dough hook as needed.

4. With mixer still running, add butter 1 piece at a time until incorporated. Continue kneading until dough is uniformly combined, 8 to 10 minutes (dough will be sticky and will not completely clear sides of bowl). Turn out dough onto lightly floured counter and knead until smooth, about 1 minute. Form dough into tight ball and transfer to greased bowl, turning to coat. Cover with plastic wrap and let rise at room temperature until nearly doubled in size, 1 to 1½ hours.

5. Grease light-colored 9-inch round cake pan, line with parchment paper, and grease parchment. Transfer dough to lightly floured counter and press into 9-inch round. Transfer dough to

prepared pan and press in even layer to edges of pan. Using fork, poke dough all over. Cover pan loosely with plastic and let rise at room temperature until puffy, 35 to 50 minutes. (After rising, dough and pan can be wrapped tightly in plastic and refrigerated for up to 24 hours. Let dough come to room temperature before baking.)

6. FOR THE TOPPING: Meanwhile, bring butter, honey, sugar, and salt to boil in small saucepan over medium heat, stirring often. Once boiling, stir in almonds and remove from heat.

7. Adjust oven rack to middle position and heat oven to 350 degrees. Spread almond mixture evenly over top of dough. Bake until topping is deep golden brown, 30 to 40 minutes, rotating pan halfway through baking. Let cake cool in pan on wire rack for 20 minutes. Remove cake from pan and let cool completely on rack, about 2 hours.

8. Stir chilled pastry cream with fork to loosen. Transfer cake to cutting board topping side up. Using long serrated knife, split cake in half horizontally. Transfer cake bottom to serving platter and spread pastry cream evenly over cut side. Cut cake top into 12 wedges and reassemble on top of pastry cream. To serve, use cuts in top layer as guide to slice cake into 12 pieces.

Cooking Class Easy Rustic Bread

With some revolutionary techniques, making your own rustic bread can be a mostly hands-off affair. We show you how to get crusty, chewy, flavorful homemade bread with minimal effort and fuss. BY REBECCAH MARSTERS

Yeast Primer

Buying, Storing, Using

Yeast is a living organism that feeds on sugar and starch. Fresh yeast (or cake yeast), which you probably won't come across in the grocery store, consists of drained and compressed yeast cells with about 70 percent water by weight. It's highly potent, fast, and reliable but also highly perishable and impractical for most home baking.

The two kinds of yeast you'll see in the grocery store are active dry yeast and instant or rapid-rise yeast. Both have been reduced to 95 percent dry matter for stability. Active dry yeast must be dissolved in a warm liquid before use, whereas instant yeast can simply be mixed directly into other ingredients, making it our first choice for most breads and baked goods. Both instant and active dry yeast are sold in ¼-ounce packets, each containing about 2¼ teaspoons of yeast, but don't rely on the packets to be perfectly accurate—always measure yourself.

Anything higher than 120 degrees will kill yeast, so avoid adding hot liquids to your dough. Keep your dry yeast in the refrigerator or freezer, where it will last for almost two years unopened.

Good to know: To substitute active dry yeast for instant, use 25 percent more active dry (if the recipe calls for 1 teaspoon of instant yeast, use 1¼ teaspoons of active dry) and dissolve it in a portion of the recipe's liquid that's been heated to 110 degrees.

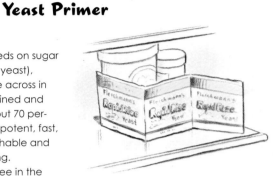

KEEP IT COLD

MEASURE FOR ACCURACY

WATCH THE HEAT

TEST KITCHEN TIPS
FOR ANY
YEASTED BREAD

Core Techniques

Maximize Gluten Development

To achieve the proper texture in a loaf of bread, gluten development is essential, but there's more than one way to go about it. The traditional technique involves physical manipulation, or kneading, during which the proteins link together to form gluten.

In our recipe, we replace elbow grease with a process called autolysis. As the dough sits at room temperature (covered) for 8 to 18 hours, enzymes naturally present in the wheat cut the proteins into smaller segments that link up readily, which means that less than a minute of kneading is sufficient to form enough gluten to make a pleasantly chewy rustic bread.

Develop (or Add) Complex Flavor

Good bakery bread has a distinctly yeasty, slightly sour flavor, which comes from a fermented starter that contains a varied assortment of yeasts. You can certainly make or purchase your own starter, but we found an easier way: beer. Adding a mild lager to our dough produces carbon dioxide, alcohol, and sulfur compounds, which together create a subtle yeasty flavor. And a tablespoon of vinegar mimics the tang of acetic acid produced by a bakery starter's bacteria.

Take Your Time

Resting the dough for a minimum of 8 hours before shaping is essential for proper hydration and gluten formation. For the rising after shaping, look for visual and tactile cues: The dough should be puffed—nearly double its original volume—and a fingertip depression in the dough should fill in slowly, not bounce back immediately. When baking, we leave nothing to chance and use the interior temperature of the loaf as our measure of doneness; 210 degrees is the optimum temperature for perfectly cooked rustic bread that has a nice crust and tender-but-chewy interior.

STEP BY STEP Ten Steps to Easy Rustic Bread

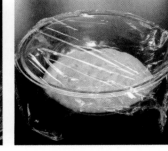

1. HAND-MIX INGREDIENTS
Combine flour, yeast, and salt; then stir in water, beer, and vinegar and fold it all together. No mixer required.
WHY? This bread will form gluten as it sits, so there's no need for a lot of mixing at the start.

2. LET REST Cover the bowl with plastic wrap and let it sit on the counter for at least 8 hours or up to 18 hours.
WHY? Much like kneading, letting the dough sit develops gluten through a process called autolysis (see "Maximize Gluten Development").

3. PREPARE PARCHMENT
Spray an 18 by 12-inch sheet of parchment paper lightly with vegetable oil spray.
WHY? You'll use the parchment to move the dough from the counter to the Dutch oven for its second rise, and to remove the bread from the pot after baking.

4. KNEAD DOUGH Transfer the dough to a floured counter and knead it just 10 to 15 times.
WHY? During the long rest, the proteins in the dough break down, making it easier to manipulate, and with less than a minute of kneading, the gluten has been sufficiently developed.

5. SHAPE AND LET RISE Form the dough into a ball, place it on the parchment, and transfer it to a Dutch oven. Then cover it and let it rise for 2 hours.
WHY? Once shaped, the dough undergoes its final rise, during which the yeast produces carbon dioxide to make the dough puff.

A covered Dutch oven helps give this bread its flavorful, chewy crust.

ALMOST NO-KNEAD BREAD

Makes 1 large round loaf

Use a mild-flavored lager, such as Budweiser (nonalcoholic lager also works). In step 3, start the 30-minute timer as soon as you put the bread in the cold oven. Don't wait until the oven has preheated to start the timer or the bread will burn. The bread is best eaten the day it is baked, but it can be wrapped in foil and stored for up to two days.

- 3 cups (15 ounces) all-purpose flour
- 1½ teaspoons salt
- ¼ teaspoon instant or rapid-rise yeast
- ¾ cup plus 2 tablespoons water, room temperature
- 6 tablespoons mild-flavored lager
- 1 tablespoon distilled white vinegar
  Vegetable oil spray

1. Whisk flour, salt, and yeast together in large bowl. Add water, lager, and vinegar. Using rubber spatula, fold mixture, scraping up dry flour from bottom of bowl, until shaggy ball forms. Cover bowl with plastic wrap and let sit at room temperature for at least 8 hours or up to 18 hours.

2. Lay 18 by 12-inch sheet of parchment paper on counter and spray with oil spray. Transfer dough to lightly floured counter and knead 10 to 15 times. Shape dough into ball by pulling edges into middle. Transfer dough, seam side down, to center of parchment and spray surface of dough with oil spray. Pick up dough by lifting parchment overhang and lower into heavy-bottomed Dutch oven (let any excess parchment hang over pot edge). Cover loosely with plastic and let rise at room temperature until dough has doubled in size and does not readily spring back when poked with finger, about 2 hours.

3. Adjust oven rack to middle position. Remove plastic from pot. Lightly flour top of dough and, using razor blade or sharp knife, make one 6-inch-long, ½-inch-deep slit along top of dough. Cover pot and place in oven. Heat oven to 425 degrees. Bake bread for 30 minutes.

4. Remove lid and continue to bake until loaf is deep brown and registers 210 degrees, 20 to 30 minutes longer. Using parchment overhang, carefully remove bread from pot; transfer to wire rack and let cool completely, about 2 hours.

ALMOST NO-KNEAD CRANBERRY-PECAN BREAD

Add ½ cup dried cranberries and ½ cup toasted pecan halves to flour mixture in step 1.

ALMOST NO-KNEAD OLIVE, ROSEMARY, AND PARMESAN BREAD

Add 2 cups grated Parmesan and 1 tablespoon minced fresh rosemary to flour mixture in step 1. Add ½ cup chopped pitted green olives to dry ingredients with water, lager, and vinegar in step 1.

ALMOST NO-KNEAD SEEDED RYE BREAD

Substitute 1 cup rye flour for 1 cup all-purpose flour. Add 2 tablespoons caraway seeds to flour mixture in step 1.

6. SLASH DOUGH Use a sharp knife or razor to cut one 6-inch-long, ½-inch-deep slit along the top of the dough.
WHY? Slashing the dough allows steam to escape so the loaf bakes evenly, preventing splits and cracks.

7. COVER UP Place the cover on the pot.
WHY? The covered pot produces a steamy environment that gives the loaf an open crumb structure.

8. START IT COLD Place the covered pot in a cold oven. Heat the oven to 425 degrees and bake the bread for 30 minutes.
WHY? Starting the bread in a cold oven ensures against burning the bottom, and the bread rises just as much as in a preheated oven.

9. REMOVE COVER Uncover the pot and continue to bake the bread until it is deep brown and its center registers 210 degrees, 20 to 30 minutes more.
WHY? After the steamy environment has created the ideal interior texture, uncovering the pot allows the crust to brown and crisp.

10. LET COOL AND SERVE Remove the bread from the pot and place it on a rack to cool for about 2 hours before slicing.
WHY? There's still a lot of moisture trapped inside the hot bread. As the bread sits, the steam escapes giving the cooled loaf just the right texture.

Slow Cooker Roast Beef with Mushroom Gravy

We had our doubts. But if you use a few tricks, your slow cooker can produce a perfectly pink roast beef—with a rich, thick mushroom gravy, too. BY DIANE UNGER

MEDIUM-RARE ROAST BEEF from the slow cooker? Not possible, I thought. Slow cookers are perfect for fatty, collagen-laden cuts like chuck roast, for which the goal is fall-apart-tender meat. A roast beef with a nicely browned exterior and a perfect pink interior cooks in a dry environment—an oven. But I'd been issued a challenge: to slow-cook a leaner, more economical cut (like a top or bottom round or an eye round) to an internal temperature of 125 degrees and achieve a beautifully seared roast that cut easily into thin slices of pink meat. And I needed to create a rich brown mushroom gravy while I was at it.

I quickly decided to use an eye-round roast, an economical cut that, unlike top and bottom rounds, has a uniform shape, which is important for even cooking. But an eye round lacks the depth of flavor found in cuts laced with more fat; I knew that it would need a boost. An early test proved that seasoning the beef just before cooking produced a dull, slightly livery flavor, so I drew on a technique that we often use in the test kitchen: salting the beef generously and letting it sit in the refrigerator overnight, which gives the salt a chance to penetrate the meat and enhance its flavor throughout.

> ▶ Every slow-cooker recipe we publish is available to our Web members. Visit CooksCountry.com/ slowcooker for more than 50 of our best.

A quick survey of existing recipes revealed very few that targeted medium-rare. And for good reason: After several hours in a slow cooker (typically our minimum amount of time for a slow-cooker recipe is 4 hours), roasts are inevitably well-done, gray and chewy, and disappointing. But if we simply reduced the cooking time, could we get a uniformly pink roast?

To zero in on cooking time, I started checking my roast's internal temperature with an instant-read thermometer just an hour after starting up the slow cooker. I knew that any more than 125 degrees and I'd lose that beautiful pink hue. At about an hour and a half, my roast was in the zone.

But while the interior was a lovely pink, the exterior was unappetizing—a battleship-gray hunk of meat. Was there a way to achieve that beautiful brown exterior? We try hard to minimize

up-front work with our slow-cooker recipes, so I experimented with several other browning tricks: sugar, soy sauce, tomato paste mixed with soy, and even Gravy Master, a commercial browning and seasoning sauce. In a four-way test for my tasters, none of these techniques came close to satisfying like a preseared roast, which looked and tasted much better than the others. I decided that a stovetop sear before putting the beef in the slow cooker was worth the extra step.

On to the gravy, which I was determined to create in the slow cooker itself to minimize post-roast work. But because the mushrooms and chopped onion were going into the slow cooker cold, the gravy had a raw, underdeveloped flavor without much muscle. Was there a way to impart richer flavor to the gravy vegetables before they went into the mix? Browning onions and mushrooms in a pan, scraping up the browned bits they leave behind, and stirring them into the mix is the best method for adding depth of flavor; the same holds true for tomato paste. As

long as I was searing the meat ahead of time, why not have the gravy ingredients pay a visit to the sauté pan as well?

After I'd situated the meat in the slow cooker, I tossed the cremini mushrooms, onion, and tomato paste into the pan to brown for about 5 minutes. To thicken the concoction, I stirred in 2 tablespoons of flour (which tasters preferred to cornstarch or tapioca) and then deglazed the pan with beef broth, carefully scraping the browned bits into the broth. Dried porcini mushrooms and fresh thyme completed the mixture. Once it came to a boil, I carefully poured it around (not over) the roast. By the time the roast was done, the gravy, with its browned vegetables and added fond, was thick and flavorful. A couple of tablespoons of butter whisked into the warm gravy just before serving introduced richness and gloss.

I may have been skeptical at the onset of my testing, but I (like my tasters) was pleasantly surprised by the results. Medium-rare roast beef and a rich mushroom gravy from the slow cooker is not only possible but delicious.

Browning the beef—and the vegetables for the gravy—in a skillet before adding them to the slow cooker builds a base of deep flavor.

SLOW-COOKER ROAST BEEF WITH MUSHROOM GRAVY
Serves 6 to 8

Trim all visible fat from the surface of the roast. Note that the roast needs to rest for at least 18 hours after salting. If your roast is less than 4 pounds, begin checking the internal temperature at 1 hour. Take the temperature as quickly as possible.

- 1 (4-pound) boneless beef eye-round roast, trimmed
  Kosher salt and pepper
- 3 tablespoons vegetable oil
- 8 ounces cremini mushrooms, trimmed, halved, and sliced thin
- 1 onion, chopped fine
- 2 tablespoons tomato paste
- 2 tablespoons all-purpose flour
- 1¼ cups beef broth
- ⅛ ounce dried porcini mushrooms, rinsed and minced
- 1 teaspoon minced fresh thyme
- 2 tablespoons unsalted butter
- 2 tablespoons minced fresh parsley

1. Sprinkle roast all over with 4 teaspoons salt. Wrap in plastic wrap and refrigerate for at least 18 hours or up to 24 hours.

2. Pat roast dry with paper towels; rub with 1 tablespoon oil and season with pepper. Heat 1 tablespoon oil in 12-inch nonstick skillet over medium-high heat until just smoking. Sear roast until browned on all sides, about 10 minutes. Set roast in slow cooker.

3. Add remaining 1 tablespoon oil to now-empty skillet and heat over medium-high heat until shimmering. Add cremini mushrooms, onion, tomato paste, and 1 teaspoon salt and cook until vegetables have softened, about 5 minutes. Stir in flour to coat vegetables and cook for 1 minute. Slowly whisk in broth until incorporated, scraping up any browned bits. Add porcini mushrooms and thyme and bring to boil. Pour broth mixture around roast. Cover and cook on low heat until meat registers 125 degrees (for medium-rare), 1½ to 2 hours.

4. Transfer roast to carving board, tent with foil, and let rest for 15 minutes. (Leave slow cooker on "warm" setting to keep gravy hot.) Whisk butter and parsley into gravy and season with salt and pepper to taste. Slice roast thin against grain and serve with gravy.

Cooking for Two Fried Chicken

To make a scaled-down version of fried chicken, we had to take the "deep" out of frying.

BY CHRISTIE MORRISON

THE BEST FRIED chicken combines an ultracrunchy coating with supermoist meat. Deep-frying the chicken in copious amounts of hot oil—at least 2 quarts—simultaneously crisps the exterior and allows the meat to cook through evenly. This time-tested process can produce enough fried chicken to feed a crowd—and a big mess in the kitchen. To make fried chicken doable for a weeknight meal for two, I knew I'd have to make it not just quicker, but cleaner.

First, I considered the deep-frying method. Most recipes call for filling a Dutch oven with anywhere from 2 to 3 quarts of oil to allow the food to be fully submerged. Moving to a smaller vessel seemed like a natural starting point; a smaller footprint would require less oil to submerge the chicken. Unfortunately, a standard 4-quart saucepan wasn't large enough to accommodate four chicken thighs or two bone-in breasts at once. Since cooking more than one batch of chicken seemed unnecessarily fussy for just two people, the saucepan was out. The chicken fit perfectly in our 10-inch skillet, but given its significantly lower sides, there was no way to fully submerge the chicken without the oil level being dangerously high.

Was it essential that the chicken be completely submerged, I wondered? As long as the oil level was high enough to reach all exposed parts of the skin

TEST KITCHEN DISCOVERY
Shallow-Fried Chicken
We use just 1½ cups of frying oil so that only half of the chicken is submerged at a time.

LESS CHICKEN = LESS OIL
When frying chicken for two, we shallow-fry.

Our crisp, moist Fried Chicken for Two is on the table in less than an hour.

during some part of the cooking process, couldn't I flip the chicken and just as effectively fry both sides? In successive tests, I reduced the amount of oil in the pan from 2½ cups to 1½ cups—just under ½ inch deep—and found that I could get perfect browning on all parts of the chicken pieces. But while the depth of the oil was adequate for browning, it didn't promote even cooking in the way that fully submerging chicken in oil did. I needed to trap the heat (and steam) in the pan so that the meat could cook through as the coating was browning. Covering the pan for the first half of cooking jump-started the process as well as contained the spattering oil. After turning the pieces over, I let them cook uncovered to ensure that the exposed coating wouldn't become soggy.

Content with my cooking method, I could examine the other part of the fried chicken equation: the composition of the coating. Thick batters were out since they tended to stick to the bottom of the skillet and burn. I scanned our archive for a coating that would work

in this new frying setup. One favorite recipe called for adding a few tablespoons of buttermilk to a seasoned flour mixture to form shaggy bits that added extra crunch to the chicken. It was a simple approach with the promise of a great exterior. But first I needed to dip the chicken in some kind of liquid to help the coating stick. We liked the flavor and texture of buttermilk best—its thick consistency had the best binding power—but we found that half-and-half was a close second, so you can use that if it's more convenient. As for flavorings, a blend of garlic powder, thyme, and cayenne pepper combined with a healthy dose of salt gave the chicken plenty of kick.

From start to finish (including a 30-minute rest in the refrigerator after applying the coating), my fried chicken for two takes less than an hour and uses a fraction of the oil called for in traditional fried chicken recipes. Don't get me wrong: Fried chicken is still an indulgence, but now it's one that you can enjoy for dinner even if it's just the two of you.

FRIED CHICKEN FOR TWO
We prefer the flavor of buttermilk in this recipe, but half-and-half also works well. Do not substitute regular milk. This recipe was engineered to work with a 10-inch skillet; if you use a skillet of a different size, you will need to adjust the amount of oil.

- 4 (5- to 7-ounce) bone-in chicken thighs, trimmed, or 2 (10- to 12-ounce) bone-in split chicken breasts, trimmed and halved crosswise
  Salt and pepper
- 1¼ cups all-purpose flour
- 1 teaspoon baking powder
- 1 teaspoon garlic powder
- ½ teaspoon dried thyme
- ¼ teaspoon cayenne pepper
- ½ cup buttermilk
- 1½ cups peanut or vegetable oil

1. Season chicken with 2 teaspoons salt and ½ teaspoon pepper. Combine flour, baking powder, garlic powder, thyme, cayenne, 2 teaspoons salt, and 1 teaspoon pepper in shallow dish. Add 2 tablespoons buttermilk to flour mixture and rub together with your fingers until liquid is incorporated and shaggy pieces form. Place remaining 6 tablespoons buttermilk in second shallow dish.

2. Set wire rack inside rimmed baking sheet. Working with 1 piece at a time, dip chicken in buttermilk to thoroughly coat, letting excess drip back into dish; then dredge chicken in flour mixture, pressing to adhere. Transfer chicken to prepared wire rack. Refrigerate for 30 minutes to 1 hour.

3. Line large plate with paper towels. Add oil to 10-inch skillet until it measures about ½ inch deep and heat over medium heat to 350 degrees. Add chicken to hot oil, skin side down. Cover and fry until deep golden brown, 6 to 8 minutes, checking for even browning and rearranging pieces as needed halfway through frying. Adjust burner, if necessary, to maintain oil temperature around 300 degrees.

4. Turn chicken pieces over and continue to fry, uncovered, until chicken is deep golden brown on second side and thighs register 175 degrees or breasts register 160 degrees, 6 to 10 minutes longer. Transfer chicken to prepared plate and let cool for 5 minutes, flipping once to evenly blot away oil. Serve.

The classic version of this rich, creamy layered Greek casserole is easy to love.
Could we say the same for the lower-fat version? BY CRISTIN WALSH

PASTITSIO, OTHERWISE KNOWN as Greek lasagna, has it all: a saucy macaroni and cheese bottom layer, a tomato-based meat sauce flavored with oregano and cinnamon sandwiched in the middle, and more cheese sauce slathered on top. But finding out how much fat and calories this diner classic boasted ruined my love affair with it. Each serving contains a whopping 790 calories and 49 grams of fat. But to never enjoy this delicious casserole again would be a tragedy, and the Greeks have plenty of those already. Instead, I set out to make a healthier version.

Greek lasagna starts with béchamel, a butter-and-flour-thickened dairy sauce, to which cheese—Parmesan or Pecorino Romano usually stands in for the traditional Greek kasseri cheese—has been added. This fat-laden cheese sauce is then divided, with half dedicated to saucing the ½ pound of pasta for the mac and cheese layer, while the other half is mixed with Greek yogurt (and sometimes eggs) to create the tangy top layer. Next, ground lamb or beef, or both, is cooked into a tomato-based sauce with warm spices and aromatics for the middle section. Once assembled, this casserole is baked until browned. It's really good.

Trying existing low-fat recipes for this diner classic proved fruitless. Invariably the leaner béchamel lacked flavor or became separated or both, and meat sauces made with low-fat ground beef or turkey were bland and chewy. Since these recipes were disappointing, I decided to try my own hand at chipping away at the full-fat recipe, hoping that some of our established test kitchen tricks could come to my rescue.

I started with the meat sauce, trying 93 percent lean ground turkey as an alternative to the fatty beef or lamb. This slashed the fat and calories, all right, but it also slashed the meaty flavor. To put back some of that flavor while keeping the calories low, I turned to mushrooms, which contain plenty of meaty flavor. I sautéed ground mushrooms along with an onion; added the traditional garlic, cinnamon, oregano, and tomato paste when the onion softened; and then poured in a can of tomato sauce before adding the turkey. Now the flavor was great, but the lean

Ground turkey, fortified with meaty-tasting sautéed mushrooms, stands in for the usual ground beef (or lamb) in our lighter Pastitsio.

turkey was pebbly and chewy. Turning to a test kitchen technique often used to tenderize meatballs, I added a panade of white bread and low-fat milk to the ground turkey before cooking. It worked. The meat sauce tasted meaty and rich and had a great texture. Now I could turn my focus to the cheese sauce.

I figured I had a good starting point. When one of my test kitchen colleagues wanted to cut calories and fat in a macaroni and cheese recipe a while back, she ditched the butter-based béchamel sauce for a more waistline-friendly sauce thickened with cornstarch. I followed suit and, while I was at it, tried using skim milk in place of whole. I sautéed the garlic in olive oil before adding 4½ cups of skim milk, bringing it to a simmer, and then stirring in a slurry of ½ cup of skim milk and 1 tablespoon of cornstarch to thicken it. The result was awful—a watery, broken mess. Not giving up, I tried other low-fat dairy options in combination with added cornstarch, finally landing on 1½ cups (one 12-ounce can) of low-fat evapo-

rated milk and 3½ cups of 2 percent low-fat milk combined with 2½ tablespoons of cornstarch. The small amount of additional fat in the low-fat milk, plus the high viscosity of the low-fat evaporated milk, was just enough to create a sauce that held together well and tasted richer and creamier to boot.

With my calorie and fat numbers in check, I was able to keep a generous 1¼ cups of grated cheese for the sauce, opting to use Pecorino for its assertive flavor. I tossed half of the sauce with elbow macaroni and the other half with low-fat Greek yogurt. Though full-fat versions often incorporate egg for the tangy top layer, we ditched the high-calorie addition and tried it sans egg. The top layer was thinner than usual, but it was no less velvety and rich, and it came out of the oven evenly browned and bubbly. With tasters conveying their approval with second helpings, there was nothing second-rate about this Greek lasagna, despite the fact that it has less than one-fourth the fat of the original.

The Numbers

Nutritional information is for one serving.

Traditional Greek Lasagna
CALORIES **790**
FAT **49 g**
SATURATED FAT **15 g**

Cook's Country Reduced-Fat Greek Lasagna
CALORIES **370**
FAT **11 g**
SATURATED FAT **4.5 g**

REDUCED-FAT PASTITSIO (GREEK LASAGNA)

Serves 8

The meat sauce can be made and refrigerated up to two days in advance. The béchamel is best made the day of use.

MEAT SAUCE
- 1 pound white mushrooms, trimmed and halved
- 1 slice hearty white sandwich bread, torn into quarters
- 2 tablespoons 2 percent low-fat milk
  Salt and pepper
- 1 pound 93 percent lean ground turkey
- 1 teaspoon olive oil
- 1 onion, chopped fine
- 2 tablespoons tomato paste
- 4 garlic cloves, minced
- 1½ teaspoons dried oregano
- 1 teaspoon ground cinnamon
- 1 (15-ounce) can tomato sauce

PASTA AND BÉCHAMEL
- 8 ounces (2 cups) elbow macaroni
  Salt and pepper
- 3 tablespoons cornstarch
- 3 cups 2 percent low-fat milk
- 1 teaspoon olive oil
- 3 garlic cloves, minced
- 1 (12-ounce) can evaporated skim milk
- 2½ ounces Pecorino Romano cheese, grated (1¼ cups)
- ⅓ cup 2 percent Greek yogurt

1. FOR THE MEAT SAUCE: Process mushrooms in food processor until coarsely chopped, about 10 pulses, scraping down sides of bowl as needed. Transfer mushrooms to bowl; set aside. In now-empty processor, pulse bread,

Making pickles at home can be a real headache. We sought an easier way.

BY ASHLEY MOORE

milk, ½ teaspoon salt, and ½ teaspoon pepper until paste forms, about 8 pulses. Add turkey and pulse until well combined, about 6 pulses.

2. Heat oil in 12-inch skillet over medium heat until shimmering. Add onion, mushrooms, ½ teaspoon salt, and ¼ teaspoon pepper and cook until liquid has evaporated, 8 to 10 minutes. Stir in tomato paste, garlic, oregano, and cinnamon and cook until fragrant and tomato paste turns rust colored, about 1 minute. Stir in tomato sauce. Add turkey mixture and cook, breaking into small pieces with spoon, until no longer pink, about 6 minutes. Remove from heat and set aside.

3. FOR THE PASTA AND BÉCHAMEL: Adjust oven rack to middle position and heat oven to 375 degrees. Bring 2 quarts water to boil in Dutch oven. Add macaroni and ½ tablespoon salt and cook until al dente. Drain in colander, rinse with cold water until cool, and then drain again thoroughly. Transfer macaroni to large bowl.

4. Whisk cornstarch together with ½ cup low-fat milk and set aside. Combine oil and garlic in now-empty pot and set over medium-high heat. Once garlic begins to brown, add evaporated milk and remaining 2½ cups low-fat milk and bring to boil, stirring occasionally to prevent scorching. Whisk cornstarch mixture to recombine, then whisk into pot. Return to boil, whisking constantly, and cook until thickened, about 1 minute. Off heat, whisk in 1 cup Pecorino. Season béchamel with salt and pepper to taste.

5. Grease 13 by 9-inch baking dish with vegetable oil spray. Stir 2 cups béchamel into macaroni until combined. Transfer sauced macaroni to prepared dish. Spread meat sauce over macaroni. Whisk yogurt into remaining béchamel, then pour over meat sauce. Sprinkle pastitsio with remaining ¼ cup Pecorino. Bake until golden brown, 30 to 35 minutes, rotating dish halfway through baking. Let cool for 20 minutes. Serve.

WHEN I THINK of pickling, I envision a harried cook bustling about a steamy, vinegar-scented kitchen, sterilizing jars and filling them with sliced vegetables and hot brine, capping the jars, boiling them again, and carefully inverting them on a towel-covered counter. While there's something appealing about the intricate process, it's also a lot of work. I wanted to make fantastic homemade pickles without breaking a sweat.

The answer was quick pickling, which nets crisp, fresh vegetable pickles with much less time and effort. The basic method is to warm up a mixture of vinegar, water, salt, sugar, and other seasonings and then pour the hot liquid over sliced vegetables stuffed into jars (no sterilization required). The jars are then covered and refrigerated until the pickles are chilled. The quick pickles don't keep nearly as long as traditional pickles, but they don't take nearly as long to make, either—as soon as they've cooled down in the fridge, they're ready to eat.

I started with a tried-and-true test kitchen recipe for bread-and-butter pickles, heating up a brine made of water, sugar, kosher salt, and two vinegars—white wine vinegar and mild rice vinegar—and pouring it over cucumber slices. Fantastic. But a test using just rice vinegar produced very nice pickles, too. Emboldened, I improvised with seasoned rice vinegar, skipping the added salt and sugar. Yes: Bread-and-butter pickles made with just the seasoned rice vinegar were also a success.

Here's the thing about quick pickling: Once you try it and see how easy it is to do (and how easy the pickles are to eat), it's hard to stop. Looking around at other fresh, colorful ingredients, I was inspired to develop recipes for other quick pickles.

Bright orange carrot sticks pickled with fresh tarragon were a crisp, invigorating hit. My tasters also loved a sweet, citrusy pickle of sliced fennel bulb flavored with orange zest.

I came up with a version of *giardiniera*, the Italian pickle-mix of cauliflower, celery, and carrot, that made for an excellent condiment for hot dogs and sandwiches. And a mix of sliced red onion and jalapeño chiles pickled along with lime zest made a great condiment for tacos—or you can eat it straight out of the jar, like I did.

Using seasoned rice vinegar helps us streamline the method for making these fast, easy, delicious pickles.

QUICK BREAD AND BUTTER PICKLES Makes 1 quart
Be sure to use seasoned rice vinegar.

1	pound pickling cucumbers, sliced crosswise ¼ inch thick
5	sprigs fresh dill
1¼	cups seasoned rice vinegar
¼	cup water
2	garlic cloves, peeled and halved
½	teaspoon turmeric
¼	teaspoon black peppercorns
¼	teaspoon yellow mustard seeds

Place cucumbers and dill in 1-quart glass jar with tight-fitting lid. Combine vinegar, water, garlic, turmeric, peppercorns, and mustard seeds in small saucepan and bring to boil. Pour brine into jar, making sure all vegetables are submerged. Let cool completely. Affix jar lid and refrigerate for at least 3 hours before serving. Pickles will keep, refrigerated, for at least 1 week.

QUICK CARROT PICKLES
Substitute 1 pound carrots, peeled and cut into 4 by ½-inch sticks, for cucumbers and 5 sprigs fresh tarragon for dill. Omit turmeric.

QUICK FENNEL PICKLES
Substitute 1 fennel bulb, stalks discarded, bulb halved, cored, and cut crosswise into ¼-inch-thick slices, for cucumbers. Omit dill and turmeric. Add two 1-inch strips orange zest and ½ teaspoon fennel seeds to saucepan with vinegar.

QUICK GIARDINIERA
Substitute 6 ounces cauliflower, cut into 1-inch florets; 1 celery rib, sliced ¼ inch thick; and 1 carrot, sliced ¼ inch thick, for cucumbers. Omit dill and turmeric. Add ½ teaspoon red pepper flakes to saucepan with vinegar.

QUICK RED ONION AND JALAPEÑO PICKLES
Substitute 1 halved and thinly sliced red onion and 2 jalapeños, sliced crosswise into ¼-inch-thick rings, for cucumbers. Omit dill and turmeric. Add two 1-inch strips lime zest and 5 allspice berries to saucepan with vinegar.

Equipment Review Slow Cookers

Slow cookers with jazzy new features promise easier, better food. Would any of them deliver? BY HANNAH CROWLEY

KEY Good ★★★   Fair ★★   Poor ★

SLOW COOKERS HAVE come a long way since Irving Naxon patented the first in 1940. According to market research firm NPD Group Inc., 83 percent of American households now have slow cookers, and usage of the appliance has doubled since the 1980s. But slow cookers have evolved. New on the market: slow cookers that slow down or speed up a recipe's cooking time, models that stir a pot or record a roast's internal temperature, and even a combo model with a stove- and ovensafe crock plus a heated base that's also a warming tray or griddle.

They sound enticing, but are any of these new technologies actually helpful? To find out, we chose seven slow cookers—all digital, all with capacities of 6 to 6½ quarts, and all costing less than $100—and pitted five that have special features against our current winner, the Crock-Pot Countdown Touchscreen Digital, along with a new slow cooker from major brand KitchenAid. We cooked pasta, chicken breasts, chili, and pork loins, evaluating each machine for its special features, as well as for overall even, accurate cooking and usability.

We looked at the most radical design first: the combo cooker. It's a metal pot that sits on a warming plate; the pot is stove- and ovensafe, and the base works as a griddle and warming tray. But like most overachievers, this model spread itself too thin (literally). Its paper-thin metal pot sits right on the heated base, which explains why this cooker scorched most of its food; we tried it on the stove and in the oven with similar results.

Next, we evaluated the two cookers that will shorten or lengthen a recipe's cooking time by revving up or slowing down the heat so that your meal is ready when you choose. The technology sounds convenient, but it came with a host of caveats. Stipulations include: The crock must be two-thirds full, recipes with short cooking times don't work (think desserts, dips, fish, chicken, and pasta), and changing a recipe's cooking time too much may cause tough or delicate cuts of meat to suffer. When we did find a recipe that we could use, the results were mixed. We stretched the cooking time of spareribs, and one cooker made ribs so overcooked that they buckled into a pile, while the second cooker produced ribs that were chewy and underdone. Forgiving dishes like chili were fine, but we found that straying too far from a recipe's published

HIGHLY RECOMMENDED	CRITERIA		TESTERS' NOTES
KITCHENAID 6-Quart Slow Cooker with Solid Glass Lid **Model:** KSC6223SS **Price:** $99.99 **Capacity:** 6 qt **Special Features:** N/A	Cooking Design	★★★ ★★★	This model made juicy and tender chicken, turkey, pork, and chili, and caramelized onions were evenly cooked. Testers liked its bright, intuitive control panel, with tactile buttons and beeps that alert you to changes. Cool-to-the-touch handles were a bonus.
RECOMMENDED			
CROCK-POT Countdown Touchscreen Digital Slow Cooker **Model:** SCVT650-PS **Price:** $89.99 **Capacity:** 6½ qt **Special Features:** Touch screen control panel	Cooking Design	★★½ ★★★	Our previous winner performed admirably again with an easily understood and attractive control panel. It made food well, but it runs slightly hot; in a runoff against our new winner, it scorched caramelized onions and made acceptable, but drier, chicken breasts.
RECOMMENDED WITH RESERVATIONS			
HAMILTON BEACH Set 'n Forget 6 Qt. Programmable Slow Cooker with Spoon/Lid **Model:** 33967 **Price:** $59.99 **Capacity:** 6 qt **Special Features:** Programmable thermometer	Cooking Design	★★½ ★★	This model's thermometer sticks through the lid and into meat. Once the meat reaches a safe temperature, the cooker switches to warming mode. But because it checks the temperature in only one spot and slow cookers often cook unevenly, it frequently shut off before the meat was fully cooked. It had a nice control panel and cooked well without the probe.
CROCK-POT Digital Slow Cooker with iStir Stirring System **Model:** SCCPVC600AS-P **Price:** $69.99 **Capacity:** 6 qt **Special Features:** Stirring mechanism	Cooking Design	★★ ★★	This cooker has a removable stirring system that made rich chili but didn't prevent scorching in a thick pasta dish because it stirs food in only the middle, not at the edges near the heat. It was hard to tell whether the machine was on if we weren't using the brightly lit timer.
CROCK-POT Slow Cooker featuring Smart Cook Technology **Model:** SCCPVM650-PS **Price:** $99.99 **Capacity:** 6½ qt **Special Features:** Lengthens or shortens recipe cooking time	Cooking Design	★½ ★★	This slow cooker had a user-friendly control panel and was the more intuitive of the two time-altering machines, but we still had mixed results. Ribs that we stretched the cooking time for were so tender that they limply fell apart. When we set the time and temperature, this cooker ran slightly hot and testers noted minor scorching.
HAMILTON BEACH IntelliTime 6 Quart Slow Cooker **Model:** 33564 **Price:** $59.99 **Capacity:** 6 qt **Special Features:** Lengthens or shortens recipe cooking time	Cooking Design	★★ ★½	This slow cooker's controls are on one round dial that you spin to set, which testers found counterintuitive because you had to flip through it like a Rolodex searching for the right setting. It cooked food well when we set the time and temperature, but the IntelliTime settings were hit or miss.
NOT RECOMMENDED			
WEST BEND VERSATILITY COOKER **Model:** 84966 **Price:** $79.99 **Capacity:** 6 qt **Special Features:** Removable crock, works in oven and on stovetop; griddle/warming tray base	Cooking Design	★ ★½	This slow cooker's crock is a metal pot that is stove- and ovensafe; its heating base doubles as a griddle and warming tray (though it's too small to do much good). Versatile but unsuccessful, it consistently scorched its contents thanks to a paper-thin pot and a piping-hot heating element.

times yielded unpredictable results.

Then we turned to the cooker with a probe that weaves through a hole in its cover and records the internal temperature of meat; you can program it based on the type, and it will switch to warming mode once a safe temperature is reached. Unfortunately, it tracks the meat in only one spot, so when making pork loin, we speared the thickest part and walked away, only to return later to find the cooker in warming mode and a pork loin with one side still too rare. (Because the heating elements are typically located on the sides of slow cookers, food doesn't cook evenly.)

After that, we tested the iStir, from Crock-Pot, which stirs its contents with a mechanism that clips onto the lid. This cooker is flawed because it stirs the middle of the pot, not the outer contents, which, sitting next to the heating elements in the walls of the cooker, are always the first to scorch. And they did. Finally, we turned to the two remaining slow cookers: the Crock-Pot Countdown Touchscreen Digital and a newer model from KitchenAid. Special features aside, these two models were the most user-friendly, with intuitive controls.

So we decided to put both through a final gauntlet: bulky bone-in turkey

breasts, finicky pasta, delicate boneless, skinless chicken breasts, 10-hour caramelized onions, and whole chickens. Both models made good food, but testers unanimously preferred the KitchenAid because it cooks food more gently and didn't have any hot spots.

None of the new technologies impressed us, but we did find a model that improved slow cooking at its core: With more even cooking and a few perks like satisfyingly clickable buttons, brighter lights, helpful beeps, and cool-to-the-touch handles, the KitchenAid 6-Quart Slow Cooker earned the top spot as our new winning slow cooker.

Taste Test Salted Butter

There are plenty of butters out there. Could we find one worth its salt?

BY LAUREN SAVOIE

THOUGH WE PREFER unsalted butter for most recipes because it allows finer control over flavor and texture, most of the butter sold in the United States is salted. We use salted butter as a condiment for foods like corn on the cob, biscuits, or toast when we want extra-salty, savory flavor. Since most of the times we use salted butter are when butter flavor needs to be front and center, we wondered: Is it worth shelling out more for "premium" salted butter?

To find out, we selected six nationally available products and one top-selling regional product (Challenge Butter, which is available in only 34 states but ranks second in total national sales). We asked 21 America's Test Kitchen staffers to sample the butters plain, spread on crackers, and melted over toast.

We tallied the scores and found that we liked all the butters we tried, but it was clear that some products were in a league of their own. What set the best butters apart? Since all the products in our lineup have simple ingredient lists of just cream and salt, we looked first into the most obvious variable: salt content. But that yielded no answers—tasters scored products with comparable levels of salt vastly differently.

As we examined nutritional labels, we noticed a handful of lower-ranked products with a shield on their box indicating a "Grade AA" rating by the U.S. Department of Agriculture (USDA). Curious why this label was absent from our favorite butters, we contacted Robert Bradley, professor emeritus of food science at the University of Wisconsin. It's often rumored that salted butter is made from lower-quality cream than is unsalted butter, but Bradley quickly dismissed that suggestion and said that the USDA doesn't require manufacturers to grade their butter (or the cream used to make it), and a rating

doesn't necessarily guarantee a better butter. "There's a lot better cream today going into butter manufacturing than we've ever had," he said. "Handling and storage conditions have greater potential for off-flavor development than the quality of the cream used."

Bradley confirmed what we learned from previous butter taste tests: Packaging has a huge impact on butter's flavor potential. "Butter, like any other fat product, is a sponge for off-flavors," he said. If not properly protected, butter quickly absorbs odors from its surroundings—usually whatever else is in the fridge. The majority of butter is packaged in either foil or wax parchment, with foil offering far greater defense from funky odors. "Parchment does next to nothing in protecting the butter," Bradley said. "Those wrappers are as porous as a summer screen on your window."

It wasn't surprising, then, that the butters wrapped in plain parchment landed at the bottom of our rankings. Tasters detected a number of off, "fridge-y" flavors in these butters even though they were well within their expiration dates. Parchment-wrapped butters also had a harder, cheese-like consistency that contrasted with the airy, almost whipped texture we preferred in our top butters. Because parchment offers minimal protection from moisture loss, butters wrapped this way are likely to harden.

Foil fared much better—four of our top five butters are foil-wrapped and tasters deemed them "fresh" and "clean," with a "soft," "rich" texture. The fifth, Land O'Lakes, is packaged in a special FlavorProtect wrapper that looks like plain parchment but contains a patented moisture and air barrier that acts like foil. Though it sounds like a marketing gimmick, Bradley told us that it's actually one of the best wrappers available and remarkably effective at keeping butter fresh. Regardless of packaging, our experts recommend buying butter with an expiration date 4 to 6 months out to minimize storage-related issues.

Not all the funky flavors we noted came from the fridge, though. Tasters were mixed on the "vegetal," "grassy," even "barnyard-y" flavors in a few of our lower-ranked products. Most dairy cooperatives don't require their farmers to pasture-graze their cows, though many farmers may choose to anyway.

A Cultural Impact

Cultured butters are made with cream that is inoculated with bacterial cultures similar to those found in yogurt and cheese. Culturing is most commonly seen in the production of unsalted European butters, and Lurpak, our taste-test winner, is one of the few companies to use the same process on its salted butter.

HIGHLY RECOMMENDED		TASTERS' NOTES
LURPAK Slightly Salted Butter **Price:** $3.59 for 8 oz ($0.45 per oz) **Wrapper:** Foil **Cultured:** Yes **Grass-Fed:** No **Salt:** 1.14%		This Danish import was "creamy" and "rich," with "intense butter flavor" and "spot-on salt." The only product in our lineup made with cultured cream, this "complex," "flowery" butter had a "sharp," "crème fraîche" tanginess that our tasters loved.

RECOMMENDED

KATE'S Homemade Butter **Price:** $4.99 for 1 lb ($0.31 per oz) **Wrapper:** Foil **Cultured:** No **Grass-Fed:** No **Salt:** 1.72%	BEST BUY	This "soft and velvety," "fresh-tasting" butter from Maine was praised for its "simple, classic" creaminess and "great dairy flavor." Tasters loved the "markedly salty," "ocean" notes in this sea-salted butter, which contains the highest percentage of salt in our lineup.
PLUGRÁ European-Style Butter **Price:** $4.99 for 8 oz ($0.62 per oz) **Wrapper:** Foil **Cultured:** No **Grass-Fed:** No **Salt:** 1.50%		American-made with a European name, this butter (from the brand that makes our favorite unsalted butter) was praised for its "sweet caramel notes," "silky-smooth" texture, and "almost spicy" aftertaste. Said one taster: "I'd love this on bread . . . or scones . . . or anything!"
LAND O'LAKES Salted Butter **Price:** $4.49 for 1 lb ($0.28 per oz) **Wrapper:** FlavorProtect Parchment **Cultured:** No **Grass-Fed:** No **Salt:** 1.24%		This best-selling butter had a "remarkably airy," almost "whipped" texture and a "mild," "milky richness" with lots of "dairy flavor." Wrapped in a special protective parchment that kept out any fridge-y aftertastes, this butter was markedly "clean," "fresh," and "bright."
KERRYGOLD Pure Irish Butter **Price:** $4.99 for 8 oz ($0.62 per oz) **Wrapper:** Foil **Cultured:** No **Grass-Fed:** Yes **Salt:** 1.25%		"Tangy," "custardy," and "very rich," this Irish import (made from the milk of all pasture-raised cows) had a pronounced "grassy" earthiness. While too "barnyard-y" for some tasters, most loved its "melt-in-your-mouth," "silky" texture.
CHALLENGE Butter **Price:** $3.15 for 1 lb ($0.20 per oz) **Wrapper:** Parchment **Cultured:** No **Grass-Fed:** No **Salt:** 1.58%		Tasters found this California-made butter "sweet," "nutty," and "almost floral," with a "silky," "cheesy texture." Some detected a "slightly sour," "off-flavor" from this parchment-wrapped butter, though most liked its "rich," "rounded" creaminess.
ORGANIC VALLEY Salted Butter **Price:** $5.99 for 1 lb ($0.37 per oz) **Wrapper:** Parchment **Cultured:** No **Grass-Fed:** Yes **Salt:** 1.05%		"Grassy, herbaceous, complex, and a little funky," this organic butter had a "vivid" yellow color and "farm-fresh" tang. "You can really taste the pasture," said one taster. Some noted "papery," "refrigerator" flavors from its parchment wrapper.

Of the brands we tried, Kerrygold and Organic Valley are the only two cooperatives that claim their butter is made entirely from the milk of cows that are grass-fed for the majority of the year. These butters were herbaceous and earthy but a little too strong for some of our tasters, who favored nuanced, milk-forward butter.

That doesn't mean that we prefer our butter bland, though. Our favorite product, Lurpak Slightly Salted Butter, had a rich, creamy texture and a unique tanginess that set it apart. That's because Lurpak is the only butter in our lineup to undergo a process called "culturing." Tasters overwhelmingly preferred the result—a complex, rich butter with tangy, yogurt-y notes.

So are premium butters worth the price tag? In the end, we couldn't find a bad butter in the bunch and recommended all seven products in our lineup, but one was clearly cream of the crop. As long as you're not baking with it (flavor nuances disappear with prolonged heating), Lurpak Slightly Salted is a rich, decadent butter well worth the splurge.

Heirloom Recipes

You have recipes you treasure—your family's handed them down for generations, and they've earned a place at your table and in your heart. Share! Visit **CooksCountry.com/magazines/home** (or write to Heirloom Recipes, *Cook's Country*, P.O. Box 470739, Brookline, MA 02447) and tell us about them! Include your name and mailing address. **If we print your recipe, you'll receive a free one-year subscription to** *Cook's Country*.

LAZY DAY POT ROAST
Serves 6

This was one of my maternal grandmother's favorite recipes; to her, it was "lazy" because it's so easy. It is in fact simple, but the unusual flavors of marjoram and caraway seeds—not to mention apples—in a pot roast take it out of the ordinary.
John Willoughby, Editorial Director, Magazines

- 1 (4- to 5-pound) boneless beef chuck-eye roast, trimmed and tied at 1-inch intervals
  Salt and pepper
- 2 tablespoons vegetable oil
- 2 onions, halved and sliced thin
- ½ cup cider vinegar
- 2 cups chicken broth
- ¼ cup packed dark brown sugar
- ¼ cup chopped fresh marjoram
- 3 bay leaves
- 1 tablespoon caraway seeds
- 4 Granny Smith apples, peeled, cored, and quartered

1. Adjust oven rack to lower-middle position and heat oven to 300 degrees. Pat beef dry with paper towels and season with salt and pepper. Heat oil in Dutch oven over medium-high heat until just smoking. Add beef and cook until well browned on all sides, about 10 minutes. Transfer to plate.

2. Pour off all but 2 tablespoons fat from pot. Add onions and cook over medium heat, stirring occasionally, until translucent, 5 to 7 minutes. Stir in vinegar, scraping up any browned bits. Stir in broth, sugar, marjoram, bay leaves, and caraway seeds. Add beef, along with any accumulated juices, and bring to simmer. Cover, transfer to oven, and cook until fork slips easily in and out of beef, about 3 hours, flipping beef once halfway through cooking.

3. Transfer beef to carving board and tent loosely with aluminum foil. Let braising liquid settle for 5 minutes, then, using shallow spoon, skim any fat from surface.

4. Bring braising liquid to boil over medium-high heat. Add apples and cook until very tender, about 20 minutes. Using slotted spoon, transfer apples to serving platter. Continue to boil sauce until reduced to about 2½ cups, about 15 minutes longer. Season with salt and pepper to taste.

5. Discard twine, slice beef against grain into ½-inch-thick slices, and transfer to platter with apples. Using slotted spoon, remove onions from braising liquid and spoon over beef. Pour 1½ cups sauce over beef. Serve, passing remaining sauce separately.

COMING NEXT ISSUE

Our holiday menu features an amazing **Porterhouse Steak**, **Butternut Squash Gratin**, and **Milk Chocolate Cheesecake**. Plus we've got the winners of our **Holiday Cookie Contest**, **Indoor BBQ Ribs**, and tons of other great recipes. Join us.

FIND THE ROOSTER!

A tiny version of this rooster has been hidden in the pages of this issue. Write to us with its location and we'll enter you in a random drawing. The first correct entry drawn will win our winning slow cooker, and each of the next five will receive a free one-year subscription to *Cook's Country*. To enter, visit **CooksCountry.com/rooster** by November 30, 2014, or write to Rooster ON14, *Cook's Country*, P.O. Box 470739, Brookline, MA 02447. Include your name and address. Colleen Palmer of Okemos, Michigan, found the rooster in the June/July 2014 issue on page 4 and won a set of our winning dish towels.

WEB EXTRAS

Free for 4 months online at **CooksCountry.com**

Classic Single-Crust Pie Dough
Classic Yellow Bundt Cake
Dakota Bread
Hard Cider Tasting (full story)
Innovative Dish Drying Racks (full story)
Potato Biscuits with Bacon
Yellow Mustard Tasting

READ US ON iPAD

Download the *Cook's Country* app for iPad and start a free trial subscription or purchase a single issue of the magazine. All issues are enhanced with full-color Cooking Mode slide shows that provide step-by-step instructions for completing recipes, plus expanded reviews and ratings. Go to **CooksCountry.com/iPad** to download our app through iTunes.

Follow us on **Pinterest**
pinterest.com/TestKitchen

Follow us on **Twitter**
twitter.com/TestKitchen

Find us on **Facebook**
facebook.com/CooksCountry

Mocha Walnut Bundt Cake

Cozy up to this humble but satisfying Bundt:
A swirled mocha and walnut cake underneath a glaze of chocolate.

To make this cake, you will need:

- **6 ounces bittersweet chocolate, chopped**
- **3 tablespoons water**
- **1 tablespoon instant espresso powder**
- **1 recipe Classic Yellow Bundt Cake* batter**
- **1½ cups walnuts, toasted and chopped fine**
- **6 tablespoons heavy cream**
- **2 tablespoons corn syrup**

FOR THE CAKE: Adjust oven rack to lower-middle position and heat oven to 325 degrees. Grease and flour 12-cup nonstick Bundt pan. Combine 2 ounces chocolate, water, and espresso powder in bowl. Microwave chocolate mixture at 50 percent power, stirring occasionally, until melted and smooth, about 1 minute; let cool slightly. Stir one-third of cake batter into melted chocolate mixture. Stir walnuts into remaining cake batter. Spoon half of walnut batter into prepared pan and smooth top. Spoon half of mocha batter over top and smooth top. Repeat with remaining walnut and mocha batters. Bake until skewer inserted in center of cake comes out clean, about 1 hour, rotating pan halfway through baking. Let cake cool in pan on wire rack for 10 minutes. Remove cake from pan and let cool completely on rack, about 2 hours.

FOR THE GLAZE: Cook cream, corn syrup, and remaining 4 ounces chocolate in small saucepan over medium heat, stirring constantly, until smooth. Set aside to cool until slightly thickened, about 30 minutes. Drizzle glaze over cake and let set for at least 10 minutes. Serve.

▶ *Go to **CooksCountry.com/yellowbundtcake** for our recipe for **Classic Yellow Bundt Cake**.

Inside This Issue

Cook's Country

DECEMBER/JANUARY 2015

Milk Chocolate Cheesecake

Thick-Cut Steaks

Holiday Cookies

Breaded Chicken Cutlets
Step-by-Step Instructions

Football Sandwiches
Perfect Game-Day Snack

Testing Hand Mixers
Speed, Power, or Innovation?

Chicken Shepherd's Pie
New Twist on a Classic

Homemade Stromboli
Quick Trick Stops Leaks

Indoor BBQ Beef Ribs
Texas-Style Short Ribs

Roasted Green Beans
Tender and Flavorful

Best Breakfast Sausage
We Test Seven Products

Chicken Imperial for Two
Simple Enough for a Weeknight

Easy Chocolate Truffles
Five Flavor Variations

CooksCountry.com
$5.95 U.S./$6.95 CANADA

All the recipes we tried for chocolate cheesecake were too dense or had a sour taste. After making dozens of versions, we figured out that switching from dark to milk chocolate was the secret to a creamy, fluffy cheesecake. PAGE 8

Cook's Country

Dear Country Cook,

When I was a kid growing up summers in Vermont, the mailbox was my only connection to the outside world. (Phone calls were party line and local.)

I once ordered a pool toy, an inflatable serpent, from the back of a *Green Lantern* comic book. Every day after milking, I made a run to the mailbox to see if it had arrived.

Those three weeks were a season of imagination. Time stood still. Dust rose up from the dirt road onto the leafy canopy. Workhorses stood fast in their stalls. Rain threatened but storms never came.

Expectation caused the world to hang in midair, like a seventh chord, the strings humming with the present and the future.

We anticipate the holidays. We hope that time will stand still once again, when a mailbox at the end of a dirt road held the promise of worlds unknown.

Cordially,

Christopher Kimball
Founder and Editor, *Cook's Country*

Cook's Country

Founder and Editor Christopher Kimball
Editorial Director Jack Bishop
Editorial Director, Magazines John Willoughby
Executive Editor Tucker Shaw
Managing Editor Scott Kathan
Executive Food Editor Bryan Roof
Senior Editors Hannah Crowley, Lisa McManus, Diane Unger
Test Kitchen Director Erin McMurrer
Associate Editors Shannon Friedmann Hatch, Christie Morrison
Test Cooks Morgan Bolling, Aaron Furmanek, Ashley Moore, Cristin Walsh
Assistant Editors Lauren Savoie, Kate Shannon
Senior Copy Editor Megan Ginsberg
Copy Editor Krista Magnuson
Executive Assistant Christine Gordon
Test Kitchen Manager Leah Rovner
Senior Kitchen Assistants Michelle Blodget, Alexxa Grattan
Kitchen Assistants Maria Elena Delgado, Ena Gudiel
Executive Producer Melissa Baldino
Co-Executive Producer Stephanie Stender
Associate Producer Kaitlin Hammond

Contributing Editors Erika Bruce, Eva Katz, Jeremy Sauer
Consulting Editors Anne Mendelson, Meg Ragland
Science Editor Guy Crosby, PhD
Executive Food Editor, TV, Radio & Media Bridget Lancaster

Managing Editor, Web Christine Liu
Senior Editor, Cooking School Mari Levine
Associate Editors, Web Jill Fisher, Roger Metcalf
Assistant Editor, Web Charlotte Wilder
Senior Video Editor Nick Dakoulas

Design Director Amy Klee
Photography Director Julie Cote
Art Director Susan Levin
Associate Art Director Lindsey Timko
Art Director, Marketing Jennifer Cox
Staff Photographer Daniel J. van Ackere
Color Food Photography Keller + Keller
Styling Catrine Kelty, Marie Piraino
Deputy Art Director, Marketing Melanie Gryboski
Associate Art Director, Marketing Janet Taylor
Designer, Marketing Stephanie Cook
Associate Art Director, Photography Steve Klise

VP, Marketing David Mack
Circulation Director Doug Wicinski
Circulation & Fulfillment Manager Carrie Fethe
Partnership Marketing Manager Pamela Putprush
Marketing Assistant Marina Tomao

Director, Project Management Alice Carpenter
Project Manager Britt Dresser
Development Manager Mike Serio

Chief Operating Officer Rob Ristagno
VP, Digital Products Fran Middleton
VP, New Product Development Michael Burton
Production Director Guy Rochford
Workflow & Digital Asset Manager Andrew Mannone
Senior Color & Imaging Specialist Lauren Pettapiece
Production & Imaging Specialists Heather Dube, Lauren Robbins
Client Services Manager Kate Zebrowski
Sponsorship Sales Associate Morgan Mannino
Senior Controller Theresa Peterson
Customer Loyalty & Support Manager Amy Bootier
Customer Loyalty & Support Reps Jessica Haskin, Andrew Straaberg Finfrock, Juliet Tierney

Director, Retail Book Program Beth Ineson
Retail Sales & Marketing Manager Emily Logan
Human Resources Manager Adele Shapiro
Publicity Deborah Broide

ON THE COVER: *Milk Chocolate Cheesecake*, Keller + Keller, Catrine Kelty
ILLUSTRATION: Greg Stevenson

Follow us on **Pinterest**
pinterest.com/TestKitchen

Follow us on **Twitter**
twitter.com/TestKitchen

Find us on **Facebook**
facebook.com/CooksCountry

Cook's Country magazine (ISSN 1552-1990), number 60, is published bimonthly by Boston Common Press Limited Partnership, 17 Station St., Brookline, MA 02445. Copyright 2014 Boston Common Press Limited Partnership. Periodicals postage paid at Boston, MA. and additional mailing offices. USPS #023453. Publications Mail Agreement No. 40020778. Return undeliverable Canadian addresses to P.O. Box 875, Station A, Windsor, ON N9A 6P2. POSTMASTER: Send address changes to Cook's Country, P.O. Box 6018, Harlan, IA 51593-1518. For subscription and gift subscription orders, subscription inquiries, or change of address notices, visit AmericasTestKitchen.com/support, call 800-526-8447 in the U.S. or 515-248-7684 from outside the U.S., or write to us at Cook's Country, P.O. Box 6018, Harlan, IA 51593-1518. PRINTED IN THE USA.

Contents

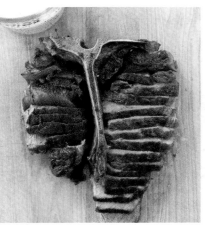

THICK-CUT PORTERHOUSE STEAKS, 4

KALE CAESAR SALAD, 13

ALMOND SPICE CHRISTMAS COOKIES, 23

Features

Departments

A Fresh Take on Family Favorites

With more than 1,200 recipes, from classic beef chili to big-batch birthday cupcakes, our latest collection, *The America's Test Kitchen New Family Cookbook*, is an indispensable resource for every home cook. Order online at **americastestkitchen. com/NewFamily.**

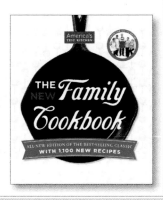

RECIPES THAT WORK®

America's Test Kitchen is a very real 2,500-square-foot kitchen located just outside Boston. It is the home of *Cook's Country* and *Cook's Illustrated* magazines and the workday destination of more than three dozen test cooks, editors, and cookware specialists. Our mission is to test recipes until we understand how and why they work and arrive at the best version. We also test kitchen equipment and supermarket ingredients in search of products that offer the best value and performance. You can watch us work by tuning in to *Cook's Country from America's Test Kitchen* (CooksCountry.com) and *America's Test Kitchen* (AmericasTestKitchen.com) on public television.

Ask Cook's Country

BY CHRISTIE MORRISON

I've seen small artichokes in the grocery store. How are they different from regular-size artichokes? Do you cook them the same way?
Marcus Williams, St. Louis, Mo.

In the United States, small or "baby" artichokes aren't really immature artichokes (unlike in Europe, where artichokes are often harvested while they're small and haven't fully matured). These minute versions actually grow on the same plants as regular artichokes; they just grow low on the stalk—below the larger artichokes—where they receive less sun and, as such, never reach more than 2 to 4 ounces (about the size of a chicken egg).

Unlike larger artichokes, the edible areas of which include only the heart, trimmed stem, and the meaty base of the tough leaves that must be scraped off with your teeth, baby artichokes never develop the fuzzy choke that must be removed from large artichokes, so they're easier to prepare with less waste.

Like the adult version, though, baby artichokes must be trimmed before being cooked. To trim baby artichokes, cut off the top quarter and snap off the fibrous outer leaves until you reach the yellow leaves. Then use a vegetable peeler or paring knife to trim the dark green exterior from the base of the artichoke, the exterior of the stem, and the stem's tough bottom. Don't forget to keep the trimmed artichokes in a bowl of acidulated water while you prepare the rest; the acid in the water will help neutralize the enzymes that cause the artichokes to oxidize and turn brown.

THE BOTTOM LINE Baby artichokes don't have the inedible choke you find in larger artichokes, but they do take some prep.

DON'T CHOKE
Baby artichokes do not have the fuzzy, inedible choke of their older brethren.

Why does my honey bottle have a warning that it's unsafe for infants? Is pasteurized honey OK?
Brenda Cahn, Eureka, Calif.

The consumption of honey by infants has been linked to infant botulism, a paralyzing and sometimes deadly illness. The spores of the botulism bacteria (*Clostridium botulinum*) can be carried in soil, dust, and, sometimes, honey. While these spores lie dormant and are harmless when ingested by people over the age of 1, an infant's still-developing intestinal tract provides an amenable place for the spores to grow and ultimately release toxins.

According to the Centers for Disease Control and Prevention, of the 145 or so cases of botulism reported each year, 65 percent of those are infant botulism—though in most of these cases the illness was contracted by swallowing microscopic dust particles rather than honey. Since the spores are heat-resistant, the pasteurization process that kills yeast strains in honey and prevents crystallization doesn't affect the spores, so pasteurized honey is no safer than raw honey when it comes to infant botulism.

THE BOTTOM LINE While honey—raw or pasteurized—isn't the only cause of infant botulism, it is one that is easily avoided. Consult your physician on this and all health matters related to diet; but in the meantime, do not feed honey to babies under the age of 12 months.

I am lactose intolerant, and I've come to love almond milk in my coffee. Will it work as a milk replacement in desserts?
Veronica Mathis, Omaha, Neb.

Almond milk is made by first soaking raw almonds in water to soften the nuts (anywhere from 4 hours to overnight). The nuts are then drained and pulverized with fresh water to make a paste. The mixture is strained to remove any unground almond bits. Some commercial almond milks add sweeteners like evaporated cane juice to balance flavor, plus stabilizers and thickeners like carrageenan and lecithin to adjust the texture and help keep the particles and proteins in suspension for a smoother and more homogenized liquid.

Since not all dairy substitutes work equally well in cooked applications, we decided to try almond milk in three different desserts: white layer cake, crème anglaise (a light custard), and rice pudding. We did our testing with unflavored almond milk so as not to introduce additional sweetness or unexpected

Recipes often call for a "medium" onion but my grocery store usually has only one general size of onion available for each variety. Is there a volume and/or weight guide? What does "medium" mean?
Valerie Bennett, Marietta, Ga.

While we usually give weights for ingredients like meats and poultry, cheeses, and baking ingredients, we tend to call for vegetables in terms of relative size unless the weight is of utmost importance to the outcome of a particular recipe. But since produce sizes can vary (especially due to seasonality), we set standards for all our recipe development and testing. Our default onion is a medium yellow cooking onion (like the ones you find in net bags in the grocery store), which is the approximate size of a tennis ball. Here's how small, medium, and large onions measure up.

SMALL ONION (like a billiard ball)	**MEDIUM ONION** (like a tennis ball)	**LARGE ONION** (like a softball)
6 ounces ¾ cup chopped	8 ounces 1 cup chopped	16 ounces 1½ cups chopped

flavors to the recipes.

Both milks performed well in the white cake, which called for a full cup. Tasters couldn't detect any difference in flavor, although the cake made with almond milk was slightly drier and more crumbly than the dairy milk version (according to our science editor, this is likely due to almond milk's lower fat content: 2.5 grams per cup versus 8 grams per cup of whole milk). In both cases, the textures of the cakes were still deemed acceptable.

We noticed a greater difference between the milks in tests with rice pudding and crème anglaise, where the flavors and textures of the milks were more apparent.

ALMOND MILK
A fine milk substitute for baking.

In the rice pudding, which uses 6 cups of milk, it was easy to tell which sample used almond milk; its beige color was a clear giveaway, and some tasters noticed a "savory flavor" that was off-putting (other tasters liked the faint, sweet almond flavor). The thickeners in the almond milk also caused the pudding to take on a thick, dense texture that one taster deemed "gloppy."

The crème anglaise was a closer contest: The flavors were similar, although the vanilla flavor came through more in the cow's-milk version and some tasters detected a "chalky" texture in the almond milk custard. Once again, the almond milk version was thicker (if not richer-tasting) than the cow's-milk custard.

THE BOTTOM LINE Reach for unflavored almond milk for a decent milk substitute in baked goods, but think twice before using it in custard sauces and puddings—as an almond milk lover, you may be satisfied with the results, but you won't be fooling anyone.

▶ To ask us a cooking question, visit **CooksCountry.com/ask**. Or write to Ask *Cook's Country*, P.O. Box 470739, Brookline, MA 02447. Just try to stump us!

Kitchen Shortcuts

COMPILED BY SHANNON FRIEDMANN HATCH

TIDY TIP
Funneling Advice
Elizabeth Strong, Tremonton, Utah

Whenever I'm making an emulsion, like homemade mayonnaise, in my blender and the recipe calls for oil to be poured through the hole in the lid while the machine is running, I end up with splattered oil all over my kitchen. Now I insert a funnel into the hole and pour the oil into that. It fits perfectly in place and keeps the oil from splashing out.

COOL TRICK
Easier Bacon Chopping
Kyle Bennett, Nashville, Tenn.

When I have to chop bacon for a recipe, I place the needed amount in the freezer for 15 minutes to firm it up. Rather than scrunching and smushing under the knife, the cold bacon holds its shape and slices neatly.

Submit a tip online at CooksCountry.com/kitchenshortcuts or send a letter to Kitchen Shortcuts, Cook's Country, P.O. Box 470739, Brookline, MA 02447. Include your name, address, and phone number. If we publish your tip, you will receive a free one-year subscription to Cook's Country. Letters may be edited for clarity and length.

RECYCLE IT
Can Dispenser
Ariel Gulasch, Sunnyvale, Calif.

I keep lots of canned beans and tomatoes on hand. To save valuable pantry space, I slide them into an empty soda or beer 12-pack box in the pantry. The box has a compact footprint—I can fit nine cans of vegetables (on their sides in the box) in the space that would normally hold just five or six. It's really convenient.

NEAT TRICK
Dredge Report
Arline Fleming, Narragansett, R.I.

I don't mind doing the work of dredging chicken or eggplant before frying, but what I do dread is the cleanup: flour on the floor, bread crumbs between the counter and stove, egg everywhere. To contain the mess, I place the dishes holding the dredging ingredients in my sink and set my casserole dish on the counter beside it. I can dredge, and any mess drips into the sink, where I can easily wash it down the drain.

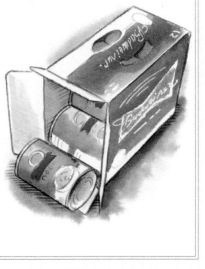

TIDY TIP
Better Cake Carrier
Joan Ross, Rochester, N.Y.

I often transport cakes in my cake carrier only to find them ruined when I arrive at my destination. I've started wrapping three or four rubber bands around the bottom of the container before placing the plate holding my cake on top. This creates traction and locks the plate in place so it doesn't smush against the side of the carrier.

HANDY TIP
Digital Recipe File
Deborah Garnett, Overland Park, Kan.

I keep a photo album on my smartphone of pictures of ingredient lists from my favorite go-to recipes. Now, if I don't remember to make a grocery list before I leave the house, I can swipe through my collection right at the store.

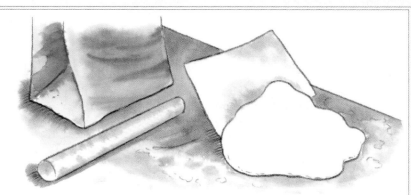

DOUBLE DUTY Pastry Peel
Joyce Rutter Kaye, Brooklyn, N.Y.

There's nothing more frustrating than carefully rolling out pie dough only to have it stick to the counter when you try to transfer it to the pie plate. I don't own a pastry cloth, but I've turned the plastic insert from one of my reusable grocery bags into a "pastry peel." It's thin enough to slide underneath the fragile dough but sturdy enough to lift it into place.

Thick-Cut Porterhouse Steaks

Mammoth porterhouse steaks are a spectacular centerpiece for the holiday table—
if you can manage to cook them properly. BY MORGAN BOLLING

THE PORTERHOUSE IS a meaty beast. The combination of a flavorful, fat-marbled strip steak and a buttery tenderloin attached to (and separated by) a great big bone is grand, expansive, and expensive—a fresh alternative to the traditional holiday roast. But with stakes this high, I knew that I needed a foolproof method to make sure I got my money's worth and to give Christmas dinner its due.

To serve eight hungry people, I'd need two 3-pound steaks, each about 2 inches thick. Cooking steaks this thick presents a serious challenge for the home cook: By the time you've given it enough heat to create a good crust and the center of the steak is a nice medium-rare, the outer edges of the meat are overcooked, with an unappetizing band of pallid gray meat.

For most boneless steaks, the test kitchen has found a way to prevent the gray band: We lay them on a wire rack set in a rimmed baking sheet and then roast them in a low, 275-degree oven before searing them in a ripping-hot pan to create a crust. The slow roasting gradually brings the steaks up to temperature, allowing for even cooking with no gray band; because the steaks are elevated on the rack, hot air can circulate all around them. This method also dries the steaks' exterior so that the final searing happens fast and furiously, further reducing the chance of overcooking.

I quickly realized that the first part of this method worked great with my big bone-in steaks (especially when I positioned them with the more delicate tenderloin portions facing each other in the center of the rack, where they were slightly insulated and thus cooked more gently than the more resilient strip portions that were positioned on the hotter outer part of the rack), but the wheels came off during the searing step.

The problem was that the meat shrank away from the bone while it was in the oven, which meant the bone now protruded beyond the surface of the meat. This prevented the full surface of each side of the steaks from coming into direct contact with the hot pan when I tried to sear them. Not good: If the steaks weren't able to lie flat against the skillet, there's no way they'd get a good, hard sear. I tried broiling the steaks in the oven as an alternative to pan searing, but it took much too long to develop a

Why so much oil? Since the bone prevents full contact between meat and pan, you need extra oil to carry the heat to the entire surface of the steaks.

decent crust, meaning that I risked overcooking the interior, or worse, inviting the ugly gray band back into the meat. I'd have to find a different way to create a dark, delicious crust in the skillet.

I took a deep breath and a step back to reconsider the process. If all the meat wasn't coming into direct contact with the heat of the pan (because the bone was in the way), then maybe I could bring the heat to the steak. But how?

By adding more oil, that's how. Oil is a perfect heat conductor; if I could use it to create a bridge between the hot pan and the roasted steaks, I'd have a win. Jumping from 1 to 3 tablespoons of vegetable oil in the skillet—turning the process into a kind of hybrid sear and pan-fry—was the fix that produced a nice, even crust on these big steaks. For good measure, I also seared the steaks on their curved edges for a few minutes

to crisp some of the exterior fat.

I was feeling pretty confident about my porterhouse steaks, and they certainly looked spectacular, but my scrupulous tasters would have the final say. It wasn't easy to let the steaks rest for about 10 minutes (an essential step to prevent the meat from being dry on the plate), so I occupied myself by whipping up a quick batch of the test kitchen's easy, elegant Blender

Béarnaise Is a Breeze
This herby, creamy sauce is easy to make and elevates any steak.

BLENDER BÉARNAISE SAUCE
Makes 1¼ cups

When making the béarnaise with an immersion blender, we prefer to make it in a 2-cup liquid measuring cup, but another container of equal volume and diameter will also work. It's important to make sure the butter is still hot (about 180 degrees) so that the egg yolks cook sufficiently.

- ½ cup white wine vinegar
- 2 sprigs fresh tarragon, plus 1½ tablespoons minced
- 1 shallot, sliced thin
- 3 large egg yolks
- 1½ teaspoons lemon juice
  Salt
  Pinch cayenne pepper, plus extra for seasoning
- 16 tablespoons unsalted butter, melted and still hot
  Hot water

1. Bring vinegar, tarragon sprigs, and shallot to simmer in small skillet over medium heat. Cook until vinegar is reduced to about 2 tablespoons, 5 to 7 minutes; remove from heat. Using fork, discard shallot slices and tarragon sprigs.

2A. FOR A BLENDER: Process egg yolks, lemon juice, ¼ teaspoon salt, cayenne, and vinegar mixture in blender until frothy, about 10 seconds. With blender running, slowly drizzle in hot butter until fully emulsified, about 2 minutes.

2B. FOR AN IMMERSION BLENDER: Combine egg yolks, lemon juice, ¼ teaspoon salt, cayenne, and vinegar mixture in 2-cup liquid measuring cup. Add hot butter. Quickly place blender in bottom of cup and blend until sauce begins to emulsify. Slowly pull blender toward surface until sauce is fully emulsified, about 30 seconds.

3. Stir in minced tarragon. Adjust consistency with hot water as needed, 1 teaspoon at a time, until sauce slowly drips from spoon. Season with salt and extra cayenne to taste.

Béarnaise Sauce. Hey, this was a holiday dinner, after all.

I carved the steaks, first separating the two sides of meat from the bone and then cutting the pieces crosswise into strips, and called over my hungry colleagues. The steaks were a picture-perfect medium-rare, pink on the inside with a gorgeous, even mahogany crust, and the sauce was creamy, herby, and flavorful. The combination was a huge hit. With a steak this special, it's quite possible that my family will never go back to roast beef for our Christmas dinner.

THICK-CUT PORTERHOUSE STEAKS Serves 8
Porterhouse steaks have a bone dividing the smaller tenderloin and the larger strip. We use kosher salt because it's easy to sprinkle evenly over the meat. Let the oil heat in the pan until it is just smoking before adding the steaks. If serving with béarnaise sauce, make the sauce while the steaks rest.

- 2 (2½- to 3-pound) porterhouse steaks, 2 inches thick, trimmed
  Kosher salt and pepper
- 3 tablespoons vegetable oil

1. Adjust oven rack to middle position and heat oven to 275 degrees. Set wire rack in aluminum foil–lined rimmed baking sheet. Pat steaks dry with paper towels and season liberally with salt and pepper. Place steaks side by side on prepared rack with tenderloins facing center, about 1 inch apart. Transfer steaks to oven. Cook until thermometer inserted sideways 3 inches from tip of strip side of steak registers 115 to 120 degrees (for medium-rare), 70 to 90 minutes, rotating sheet halfway through cooking.

2. Pat steaks dry with paper towels. Heat oil in 12-inch skillet over high heat until just smoking. Place 1 steak in skillet and sear until well browned, about 2 minutes per side, lifting occasionally to redistribute oil. Using tongs, stand steak upright to sear edges, 1 to 2 minutes. Return steak to wire rack, tent loosely with foil, and repeat with remaining steak. Let steaks rest for 10 minutes.

3. Transfer steaks to carving board. Carve strip steaks and tenderloins from bones. Place T-bones on platter. Slice steaks thin against grain, then reassemble sliced steaks on both sides of bones. Season with salt and pepper to taste. Serve.

TASTING FROZEN DINNER ROLLS: LESS IS MORE

Frozen rolls pale in comparison with good homemade ones, but they do keep for months in the freezer, so you can always have bread on hand. And you can bake only what you need. We've tasted frozen rolls before and found them to be acceptable in a pinch. Our previous winner was discontinued, so we returned to the freezer aisle and found new products touting "stone baked," "artisan," "crusty," and "French" rolls. They certainly sound better—are they? We gathered a few nationally available products, prepared them according to their package directions, and assembled a tasting panel of 21 editors and test cooks. Tasters wanted rolls that were crusty outside and tender inside. The top product nailed this, but the bottom-ranking product was "gummy" and "dense."

We compared labels and saw that the losing roll had 17 different ingredients, including vital wheat gluten, guar gum, and xanthan gum—all of which retain moisture and create a gummy texture. These rolls were also the only ones to include some whole-wheat flour, which makes for denser bread. Our favorite product had only seven ingredients and earned extra points for tasting "homemade." They're also the only product that's fully cooked at the factory, so they're especially light and crisp. Visit **CooksCountry.com/jan15** for the complete story and product chart.
—HANNAH CROWLEY

HIGHLY RECOMMENDED

PEPPERIDGE FARM Stone Baked Artisan French Dinner Rolls
Price: $3.99 for 8 rolls, 14 oz ($0.50 per roll, $0.29 per oz)
Sodium: 300 mg per 50-g serving
Ingredients: Unbromated unbleached enriched wheat flour, water; Less than 2% of salt, white rice flour, malt syrup, yeast, sesame seed meal

Comments: These rolls were "surprisingly good," "wheaty," and "yeasty," with a perfect, flavorful hint of salt. They were "supercrispy" outside and "chewy" yet "tender" inside. As one taster put it: "I respect this roll. It can come to dinner with me."

NOT RECOMMENDED

ALEXIA Artisan French Rolls
Price: $2.99 for 8 rolls, 12 oz ($0.37 per roll, $0.25 per oz)
Sodium: 267 mg per 50-g serving
Ingredients: Wheat flour, whole wheat flour, water, rye flour, yeast, sea salt, vital wheat gluten, rye sourdough culture (rye flour, water, salt, starter culture), cane sugar, fava bean flour, malted barley flour, guar gum, xanthan gum, organic dried cane syrup, malt extract, sunflower lecithin, enzymes

Comments: The sourdough starter in these rolls made them taste "fermented" and "weirdly funky." Worse, inside they were "gummy" and "sticky" and seemed "underbaked," even when we cooked them far longer than recommended.

Butternut Squash Gratin

Did a gratin made with sweet, rich butternut squash really need cheese and cream to make it delicious?

BY CHRISTIE MORRISON

WHEN I SET about developing a recipe for a gratin made with butternut squash, I wasn't about to obscure its nutty, sweet flavor with a thick cloak of heavy cream and cheese, as many recipes do. After all, a gratin really just refers to a dish topped with a browned crust. I also wanted to avoid the traditional step of precooking the squash before assembling and baking the gratin.

After my initial research, I started my gratin by softening thinly sliced onions over medium heat to build a savory base and then added a few garlic cloves and a bit of sage for earthy depth. I transferred the mixture to a 13 by 9-inch dish and turned to the squash.

I knew that if I wanted the squash to bake evenly without precooking, I'd need to slice it on the thin side— ¼-inch-thick slices cut from squash halves. I tossed the slices with olive oil, more sage, salt, and pepper and shingled them over the onions. I then covered the dish with foil to keep it from drying out and baked it until the squash was just tender, about 40 minutes. Next I removed the foil, sprinkled on some crunchy panko bread crumbs mixed with olive oil and parsley, and baked 15 minutes longer to brown the top.

But after almost an hour of cooking, some of the squash was still underdone. And while the browned onions did add flavor, they also contained enough moisture to give the dish a steamed, rather than roasted, taste. Plus, the crumbs seemed sandy—not the crisp contrast the tender squash needed.

For my next round, I quartered the squash lengthwise before cutting it into ¼-inch-thick slices for smaller (and quicker-cooking) pieces. I decided to fully caramelize the onions to add a more intense flavor as well as to drive off excess moisture. (At the end, I introduced a little water to loosen the flavorful fond from the bottom of the pan.) I also doubled the amount of onions so I could layer the onions with the squash rather than just put the squash on top of the onions. Finally, I toasted the panko in oil in the skillet for a few minutes to jump-start the browning and ensure crunch.

Much better. My gratin had intense roasted flavor and good textural contrast. A bit of chopped parsley and lemon zest brought it all into balance.

A finishing sprinkle of fresh parsley and grated lemon zest brightens up this earthy dish.

BUTTERNUT SQUASH GRATIN Serves 8

Avoid buying prepeeled or chunked butternut squash for this dish.

- 6 tablespoons extra-virgin olive oil
- ¼ cup panko bread crumbs
  Salt and pepper
- 2 pounds onions, halved and sliced thin
- ¼ cup water
- 4 teaspoons chopped fresh sage
- 2 garlic cloves, minced
- 4 pounds butternut squash
- ¼ cup minced fresh parsley
- 1 teaspoon grated lemon zest

1. Adjust oven rack to middle position and heat oven to 425 degrees. Grease 13 by 9-inch baking dish. Combine 1 tablespoon oil and panko in 12-inch skillet and toast over medium-high heat, stirring frequently, until golden brown, about 3 minutes. Transfer to bowl and stir in ½ teaspoon salt and ¼ teaspoon pepper; set aside.

2. Heat 3 tablespoons oil in now-empty skillet over medium heat until shimmering. Add onions, ½ teaspoon salt, and ¼ teaspoon pepper and cook, stirring frequently, until soft and golden brown, about 30 minutes. Add 2 tablespoons water and cook, scraping up any browned bits, until water is evaporated, about 5 minutes. Add remaining 2 tablespoons water and cook until onions are caramelized and water is evaporated, about 5 minutes longer. Add 2 teaspoons sage and garlic and cook until fragrant, about 30 seconds; set aside.

3. Trim ends from squash and peel. Cut in half lengthwise, then quarter each half lengthwise and remove seeds. Cut each piece into ¼-inch-thick slices (you should have 11 cups). Toss squash, remaining 2 tablespoons oil, remaining 2 teaspoons sage, 1 teaspoon salt, and ¾ teaspoon pepper together in large bowl. Arrange half of squash evenly in prepared dish. Spread half of onion mixture evenly over squash. Arrange remaining squash evenly over onion mixture. Spread remaining onion mixture evenly over squash.

4. Cover dish with aluminum foil and bake until squash is nearly tender, about 40 minutes. Sprinkle panko mixture over top and continue to bake, uncovered, until squash is tender, about 15 minutes longer. Transfer dish to wire rack. Combine parsley and lemon zest in bowl and sprinkle over gratin. Serve.

TEST KITCHEN TECHNIQUE **Cutting Butternut Squash**

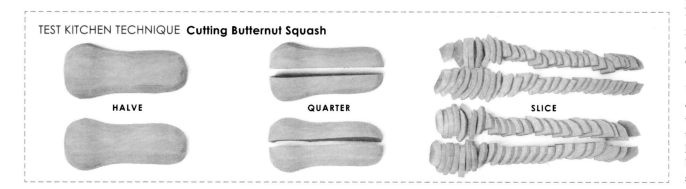

HALVE   QUARTER   SLICE

Roasted Green Beans

Roasted green beans should be earthy and sweet, not drab and leathery. Time to find a foolproof method.

BY CRISTIN WALSH

REGARDING ROASTED GREEN beans: I had always assumed that tossing them in olive oil, salt, and pepper and then sending them on a short swing through a hot oven would net me a rustic, fresh-tasting side dish of bright, perfectly cooked green beans with rich brown blisters. Imagine my disappointment when the beans I pulled out of the oven were limp, pale, and leathery. Where did I go wrong?

In search of an easy salve, I collected an array of recipes, all suggesting variations on the same concept. Some recommended higher temperatures (up to 500 degrees) and shorter cook times; others promised good results with gentler oven temperatures and longer cook times. I tried several of these recipes with fresh batches of beans. No luck. Higher oven temperatures produced nicely colored but dry and leathery beans, while lower temps resulted in wilted, stringy, olive-green beans. It was clear that this simple dish needed a fresh approach.

I considered blanching the beans in salted water before roasting them, but this seemed like too much work (and too much dirty cookware) for a dish of beans. Ditto a preroast visit to the microwave.

Was the answer right under my nose in the test kitchen? In the past, my coworkers have used a hybrid roasting technique with other vegetables like cauliflower, first cooking them on a sheet pan under an aluminum foil cover, essentially steaming them during the first few minutes in the oven, and then removing the foil to expose the beans to dry heat and achieve a light browning. Could the two-fold process work on green beans, too?

I gave it a shot, roasting 1½ pounds of beans covered for 10 minutes at 475 degrees and then uncovered for another 15 minutes, until they had adequate

Shreds of salty, sharp Pecorino Romano cheese add a lively bite to these flavorful beans.

browning. Much to my dismay, the beans were overcooked.

Down but not out, I tried it again with just 10 minutes of uncovered roasting. These beans had better texture but lacked the deep brown blisters and caramelized flavor that define the best roasted vegetables.

Sugar is usually the first ingredient we turn to when we need a browning boost, and my next test confirmed its worth: When I tossed a bit of sugar into the beans, they emerged speckled with brown.

While they were in the oven, I had just enough time to whisk together a light dressing of olive oil, garlic, Dijon mustard, and lemon juice and zest. I drizzled the beans and then tossed them with a bit of minced basil, toasted pine nuts, and salty grated Pecorino Romano. The add-ons elevated the dish and brought everything into balance. Inspired, I created two variations, one with almonds and mint and one with goat cheese and hazelnuts.

TEST KITCHEN TECHNIQUE Steam and Then Roast Uncovered

For tender green beans with a hint of flavorful browning, we found that a hybrid moist-then-dry roasting method worked best. First we roast the beans covered with foil, which traps steam and helps them cook through quickly. Then we remove the foil to allow the beans to brown in the dry heat.

ROASTED GREEN BEANS WITH PECORINO AND PINE NUTS
Serves 4 to 6

High-quality olive oil makes a difference here. Shred the Pecorino Romano on the large holes of a box grater.

- 1½ pounds green beans, trimmed
- 5½ tablespoons extra-virgin olive oil
- ¾ teaspoon sugar
  Kosher salt and pepper
- 2 garlic cloves, minced
- 1 teaspoon grated lemon zest plus 4 teaspoons juice
- 1 teaspoon Dijon mustard
- 2 tablespoons chopped fresh basil
- 1½ ounces Pecorino Romano cheese, shredded (½ cup)
- ¼ cup pine nuts, toasted

1. Adjust oven rack to lowest position and heat oven to 475 degrees. Combine green beans, 1½ tablespoons oil, sugar, ¾ teaspoon salt, and ½ teaspoon pepper in bowl. Evenly distribute green beans on rimmed baking sheet.

2. Cover sheet tightly with aluminum foil and roast for 10 minutes. Remove foil and continue to roast until green beans are spotty brown, about 10 minutes longer, stirring halfway through roasting.

3. Meanwhile, combine garlic, lemon zest, and remaining ¼ cup oil in medium bowl and microwave until bubbling, about 1 minute; let mixture steep for 1 minute. Whisk lemon juice, mustard, ¼ teaspoon salt, and ¼ teaspoon pepper into garlic mixture.

4. Transfer green beans to bowl with dressing, add basil, and toss to combine. Transfer to serving platter and sprinkle with Pecorino and pine nuts. Serve.

ROASTED GREEN BEANS WITH ALMONDS AND MINT

Substitute lime zest and juice for lemon zest and juice; ¼ cup torn fresh mint leaves for basil; and whole blanched almonds, toasted and chopped, for pine nuts. Omit Pecorino.

ROASTED GREEN BEANS WITH GOAT CHEESE AND HAZELNUTS

Substitute orange zest for lemon zest; 2 teaspoons orange juice for 2 teaspoons lemon juice; minced fresh chives for basil; ½ cup crumbled goat cheese for Pecorino; and hazelnuts, toasted, skinned, and chopped, for pine nuts.

Milk Chocolate Cheesecake

Replacing deep, dark chocolate with mild-mannered milk chocolate unlocked the secret to a fluffy, creamy chocolate cheesecake. BY ERIKA BRUCE

CHOCOLATE MAKES EVERYTHING better, right? This misguided thinking has caused me to repeatedly order chocolate cheesecake at restaurants and cafés in expectation of something akin to a flourless chocolate tart, only fluffier, creamier, and even richer. Instead, too often I bite into a disappointingly dense or sour wedge. Chocolate's bitter side, usually considered a good thing, can really clash with, rather than complement, the tangy flavor of cream cheese.

Call me an optimist, but something that sounds so good shouldn't have to be bad. To prove it, I loaded myself up with cream cheese, chocolate bars, and a handful of promising recipes and headed into the kitchen.

While none of the recipes I had collected produced the chocolate cheesecake of my dreams, each held a glimmer of promise. Some showed restraint in the amount of chocolate to keep its bitterness to a minimum, while others had the foresight to call for first melting the chocolate with heavy cream to mute its bite and produce a creamier texture. Good ideas, but none struck the perfect balance.

Crusts were all over the map, varying from crushed graham crackers to pie dough pastry. One inspired recipe used crushed Oreo cookies. My tasters were especially enthusiastic about this one, so I stuck with it.

The most interesting thing I observed was that many of the recipes didn't bother with a water bath when baking the cake. I'd always thought that the steady, gentle heat produced by placing a foil-wrapped springform pan into a roasting pan half-full of water was essential for a smooth, evenly baked cheesecake. But I was intrigued by the freedom of baking without a water bath, if I could only make it work.

Using four eggs, 1½ pounds of cream cheese, and 4 ounces of bittersweet chocolate, I made three cheesecakes and baked them at 225, 250, and 275 degrees, respectively. At 225 degrees the cheesecake emerged with no cracks, but it took longer than 2 hours to bake (too long for me). At 275 degrees my cheesecake looked like a relief map of the American Southwest. But at 250 degrees, while I still had to exercise some patience, the cake came out with no cracks at all.

But my work was nowhere near done. There were flavor challenges—most

A crunchy, chocolaty crust made from ground Oreos, melted butter, and a little sugar is the perfect base for this creamy cheesecake.

notably a subtle, lingering bitterness from the bittersweet chocolate. Adding cream helped soften the sharpness, but only slightly. I tried semisweet chocolate in place of bittersweet; this was an improvement, but only a modest one. I needed a dramatic change.

So I got to thinking—what if I used mild-mannered milk chocolate? Milk chocolate gets its gentle, milky character from the milk powder added to the

basic ingredients of chocolate liquor and cocoa butter, and it delivers almost no bitterness. Could this often-maligned ingredient be my salvation for chocolate cheesecake?

I made my next cake with 6 ounces of milk chocolate. Its sweet milky flavor was an ideal counterpoint to the tangy cream cheese, and with one taste I knew I had the makings of a winner. But switching to milk chocolate created an

obvious problem. The cake now needed more complex, deep, and round chocolate flavor.

Luckily, the fix was relatively easy: Adding cocoa powder provided chocolate nuance—just 2 tablespoons was enough to add some complexity without compromising the texture or welcoming back the bitterness.

I was almost there—no cracks, a light consistency, a fully realized chocolate

1. TAP After you've poured the batter into the prebaked crust, gently tap the pan on the counter to release air bubbles.

2. TEMP Use an instant-read thermometer to determine when the cheesecake is perfectly baked; it should register 150 degrees.

3. SLICE For the neatest pieces, heat your knife by running it under hot water, quickly dry it with a cloth, and slice the cheesecake.

---

flavor—but a tough, dry skin was forming on top of my cheesecake. So I did what I usually do to keep things from drying out in the oven: I covered the pan tightly with a piece of aluminum foil. This kept the top moist while also reducing the baking time by about 15 minutes, to about an hour and a half. The only downside was that the cheesecake's top was too moist from its own steam when I took it out of the oven. I solved this issue by removing the foil after an hour in the oven to give the top some time to dry out and set up.

The result? Spectacular. The key to a successful chocolate cheesecake turned out to be an exercise in matchmaking—finding the right kind of chocolate to pair with the tangy cream cheese. Not only had the switch to milk chocolate helped solve my chocolate cheesecake conundrum, but it had transformed the dessert. I had a showstopper of a cheesecake, fluffy and creamy, with a soothing milk chocolate flavor (one taster described it as a giant, creamy, slightly tangy malted milk ball) and no cracks.

And with such a straightforward, no-water-bath baking method, who needs disappointing restaurant versions? I'll be making this milk chocolate cheesecake at home from now on.

TEST KITCHEN TIP
Melt Milk Chocolate Carefully
Because milk chocolate contains milk solids, its protein content is generally higher than that of dark chocolate. The extra protein means that milk chocolate melts at a slightly lower temperature than dark; what's more, when you add heat to protein and sugar, new molecules may form, introducing unwelcome scorched or burned flavors. Microwaves are generally gentle, but notoriously inconsistent, so choose 50 percent power, keep a close eye on the chocolate, and give it a stir every 15 seconds.

MILK CHOCOLATE CHEESECAKE
Serves 12
Our favorite milk chocolate is Dove Silky Smooth Milk Chocolate. For the crust, use the entire Oreo cookie, filling and all. The cheesecake needs to be refrigerated for at least 8 hours before serving.

- 16 **Oreo sandwich cookies, broken into rough pieces**
- 1 **tablespoon sugar plus ½ cup (3½ ounces)**
- 2 **tablespoons unsalted butter, melted**
- 8 **ounces milk chocolate, chopped**
- ⅓ **cup heavy cream**
- 2 **tablespoons unsweetened cocoa powder**
- ¼ **teaspoon salt**
- 1½ **pounds cream cheese, softened**
- 4 **large eggs, room temperature**
- 2 **teaspoons vanilla extract**

1. Adjust oven rack to middle position and heat oven to 350 degrees. Grease bottom and sides of 9-inch nonstick springform pan.

2. Process cookies and 1 tablespoon sugar in food processor until finely ground, about 30 seconds. Add melted butter and pulse until combined, about 6 pulses. Transfer crumb mixture to prepared pan and press firmly with bottom of dry measuring cup into even layer in bottom of pan. Bake until fragrant and set, about 10 minutes. Let cool completely on wire rack.

3. Reduce oven temperature to 250 degrees. Combine 6 ounces chocolate and cream in medium bowl and microwave at 50 percent power, stirring occasionally, until melted and smooth, 60 to 90 seconds. Let cool for 10 minutes. In small bowl, whisk cocoa, salt, and remaining ½ cup sugar until no lumps remain.

4. Using stand mixer fitted with paddle, beat cream cheese and cocoa mixture on medium speed until creamy and smooth, about 3 minutes, scraping down bowl as needed. Reduce speed to medium-low, add chocolate mixture, and beat until combined. Gradually add

eggs, one at a time, until incorporated, scraping down bowl as needed. Add vanilla and give batter final stir by hand until no streaks of chocolate remain.

5. Pour cheesecake mixture into cooled crust and smooth top with spatula. Tap cheesecake gently on counter to release air bubbles. Cover pan tightly with aluminum foil (taking care not to touch surface of cheesecake with foil) and place on rimmed baking sheet. Bake for 1 hour, then remove foil. Continue to bake until edges are set and center registers 150 degrees and jiggles slightly when shaken, 30 to 45 minutes. Let cool completely on wire rack, then cover with plastic wrap and refrigerate in pan until cold, about 8 hours. (Cake can be refrigerated for up to 4 days.)

Drizzling Chocolate
We've found that a plastic zipper-lock bag with a corner snipped off is an effective tool for drizzling melted and cooled chocolate.

To create even drizzles, hold the bag at least 8 to 12 inches above the cheesecake and swipe back and forth in long, smooth gestures, draping lines of chocolate over the cake.

6. To unmold cheesecake, remove sides of pan, slide thin metal spatula between crust and pan bottom to loosen, and slide cake onto serving platter. Microwave remaining 2 ounces chocolate in small bowl at 50 percent power, stirring occasionally, until melted, 60 to 90 seconds. Let cool for 5 minutes. Transfer to small zipper-lock bag, cut small hole in corner, and pipe chocolate in thin zigzag pattern across top of cheesecake. Let cheesecake stand at room temperature for 30 minutes. Using warm, dry knife, cut into wedges and serve.

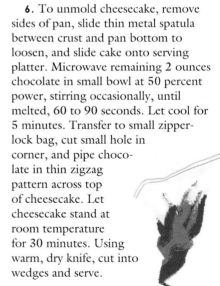

A Fresh Take on Shepherd's Pie

For a lighter, brighter shepherd's pie, use chicken instead of beef.
But it takes more than a straight swap to get good results. BY JEREMY SAUER

SHEPHERD'S PIE IS a case study in rib-sticking, belly-filling comfort food. This classic casserole features ground beef (or lamb) that is browned with aromatic vegetables and then stewed in a rich gravy before being topped with buttery mashed potatoes and broiled until golden. Delicious? Sure. Nap-inducing? Absolutely. Would swapping white meat (chicken) for the red meat (lamb or beef) produce a shepherd's pie that was hearty without being heavy?

I hit our cookbook library, searching for a chicken shepherd's pie recipe that was fresh and full-flavored. Unfortunately, I found no such thing. What I did find were two types of recipes for this dish: "healthy" pot pies that used low-fat ingredients (like skim milk, low-fat sour cream, etc.) to unsatisfying effect and thick, gloppy casseroles heavy on condensed soup, stodgy béchamel, and canned chicken and vegetables. Clearly I wasn't going to find my ideal recipe—I was going to have to develop it myself in the test kitchen.

▶ Want to see all our chicken recipes in one place? Visit **CooksCountry.com/chicken**.

Starting with a clean slate, I made *Cook's Country*'s much-loved shepherd's pie recipe using ground chicken breast in place of the ground beef. Almost immediately, it was obvious that this approach wouldn't work. The base recipe—chock-full of malty beer, tomato paste, and soy sauce—completely overwhelmed the subtle taste of the chicken. But the texture of the dish was an even bigger problem. The chicken was dry and chalky, and the lean meat left the filling watery, a far cry from the silky and rich ground beef gravy.

Thinking the lean white meat was the problem, I switched to ground thigh meat in hopes that the higher fat content would improve the texture. Although the flavor of the dark meat was far superior, the texture was still disappointing. Clearly, ground chicken wasn't going to cut it. Next I tried cutting boneless, skinless thighs into bite-size chunks that I browned and simmered until tender. The browned thigh meat tasted great and stayed quite moist, but instead of creating a cohesive filling, the chunks just bobbed around

This is not the usual crown of mashed potatoes—but our unmashed topping is just as delicious and much easier to make.

in the sauce like ice cubes in a glass of water. I had better luck with whole bone-in, skin-on thighs that I seared and then braised until tender. From here, I shredded the meat into bite-size pieces (discarding the skin and bones) so that it would soak up some of the liquid and make a moist, cohesive filling. It's a little more work than using ground chicken, sure, but the vastly superior results proved well worth it.

With the texture of the chicken under wraps, I turned my focus to flavor. Using bone-in, skin-on thighs gave me a great start, especially when I browned the thighs in a tablespoon of butter to render the fat and create a flavor-rich fond on the bottom of the pan. To allow the chicken to shine through, I built the filling with a base of chicken broth and a little reduced sherry rather than the beef broth and

tomato paste used in a standard recipe. As for the vegetables, I stuck with tradition: onion, carrots, and peas, with a couple of garlic cloves thrown in for good measure. For an herbal touch, I chose thyme (a classic seasoning for chicken), and I added a squeeze of lemon juice for brightness. While the flavor was spot on, my tasters thought the filling was still a bit loose. Stirring in a slurry of cornstarch and water solved the problem and left me with a nicely thickened sauce.

Of course, no shepherd's pie is complete without a rich, buttery, browned potato topping. But boiling, mashing, and piping the potatoes on top of the filling was a lot of work. Could I find an easier way? Yes I could: After several tests, I found that I could boil the chunks of peeled potato, drain them, stir in some butter, and be done with it—no mashing or piping required, and no extra milk or cream to cloud the savory chicken flavor. Brushing the chunks of potatoes with egg wash before baking added extra richness and ensured that they browned nicely. The rustic potato topping was easy and delicious.

I finally had my ideal recipe, a hearty—but not heavy—chicken shepherd's pie.

CHICKEN SHEPHERD'S PIE Serves 6
You will need a 10-inch ovensafe skillet for this recipe. You can use dry white wine in place of the sherry. Swanson Chicken Stock is our taste-test winner. Make sure to use russet potatoes here.

- 2 pounds bone-in chicken thighs, trimmed
  Salt and pepper
- 6 tablespoons unsalted butter, cut into 6 pieces
- 1 onion, chopped
- 3 carrots, peeled, halved lengthwise, and cut crosswise ½ inch thick
- 2 garlic cloves, minced
- 1½ teaspoons minced fresh thyme
- ¼ cup dry sherry
- 2 cups chicken broth
- 2 pounds russet potatoes, peeled and cut into 1-inch chunks
- ¼ cup cornstarch
- 1 cup frozen peas, thawed
- 1 tablespoon lemon juice
- 1 large egg, lightly beaten

1. Adjust oven rack to upper-middle position and heat oven to 375 degrees. Pat chicken dry with paper towels and season with salt and pepper. Melt 1 tablespoon butter in ovensafe 10-inch skillet over medium-high heat. Cook chicken until well browned, about 5 minutes per side (skillet will be crowded). Transfer chicken to plate and pour off all but 2 tablespoons fat from skillet.

2. Return skillet to medium-high heat, add onion and carrots, and cook until golden brown, about 5 minutes. Add garlic and thyme and cook until fragrant, about 30 seconds. Add sherry and cook until pan is nearly dry, scraping up any browned bits, about 1 minute. Stir in broth.

3. Return chicken to skillet, skin side up, along with any accumulated juices, and bring to boil. Cover, reduce heat to medium-low, and simmer until chicken registers 175 degrees, 12 to 14 minutes. Remove skillet from heat and transfer chicken to plate. Once cool enough to handle, shred chicken into bite-size pieces; discard skin and bones.

4. Meanwhile, place potatoes and 1 tablespoon salt in large saucepan and cover with water by 1 inch. Bring to boil over high heat, reduce heat to medium, and cook at strong simmer until tender, 15 to 18 minutes. Drain potatoes and return to saucepan. Place saucepan over low heat and cook to drive off any remaining moisture from potatoes, about 1 minute. Off heat, gently fold remaining 5 tablespoons butter, ¼ teaspoon salt, and ½ teaspoon pepper into potatoes. Cover and set aside.

5. Whisk cornstarch together with ¼ cup water in bowl. Bring broth mixture in skillet to boil and whisk in cornstarch mixture. Return to boil and cook until thickened, about 1 minute. Remove from heat and stir in peas, lemon juice, and shredded chicken. Season with salt and pepper to taste.

6. Spoon potatoes over entire surface of filling. Brush potatoes with egg. Transfer to oven and bake until pie is bubbling, about 15 minutes. Turn oven to broil and cook until potatoes are golden brown, 5 to 7 minutes. Let cool for 15 minutes. Serve.

TEST KITCHEN DISCOVERY **No Masher (or Pastry Bag) Required**
Mashed potatoes make a fine cap for shepherd's pie, but many recipes call for using a pastry bag to pipe the hot potatoes on top of the stew so that the spuds don't sink in. We wanted to find a simpler way. We found that just boiling potato chunks, draining them, and stirring in some butter made for a rustic, delicious topping that was easily spooned over the stew. Brushing the potato topping with beaten egg ensured that it browned well in the oven.

OUR EASY, RUSTIC TOPPING
You may never mash again.

Braised Red Cabbage

We wanted to transform humble cabbage into a dish that would not be out of place on the holiday table.

BY MORGAN BOLLING

A FRIEND RECENTLY told me about the "amazing" sweet-and-sour braised red cabbage that she remembered from her German American grandmother's holiday table. "Amazing" is a word I usually cringe at, but my curiosity was piqued, and although my friend couldn't provide a recipe, a little research unearthed several possibilities. Some recipes were as basic as cabbage, vinegar, and sugar, while others had close to 20 components.

To figure out a good starting point, I prepared a half-dozen representative recipes and lined up tasters for what we hoped would be a delicious sampling. Unfortunately, these dishes ran the gamut from mushy and bland to one so vinegary that a taster described it as "pickled." They did, however, give me some insights.

Our favorite recipe from the initial tests started with a sliced onion and used a braising liquid of equal parts orange juice and red wine, so I'd incorporate those elements into my working recipe. Throughout several days of testing, I made some important discoveries.

While the version with orange juice was good, I found that using orange juice concentrate boosted the dish's flavor and helped it cook faster (since I didn't have to wait for the concentrate to, well, concentrate). Leaving the lid on the pot the entire time resulted in too much liquid in the pot when the cabbage was done.

A better method was to braise the cabbage for 45 minutes, covered, and then remove the cover and simmer the cabbage for another 25 to 30 minutes. This gave me perfectly tender cabbage that was nicely coated in the sweet, sour, and syrupy glaze. And finally, including a little brown sugar and finishing the dish with a chopped Granny Smith apple for freshness, some fresh parsley, and butter brought everything together. Amazing.

Wine and orange juice concentrate make this cabbage unexpectedly lively.

BRAISED RED CABBAGE
Serves 4
We developed this recipe with inexpensive Cabernet Sauvignon, but any dry red wine will work. Our favorite frozen orange juice concentrate is Minute Maid Original Frozen Concentrated Orange Juice.

- 3 tablespoons unsalted butter
- 1 onion, halved and sliced thin
- 1 head red cabbage (2 pounds), cored and sliced ½ inch thick
- 1 cup red wine
- ½ cup frozen orange juice concentrate
- 1½ tablespoons packed brown sugar
  Salt and pepper
- 1 Granny Smith apple, peeled, cored, and cut into ¼-inch pieces
- 3 tablespoons minced fresh parsley

1. Melt 2 tablespoons butter in Dutch oven over medium heat. Add onion and cook until golden, 7 to 9 minutes. Stir in cabbage, wine, orange juice concentrate, sugar, 1¼ teaspoons salt, and ½ teaspoon pepper and bring to boil. Cover, reduce heat to low, and simmer for 45 minutes.

2. Stir in apple. Increase heat to medium-low and continue to simmer, uncovered, until cabbage is tender and liquid is syrupy, 25 to 30 minutes longer.

3. Off heat, stir in parsley and remaining 1 tablespoon butter. Season with salt and pepper to taste. Serve.

Stromboli

We set out to make stromboli—the calzone's more stylish cousin—simple enough for a weeknight supper. BY CRISTIN WALSH

IMAGINE AN ITALIAN cold-cut sandwich rolled up in pizza dough and baked into something akin to a savory jelly roll, and you've pictured a stromboli. The fillings can be various meats, cheeses, and vegetables.

I tested a handful of recipes and was disappointed. Leaking cheese, gummy dough, poorly distributed fillings: I had plenty of work to do.

Store-bought pizza dough made my tasters just as happy as homemade, so I chose the convenient route. I rolled pizza dough into a 12 by 10-inch rectangle and layered it with 4 ounces of provolone, 2 ounces of salami, and 4 ounces of mozzarella. For a vegetable, my tasters voted for broccoli rabe over other contenders; its slight bitterness nicely complemented the rich meat and cheese. But when I rolled the stuffed dough into a log, I got a leaky mess.

> Visit CooksCountry.com/jan15 for our Vegetable Stromboli and Spicy Sausage Stromboli.

Professional bakers often use a "letter fold" when filling pastry. It's a simple technique of folding the dough into thirds like a business letter. I tried it here, tucked the edges under, and baked the stromboli with fingers crossed. Alas, it exploded. But there was one significant improvement: The filling was nicely distributed throughout the bread.

For my next round, I took extra care to create a tighter package, brushing beaten egg at the edges of the dough before pressing firmly to create a stronger seal. Success. No explosion.

Just one problem remained—the underbaked interior. I tried dropping the oven temperature from 475 to 375 degrees. Although this extended the baking time from 15 to 30 minutes, the gentler heat gave the interior time to properly bake without overbrowning the exterior.

BROCCOLI RABE AND SALAMI STROMBOLI Serves 4

You may substitute broccoli florets for the broccoli rabe. Serve with our Basic Pizza Sauce: CooksCountry.com/pizzasauce.

- 1 teaspoon olive oil
- 2 garlic cloves, minced
- ¼ teaspoon red pepper flakes
- 6 ounces broccoli rabe, trimmed and cut into ¼-inch pieces
- 2 tablespoons water
- 1 pound store-bought pizza dough
- 4 ounces thinly sliced aged provolone cheese
- 2 ounces thinly sliced Genoa salami
- 4 ounces mozzarella cheese, shredded (1 cup)
- 1 large egg, lightly beaten
- 1 teaspoon sesame seeds

1. Adjust oven rack to middle position and heat oven to 375 degrees. Line rimmed baking sheet with aluminum foil and grease foil. Heat oil in 12-inch nonstick skillet over medium heat until shimmering. Add garlic and pepper flakes and cook until fragrant, about 30 seconds. Add broccoli rabe and water, cover, and cook until just tender, about 1 minute. Uncover and cook until liquid has evaporated, about 1 minute longer. Transfer broccoli rabe to dish towel; gather corners of towel and squeeze out excess moisture.

2. Roll dough into 12 by 10-inch rectangle on lightly floured counter with long side parallel to counter edge. Shingle provolone evenly over dough, leaving ½-inch border along top and sides. Layer salami over provolone. Sprinkle mozzarella and broccoli rabe evenly over salami.

3. Brush borders with egg (reserve remaining egg for brushing top of stromboli). Fold bottom third of stromboli in toward middle. Fold top third of stromboli down to cover first fold, creating log. Pinch seam firmly to seal.

We like to serve the stromboli slices warm, with tomato sauce on the side.

Transfer stromboli to prepared sheet, seam side down. Pinch ends firmly to seal and tuck underneath.

4. Brush top of stromboli with remaining egg. Using sharp knife, make 5 evenly spaced ½-inch-deep slashes, 2 inches long, on top of stromboli.

Sprinkle with sesame seeds. Bake until crust is golden and center registers 200 degrees, 30 to 35 minutes, rotating sheet halfway through baking. Transfer stromboli to wire rack and let cool for 10 minutes. Transfer to cutting board and cut into 2-inch-thick slices. Serve.

TEST KITCHEN TECHNIQUE **Constructing Stromboli**

FILL AND FOLD
Layer the filling ingredients over the dough, leaving a ½-inch border along the entire perimeter. Brush perimeter with beaten egg. Fold the bottom third in toward the middle.

FOLD AGAIN, SEAL, AND INVERT
Carefully fold the second side down over the first fold. Pinch the seam firmly to seal the stromboli. Invert onto baking sheet, pinch ends to seal, and tuck ends under. Brush with egg, cut vent holes, and sprinkle with sesame seeds.

Kale Caesar Salad

We had a hunch that kale greens and Caesar dressing could make a happy match, if we could only get the kale to relax (without a massage). BY MORGAN BOLLING

KALE, FOR ALL its popularity, is not a leaf I think of when I think of salad. But on a recent trip to the farmers' market, I couldn't help noticing the massive piles of emerald green kale beckoning to me.

One of the farmers told me how his wife has started using kale in her Caesar salads. Say what? Both kale, with its bitter earthiness, and Caesar dressing, with its savory tang, have powerful flavors. Could the two really work in a way that would allow the strong flavors to complement each other without knocking each other out?

To find out, I pulled a test kitchen Caesar salad recipe that I knew to be well seasoned and flavorful. Doubtful but hopeful, I swapped curly kale, stemmed and cut, ounce for ounce for romaine. No dice. Without being cooked, fibrous kale can be, as one taster commented, like "trying to chew on tree branches." Plus, the bitterness of the green did not allow the signature garlic, lemon, Parmesan, and anchovy flavors of the Caesar to shine through.

Simply cutting the tough kale leaves into smaller pieces didn't solve the chewability problem. I tried a variety of cooking methods—sautéing, steaming, and boiling—to soften it, but these took away any sense of freshness. I tried salting it, soaking it in a brine, and even, skeptically, massaging it (a technique that is enjoying a vogue among kale fans). Each of these methods helped with texture, but the first two made my salad too salty and massaging the kale was just too much work.

Beleaguered, I reached out to our science editor. He explained to me that these methods were all causing the cell walls of the kale leaves to break down,

Kale has a stronger flavor than the traditional romaine, so it requires a more assertive dressing.

making for a tender, easy-to-chew leaf. Surely, I said, there's an easier way. He suggested a softer approach: soaking the kale in a warm water bath. Not scalding hot, just warm. He suspected that it would have the same effect.

He was right. Soaking the kale in warm tap water (110 to 115 degrees) for just 10 minutes relaxed the leaves just enough for a salad. No extra heat (or massaging) necessary. And there was a bonus: This warm water bath could double as my washing step. I wouldn't need to prerinse the leaves.

The temperature of the water, however, created a new problem. When I went to serve my salad, the kale was still warm. I needed to refrigerate the kale to cool it back down and restore some

fresh crispness. A colleague suggested that I toss the kale in the dressing before cooling it to allow the flavors to meld together. Twenty minutes in the fridge worked like a charm.

About that dressing: The test kitchen's Caesar dressing recipe is delicious with romaine, but kale has a more powerful flavor that requires a more intense match. After a couple of tests finagling different ingredients and amounts, I decided to increase the number of anchovies and the volume of lemon juice to add to the dressing's pungency. An extra sprinkle of Parmesan and a few crunchy croutons (made while my salad was chilling) and I had a balanced, satisfying salad that changed my mind about kale.

TEST KITCHEN DISCOVERY
Softening Kale
To soften raw kale enough for it to be enjoyed in a salad, first soak stemmed, cut leaves in warm tap water for 10 minutes. Then, after drying the leaves, dress them and refrigerate the salad for at least 20 minutes (or up to 6 hours); during the refrigerating phase, the oil in the dressing "wets" the waxy, water-repelling surface of the kale leaves, which causes them to soften further.

KALE CAESAR SALAD Serves 4

The kale leaves must be dressed at least 20 minutes (or up to 6 hours) before serving.

SALAD
- **12 ounces curly kale, stemmed and cut into 1-inch pieces (16 cups)**
- **1 ounce Parmesan cheese, grated (½ cup)**

CROUTONS
- **3 ounces baguette, cut into ¾-inch cubes (3 cups)**
- **2 tablespoons extra-virgin olive oil**
- **¼ teaspoon pepper**
- **⅛ teaspoon salt**

DRESSING
- **½ cup mayonnaise**
- **¼ cup grated Parmesan cheese**
- **2 tablespoons lemon juice**
- **1 tablespoon white wine vinegar**
- **1 tablespoon Worcestershire sauce**
- **1 tablespoon Dijon mustard**
- **3 anchovy fillets, rinsed**
- **1 garlic clove, minced**
- **½ teaspoon salt**
- **½ teaspoon pepper**
- **¼ cup extra-virgin olive oil**

1. FOR THE SALAD: Place kale in large bowl and cover with warm tap water (110 to 115 degrees). Swish kale around to remove grit. Let kale sit in warm water bath for 10 minutes. Remove kale from water and spin dry in salad spinner in multiple batches. Pat leaves dry with paper towels if still wet.

2. FOR THE CROUTONS: Adjust oven rack to middle position and heat oven to 350 degrees. Toss all ingredients together in bowl. Bake on rimmed baking sheet until golden and crisp, about 15 minutes. Let croutons cool completely on sheet. (Cooled croutons can be stored in airtight container at room temperature for up to 24 hours.)

3. FOR THE DRESSING: Process mayonnaise, Parmesan, lemon juice, vinegar, Worcestershire, mustard, anchovies, garlic, salt, and pepper in blender until pureed, about 30 seconds. With blender running, slowly add oil until emulsified.

4. Toss kale with ¾ cup dressing in large bowl. Refrigerate dressed kale for at least 20 minutes or up to 6 hours. Toss Parmesan and croutons with dressed kale. Serve, passing remaining ¼ cup dressing at table.

Indoor Texas-Style Beef Ribs

Could we get big, bold, smoky barbecue flavor in beef short ribs . . . in the oven?

BY MATTHEW CARD

IN CENTRAL TEXAS barbecue, beef reigns supreme. Think gargantuan beef ribs, tender brisket, and, in certain circles, English-style short ribs. The block-like hunks of meat take to the pit like a duck to water, turning succulent and flavorful in the low, smoky heat. You will pay top dollar for smoked short ribs at such vaunted Texas barbecue haunts as Louie Mueller Barbecue and Franklin Barbecue—and they are worth every penny (and the interminable wait you will likely endure).

Could I get similar results on a faster timetable from the oven? I wanted authentic Texas-style results: tender meat coated with a thick, peppery "bark"—the true signifier of good 'cue.

Most recipes call for roasting the ribs and then slathering them with smoky-tasting sauce or liquid smoke. This approach works fairly well, but I wanted more resonant flavor. In a recipe search I uncovered a few unexpected ideas, including simmering the ribs with wood chips or thick slabs of bacon (neither proved effective). Most promising was a method in which the ribs were slowly braised in a seasoned liquid to tenderize and render their fat, and then drained, coated in spices, and finished in the oven. When I tried it, the ribs readily absorbed flavors from the braising liquid and the final roasting step worked well, especially when I sprinkled on a Texas-style spice crust that was heavy on the black pepper.

With a general method in hand, I pressed on. Six pounds of English-style ribs, sawed into 4- to 5-inch lengths, would serve four. Once trimmed, they fit easily into a large roasting pan. I cooked the ribs sealed tightly under foil at temperatures ranging from 250 to 400 degrees and found the best compromise between time and tenderness at 300 degrees. In 3 hours, the ribs were tender and nearly falling off the bone.

My braising liquid started out simple: water, a tablespoon of liquid smoke, and salt. It did the job, but I knew I could do better. I stuck with a base of water—beef broth surprisingly provided very little flavor enhancement—but increased the liquid smoke to a whopping ¼ cup. I added Worcestershire sauce and some bottled barbecue sauce. Brown sugar, combined with a pinch of ground clove, emphasized the smokiness. Coffee is common in barbecue sauces, and adding a few tablespoons of instant espresso

powder to the braising liquid had a galvanizing effect. The ribs didn't taste of coffee, just smokier and more satisfying.

These fully seasoned, ultratender ribs were now ready for a topcoat of baked-on spice rub. Spice rubs in central Texas are traditionally kept to a minimum, usually just coarse-ground black pepper, chili powder, paprika, garlic powder, and brown sugar. I tested a handful of rubs before settling on one made from black pepper, salt, chili powder, and brown sugar (cayenne appealed to some of my tasters but left others gasping, so I'll leave that option up to you).

To get the spice rub to cling more readily, I coated the ribs with a liquid smoke–enhanced swipe of barbecue sauce before applying the rub. I found that roasting the ribs for 30 minutes at 425 degrees crisped the exterior without drying out the meat or causing the sugar in the spice rub to burn. These indoor-cooked ribs now looked like they had spent the day in a Texas smoker despite taking less than 4 hours and requiring minimal hands-on effort.

INDOOR BARBECUE BEEF SHORT RIBS Serves 4 to 6
Our favorite store-bought barbecue sauce is Bull's-Eye Original Barbecue Sauce.

- 4 cups water
- ¾ cup barbecue sauce, plus extra for serving
- ¼ cup plus ½ teaspoon liquid smoke
- ¼ cup Worcestershire sauce
- 5 tablespoons packed brown sugar
- 2 tablespoons instant espresso powder
  Salt and pepper
- ¼ teaspoon ground cloves
- 6 pounds bone-in English-style short ribs, bones 4 to 5 inches long, 1 to 1½ inches of meat on top of bone, trimmed
- 2 teaspoons chili powder
- ¼ teaspoon cayenne pepper (optional)

1. Adjust oven rack to middle position and heat oven to 300 degrees. Bring water, ¼ cup barbecue sauce, ¼ cup liquid smoke, Worcestershire sauce, 3 tablespoons sugar, espresso powder, 1 teaspoon salt, and cloves to boil in medium saucepan over medium-high heat. Remove from heat once boiling.
2. Arrange ribs meat side down in large roasting pan. Pour hot water mixture over ribs. Wrap pan tightly with

These ultratender, silky short ribs are infused with smokiness.

aluminum foil and transfer to oven. Roast until ribs are easily pierced with paring knife, about 3 hours.

3. Remove pan from oven and increase oven temperature to 425 degrees. Line rimmed baking sheet with foil. Combine remaining ½ cup barbecue sauce and remaining ½ teaspoon liquid smoke in small bowl. In separate bowl, combine chili powder; cayenne, if using; 2 teaspoons pepper; 1½ teaspoons salt; and remaining 2 tablespoons sugar.

4. Place ribs meat side up on prepared sheet. Brush ribs liberally with barbecue sauce mixture, then sprinkle tops and sides with spice mixture. Roast until ribs are crispy and dark brown, about 30 minutes. Let ribs rest for 15 minutes. Serve, passing extra barbecue sauce separately.

Savory Noodle Kugel

While this traditional baked dish often takes a sweet route,
we were looking for a salt-and-pepper version to serve as a side. BY CHRISTIE MORRISON

THOUGH NOODLE KUGEL is often served as a sweet dish for Jewish Shabbat or holiday meals, kugel can also be an excellent savory side. But it shouldn't be saved for only special occasions. On the contrary, a savory kugel is an excellent side dish to a weeknight meal; think of it as a simple, rustic egg-noodle casserole.

Like other eastern European dishes such as pierogi or *haluski*, kugel uses a handful of inexpensive ingredients—in this case egg noodles, onions, and eggs—to make a filling casserole. Traditionally, onions are sautéed until they're soft and brown; tossed with cooked egg noodles, beaten eggs, salt, and pepper; and baked until the eggs are just set and the top layer of noodles has become browned and crisp.

The recipes I began my experiments with varied on the type of fat used to cook the onions; some called for schmaltz, or rendered chicken fat (often flavored with onion), for richness and depth. And while versions I made with schmaltz were deeply satisfying, I found that I could use more readily available olive oil in its place without compromising the basic mechanics of the recipe. (Due to kosher dietary restrictions, butter isn't traditionally used in a kugel served as a side dish to meat.) I did take issue with the amount of fat used in many recipes, however. One called for almost a cup of fat; I found that 3 tablespoons was plenty to add richness and effectively cook the onions without being greasy.

While sweet kugel casseroles frequently use cottage cheese and sour cream to bind the noodles together, savory kugel relies on eggs alone to provide sticking power and cohesion. And therein lies the rub: Too few eggs and the noodles remain separate in the dish; too many and the dish tastes and looks like a very lumpy quiche. I began by beating two eggs and tossing them with 1 pound of cooked, drained, and cooled egg noodles, working my way up. Three eggs, then four, and so on. After several kugels, I determined that six eggs for a pound of noodles yielded just the right density.

The trick was keeping the eggs evenly distributed while the casserole baked. In a few tests, the eggs sank to the bottom, creating two distinct layers of noodles: The top was loose and separate,

New to kugel? Think of it as a simple, rustic egg-noodle casserole.

while the bottom was thick and dense and eggy. How could I encourage the eggs to cling to the top? I learned that letting the noodles cool for a bit first and then tempering the egg mixture with just 3 tablespoons of the starchy noodle cooking water caused the eggs to thicken slightly and cling solidly. The resulting casserole had a more uniform consistency from top to bottom.

Many recipes achieve the characteristic browned, crunchy layer of noodles by prolonged baking in a hot oven, but too often this nets a dry, rubbery, overcooked kugel. I opted for a quick pass under the broiler after the dish had set to achieve the same effect without overcooking this classic, comforting casserole.

SAVORY NOODLE KUGEL
Serves 8 to 10
It's important to combine the egg mixture with warm noodles. Use a broiler-safe dish for this recipe. Look for rendered chicken fat (schmaltz) in the frozen food section of larger supermarkets. Pennsylvania Dutch Wide Egg Noodles are the test kitchen's taste test winner.

- 3 tablespoons rendered chicken fat (schmaltz) or extra-virgin olive oil
- 3 onions, chopped fine
  Salt and pepper
- 6 large eggs
- 2 tablespoons minced fresh parsley
- 1 pound wide egg noodles

1. Adjust 1 oven rack to middle position and second rack 6 inches from broiler element. Heat oven to 350 degrees. Grease broiler-safe 13 by 9-inch baking dish. Heat rendered chicken fat (schmaltz) in 12-inch skillet over medium-low heat until shimmering. Add onions and ½ teaspoon salt and cook, stirring occasionally, until caramelized, 30 to 40 minutes. (Caramelized onions can be refrigerated for up to 3 days.)

2. Transfer onions to large bowl and let cool for 10 minutes. Whisk eggs, parsley, 1 teaspoon salt, and ¾ teaspoon pepper into onions; set aside.

3. Bring 4 quarts water to boil in large pot. Add noodles and 1 tablespoon salt and cook, stirring often, until al dente. Reserve 3 tablespoons cooking water, then drain noodles and let cool for 5 minutes. Whisk reserved cooking water into onion mixture. Stir still-warm noodles into onion mixture until well combined.

4. Transfer noodle mixture to prepared dish. Bake on middle oven rack until set, about 20 minutes. Remove kugel from oven and heat broiler. Once broiler is hot, broil kugel on upper rack until top noodles are browned and crisp, 1 to 3 minutes, rotating dish as needed for even browning. Serve.

TO MAKE AHEAD
Kugel can be fully assembled, covered, and refrigerated up to 24 hours in advance. Extend baking time to 25 minutes.

Getting to Know Cooking Wines and Spirits

Wines and other spirits can add acidity, sweetness, or complex flavor to an array of dishes—both sweet and savory. Here are the ones that we like to keep handy. BY CHRISTIE MORRISON

Red Wine
BODY BUILDER

Along with acidity, red wine contributes flavor and complexity to foods. We usually find that cooking or reducing the wine allows some of the alcohol to evaporate and mellows the flavor. Mild-flavored wines work best for cooking; we use balanced table wines like French Côtes du Rhône for braises and pan sauces like our Basic Red Wine Pan Sauce: **CooksCountry.com/basicpansauce**.

White Wine
CRISP AND CLEAN

White wine's acidity and complex flavors can be a boon to pan sauces and casseroles. Avoid oaky, buttery Chardonnays—they can overwhelm subtle flavors—in favor of crisp, clean, dry Sauvignon Blancs. Don't spend an arm and a leg; a $10 wine is fine for cooking. Just be sure to avoid "cooking wines" in supermarkets—what these low-alcohol impostors lack in flavor, they overcompensate for with sodium and unpalatable acidity.

Beer
BATTERED AND FRIED

Sometimes we turn to beer to add hoppy or malty flavor to dishes like our Brisket Carbonnade or Guinness Beef Stew. But other times it's also the carbonation in beer that makes it essential to recipes like beer-battered onion rings and our tempura-style fish tacos: **CooksCountry.com/fishtacos**. As the batter cooks, the escaping bubbles add lift and help inhibit gluten development, keeping the batter more tender and less bready.

Marsala
SWEET FORTIFICATION

This Sicilian import is a fortified wine—a wine that has been supplemented with brandy or another distilled spirit. This process not only extends the shelf life of the wine but also allows winemakers to manipulate the flavors. Marsala has a smoky flavor and a range of sweetness levels: dolce (sweet), semisecco (semi-sweet), and secco (dry). We use sweet Marsala in our Chicken Marsala recipe: **CooksCountry.com/chickenmarsala**.

Dry Vermouth
PINCH HITTER

While it was originally produced in France, this fortified white wine (also known as French Vermouth) is now made in countries across Europe and in the United States. A classic ingredient in martinis, dry vermouth works equally well as a cooking wine. Flavored with herbs, spices, and other botanicals, it adds a subtle range of flavors. Plus, its longer shelf life (three to nine months if refrigerated) makes it a more convenient option than white wine, which starts to decline in a few hours.

Sherry
SPANISH SIPPER

Sherry is a Spanish fortified white wine that has oxidized, giving it a caramel, nutty flavor. It is produced in different styles: Fino is the least oxidized and has the lightest, driest flavor. Amontillado is slightly heavier and sweeter. Oloroso, also known as cream sherry, is the most expensive and highest in alcohol (at 24 percent); it is highly concentrated, sweet, and dark brown. We use dry sherries in savory recipes and save the sweet stuff for desserts like our Tipsy Squire: **CooksCountry.com/tipsysquire**.

Mirin
FERMENTED BREW

Mirin is a low-alcohol Japanese wine made from a blend of rices and alcohol and then fermented. While it is served as an aperitif in Japan, in the United States, it is most often used in Asian-inspired marinades and sauces to add sweet, acidic tang. Available in most grocery stores, it is sometimes labeled "sweetened sake" or "Aji-Mirin," though it is made from a different variety of rice than sake. Our Best Buy supermarket mirin is Eden Mirin Rice Cooking Wine.

Port
WORLD TRAVELER

Port is wine (usually red) from Portugal's Douro Valley that has been fortified with brandy. It is slightly sweet, as producers stop fermentation early while much of the grape sugar is still left in the wine. It is then aged anywhere from two to 50 years. We use ruby port (which is fruity and aged only about two years) in most recipes because it is less expensive and more visually appealing than older tawny port.

Bourbon
BARREL AGED

True bourbon is made in the United States from a fermented grain mash of corn (at least 51 percent), wheat, rye, and malted barley. It is aged in charred oak barrels that contribute bourbon's characteristic flavors of vanilla, caramel, and toasted nuts. We use the spirit in sauces, marinades, and desserts like our New Orleans Bourbon Bread Pudding: **CooksCountry.com/neworleansbreadpudding**.

Brandy
DISTILLED FRUIT

Brandies like cognac and Armagnac are distilled from wine made from neutral grapes (usually Ugni Blanc) and then aged—sometimes upwards of 60 years—to develop their flavors. Some brandies are made from other fruits; Calvados is a famous brandy of northern France made from apples. Their high alcohol percentage (about 40 percent) gives brandies a long shelf life.

Rum
SUGAR SPIRIT

Rum is usually distilled from fermented sugarcane juice or molasses; different distillation and aging methods produce light rum and dark rum. Both types are used in baking; we use light rum in our Holiday Rum Cake (**CooksCountry.com/holidayrumcake**) and dark rum in our Pumpkin Cake with Rum-Raisin Frosting (**CooksCountry.com/pumpkincake**).

Vodka
SECRET WEAPON

Vodka performs a vital role in our recipe for foolproof pie dough. We replace some of the water (which helps develop the gluten that makes pie dough tough) with vodka, which is 40 percent alcohol (and doesn't promote gluten development). This way, we're able to add enough liquid to make a rollable pie dough without developing the gluten that makes it tough.

**PAN-SEARED SWORDFISH
WITH CREAMY DIJON-CAPER SAUCE**

SKIRT STEAK WITH PINTO BEAN SALAD

**PENNE WITH CHICKEN, CHICKPEAS,
AND RADICCHIO**

**ROASTED CHICKEN WITH ARTICHOKE HEARTS
AND PANCETTA**

SKIRT STEAK WITH PINTO BEAN SALAD

Serves 4

WHY THIS RECIPE WORKS: Because skirt steak is thin, it's an ideal cut for a quick weeknight meal. Lime juice brightens up the pinto bean salad, and the chipotle provides subtle spicy and smoky notes.

- 2 (15-ounce) cans pinto beans, rinsed
- ½ cup finely chopped red onion
- ¼ cup chopped fresh cilantro
- 2 tablespoons lime juice
- 2 tablespoons vegetable oil
- 2 teaspoons minced canned chipotle chile in adobo sauce
  Salt and pepper
- 1 (1-pound) skirt steak, trimmed and cut into thirds
- 1 teaspoon paprika

1. Combine beans, onion, cilantro, lime juice, 1 tablespoon oil, chipotle, ½ teaspoon salt, and ½ teaspoon pepper in bowl. Transfer to platter.

2. Pat steak dry with paper towels, sprinkle with paprika, and season with salt and pepper. Heat remaining 1 tablespoon oil in 12-inch skillet over medium-high heat until smoking. Cook steak until well browned and meat registers 120 to 125 degrees (for medium-rare), about 2 minutes per side. Transfer steak to carving board, tent loosely with foil, and let rest for 5 minutes. Slice steak thin against grain and arrange on top of bean salad. Serve.

TEST KITCHEN NOTE: Be sure to slice the steak thin against the grain or it will be very chewy.

PAN-SEARED SWORDFISH
WITH CREAMY DIJON-CAPER SAUCE Serves 4

WHY THIS RECIPE WORKS: Slim ¾-inch-thick swordfish steaks cook quickly in the skillet. Crème fraîche cooks down to a slightly tart, creamy pan sauce.

- 4 (6-ounce) swordfish steaks, about ¾ inch thick
  Salt and pepper
- 1 tablespoon vegetable oil
- 1 shallot, minced
- 12 ounces cherry tomatoes, halved
- ½ cup crème fraîche
- 2 tablespoons Dijon mustard
- 2 tablespoons capers, rinsed
- 1 tablespoon chopped fresh tarragon

1. Pat fish dry with paper towels and season with salt and pepper. Heat oil in 12-inch nonstick skillet over medium-high heat until shimmering. Cook fish until golden brown and registering 140 degrees, about 5 minutes per side. Transfer fish to platter and tent loosely with foil.

2. Add shallot to now-empty skillet and cook until softened, about 3 minutes. Stir in tomatoes and cook until just softened, about 1 minute. Stir in crème fraîche, mustard, and capers and cook until slightly thickened, about 2 minutes. Season with salt and pepper to taste. Top fish with sauce, sprinkle with tarragon, and serve.

TEST KITCHEN NOTE: Halibut or salmon steaks of a similar thickness are good alternatives to swordfish.

ROASTED CHICKEN WITH ARTICHOKE HEARTS
AND PANCETTA Serves 4

WHY THIS RECIPE WORKS: Cooking the chicken skin side down in a 450-degree oven nicely crisps and browns the skin. Frozen artichokes and pancetta combine for a quick-cooking, flavorful side dish.

- 3 pounds bone-in chicken pieces (split breasts cut in half, drumsticks, and/or thighs), trimmed
  Salt and pepper
- 1 tablespoon olive oil
- 2 ounces pancetta, chopped fine
- 18 ounces frozen artichoke hearts, thawed, patted dry, and quartered
- 3 garlic cloves, minced
- 2 teaspoons minced fresh thyme
- ½ cup chicken broth
- 2 teaspoons lemon juice

1. Adjust oven rack to middle position and heat oven to 450 degrees. Pat chicken dry with paper towels and season with salt and pepper. Heat oil in 12-inch skillet over medium-high heat until shimmering. Add chicken, skin side down, and cook until well browned, about 5 minutes. Transfer skillet to oven and roast until breasts register 160 degrees and drumsticks/thighs register 175 degrees, about 15 minutes. Transfer chicken to platter, skin side up, and tent loosely with foil.

2. Add pancetta to now-empty skillet (skillet handle will be hot) and cook over medium-high heat until crisp, about 4 minutes. Add artichokes and cook, without stirring, until browned, about 2 minutes. Stir in garlic and thyme and cook until fragrant, about 30 seconds. Add broth and lemon juice, scraping up any browned bits, and cook until slightly thickened, about 2 minutes. Season with salt and pepper to taste. Spoon artichoke mixture around chicken and serve.

TEST KITCHEN NOTE: In step 2, be mindful of the hot skillet handle.

PENNE WITH CHICKEN, CHICKPEAS,
AND RADICCHIO Serves 4

WHY THIS RECIPE WORKS: A bold balsamic vinaigrette unites the flavors of the chicken, nutty chickpeas, and bitter radicchio. A hefty amount of basil adds freshness.

- 1 (14-ounce) can chickpeas, rinsed
- 1 small head radicchio (6 ounces), halved, cored, and sliced ¼ inch thick
- 1 ounce Pecorino Romano cheese, grated (½ cup), plus extra for serving
- 5 tablespoons balsamic vinegar
- ¼ cup extra-virgin olive oil, plus extra for drizzling
  Salt and pepper
- 2 (6-ounce) boneless, skinless chicken breasts, trimmed
- 8 ounces penne
- ½ cup chopped fresh basil

1. Combine chickpeas, radicchio, Pecorino, vinegar, 3 tablespoons oil, ½ teaspoon salt, and ½ teaspoon pepper in large bowl.

2. Pat chicken dry with paper towels and season with salt and pepper. Heat remaining 1 tablespoon oil in 10-inch nonstick skillet over medium-high heat until shimmering. Cook chicken until golden brown and thickest part registers 160 degrees, about 6 minutes per side. Transfer to carving board, tent loosely with foil, and let rest for 5 minutes. Slice chicken ½ inch thick and add to chickpea mixture.

3. Meanwhile, bring 4 quarts water to boil in large pot. Add pasta and 1 tablespoon salt and cook, stirring often, until al dente. Drain pasta and add to chickpea mixture. Transfer to platter and sprinkle with basil and extra Pecorino. Drizzle with extra oil before serving.

TEST KITCHEN NOTE: You can use fusilli or another short, tubular pasta in place of the penne.

**CRISP PORK CUTLETS
WITH ARUGULA AND APPLE SALAD**

**FENNEL-CRUSTED PORK CHOPS
WITH PRUNE COMPOTE**

STEAK TIPS WITH ROASTED FETA POTATOES

MUSHROOM AND GRUYÈRE CROSTATA

FENNEL-CRUSTED PORK CHOPS WITH PRUNE COMPOTE
Serves 4

✓ **WHY THIS RECIPE WORKS:** We cook the compote in the skillet after browning the chops, which minimizes cleanup while maximizing taste, as the pork drippings help flavor the compote.

- 4 (8- to 10-ounce) bone-in pork rib chops, ½ inch thick, trimmed
  Salt and pepper
- 1 tablespoon ground fennel
- 1 tablespoon vegetable oil
- 2 tablespoons minced shallot
- 1 cup pitted prunes, chopped
- ½ cup port
- ¼ cup cider vinegar
- ½ teaspoon grated orange zest plus ¼ cup juice
- ⅛ teaspoon cayenne pepper

1. Pat pork dry with paper towels and season with salt, pepper and 2 teaspoons fennel. Heat oil in 12-inch skillet over medium-high heat until just smoking. Add pork and cook until well browned and meat registers 140 degrees, about 4 minutes per side; transfer to platter and tent loosely with foil.

2. Add shallot to now-empty skillet and cook until softened, about 2 minutes. Add prunes, port, vinegar, orange zest and juice, cayenne, and remaining 1 teaspoon fennel and bring to boil. Reduce heat to medium-low and simmer until syrupy and reduced to 1 cup, about 8 minutes. Add any accumulated pork juices to compote and season with salt and pepper to taste. Spoon compote over pork and serve.

TEST KITCHEN NOTE: To prevent the pork chops from curling while they cook, cut two slits about 2 inches apart through the fat and connective tissue on one side of each chop.

CRISP PORK CUTLETS WITH ARUGULA AND APPLE SALAD
Serves 4

✓ **WHY THIS RECIPE WORKS:** For tender pork cutlets with a golden crust, we coated pork tenderloin cutlets with panko bread crumbs. A simple salad of peppery arugula and crisp apple complements the pork.

- 2 tablespoons lemon juice
- 1 tablespoon extra-virgin olive oil
  Salt and pepper
- ½ cup all-purpose flour
- 2 large eggs
- 1 cup panko bread crumbs
- 1 (16-ounce) pork tenderloin, trimmed, cut into 4 pieces, and pounded ¼ inch thick
- 1 cup vegetable oil
- 4 cups baby arugula
- 1 apple, cored, quartered, and cut into ¼-inch slices

1. Whisk lemon juice, olive oil, ½ teaspoon salt, and ½ teaspoon pepper together in bowl; set aside. Place flour in shallow dish. Beat eggs in second shallow dish. Place panko in third shallow dish. Pat pork dry with paper towels and season with salt and pepper. Working with one at a time, coat cutlets lightly with flour, dip in egg, and dredge in crumbs, pressing to adhere. Transfer cutlets to large plate and let dry for 5 minutes.

2. Heat vegetable oil in 12-inch nonstick skillet over medium heat until just smoking. Add pork and cook until golden brown and crisp, about 2 minutes per side. Transfer pork to paper towel–lined plate, tent loosely with foil, and let rest for 5 minutes. Just before serving, gently toss arugula and apple with dressing and serve with pork.

TEST KITCHEN NOTE: Ian's makes the test kitchen's favorite panko bread crumbs.

MUSHROOM AND GRUYÈRE CROSTATA Serves 4

✓ **WHY THIS RECIPE WORKS:** Using store-bought pie crust is easier than making your own. Browning the mushrooms and leeks in the skillet gives the tart depth of flavor.

- 1 (9-inch) store-bought pie dough round
- 2 tablespoons unsalted butter
- 6 portobello mushroom caps, gills removed, halved, and sliced crosswise ¼ inch thick
- 1 pound leeks, white and light green parts only, halved lengthwise, sliced thin, and washed thoroughly
  Salt and pepper
- 2 garlic cloves, minced
- 1 teaspoon minced fresh rosemary
- 2 ounces Gruyère cheese, shredded (½ cup)
- 1 large egg, lightly beaten
- 1 tablespoon minced fresh chives

1. Adjust oven rack to middle position and heat oven to 425 degrees. Line rimmed baking sheet with parchment paper. Roll dough into 14-inch circle on lightly floured counter; transfer to prepared sheet.

2. Melt butter in 12-inch nonstick skillet over medium-high heat. Add mushrooms, leeks, and ½ teaspoon salt and cook until beginning to brown, about 10 minutes. Stir in garlic and rosemary and cook until fragrant, about 30 seconds.

3. Transfer vegetables to prepared dough, leaving 2-inch border around edge. Sprinkle with Gruyère and fold border over filling, pinching pleated dough to secure. Brush dough with egg. Bake until crust is deep golden brown, 15 to 18 minutes, rotating halfway through baking. Sprinkle with chives. Cut into wedges and serve.

TEST KITCHEN NOTE: The test kitchen prefers Wholly Wholesome 9" Certified Organic Traditional Bake at Home Rolled Pie Dough.

STEAK TIPS WITH ROASTED FETA POTATOES Serves 4

✓ **WHY THIS RECIPE WORKS:** The browned bits (or fond) left behind in the skillet add valuable flavor to the vinegar sauce. Lining the rimmed baking sheet with parchment prevents the potatoes from sticking to the pan and makes cleanup easy.

- 1½ pounds Yukon Gold potatoes, unpeeled, sliced ¼ inch thick
- 3 tablespoons vegetable oil
  Salt and pepper
- 2 ounces feta cheese, crumbled (½ cup)
- 4 scallions, white and green parts separated and sliced thin
- 1½ pounds sirloin steak tips, trimmed and cut into 2-inch pieces
- ½ teaspoon dried oregano
- ¼ cup red wine vinegar

1. Adjust oven rack to upper-middle position and heat oven to 475 degrees. Line rimmed baking sheet with parchment paper. Toss potatoes with 2 tablespoons oil, 1 teaspoon salt, and 1 teaspoon pepper and arrange in single layer on prepared sheet. Roast potatoes until spotty brown and tender, about 20 minutes. Sprinkle potatoes with feta and scallion greens and continue to bake until cheese is just melted, about 5 minutes.

2. Meanwhile, pat steak dry with paper towels and season with salt and pepper. Heat remaining 1 tablespoon oil in 12-inch skillet over medium-high heat until just smoking. Add steak and cook until well browned all over and meat registers 125 degrees (for medium-rare), 5 to 7 minutes. Transfer to plate and tent loosely with foil.

3. Add scallion whites and oregano to now-empty skillet and cook until softened, about 30 seconds. Add vinegar and cook until slightly thickened, about 1 minute. Pour sauce over steak and serve with potatoes.

Football Sandwiches

Brushed with a butter sauce and baked, these hot sandwiches are a game-day favorite.

BY DIANE UNGER

FOOTBALL SANDWICHES ARE a staple at Southern football parties and a popular recipe in Junior League cookbooks. Slider-size, they're made from soft (usually square) white dinner rolls that are split and filled with sliced deli ham and Swiss cheese.

But that's only half the story. What makes these little sandwiches special is the savory poppy-seed sauce that's poured over the sandwiches before they're baked. Made from butter (lots of butter), poppy seeds, mustard, onion, and Worcestershire sauce, the sauce is absorbed into the sandwiches, which are then baked until the cheese just begins to melt and the sandwiches are all hot and toasty. Sounds like a winning idea, right? Not so much. After baking my way through several existing recipes, it was clear: There was something wrong with the game plan.

A few of the recipes I tested early on called for a stick and a half of butter for a dozen sandwiches—1 tablespoon of butter per tiny sandwich. I love butter as much as anyone, but this was excessive. Those early tests produced soft, squishy sandwiches that were coat-your-fingers greasy—and for all that fat, they fell remarkably short on flavor.

Working with 12 sandwiches (two per serving), I was able to whittle the amount of butter from 12 tablespoons

By bathing the rolls in a supersavory butter sauce, we transform ordinary sandwich ingredients into something spectacular.

all the way down to four without a significant loss of flavor.

Some recipes I tried called for chopped raw onion, but my tasters found its bite just too strong. To take the edge off the onion and to enhance the flavor of the poppy seeds, I microwaved them along with the butter I was already melting. And to amp things up in the savory department, I doubled the amount of savory-sweet Worcestershire sauce and added some garlic powder to the mix.

Spreading the rolls with butter or mayonnaise before piling on the meat and cheese was a common technique, but my tasters decided that this was overkill. Instead, I spread the rolls with yellow mustard (about 1 teaspoon per

roll) before loading them up with a full slice each of deli sliced Black Forest ham and a good-quality deli sliced Swiss cheese, carefully folded and stacked onto the rolls to keep things neat.

After brushing the sandwiches with the poppy-seed sauce and then carefully pouring the remaining sauce over the top, I gave them a short time-out to soak it all in.

Filled and sauced, my sliders were ready for the oven. I baked the sandwiches covered for 20 minutes to help the cheese melt and then uncovered for another 7 to 9 minutes. This gave the tops of the sandwiches a chance to crisp up a bit. Buttery, savory, and ready for game day, my Ham and Swiss Football Sandwiches were a hit.

Sandwich Construction

Big flavors come in small packages. To make the most of our football sandwiches, precise construction is key. Here's how we build them.

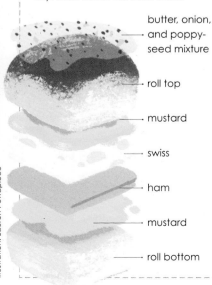

- butter, onion, and poppy-seed mixture
- roll top
- mustard
- swiss
- ham
- mustard
- roll bottom

Illustration: Lauren Pettapiece

HAM AND SWISS FOOTBALL SANDWICHES
Serves 6

We prefer the soft white dinner rolls found in the bakery section of your supermarket, but dinner-size potato rolls will also work in this recipe.

- 12 square soft white dinner rolls
- 6 tablespoons yellow mustard
- 12 thin slices deli Black Forest ham (8 ounces)
- 12 thin slices deli Swiss cheese (8 ounces)
  Pepper
- 4 tablespoons unsalted butter
- 2 tablespoons finely chopped onion
- 1 tablespoon poppy seeds
- 2 tablespoons Worcestershire sauce
- 1 teaspoon garlic powder

1. Adjust oven rack to middle position and heat oven to 350 degrees. Slice rolls in half horizontally. Spread 4 tablespoons mustard on cut sides of roll tops and bottoms. Arrange roll bottoms, cut side up and side by side, in 13 by 9-inch baking dish. Fold ham slices in thirds, then once in half; place 1 slice on each roll bottom. Fold Swiss like ham, then place over ham. Season with pepper and cap with roll tops.

2. Combine butter, onion, and poppy seeds in bowl. Microwave until butter is melted and onion is softened, about 1 minute. Whisk Worcestershire, garlic powder, and remaining 2 tablespoons mustard into butter mixture until combined. Generously brush tops and edges of sandwiches with all of butter mixture. Spoon any remaining solids over sandwiches.

3. Cover dish with aluminum foil and let sit for 10 minutes to allow sandwiches to absorb sauce. Bake for 20 minutes. Uncover and continue to bake until cheese is melted around edges and tops are slightly firm, 7 to 9 minutes. Let cool for 10 minutes. Serve.

TO MAKE AHEAD

Sandwiches can be brushed with sauce, covered, and refrigerated up to 1 day in advance. Bring to room temperature before cooking.

▶ How about a version with pastrami and Swiss? Visit CooksCountry.com/jan15 for the recipe.

Reviving Mulligan Stew

Mulligan stew was once a catchall supper used to clean out the fridge (and pantry).
We refined it into a dish all its own. BY BRIDGET LANCASTER

I GET THE IDEA of "kitchen sink" recipes—the higgledy-piggledy approach to using any and all on-hand ingredients in a dish can be both practical and economical but not always successful. Sure, the folks at the table will be filled up, but happy? That's another question. Meet mulligan stew, aka "hobo stew," "bachelor's stew," or (shudder) "mystery stew."

It's difficult to call this dish a recipe. A stew born from thriftiness, the commonest ground from one mulligan recipe to the next is a roster of inexpensive and easily procured ingredients: beef (round) as the base; cheap vegetables like onion, potatoes, and carrots; and, least pricey of all, water for the stewing liquid.

From there, it's anything goes. I could add pork, chicken, lamb, beef stew bones, celery, cabbage, Brussels sprouts, turnips, rutabaga, parsnips, green beans, lima beans, peas, corn, rice, barley, or tomatoes and still call it mulligan. Or I could go the bachelor route and use canned versions of everything, including condensed tomato soup (or ketchup) and tinned meat, for a dump-and-stir solution. I picked the former "fresher" approach.

I tried a handful of published recipes, but no matter the method, the results were full of unfulfilled promise: When you throw everything in a pot together and simmer it for hours, you'll get a murky, mashed-up stew with over-cooked vegetables, blown-out grains, and, despite the panoply of ingredients, very little depth of flavor. Uninspiring. Lackluster. Dull. Clearly, mulligan needed a do-over.

I was determined to stick with water as the cooking liquid; its essential thriftiness is the very soul of mulligan stew. To make the most of it, I'd need flavorful ingredients, especially meat that could hold up to long simmering. Instead of a lean and potentially tough cut of beef round, I chose a meaty, marbled chuck-eye roast. This still-inexpensive shoulder cut slow-cooks into moist and tender bites.

I browned the beef in batches, which produced flavorful browned bits known as fond on the bottom of the pot. Later, I would scrape up the fond into the liquid to help create a richer broth and more robust stew.

From there, I refined the vegetable

What you can't see: the rich flavor imparted by a smoky ham hock.

list. Channeling the not-so-subtle Irish "mulligan" moniker, I kept potatoes, carrots, and, of course, onions. I chose mustardy turnips over parsnips and rutabaga, nixed the bitter celery stalks, picked hearty green cabbage over quick-wilting Brussels sprouts, and passed over the sweet corn and limas for fresh green beans.

To ensure that the vegetables emerged with the right texture,

I cooked them in stages. Onions and long-cooking carrots went in near the start so they'd have time to soften and yield their texture and aromatic flavor to the dish.

Next, tomatoes. I really, really wanted to like fresh chopped tomatoes in the stew, but their presence was pretty much null and void, despite the extra, careful work it took to peel, seed, and chop them. On the other hand, I wanted to

despise the addition of canned tomato soup, but although it was sweet and artificial, there was something about the long-cooked tomato flavor that was appealing. To get the depth without the artifice, I split the difference and reached for a can of tomatoes packed in juice. By condensing them myself—cooking down the pulp and juice in the pot until almost dry—I added a subtly sweet tomato flavor that warmed up the dish, especially when I introduced a smidge of pungent allspice to the equation.

My mulligan was really shaping up. Tasters clearly preferred the inclusion of chewy, malty pearl barley over rice, as the barley retained its texture better during the long cooking and added a bit of body to the stew.

After simmering the rest of the stew for a spell, I added a cut-up turnip and a pound of cubed (but not peeled) Yukon Gold potatoes (chosen for their buttery flavor and stalwart texture). I tossed in a handful of trimmed fresh green beans and let it all bubble slowly for another hour until the turnips and potatoes were soft and the beans were tender and silky. The cabbage, added at the very end, held on to a bit of crunch.

But there was something missing—something that would take the stew over the top in flavor and richness. I remembered that so many recipes used multiple cuts of meat and/or beef bones to boost the flavor. I wasn't crazy about cutting up more meat for the stew, so I tried bones—beef shin bones, knuckles, and oxtail, all of which I had to special-order from the butcher, plus one that was readily available (and not bovine): smoked ham hock.

Happily, the hock prevailed and then some. The savory smoked bone provided incredible flavor and richness, but the best part? After fishing out the hock and letting it cool a bit, I picked off the soft shreds of stewed ham from the bone and stirred those morsels of meat back into the stew.

This was the new mulligan stew—complete with its own contemporary identity. And although its ingredient list had been shortened, its flavor was bigger than ever.

TEST KITCHEN TECHNIQUE
Dividing a Chuck-Eye Roast

You'll find a natural seam in the center of your eye roast. But the best tool for separating the roast at this seam (so you can trim away the excess fat) isn't a knife—it's your hands. Carefully work your fingers into the seam and ease the two sides apart before cutting it into 1½-inch pieces.

MULLIGAN STEW
Serves 8

Be sure to use a smoked ham hock for this recipe. You should have about 2¾ pounds of beef after trimming and cubing.

- 1 (4-pound) boneless beef chuck-eye roast, pulled apart at seams, trimmed, and cut into 1½-inch pieces
  Salt and pepper
- 3 tablespoons vegetable oil
- 4 carrots, peeled and cut into 1½-inch lengths (2 cups)
- 1 large onion, chopped
- ½ teaspoon ground allspice
- 1 (14.5-ounce) can diced tomatoes
- 5½ cups water
- 1 (12-ounce) smoked ham hock
- ½ cup pearl barley
- 2 teaspoons minced fresh thyme
- 1 pound Yukon Gold potatoes, unpeeled, cut into 1-inch pieces
- 1 (8-ounce) turnip, unpeeled, cut into 1-inch pieces
- 8 ounces green beans, trimmed and cut into 1-inch lengths
- 1½ cups coarsely chopped green cabbage

1. Adjust oven rack to lower-middle position and heat oven to 300 degrees. Pat beef dry with paper towels and season with salt and pepper. Heat 1 tablespoon oil in large Dutch oven over medium-high heat until just smoking. Add half of beef and cook until well browned on all sides, about 8 minutes, reducing heat if pot bottom becomes too dark. Transfer beef to plate. Repeat with 1 tablespoon oil and remaining beef.

2. Add remaining 1 tablespoon oil, carrots, onion, and allspice to now-empty pot. Cook over medium heat, scraping up any browned bits, until onion is just softened, about 2 minutes. Add tomatoes and their juice and cook until nearly dry, about 8 minutes. Add water, ham hock, barley, thyme, beef and any accumulated juices, and 1 teaspoon salt. Increase heat to high and bring to simmer. Cover, transfer to oven, and cook for 1¾ hours.

3. Remove pot from oven; stir in potatoes, turnip, and green beans. Cover, return to oven, and cook until potatoes and turnips are nearly tender, about 45 minutes. Remove pot from oven, then remove ham hock from stew and let cool for 5 minutes. Using 2 forks, shred meat from ham hock, discarding skin and bones.

4. Stir cabbage and ham hock meat into stew. Cover, return to oven, and cook until all vegetables are tender, about 15 minutes longer. Season with salt and pepper to taste. Serve.

The American Table
Stews for Crews

The barn's been raised, the stump speech spoken, the sermon delivered. What's an American cook faced with a hungry horde to do? Fire up the stew pot. What you call your concoction has as much to do with where you are as what's cooking.

Mulligan: The catchall term for catchall stews, "mulligan" has imprecise origins. Mulligan stew's similarity to Irish stew (mutton, potatoes, and vegetables) suggests a connection to Ireland, where "Mulligan," according to linguist Henry Hitchings, is used as a generic (and often negative) term for Irishmen: He told us, "I've heard the name used derisively in Ireland—in a statement along the lines of 'Oh, it was one of those Mulligan fellas' when in truth no one called Mulligan was involved in the outrage under discussion."

Brunswick: Brunswick, Virginia; Brunswick, Georgia; and Brunswick County, North Carolina all lay claim to this stew, but food historian John Egerton dismissed them all in his book *Southern Food*: "There was Brunswick stew before there was a Brunswick." Native Americans had been stewing squirrel, rabbit, and other typical Brunswick ingredients for centuries.

Burgoo: A Works Progress Administration study set this Kentucky stew's origins in the 19th century, hailing a crafty Confederate army cook who put "potatoes, tomatoes, onions, some cabbage, twenty-nine blackbirds, three crows, a goose, several hens, and a shoat (a young pig)" in a powder kettle and set it to simmer.

Booya: Walloon-speaking Belgian immigrants settled the area around Green Bay, Wisconsin, in the 1850s, where they started serving this stew of oxtails, beef, chicken, cabbage, beans, kohlrabi, and rutabaga.

Slumgullion: Miners in the Rockies called their stew slumgullion, a word also used to describe the muddy slough left behind after gold-panning. In Colorado's San Juan mountains, a slow-moving landslide so reminded miners of the stew that they dubbed it Slumgullion Slide. Its footprint is still visible from nearby Slumgullion Pass.

INGREDIENT SPOTLIGHT **Barley**

Barley, by and large, is used for two things in the United States: animal feed and beer. But a century ago, it was a cheap and ubiquitous pantry staple, eaten at all three meals. Barley, still cheap, is enjoying a quiet comeback today. Most supermarkets carry two types of barley: pearl barley, which has had both the outer hull and bran removed for quicker cooking, and hull-less (or hulled) barley, with the bran still intact. We use the more common pearl barley in mulligan stew for its softer texture and subtle flavor and also for the starch it releases into the soup, gently thickening the broth as it cooks.

PEARL BARLEY   **HULL-LESS BARLEY**

Christmas Cookie Contest

It's prime season for cookie baking, so we turned to our greatest resource for fresh ideas: you.

What makes a winning cookie? Ask a dozen judges and you'll get a dozen answers. Our annual holiday contest stirred passions and inspired feverish debate. In the end, we put it to a vote. Who knew the democratic process could be so . . . sweet?

CHOCOLATE CROISSANT COOKIES Makes 20 cookies

Karen Cope, Minneapolis, Minn.

Plan ahead: The dough needs to chill for at least 1 hour before baking. Be sure to use Hershey's bars, as the size of the chocolate pieces is important for these cookies.

- 1 cup (5 ounces) all-purpose flour
- ⅛ teaspoon salt
- 8 tablespoons unsalted butter, softened
- 4 ounces cream cheese, softened
- 2 tablespoons granulated sugar
- ½ teaspoon vanilla extract
- 6 (1.55-ounce) Hershey's milk chocolate bars
- 1 large egg, lightly beaten
- 3 tablespoons white sanding sugar

1. Whisk flour and salt together in bowl. Using stand mixer fitted with paddle, beat butter, cream cheese, and granulated sugar on medium-high speed until light and fluffy, about 3 minutes. Add vanilla and beat until incorporated. Reduce speed to low and add flour mixture in 2 additions, until just combined, scraping down bowl as needed. Form dough into 6-inch disk. Wrap disk in plastic wrap and refrigerate for at least 1 hour or up to 24 hours.

2. Adjust oven racks to upper-middle and lower-middle positions and heat oven to 350 degrees. Line 2 baking sheets with parchment paper. Break 5 chocolate bars crosswise along their 3 seams to yield 4 rectangles. (You should have 20 chocolate pieces in total.) Roll dough into 20 by 8-inch rectangle on lightly floured counter. Cut dough into twenty 4 by 2-inch rectangles. Working with 1 dough rectangle at a time, place 1 chocolate piece crosswise across dough so chocolate overhangs edges. Fold dough around chocolate. Repeat with remaining 19 pieces of dough and chocolate and place cookies seam side down, 1½ inches apart, on prepared

$1,000 grand-prize winner

sheets (10 per sheet). Brush tops with egg and sprinkle with sanding sugar.

3. Bake until golden brown, 18 to 20 minutes, switching and rotating sheets halfway through baking. Let cookies cool on sheets for 5 minutes, then transfer to wire rack and let cool completely.

4. Break remaining 1 chocolate bar into pieces and microwave in bowl at 50 percent power, stirring occasionally, until melted, about 1 minute. Using spoon, drizzle chocolate over tops of cookies. Let set for at least 30 minutes before serving.

KEY STEP **Wrap 'em Up**
While Hershey's isn't the test kitchen's favorite milk chocolate (that would be Dove Silky Smooth Milk Chocolate), it is essential in this recipe. Why? Because these cookies were engineered to work with three-rectangle blocks of this iconic milk chocolate. Place one chocolate rectangle in the center of each 4 by 2-inch piece of dough, fold the edges over, and bake seam side down.

RASPBERRY-FILLED ALMOND TORTE COOKIES Makes 36 cookies

Patricia Harmon, Baden, Pa.

A small offset spatula makes it easy to spread the frosting over the cookies.

TOPPING
- ½ cup sliced almonds
- 2 tablespoons turbinado sugar
- 1 tablespoon water

COOKIES
- 3 cups (15 ounces) all-purpose flour
- 1 teaspoon baking powder
- ⅛ teaspoon salt
- 16 tablespoons unsalted butter, softened
- 1 cup (7 ounces) granulated sugar
- 3 ounces cream cheese, softened
- 1 large egg
- 2 tablespoons sour cream
- ½ teaspoon vanilla extract
- 6 tablespoons seedless raspberry jam

FROSTING
- 8 tablespoons unsalted butter, softened
- 2 cups (8 ounces) confectioners' sugar
- 3 tablespoons heavy cream
- ¼ teaspoon almond extract

1. FOR THE TOPPING: Adjust oven racks to upper-middle and lower-middle positions and heat oven to 350 degrees. Line 2 baking sheets with parchment paper. Combine almonds, sugar, and water in bowl. Spread almond mixture in single layer on 1 prepared sheet. Bake on upper rack until lightly browned, 10 to 12 minutes. Let topping cool completely on sheet. Break into small pieces and transfer to bowl. Leave parchment on sheet.

2. FOR THE COOKIES: Increase oven temperature to 375 degrees. Combine flour, baking powder, and salt in bowl. Using stand mixer fitted with paddle, beat butter, sugar, and cream cheese on medium-high speed until pale and fluffy, about 3 minutes. Add egg, sour cream, and vanilla and beat until combined. Reduce speed to low and add flour mixture in 3 additions until just combined, scraping down bowl as needed. Transfer dough to bowl, cover with plastic wrap, and refrigerate until slightly firm, about 20 minutes.

3. Working with 2 tablespoons dough at a time, roll into 36 balls and space 1 inch apart on prepared sheets (18 cookies per sheet). Bake until dry on top but not browned, 10 to 12 minutes, switching and rotating sheets halfway through baking. Let cookies cool on sheets for 5 minutes, then transfer to wire rack and let cool completely.

4. FOR THE FROSTING: Using stand mixer fitted with paddle, beat butter on medium-high speed until fluffy, about 30 seconds. Reduce speed to low and add sugar in 2 additions until combined. Increase speed to medium-high and beat until pale and fluffy, about 2 minutes, scraping down bowl as necessary. Reduce speed to medium-low and add cream and almond extract; mix until combined.

5. Using serrated knife, cut off tops of cookies and reserve. Spread ½ teaspoon raspberry jam over 1 cookie bottom; replace top. Spread 1 heaping teaspoon frosting on cookie top; sprinkle with almond topping. Repeat with remaining cookies.

JEWELED PYRAMIDS Makes 24 cookies

Beth Esser, Friendship, Wis.

If you're unable to find Kraft caramels, any soft caramel candy may be substituted.

- 2½ cups (12½ ounces) all-purpose flour
- 2½ cups (10 ounces) pecans, chopped fine
- 16 tablespoons unsalted butter, cut into small pieces and chilled
- ½ cup packed (3½ ounces) light brown sugar
- 2 teaspoons vanilla extract
- ¼ teaspoon salt
- 26 Kraft caramels
- ¼ cup milk

1. Adjust oven rack to upper-middle and lower-middle positions and heat oven to 325 degrees. Line 2 baking sheets with parchment paper. Pulse flour, 1 cup pecans, butter, sugar, vanilla, and salt in food processor until combined and dough holds its shape when squeezed together, about 20 pulses. Transfer to counter and press together to form cohesive dough.

2. Divide dough into 24 balls, form each into pyramid shape, and space evenly on prepared sheets (12 cookies per sheet). Bake until cookies are light golden, 20 to 25 minutes, switching and rotating sheets halfway through baking. Let cookies cool on sheets for 5 minutes, then transfer to wire rack and let cool completely. (Do not discard parchment on baking sheets.)

3. Microwave caramels and milk in bowl, stirring occasionally, until melted and smooth, about 3 minutes. Place remaining 1½ cups pecans in shallow dish. Dip point of each pyramid in caramel to coat, then lightly press into pecans. Return to sheets and let cookies set for at least 20 minutes before serving.

KEY STEP **Forming Pyramids**
To shape the balls of dough into pyramids, place one ball on an unfloured counter and press down firmly to flatten the bottom. Then pinch the top and sides, using increasingly more pressure at the top, until you have a three-sided triangle, Use both hands to finish the shaping, pushing with equal pressure on opposite sides. Repeat with remaining balls.

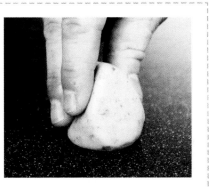

CHOCOLATE 'MALLOW COOKIE CUPS Makes 20 cookies

Pam Correll, Brockport, Pa.

If you do not have a mini muffin tin, use mini foil cups placed on a baking sheet.

- 1½ cups (7½ ounces) all-purpose flour
- ½ cup (1½ ounces) unsweetened cocoa powder
- ¼ teaspoon salt
- ¼ teaspoon baking soda
- ¼ teaspoon baking powder
- 1 cup (7 ounces) sugar
- 8 tablespoons unsalted butter, softened
- 1 large egg
- 1 teaspoon vanilla extract
- ⅔ cup marshmallow crème
- ¼ cup (½ ounce) sweetened flaked coconut
- ¼ cup milk chocolate chips

KEY STEP Filling Cookie Cups

Once the chocolaty dough is divided and rolled into 3-inch circles, place 1 teaspoon of the marshmallow-coconut filling in the center of each circle. Then fold the dough around the filling, pinching to seal; gently roll the filled dough into a ball; and bake in a lined mini muffin tin.

1. Adjust oven rack to middle position and heat oven to 350 degrees. Line mini muffin tin with 20 paper or foil liners. Whisk flour, cocoa, salt, baking soda, and baking powder together in bowl; set aside.

2. Using stand mixer fitted with paddle, beat sugar and butter on medium-high speed until pale and fluffy, about 3 minutes. Add egg and vanilla and beat until combined. Reduce speed to low and add flour mixture in 2 additions until well combined, scraping down bowl as needed.

3. Combine marshmallow crème and coconut in small bowl; set aside. Divide dough into 20 heaping tablespoons and roll into balls. On lightly floured counter, press each ball into 3-inch circle. Place 1 teaspoon of marshmallow mixture in center of each circle and wrap dough around mixture, pinching to seal. Roll into smooth ball and place in liners in muffin tin.

4. Bake until just set, 10 to 12 minutes, rotating muffin tin halfway through baking. Let cookies cool in muffin tin for 15 minutes, then transfer to wire rack and let cool completely.

5. Microwave chocolate chips in bowl at 50 percent power, stirring occasionally, until melted, about 1 minute. Spread chocolate over cookies and let set for at least 20 minutes before serving.

SPICY NUTTY PEPPERY JAWBREAKERS Makes 36 cookies

Susan Asanovic, Wilton, Conn.

Mixed peppercorns—a combination of black, white, and red—can be found in most grocery stores; however, black pepper can be used exclusively.

- 1 cup plus 3 tablespoons (7⅛ ounces) whole-wheat pastry flour
- 2 teaspoons grated orange zest
- 1 teaspoon ground cinnamon
- 1 teaspoon ground mixed pepper
- ½ teaspoon baking powder
- ¼ teaspoon baking soda
- ¼ teaspoon ground nutmeg
- ⅛ teaspoon salt
- 1 cup unsalted mixed nuts, toasted
- ⅔ cup (4¾ ounces) turbinado sugar
- 2 tablespoons unsalted butter, softened
- ⅓ cup molasses
- ¼ cup minced crystallized ginger
- 2 large egg yolks
- 8 ounces white chocolate, chopped fine
- 2 teaspoons vegetable oil
- ⅛ teaspoon peppermint extract Sanding sugar

1. Whisk flour, orange zest, cinnamon, pepper, baking powder, baking soda, nutmeg, and salt together in bowl. Pulse nuts in food processor until finely ground, about 10 pulses; add to bowl with flour mixture.

2. In now-empty food processor, pulse turbinado sugar and butter until combined, about 15 pulses. Add molasses, ginger, and egg yolks and pulse until combined, about 7 pulses. Add flour mixture and pulse until dough forms, about 5 pulses. Transfer to bowl, cover, and refrigerate for at least 1 hour or up to 24 hours.

3. Adjust oven rack to middle position and heat oven to 325 degrees. Line 2 baking sheets with parchment paper. Working with 1 tablespoon dough at a time, roll into ¾-inch balls and space 1 inch apart on prepared sheets (18 cookies per sheet).

4. Bake 1 sheet at a time until cookies are firm and lightly browned with cracked tops, 15 to 20 minutes, rotating sheet halfway through baking. Let cookies cool on sheet for 5 minutes, then transfer to wire rack and let cool completely.

5. Microwave chocolate in bowl at 50 percent power, stirring occasionally, until melted, about 2 minutes. Stir in oil and peppermint extract until smooth. Drizzle chocolate over surface of cookies and immediately decorate with sanding sugar. Let set for at least 30 minutes before serving.

finalist

ALMOND-SPICE CHRISTMAS WREATH COOKIES Makes 40 cookies
Elsa Escobar, Tulsa, Okla.

Dried cherries can be substituted for maraschino cherries in this recipe.

COOKIES
- 4 cups (18 ounces) almond flour
- 2 tablespoons grated orange zest (2 oranges)
- 1 tablespoon ground coffee
- 1 teaspoon ground cinnamon
- 1 teaspoon ground ginger
- ½ teaspoon ground cardamom
- ¼ teaspoon salt
- 3 large egg whites
- 1½ cups (10½ ounces) granulated sugar
- 2 teaspoons almond extract
- 1 teaspoon vanilla extract
- 3 tablespoons orange marmalade

TOPPING
- 2 large egg whites
- 2 cups (7 ounces) sliced almonds
- 40 maraschino cherries (combination of red and green), quartered
- Confectioners' sugar

1. FOR THE COOKIES: Whisk almond flour, orange zest, coffee, cinnamon, ginger, cardamom, and salt together in bowl. Using stand mixer fitted with whisk, whip egg whites on medium-low speed until foamy, about 1 minute. Increase speed to medium-high and whip whites to soft, billowy mounds, about 1 minute. Gradually add sugar and whip until glossy, soft peaks form, 2 to 3 minutes. Whip in almond and vanilla extracts.

2. Fold almond flour mixture into whipped whites in 2 additions until few white streaks remain. Fold in marmalade until no white streaks remain. Divide dough in half and wrap each half in plastic wrap. Refrigerate until firm, at least 1 hour or up to 24 hours.

3. FOR THE TOPPING: Adjust oven rack to upper-middle and lower-middle positions and heat oven to 300 degrees. Line 2 baking sheets with parchment paper. Whisk egg whites in shallow dish until frothy. Place almonds in second shallow dish.

4. Divide 1 dough half into 20 pieces. On lightly floured counter, roll each piece into 5-inch rope, shape into circle, and press ends together to seal. Dip 1 side of each wreath into egg whites, letting excess drip off, then press gently into almonds. Place, almond side up, on prepared sheets (10 cookies per sheet). Press 4 cherry pieces into each wreath.

5. Bake until firm and golden brown, 20 to 25 minutes, switching and rotating sheets halfway through baking. Let cookies cool on sheets for 5 minutes, then transfer to wire rack and let cool completely. Repeat with remaining dough, egg whites, almonds, and cherries, letting sheets cool between batches. Dust with confectioners' sugar before serving.

DORIS'S COCONUT LEMON MELTS Makes 36 cookies
Cindy Beberman, Orland Park, Ill.

If you can't find superfine sugar, process granulated sugar in a food processor for 30 seconds. Instead of a tablespoon measure, a #60 scoop can be used for portioning the dough.

- 2½ cups (12½ ounces) all-purpose flour
- ¼ teaspoon baking powder
- 1 cup macadamia nuts, toasted
- 1 cup (2 ounces) sweetened flaked coconut, toasted
- 16 tablespoons unsalted butter, softened
- 1 cup (7 ounces) plus 2 tablespoons superfine sugar
- ½ teaspoon salt
- 1 large egg plus 1 large yolk
- 1 tablespoon grated lemon zest plus 4 teaspoons juice
- 1 teaspoon vanilla extract
- 12 ounces white chocolate, chopped
- ⅛ teaspoon lemon oil
- 6 ounces semisweet chocolate, chopped

1. Adjust oven rack to middle position and heat oven to 375 degrees. Line baking sheet with parchment paper. Whisk flour and baking powder together in bowl. Pulse nuts in food processor until finely ground, about 10 pulses; add to flour mixture. In now-empty food processor, pulse coconut until finely ground, about 5 pulses; add to flour-nut mixture.

2. Using stand mixer fitted with paddle, beat butter, sugar, and salt on medium-high speed until pale and fluffy, about 3 minutes. Add egg and yolk, lemon zest and juice, and vanilla and beat until combined. Reduce speed to low and add flour mixture in 2 additions until just combined, scraping down bowl as needed.

3. Using 1-tablespoon measure, scoop 12 portions of dough, roll into smooth balls, and evenly space on prepared sheet. Press dough to ¼-inch thickness using bottom of greased measuring cup or flat-bottomed glass.

4. Bake until golden brown around edges, 8 to 10 minutes, rotating sheet halfway through baking. Let cookies cool on sheet for 5 minutes, then transfer to wire rack and let cool completely. Repeat twice more with remaining dough, letting sheet cool between batches.

5. Microwave white chocolate in bowl at 50 percent power, stirring occasionally, until melted, 2 to 3 minutes. Stir in lemon oil. Dip half of each cookie into melted white chocolate, letting excess drip back into bowl, and place on parchment-lined sheet. Let chocolate set for 30 minutes.

6. Microwave semisweet chocolate in bowl at 50 percent power, stirring occasionally, until melted, about 2 minutes. Dip fork into chocolate and wave back and forth over white chocolate–coated half of cookies to create lines. Let chocolate set for at least 30 minutes before serving.

finalist

Cooking Class Breaded Chicken Cutlets

Breaded cutlets promise a moist, tender interior and crunchy, crisp exterior. But to get there, you have to follow the rules. BY BRYAN ROOF

CRISP BREADED CHICKEN CUTLETS

Serves 4

Make sure to remove the tenderloin from each breast so the cutlets will be a uniform shape and will cook evenly; reserve tenderloins for another use. Don't substitute store-bought bread crumbs for the fresh bread crumbs.

- 4 (6- to 8-ounce) boneless, skinless chicken breasts, tenderloins removed, trimmed
  Salt and pepper
- 4–6 slices hearty white sandwich bread, crusts removed, torn into 1½-inch pieces
- ¾ cup all-purpose flour
- 2 large eggs
- ¾ cup vegetable oil
  Lemon wedges

1. Adjust oven rack to lower-middle position and heat oven to 200 degrees. Cover chicken breasts with plastic wrap and pound to even ½-inch thickness with meat pounder. Pat cutlets dry with paper towels and season with salt and pepper.

2. Process bread in food processor to fine crumbs, 20 to 30 seconds (you should have 1½ cups bread crumbs). Transfer bread crumbs to shallow dish. Place flour in second shallow dish. Lightly beat eggs in third shallow dish.

3. Working with 1 cutlet at a time, dredge in flour, shaking off excess; dip in egg mixture, allowing excess to drip off; and coat with bread crumbs, pressing gently to adhere. Transfer to plate and let sit for 5 minutes.

4. Set wire rack in rimmed baking sheet and cover half of rack with triple layer of paper towels. Heat oil in 12-inch non-stick skillet over medium-high heat until shimmering. Place 2 cutlets in skillet and cook until deep golden brown and crisp and chicken registers 160 degrees, about 2½ minutes per side, gently pressing on cutlets with spatula for even browning.

5. Place cutlets on paper towel–lined side of prepared wire rack to dry, about 15 seconds per side. Move cutlets to unlined side of wire rack and transfer to oven to keep warm. Repeat with remaining 2 cutlets. Serve with lemon wedges.

CRISP BREADED CHICKEN CUTLETS WITH GARLIC AND OREGANO
Lightly beat 3 tablespoons minced fresh oregano and 8 minced garlic cloves into eggs.

CRISP BREADED CHICKEN CUTLETS WITH PARMESAN (CHICKEN MILANESE)
Mix ¼ cup grated Parmesan cheese with bread crumbs in shallow dish.

DEVILED CRISP BREADED CHICKEN CUTLETS
Rub each breast with generous pinch cayenne pepper before dredging in flour. Lightly beat 3 tablespoons Dijon mustard, 1 tablespoon Worcestershire sauce, and 2 teaspoons minced fresh thyme into eggs.

STEP BY STEP **Ten Steps to Crisp Breaded Chicken Cutlets**

1. POUND IT OUT
Remove the tenderloins and pound the breasts to a ½-inch thickness.
WHY? The tenderloins will likely detach during cooking, and pounding ensures that the breasts will cook evenly before the breading gets too dark.

2. STAY DRY
Pat the chicken dry with paper towels.
WHY? Both the seasoning and breading will adhere better to dry chicken.

3. SEASON
Shower the chicken liberally with salt and pepper.
WHY? Seasoning the chicken instead of the breading, as most recipes call for, ensures that the finished cutlets won't be shy on flavor.

4. MAKE THE CRUMBS
Process decrusted, torn sandwich bread to fine crumbs.
WHY? Homemade bread crumbs provide a subtle sweet flavor and light, crisp texture.

5. DREDGE AND DRENCH
Dust the cutlets with a light coating of flour and then dip them in egg wash.
WHY? Flour helps the beaten egg coating adhere by giving it a surface to cling to, and the egg works as a glue to make the crumbs stick.

Core Techniques

Proper Pounding

"Pounding" meat may be a too-aggressive term for what you're really trying to do, which is flatten it—relatively gently—to a uniform thickness. This ensures that the meat cooks evenly. A meat pounder is your best tool option, though in a pinch a small saucepan or a rolling pin will do the trick. Start at the thick end and pound gently (don't take your aggression out on it) until the cutlet is a consistent shape. Covering the meat with plastic wrap keeps it from sticking to your utensil and helps prevent splattering, too.

Three-Tiered Approach

A classic bound-breading technique works with most cuts of meat. A very thin layer of flour creates a dry surface on the meat, which allows the egg to adhere evenly. The beaten egg, in turn, gives the bread crumbs something to stick to. This technique is the surest route to crisp, unsoggy breaded cutlets.

Shallow Frying

Deep frying is a popular and reliable way to get a moist-on-the-inside, crisp-on-the-outside result for many foods. But shallow frying, which uses much less oil and can be done in a skillet, works for thin cuts like these because the meat doesn't need to be fully submerged to cook through.

Cutlet Know-How

Make Your Own Bread Crumbs

Bread crumbs have a handful of primary uses for home cooking: They make a crisp coating (as in the recipe for chicken cutlets on these pages), they help bind together meats (as in meatballs or crab cakes), and they create a crunchy topping on baked dishes (think macaroni and cheese or baked fish). Bread crumbs also add texture when sprinkled over pasta, meats, and salads.

Premade bread crumbs abound at the supermarket, but shop with care. In tastings, we found traditional packaged bread crumbs dusty and artificial-tasting, and they don't cling well to meat. Japanese-style panko bread crumbs fared better: Some brands produced a crisp crust on breaded meats (our favorite supermarket option is Ian's Panko Breadcrumbs, Original Style).

But the advantages of fresh bread crumbs far outweigh the convenience of premade. They're much less expensive, they adhere better to the meat, they cook up crunchy, and they're easy to make.

DON'T MAKE THIS MISTAKE
Breading That Doesn't Stick

PATCHY, PEELING COATING
Our techniques help you steer clear of this mess.

Getting a crisp, crunchy coating that sticks to the cutlets isn't hard if you follow our technique for a bound breading (see "Three-Tiered Approach" at left). And one more thing: Be patient. If you try to cook the cutlets immediately after applying the coating, it still has a tendency to fall off. Instead, let the breaded cutlets rest for 5 minutes before frying so the coating has a chance to stabilize.

ESSENTIAL GEAR
Meat Pounder

Our favorite meat pounder is the Norpro GRIP-EZ Meat Pounder. The shape and heft of this vertical-style model provide the right combination of control and force to produce nearly flawless cutlets.

POUND FOR POUND CHAMP
Our favorite model from Norpro ($17.50).

6. COAT
Use your hands to press the crumbs gently onto the cutlets.
WHY? Gentle pressure helps the crumbs adhere to the chicken.

7. LET REST
Move the cutlets to a plate and let them sit for 5 minutes.
WHY? The resting time allows the coating to set up, meaning that it will better adhere and stay put during frying and eating.

8. DOUBLE UP
Shallow-fry the cutlets, just two at a time.
WHY? Frying two cutlets at a time (rather than four) reduces the amount of steam in the skillet, allowing the breading to crisp evenly.

9. PRESS
Using a spatula, gently press the cutlets flat as they fry.
WHY? This action promotes even browning.

10. DECREASE THE GREASE
Line half of a wire rack with a triple layer of paper towels and set the cutlets on top before moving them to the unlined rack.
WHY? Paper towels wick away excess oil, and moving the cutlets to the unlined part of the rack keeps the coating crisp.

Slow Cooker Loaded Baked Potato Soup

Hearty potato soup loaded with bacon, cheese, chives, and sour cream should be a winner. But to get it right in the slow cooker, we had to rethink the potato. BY DIANE UNGER

THERE'S MUCH TO love about a baked russet potato loaded with crispy bits of savory bacon, shreds of cheddar cheese, crunchy pieces of chopped chive, and a creamy dollop of sour cream. We've transformed these ingredients into a flavorful stovetop soup before, but we wanted a reliable slow-cooker method. So to start, I gathered up existing slow-cooker recipes for baked potato soup, grabbed a vegetable peeler, and hit the kitchen.

After I put my tasters through a thorough five-way test of existing slow-cooker recipes, it was clear that this soup needed help. Most of the samples emerged from the cooker thick, gloppy, and burdened with an unpleasant graininess. And the "loaded" part of the concept consistently backfired: rubbery bits of bacon, stringy clumps of cheese, and curdled sour cream. Five samples, five failures. Not a promising start. But I was determined to produce a silky-smooth potato soup and to have all the necessary fixings—cheddar cheese, bacon, sour cream, and chives—hold up. It had to be possible.

My first challenge was to find the right potato. For my initial tests, I stuck with russets, because that's what most baked potatoes are. But my soups were consistently grainy. Was I using the

> Want to see all our slow-cooker recipes in one place? Visit CooksCountry.com/slowcooker.

Sour cream and crisp bacon are the perfect garnishes for this satisfying soup.

wrong potato? A three-way test comparing russets, Yukon Golds, and Red Bliss potatoes showed me the light: Waxy Red Bliss potatoes, which you'd never think of for baked potatoes, emerged the clear winner. While the high-starch russets and medium-starch Yukon Golds made the soup too grainy, the Red Bliss potatoes, with their lower starch content, produced a velvety soup with big potato flavor and zero graininess.

Next up: the adjunct flavors. A baked potato can't be called fully loaded without bacon. I wanted bacon flavor throughout the soup, but I knew that slow-cooking bacon all day was a nonstarter—I'd just end up with chewy little pieces of overcooked meat. Instead, I'd sauté my bacon garnish early in the process and then use some of its rendered fat to cook my onions and garlic to ensure that bacon flavor infused the finished soup. I'd set the crunchy little bacon bits aside for now.

In a side-by-side test pitting water against chicken broth as my cooking liquid, I found that broth seasoned with salt and a bit of dried thyme gave my soup a much deeper flavor than water, and was well worth the expense.

You'd think that finishing off the soup should be easy enough: Just whisk in some heavy cream to add richness, toss in some shredded cheddar cheese, and stir in the garnishes, right? Who cares what order they go in?

My tasters did, that's who. I found that when I added the heavy cream to the soup before adding the cheese, the cream cooled the soup just enough to keep the cheese from fully melting. Sour cream, when I incorporated it thoroughly into the soup, made the soup too sour. And bacon added too early became soggy and chewy.

Turns out the ideal order for introducing the add-ins was this: first, cheddar cheese, whisked into the soup until fully melted. Next, heavy cream and chives, stirred into the soup for velvetiness and flecks of green. And finally, a spoonful of sour cream and some reheated bacon bits as a topping.

Bingo. With a few small tricks, I had a fully loaded slow-cooker "baked" potato soup as satisfying as its namesake.

SLOW-COOKER LOADED BAKED POTATO SOUP
Serves 6 to 8

The easiest way to puree this soup is with an immersion blender. Our favorite model is the KitchenAid 3-Speed Hand Blender. If using a standard blender, let the soup cool for 5 minutes before pureeing. Puree in batches, holding lid in place with a dish towel. Buy large potatoes so there are fewer to peel.

- 8 slices bacon, chopped
- 2 onions, chopped
- 2 garlic cloves, minced
- ½ teaspoon dried thyme
- 5½ cups chicken broth
- 3 pounds Red Bliss potatoes, peeled and sliced ½ inch thick
  Salt and pepper
- 8 ounces white sharp cheddar cheese, shredded (2 cups)
- 1 cup heavy cream
- ¼ cup minced fresh chives
  Sour cream

1. Cook bacon in large saucepan over medium heat until crispy, 8 to 10 minutes. Using slotted spoon, transfer bacon to paper towel–lined plate and refrigerate until soup is ready. Pour off all but 2 tablespoons fat from pot.

2. Add onions to fat in pot and cook until softened and lightly browned, 7 to 9 minutes. Stir in garlic and thyme and cook until fragrant, about 30 seconds. Add broth, scraping up any browned bits, and bring to boil over high heat.

3. Combine potatoes and 1½ teaspoons salt in slow cooker. Pour hot broth mixture over potatoes; stir to combine. Cover and cook until potatoes are tender, 5 to 6 hours on high, or 6 to 7 hours on low.

4. Puree soup with immersion blender until smooth, about 1 minute. (Alternatively, puree soup in batches in blender until smooth; transfer to Dutch oven and keep warm over low heat.) Whisk cheddar into soup until melted. Whisk in cream, chives, and 1 teaspoon pepper. Season with salt to taste.

5. Microwave bacon until hot and crispy, about 30 seconds. Serve soup, garnished with bacon and sour cream.

Cooking for Two Chicken Imperial

Reworking this weeknight classic to serve two meant cutting back on prep time, but not on flavor. BY AARON FURMANEK

CHICKEN IMPERIAL, WITH its buttery bread-crumb topping and elegant sauce, is a dish kingly enough for company. But why should guests have all the fun? I wanted to adapt the test kitchen's existing recipe for this retro classic to serve two diners. But rather than just halving the recipe, I decided to see where I could cut back on time and effort—without, of course, cutting back on flavor.

Our existing recipe goes something like this: Use a food processor to whiz French bread into crumbs, combine the crumbs with butter and flavorings, pile the crumbs generously atop four chicken breasts, nestle the crumb-topped breasts in a 12-inch ovensafe skillet, surround them with a sauce of cream and wine, bake until the chicken's done, and, finally, cook down the sauce on the stovetop until it's luxuriously thick and velvety. It's a winning recipe, but could I make it even easier?

Fresh bread crumbs are fairly easy to create in the food processor, but if I could avoid using the extra machinery, I could cut down a bit on time and cleanup. Unfortunately, most prefab bread crumbs taste stale and look like sawdust. Panko crumbs proved to be the answer. These crackly Japanese crumbs have good flavor, hold up well in the oven, and are available in any supermarket—and the only equipment I'd need to prepare them would be a fork and a bowl to toss them with the butter and seasonings.

When we developed our Chicken Imperial recipe, testers considered various chicken parts before settling on boneless, skinless breasts. Though chicken breasts run the risk of blandness, a sprinkle of salt followed by a 30-minute rest imparts deep seasoning. Also, the breasts' larger surface area allows for more of the bread-crumb topping to adhere.

Our original recipe, which serves four people, calls for reducing the sauce on the stovetop after baking the chicken, but I wondered if I could just reduce the sauce in the oven—it was already hot, so why not take advantage of the heat and save myself a step? I switched to a 13 by 9-inch baking dish to increase the surface area for better evaporation (and reduction); then after baking the chicken and transferring it to a serving platter,

I slid the dish with the cream sauce back into the hot oven. Just a few minutes later I had a smooth, velvety sauce.

With these easy revisions, I was able to keep the signature richness of chicken imperial while trimming the amount of work. More time to eat.

CHICKEN IMPERIAL FOR TWO

Use chicken breasts of equal size so they cook at the same rate. Ian's Panko Breadcrumbs, Original Style won a recent test kitchen taste test of bread crumbs.

- 2 (6- to 8-ounce) boneless, skinless chicken breasts, trimmed
  Salt and pepper
- ½ cup panko bread crumbs
- 2 tablespoons grated Parmesan cheese
- 1½ tablespoons unsalted butter, softened, plus 1 tablespoon melted
- 1 tablespoon minced fresh parsley
- 1 teaspoon minced fresh thyme
- 1 garlic clove, minced
- ½ cup heavy cream
- ⅓ cup chicken broth
- ¼ cup dry white wine
- 1 small shallot, minced
- 1 teaspoon Dijon mustard

1. Season chicken all over with ½ teaspoon salt. Cover with plastic wrap and refrigerate for 30 minutes. Adjust oven rack to middle position and heat oven to 425 degrees.

2. Meanwhile, combine panko, Parmesan, softened butter, 1½ teaspoons parsley, thyme, garlic, and ¼ teaspoon pepper in bowl with fork until butter is fully incorporated into crumbs.

3. Pat chicken dry with paper towels

and season with pepper. Arrange chicken, skinned side up, in 13 by 9-inch baking dish, side by side with narrow ends of breasts opposite each other. Brush tops of breasts with melted butter. Top each breast with equal amount panko mixture, pressing firmly to adhere.

4. Whisk cream, broth, wine, shallot, and mustard together in 2-cup liquid measuring cup. Carefully pour cream

mixture around chicken breasts, taking care not to wet crumbs. Transfer dish to oven and bake until chicken registers 160 degrees, 17 to 20 minutes.

5. Using spatula, transfer chicken to platter. Return dish to oven and continue to cook until sauce is thickened slightly, 1 to 3 minutes. Season with salt and pepper to taste. Spoon sauce around chicken, sprinkle with remaining 1½ teaspoons parsley, and serve.

Chicken breasts get the "imperial" treatment with a crunchy, buttery crumb topping and a savory cream sauce.

RECIPE REVAMP Downsizing Chicken Imperial
Rethinking the process helped us reinvent this dish for two.

BAKE CHICKEN IN SAUCE
Pour the sauce around the chicken without getting the crumbs wet. Then bake the chicken in the sauce to maximize flavor transfer.

REDUCE SAUCE SOLO
Once the chicken is done, remove it from the baking dish and return the sauce to the oven to reduce. The large baking dish helps this happen quickly.

Recipe Makeover Funeral Potatoes

Would slimming down this cheesy potato casserole slim down the flavor, too? Not if we could help it. BY CRISTIN WALSH

WHETHER YOU CALL it "funeral potatoes" or "hash brown casserole," this cheesy, creamy, crunchy potato dish, often found on funeral buffets, always disappears quickly. But with 430 calories and 27 grams of fat, it could use a little slimming down.

The test kitchen has a well-loved funeral potatoes recipe in its collection that would serve as a good starting point. The recipe begins with calling for creating a butter-and-flour roux for thickening and then adding chicken broth, half-and-half, cheddar cheese, and sour cream and, to really seal the deal, 4 cups of potato chips—sour cream and onion flavor—crumbled over the top. It's a full-fat recipe that's also full of flavor. Would a lower-fat, lower-calorie version still deliver?

If only it were as easy as swapping out the full-fat dairy items in favor of lower-fat counterparts. I tried, replacing the half-and-half with skim milk and the cheddar cheese and sour cream with reduced-fat versions, but as I suspected, my experiment resulted in a dull, listless sauce with almost no creaminess. I decided to reintroduce some fat into the mix: I tried low-fat milk, whole milk, and—taking a cue from earlier test kitchen experiments—evaporated milk, an ingredient we've used in the test kitchen before to create a creamy casserole sauce. A version using both 2 percent low-fat and regular evaporated milks had enough body to create a creamy sauce. As a bonus, I was able to thicken the sauce by stirring cornstarch into some of the cold milk, allowing me to say goodbye to the caloric butter-based roux.

Creamy sauce solved. But the low-fat cheese was still low in flavor. Inspiration struck: I'd scrap the low-fat cheese

Replacing sharp cheddar with extra-sharp allows us to use less cheese without sacrificing flavor.

and go back to full-fat, but I'd use less. Instead of 8 ounces of sharp cheddar, I tried 4 ounces of extra-sharp cheddar, boosted by a small portion of flavorful Parmesan cheese. The dish was now undeniably cheesy and creamy, but what about the crunchy topping? My tasters demanded it.

I tried several low-fat topping options including corn flakes, rice cakes, crackers, and bread crumbs, but nothing compared with the beloved sour cream and onion potato chips. Unfortunately, they were out of bounds. I tried the

casserole topping with half the original amount of potato chips but using plain-flavored low-fat chips and crossed my fingers. Tasters loved the crunch (and were OK with the reduced amount), but the plain chips disappointed. "Where's the tang?" they asked. When a search for a worthy low-fat flavored chip turned up empty, a coworker suggested seasoning plain reduced-fat chips with ranch-flavor salad dressing mix, which is low in fat. For the next casserole, I crushed the plain low-fat chips with a packet of ranch flavoring. This time, victory.

KEY INGREDIENTS Reduced-Fat Chips and Ranch Dressing Mix

Our full-fat recipe uses crushed sour cream and onion potato chips, but our favorite reduced-fat chips, Cape Cod 40% Reduced Fat Potato Chips, don't come in that flavor. So we crushed our favorite chips (which are so good that some of our tasters mistook them for full-fat) with a flavorful ranch salad dressing mix. This gave us a "homemade," lower-fat version of sour cream and onion potato chip crumbs to use for the signature crunchy topping.

The Numbers

Nutritional information is for one serving.

Traditional Funeral Potatoes
CALORIES **430**
FAT **27 g** SATURATED FAT **15 g**

Cook's Country **Reduced-Fat Funeral Potatoes**
CALORIES **310**
FAT **12 g** SATURATED FAT **4 g**

REDUCED-FAT FUNERAL POTATOES Serves 8

Be sure to buy shredded, not cubed, frozen hash brown potatoes. If the potatoes are frozen in one big block, whack them on the counter to break them up; they do not need to be thawed for this recipe.

- 3 ounces (2 cups) reduced-fat potato chips
- 1½ tablespoons ranch-flavor salad dressing mix
- 1½ cups 2 percent low-fat milk
- 1 tablespoon cornstarch
- 2 teaspoons olive oil
- 2 onions, chopped fine
- 3 garlic cloves, minced
- 1¾ teaspoons salt
- ½ teaspoon dry mustard
- ½ teaspoon dried thyme
- ¼ teaspoon pepper
- 1 (12-ounce) can evaporated milk
- 30 ounces (8 cups) frozen shredded hash brown potatoes
- 4 ounces extra-sharp cheddar cheese, shredded (1 cup)
- ½ cup low-fat sour cream
- ¼ cup grated Parmesan cheese

1. Adjust oven rack to middle position and heat oven to 350 degrees. Place potato chips and salad dressing mix in 1-gallon zipper-lock bag, seal, and crush chips to fine crumbs with rolling pin; set aside. Whisk ¼ cup low-fat milk with cornstarch in bowl; set aside.

2. Heat oil in Dutch oven over medium heat until shimmering. Cook onions until just beginning to brown, about 5 minutes. Stir in garlic, salt, mustard, thyme, and pepper and cook until fragrant, about 30 seconds. Add evaporated milk and remaining 1¼ cups low-fat milk and bring to boil, stirring occasionally.

3. Stir in potatoes and cornstarch mixture. Cover and cook over medium heat, stirring occasionally to prevent scorching, until mixture has thickened, about 8 minutes. Off heat, stir in cheddar, sour cream, and Parmesan until melted and combined.

4. Transfer potato mixture to 13 by 9-inch baking dish. Sprinkle potato chip mixture over top. Bake until bubbling around edges and golden brown on top, 40 to 45 minutes, rotating dish halfway through baking. Let cool for 10 minutes. Serve.

Chocolate truffles are gone in a flash, but creating them can take all afternoon. We sought a faster, easier way. BY ASHLEY MOORE

THE IDEA IS EASY, but the act of making chocolate truffles is often not. The process of creating a chocolate ganache base, waiting for it to firm up, shaping it into balls, waiting again, and coating the balls with cocoa or nuts can eat up an entire afternoon. I wanted a quicker method that would work every time.

Truffles start with ganache, a thick chocolate-and-cream mixture that's pliable enough to be formed into balls but stiff enough to hold its shape. In the past, the test kitchen has developed a reasonable approach to making ganache using chocolate, cream, butter, corn syrup, and vanilla. Now, though, I wondered if I could streamline things even further by reducing the number of ingredients and speeding up the process, yet still produce holiday-worthy truffles.

My first target was the ingredient list. Could I trim it down without sacrificing that silky texture? I knew that chocolate and cream were must-haves, but I found many recipes that didn't call for corn syrup (which acts as a preservative and helps smooth out the texture) or butter. Several tests without corn syrup or butter revealed that, after tweaking the ratio of heavy cream to chocolate, I could still achieve the ganache texture that I wanted. Vanilla, too, proved optional. But a side-by-side test confirmed that salt, which amplifies chocolate's complex flavors, was essential to bring out the truffles' full flavor.

Careful mixing was also necessary. While it was tempting to grab a whisk to

Using the microwave to melt the chocolate helps lighten the labor for these easy truffles.

thoroughly combine the ganache ingredients, earlier test kitchen tests showed that a whisk invites too much air into the mixture, resulting in a grainy truffle. The ideal utensil for this application is a rubber spatula.

Now that I had simplified my ingredients, I wanted to chip away at the time. Some recipes call for cooling the ganache for up to 4 hours before shaping it into balls, but I found that 45 minutes in the refrigerator worked just fine. After I portioned out the mixture using a teaspoon measure, another short chill of just 30 minutes was all the ganache needed before being rolled quickly into balls (a pair of disposable gloves kept my hands clean). I finished my truffles with a light cocoa coating.

The truffles were so good that I decided to create four variations. Almond extract and a chopped, toasted almond coating gave the truffles a nutty sweetness. A variation that included cinnamon and cayenne was reminiscent of Mexican chocolate. Ground ginger added a subtle spiciness, and a version with a bit of lemon zest packed a bright punch.

with rubber spatula, until melted, about 1 minute. Stir truffle mixture until fully combined; transfer to 8-inch square baking dish and refrigerate until set, about 45 minutes.

2. Using heaping teaspoon measure, scoop truffle mixture into 24 portions, transfer to large plate, and refrigerate until firm, about 30 minutes. Roll each truffle between your hands to form uniform balls (balls needn't be perfect).

3. Transfer truffles to cocoa mixture and roll to evenly coat. Lightly shake truffles in your hand over pie plate to remove excess coating; transfer to platter. Refrigerate for 30 minutes. Let sit at room temperature for 10 minutes before serving. (Coated truffles can be refrigerated along with excess cocoa mixture in airtight container for up to 1 week. Shake truffles in your hand to remove excess coating and let sit at room temperature for 10 minutes before serving.)

CHOCOLATE-ALMOND TRUFFLES
Substitute 1 cup sliced almonds, toasted and chopped fine, for cocoa mixture coating. Add ½ teaspoon almond extract to chocolate mixture before microwaving.

CHOCOLATE-CINNAMON TRUFFLES
Sift ¼ teaspoon ground cinnamon with cocoa powder and sugar for coating. Add 1 teaspoon ground cinnamon and ⅛ teaspoon cayenne pepper to chocolate mixture before microwaving.

CHOCOLATE-GINGER TRUFFLES
Add 2 teaspoons ground ginger to chocolate mixture before microwaving.

CHOCOLATE-LEMON TRUFFLES
Add 1 teaspoon grated lemon zest to chocolate mixture before microwaving.

BASIC CHOCOLATE TRUFFLES
Makes 24 truffles
Wear latex gloves when forming the truffles to keep your hands clean.

- ¼ cup (¾ ounce) unsweetened cocoa powder
- 1 tablespoon confectioners' sugar
- 8 ounces bittersweet chocolate, chopped fine
- ½ cup heavy cream
  Pinch salt

1. Sift cocoa and sugar through fine-mesh strainer into pie plate. Microwave chocolate, cream, and salt in bowl at 50 percent power, stirring occasionally

---

KEY INGREDIENT
Cocoa Powder
In our most recent taste test of cocoa powder, supermarket stalwart Hershey's came out on top. Our tasters praised its "assertive" chocolate flavor underlined by hints of "coffee," "orange," and "cinnamon." Sometimes you don't have to pay more to get the best product.

Equipment Review Handheld Electric Mixers

We whipped ourselves into a frenzy looking for the best mixer. BY ADAM RIED

KEY Good ★★★ Fair ★★ Poor ★

WHILE WE USE stand mixers for heavy-duty tasks like kneading bread, a good handheld mixer helps if you don't want to lug out the stand mixer every time you need to whip ½ cup of cream. Our previous winning model, the Cuisinart Power Advantage 7-Speed, is powerful. But some newer models have innovations like bowl-scraping beaters, timers, or "turbo" and "power boost" options. Others have three simple speeds—low, medium, and high. Still others have a whopping 16 different speeds. So what's the best handheld mixer on the market?

We chose a lineup of seven mixers priced from roughly $27 to $100, with a range of speeds. We ran them through a series of tests that covered light, medium, and heavy mixing tasks: We timed how long it took them to whip heavy cream, in both ½-cup and 1½-cup amounts, and to cream softened butter and sugar. We incorporated flour, oats, and raisins into the creamed mixture to make heavy oatmeal cookie dough. To help assess mixing efficiency, we tinted cooked potatoes with drops of blue and yellow food coloring and timed how long it took the mixers to whir them into a uniform green color.

After weeks of testing, we concluded that the new features were a bust. The Hamilton Beach's self-scraping beaters are coated in silicone and designed to clear food away from the sides of the bowl, but they didn't work. Worse, they splattered whipped cream everywhere. The Breville's timer sounds like a great idea, but the design was all wrong; it was hard to see the clock and it automatically resets when you switch off the mixer. The power burst or turbo functions didn't impress either. Testers repeatedly activated these buttons accidentally on the Breville and Hamilton Beach mixers, and the extra power proved unnecessary.

So what makes a great basic handheld mixer? Testing confirmed our strong preference for open beaters. A classic beater has four metal tines surrounding a center post. This post is problematic because it traps food; when it jams, you have to stop, detach the beaters, and clear them out. Open beaters have no central post, just the outer metal tines (similar to a whisk), so food moves smoothly in and out as it is mixed—a much more efficient system.

After looking at beaters, we turned to weight. We weren't searching for lighter mixers, but once we had them in hand,

HIGHLY RECOMMENDED		CRITERIA		TESTERS' NOTES
KITCHENAID 5-Speed Ultra Power Hand Mixer **Model:** KHM512 **Price:** $69.99 **Speeds:** 5 **Weight:** 1 lb, 15½ oz		Design Heavy Mixing Moderate Mixing Light Whipping	★★★ ★★★ ★★★ ★★★	This felt like the sports car of the group: light, maneuverable, and efficient. Its five speeds were powerful and well calibrated, nicely covering the range called for in recipes.
RECOMMENDED				
CUISINART PowerSelect 3-Speed Hand Mixer **Model:** CHM-3 **Price:** $26.77 **Speeds:** 3 **Weight:** 2 lb, 2 oz	BEST BUY	Design Heavy Mixing Moderate Mixing Light Whipping	★★ ★★★ ★★★ ★★★	Comfortable to hold and plenty powerful, this unit had three fast speeds. It made quick work of all the tests but doesn't have medium-low or medium-high settings; a good simple mixer for basic tasks like whipping cream.
CUISINART Power Advantage 7-Speed Hand Mixer **Model:** HM-70 **Price:** $59.00 **Speeds:** 7 **Weight:** 2 lb, 6 oz		Design Heavy Mixing Moderate Mixing Light Whipping	★★ ★★★ ★★ ★★★	This unit was powerful, with well-calibrated speeds that covered all the bases with a few to spare. Our previous winner, this mixer was edged out of the top spot in favor of lighter, more pared-down models.
BODUM Bistro Electric Hand Mixer **Model:** 11532 **Price:** $72.00 **Speeds:** 5 **Weight:** 2 lb, 1⅛ oz		Design Heavy Mixing Moderate Mixing Light Whipping	★ ★★★ ★★★ ★★★	This mixer started fast, causing a light flour spray; otherwise, its power levels were sufficient. The power cord faces downward from the mixer's body, which causes it to catch on the edge of the bowl and collect food while you work.
RECOMMENDED WITH RESERVATIONS				
KITCHENAID 9-Speed Hand Mixer **Model:** KHM926 **Price:** $99.99 **Speeds:** 9 **Weight:** 2 lb, 2¼ oz		Design Heavy Mixing Moderate Mixing Light Whipping	★★★ ★★ ★★ ★★	This machine felt light and balanced and the digital controls responded quickly. Testers found themselves wanting a bit more oomph; we had to scroll through too many similar middle speeds to get enough power.
NOT RECOMMENDED				
BREVILLE Handy Mix Digital **Model:** BHM500X **Price:** $79.95 **Speeds:** 16 **Weight:** 2 lb, 4 oz		Design Heavy Mixing Moderate Mixing Light Whipping	★ ★½ ★★★ ★★★	This model's 16 speeds were unnecessary and often redundant. Its center-posted beaters clogged with dough, its digital controls were slow, and its power boost button was easily hit by mistake. The timer was hard to see.
HAMILTON BEACH SoftScrape 6 Speed Mixer with Case **Model:** 62637 **Price:** $32.20 **Speeds:** 6 **Weight:** 2 lb, 11½ oz		Design Heavy Mixing Moderate Mixing Light Whipping	★ ★★★ ★★★ ★	This mixer was very beater-heavy, which caused testers to move their hands closer to the front of the mixer to maintain balance. That, in turn, accidentally engaged the power boost button. The self-scraping beaters produced no benefit and, in fact, caused excessive whipped cream splatter.

we were charmed. Both the KitchenAid 5-Speed and the Cuisinart 3-Speed weigh about 2 pounds and testers found them agile, quick, and light. Our old winner, the Cuisinart 7-Speed (2 pounds and 6 ounces), and a new model, the Hamilton Beach (just under 2 pounds and 12 ounces), felt more cumbersome.

We next examined the array of speed options in our lineup; our mixers offered from three to 16 speeds. Recipes typically reference five speeds: low, medium-low, medium, medium-high, and high. We've never found a reason for more; extra speeds only hindered us and left us wondering if medium-high would be a 6 or a 7 on a nine-speed mixer. Furthermore, more speeds don't

equal more power; they simply mean more steps between low and high. The mixer with only three speeds felt sufficiently powerful. When working with the 16-speed mixer, it was hard to tell a difference between, say, speed 14 and speed 15, and the result in the bowl was negligible.

We wanted numbers to back up the power levels we could feel, so we tested each mixer's speeds with a tachometer, which measures revolutions per minute (rpm). The test showed that starting power levels varied greatly among machines: The mixer with the slowest speed 1 reached 230 rpm and the mixer with the fastest starting speed hit 757 rpm—a 70 percent difference in power.

At their highest speeds the range was smaller, from 1,064 rpm to 1,321 rpm, a 20 percent increase in power.

So how did these differences translate in real world kitchen tests? At the highest setting, all the mixers had sufficient oomph. However, at the lowest speeds, we actually preferred mixers with less power—mixers with too much power at the lowest setting made a mess by throwing ingredients out of the bowl. More power isn't always better.

Our winner, the KitchenAid 5-Speed Ultra Power Hand Mixer, was comfortable to use, with five logical, calibrated speeds that covered all our recipe needs. Our Best Buy is the Cuisinart PowerSelect 3-Speed Hand Mixer.

Taste Test Frozen Breakfast Sausage Links

What makes great breakfast sausage? We link it all together. BY LAUREN SAVOIE

PLUMP AND JUICY with hints of sweetness and spice, sausage links are a staple of a hearty breakfast. We've tasted both fresh and frozen sausage over the years and have always sung the same tune: frozen trumps fresh. In previous taste tests we learned that freezing adds an extra level of protection against oxidation, so frozen sausage retains its meaty flavor and stays tender better than fresh sausage. With that in mind, when we found out our winning breakfast links were reformulated, we focused on frozen in our search for a new favorite.

We gathered six top-selling sausage products and included the new version of our previous winner, Farmland Fully Cooked Sausage Links, even though it's now available in only 11 states. Most frozen sausage is precooked, but we included the one raw frozen sausage we found to see how it compared. Cooking each according to its package instructions, we served up sausage links to 21 America's Test Kitchen staffers.

One product immediately stood out—and not in a good way. Bright white and oddly chunky, Hormel Little Sizzlers Pork Sausage was the sole raw frozen offering and cooked up rubbery and pasty. Our science editor explained that freezing raw sausage often gives it a dry, rubbery texture because water is pushed out of the raw meat as it freezes and is usually not reabsorbed during heating. By contrast, precooking at the factory locks protein molecules in place and traps liquids, so links retain their juicy texture after freezing.

But even fully cooked products were rife with texture differences: some were "tender" and "juicy," while others were "tough" or "mushy." To learn how good sausage gets its juiciness, we talked to Edward Mills, an associate professor of meat science at Penn State University, who told us that an ideal texture is a delicate balance of protein, fat, and water. Manufacturers make sausage by combining meat trimmings of varying fat levels to achieve their desired fat-to-protein ratio. The meat mixture is then blended with water, spices, and any other additives or preservatives. To get a better idea of each product's composition, we sent the sausages to an independent lab for an analysis.

The lab results agreed with the nutrition labels: Tasters preferred fattier sausage. While most products had comparable percentages of protein, fat varied

widely—our favorite "moist" sausages were more than 39 percent fat, while bottom-ranked "gristly" and "rubbery" links contained anywhere from 17 percent to 34 percent fat. Fat not only adds flavor but is also the key to tender, juicy texture, as it helps keep meat fragments from sticking together and becoming tough during cooking.

But too much fat makes for oily sausage, so water is equally important in creating moist, juicy links that aren't bogged down by grease. The more moisture the sausage loses during cooking, the tougher and chewier it becomes. It would stand to reason that the more water the better, but our lab results showed no link between the percentage of water in uncooked links and our tasters' preferences.

Mills told us that moisture loss isn't necessarily determined by the amount of water the links start out with, but by how well the complicated network of protein retains that water during cooking. Fat and water typically don't mix, which is why sausage is considered an emulsion, like mayonnaise, where fat and water are suspended in a web-like matrix of protein. During cooking, that matrix starts to break down, releasing water and fat. We saw top-rated brands use only pork in their sausages, while bottom-ranked products use both pork and turkey. According to Mills, turkey can make for tough sausage because its protein structure is weaker, causing it to break down and release more water during cooking. Tasters enjoyed the "meatier," "juicer" all-pork sausages.

Our top manufacturers also combat moisture loss by adding two special salts to their sausage. One kind, phosphates, raises the pH of the meat, causing the sausage to hold on to more water, thus keeping the sausages moist and tender. The second salt, monosodium glutamate (MSG), heightens the perception of savory flavors in foods: Tasters said sausages that included it were "meatier" and more "porky" than those that rely on salt, sugar, and spices alone.

Our top product nailed the ideal ratio of fat, protein, and additives. Made from all pork, Jimmy Dean Fully Cooked Original Pork Sausage Links were "fatty," "rich," "plump," and "juicy." This brand also makes our favorite frozen sausage patties, so for tender, flavorful breakfast sausage, we'll be sticking with Jimmy Dean.

RECOMMENDED

	TASTERS' NOTES

JIMMY DEAN Fully Cooked Original Pork Sausage Links
Price: $4.99 for 9.6 oz ($0.52 per oz)
Fat: 39.1%
Ingredients: Pork, water, contains 2% or less: potassium lactate, salt, spices, sugar, sodium phosphates, dextrose, monosodium glutamate, sodium diacetate, caramel color

This sausage was "fatty but not too greasy," with a "meaty chew" and a "crisp," "golden" crust. "Nice and plump," with hints of "maple," this "very juicy" sausage balanced "sweet" and "spicy" for a "rich pork taste."

ODOM'S Tennessee Pride Fully Cooked Original Sausage Links
Price: $4.78 for 9 oz ($0.53 per oz)
Fat: 39.3%
Ingredients: Pork, water, salt, spices and flavoring, sodium phosphate, sugar, monosodium glutamate, BHT, propyl gallate, citric acid, and caramel color

With just a "hint of heat" and a "strong herby flavor," these "porky" links were favored for their "loose" texture and "rich," "mild" sweetness. "Nice balance of seasoning and pork," summarized one taster.

BOB EVANS Fully Cooked Original Pork Sausage Links
Price: $3.29 for 8 oz ($0.41 per oz)
Fat: 25.0%
Ingredients: Pork, water, seasoning (salt, spices, dextrose, monosodium glutamate), formed in a collagen casing

Though it's lower in fat than other products, tasters enjoyed the "snappy," "chewy" texture of this sausage—the only product with a casing, which helps keep in moisture. "Meaty" and "mild," this sausage's "traditional" flavors were "completely familiar and quite satisfying."

RECOMMENDED WITH RESERVATIONS

JONES All Natural Golden Brown Mild Pork Sausage Links
Price: $3.39 for 7 oz ($0.48 per oz)
Fat: 41.9%
Ingredients: Pork, water, salt, spices, sugar

While some tasters felt that these "mushy" links were "more greasy than porky," most enjoyed the "balanced" sweetness and "maple-y" notes in this preservative-free sausage.

NOT RECOMMENDED

FARMLAND Fully Cooked Sausage Links
Price: $4.91 for 9.6 oz ($0.51 per oz)
Fat: 17.4%
Ingredients: Pork, mechanically separated turkey, water, contains 2% or less of salt, spices, corn syrup solids, dextrose, spice extractives, potassium lactate, potassium acetate, sodium diacetate

The reformulated version of our previous winning sausage links, this product adds turkey and a whole lot of extra water. The result is a "soggy," "mushy interior" and "bland," "unremarkable" flavor. "Tastes and feels like it's been microwaved straight from the freezer," said one taster.

BANQUET Brown 'N Serve Original Sausage Links
Price: $2.49 for 6.4 oz ($0.39 per oz)
Fat: 33.2%
Ingredients: Pork, mechanically separated turkey, water, soy protein concentrate; contains 2% or less of salt, flavorings, dextrose, citric acid, BHA, BHT

The mix of turkey and soy protein in this sausage perplexed tasters, who compared its "rubbery," "spongy" texture to "hot dogs" and vegetarian "tofurkey." Equally off-putting was its "aggressive" spiciness and "really processed," "sour" flavor.

HORMEL Little Sizzlers Pork Sausage
Price: $2.39 for 12 oz ($0.20 per oz)
Fat: 34.3%
Ingredients: Pork, water, salt, sugar, dextrose, flavoring, THBQ, BHT, citric acid

This raw frozen sausage was "rubbery," like "Styrofoam," and "weird" and "pale" in color. "I know pork is the other white meat, but this is creepily white," said one taster. Summarized another: "I would skip breakfast rather than eat this."

Heirloom Recipe

Share your family's treasured recipes at **CooksCountry.com/magazines/ home** (or write to Heirloom Recipes, *Cook's Country*, P.O. Box 470739, Brookline, MA 02447). Include your name and mailing address. **If we print your recipe, you'll receive a free one-year subscription to *Cook's Country*.**

SAUSAGE-SAUERKRAUT BALLS
Makes 3 dozen

Sheila Adler of Fort Wayne, Ind., says "I loved these as a kid growing up in a big German family outside Columbus, Ohio."

Serve with Dijon mustard.

- 1 pound bulk pork breakfast sausage
- 1 onion, chopped fine
- 1 teaspoon caraway seeds
- 1 teaspoon ground fennel
- 3 tablespoons plus 1 cup all-purpose flour
- 2 cups sauerkraut, drained and chopped coarse
- 4 ounces cream cheese, softened
- 1 tablespoon Dijon mustard
    Salt and pepper
- 1 large egg, lightly beaten, plus 3 large eggs
- ¼ cup minced fresh chives
- 3 cups fresh bread crumbs
- 2 quarts peanut or vegetable oil

1. Line rimmed baking sheet with parchment paper. Cook sausage, onion, caraway seeds, and fennel in 12-inch nonstick skillet over medium heat, breaking sausage into small pieces with spoon, until no longer pink, 6 to 8 minutes. Stir in 3 tablespoons flour until incorporated.

2. Off heat, stir in sauerkraut, cream cheese, mustard, and 1 teaspoon pepper until cream cheese melts. Let mixture cool for 10 minutes, then stir in beaten egg and chives. Divide mixture into 36 portions, about 1 heaping tablespoon each. Roll into balls and transfer to prepared sheet.

3. Place remaining 1 cup flour in shallow dish; beat remaining 3 eggs in second shallow dish; and place bread crumbs in third shallow dish. Season bread crumbs with 1 teaspoon salt and 1 teaspoon pepper.

4. Working with 6 balls at a time, roll in flour, dip in eggs, and coat with bread crumbs, pressing gently to adhere. Divide balls between 2 large plates and freeze until firm, about 30 minutes.

5. Set wire rack in rimmed baking sheet. Add oil to large Dutch oven until it measures about 1½ inches deep and heat over medium-high heat to 350 degrees. If balls have flattened on bottom during freezing, reshape to round. Add 12 balls to oil. Adjust burner, as necessary, to maintain oil temperature between 300 and 325 degrees. Fry until deep golden brown, 3 to 5 minutes. Transfer balls to wire rack. Return oil to 350 degrees and repeat with remaining balls in two batches. Serve.

U.S. POSTAL SERVICE STATEMENT OF OWNERSHIP, MANAGEMENT AND CIRCULATION

1. Publication Title: Cook's Country; 2. Publication No. 1552-1990; 3. Filing Date: 9/16/14; 4. Issue Frequency: Dec/Jan, Feb/Mar, Apr/May, Jun/Jul, Aug/ Sep, Oct/Nov; 5. No. of Issues Published Annually: 6; 6. Annual Subscription Price: $35.70; 7. Complete Mailing Address of Known Office of Publication: 17 Station Street, Brookline, MA 02445; 8. Complete Mailing Address of Headquarters or General Business Office of Publisher: 17 Station Street, Brookline, MA 02445; 9. Full Names and Complete Mailing Address of Publisher, Editor and Managing Editor: Publisher: Christopher Kimball, 17 Station Street, Brookline, MA 02445; Editor: Jack Bishop, 17 Station Street, Brookline, MA 02445; Managing Editor: Scott Kathan, 17 Station Street, Brookline, MA 02445; 10. Owner: Boston Common Press Limited Partnership, Christopher Kimball, 17 Station Street, Brookline, MA 02445; 11. Known Bondholders, Mortgagees, and Other Securities: None; 12. Tax Status: Has Not Changed During Preceding 12 Months; 13. Publication Title: Cook's Country; 14. Issue Date for Circulation Data Below: August/September 2014; 15a. Total Number of Copies: 416,308 (Aug/Sep 2014: 398,556); b. Paid Circulation: (1) Mailed Outside-County Paid Subscriptions Stated on PS Form 3541: 324,393 (Aug/Sep 2014: 332,695); (2) Mailed In-County Paid Subscriptions Stated on PS Form 3541: 0 (Aug/Sep 2014: 0); (3) Paid Distribution Outside the Mails Including Sales Through Dealers and Carriers, Street Vendors, Counter Sales, and Other Paid Distribution Outside the USPS: 25,638 (Aug/Sep 2014: 19,714); (4) Paid Distribution by Other Classes of Mail Through the USPS: 0 (Aug/Sep 2014: 0); c. Total Paid Distribution: 350,031 (Aug/Sep 2014: 352,409); d. Free or Nominal Rate Distribution: (1) Free or Nominal Rate Outside-County Copies Included on PS Form 3541: 2,609 (Aug/Sep 2014: 2,555); (2) Free or Nominal Rate In-County Copies Included on Form PS 3541: 0 (Aug/Sep 2014: 0); (3) Free or Nominal Rate Copies Mailed at Other Classes Through the USPS: 0 (Aug/Sep 2014: 0); (4) Free or Nominal Rate Distribution Outside the Mail: 515 (Aug/Sep 2014: 515); e. Total Free or Nominal Rate Distribution: 3,124 (Aug/Sep 2014: 3,070); f. Total Distribution: 353,155 (Aug/Sep 2014: 355,479); g. Copies Not Distributed: 63,153 (Aug/Sep 2014: 43,077); h. Total: 416,308 (Aug/Sep 2014: 398,556); i. Percent Paid: 99.12% (Aug/Sep 2014: 99.14%).

RECIPE INDEX

FIND THE ROOSTER!

A tiny version of this rooster has been hidden in the pages of this issue. Write to us with its location and we'll enter you in a random drawing. The first correct entry drawn will win our winning handheld mixer, and each of the next five will receive a free one-year subscription to *Cook's Country*. To enter, visit **CooksCountry.com/rooster** by January 31, 2015, or write to Rooster DJ15, *Cook's Country*, P.O. Box 470739, Brookline, MA 02447. Include your name and address. Sara Morandini of Aurora, Colorado, found the rooster in the August/September 2014 issue on page 6 and won our winning vacuum sealer.

WEB EXTRAS

Free for 4 months online at **CooksCountry.com**

Basic Pizza Sauce
Basic Red Wine Pan Sauce
Chicken Marsala
Chocolate Layer Cake
Fish Tacos
Frozen Dinner Roll Tasting (full story and chart)
Holiday Rum Cake
New Orleans Bourbon Bread Pudding
Pastrami and Swiss Football Sandwiches
Pumpkin Cake with Rum-Raisin Frosting
Spicy Sausage Stromboli
Tipsy Squire
Vegetable Stromboli

READ US ON iPAD

Download the *Cook's Country* app for iPad and start a free trial subscription or purchase a single issue of the magazine. All issues are enhanced with full-color Cooking Mode slide shows that provide step-by-step instructions for completing recipes, plus expanded reviews and ratings. Go to **CooksCountry.com/iPad** to download our app through iTunes.

Follow us on **Pinterest**
pinterest.com/TestKitchen

Follow us on **Twitter**
twitter.com/TestKitchen

Find us on **Facebook**
facebook.com/CooksCountry

Hot Cocoa Cake

We transformed a favorite winter warmer into a rich chocolate layer cake with marshmallow crème filling, cocoa frosting, and a mountain of marshmallows.

To make this cake, you will need:

- 1 teaspoon plain gelatin
- ¼ cup cold water
- 6 tablespoons unsalted butter, softened
- 1 teaspoon vanilla extract
  Pinch salt
- 2 cups marshmallow crème
- 1½ cups heavy cream
- 3 tablespoons Dutch-processed cocoa powder, plus extra for dusting
- ½ cup white chocolate chips
- 3 (8-inch) chocolate cake layers*
- 24-36 large marshmallows

FOR THE FILLING: Sprinkle gelatin over water in large bowl and let sit until softened, about 5 minutes. Microwave mixture until bubbling around edges and gelatin dissolves, about 15 seconds. Stir in butter, vanilla, and salt until combined. Let mixture cool until just warm to touch, about 5 minutes. Whisk in marshmallow crème until smooth; refrigerate marshmallow filling until firm enough to spread, about 30 minutes.

FOR THE FROSTING: Bring ½ cup cream and cocoa to simmer in small saucepan over medium-high heat, whisking until smooth. Pour cream mixture over white chocolate chips in small bowl and whisk until melted and smooth. Let white chocolate mixture cool completely,

about 30 minutes. Using stand mixer fitted with whisk, whip remaining 1 cup cream with cooled white chocolate mixture on medium-high speed until soft peaks form, 60 to 90 seconds.

TO ASSEMBLE: Place 1 cake layer on plate or pedestal. Spread half of filling in even layer over top. Top with second cake layer and remaining filling. Place third cake layer on top. Spread top and sides of cake with even layer of frosting. Arrange marshmallows on top in large mound; dust with extra cocoa. Serve.

▶ *Go to **CooksCountry.com/chocolatelayercake** for our **Chocolate Layer Cake** recipe.

Inside This Issue